CONFIDENCE
MAN

CONFIDENCE MAN

THE MAKING
OF DONALD TRUMP
AND THE
BREAKING OF AMERICA

Maggie Haberman

RANDOM HOUSE
LARGE PRINT

Cover design: Christopher Brian King
Cover photographs: (front) Bill Truran / Alamy Stock Photo; (back) Tasos Katopodis / Getty Images
Photo research by Toby Greenberg
Illustration credits appear on page 955.

The Library of Congress has established a Cataloging-in-Publication record for this title.

ISBN: 978-0-593-63272-7

www.penguinrandomhouse.com/large-print-format-books

FIRST LARGE PRINT EDITION

Printed in the United States of America

1st Printing

This Large Print edition published in accord with the standards of the N.A.V.H.

For my family

Contents

CONFIDENCE MAN

Prologue

W hat do you need me to say?"

It was May 5, 2016, two days after the Republican primary in Indiana. I sat in the back of a yellow taxicab as it rolled down Fifth Avenue, my computer open on my lap and a phone held to my ear.

The likely Republican nominee for president was on the other end of the call. I had reached out to his staff for comment about a fresh round of support he had received from David Duke, a former Ku Klux Klan grand wizard and onetime Louisiana politician, who had recently alleged that opposition to the Trump campaign came from "Jewish extremists" and "Jewish supremacists." The Anti-Defamation League, as it did at other points during that campaign, called on the candidate to "make unequivocally clear" that he rejected Duke's statement.

Donald Trump greeted me and then cut quickly to his point.

"I'm here with my two Jewish lawyers," he said, appearing to refer to David Friedman and Jason Greenblatt, both of whom handled matters for his company, the Trump Organization.

"I have a statement. Are you ready?" he asked. I waited, my fingers hovering over the keyboard. "Antisemitism has no place in our society, which should be united, not divided," he said, as I typed his words. Then a pause. A pause that went on a beat too long.

"That's it?" I asked.

Another pause. Then Trump asked, "What do you need me to say?"

Trump was notorious for seeking cues that would help him please his audience, but in this context, his uncertainty threw me. Knowing what to say to show you wanted to separate yourself from the nation's most famous white supremacist should not be hard. I reiterated what I had told his campaign aides, that I was seeking a response or reaction to Duke's antisemitic remarks about "Jewish extremists"; Trump seemed to realize why his initial statement was deficient, and added that he "totally disavows" what Duke said. A few seconds later, we hung up.

What do you need me to say?

In some ways, it was the question that informed all Trump had done as a businessman, where success had made him a recurring character in New York City's tabloid newspapers. Young Donald Trump had been athletic as a teenager, and then aspired to a career in Hollywood. He ultimately fulfilled his father's desire for a successor in the family business: real estate. But what the son really always wanted was to be a star.

So that question guided Trump to cast himself as

he preferred to be seen—a take-charge billionaire in a leather-backed seat on the reality television show **The Apprentice.** He was usually selling, saying whatever he had to in order to survive life in ten-minute increments. He was also guided by a belief in repetition; over and over he would convey to employees and friends a version of the same idea: if you say something often enough, it becomes true. Together these instincts helped him to evade public and private danger over the course of nearly fifty years, and then became the foundation for his approach to politics, as a candidate and then a president and a former president.

Though some of his confidants held out hope that the weight of the presidency would change Trump, that was never a likely outcome. Over the years, those who got closest to him and chose to stay there often suggested they had been sucked in by a version best described as the "Good" Trump. The Good Trump was capable of generosity and kindness, throwing birthday parties for friends and checking on them repeatedly when they fell ill, calling the daughter of a political ally who was suffering from breast cancer for a surprise chat from the White House. The Good Trump could be funny and fun to be around, solicitous and engaged, able to at least appear interested in the people in his company. The Good Trump could heed advice from aides hoping to curb his self-destructive impulses and could seem vulnerable. That version of Trump won the loyalty of many people over decades.

Being close to Trump was like "being friends with a hurricane," one longtime friend told me. "It was very exciting, but you kind of don't know which way the wind was blowing."

In the White House, those who met Trump for the first time were often disarmed, seeing someone not at all like the angry voice of his Twitter feed or the fuming boss portrayed in innumerable news accounts. In some respects, he benefited from that media coverage and social media persona; he was often calmer in person in initial interactions, leading people to question the veracity of what they had read. (The all-capitalized tweets that projected anger were sometimes sent while he was laughing about the same topic.) He is charismatic and can be charming, and in those initial encounters, he would ask people questions about themselves, zeroing in on them, giving them the sense that they were the only person in the room.

But even those who rationalized staying close to him acknowledged that a "Bad" Trump always revealed himself. That was the man who made racist comments and then insisted people had misunderstood him, giving his allies cover by which to defend him. He was interested primarily in money, dominance, power, bullying, and himself. He treated rules and regulations as unnecessary obstacles rather than constraints on his behavior. He lost his temper suddenly, and abusively, directing his ire at one aide in a roomful of others, before moving on from a burst of anger that instilled fear in everyone that they could be its next target. Occasionally, he would recognize that he had gone too far, but instead of apologizing, he would be effusive toward his target the next time they saw each other. He sought an endless stream of praise, prompting a range of aides to offer it in his presence or on television. He created an environment perpetually beset by rivalries, where those in his circle became fixated on tearing down whoever had begun to win his favor. He disregarded the advice of long-serving government employees and business professionals and his own lawyers. He encouraged people to take risky actions in his name, and demanded they prove themselves to him over and over; many were so eager for his approval that they obliged. His thirst for fame seemed to grow each time he tasted more of it, and his anger at being wounded, which was often met only with an outsize reaction against the person he blamed for the injury, was always there. Trump almost always foreclosed few options until the last possible minute and modulated his behavior only when he had to; more often than not, he waited out people and institutions who posed resistance, ultimately bending them to his will through inertia. That version of Trump was the one who was most often seen in the eight weeks leading to the violent aftermath of his 2020 loss on January 6, 2021. After he left office, some of his closest aides and supporters privately described themselves and his political movement as having been held hostage to his refusal to cede the stage; independently, those people said the only thing that would change the situation was Trump's passing.

Trump did not produce the intense polarization that has riven the country since at least the 1990s, when President Bill Clinton and Speaker Newt Gingrich were pitted in a zero-sum partisan conflict amid increasingly virulent culture wars. A sequence of traumas followed: impeachment trial, close presidential election decided by the Supreme Court, catastrophic and world-altering terrorist attack, two seemingly endless and costly overseas conflicts, a devastating hurricane that lay bare racial disparities, a fiscal crisis that left millions in financial ruin with no one held accountable. But he did capitalize on the aftermath of those events, adding accelerant to existing trends and exploiting the cultural divide, defined in part by anger at government and financial elites, and by resentment among white voters at the country's shifting demographics. In a celebrity-obsessed country that over many years treated politics as a wrestling match or a game, Trump found his moment, fueling and benefiting from the collapse of cultural and political identities into one another as the country cleaved along the lines of whom you hate, or who hates you back.

Trump had spent decades surviving one professional near-death experience after another, and after a lifetime of bluffing and charming and cajoling and strong-arming his way through challenging situations, he saw no need to change after winning the White

House in 2016. By any objective measure, Trump had already led a remarkable life by the time he got there. He had been a famous figure for decades, defining an in-your-face approach to wealth that helped enmesh him in the pop culture fabric of movies and television. He was unrivaled in his ability to reinvent himself just when he approached the brink of personal disaster, often owing to his own behavior.

By the end of his presidency, he had assembled a record of historical consequence, changing the Republican Party's policy orientation toward anti-interventionism, nativism, and confrontation with China. He had accumulated a list of legacy accomplishments, including a dramatic reshaping of the U.S. Supreme Court with conservative appointees, a revision of the tax code, peace accords in the Middle East, and an economy that his predecessor had rebuilt and which Trump grew, with record-low unemployment numbers. But none seemed as significant to him as the prize he lost—a second term.

When eighty-one million voters rejected him, revoking the job that brought the most sustained attention he had ever experienced, Trump attacked the democratic processes that brought him to power in the first place. For weeks, he insisted ballots cast against him were fraudulent without providing evidence, as his allies loaded up specious lawsuits. Trump, who routinely conflated legal and public relations problems, appeared to expect law-enforcement officers and judges to reflexively take his side. He wanted to promote a conspiracy theorist lawyer as a chief adviser in the White House and considered pushing the attorney general to appoint a special counsel to investigate her claims, while entertaining a suggestion that the government be dispatched to seize voting machines.

All was in the service of seeing how far he could take what he often called "the fight." He pursued a scorched-earth strategy even as his private actions after the election conceded the bleak reality of his situation. In public he echoed the "Stop the Steal" rallying cry conceived years earlier by one of his oldest advisers. In private, Trump renovated his post-presidential home in Florida and at least acted as though he were debating whether to attend Joe Biden's inauguration. Some allies discussed whether any lawyers would be willing to negotiate a global settlement to let him avoid criminal charges that loomed upon leaving office (the idea went nowhere).

When he ran out of other options, Trump encouraged his supporters to march to a branch of the federal government that was beyond his control and initially stood back, watching television while they launched a violent uprising, stormed through the Capitol building, and interrupted the certification of the election he had lost.

Trump possess [sic] a unique base of support among young people, executives, middle-level white collar workers and minorities," read the executive summary of the Report to Donald Trump on Public Opinion in America, delivered to him in October 1988 by the research firm Penn and Schoen Associates, Inc.

"Regarding issues which detract from his support," wrote the pollster who conducted the survey, Doug Schoen, "only one really impacts a large number of voters: Trump's lack of experience in government. This, however, can be overcome, and we have outlined a plan in that regard later in this memo."

The 95-page report was completed eleven months after Trump published **The Art of the Deal,** the bestselling book that elevated a real estate developer largely unknown outside New York into the American standard of aspirational success. At that point in his life, Trump was getting his first taste of fame, the drug that would sustain him and of which he seemed to require increasing doses over time. A quarter century later, Trump experienced the ultimate high: in the White House, he received as much attention as the world can offer a single human being.

Before he sought office, the biographers Wayne Barrett, Tim O'Brien, Gwenda Blair, Harry Hurt, and Michael D'Antonio put significant work into chronicling Trump's rise, his family, his business ties, and his fame. He became the subject of more books during and immediately after his presidency than almost certainly any other one-term president, with the possible exception of John F. Kennedy. These books, some written by my colleagues and competitors on the White House beat, have explored Trump's moods, his dysfunctional management style, and how he reached decisions on critical policy matters. Their chapters have been filled with fly-on-the-wall anecdotes, insights from disaffected staffers, and scoops that often left me kicking myself for not having had them. But they almost always start sometime in the White House, or with the launch of his presidential campaign, when Trump presented himself as an ingenue to politics.

The reality is quite different. Trump had considered campaigns for the presidency, sometimes with more intensity than he let on in real time, throughout much of his adult life. It was partly an effort at brand enhancement, but the idea of becoming a celebrated national figure with immense power captured his imagination in the late 1980s. Even in the decades when he chose not to seek office, he was being shaped for it. He did not act in a way that most political strategists would have recognized as serious ahead of a campaign, but his interest level was.

But the work of the presidency itself rarely matched the thrill of standing in the center of an excited convention crowd as balloons dropped cinematically on him as a party's nominee. As other presidents have, Trump discovered the limited powers of the office were not commensurate with the grand title. Most of the powers that come with the presidency did not actually interest him; he alternated between unfocused involvement in minutiae and appearing to pass the time. During one late-day session with aides to focus on the music played at his rallies, Trump had the group search through Spotify for specific songs from the Who's rock opera **Tommy** for more than an hour because he was trying to find one that he insisted existed. (The aides couldn't find it.)

This book is an effort to find the threads that weave those two worlds together. It is not intended as an exhaustive review of the White House years, or of matters related to the investigations into whether there was a conspiracy between Russians and the Trump campaign in 2016, or of the final ten weeks of the Trump presidency. It is an examination of the world that made Trump and the personality and character traits he possessed as he emerged from it, and how they shaped and defined his presidency.

My task became easier after January 6, 2021. The riot at the Capitol was, for a time, too much to take for a number of Trump aides, allies, advisers, and associates. Some declined to speak, either because they felt lingering gratitude toward him for professional or personal reasons or because they remained fearful of him. But, especially with Trump out of office, others were willing to offer a fuller portrait than they had been at any previous point. I spoke to more than 250 people specifically for this book. Conversations, information, and scenes described here are based on detailed notes and recordings, as well as contemporaneous observations and recollections. (Trump, responding to a lengthy list of questions about some of the reporting in the book, dismissed most as "fake news," "false," or "fantasyland.") It became clear over the course of those interviews that much of what happened during the presidency was foretold by the earlier parts of Trump's life.

The New York from which Trump emerged was its own morass of corruption and dysfunction, stretching from seats of executive power to portions of the media to the industry in which his family found its wealth. Late twentieth-century New York was a place in which tribal racial politics dominated aspects of public life, keeping Black officials locked out of citywide government power until 1989, informing news coverage of crime and public services, and dictating what got built where and who paid for it. The world of New York developers was filled with shady figures and rife with backbiting and financial knife fighting; engaging with them was often the cost of doing business. But Trump nonetheless stood out to the journalists covering him as particularly brazen; they were hard-pressed to point to another developer who would do something like breezily admitting to using an alias while under oath in a lawsuit about the underpaid, undocumented workers who'd built his eponymous tower.

It was his desire to see how far he could take a presidential campaign that defined the later years of his life. For all the previous times he had toyed with running, and all the scut work he did to develop relationships in key primary states, aides conceded that he never gave much thought ahead of time about what the job itself entailed. Without understanding how the federal government worked, and with little interest in learning, he recreated around him the world that had shaped him.

During two campaigns and four years in office, he treated the country like a version of New York City's five boroughs. Trump aides soon realized in 2017 that he had imagined a presidency that functioned like one of the once-powerful Democratic Party machines in those boroughs, where a single boss controlled everything in his kingdom and knew his support alone could ensure electoral success for others, and where "us" versus "them" defined a city where racial dynamics changed from one block to the next.

When he arrived in Washington, Trump defaulted to the accumulated wisdom gathered over decades of boom-and-bust cycles in his business and his personal life. In his earliest days, he had a handful of key advisers and mentors. Norman Vincent Peale, who preached the "power of positive thinking" and a proto-prosperity gospel, gave Trump a belief that he could will something into existence; when a situation worked out in his favor, Trump often attributed it to mental force. From the temperamental owner of the New York Yankees, George Steinbrenner, whose habit of theatrical firings mesmerized fans and made him as much a focal point of press attention as the team's on-field doings, Trump found a display of hypermasculinity he often emulated during the fragile era when the AIDS virus terrified the country in the 1980s. From Ed Koch and Rudy Giuliani, he learned about showmanship in elected office. And from Meade Esposito, the ironfisted Brooklyn Democratic Party boss, he learned how he thought powerful political allies were supposed to behave. The provocateur and political flamethrower Roger Stone, who spent years helping to groom Trump for political office, starting with that first 1988 poll, was key to mapping Trump's political rise. Other than his father, the most important influence on the future president was Roy Cohn, who taught him how to construct an entire life around proximity to power, avoiding responsibility, and creating artifice through the media. How much of Trump's displays of brute personality have been a function of keeping people from seeing through the artifice is unknowable, perhaps even to him.

Just as he was guided by old models, he was motivated by dated rivalries and grudges. Those who had been around him awhile often recognized, in the many personalized feuds that occupied his time in office, threads of grievances related to the Trump Organization's business. Two of his favorite targets, Senator John McCain and New York representative Jerry Nadler, had opposed Trump's access to a federal loan program in the 1990s for construction on Manhattan's West Side, while another, Representative Debbie Dingell, had been married to a late congressman who wanted one of Trump's casino-related actions investigated.

Yet for all the intrigue that is part of the Trump mythos—the talk of his unpredictability or descriptions of him as an agent of chaos—the irony, say those who have known him for years, is that he has had only a handful of moves throughout his entire adult life. There is the counterattack, there is the quick lie, there is the shift of blame, there is the distraction or misdirection, there is the outburst of rage, there is the performative anger, there is the designed-just-for-headlines action or claim, there is the indecisiveness masked by a compensatory lunge, there is the backbiting about one adviser with another adviser, creating a wedge between them. The challenge is figuring out at any given moment which trick he is using.

When assessing others, Trump is usually focused above all else on whether something or someone has "the look," reflecting his view of life as a show he was casting. Obsessed with other people's secrets, Trump is expert at finding their weaknesses and exerting pressure on those weak points, as well as encouraging people to try to please him by taking risks on his behalf so that he can claim to be at a remove from the fallout. For all the talk of how he values loyalty, he has been most abusive to those who readily offer it, and he enjoys watching people who had previously criticized him grovel in search of his forgiveness or approval. Yet people also describe him as lonely, and often a people pleaser as much as he is a fighter, frequently allergic to direct interpersonal conflict.

He is incredibly suggestable, skimming ideas and thoughts and statements from other people and re-packaging them as his own; campaign aides once called him a "sophisticated parrot." He has shown a willingness both to believe anything is true, and to say anything is true. He has a few core ideological impulses, but is often willing to suppress them when it's useful for another purpose. He makes vague state-ments that allow people to project what they want onto his words, so two sides of the same issue could claim his support. More often than not, Trump is re-acting to something instead of having an active plan, but because he so disorients people, they believe there must be a grander strategy or secret scheme at play. Whatever he's up to is often part of what he sees as a game, whose rules and objectives make sense only to him.

His need to live in the eternal now usually out-weighs any ability to think of the long term. But Trump also lives in the eternal past, constantly drag-ging a deep raft of old grievances—or impressions of better days lost—into the present, where he tries to force others to relive them along with him. His will-ingness to take a course of action that he knows will inflame critics and lead to him being seen as tough has guided him for decades.

Among his most consistent attributes are a desire to grind down his opponents; his refusal to be shamed, or to voluntarily step away from the fight; his pro-jection that things will somehow always work out in his favor; and his refusal to accept the way life in business or politics has traditionally been conducted. These qualities have been his edge, as is wearing on his sleeve that which other people strive to keep hidden. He grew angrier over time, especially when he faced one investigation after another, from prosecutors but also from political opponents. Yet precisely what was causing that anger was often beside the point. A core tenet of the Trump political movement has been finding publicly acceptable targets to serve as receptacles for preexisting anger. That anger helped signal his supporters, who are bound to him more by common enemies—liberals, the media, tech companies, government regulators—than shared ideals. Employees and advisers who wrapped their identities in him felt more bonded to him when he was under attack. (In the White House, aides who had not known him previously were struck by the projection of confidence at all **Times,** even when he seemed to be at low points.) His most ardent fans saw pieces of themselves in him, or something they wanted to be like.

His entire business career prior to the presidency was not a mirage. He built a giant tower on Fifth Avenue and owned three casinos in Atlantic City, convincing banks and government officials to help him do it. He bought up major properties and forced those in power to deal with him. He developed a portfolio of holdings. But he was never a businessman on the scale of titans of finance and real estate in

New York that he tried to appear commensurate with. Executives in Trump's hometown scoffed that he was playacting at having a bigger bank account and bigger real estate portfolio than he did, mocking his eventual willingness to lend his name to almost any licensing deal. And the matter of whether he inflated the value of his properties to deceive lenders was at the heart of a criminal investigation into his company after he left office. But outside the bubble of New York City, he had been synonymous with wealth for decades; across the country he was merely someone who'd built big towers branded with gold letters.

To fully reckon with Donald Trump, his presidency and political future, people need to know where he comes from.

I was born in New York City the same month that Donald Trump first tangled with the federal government, to parents who met while working at the **New York Post,** one of the tabloid newspapers that Trump came to identify with. At my public elementary school on Manhattan's Upper West Side, one field trip was to see the public lobby of the new architectural marvel known as Trump Tower. I have lived for most of my adult life in the borough where Fred and Donald Trump learned how political power worked. My career has been spent at the news outlets Trump cared most about.

For much of the last decade, as Trump went from

being a primarily local to a national and international story, reporting on him has been my full-time job as a correspondent for **The New York Times.** I have found myself on the receiving end of the two types of behavior he exhibits toward reporters—his relentless desire to hold the media's gaze, and his poison-pen notes and angry statements in response to coverage. The opportunities that his rise presented to a journalist were manifold, in terms of both unending stories and increased interest level in my work. But so were the downsides of being forcibly cast as one of the characters in the movie he was forever scripting with his life.

Over time, Trump has had both the thickest skin and the thinnest skin of any public figure I have ever covered, sloughing off a barrage of negative coverage in one moment, while zeroing in on a perceived minor slight made against him by a talking head on television in the next. From his earliest days through the present, Trump has always had enforcers, informants, and people willing to spy on one another scattered throughout his orbit, to create a sense of menace and a threat of attacks to try to force people to engage with them on their terms. Many have been willing to use his inherent paranoia and thin interest in details to bend him for their own ends. Trump often encouraged their tactics.

Republicans' rejection of the mainstream media intensified during the Obama presidency and then dovetailed with Trump's anger, except for him it was all more personal than it was to his copartisans. He considered himself part of the media after ingratiating himself as a frequent television commentator and radio guest for years, and he treated coverage he did not like as a betrayal.

One of the most peculiar aspects of Trump over time has been his ability, not always intentional and often not stated explicitly, to get the people around him to adopt his behavior. Many in his world have started to practice qualities that only Trump has been able to get away with. As the head of what was ultimately a privately owned family business, the number of people subject to that pull had been limited. As a candidate for president, and then as commander in chief, the circle expanded dramatically, and came to include even some of his Republican critics who started to act like him.

But so did many critics who remained in opposition to him, adopting his habit of personal insults or making claims that exceeded what the facts demonstrated, or refusing to apologize for errors or believing the ends justify the means of their attacks. Over two decades, the political tide had lowered for what was considered acceptable public behavior, pulling down everyone in the process. Trump was very comfortable navigating the changing waters.

Even if so much about Trump's Washington years—the personalities, the style, the approach to power—was familiar to me, permanently examining his world left me often questioning whether even the most minute of facts were true, much as many of the people who worked for him in the White House found themselves doing.

Ultimately, as both a candidate and president, Trump spoke to me more often than he claimed, but nowhere near as much as some Democrats and some Trump aides convinced themselves was the case. In the White House, he tweeted about me repeatedly and mentioned my name, unprompted, in meetings with advisers. One time, it followed having seen me mention during a PBS interview that Trump watches several hours of television a day; he complained about my remark, ignoring the fact that he had learned of it only because he had been watching television. He derided my appearance to aides, saying to one, "Did you ever notice that her glasses are always smudged?"

Shortly after his election in 2016, someone who had known Trump for years, in shock at the result, told me, "The country's elected Chauncey Gardiner and nobody realizes it," referring to the protagonist of **Being There.** The book was adapted to a movie in which Peter Sellers plays a dim man named Chance, a gardener, who through a series of misunderstandings ends up being confused for an upper-crust genius named Chauncey Gardiner. But that missed the mark; Trump was not especially knowledgeable of much beyond real estate deals, building construction, sports, movies, and television, but he was shrewd and smarter than his critics gave him credit for, possessed of a survival instinct that was likely unmatched in

American political history. He also was not, as Chance the gardener was, harmless; Trump's zero-sum mentality ensured someone else would often have to pay the price for his success.

A single fact in a story that I cowrote with three colleagues the weekend before the election in 2016 about the missteps by the Trump campaign had infuriated the candidate: we wrote that advisers had removed the Twitter app from his cell phone. Hours after the polls closed on November 8, 2016, and as a key state was being called for Trump, a **Times** colleague, Patrick Healy, tried his cell phone.

Mr. Trump, Patrick said, seeking a comment, **you're about to become the president of the United States.** "Thank you, thank you—great honor. You tell Maggie," he replied, "that nobody took my Twitter away."

A different colleague—this one a veteran of the paper's Washington bureau, Adam Nagourney—sent me a note about what Trump's win meant for my career. "This is great for you," he said, alluding to the typical route for a campaign reporter who follows a winning candidate to the White House, and the fact that I had covered Trump longer than other reporters.

I had just followed a slashing, often dysfunctional, retribution-minded campaign, shaped at every moment by the candidate's impulse for control—of his news coverage, his supporters, and his aides—alongside an innate drive to test the limits of transgressive behavior and a dangerous disregard for democracy and civil rights. Now an entire government would be in his hands, his strongman impulse joined for the first time with expansive power over the lives of millions of people. I typed back my immediate reaction: You have no idea what is coming.

CHAPTER 1

The Power of Negative Thinking

On the morning of November 21, 1964, the eighteen-year-old Donald Trump accompanied his politically well-connected father to the dedication ceremony of the Verrazano-Narrows Bridge linking Brooklyn's Bay Ridge to Staten Island. Before the 11:00 a.m. ceremony, fifty-two limousines carrying an array of politicians and influential figures snaked through the Bay Ridge neighborhood to the Brooklyn side of the bridge.

At the front of the worthies crowded behind the ribbon was Robert Moses, the head of the Triborough Bridge and Tunnel Authority, whose ironfisted approach to consolidating power and forcing through construction plans was admired by both the teenager and his father. Even by Moses's standards, this project was a particularly heavy lift; it had come to fruition only after decades of failed attempts to link the two boroughs. Five men were ultimately handed sets of golden scissors, including New York's mayor, governor, and Moses, the designated master of ceremonies.

The men followed a signal to clip the ribbon, and then the procession drove over the bridge to the

Staten Island side, where the official program was held. There, the engineer who had designed the long-delayed suspension bridge project, Othmar Ammann, disappeared into the grandstand.

Donald Trump later would describe the eighty-minute ceremony as a "sad experience" that was foundational for him. In his telling, it rained heavily that day, and he watched Ammann standing by himself while others talked about his creation and all but ignored him. "The rain was coming down for hours while all these jerks were being introduced and praised," Trump recalled in 1980 to **New York Times** reporter Howard Blum. "But all I'm thinking about is that all these politicians who opposed the bridge are being applauded. Yet, in a corner, just standing there in the rain, is this man, this 85-year-old engineer who came from Sweden and designed this bridge, who poured his heart into it, and nobody even mentioned his name.

"I realized then and there that if you let people treat you how they want, you'll be made a fool," Trump told Blum. "I realized then and there something I would never forget: I don't want to be made anybody's sucker."

Trump's view of the day appeared to be singular. "The sun shone, the sky was cloudless" were the first lines of Gay Talese's next-day **Times** dispatch about the 1964 ceremony. There was no rainfall. Ammann was Swiss, not Swedish, and he had lived in the

United States for decades before the bridge's completion, having emigrated from Switzerland in 1904.

And in fact, Ammann was among the first people Moses called on to be acknowledged with applause during the ceremony. "I now ask that one of these significant great men of our times—modest, unassuming, too often overlooked on such grandiose occasions, stand and be recognized. It may be that in the midst of so many celebrities, you don't even know who he is," Moses said at the microphone. "My friends, I ask that you now look upon the greatest living bridge engineer, perhaps the greatest of all time. A Swiss who has lived, lived and labored magnificently, sixty years in this country." Ammann stood and received a loud ovation from the crowd. Moses forgot one thing—his name, in what appeared to be an inadvertent slip. Perhaps that was the germ of Trump's story, the rest of which was mostly a confection. Trump's remark suggesting that Ammann had been made a "sucker" revealed a belief that people were looking for ways to get him, that if he felt harmed, it wasn't done accidentally. Whatever the reasons he seized on this incident and turned it into an origin story, he revealed himself to be an unreliable narrator of his own history from its early moments. His comments went unchecked for years, but for good reason: why would anyone think such details might be untrue?

Even without embellishment, there was plenty of power for Trump to soak up that day. The people who ran the world Trump's father had aspired to join were all there, describing their own roles in getting the project accomplished. But Trump's main interest at the time was not about the kind of power, ingenuity, or clout that led to invitations to ribbon cuttings for construction projects, even as he told people that he wanted to own plum real estate in New York City. It was about becoming a star.

On that crisp November morning, Trump was a freshman at Fordham University in the Bronx. The school, a Jesuit college not considered an elite academic institution, had not been his first choice. Trump would ultimately brag about attending the University of Pennsylvania's Wharton School of business, but he had toyed with studying film at the University of Southern California. Trump has told people privately over the years that his father did not want him to do so, preferring that he join him in the family business. He insisted otherwise when I asked him about it. "He was never much involved in that because I never really told him about that," he told me. "And it was early on, but I always loved the motion picture. I'm glad I didn't do it."

Trump would maintain a lifelong obsession with the movies, even as he pursued a career in the less glamorous, often shady world of New York City real estate. When he did conceive of large properties, they were almost always on an excessively grand scale. "I wanted to make it more exciting, and you know, I always loved show business and I loved other things, but I think we put some show business into the real estate business," Trump said later. He ultimately realized that he could win as much press for projects he never completed as those he did.

Donald had learned some of this from his father. Fred Trump had his own flair for the dramatic and for getting press attention, although he did not seem to crave it the way his son did. Fred Trump periodically used an alias, Harry Green, to keep contractors honest; he believed they would be more likely to raise prices if they knew his true identity. When Donald later adopted the practice of pseudonymity, referring to himself at various points as John Barron and John Miller, it was in his business endeavors, but also to act as his own publicist when dealing with reporters on relatively trivial matters, such as ones pertaining to his dating life.

Fred Trump was, above all else, an effective businessman who created expansive middle-class housing. He knew how to cut corners and make beneficial political connections. With little use for the services that tax dollars helped to provide people of lesser means, Fred treated the government as if it existed to cater to businessmen—when it was not harassing and menacing those same businessmen.

Many of the New York real estate companies of the day were family concerns, some led by patriarchs cultivating their children to take over. Unlike some of his New York real estate peers, who derided their scions in front of others, Fred always boasted about Donald publicly. But Fred's private approach to fatherhood—described by family members and associates as undermining, pitting his children against one another, with his attention singularly focused on building an empire of financial mechanisms to maximize profits—was better suited to overseeing a business than a home. That way of being was something Fred Trump passed on to his son, without the striver work ethic of the first-generation American who began scrapping for all he had while still a teenager.

Fred Trump's parents were accidental permanent American residents. His father, Friedrich Trump, came to the United States from Germany, where he had worked as a barber but could not find enough work to sustain himself. In his search for new employment, he abandoned the country's compulsory military service for teenagers and found himself fleeing, in the words of the biographer Gwenda Blair, "three centuries of barbaric European history."

Friedrich disembarked from the SS **Eider** in New York Harbor in 1885, moving in with a sister who had done so a year earlier. After six years of working as a barber as he shuffled among New York apartments, he decided he wanted more from life, and traveled west to capitalize on the aftermath of the Klondike Gold Rush. Instead of mining for gold himself, he opened businesses catering to others who had arrived in Yukon frontier towns seeking treasure. There is no clear evidence he operated brothels in those towns, but Blair found evidence to suggest that he tolerated and possibly even encouraged prostitution at his properties.

He became an American citizen in 1892, but on a trip home to Germany nine years later began a romance with the daughter of his family's neighbors. He and Elizabeth Christ married in 1902, and she returned with him to New York, but she did not want to remain in the United States. So in 1904, they went back to Germany, but not for long. Because Friedrich had ducked military service, he was not allowed to stay in Germany and was ultimately expelled. The couple returned to the United States for good on June 30, 1905. Elizabeth was pregnant with their second child at the time, and the family settled in the Bronx, where Frederick Christ Trump was born later that same year. The household spoke German.

After establishing his family in New York, Friedrich Trump met an early end, at age forty-nine, a casualty of the flu pandemic of 1918. Feeling sick while out walking with his twelve-year-old son, Fred, Friedrich went home and went to bed. "Then he died," Fred told Blair. "Just like that."

Friedrich Trump left behind a fortune valued at more than a half million dollars in today's money, collected from his prospecting-town holdings and small parcels of land he had purchased in Queens. Friedrich's widow, Elizabeth, took over the real estate portfolio, incorporating it in 1927 as E. Trump &

Son. She worked with her young son, Fred, who was not old enough to sign checks, on expanding the business.

Fred struggled to find his footing. Upon his high school graduation, he went to work as a carpenter, but when the Great Depression hit was forced to run a Queens supermarket to stay afloat. In 1927, he was arrested at a Ku Klux Klan rally intended to protest "Roman Catholic police of this city" guilty of "assault" against "Native-born Protestant Americans" trying "to protect one flag, the American flag; one school, the public school; and one language, the English language," according to flyers. The event drew a crowd of one thousand people; Fred was among several charged with failing to disperse after being ordered to do so by police.

Fred pursued the political connections one needed to become truly successful at scale in New York real estate. The Kings County Democratic County Committee, as the Brooklyn Democratic Party was formally known, represented a model machine organization, with unrivaled dominance of government and politics in the most populous of the city's five boroughs. Fred ingratiated himself with Frank V. Kelly, who as a district leader had been a key local supporter of Franklin D. Roosevelt's campaign for president, just as Kelly was making a play to become the county party boss, which would give him control over patronage jobs, influence over judges in the borough, and a hand in city zoning decisions.

The value of Trump's nascent relationship with Kelly soon became clear. For decades, Julius Lehrenkrauss had been Brooklyn's most powerful mortgage investor. His firm, known around New York as the House of Lehrenkrauss, issued roughly $26 million in mortgages to forty thousand homes in the city over the course of a half century. In 1934, the sixty-six-year-old and two others were indicted by the Kings County district attorney for extensive mortgage theft.

The indictments jolted the Brooklyn political establishment and, through the courts, forced a sell-off of the company's mortgage business. For twenty-nine-year-old Fred Trump, acquiring the mortgage servicer was an appealing addition to the moribund business his mother had incorporated, as it would deliver automatic fees on other people's monthly payments, as well as provide a window into properties headed to default and sale at auction. Recognizing that he would likely not be able to match the bids made by his competitors, Trump aligned with another bidder to improve his standing. Still, according to the most dogged journalistic chronicler of Donald Trump's rise, the Brooklyn court managing the Lehrenkrauss bankruptcy may have awarded Fred Trump and his partner the victory for reasons other than the quality of their bid. Associates of Kelly had thrown their considerable weight behind them. "The vigorous support he received from the Democratic Party players," wrote Wayne Barrett, "suggests that he was their designated winner, making

Lehrenkrauss the introductory venture for an alliance between Trump and the Brooklyn organization that would last a lifetime."

Throughout the 1930s, Fred Trump built houses across Brooklyn at a brisk pace, including hundreds of bungalows on an East Flatbush site recently vacated by the Barnum & Bailey Circus. At the same time, he probed the array of influential political clubs representing the borough's neighborhoods for further points of entry into the county machine. In Flatbush, he entered the orbit of Irwin Steingut, who delicately balanced the interest of Brooklyn's diverse ethnic minorities into a common political force. In Coney Island, he encountered Kenny Sutherland, who ruled the oceanfront redoubt with an iron fist. The most enduring and valuable relationships were made through the Madison Club in central Brooklyn, where Trump encountered the lawyer Abraham "Bunny" Lindenbaum. Through Lindenbaum, Trump met the accountant Abraham Beame, who the next decade would enter government as New York City's deputy budget director. Another alumnus of the club was Hugh Carey, who became New York's fifty-first governor.

But the United States' entry into World War II ended a federal home-finance program that had been Trump's economic lifeline. So he reinvented himself, moving his family to Virginia in 1942, after being tasked by the federal government to erect wartime housing near the naval base in Norfolk. The terms of the deal let Fred Trump maintain ownership in what he built and enabled him to start building on a far larger scale. By the time he moved back to New York City in 1944, he had significantly more experience with which to impress his Brooklyn political contacts.

Martha Burnham's baby Dennis had been in the backyard playpen behind their house for only a short time, while she sat inside with a neighbor, chatting. Startled by little Dennis's sudden screams, Martha raced outside. Dennis was still in his playpen, being pelted by rocks. They were being thrown by a five-year-old neighbor, who stood by the fence separating his home from the Burnhams'. As Martha Burnham retold the story to her son years later, she dragged Donald Trump to his house by the collar and told his mother what had happened.

Mary Anne MacLeod, a Scottish immigrant who worked as a domestic servant upon her arrival in New York, met Fred Trump in 1935 at a party in Queens, and following a quick courtship, they married at an Upper East Side church; their honeymoon was either in Atlantic City or Niagara Falls, depending on the telling. The next year, Mary gave birth to Maryanne, the first of five children.

The family settled into life in a house that Fred had built on Midland Parkway in Jamaica Estates. An older Donald Trump would describe the area as an "oasis" from the "rough" areas throughout Queens.

The children were coddled in ways that others on the street were not. Servants tended to the home, with a chauffeur at the ready; neighbors recalled Donald being driven along his paper delivery route when the weather was poor. Two cars sat in the driveway, both with vanity plates bearing Fred Trump's initials.

To one-off visitors, the family was charming. But the Trump home was not, according to neighbors, a warm household. Even at home, Fred Trump was as formal as the business suit he always wore: cold, stiff, and resistant to small talk, unwilling to tolerate errors or imperfections and often emphasizing negatives over positives. Mary Trump was remembered as social while at her husband's side, at parties and events, and loving the glamour associated with the British crown. But closer to home, neighbors knew her as an emotionally reserved presence in a house dominated by Fred.

After the birth of the Trumps' youngest son in 1948, Mary Trump had an emergency hysterectomy. Maryanne recalled to Blair, the family biographer, that she was told by her father that her mother was in the hospital and might not survive. Nevertheless, Fred instructed, she should go to school as normal each day, and he would call if something happened—a demonstration of emotional detachment that encapsulated the family ethos about pushing through and all but ignoring illness, bad news, and danger.

As a schoolboy, Donald became known for an aggressive temper and a bullying instinct. It extended to the younger brother, Robert, who was often his target. Years later, Donald would proudly recall gluing Robert's toy blocks together to build his own block tower, leaving his brother without his toys.

When Donald was eight, his father faced the first of two searing encounters with government officials. In 1954, Fred Trump was forced to testify before Congress about a Federal Housing Authority loan he had taken for far more money than the project had in fact required. In the end, Fred Trump was banned from receiving any future funds from the program, and he received a level of negative publicity that he could ill afford. The experience left the family embittered by the awareness that the same government that could be a source of one's wealth could swiftly take it away.

Despite his impulsivity and outbursts in school, some friends remembered young Donald Trump as sweet and fun to be around. While attending the private elementary Kew-Forest School, Donald developed a close relationship with a boy named Peter Brant. They shared a love of baseball, and during the World Series would sneak a transistor radio into school with a small earpiece snaked through their sleeves so they could listen to games during class. They gathered at the schoolyard fence one day to watch Dwight Eisenhower's motorcade pass as the former president made a trip to New York City. Brant often had his friend sleep over, and would recall Donald commenting earnestly about how wonderful the bedsheets in his home were.

As preteens, they went to Manhattan together on the subway. Brant later described those excursions as introducing the pair to the world outside their enclaves in Queens, tantamount to a journey to "the jungle." They ventured into Times Square and its novelty stores, returning home with foreign wares like gag hand buzzers and pocket knives. The friendship was close until seventh grade, when Fred Trump discovered his son's collection of the knives the boys had purchased together. It was at that point, in Brant's telling, that Fred sent Donald to New York Military Academy in Cornwall, New York, roughly seventy miles to the north. The thirteen-year-old had been pulled out of the family and, after years of being surrounded by every comfort he could imagine, was suddenly far from home and all alone, away from one of the best friends he had known.

Brant was at a loss to explain his friend's sudden departure. The real reason that Trump disappeared always seemed elusive. "I always said to myself, is there something I didn't know about his past that would make his father send him to military academy?" he told **The Washington Post** in 2016. "He wouldn't be sent to military academy today for doing what he did."

Some of the academy's students were in the care of Major Theodore Dobias, a World War II veteran known for smacking kids to keep them in line; Donald was subjected to physical abuse like slaps and punches. While Donald was at the military academy, his father's influence remained omnipresent, even from a hundred miles away. "The only thing Trump ever talked about," his classmate George White recalled, "was, 'I gotta win.' What Fred put into his head was he had to win at all cost and other people didn't matter. Other people he treated like crap."

In Trump's senior year, the school administration gave Trump a promotion to captain of A Company. Classmates questioned whether he deserved the prestigious post, and they suspected it was granted to him because of his father's influence at the school. As the captain, Trump was charged with leading other boys in the unit. But he did so "at a remove," a former classmate named Sandy McIntosh wrote; when one student in A Company was brutally hazed by another, the story at school was that Donald Trump stayed in his room, listening to his record player. The hazed student complained to his parents, and Trump was removed from his position. Trump refused to concede defeat, insisting that he had really been given a promotion to another title.

Girls came to see Trump on weekends when visitors were allowed, classmates recalled, although it was not clear if he had a romantic relationship with any of them. In a book about his experience with the man who became president, a classmate named Peter Ticktin appeared at least somewhat aware of Trump's need for praise; he explained how a coveted superlative ended up next to Trump's picture in their senior yearbook. "We gave Donald the designation of Ladies' Man," Ticktin wrote, "because we wanted to give him something to let him know that he was well liked, respected, and deserved some recognition."

By the fall of 1964, Trump had enrolled at Fordham University in the Bronx, a lengthy commute from the house in Jamaica Estates. His attendance at the Jesuit school did not seem to be by design. "That's where he got in," Trump's sister Maryanne told Blair. He never settled there, wandering campus aloofly in suit and tie and making little effort to participate in group activities that would introduce him to others. He joined the Army Reserve Officers Training Corps his first year, but withdrew as other students were being drafted to serve in the Vietnam War.

Trump left only scattered impressions on classmates. One recalled Trump somehow managing to avoid paying the Triborough Bridge's twenty-five-cent toll and leaving it to a friend with considerably less economic means to pay each time. Another recalled Trump's focus on other students' ethnic backgrounds. "He complained to me on one of our rides to school that there were too many Italian and Irish students at Fordham. He wanted me to know that I was excluded from that comment," a schoolmate with the Irish last name Fitzgibbon recalled.

While Trump navigated his new life at Fordham, Fred was facing down a second crisis related to his government subsidies. In 1957, he had started the process of obtaining tracts of land in Coney Island, the coastal Brooklyn neighborhood famed for its beach and its amusement park. He began to plan for Trump Village, a seven-building complex with rental apartments subsidized by a New York State program called Mitchell-Lama. Trump started on the project before he had secured mortgages for the buildings; with his old friend Abe Beame, who as city comptroller acted as its chief financial officer, he had every reason to count on everything coming together.

But private financing eluded Fred Trump, making him reliant on government largesse. The state was lending him money to pay for the next sections of needed land as he went, but an auditor later found that Fred was estimating his land costs—set by Brooklyn courts, run by his cronies in the county's Democratic machine—at a much higher premium than what he actually paid. (While he donated aggressively to Democrats locally, Fred was registered as a Republican to vote.) Despite the findings of the audit, officials including Beame made no changes to the process.

State Investigations Commission officials eventually started asking questions about Fred Trump's profiteering. Finally, in January 1966, he was called to a public commission hearing to account for what had happened at Trump Village. His answers did not satisfy his interrogators. Twelve years after the U.S. Senate hearings had left him more or less blacklisted from federal programs, Fred Trump found himself shut out of government funding.

As his father faced this latest crisis, Donald left New York. After two years at Fordham, he transferred to Wharton, the University of Pennsylvania's business school. Its prestige appealed to the Trumps, certainly; the eldest son, Fred Jr., known to friends and family as Freddie, had been rejected there, attending Lehigh University instead. Trump did not leave any more lasting mark on his Wharton classmates than he did those at Fordham. (He is not pictured in the yearbook from his senior year, listed only as "not photographed.") An exception was a classmate, Louis Calomaris, who witnessed Trump declare in class one day, "I'm going to be the king of New York real estate."

The debacle with the State Investigations Commission ended Fred Trump's ability to get public funds for Trump Village, but that was not the only governmental barrier to his plans for Coney Island. In 1965, he acquired a tract of land that had previously housed Steeplechase Park, a nineteenth-century amusement park whose famous showcase Pavilion of Fun, with an iconic grinning visage painted on its glass front, was filled with indoor rides. New York had just enacted its first law protecting historic landmarks that year, and Fred feared that the city could declare the property a landmark, blocking him from constructing new buildings there. He sent out invitations to a "V.I.P. Farewell Ceremony" for the Pavilion at noon on September 21, 1966. Alongside four fashion models he had hired—two wearing dresses, two in bikinis, all in hard hats—Fred Trump handed out bricks for people to toss at the glass front of the Pavilion, known as Funny Face. After the party was over, the heavy machinery moved in and leveled Steeplechase Park to the ground.

But Fred Trump never got the chance to build on the site. It had not been zoned for residential use, and after Beame lost the 1965 mayoral election to reform-minded moderate Republican John Lindsay, Trump lacked the connections necessary to wire the situation in his favor. The site sat undeveloped for years.

As Donald prepared to graduate from Wharton, none of these challenges to the family business fazed him, according to Barrett. If anything, he was left with confirmation of his chosen life path: he saw that Fred needed a successor to keep his work going. But Fred had not yet made clear the preferred heir. He had initially hoped that it would be his namesake son who would join him in the real estate business, seeking an extension of, and reflection of, himself that could continue into the future.

The competition for their father's favor fueled an ugly rivalry between Donald and Fred Jr., nearly eight years apart in age and dissimilar in temperament, that the elder Fred was said to be happy to stoke. Of all his children, Fred Trump zeroed in most aggressively on his two older sons for interest, ridicule, and cajoling. Instead of motivating Freddie, his father's exacting nature proved crippling. Soon after graduating from Lehigh, Freddie—tall, good-looking, easygoing, and friendly—went to work on the Trump Village project. His father railed at him for choosing building materials he considered wasteful and too expensive. The experiences helped drive Fred from the construction business and into a career as a commercial pilot, bitterly disappointing his father.

Donald echoed his father's derision of Freddie's life choices, goading him to do something better, and bigger, with his life than flying planes. Even as he mocked his older brother, Donald would be scarred by his example. Freddie's drinking problem would eventually help kill him at the age of forty-two, an outcome Donald would cite for decades as the reason why—for all his excesses—he abstained from alcohol. "I watched him," Trump later told a reporter of his brother's fall. "And I learned from him." To friends, Trump was more candid later in life, telling close associates that he drew a direct line between Freddie's death and their father's treatment of him.

Even after joining the family firm, Donald could not shake his youthful interest in show business and the faster track to fame that it offered. In 1969, he strolled into the producer David Black's office, above the Palace Theatre, and inquired about becoming a producer himself. Over lunch, Trump made clear he had researched Black's next production, a comedy called **Paris Is Out!,** and was ready to invest. In exchange for providing half the budget, Trump asked that his name be featured on the show's posters and in the playbill. The show was canceled after 112 performances in early 1970—hardly a disaster, but it cost Trump most of his investment.

Donald Trump concentrated on real estate, but his aspirations were flashier than his father's from the start. He began work on plans to rebrand the outer-borough family enterprise "The Trump Organization," making it sound grander and bigger and more established than it was. That was just one step in a broader effort to shake the small-town aspects of life with his mother and father. In 1971, he moved into a rent-stabilized apartment of his own on the Upper East Side and became a fixture at Manhattan's elite nightclubs.

The goal for Trump was to make an impression. He often appeared with conventionally beautiful women on his arm, trophies that would raise his profile. "He really wasn't the playboy he made himself appear to be. That was part of the act," Rudolph Giuliani, then a politically active New York lawyer, said decades later. "This is a guy who doesn't drink, doesn't smoke, and likes to go to bed at home at night." He nevertheless made himself known at places like Le Club, a hidden gathering place in a Midtown Manhattan stucco building with a small plaque in front that read

MEMBERS ONLY. Trump's efforts to join the club were repeatedly rebuffed before he was eventually accepted.

Trump's early days at the family business were consumed by difficulties. In October 1973, the Housing Section of the federal Justice Department served notice to Trump Management, Inc., that they were being sued for discriminatory rental practices against Black tenants, naming both Fred Trump, the company's chairman, and Donald, its president, in the suit.

The federal government and civil rights groups had been investigating the Trumps for years, beginning when Donald was in college. In Trump Village, Fred Trump's sprawling complex of 3,700 apartments, state investigators recorded just seven Black families. This was not an accident: prospective Black tenants told authorities stories of being blocked by a building superintendent or being denied the same apartment repeatedly. The Trumps were not unique among landlords in such practices. The prominent New York developer Samuel LeFrak, a Trump friend, was also sued for violating the Fair Housing Act of 1968. But LeFrak chose to settle quickly with the government, offering a month's free rent to help fifty Black families move into buildings mostly occupied by white tenants.

Donald, however, was getting his advice from Roy Cohn. As a New York–born child of privilege and then federal prosecutor in Washington, D.C., Cohn had been deeply involved in the 1951 convictions of Julius and Ethel Rosenberg, executed as traitors for committing espionage on behalf of the Soviet Union. That led Cohn to a job as chief investigator for Senator Joseph McCarthy, whose investigative subcommittee was busy stoking the Red Scare, the nationwide fear of Communism, and of merely being called a Communist. McCarthy and Cohn followed with a lesser-known effort to purge gay people from government employment, arguing they were susceptible to blackmail. Their work, which historians later dubbed the Lavender Scare, prompted Eisenhower to sign a 1953 executive order essentially approving of the investigation and firing federal workers who were believed to be gay.

By the time he entered Donald Trump's life two decades later, Cohn was firmly ensconced in New York as a lawyer in private practice, with a town house on Manhattan's East Side. Since leaving government service, he had had his taxes audited, escaped four indictments, represented mobsters and celebrities, placed demands on politicians, and intimidated reporters, doing nearly all of it in public view. He was an expert practitioner at accessing what journalist Marie Brenner called the "Favor Bank" of New York City. It brought a mob-like vibe to his approach in practicing law. People who crossed him had reason to fear he might find a way to smear them if he found it necessary to win a battle or to settle a score. To the degree he followed rules, they involved a vague, menacing concept of "friendship." In 1978, Cohn laid out to the journalist Ken Auletta how far he would go to protect those he saw as friends. "I wouldn't lie under any circumstances. But I'd do everything I could, within the bounds of legal propriety, not to hurt someone whose friendship I had accepted," he said.

Cohn was about five foot eight, and slight, with closely cropped hair marked by a receding hairline. His face was scarred, and he had a habit of sliding his tongue over his lips midsentence. His eyes looked as if he always needed rest. He was known to sleep with men, even as one of his greatest career achievements was motivated by deep homophobia.

His singular talent was for emotional terrorism; being known as a terrible person only seemed to make Cohn happier. "It's given me a reputation for being tough, a reputation for being a winner," he said. What does an adversary do with someone who is willing to jump in his face and, using language they have rarely heard in their lives, keep screaming until the other party relents?

Cohn was also charming, gracious, and generous with friends, viewed affectionately as little more than a scamp with a dark past by some of the gossip columnists and nightclub owners and media executives and politicians who indulged and feared him. Cohn was perceived as powerful, and having access to that power or fame proved most important for the people he dealt with. Cohn became close to the television anchor Barbara Walters, worked with media mogul Rupert Murdoch, and had been thanked by

Nancy Reagan for his efforts on her husband's behalf in 1980.

Trump's story of how he met Cohn changed in different tellings, but the most consistent version, which appeared in his first book, **The Art of the Deal,** has it that they met in 1973 at Le Club, shortly after the federal government filed its housing-discrimination suit. Other lawyers had told him he couldn't win, Trump claimed. But Cohn gave him the answer he wanted. "Tell them to go to hell," Cohn said, "and fight the thing in court."

In nearly any other setting later in his life, the man who became obsessed with the "central casting" looks of White House advisers and cabinet appointees likely would have been repulsed by Cohn's reptilian physical presence. Yet if that bothered Trump, he never showed it publicly. "I was very young and Roy was a very political guy," he told me later. Trump said Cohn was "a different kind of guy," without explaining what that meant.

A central lesson Trump would take from his mentor was that literally everything could be treated as a transaction. Even a seemingly neutral job like that of an attorney, in theory hired to serve a client's interests, could be transformed into something akin to a machine boss or a Mafia don. A person's worth would be determined by whether they were liked or what they owed you. "Roy would be effective if he liked you," Trump told me. "If he didn't like people, I mean, I think, I don't know, he would have some clients that

he didn't like. I think he'd sell them down the tubes.
You know Roy. You understand that? He really had
to like somebody."

Throughout his presidency, Trump had one complaint about the lawyers who served him—White
House counsel, outside firms, and three attorneys
general—and he believed had failed to protect him
from enemies when the stakes were highest. None, he
repeated often, was "like Roy Cohn."

CHAPTER 2

Welcome to Fear City

You get the fuck out of here before I count to three, or I'm going to have you arrested."

Richard Ravitch was furious. Not long after taking over as chairman of the New York State Urban Development Corporation in February 1975, he received a call from Louise Sunshine, a well-connected Democratic fundraiser whom he knew through their children's shared elementary school. She had asked him to take a meeting with a new consulting client of hers, a young developer with big plans for himself and New York City. Ravitch agreed, and at the designated time, Sunshine arrived at his Midtown Manhattan office with Donald Trump. He was developing a once great but crumbling nearby property, the Commodore Hotel, and was struggling to get financial backing because of the taxes involved. As chairman of the Urban Development Corporation, Trump explained, Ravitch could help by granting the project a tax exemption.

It was an especially brutal year for New York, mired in its worst fiscal crisis since the Great Depression. To win political support in Albany for the massive tax hike necessary to prevent a further slide, Mayor Abe Beame—as head of a city almost entirely dependent on the state legislature for its taxing power—had laid off forty thousand public employees. The austerity measures inspired worker protests, including a strike by sanitation workers that left trash piling up on the streets. As essential services were neglected across the five boroughs, New York struggled to maintain its appeal to tourists and to retain its residents.

But Trump was eager to build, and to get government help to do so. "I want a tax exemption," Trump repeated. Ravitch wondered why Trump was unable to secure financial backing from lenders. "Who turned you down?" he asked. Trump talked around the question without answering it. "Give me the numbers," Ravitch said, hoping to hear an analysis of projected revenues and depreciation schedules. Instead, what he got was a sales pitch about how fortuitous it would be for a city in such terrible shape to have such a beautiful new project on Forty-Second Street. When Ravitch was unmoved, Trump shifted to intimidation. "If you don't give me the tax abatement, I'm gonna have you fired," he warned. That is when Ravitch responded with the threat of arrest. Trump left without getting what he wanted, but the setback was only temporary.

Trump was incapable of long-term planning, but he loved nothing more than grinding down a rival or critic. If he was emboldened in pursuing this strategy, it was because he had just seen it work against the federal government. Trump's response to the HUD suit filed against him set a behavioral template for nearly every fight Trump faced over the next fifty years, regardless of its size or stakes: Trump would defend himself against accusations of wrongdoing with a furious mix of outright falsehoods and complaints that he was the true victim. He wrote in **The Art of the Deal** that "the idea of settling drove me crazy." He described it as a matter of both instinct and strategy. "I'd rather fight than fold, because as soon as you fold once, you get the reputation of being a folder."

So in December 1973, with the aid of his new lawyer, Roy Cohn, Trump countersued the federal government for $100 million in damages. At a press conference announcing the suit, Trump delivered a lawyerly defense. "I have never, nor has anyone in our organization ever, to the best of my knowledge, discriminated or shown bias in renting our apartments," he said. Trump said he was rejecting a federal consent decree that, by forcing the company to rent to welfare recipients, would lead to a "massive fleeing from the city of not only our tenants, but communities as a whole." A reporter asked Trump why he believed a consent decree would require him to rent to those on welfare. Trump explained that he had observed such an outcome when his father's friend Sam LeFrak was sued by the federal government two years earlier. (LeFrak's son, Richard, said at the time that was not an accurate description.)

Cohn submitted his own affidavit in the case, one

that appeared to be written for media consumption as much as anything else. Cohn said at one point that no matter how the $100 million countersuit fared, "I suppose the damage is never going to be completely undone because you are never going to catch up with these initial headlines."

The Justice Department and Cohn spent the next twenty-one months going back and forth, with Cohn's goal often appearing to be little more than dragging out the proceedings and intimidating the inexperienced lawyer representing the government. In one cross-examination, Cohn attacked the key witness against Trump, a former employee who described the code used to flag rental applications from Black prospective tenants; Cohn claimed that he had been coerced into testifying. For Cohn, no analogy went too far. The government had conducted a "gestapo-like interrogation" of the Trump employee, Trump's team wrote in one court filing, and federal officials were "descending upon the Trump offices with five stormtroopers."

As a matter of public relations the tactics were relatively successful, but they fell short in legal terms. After moving to have the opposing attorney held in contempt, Cohn was scolded by the judge for making baseless statements. Eventually, Cohn faced the inevitable and quietly moved to settle the case. In June 1975, Trump signed a consent decree promising not to discriminate in renting practices, with specific consequences for each violation. The company agreed to buy local advertisements informing people of color they were welcome to rent in Trump buildings.

Trump had survived his first encounter with the fearsome power of the federal government. It was essentially a defeat, but for decades, whenever asked about the case, he pointed to one specific aspect of the settlement that felt like victory: the consent decree made clear that there would be no admission of wrongdoing by the Trumps.

For his role, Cohn established himself as a central figure in Donald's life, a rival in importance to Trump's father. Fred had been able to take Donald a certain distance within the power grid of Brooklyn and Queens, but now Roy was about to unlock a bigger world for him. He would provide Donald not just with a form of lead-pipe protection, but access to previously unreachable contacts in sports, politics, the media, as well as a seamier roster of clients. Trump always had enjoyed fighting, but Cohn tried to teach him how to do it more strategically, rather than by instinct alone.

As they grew closer, Cohn helped to steer Trump's increasingly ambitious efforts to grow his business in a New York City that little resembled the idyllic Queens enclave of Trump's nostalgized youth. By 1975, years of fiscal mismanagement and budgetary flimflam had caught up with City Hall, which was essentially bankrupt and on the verge of defaulting on the bank loans it needed to stay afloat. To win political support in Albany, Beame slashed the public payroll, with more than five thousand of those laid off being uniformed police.

Public safety unions worked to pressure Beame to drop the plan. As trash piled up on the streets, striking union members positioned themselves at transit hubs and hotels to hand out pamphlets—adorned with skulls and a thick black border—cautioning tourists to avoid a city ravaged by a crime wave with no end in sight. Long after the conflict over layoffs had ended, the pamphlets' title endured: WELCOME TO FEAR CITY—a mocking echo of the nickname "Fun City" bequeathed in the late 1960s by then mayor John Lindsay. For a businessman like Trump, trying to win public backing for his projects at a moment of intense vulnerability for New York, the cynical epithet Fear City would prove more useful.

While the federal housing-discrimination suit demonstrated to Donald Trump that the government could be a potential threat to his business, he appreciated, as his father had, that it could also be a gatekeeper to new wealth. This was underscored by the 1970 bankruptcy of the Penn Central Transportation Company, which forced a sell-off of the railway's vast property holdings nationwide. New York developers had their eyes on one asset in particular: the company's West Side rail yards, among the largest undeveloped parcels remaining in Manhattan.

It was an especially appealing piece of land to

Trump. After he had found a footing in the real estate business, a key goal became differentiating himself from his father, a "mere" developer of middle-class housing in Brooklyn. Empty swaths of land abutting Midtown skyscrapers, Broadway theaters, and luxurious Riverside Drive apartment buildings would be the perfect canvas for the twenty-seven-year-old to show what he was capable of accomplishing on his own.

Trump courted executives representing Penn Central, but waited for power to change in City Hall to make his move, as Beame succeeded Lindsay in office in January 1974. Fred was written into contracts as Donald's not-quite-silent partner, as reassurance to city officials that the project could not go belly-up. Donald then arranged for a meeting with the mayor and the manager of the railroad's non-rail real estate holdings in New York, at which Beame proclaimed, "Whatever Donald and Fred want, they have my complete backing," wrapping his short arms around both Trumps for show.

As part of his efforts to get the necessary approvals, Trump encountered a lawyer named David Berger, who represented Penn Central shareholders and had been vocally skeptical of a sale to Trump. Berger informed Trump of a suit he planned to file on behalf of New York residential landlords accusing energy companies of fixing prices on the heating oil that warmed their buildings. Berger would get one third of any settlement, the size of which would be determined by how many apartments were collectively represented in the suit; Trump would later join, swelling Berger's potential gain. A few days before a key November 1974 court hearing on the Penn Central land, Trump went to see the lawyer at his Philadelphia town house. By the time Trump returned to New York, Berger had dropped his opposition to a sale. Trump came away from the bankruptcy with two separate parcels from Penn Central's West Side rail yards. One stretched from West Thirtieth to West Thirty-Ninth streets in Midtown, where Trump proposed a new convention center, and another to the north, from West Fifty-Ninth to West Seventy-Second streets, where he envisioned massive new apartment blocks.

As Trump learned how difficult zoning rules would make it to actually build there, his attention turned to another item in the Penn Central portfolio: the grand Commodore Hotel attached to Grand Central Terminal. For much of the twentieth century, the station had served as the primary gateway in and out of New York, but it struggled with the decline of intercity travel by passenger rail. When he approached government officials with a vision of a new hotel breathing life into the decrepit East Side of Midtown, Trump claimed he had tentative interest from the Hyatt company to partner on the project. But no bank or investor was willing to finance a massive redesign of the Commodore without being promised that the mortgage payments could be made, and Trump maintained that the city's high taxes made the math impossible. He tried first to secure a multidecade break on the building's property taxes through the state legislature, relying on his father's Brooklyn machine ties to the assembly speaker. When those efforts to work the system in Albany stalled, he made his appeal for a tax abatement to city officials, often misrepresenting not just his support from a possible long-term financial backer, but his legal claim to the property overall. He was quoted in May 1975 saying he had a "purchase contract" with Penn Central for the hotel, then a year later told **The New York Times** he had "an option—with no particular time limit—to buy the Commodore for $10 million from the railroad trustees."

When city officials asked Trump to show them the option he claimed to possess, he sent along a piece of paper bearing only his signature. A signed option from the hotel did not arrive for another year. Penn Central representatives, interested in preserving the relationship with Trump, indicated to city officials that they intended to sell him the Commodore, making the paperwork matter easier to overlook. No one saw it in their interest to challenge Trump's claim.

Over the course of the negotiations, Trump developed something akin to friendship with the development-agency official on the other end of the talks, Michael Bailkin. They would get drinks at a Third Avenue bar, where Trump would occasionally offer Bailkin a glimpse into his inner life, such as it was, by talking about his brother Freddie's struggles with alcoholism. During one conversation Bailkin told Trump, "You're a very shallow person." Trump replied, "Of course. That's one of my strengths. I never pretend to be anything else."

This was less an admission from Trump about his emotional or intellectual depth than a concession that his focus was solely on business matters, and he would use any means necessary to get what he wanted. When it came to charming Bailkin, Trump succeeded. Impressed by his hustle, the bureaucrat worked to steer the tax-abatement proposal through the government approval process. Bailkin devised a scheme for Trump to donate the Commodore property to the city after he obtained it from Penn Central, then have the city lease it back to him for a ninety-nine-year term. Then Bailkin came up with the idea of securing the forty-year tax abatement through the Urban Development Corporation, which fell under the purview of Governor Hugh Carey, the Brooklyn Democrat to whom Fred Trump was a major donor, not the city government. Fred committed to officials that he would "provide financial credibility" to his son's undertaking.

By the time he visited the corporation's offices to meet its chairman, in December 1975, Trump seemed to believe he had everything wired in his favor. But unlike other public officials, Richard Ravitch refused to let himself be dazzled or bullied by Trump. Ravitch was offended by Trump's sense of entitlement, and found it unseemly that he arrived with a political fundraiser who worked for the governor. Ravitch set about trying to defeat the abatement, warning City Hall that a tax break on such a hotel project amounted to an unreasonably big giveaway to a private business and enlisting City Council members to challenge it.

Bailkin, who would soon leave city government to start a law practice, proposed a different arrangement: in exchange for the tax break, Trump would give the city a cut of his hotel profits. Trump balked at first, but ultimately used the compromise as the basis for fresh overtures to resistant City Council members. The concept loosened the political resistance to the Commodore project. In the spring of 1976, Trump finally won preliminary approvals from the city Board of Estimate and an initial vote by Ravitch's agency. In securing the tax break, Trump mixed charm and threat in a way that would become a lifelong hallmark of his interactions with legislators.

Even when the major political work was done, Trump still had to win final approvals before his construction crews could break ground. With Bailkin gone, Roy Cohn brought Stanley Friedman, a deputy mayor to Beame, into Trump's fold. Friedman had found his way into City Hall after years rising through the ranks of the Bronx Democratic Party, a weaker counterpart to the Brooklyn machine. Friedman remained a machine politician, amassing chits and, according to prosecutors years later, using the levers of bureaucracy to enrich his friends and associates. The final package he secured on the Commodore project, in September 1976, delivered Trump forty-two years of property tax relief, worth about $168 million, with the condition that he had to give a portion of profit back to the city.

Trump's quest for the Penn Central properties presented an opening to reinvent himself in the press. He aligned himself with the public relations executive Howard Rubenstein, who helped orchestrate press conferences promoting Trump's plans for the convention center and the Commodore. Before the first one, Trump was nervous as he stepped in front of the cameras. But if Trump had begun with a visible ambivalence about starring in such a performance, he left it hooked. "That was great," he told Rubenstein. "Let's do that again."

With Rubenstein guiding his image, Trump was the focus of a November 1976 story in **The New York Times** that portrayed him as a well-liked wunderkind whose hustle was appreciated by his rivals. The story did not describe him as a developer so much as a "real estate promoter." The **Times** reporter who followed Trump around for a day in a chauffeured limousine, Judy Klemesrud, relayed, without overtly acknowledging the laughability of it, Trump's claim that he was "publicity shy." The only place the chatty developer went quiet was at the Trump Organization's Brooklyn offices, where Donald met with his father. "Face to face, the son seemed affectionately intimidated by the older man," wrote Klemesrud.

She watched Trump at the "21" Club, a favorite Cohn spot, where Trump talked to two men whose

Jewish hospital was about to honor Trump as its Man of the Year. "I'm not even Jewish, I'm Swedish," Trump explained to the reporter. "Most people think my family is Jewish because we own so many buildings in Brooklyn. But I guess you don't have to be Jewish to win this award, because they told me a gentile won it one other year."

Trump was neither Jewish nor Swedish; Fred Trump, a first-generation American born to German parents, had developed the habit of telling people the family was Swedish because they had so many Jewish tenants and, after World War II, he did not want to repel them. Donald perpetuated the fiction for many years.

Trump had told confidants that he did not plan to marry, one biographer recounted. But now he was beginning to say that if he met the right woman, he would consider doing it. It was a propitious moment in his still-young business career. His foray into Manhattan was well under way. Construction was eventually set to begin on the Commodore. Trump would eventually learn to promote himself as a brand, so that in the public eye his real estate projects would be as much about the builder as the buildings.

And then he met the right woman. Trump was genuinely infatuated with Ivana Marie Zelnickova; she appealed to him on several levels. She was a tall, striking blonde—at one point she had done some low-level modeling—with Eastern European roots and a thick accent that struck him as exotic and worldly. But if he thought he was getting an obedient wife who would be willing to quietly take his arm and say little, he misunderstood. Ivana had established an entire life of her own before she married Donald. As a young woman growing up in Communist Czechoslovakia, she had been both a competitive skier and a child actress. In 1971, at the age of twenty-two, she married a platonic friend, Austrian ski instructor Alfred Winklmayr, in order to use her new Austrian citizenship to escape the Eastern Bloc. They were divorced in 1973, and Ivana followed another boyfriend to Canada, where she worked as a part-time ski instructor. Then she met Trump.

Shortly after they met, Trump excitedly described her to Bailkin as a top model in Canada and a former member of the 1972 Czech Olympic ski team. Neither was quite true. Ivana had done some local modeling in Canada and for publicity shots related to the 1976 Montreal Summer Olympics, according to Barrett. Years into their marriage, Trump's tormentors at **Spy** magazine tried to find evidence that she had been an alternate on the Olympics team, as she later said, and came up with none. Ivana eventually said in a deposition that she had tried out for an Olympics team but did not make it, according to Barrett, and she blamed others for spreading the exaggeration.

The courtship was relatively brief. Ivana, still living in Canada, made weekend trips to New York

City, meeting Donald's parents at the Jamaica Estates house. He used the same tactics on her that had helped him get his way on the Commodore deal. "If you're not going to go marry me, you're going to ruin your life," he told her, as Ivana recalled it.

Before they married, however, Roy Cohn intervened to protect Trump's interests once again. After advising him, futilely, not to get married—"I don't know why you want to do this"—Cohn persuaded Trump to get his fiancée to sign a prenuptial agreement. One version included a bonus for each child she had; that provision was excised from the signed deal. Another called for her to return any gifts Trump gave her during the marriage if they divorced, a stipulation that pushed her away from the negotiating table. She eventually returned once the terms were changed.

The agreement included a phrase that seemed to codify Trump's professed uninterest in personally living the high life by establishing that his current preferences were neither "opulent nor extravagant." In fact, the way he lived would become ostentatiously opulent and extravagant, but it was already the opinion of Cohn—and possibly Trump too—that Ivana craved a more expensive lifestyle, and the prenuptial agreement was essentially, according to Barrett, a "gold-digger warning."

The wedding ceremony was held at Marble Collegiate Church on Fifth Avenue in April 1977, a church where Trump and his parents had become frequent attendees. Norman Vincent Peale, the church's pastor and author of the bestselling **The Power of Positive Thinking,** officiated. Donald's sisters were bridesmaids. Bailkin was part of the wedding party, and Abe Beame was there as a guest. A reception followed at the "21" Club on West Fifty-Second Street, just off Fifth Avenue, Cohn's spot and now Trump's.

Ivana was barely represented at the event. There were a handful of her friends from Canada, and her parents, but otherwise the entire wedding amounted to a Trump society event. She later realized she had married into a family in which what Fred Trump said carried weight above all else. Fred was a "really brutal father," she recalled years later. She pointed to a family brunch at Tavern on the Green, the famous restaurant in Central Park, where the patriarch ordered a steak. His children, all adults, followed suit and ordered steak. When Ivana asked for filet of sole, Fred told the waitress, "No, she's going to have a steak." She insisted on the fish, because if she permitted Fred to roll "right over me, it would be all my life."

Being married did not dampen Trump's desire to remain part of New York City nightlife. A new club, Studio 54, opened the year he got married, and Trump would make sure to be seen there. He would claim to recall in graphic detail the debauchery at the club, and describe himself as a voyeur taking it in. "I would watch supermodels getting screwed, well-known supermodels getting screwed on a bench in the middle of the room," Trump claimed to his biographer Tim O'Brien. "There were seven of them and each one was getting screwed by a different guy. This was in the middle of the room."

The year Trump married Ivana, Wayne Barrett entered his life, and he would prove much harder to separate from. Barrett was a muckraking, old-school journalist: his career would be defined by landscape-altering exposés and, in the minds of his critics, at times connecting dots that did not merit connecting. In 1973, he joined **The Village Voice,** a fabled alternative weekly with its roots in the Greenwich Village counterculture; its New Left politics mixed progressive values with deep disdain for a self-serving Democratic Party apparatus that governed New York with little consistent opposition. The paper's leading political reporter at the time, Jack Newfield, was a Brooklyn native who grew up in poverty and maintained a lifelong anger at the unfairness and racial injustice in his hometown's financial and political systems. He enjoyed pointing fingers at those responsible. Newfield became a mentor to Barrett, and alerted him to the ascendant real estate developer who had just succeeded in convincing New York to grant him an unprecedented tax break. With his father's money and connections alongside his persistent self-promotion, Newfield advised, Donald Trump was someone to take seriously.

In 1978, Barrett began gathering reams of documents from government sources, and filled legal pads with long, numbered daily to-do lists of people he wanted to interview. He assembled facts into meticulous timelines that mapped Trump's path to the Penn Central rights and political support for the Commodore transformation. Barrett had been planning to wait until he was further along in his research to make contact with Trump. But one day while sitting alone in an Urban Development Corporation conference room reviewing its files on the Commodore deal, the phone rang. "Wayne!" boomed the voice on the other end. "It's Donald! I hear you're doing a story on me!" The two men eventually spent hours talking; at the initial interview, Trump greeted the first reporter to dig deeply into his life with a solicitation. "You know, Wayne, you don't have to live in Brownsville," Trump said. "I can get you an apartment."

CHAPTER 3

Fifth Avenue Frieze-Out

On January 15, 1979, Wayne Barrett's first piece on Donald Trump was published on the front page of **The Village Voice** beneath a headline that read, LIKE FATHER, LIKE SON: ANATOMY OF A YOUNG POWER BROKER. It was the first of two long installments from Barrett on Trump and his way of doing business, and it made public the full story of how he won control of the West Side rail yards. To a reader, Barrett's blow-by-blow reconstruction of bureaucratic processes could at times be hard to follow and even dull to wade through. But for a prosecutor, his Trump stories served as a road map for an investigation.

The U.S. attorney for New York's Eastern District, Edward R. Korman, opened a criminal investigation into the circumstances behind the court's decision to award Donald Trump the option on the West Side rail yards. Korman's Brooklyn office spent roughly six months probing whether Trump may have gotten his way only by inducing the lawyer David Berger to trade his support in exchange for Trump's joining his price-fixing lawsuit against oil companies.

For Trump, the Penn Central properties had yielded

mixed results. The redesign of the Commodore into a Grand Hyatt moved along, with sleek glass replacing the staid masonry front. Trump was dismissive about the history being lost. "Here," he said, handing off a brass doorknob to someone touring the construction site with him, "take this souvenir of this crappy, dumpy hotel." And though he did not win the job to build a giant convention center on his Midtown parcel, he did secure a windfall in fees when his location was chosen as the site. On the Upper West Side, meanwhile, community opposition to Trump's proposals for new apartment blocks ground progress to a stop, forcing him to let his option to build there lapse.

When Korman's office began its investigation, Roy Cohn sat down with the U.S. attorney to assess the potential danger. Korman told Cohn that both Trump and David Berger were "subjects of the inquiry," Barrett wrote years later, and that it would be a "short and quiet" investigation. Cohn offered his client up for an interview, and Korman sent an investigator to meet Trump at Fred's nondescript office on Avenue Z in Coney Island, a very different environment from the Crown Building, on Manhattan's Fifth Avenue, where his son had headquartered the Trump Organization.

Over ninety minutes, the investigator heard Trump insist, without a lawyer present, that there was no improper arrangement with Berger. The case ultimately relied on a weak witness and a looming statute of limitations for a potential fraud charge. The existence of the investigation never leaked into the press, a fact that thrilled Trump and his lawyer. Cohn praised Korman for his discretion. Trump, however, started telling people about the ordeal he'd endured. Trump blamed Barrett, calling it a "noncase, and the whole thing was dropped and done with before I, in my na-ivete, really got a handle on exactly what was happening." (Full disclosure: I covered the Brooklyn federal courthouse in 2000 when Korman was serving as its chief justice. He performed my wedding ceremony three years later at my request. I was unaware of his role in the rail yards investigation until I was covering Trump as president.) "In retrospect, though, I'm glad I had the experience," Trump wrote in his 1990 book, **Surviving at the Top,** "because I learned that as soon as you reach an even slightly prominent position in life, people will try to make a name for themselves by knocking you down."

But Trump was presented with an even more use-ful lesson from the episode: the value of appealing to prosecutors or officials, trying to talk to them directly, to avoid trouble before it could grow out of control. The mere taint of an investigation could be problem-atic, as his father had learned in the 1950s. Donald and Fred already had a line into the prosecutor's of-fice in Brooklyn, where Democratic machine leaders helped to elect the district attorney and installed their preferred judges in state courts. Party boss Meade Esposito was so dominant that on weekends political leaders from across the city would bring pastries to his mother's home; Esposito held court with the leaders in the basement. A visitor to Esposito's Brooklyn Heights office recalled the walls being adorned with well-known quotes, one attributed to Albert Camus, which Esposito pointed to during a negotiation: "Don't walk behind me, I may not lead. Don't walk in front of me, I may not follow. Just walk beside me and be my friend."

By the late 1970s, a reform movement in Manhattan had shaken up the type of party politics that prevailed in Brooklyn. As he moved his business into Manhattan, Donald seemed to realize he had to build new relationships. A few years later, Trump appeared as a cochairman at a fundraising event for the New York City Police Athletic League, which, among other things, arranges for cops to coach youth sports. The charity was dear to Robert Morgenthau, a former federal prosecutor who in 1974 had been elected district attorney for Manhattan. Morgenthau was at the center of elite power in New York City, and that was part of his appeal, but the relationship also gave Trump access to a top law-enforcement official. Not long thereafter, Trump forged a separate connection with a prosecutor who was one of Morgenthau's successors atop New York's Southern District: Rudolph W. Giuliani.

Roger J. Stone Jr., twenty-seven years old, immaculately dressed and with a shock of sandy hair, stepped into the elevator of his apartment building at 25 Central Park South and ran into his neighbor Sheila Mosler. Mosler, a wealthy divorcée, told Stone she was planning a dinner party. "Why don't you come?" she asked. He accepted, with an eye to meeting one guest in particular: Mosler's divorce lawyer, Roy Cohn.

Not nearly as well known as Cohn yet, Stone had already cultivated a raffish mystique, partly informed by his knowledge of political history. At age nineteen, Stone had, at his boss's direction, made a donation in the name of the Young Socialist Alliance to Pete McCloskey, a moderate Republican challenging Richard Nixon in the 1972 New Hampshire primary—and then provided a receipt to a local newspaper there. Stone's role was revealed the next year during the Watergate hearings. Unlike others tied up in the scandal, Stone never repented for his actions. In fact, his relatively minor association with Nixon's "dirty tricks" regime became a crucial element in his professional biography. Stone was a Republican with libertarian leanings whose specialties included wedge issues in campaigns. He ultimately became someone whom Democrats and Republicans along the East Coast engaged with, and feared. His early experiences in the Nixon era informed a brand of politics—combative, smoke and mirrors, that was sometimes described as a gag, combined with a mix of retribution, menace, and periodic overstatement of his involvement in controversies—that Stone would practice for the rest of his life, with ever-higher stakes.

In 1980, Stone inaugurated a partnership with two other up-and-coming Republican operatives, Paul Manafort and Charlie Black. Soon after it opened, the trio's small, Washington-based political consultancy morphed into a pioneering firm that made money not just by putting politicians in office but lobbying them once they were there. Stone spent much of the year based in New York while raising money for Reagan in the surrounding region.

At the dinner party, Stone approached Cohn, who took stock of Stone's age and smirked to another attendee, "Reagan's in big trouble." Cohn then asked what he could do to help the campaign. Stone ticked through a menu of needs, including a local headquarters that could be leased at a reasonable price. Cohn told Stone to visit his East Side town house the next day. In Stone's recounting, he waited for about forty-five minutes to be summoned up to the second floor. There Cohn sat at the head of a long dining table, visibly shirtless in a silk robe and pajama bottoms, picking at food with his fingers. He introduced the man sitting to his left as "Fat Tony" Salerno.

Cohn described one of his clients who could be a good fit to help with both headquarters and fundraising, but advised that Stone should probably first meet with the client's father. Stone trekked out to Coney Island, where Fred Trump greeted him by proudly pulling out an old letter from Barry Goldwater, the hard-right Republican nominee for president in 1964, thanking him for a donation.

(Stone also recalls being shown a thank-you note to Fred Trump from Robert Welch, whose John Birch Society defined the extreme-right fringe of paranoid Cold War conservatism. There is no other record of a connection between the two men.) Fred made clear that while he had to play with Democrats for local political reasons, his personal politics were far more conservative. He liked Reagan, he told Stone, and would be happy to talk to his son about helping.

After that meeting, Cohn arranged for Stone to visit Donald's Manhattan office. The two instantly hit it off. Trump peppered Stone with questions about the weaknesses of President Jimmy Carter and whether Reagan had what it took to beat him. To Stone, Trump represented a potential client for his burgeoning firm. In Stone, Trump sized up another addition to his collection of useful people, one who understood politics more deeply than he did and could provide him with a path to the national stage.

From 1978 through 1980, as the Commodore redesign was under way, Donald Trump began to fulfill two other dreams. He started building in the heart of the wealthiest enclave of Manhattan, on Fifth Avenue near the Plaza Hotel, and farther south, in Atlantic City, on the New Jersey Shore.

On Fifth Avenue, he wanted to build a mixed-use skyscraper including apartments, offices, and shops. He staked a claim to the struggling Bonwit Teller department store, and then to maximize the space available, acquired the air rights—the unused space above a structure—over its neighbor, the legendary Tiffany jewelry store. What Trump started calling Tiffany Tower soon became known as Trump Tower, an early indication that despite the builder's interest in the location's prestige, he would show little deference to his surroundings.

As Trump prepared to demolish the Bonwit Teller building, officials at the Metropolitan Museum of Art implored him to preserve historic sculptures studding the facade of the otherwise bland art-deco building. Trump agreed, provided the cost to him remained manageable. But when he faced a delay and potential additional fees for removal, Trump had his crews proceed with destroying the frieze. Despite the echo of Fred Trump's party to smash a historic glass pavilion at Steeplechase Park, Donald's new project required a different relationship with the city's cultural elite. In promoting Fifth Avenue apartments with grand western views over Central Park, Trump's market was wealthy people, in a part of town that prized its class and aesthetic restraint. As the building approached completion, Trump mounted an aggressive advertising campaign that included a false rumor that the British royal family was interested in purchasing apartments there.

Yet Trump could never decide what he wanted from New York's social aristocracy, and would spend the rest of his days both seeking its validation and, feeling alienated, congratulating himself for rejecting it. "Let's say that I had given that junk to the Met. They would have just put them in their basement," Donald reflected on the Bonwit Teller frieze fiasco to journalist Marie Brenner nearly a decade later. "I'll never have the goodwill of the Establishment, the tastemakers of New York. Do you think, if I failed, these guys in New York would be unhappy? They would be thrilled! Because they have never tried anything on the scale that I am trying things in this city. I don't care about their goodwill."

As the new gold-plated, black-glass edifice rose from the ground, Ivana became a frequent presence on the site, where she often butted heads with Fred Trump as both issued directives to construction crews. (Fred had no real role to play but used the opportunity to relive his headier days as a builder and try to demonstrate that he still had power.) Donald was interested in speeding along construction, hiring a contractor who employed undocumented Polish immigrants for demolition (and allegedly underpaid them) and building the tower primarily out of concrete, a material that was quicker to use than steel.

That choice of material meant dealing with one of New York's most mobbed-up industries. In the 1954 Senate hearings over his housing loans, Fred Trump acknowledged that his minority partner in the Beach Haven venture was a contractor with known ties to the Genovese crime family. Some of Fred's peers were outspoken about trying to drive out the Mafia from their industry, and others just quietly followed guidance from law-enforcement officials about which businesses to avoid. While Donald Trump has over time given conflicting answers about how aware he was of working with mob-linked people, both his actions and words make clear he accepted their presence as an essential component of the local real estate economy. "Well, anybody that built in New York City, whether you dealt with them indirectly, or didn't even know they existed, they did exist," Trump told me. "You had contractors and you don't know if they were mob or controlled or maybe not controlled, but I will tell you getting bids sometimes is very tough. You'd get one bid, it'd be a high-end disappointing bid. And then there was nobody else to bid."

In the case of his eponymous tower, Trump had to do business with Teamsters Local 282, a powerful building trades union whose members handled cement and other construction materials at the site. The union's president, John Cody, was a Cohn associate supposedly friendly with the Gambino mob family and a survivor of several indictments by the time the Trump Tower job came his members' way. He was famous for threatening strikes on work sites if developers did not submit to his demands.

In the summer of 1980, Trump was subpoenaed by FBI agents investigating Cody. They told him that they were following a tip that Trump had agreed to give the union boss an apartment in the tower as a payoff to avoid work slowdowns during construction.

Trump denied there was such a deal, and agents had no way to prove the quid pro quo, because the building had not yet opened. But it was completed without major hassles from the trade unions. Two years later, a stunning and mysterious woman close to Cody named Verina Hixon occupied six apartments, worth $10 million, near the top of Trump Tower; she later said Trump helped her acquire a mortgage after Cody's intervention. She hit financial trouble, however, and sometime after Cody went to prison in 1984 for racketeering, Trump's interest in granting Hixon leeway on her finances suddenly stopped.

Atlantic City was a less obvious location for Trump to stake his ambition. He had previously spoken wishfully about swooping into Las Vegas—which he associated with Old Hollywood glamour and glitz—but he lacked the capital or connections to plant himself in a region of the country where his father had not tilled the political soil for decades before him. While he initially supported the idea of gambling in New York State, and even envisioned slot machines in the lobby of his Grand Hyatt, Trump changed his mind when elected officials made clear they were against it.

So he turned his interest instead to a spot closer to home, reachable within forty-five minutes or so by helicopter. New Jersey had legalized gambling in 1976 specifically in Atlantic City, a once vibrant resort town, and Trump had his eyes on leasing a site near the beachfront boardwalk that looked out upon the Atlantic Ocean. Like in New York City, a budget crisis motivated the local government to satisfy the demands of a developer regardless of his shortcomings. Atlantic City officials were desperate for outside investment. And like in New York, local institutions were already set up to benefit wealthy developers.

To navigate the unfamiliar political environment, Trump started building relationships in and around Atlantic City. He relied heavily on two people, the well-connected local lawyer Nick Ribis and the Atlantic City power broker Patrick McGahn, to help navigate the city. McGahn—whose nephew, by coincidence, would become Trump's campaign lawyer and then White House counsel—was another gruff, aggressive enforcer whose behaviors Trump mimicked over time. Patrick, known as Paddy, was useful for greasing a number of skids for Trump in his quest to build a casino. When he needed to purchase an additional piece of land for a parking garage, Trump purchased the property from two mob-connected brothers in McGahn's secretary's name before transferring it to his own.

In the hope of keeping their gambling colony free of the organized crime that had underpinned Las Vegas's casino industry, New Jersey state regulators had erected steep hurdles to newcomers. In Atlantic City, both a casino's operator and its landowner had to be licensed by New Jersey's Division of Gaming Enforcement and its Casino Control Commission, ensuring a degree of scrutiny Trump had never encountered in New York. Trump omitted to inform them about his inquiry from the Eastern District prosecutors just a few years earlier, despite their explicit questions about whether he had ever been the subject of an investigation by a government agency at any point.

The landowners had to win a license, too, tying Trump's fortunes to a motley trio who controlled the oceanfront parcel: a pair of Philadelphia scrap-metal dealers and a garrulous fixer named Daniel Sullivan, who, as Wayne Barrett wrote, "had been characterized as everything from Jimmy Hoffa's mortal enemy to his close ally, and everything from a mob associate to a mob-busting FBI informant." Trump had a history with Sullivan: he brought him into the Grand Hyatt to help deliver a contract with the hotel workers union outside of normal negotiating channels, and he would entrust him to mediate a dispute with the undocumented Polish immigrants working on the Trump Tower demolition.

Over several months, Trump, Sullivan, and a pair of FBI agents participated in an odd dance. Sullivan informed the FBI agents he was working with Trump, and Trump claims he relied on them to vouch for Sullivan's credibility as a business partner. The agents advised Trump to be alert to the presence of organized crime in Atlantic City if he did open a casino there. Trump, who professed naivete about the matter, returned to the FBI with an offer to cooperate, including possibly nesting agents within the casino. There is no indication that the idea went anywhere.

In March 1982, Trump got his casino license and began construction a few months later, putting his younger brother in charge of the Atlantic City operation. Genial, easygoing, and less passionate about the real estate game, Robert Trump was unlike his older brother in many ways, but he threw himself into the project. When Donald wanted approval for extra-large signage for the Trump Plaza, as the casino would become known, Robert pulled strings to get the mob-connected leader of the hotel workers union local to show up for the vote, according to Barrett.

One of Trump's casino executives, Jack O'Donnell, would recall being told that one man was key to the Trump Plaza's success: Robert LiButti. LiButti openly told O'Donnell that he worked for John Gotti, the Gambino crime family boss, and that one of his roles was gambling money on Gotti's behalf. Trump nurtured a relationship with LiButti, letting the gambler fly on his helicopter and personally introducing him to the Trump Plaza's president, Steve Hyde. LiButti would ultimately spend more than $11 million at the casino. LiButti's appalling behavior toward Black and female workers at the casino earned him a lifetime ban from all gambling facilities in the state, and the Trump Plaza a six-figure fine for accommodating some of LiButti's requests. Years later, Trump claimed not to recognize him.

• • •

Trump had begun construction on Trump Tower before securing the tax break he insisted he needed to make its finances work. But as he demanded an abatement similar to the one he had won on the Commodore project, he now had no one on the inside clearing a path for his application.

In 1977, the reform-minded liberal Manhattan congressman Ed Koch had defeated the Trumps' Brooklyn ally Abe Beame in the Democratic mayoral primary. Koch, whose ego and need for attention rivaled Trump's, quickly grew tired of the developer's gamesmanship around the Commodore—a fight over a subway easement that Trump was supposed to grant led to an early rift between the two—and was uneager to do him any favors on his next major New York project. Trump's request for a tax break on Trump Tower, under a program meant to incentivize housing constructed on "underutilized" sites, went before Koch's Department of Housing Preservation and Development. The department's commissioner, Anthony Gliedman, did not think the Fifth Avenue property qualified for the abatement, and was under pressure from Koch not to grant it. In March 1981, Gliedman called Trump and told him the city was denying the tax break.

Trump called Gliedman back ninety minutes later. "I don't know whether it's still possible for you to change your decision or not," Trump said, according to a memo Gliedman wrote memorializing the conversation. "But I want you to know that I am a very rich and powerful person in this town and there is a reason I got that way. I will never forget what you did." Trump then called Koch and told him there was a "miscarriage of justice being done." The mayor invited him to take the matter to court, which Trump promptly did. He also sued Gliedman in his private capacity, for such an exorbitant amount that Gliedman later told Trump it was hard to take seriously.

The lawsuits dragged on for three years. Early one morning about a year into the litigation, Gliedman's wife, Ginny, received a mysterious phone call at their home in Fiske Terrace, Brooklyn. A man identified himself as Vinny and said he wanted to speak to Tony. It did not seem especially unusual, given that as housing commissioner Gliedman often received urgent off-hours calls on his home number about code enforcements and building collapses. Tony took the phone; Ginny heard him respond only in brief sentences. He hung up soon after and said nothing about the conversation, and they both left for work as usual in Lower Manhattan. At the end of the day, Tony called Ginny and told her not to leave work without him. When Gliedman reached her office, a man was with him in the car. Gliedman said little until they got within a block of their house. The call he had received that morning was a death threat, he said. When Gliedman had reported the call to police, the NYPD's commissioner advised him to "take it seriously." For several weeks, the family lived under twenty-four-hour police protection.

FBI records later revealed more than Gliedman knew at the time. The day after Gliedman heard from Vinny, Trump called the FBI and said he, too, had received a mysterious phone call. In his case, it was someone who read about his "tax abatement problem with Commissioner Gliedman," Trump told the FBI. The caller, Trump went on, insisted that Trump had been "shafted" by Gliedman and that the caller would retaliate. According to the records, Trump claimed to have received a second call from the person a short time later, in which the man threatened to "kill" him "if Mr. Trump told the authorities anything concerning their prior conversation." Trump told the FBI that he was "merely passing on this information not only for his own safety but for the safety of" Gliedman, according to the bureau's records. If Trump actually felt threatened, there was little public evidence of it.

Trump and Gliedman continued to fight in court. Twice, Gliedman's department denied Trump the abatement. Trump kept the legal challenge going until 1984, when the New York State Court of Appeals ruled conclusively that the city had overstepped its authority in denying the abatement. Trump crowed about the victory and accused Koch of engaging in class warfare at Trump's expense. "Because Trump Tower is housing the most successful and wealthiest people in the world, the city decided to take a stand," he said. "It was unfair, and the courts have concurred."

But winning was not enough. Trump had another idea in mind for how to dominate Gliedman and, by extension, Koch. Gliedman had grown weary of his job as commissioner, in part because being used as a cudgel against Trump during the abatement fight had strained his relationship with the mayor. In January 1986, he received a call from Trump, inviting him to breakfast at the "21" Club. The opulent Midtown establishment was out of a bureaucrat's price range, so instead they went to a modest Italian restaurant for lunch. (Trump would adopt one of Cohn's habits at meals: plucking food from the plate of his dining companion.) In Gliedman's later recounting of the meeting to a friend, Trump asked him what he wanted to do when he left the city. "I want to run something," Gliedman responded. "Well, you could have an exciting time with me," Trump said.

Koch was astonished when Gliedman told him he was going to work for Trump, given how angry Gliedman had been about the threat that Trump had lobbed years earlier. But Gliedman had two small children and was running out of years in which he could significantly boost his income. Trump was a compromise that he felt he could live with.

There would be a few outstanding matters to settle before Gliedman could work for Trump. One was the three-year-old lawsuit still kicking around the courts. Gliedman told Trump he could not work for him as long as the suit was pending. Trump had his own ask of his potential hire: the rotund Gliedman had to lose weight.

By the mid-1980s, Donald Trump was often described by newspapers as a sui generis phenomenon, minimizing his family's role in launching him to the heights of the region's real estate industry. "My father was successful, but it was a different kind of success," he told **The Washington Post** in 1984. "I didn't grow up like this. When I played golf I played at the public course. I'd go to the state park and wait four hours to tee off when I was 14."

But Donald continued to rely on his father's help in ways the public did not see. Fred Trump passed along hundreds of millions of dollars, in part through questionable tax schemes that would be revealed decades later by **The New York Times.** He was the reason Donald had been viewed with credibility by most city and state officials he had needed to win over to achieve his ends, along with some of the financial institutions who lent him money. Fred had been key to obtaining the Commodore Hotel, the two Penn Central parcels, as well as land for the first casino. In Atlantic City, Fred had to add his signature to leasing papers because Donald did not yet have any successful deals to show creditors.

As he eclipsed his father in public acclaim, Trump never seemed to shake off the feeling that he required the patron's authorization, even long after Fred passed away. In an interview during the 2016 campaign, **New York Times** reporter Jason Horowitz asked Donald Trump how his father would have felt about him running for president. The seventy-year-old replied, with no sense of irony: "He would have absolutely allowed me to have done it."

CHAPTER 4

Blind to the Beautiful Mosaic

Like many of Donald Trump's possessions, the Puma helicopter idling next to the Hudson River served as an advertisement for its owner. On the vehicle's black body a stack of red racing stripes stretched from the cockpit to the bold white letters of TRUMP on the tail. It was, Trump would later tell a journalist from **Paris Match** who inquired about his choice of a French vehicle over an American one, "the most beautiful helicopter in the world. I love to look at it."

Within a few years, a fleet of TRUMP-emblazoned helicopters would be moving passengers seven times daily from the heliport on Manhattan's West Side to one on Atlantic City's Steeplechase Pier, promising civilians the ability to bypass traffic on the Garden State Parkway en route to the casino floor. But on this day the future chief executive of Trump Air was personally waiting on just two passengers.

One was Don King, a onetime Cleveland bookie and aspiring boxing promoter who had been convicted of manslaughter years earlier in a fight over a gambling debt. After his release, King put on the "Rumble in the Jungle" bout that pitted Muhammad

Ali against George Foreman. It helped to make him the most prominent boxing promoter of his day. King's career was marked by headline-making boxing matches, as well as business practices often described over the years as less than ethical. (He was pardoned by Ohio's governor on the manslaughter charges.)

The other passenger was the Reverend Al Sharpton, a Baptist minister from the largely Black and poor Brownsville, Brooklyn. Sharpton was said to have preached his first sermon at the age of four, and became a civil rights organizer working for the Reverend Jesse Jackson and Congresswoman Shirley Chisholm, who both sought the presidency. He then spent seven years as the singer James Brown's tour manager before returning to New York for an effort he had launched called the National Youth Movement. In 1981, Brown and Muhammad Ali brought Sharpton on Tom Snyder's national late-night talk show to anoint him as a leader in the modern civil rights era and to introduce him as a model for other young people. "He's about teaching them how to get out and fight for themselves," Brown said.

King and Sharpton had come to prominence in very different ways, but both would become iconic Black figures of the era, whose prevalence amid controversies made for frequent tabloid fodder.

When Sharpton climbed into the helicopter, a mobile palace of heavily lacquered wood-grain surfaces and gold-plated fixtures, he saw Trump and King sitting alongside each other, both facing forward.

Sharpton took a seat in a matching camel-leather chair across from them, and then watched as the pair talked nonstop, neither listening to the other, for the roughly forty-five-minute southbound flight.

When they reached Atlantic City, Trump called out for the pilot to circle around the Boardwalk. Suddenly Sharpton was the object of his attention. "I want to show you what I'm doing," Trump explained, drawing Sharpton's attention to the large rectangular picture windows by their sides. Gesturing to the urban landscape below, Trump proceeded to try to sell Sharpton on his successes in a city where he had first arrived just a half decade earlier. There was the Trump Plaza, he said, pointing. He said he had plans to buy another hotel constructed by the Hilton company, which would become the Trump Castle.

"You're lucky I'm not down here because I'd be organizing" against your plans, Sharpton said. King anticipated Trump's negative reaction and interjected, saying that Sharpton meant no offense. "He doesn't know you yet," King said to Trump.

Up to that point in his life, Trump had had few meaningful interactions with New Yorkers of color. When he was a child, in the decades after World War II, the city's segregated neighborhoods were cauldrons of bigotry and resentment, cleaved off into "us" versus "them." His childhood home in Jamaica Estates was just a seven-minute drive from Hollis,

Queens, which had primarily been settled by Black residents since after the Korean War, but the two may as well have been many miles apart. The borough was on its way to becoming one of the most racially and ethnically diverse places on earth, but Trump never appeared to value the unique multiculturalism of his surroundings.

Black people were not known to be part of Fred Trump's circle of influence, save for moments such as his attempt to hire Ed Brooke, the first Black man popularly elected to the U.S. Senate since the nineteenth century, to lobby a fellow Republican, the Department of Housing and Urban Development's Black secretary, Samuel Pierce, over an issue related to his projects. Fred Trump wanted Brooke to "cut through the red tape," a former colleague of Brooke recalled, and grew angry when the lobbyist refused to handle the matter in the way Fred demanded. Fred Trump disparaged him in racial terms. Brooke's colleague returned Fred Trump's check.

Donald himself spoke favorably about Black people who succeeded in entertainment or sports. But he would recount that Roy Cohn had advised him to hope for a Black judge, with the implication being that they could be manipulated, and associates recalled Trump musing about having Black judges preside over his cases. He told associates that one of his security guards disliked Black people and was aggressive when they got too close to Trump. (Trump called both statements false.) And he continued throughout his life to identify ethnic groups with the article "the," as in a 2011 radio interview in which he declared, "I have a great relationship with the Blacks." Over my years of reporting in New York City, Trump was the only political figure other than another Queens-born politician, Andrew Cuomo, I ever heard publicly use that specific phrase. It reflected not just a minimizing, reductive view but a transactional one: ethnic and racial groups were simply discrete units to be won over as allies in elections, or in real estate or zoning battles.

Trump publicly demonstrated little interest in the civil rights movement, though his college years coincided with one of the most intense and geographically widespread moments for race relations in our country's history. Decades of migration by Black people from the South to the North, the West, and the Midwest changed the demographic complexion of major cities such as New York and Philadelphia. White residents often reacted with resentment, with issues related to housing and policing the most common flash point. In July 1964, New York erupted in five days of riots that a Black leader called "New York's night of Birmingham horror," sparked by the shooting of a fifteen-year-old Black child by a white police officer on the Upper East Side. Riots inspired by incidents of police violence broke out the following month in North Philadelphia.

Just six weeks before Trump graduated from Wharton, Martin Luther King Jr. was assassinated, catalyzing a new round of riots in American cities.

But this time, Philadelphia was notably quiet. Many white residents credited the calm to a new police commissioner, Frank Rizzo, and the aggressive tactics his officers aimed at Black protesters. Trump would later adopt a phrase spoken at the time by Rizzo's counterpart in Miami—"When the looting starts, the shooting starts"—as his own.

Donald had returned from Wharton to a changed political landscape in New York. In a local concession to ascendant Black clout, Democratic politicians granted an electoral slot or two to candidates of color. That power was most prominently concentrated among a few Black officials from Harlem who became known as the Gang of Four—Percy Sutton, David Dinkins, Basil Paterson, and Charlie Rangel. "People in power who were white dealt with us on a transactional basis," Sharpton told me. "It was a segregated city that was always on the threshold of some kind of spark or incident that would bring that to light."

Trump experienced that racial tumult at a remove. When Tony Gliedman arrived at the Trump Organization in 1986, he insisted on bringing along his assistant at the city's housing agency, a young Jamaican immigrant named Jacqueline Williams. At the time, Trump was known to invoke stereotypes of Black people, such as laziness. Trump's assistant, Norma Foerderer, initially expressed anxiety at the suggestion of hiring Williams. Foerderer told Gliedman that they'd never had a Black person working on the executive floor, a comment that was later shared with Williams. Foerderer requested that Williams interview with her before she could join the staff. "Wow," Foerderer exclaimed when they met. "You're beautiful anyway, so you'll fit right in." Given little to do after an initial project in her first year there, Williams grew bored and left.

Trump's most sustained encounters with Black people came as he pushed beyond real estate and into the sports business. In 1983, Trump purchased a team in the newly established United States Football League, the New Jersey Generals. More than half of his roster was Black. Trump cultivated relationships with the players, most notably Herschel Walker, the Heisman Trophy winner whose decision to join the Generals from the University of Georgia gave the upstart league instant credibility. "For the first two weeks of the season Herschel simply wasn't being utilized," Trump later wrote in **The Art of the Deal.** "He'd call me up in my office, depressed, and say, 'Mr. Trump, I can run over these guys, if they'd just give me the ball.' I ranted and raved to our coach, Walt Michaels, but it wasn't until I literally threatened to fire him that he got the point."

Soon after Trump established his presence in Atlantic City, one of his executives encouraged him to host prizefights as a lure to guests, at a time when most of boxing's top stars were Black. It was in Atlantic City, too, that he was forced to contend with Black political power. Upon acquiring the rights to the Atlantic

City Convention Center Hall, adjacent to his Trump Plaza Casino and Hotel, Trump was worried that resistance from City Council members could interfere with his ability to continue building there. The city elected its first African American mayor in 1984. As Trump looked at the local elected officials he knew he would have to placate, Sharpton recalled, Don King told Sharpton that they had to meet.

For his part, according to Sharpton, King had another motive for connecting the two. He knew Sharpton had a relationship with the hottest young boxer in the country: eighteen-year-old Mike Tyson, who also hailed from Brownsville, and had made his professional fighting debut in March 1985 with a first-round knockout in Albany, New York. Trump would benefit if Sharpton could encourage Tyson to commit to a prizefight in Atlantic City.

The new proximity to Black athletes, celebrities, and political figures did little to change how Trump talked with people about race. Trump had seemed a largely oblivious bystander to so many of the social and cultural revolutions that defined the young-adult years of many of his peers. But as new opportunities pushed Trump beyond the lily-white milieu of his adolescence, his social ambitions pulled him from the facade of traditionalist domesticity that Fred Trump had erected in Jamaica Estates, and toward a world where sex seemed to be at the forefront of everything.

• • •

In the years that he was single, Trump reveled in the image of a sexually voracious man-about-town. He talked about sex frequently with associates. When he took women on dates, he made a point of doing so very visibly, often at events with lots of paparazzi on hand, and leaked word of his exploits to the gossip pages; some of the high-profile women he claimed to have relationships with, such as the former model Carla Bruni, later denied it.

Even after Trump married, he did not ease up on his constant talk about women, often with a clinical focus. The Trump Organization was notably progressive in its sector for the number of women in its executive ranks, but Trump still let routine conversation devolve into lurid detail. Nearly thirty years later, after more than a dozen allegations of sexual harassment emerged, as well as a tape of him talking with a TV host about grabbing women's genitals, Trump would call it "locker-room talk" and not indicative of who he was. But his discussion of people's looks and behavior in coarse detail was a constant through his adult life. Those who heard him speak were often struck by the fact that he appeared to be trying to shock. Trump was seated next to Tony Gliedman's wife and across the table from Ivana at a charity dinner in the late 1980s, when the conversation somehow turned to Brazilian women. "They have so much pussy hair," Trump said abruptly. Ginny Gliedman stared at him as he continued to talk about how much waxing they required, then looked across the way to see if Ivana had any reaction. If Ivana had heard her husband, she did not react.

Some former employees recalled him brandishing photos of scantily clad women with whom he claimed to have been involved. He appeared to keep the photos on hand to illustrate his boastful rendering of masculinity.

They also recalled Trump mocking gay men, or men who were seen as weak, with the words "queer" or "faggot." If someone gay was of use to Trump personally or for a business purpose, Trump appeared open to the person, but it did not exempt them from private scorn. In front of one openly gay executive, Trump was nothing but pleasant and accepting, even taking him and his husband for Florida weekend getaways on his private jet and calling the executive's husband for advice on orthodontia for Trump's children. Behind the executive's back, however, a former Trump Organization consultant named Alan Marcus said, Trump belittled him as a "queer" and bragged that he paid the executive less than he would have to otherwise because of it, a claim about compensation that appeared to be untrue.

The homophobia that had existed throughout the country for decades intensified around the AIDS virus. **The New York Times** carried its first, brief report of a RARE CANCER SEEN IN 41 HOMOSEXUALS, as the headline put it, in July 1981. The mysterious condition, which became known as AIDS, had what was at first an uncertain transmission but was identified as circulated through sexual contact and drug use. Yet for years polls showed Americans casting judgment on people who got infected. New York City became an epicenter of the disease. Ed Koch, who never married and whose sexuality was a source of speculation over his time in office—posters that cropped up during Koch's gubernatorial race against Mario Cuomo in 1982 read VOTE FOR CUOMO, NOT THE HOMO—was widely seen as late in trying to mobilize public awareness of the virus. A city's carefree attitude toward sex quickly turned dark, curtailing the greatest excesses of the club scene where Trump had once enjoyed being visible.

A country that was slow to react moved to action as the disease suddenly began impacting celebrities and heterosexuals. President Ronald Reagan made his first public reference to AIDS in 1985, years after it became an epidemic, and by which time panic about the virus was everywhere. Trump was plainly terrified of the disease, which seemed to elevate his fear of germs and illness to an almost pathological level. He told one friend after another that he wore two condoms to protect himself, and he announced publicly that he would require prospective dates to take an AIDS test. "It's one way to be careful. There are a lot of ways," he told an interviewer. "I'm saying, take all of those ways and double them, because you will need them."

Among straight New Yorkers, fear of AIDS also increased speculation about sexual orientation—musing about who might be gay and who wasn't, including about Koch—that was often homophobic in its effect. Trump was far from alone among prominent men in New York City experiencing some level of that panic, but for him, the anxiety was pronounced. He called reporters to inquire if people with whom he had just met might be gay, worried simply because they had just exchanged a handshake.

The guessing turned time and again to Roy Cohn, Trump's longtime guide to New York's power circuit. Cohn had never married, and often squired men around, and was known to have slept with some of them, but he also made efforts to pretend he dated women. He claimed to have proposed to Barbara Walters, and few spoke openly to him about his sexuality. When asked whether he was gay by journalist Ken Auletta, Cohn would not address the matter directly, but appeared to deny it. "Anybody who knows me, or knows anything about me, or who knows the way my mind works, would have an awfully hard time reconciling that with any kind of homosexuality. In other words, every facet of my personality, my aggressiveness, my toughness . . . is just totally incompatible with anything like that," he said. Cohn was immortalized in the Tony Kushner play **Angels in America** as a closeted gay man in the AIDS era who believed people were defined purely by how they wielded power. Cohn's homophobia was widely seen as something of a mask for his own sex life. Trump had insisted to some people who knew them both that he simply didn't believe his mentor was gay.

Starting in the early 1980s, Cohn began telling people he was sick, fighting liver cancer, steadfastly refusing to acknowledge that he had AIDS and had likely contracted it through sex with another man. He could not, however, deny that the disease was spreading around him. Cohn's friend Russell Eldridge had contracted the virus and was dying. Eldridge had been working out of Cohn's East Side town house, Cohn's former assistant, Susan Bell, said. "Cohn called Donald," she said, "and said we need a room for Russell, whom Donald knew." Trump helped place Eldridge in a hotel suite in an Upper East Side building he had recently acquired, the Barbizon Plaza, where he was cared for by nurses. But as always, there was the issue of who was paying. Bell remembered Norma Foerderer, reaching out to her about the billing for Eldridge's stay. "She called and said, 'Susan, we sent Roy bills for Russell's bills. He hasn't paid them.' I said, 'Guess what, Norma? He's not going to.' And she kind of knew it," Bell said. "And, he didn't."

Cohn spent his final year fighting in vain to keep his law license, against charges of improper conduct. (One allegation involved having coerced a senile, wealthy man, while on his deathbed, into signing papers that made Cohn the coexecutor of his estate.) Trump came to his defense in the disbarment hearings, a product of their lengthy relationship, but he had already started to seek his distance. "I can't believe he's doing this to me," Cohn told associates, according to Barrett.

Trump seemed to believe he did not need Cohn the way he once had. He had fully absorbed Cohn's key lessons, such as the one the lawyer once recounted to the columnist William Safire: "I bring out the worst in my enemies and that's how I get them to defeat themselves." Trump had established his own political profile and ties to elected officials, bolstered in large part by profligate campaign contributions. Once he decided it was prudent to develop a relationship with Manhattan district attorney Robert Morgenthau, who had tried to convict Cohn in the past, putting distance between himself and Cohn became even more advisable.

Cohn died in August 1986, less than two months after being disbarred. At a memorial service held at Town Hall in Midtown Manhattan, the eulogies ranged from deprecating to bitter. The luminaries in the crowd who felt a connection to Cohn were many: Beame was there, as were former Brooklyn Democratic Party boss Meade Esposito, makeup mogul Estée Lauder, and media magnate Rupert Murdoch. Looking out at the city's elite from the stage, businessman Bill Fugazy condemned the "whispering campaign" about Cohn's personal life.

Trump was not among the speakers. According to Barrett, he stood at the back of the room. "When Trump dumped him, he dumped him," Susan Bell said.

Two years after Cohn's death, Trump gave the commencement speech at Lehigh University in Bethlehem, Pennsylvania, a rolling campus with a sprawling sports complex, and his brother Freddie's alma mater. Upon collecting an honorary degree, Trump shared his wisdom with the class of 1988. "I could stand up here and talk for twenty minutes about how important" the parents of the graduates are, Trump said. "But I think we all know that. I really wanted to talk a little bit about the negative, and that's the obstacles, the obstacles in your way, in my way. But the obstacles. And you are going in and you're really one of the earliest group to go into a class, into a class of this world and get out there and fight a new obstacle, one which is just come on board and one which is probably going to be by the time it finishes, one of the great disasters, and that's AIDS."

Trump was not finished. "So many articles are written about me and they say, 'Donald Trump believes in the power of positive thinking,'" he explained. "The real fact is, I love positive thinking. But it can only get you in trouble, to a large extent. You've got to be aware of the downside, you've got to think negative."

The dynamics that defined New York City in the 1980s stayed with Trump for decades; he often seemed frozen in time there.

In the world of New York's broader racial politics, Trump was extreme, but not so completely out of sync with other whites—both the white ethnic working class of his native Queens and the elite of his adopted Upper East Side, who were perhaps less overt about expressing their prejudices—as to stand out glaringly in day-to-day conversations. Koch's relationships with some Black leaders were famously contentious, beginning with the closure of a hospital in Harlem and right into his final reelection campaign; he made controversial statements and then complained that Black leaders and voters reacted to them. "It's been my impression there is a lot of anti-Semitism amongst substantial numbers of black leaders—not all," Koch said during his 1985 reelection campaign, sparking a furious reaction. ("The Mayor's combative, 'let-Koch-be-Koch' approach to public life has long been simultaneously his greatest strength and his greatest source of vulnerability," wrote Joyce Purnick in **The New York Times** in 1985.)

Over time, the calcified racial politics of New York City began to loosen, transformed by demographic and cultural change, but Trump's own views did not seem to. As he built his Manhattan real estate empire, the "Fear City" moniker that public-sector union leaders had used to pressure City Hall a decade earlier had come to describe a city where crime rates had stayed historically high for ten years. There were nearly 2,000 murders in 1980 and 1981, and violent crime reports overall exceeded 180,000 both years. By the mid-1980s, New York was plagued by the crack cocaine epidemic. In the city, street crime exploded as users of the drug robbed people to pay for the next cheap hit. Tensions over crime and policing provoked a series of racial conflagrations with a uniquely New York character.

In 1984, a subway vigilante named Bernie Goetz shot four Black teenagers during what he claimed was an attempted mugging on a subway. Instead of being roundly rejected for the brutal act, Goetz found support among residents and indeed across the country. A majority of Americans supported what Goetz did, and locally, the **New York Post** applauded him. "The editors and reporters of this newspaper understand your anger and frustration," the paper's editorial writers wrote the day after the shooting. "We endure the same fear and anger that exploded in you Saturday."

Four and a half years after Goetz shot the four unarmed Black teens on the downtown Seventh Avenue Express subway train, Trisha Meili, a twenty-eight-year-old white woman, took a jog through Central Park after getting home from work. Elsewhere that evening were about thirty Black and Latino teenagers roaming the park together, taunting the homeless and harassing people riding by on bicycles. Meili, a banker at the Wall Street firm Salomon Brothers, was found sometime around midnight in a ravine near 102nd Street, her body savagely beaten and raped. She was rushed to a hospital, where doctors tried to save her life, unsure if that would be possible.

The NYPD arrested eight teenagers and indicted six in connection with the crime. All were Black or Latino and under the age of seventeen. Kevin Richardson, Yusef Salaam, Raymond Santana, Korey Wise, and Antron McCray became instant household names in New York City; the press called them the Central Park Five. Relying on confessions that police said they had extracted from the teenagers, Koch decried them, comparing the crime's gruesomeness to the film **A Clockwork Orange,** in which a marauding gang in England commits depraved acts of pure nihilism. Newspapers editorialized about the act's utter callousness. Meili, known only as the "Central Park Jogger," received support from celebrities such as Frank Sinatra, who sent her flowers. The case broke through the local crime blotter to win national media attention, a symbol of urban rot.

Trump saw in the backlash an opportunity for media attention for himself. Twelve days after the attack, he placed a full-page ad in all four major New York papers. BRING BACK THE DEATH PENALTY. BRING BACK OUR POLICE! read the giant-typeface headline on the ad. Trump built his ad copy around a lament for a bygone culture of law and order whose brutality he glamorized. "When I was young, I sat in a diner with my father and witnessed two young bullies cursing and threatening a very frightened waitress," he claimed in the ad. "Two cops rushed in, lifted up the thugs and threw them out the door, warning them never to cause trouble again. I miss the feeling of security New York's finest once gave to the citizens of this City."

Police, Trump said, needed to be let loose. "Unshackle them from the constant chant of 'police brutality' which every petty criminal hurls immediately at an officer who has just risked his or her life to save another's. We must cease our continuous pandering to the criminal population of this City." The primary target of Trump's ire was Koch, who had instructed citizens not to carry "hate and rancor" in their hearts. "I want to hate these muggers and murderers," the ad continued. "They should be forced to suffer and, when they kill, they should be executed for their crimes. They must serve as examples so that others will think long and hard before committing a crime or an act of violence. Yes, Mayor Koch, I want to hate these murderers and I always will. I am not looking to psychoanalyze or understand them, I am looking to punish them."

It was as clear a guiding ethos for his life as Trump seemed to have: hate should be a civic good. He sat with a handful of reporters to underscore his message that hate could be a uniting force for the city. "You better believe that I hate the people that took this girl and raped her brutally," he said. "I want society to hate them."

The case increased Trump's visibility as a commentator on topics well outside his area of business expertise. On CNN's **Larry King Live,** he spoke about what he characterized as the weakness of policing tactics, a subject that did not at all relate to the specifics of the Central Park Jogger case. (On air, Trump scooted back from King and said he found the host's breath to be unbearable.) "The problem we have is we don't have any protection for the policeman," Trump said. "The problem with our society is that the victim has absolutely no rights and the criminal has unbelievable rights, unbelievable rights, and I say it has to stop."

Trump was hardly the lone voice furious about the crime, or even the lone voice demanding swift justice. (Some white liberals, living in a terrified city that had seen record crime increases over more than a decade, agreed with Trump's general sentiment more than they would be comfortable admitting publicly.) But none called for brutality in response quite as Trump did. **New York Newsday** columnist Thomas Collins called Trump's ad "high-priced graffiti" for which the city's media outlets were rewarding him with attention. Collins spotted a tic in Trump's style of argumentation, one that became a hallmark of his public commentary on controversial topics: walking right up to the line of saying something transgressive but stopping just short of articulating it directly, so as to make it hard for anyone to pin him down. "True to his ilk, Trump appeared to be saying one thing in the ad—kill the kids—while leaving room to weasel out of it if pressed. That is what he did on one of the news shows the other night," Collins wrote. "Since some of the kids involved in the attack are 14 and 15 years old, it might appear too bloodthirsty of him to demand the death penalty outright, as would happen in more barbarous lands. So he half denied that was his intention. Yet the ad dwells at length on 'roving bands of wild criminals' who 'rape a helpless woman and laugh at her family's anguish.' So there is not much doubt who he had in mind, disclaimers to the contrary."

Years later, officials acknowledged what the teens said soon after the confessions: that their words had been coerced during police interrogations. The convictions were vacated in 2002, after a new confession, supported by DNA evidence, identified an entirely different perpetrator. The men had all completed their sentences by that point. They had lost their youth and a good part of their adulthood. Yet even then, Trump refused to back away from his 1989 comments.

The same year as the Central Park assault, Trump appeared on an NBC News special focused on race relations, along with other guests including the filmmaker Spike Lee, poet Maya Angelou, home-entertaining celebrity Martha Stewart, and conservative commentator Pat Buchanan. The guests were asked to speak about affirmative-action policies and their impact on economic opportunity in the United States. "A well-educated Black has a tremendous advantage over a well-educated white in terms of the job market," said Trump, whose father's connections and money shaped nearly every aspect of his career. "And, I think, sometimes a Black may think that they don't really have the advantage or this or that but in actuality today, currently, it's, uh, it's a, it's a great.

I've said on occasion, even about myself, if I were starting off today I would love to be a well-educated Black because I really believe they do have an actual advantage today."

Lee, whose recent film **Do The Right Thing** portrayed the era's block-by-block racial strife in his native Brooklyn, was in shock. "Well, I certainly don't agree with that garbage that Donald Trump said, that if he could be reborn or reincarnated, he'd want to come back as an educated Black, because we start off . . ." his voice drifted off. "I didn't believe he said that, that's crazy."

Four months later, a Black teenager named Yusef Hawkins was chased and killed by a mob of as many as thirty white attackers as he visited the heavily white, Italian Bensonhurst section of Brooklyn in the hopes of buying a used car. "Let's club the [expletive] n**$er," witnesses heard one of the attackers say. In the days after the murder, a group of 300 Black people marched through Bensonhurst, led in part by Sharpton. "N**$ers go home," the white residents called out to the marchers. "Central Park, Central Park!" was another chant from the white residents, referring to the case from which the city was still reeling. Some held up watermelons. "You couldn't get any uglier scene than this in Mississippi," Sharpton said at the time.

Three months after Hawkins's killing, New York elected David Dinkins as its first Black mayor. He beat out Giuliani, the candidate whom Trump had backed until it became clear he was likely to lose. The coalition that elected Dinkins, then the Manhattan borough president and a veteran of the city's clubhouse politics, was the first in city history that successfully united Black and Latino voters, along with Upper West Side white liberals and Jewish voters. In his inaugural address, Dinkins celebrated "New York as a gorgeous mosaic of race and religious faith, of national origin and sexual orientation."

Giuliani, who painted himself as an outsider shaking up the system, did not go quietly. After narrowly losing by roughly fifty thousand votes, he complained bitterly that he had been cheated by a shadowy "they" who supported the Black mayor. "They stole that election from me," he told journalist Jack Newfield in 1992. "They stole votes in the Black parts of Brooklyn, and in Washington Heights." City officials investigated claims of fraud that year but never produced anything to suggest they were substantiated.

While crime rates began to shrink at the end of Dinkins's four-year term, it did not come quickly enough for many of the city's voters. DAVE, DO SOMETHING! the **New York Post** front page cried out in September 1990. A series of localized eruptions gave life to the **Post**'s depiction of a "crime-ravaged city." The next year, three days of riots pitted Blacks against Orthodox Jews in the Brooklyn neighborhood of Crown Heights, after a Hasidic driver killed a seven-year-old Black child and a crowd of Black men stabbed and killed a visiting Orthodox man from Australia as retaliation. The relationship between Dinkins and the mostly white NYPD curdled after police killed a man in northern Manhattan in July 1992, leading to violent riots across Washington Heights.

When Dinkins proposed an independent civilian agency to review complaints against police, thousands of off-duty officers swarmed City Hall for what had been described as a rally. By the time they stormed the Brooklyn Bridge it had clearly become a riot. Among those addressing the crowd was Giuliani, well into his effort to challenge Dinkins in a 1993 rematch. His suit jacket off, Giuliani mocked Dinkins's uncertainty about the sources of poor morale in the police department. "He blames it on me. He blames it on you," Giuliani bellowed into a microphone. "Bullshit!" He went on, "The reason the morale of the police department in the city of New York is so low is one reason and one reason alone: David Dinkins!" The crowd roared. "Take the hall!" some cried, banging on the windows of the seat of city government. One of the officers called a Black city councilwomen trying to enter the building, Una Clarke, a "n**$er." The following year, Giuliani's coalition largely held, and voters moved to his column as well. The city's politics were cleaved along racial lines, and would stay that way for many years.

This was the period when Trump first somewhat seriously entertained running for office himself. From the outset, it was clear that he would incorporate racial paranoia into his public persona and his views of civic life. The first time I saw Trump after he left office, in an interview for this book, I asked him how he thought racial politics in New York were different than in the rest of the country. "I think they're more severe," he replied. When I asked in what way, he said only, "I don't know why. I think it's more severe. I think it's a tougher game." He added, "Racial is more severe in New York than it is anywhere else that I can think of."

That was the lens through which Trump seemed to view the entire country, if not the world: tribal conflict was inevitable. One day in the 1990s, Alan Marcus brought up a news item he had just seen about the changing demographics of the United States, projecting that nonwhites would one day be the majority population, intentionally trying to get a rise out of Trump by raising a subject he knew would needle him.

That won't happen, Trump said. First, he insisted, there would be a revolution. "This isn't going to become South Africa," he said.

Like Trump, Sharpton emerged during the 1980s as a permanent fixture of the city's political life and a nationally recognized symbol of New York. He was best known for his 1987 advocacy of Tawana Brawley, a teenage girl from upstate New York who claimed to have been brutalized and left in a trash bag, smeared with feces. Sharpton helped lead the effort to denounce the county prosecutor in the case, Steven Pagones, whom Sharpton and Brawley alleged was one of the attackers. Pagones eventually won a defamation case against them. Even after the Brawley case fell apart, Sharpton for years refused to apologize. "What do I have to apologize for? I believed her," Sharpton said in 2013, saying he regretted "name-calling" and that it changed his approach to his role.

Sharpton and Trump would in some ways prove to be mirror images of each other: outer-borough players who muscled their way into headlines and, albeit in different timeframes, into new, more glamorous lives. Both had redefined themselves in Manhattan and refused to be thrown out of their new ring, no matter how much antipathy they drew from different segments of the city's establishment. While Sharpton and Trump did not become friends, they repeatedly interacted over decades, until an extensive rupture after the 2016 presidential campaign.

Trump's relationships with King and Tyson ultimately proved more durable. Despite the conflict of interest in representing someone whose fights were held at his casinos, Trump eventually wrangled his way to becoming a paid adviser to Tyson, before Tyson began to rely more heavily on King instead. Tyson at one point accused Trump of sleeping with Tyson's wife, the actress Robin Givens, a story Trump told over the years to different people. ("Think I could take him?" Trump asked a stunned associate.) Trump stood by the boxer when he was jailed for a rape conviction. At one point, he interrupted a Trump Tower office meeting with a Manhattan planning official to phone Tyson and ask, clearly to show off to his guest, "Champ, did you rape her?"

A year after he was released from prison in March 1995, Tyson moved into a new mansion in Farmington, Connecticut, an upscale suburb of Hartford. When Sharpton arrived for a party there, he followed a winding staircase to a terrace overlooking the pool, where he found Don King chatting with Trump. The topic of their discussion: Tyson's white neighbors were petitioning to get him out of the community, and they were speculating about how much money Tyson could demand from them if he obliged by moving out.

"When Trump got elected, that's what occurred to me: if Donald Trump had been born Black, he would have been Don King," Sharpton said. "Because both of them—everything was transactional."

CHAPTER 5

On the Way Up

Some mornings, Donald Trump would exit the side-street residential entrance to Trump Tower and, instead of getting into his car, would turn right and walk a half block to the corner of Fifth Avenue. Then he would stand there, amid the streams of commuters, shoppers, and tourists, beneath the glistening tower with his name on it.

When people passed, Trump planted himself near them, peering into their faces to see if they recognized him. Sometimes they did not, perhaps seeing just another oddball crowding a Midtown sidewalk. But sometimes they did. For a man who swore off smoking and alcohol, this was the best possible narcotic. It was not as explicit an appeal for validation as Mayor Ed Koch's famous routine of asking, "How'm I doin'?" to residents as they entered and exited the subway, but it derived from a comparable impulse. Trump wanted feedback, affirmation, proof not just that he was on his way to stardom, but that he had arrived.

In the 1980s, Trump graduated from being a locally prominent businessman to a nationally recognizable figure who bridged the worlds of finance, entertainment, and politics. It was not merely his ego that was satisfied by discovering an audience that did not know the name Fred Trump, let alone see his son as an extension of him; Donald's appetite for attention was satisfied by it too. Over a few years, Trump's new fame would manufacture business opportunities and personal ambitions unimaginable for him at the start of the decade, and which he would eventually struggle to manage.

Yet Trump was still dogged with an unfulfilled obsession with building on the Upper West Side of Manhattan. It had nagged at him since he began his effort to acquire the northern tract of rail yards from Penn Central's bankruptcy. While long-term planning was not in him, Trump was well versed in the habit of obsessive thought, a continued private focus on something from which others had long ago moved on. In the case of the rail yards, the hope for a chance to win back control after he let the option expire in 1979 stayed with him.

Three years later, the opportunity presented itself. Developer Abe Hirschfeld's purchase of the option had done little to brush Trump away from it; if anything, he saw the fact that control of the site had gone to a parking-garage magnate friendly with his father to be a positive outcome. In 1980, Hirschfeld sold a controlling stake and management control to

Francisco Macri, an Argentine developer with a record of successful public-works projects in his home country. But neither Macri nor Hirschfeld had the local pull to push through what they envisioned as a series of condos called Lincoln West.

As Macri found himself unable to move forward with the project, Trump came back to him several times between 1982 and 1984. Macri later described a sensation of being not just ground down by Trump, but looked down on by him. "He spoke as if I did not have experience and that I had only built bridges and dams, when in reality I had constructed many more millions of cubic meters in housing than Donald Trump will construct in his lifetime," Macri said to Barrett later. "He spoke as if I was a South American banana farmer. I wasn't a dummy, and he was very young."

By December 1984, after agreeing to a price of $95 million, Trump had his prized option on the land back, calling the large cluster of undeveloped acres the "greatest piece of land in urban America." At a press conference the next year, held at the revamped Commodore Hotel, Trump explained that he intended to create not just a new building, but an entirely new neighborhood. Television City would feature a 150-story triangular tower serving as the hub of a sprawling complex of retail shops, apartments, and broadcast studios. It was not Trump's first effort to build something he could brand the "world's tallest," but unlike a previous attempt in Lower

Manhattan, here he had a vast, untouched section of the island whose underuse had vexed city officials for decades. "The television industry desperately needs in this city large spread-out space," he told reporters as the cameras clicked. "The New York City dream is having this development, and we plan to build it."

Trump's pitch to create a city within a city came at a moment of heightened fear in the five boroughs. The murder rate was still relatively high, and even after the country emerged from the economic recession of the early 1980s, New York was still finding its financial footing. If anything, the gap between the haves and the have-nots in the city grew during a decade when Wall Street was glorified and the chase for wealth was an ideal.

Trump more than anyone became a public symbol of that greed, that consumption. He was happy to show off as a Successful Man, despite a comparatively light record. His new plans for the rail yards matched his desire for dramatic flair with a newfound sense of grandiosity. "The West Side development," **The New York Times** editorial page observed, "is his bid for immortality."

The Trump projects that actually came to fruition were often less ambitious. For as long as Trump Tower had been occupied, the northwesterly view from his twenty-sixth floor corner office included a glaring eyesore. In 1980, Wollman Rink, a compact city-run ice-skating facility that had stood for years as one of Central Park's beloved attractions, was closed down for what was supposed to be a two-and-a-half-year renovation costing $9.1 million. But the project sprawled well beyond both estimates, as construction produced one debacle after another, including a new refrigeration system that sprang leaks.

After the city forecast in 1986 yet another two years to complete the project, Trump decided to offer himself up as the answer to the city's problems, promising to accomplish a job that its bureaucrats could not. It would not require complex design expertise or a major engineering feat. The chance to redo the rink could supply endless free publicity, with the added bonus of upstaging Koch.

Trump's guide to the Koch administration was its former housing commissioner, Tony Gliedman, who steered him through drafts of a "Dear Ed" letter expressing interest in taking over the project. (After a first draft, which Gliedman found unserious, he recalled to a friend that he had asked Trump, "Donald, if I were Ed Koch, and I got this letter, do you think I would be predisposed to having you do the project?") "Building the Wollman Skating Rink, which essentially involves the pouring of a concrete slab, should take no more than four months time," Trump wrote on May 28. In exchange for completing construction, Trump asked for the rights to operate the rink, insisting he could transform it into a profitable venture.

Even as some city officials were perplexed as to why

Trump appeared to want something so small bore, Koch was receptive to the offer. He set conditions: he did not want Trump running the facility, and wanted to keep Trump from renaming it after himself. (In his letter to Trump, Koch had written: "Remember the Bible says that those who give charity anonymously or, if not anonymously, then without requiring the use of their names, are twice blessed.") Trump let go of his demand to operate the rink and assured Koch it would keep its name. Discussions moved forward.

With Gliedman, Trump headed to Lower Manhattan for meetings with city officials to iron out the details of the agreement. Trump wanted to pay for the construction work himself, something that would have given him an entry point to claim the rink was his. Koch rejected that idea; instead, they agreed that the city would fund those expenses. Riding back to Trump Tower from meetings with the city officials, Trump was like a child, seeking affirmation. He repeatedly asked Gliedman a single question: "Do you think they liked me?"

The Wollman Rink was just one of the projects for which Trump put to use a former city official. Trump also hired as his general counsel Susan Heilbron, a former Koch administration commissioner who had an array of contacts. Heilbron and Gliedman were both taken aback, after joining what appeared on the outside to be a major business, to discover how slapdash Trump's operations actually were. He made plans and then changed them in an instant, and put one official in charge of a project only to have that person discover he had also tasked someone else with the same job. Trump's tirades often interfered with productivity. He was abusive to Gliedman, haranguing him over new projects and calling him a "fat fuck" in front of other people. For Barbara Res, executive vice president in charge of construction, a significant problem was that she worked in the area Trump understood best—which meant she got intense attention from the boss and often felt the brunt of his aggression. Trump seemed to enjoy fostering conflict between Res and Ivana over the Atlantic City projects. Among themselves, company executives referred to the firm as the Trump Disorganization.

The Wollman Rink deal was announced by Koch in June 1986, with Trump's promise of completion by December. In the end, Koch had recognized that Trump was able to operate outside the city processes that were far more cumbersome than what private developers faced. When Koch refused to grant him outright a contract to operate the rink and attached restaurant, Trump made clear he would submit bids to win one.

Trump's reasons for so aggressively pursuing the rink project became clear as soon as he started summoning the press to watch the progress. Trump held more than a half dozen press conferences related to the rink in roughly six months. It didn't matter that there was little actual news value to them—one revealed a new Zamboni that would resurface the ice—or even that some drew only a small number of cameras. The press conferences were about trumpeting this as a civic-minded endeavor that highlighted Trump's ability to do what the city could not. Ahead of one press conference, New York City Parks Department commissioner Henry J. Stern received an invitation to attend from one of Trump's outside publicists. "Thank you for inviting me to my park," he replied. Once Stern arrived at the rink for one of the media events to discover a sign listing: OWNER: TRUMP ICE INC. He ordered officials to take it down and put up a new one that made clear that the rink belonged to the city.

Trump could not have cared less about the emotions of government officials. His name was at the center of every good-news story about an iconic city location, and he was being credited for its turnaround. It more than offset the negative coverage he had received about an apartment building on the other side of Central Park South, where Trump worked with remarkable creativity over several years to force out residents so he could raze the structure and build a new one on the site. He allegedly forced tenants to use the service elevator, cut off heat and water during winter months, and placed newspaper ads suggesting empty apartments could be used to shelter the homeless. "Some people think I'm just doing a number on the people in the building," he claimed to **The New York Times.** "That's not true. I just want to help with the homeless problem."

Trump's contractors completed their work on the

rink by November, a month ahead of the arbitrary schedule Trump had set. At a ceremony to celebrate its reopening, Trump was joined by Olympic skaters, the mayor and other city officials, and representatives from HRH Construction, the firm he had challenged for control of the West Side rail yards but then hired for the Wollman project. But it was immediately clear that he planned to claim all the credit for the successful completion of the rink himself. He did not give Koch much attention in his remarks at the ceremony. Nor did he mention HRH Construction or other contractors. Art Nusbaum, then the head of HRH, stopped working with Trump after the display of narcissism. "He can't have two people standing on the podium. He can't have somebody even getting the silver and the bronze," Nusbaum said later. "He's gotta get the gold, the silver, and the bronze all at one time."

There was another political force ascendant on the horizon—one potentially useful to Trump at the time, and with whom he would develop a decades-long connection that ultimately defined the later years of both their lives.

Rudy Giuliani had been born two years before Trump, to a barkeep father in East Flatbush, Brooklyn, a neighborhood heavily populated by Italian immigrants. He later attended Catholic school and considered becoming a priest. He chose law school instead and, after leaving the Democratic Party, found his way into Ronald Reagan's Justice Department. He served as associate attorney general, the third-highest department official, and then maneuvered to win an appointment as U.S. attorney for the Southern District in New York. The Manhattan-based district is home to the highest-profile federal prosecutor in the country, whose prominent cases can be a launching pad for a career in elected office.

Giuliani, who had crafted a personal brand of moral rectitude, would bust Wall Street executives for insider trading, but really made his name by cracking down on the Mafia, targeting the heads of all five organized-crime families in New York. He made frequent use of the "perp walk," parading people whom he'd indicted before the news cameras after they were arrested, a tactic that even some of his supporters considered overkill.

Even before Koch was sworn in for his third term in January 1986, Giuliani's investigators had dug deeply into city government, and Koch's allies outside it. They started by looking into claims of corruption at the Parking Violations Bureau, but within eight weeks of the inauguration their probe had blossomed into a baroque scandal involving kickbacks and rigged contracts that well-connected political officials used to enrich themselves.

Giuliani's biggest trophy was Stanley Friedman, the former Bronx Democratic boss and law partner to Roy Cohn, who had helped with approval of Trump's

Commodore project. In November 1986, Friedman was found guilty, along with three others, of violating the Racketeer Influenced and Corrupt Organizations Act. Giuliani said he found their conviction "heartwarming." "This verdict is a very significant victory for the honest and decent citizens of New York City, who have had to labor under the yoke of people like Stanley Friedman for too darn long," he said. He called for Friedman to step down from his party post. Friedman did so roughly a week later, but he helped pick his successor. "It's outrageous that a man who's been convicted of racketeering remain in political office." Friedman went to prison on a twelve-year sentence. Associates of Friedman had always believed Trump gave financial support to Friedman's family while he was in prison. When I asked Trump about this, he replied, "Stanley was a good man with great courage."

Not long thereafter, one of Giuliani's investigators was asked whether he might like to learn more about Donald Trump. The offer came from a lawyer representing a corrupt mortgage broker named Frank LaMagra, whom federal prosecutors in Brooklyn had charged with forging a tax return for a Bonanno family captain named Louie "Ha Ha" Attanasio. After LaMagra's conviction, he hoped to avoid jail by offering information to prosecutors.

A few years earlier, LaMagra had helped a man named Robert Hopkins purchase a Trump Tower duplex while the building was still under construction.

Hopkins had no legitimate source of income, yet he managed to secure a mortgage in part based on a letter from Roy Cohn's firm that invoked Trump's name. (Hopkins was said to have brought a suitcase with more than one hundred thousand dollars in cash to the closing.) In 1986, while living in the apartment, Hopkins was arrested for running a gambling ring and for a gangster's murder; the murder charge was thrown out.

LaMagra's lawyer, a former prosecutor named Michael Pollack, claimed to Giuliani's office that the Hopkins arrest was a window into other illicit financial activity at Trump Tower. His client had details to share, Pollack said, provided he was given a deal to cooperate that would end his jail time.

The entire story still remains hazy. Investigator Anthony Lombardi would confirm to Wayne Barrett that he questioned Trump and claimed that Trump had delivered satisfactory answers. Lombardi also told Barrett that he briefed both Giuliani and his deputies on the matter, and that he found LaMagra not to be credible. No formal case was ever opened. Shortly after his interview with Lombardi, according to Barrett, Trump publicly said he could raise significant donations for Giuliani's first campaign for elected office.

When I spoke with LaMagra's lawyer Pollack years later, he said that Lombardi, who had since passed away, told him directly that the U.S. Attorney's Office wasn't going to follow the information. The reason, he explained, was that Giuliani was planning to run for mayor the following year and did not want to alienate Trump, who could be an influential fundraiser. And Lombardi seemed to benefit from the encounter with Trump: within months, he received tickets to see Mike Tyson box in Atlantic City and was telling associates that Trump had hinted at hiring him to be head of security.

There are other reasons that Giuliani may have chosen not to pursue a case, such as doubting a tale from a convicted felon. But the notion that a prosecutor obsessed with chasing the Mafia appears to have done little to follow a lead about possible money laundering was a reminder that politically connected figures in New York often were immune to scrutiny. Whatever the reason the tip went nowhere, Trump ended up backing Giuliani when he unsuccessfully ran for mayor in 1989.

Trump continued to cultivate Manhattan's other prosecutor too. Trump for years supported Robert Morgenthau's pet charitable cause. Over time, a member of one of Trump's private clubs recalled seeing Morgenthau there, and Trump would open his Trump Tower apartment to host a campaign fundraiser. According to their associates, both men were at peace with the mostly transactional nature of the relationship.

Elsewhere in Manhattan, Trump continued to try to push Koch to back his most ambitious project

yet, Television City. The key to its success was luring
NBC to be a featured tenant in the new neighborhood. The broadcast network was ready to abandon
its Rockefeller Center home for either new or re-
furbished space elsewhere, but the Trump proposal
had to compete with other opportunities, including
a move to New Jersey, where taxes would be lower.
City Hall would have to help give NBC a reason
to stay in New York for Trump's West Side dreams to
become reality.

The three sides began what would be years of formal
and informal discussions. NBC executives wanted to
guarantee their rent would stay at a certain range,
and in order to do that, Trump said he required a tax
abatement from the city. But he did not want one
just for the nine acres that NBC would be occupy-
ing; he demanded it cover the full site. Koch resisted
this, because it would be seen as a huge giveaway
to a wealthy developer, the type of move the politically imperiled Koch was trying to avoid. "You and
your immediate staff's total lack of cooperation will
make it impossible for NBC to build in New York,"
Trump wrote the mayor in a private letter.

Stories began appearing in the press about Trump's
plans for NBC, offering a suspiciously rosy assessment of the developer's ideas. City Hall officials
believed Trump had planted the stories to increase
the pressure on Koch and shift blame to him should
NBC flee to New Jersey. To fight back, the mayor's
office released private correspondence in which the

developer had accused Koch of refusing a deal simply because Trump would profit. Trump responded by calling Koch a "moron" to reporters.

Koch responded with a City Hall press conference in which he explained his rationale for opposing the tax break: Trump's request would essentially be unfair to the companies that had already agreed to remain in New York. He also read aloud praise from Trump, made just before the "moron" comment. "Will the real Donald Trump please stand up?" Koch asked.

Trump accused Koch of trying to milk the situation to squeeze more money out of him. "They sat around for four days, scratching their heads, saying, 'Maybe we can get more,'" Trump said. "Then I wrote a strong letter to Koch, saying I wanted to move on this. Then what happened is that Koch takes this deal and throws NBC over to New Jersey in order to make a preemptive strike on me."

The insults went back and forth. Koch called Trump a "lightweight," a pejorative Trump later began to use himself to dismiss critics. Other than having called Koch a moron, Trump, still relatively new to the art of public insults, could only muster that Koch was capable of mere "Henny Youngman one-liners, but Henny Youngman does them better."

People tried to comprehend Trump's public tantrum, assuming he was planning to run for mayor himself, because little else about attacking people who controlled the fate of his project made sense if the businessman was serious about getting a deal. Koch didn't buy that theory. "I believe it's his personality, so there's no excuse," Koch said. Trump, he explained, was "greedy, greedy, greedy" and "piggy, piggy, piggy."

Koch was a decades-long public servant, and aspects of his worldview were quite different from Trump's. Years later, when Trump began his own political career, it became clear how much of Koch's style he had absorbed. But at that moment, Trump was less focused on brinkmanship for the sake of it than on his own growing financial pressure and his lack of an anchor tenant for his unbuilt site.

In January 1987, Trump received a letter from the Soviet ambassador to Washington. "It is a pleasure for me to relay some good news from Moscow," it began, according to Trump's account. The "good news" was that Goscomintourist, the Soviet Union's state agency for international tourism, was interested in collaborating with Trump on a joint project, building and managing a hotel in Moscow.

Trump was already beginning to get serious notice beyond his hometown, stoked by the perception of his acumen, not just in the construction trade but in business more broadly. In 1982, he appeared toward the bottom among real estate developers on the first-ever Forbes 400 list of the country's wealthiest people, alongside his father as a coequal in the family business. Over the next two years, Roy Cohn and Trump himself, posing as a publicist at times and making false claims about the business's worth and his stake in it, tried to push himself further up the list. In 1985, Trump made his first appearance alone, with Fred dropping off. That same year, he purchased Mar-a-Lago, the sprawling Palm Beach estate and historic landmark built by cereal heiress Marjorie Merriweather Post. A few years later he would purchase a superyacht for $29 million that had previously been owned by Saudi arms dealer Adnan Khashoggi. During that period, he launched a condominium project in West Palm Beach, Florida, whose investors included automotive executive Lee Iacocca, the country's most well-known corporate boss. In an effort to expand his footprint in the gambling industry, Trump sought a Nevada gaming license and began buying up shares of other casino operators, including Bally, Resorts International, and Holiday Corp., which also managed the Holiday Inn chain. The maneuvers helped to define Trump in national business media not merely as an accomplished builder but a "takeover artist," as **The Wall Street Journal** called him in 1987.

While some news stories took note of his propensity for exaggeration and, in some cases, his failure to fully meet commitments, such as barely attending meetings for the New York Vietnam Memorial Commission to which he had been appointed, those were usually not the dominant themes. Two years after some of his big moves to acquire Bally and Holiday stock, the Federal Trade Commission filed charges that Trump had violated federal law by failing to report some of the trades. He claimed he had been assured by "well-respected lawyers" that he didn't have to report the trades at the time, but he agreed to pay a $750,000 fine to avoid a civil suit for up to twice as much and admitted no wrongdoing. It received relatively little press coverage.

When, in October 1987, global stock exchanges experienced their biggest-ever one-day decline in value, Trump rushed to tell reporters that he had cleared $175 million in profit by having pulled his money out of the market before it collapsed. Everyone seemed to take him at his word. As the world wondered whether it was on the cusp of another Great Depression, Trump managed to make headlines about his investing savvy: BAIL-OUT MADE TRUMP MILLIONS (**New York Post**) and EARLY SELL-OFFS LEAVE TRUMP IN THE BLACK (**Press of Atlantic City**). "Premonition, luck, call it what you want, I had very negative instincts about the stock market, a feeling that things were not going to go well for the country," he explained to a **New York Times** reporter. On the day of the crash, **The Wall Street Journal** published two distinctly different accounts from Trump. "I sold all my stock over the last month," Trump was quoted as saying in one story, while insisting in the other that "I haven't played the market for the last couple of months." In fact, subsequent filings with federal regulators showed that rather than having sold out of one of his largest holdings—Alexander's, a struggling chain of New

York–based department stores in which he already owned around 20 percent of shares—Trump spent Black Monday buying up more.

Some reporters acknowledged privately over time that they knew Trump lied a lot, and yet for years many of his statements ran unchecked in print and on television. The impulse for reporters to give a subject the benefit of the doubt, and the difficulty in disproving some of his claims, gave way to so many "How does he do it, folks!" types of stories about his supposed business prowess that they can't easily be tallied. Trump's own staff were mesmerized too. Many became unwitting characters in the news stories painting him as a man of purpose. Res, Heilbron, and another top Trump Organization executive named Blanche Sprague were photographed with Trump for a cover story in **Savvy Woman** magazine. He was among the few chief executives putting so many women in top roles at the time, and the magazine became a campaign talking point years later. Many of his executives, male and female, were exhausted by him, and fascinated by the extent of his lying, and even disgusted by it, but they marveled at his willingness to come up with grand schemes and to try to bend others to his will.

That included an unending series of feints, teases, and stunts. Not long after completing the Wollman Rink renovation, Trump offered to repair the decaying Williamsburg Bridge that linked Manhattan and Brooklyn, which he made a show of inspecting with a local state assemblyman in a visit "heavily promoted by his public relations staff," as the **Times** described it. "It's a very, very important artery in this city and certain things fascinate me. This fascinates me," Trump told a reporter. "The Wollman Rink fascinated me. It was closed for seven years, almost seven years and somehow it captured my imagination. This captures my imagination." That "send me" attitude belied the fact that Trump privately hoped that he would not be picked, well aware he lacked the experience necessary to pull off a large public-works project. But he had found a way to get coverage not only for the things he had done but those he only said he could do.

The national media was beginning to learn what New York journalists already knew: there was something magnetic about Trump. It wasn't simply that his instinct for colorful drama made for good copy. He was mesmerizing to watch, his speech fast and cocky and self-assured, with the ability to be both funny and cutting, both charming and derisive, often in the same sentence. He drew viewers: people either liked him or liked to hate him. News outlets, in that decade and in the years after, often treated Trump as if he were born anew with every story, his previous misdeeds or misstatements or lies basically washed away.

No story had more of an impact than a 1984 profile in **GQ,** which put him on the cover with a cherubic portrait and the line: "Success: How Sweet It Is; Men Who Take Risks and Make Millions." The issue sold so well for the men's magazine that S. I. Newhouse, the media mogul who controlled both **GQ**'s parent company, Condé Nast, and book publisher Random House, took notice. The article had treated Trump as a curiosity—"to the gray world of New York real estate," writer Graydon Carter observed, "Trump has infused a brand of freewheeling self-aggrandizement"—but Newhouse believed readers might want real business guidance from him. He offered Trump a book deal.

Even as Trump eagerly asked aides to relay information from newspaper headlines, including whether his name was mentioned, he had never shown much interest in books. A cabinet next to his bedside contained a book that Ivana later said she saw him occasionally leafing through: an anthology of Adolf Hitler's speeches called **My New Order.** ("It was my friend Marty Davis from Paramount who gave me a copy of **Mein Kampf,** and he's a Jew," Trump claimed when pressed about it by journalist Marie Brenner. Davis, however, said that he was not Jewish and gave Trump the book **My New Order** because he thought he would find it "interesting.")

Trump accepted Newhouse's offer and made the rare acknowledgment that writing his story was something he was incapable of doing on his own. He hired a collaborator, a young writer named Tony Schwartz. The book described Trump's typical day, his interactions, and his approach to business. It was Schwartz who came up with the volume's title: **The Art of the Deal.** A new version of Trump was about to be introduced to the country.

Trump's interest was clearly piqued by the January 1987 invitation to explore a Moscow hotel project, even as other company employees thought he was almost comically naive about how treacherous doing business there could be. Tony Gliedman, who met separately with Russians hoping to lure Trump into a project, warned him at one point, "Donald, if you put your money into Russia, it's hard to get it out." Yet Trump made the trip in July, along with Ivana and her personal assistant.

Trump had limited curiosity about the complexities of global affairs, but the tense standoff at the heart of the Cold War presented an opportunity to write himself into a much larger story. In 1984, Roy Cohn told a **Washington Post** reporter that she should profile Trump, because he was interested in getting into politics and believed he had the skills to be Reagan's arms negotiator. The reporter, Lois Romano, was skeptical of Trump's bluster but believed he could be fodder for a good story for the Style section. When it came time to discuss his actual ideas about negotiating a high-stakes treaty, Trump assured Romano that he would only need "an hour-and-a-half to learn everything there is to learn about missiles."

A claim began to spread that Trump was in fact having high-level discussions with officials in the Reagan White House about a "deal" that could solve the problem of the two growing nuclear stockpiles. One writer, Ron Rosenbaum, who was concerned that people in power were not paying enough attention to the nuclear threat, took the idea somewhat seriously and asked to meet with Trump.

They went off to the "21" Club to discuss denuclearization. Trump was critical of "defense professionals," talked about a book by Strobe Talbott called **Deadly Gambits** as if he had carefully read it, and appeared to sway Rosenbaum that he was thinking about the nuances of how the United States had arrived at such a perilous moment and how it could be averted.

Rosenbaum tried to get into the details. There were not many. "Most of those [prenuclear] countries are in one form or another dominated by the U.S. and the Soviet Union," Trump told him. "Between those two nations you have the power to dominate any of those countries. So we should use our power of economic retaliation and they use their powers of retaliation and between the two of us we will prevent the problem from happening. It would have been better having done something five years ago.

"But I believe even a country such as Pakistan would have to do something now. Five years from now they'll laugh," he said. "You think Pakistan would just fold? We wouldn't have to offer them anything in return?" Rosenbaum asked.

"Maybe we should offer them something," Trump said. "I'm saying you start off as nicely as possible. You apply as much pressure as necessary until you achieve the goal. You start off telling them, 'Let's get rid of it.' If that doesn't work you then start cutting off aid.

And more aid and then more. You do whatever is necessary so these people will have riots in the street, so they can't get water. So they can't get Band-Aids, so they can't get food. Because that's the only thing that's going to do it—the people, the riots."

Rosenbaum asked about the French, who were already in possession of the bomb. "I'd come down on them so hard," Trump said. Rosenbaum pressed some more. "They've got the bomb, but they don't have it now with the delivery capability they will have in five years," Trump replied. "If they didn't give it up—and I don't mean reduce it, and I don't mean stop, because stopping doesn't mean anything. I mean get it out. If they didn't, I would bring sanctions against that country that would be so strong, so unbelievable . . ."

Rosenbaum conceded to his readers that the "Trump Plan" was "a little crude at this point." But elsewhere in the piece, he said that off the record Trump dropped enough names of Washington elites to appear to know what he was talking about.

Trump was working hard to have names to drop. In 1987, Trump had a brief meeting with Mikhail Gorbachev, the leader of the Soviet Union, at a state dinner when Gorbachev traveled to the U.S. Trump told Maureen Dowd of the **Times** that he was skeptical of Gorbachev, but that the Soviet leader praised Trump Tower and expressed interest in one of his own. A year later, when Gorbachev planned a U.S. visit, Trump quickly sent a note inviting him to tour Trump Tower. (Trump's main spokesman in

Howard Rubenstein's office at the time, Dan Klores, said that at the state dinner Trump and Gorbachev chatted about economic matters and the possible Trump hotel.) Gorbachev ultimately did not include Trump Tower on his itinerary, but when a Gorbachev impersonator was loitering outside Trump Tower, Trump came downstairs to greet him, appearing to mistake him for the real thing.

For some of Trump's advisers, there was a different objective beyond the developer's self-aggrandizement. Roger Stone had emerged in the years since as a well-known Republican Party consultant. Even within the ranks of political operatives, Stone had developed an unusual reputation as a schemer; he was seen as either a genius at the political game, a devil corroding public life with his methods, or both. His lobbying firm, Black Manafort Stone & Kelly, represented the Trump Organization's interests in Washington, and Stone had become an increasingly important source of strategic advice for Trump. By early 1987, he had helped hatch a plan to increase publicity for Trump and his business interests: using **The Art of the Deal**'s publication as a launchpad for a potential presidential campaign.

Stone, who was formally advising the presidential campaign of upstate New York congressman Jack Kemp, did not necessarily expect Trump to actually run in 1988. (For his part, Trump had already made contributions to two Democrats and two Republicans in the race, including Kemp.) But Stone had started telling people two years earlier that he believed Trump would be president someday. And by wrapping the tease of Trump's run around the release of **The Art of the Deal,** he could maximize interest in both events. As the book approached publication, Stone persuaded Trump to take a trip to New Hampshire, site of the first nominating primary, to see how he would be received. To generate the impression of organic local interest, Stone said he worked with a local activist named Mike Dunbar, who told reporters he was collecting signatures to qualify Trump for the primary ballot.

In September, Stone helped craft a full-page ad in the **Times** and other papers labeled an "open letter from Donald J. Trump . . . to the American people." The text laid out the developer's policy-light but slogan-based impulses on a single theme: foreigners are ripping off the United States, making the country an international laughingstock. "For decades, Japan and other nations have been taking advantage of the United States," read the letter. "The saga continues unabated as we defend the Persian Gulf, an area of only marginal significance to the United States for its oil supplies, but one upon which Japan and others are almost totally dependent." He added, "The world is laughing at America's politicians as we protect ships we don't own, carrying oil we don't need, destined for allies who won't help."

The piece set the stage for an invitation to address the Portsmouth Rotary Club, near Dunbar's home, a month and a half later. He flew the TRUMP-emblazoned helicopter from New York, along with Stone. (Given the awkwardness of having committed to working with another presidential candidate, Stone wore a Groucho Marx disguise and hung back on the helicopter.) "I'm tired of nice people already in Washington," Trump said. "I want someone who is tough and knows how to negotiate. If not, our country faces disaster." He also made clear, to Dunbar's disappointment, that he was not there to announce he was running for president.

When **The Art of the Deal** was published in November 1987, Trump did what he could to ensure the book made it onto the bestseller list. He directed aides to buy up copies where they could find them, specifying that his casino executives were responsible for four thousand for each casino. When they could not be sold, they were given away. Even without the help, the book did well, rising to the top of **The New York Times** bestseller list and staying there for nearly a year, validating him almost instantly as a business genius despite his relatively light record of achievement. On Phil Donahue's popular television show, he depicted himself as a significant philanthropist and boasted that he had surpassed his father, while insisting he didn't want to brag about himself. He did not gamble at his casinos, he said, although they were the only place he would gamble because they're "the best." Then the slight raise of the eyebrows, a Cheshire-cat grin at the studio audience, the vaguest hint to fans that it was all a game and he was in on the joke.

Among those taking note was a former first lady. Trump and Richard Nixon had first crossed paths one evening at the "21" Club five years earlier, and the two men had initiated a casual correspondence. Trump praised the disgraced former president as "one of this country's great men" and insisted "one of my great ambitions is to have the Nixons as residents in Trump Tower," while Nixon returned advice on Trump's management of the New Jersey Generals football franchise. When the two men briefly shared a stage in early 1989 at an event honoring the wife of former Texas governor and treasury secretary John Connally, Trump's presence was so relatively inconsequential that photos of him did not get used in news write-ups. Yet when Nixon's wife, Pat, saw Trump on **Donahue,** it was not implausible to suggest him as a candidate for higher office. "As you can imagine," Nixon wrote, "she is an expert on politics and she predicts that whenever you decide to run for office you will be a winner!"

Even after it had grown too late in the calendar for Trump to run in 1988, Stone decided to take advantage of the election year, not to sell the country on Trump so much as to sell Trump on a future in national politics. Stone commissioned Doug Schoen, a New York pollster who advised Democrats including

Koch, to survey American public opinion toward Trump. Around the same time, a onetime Stone business partner serving as Bush's chief strategist, Lee Atwater, had a conversation with Trump about the possibility of joining the Republican ticket as the party's vice-presidential nominee. ("If it works, I would certainly consider it," Trump recalled telling Atwater.) Few viewed the conversation as a serious overture, and more as an effort to lure Trump as a donor.

Still, after that exchange, Trump decided at the last minute that he wanted to attend the Republican convention in New Orleans, where another Stone partner, Paul Manafort, served as the deputy convention director. Housing was secured for Trump at a low-scale hotel, and accommodations were made for him to sit in the first lady's box and visit the convention floor, including when Bush would formally accept the nomination.

To pass the time before the main event, Trump flew in a stunning blonde from Georgia whom he had been seeing in ways that had grown less and less discreet. Marla Maples stepped off a private plane and was whisked to Trump's quarters, where she holed up with him for hours. Even a call from Frank Sinatra to Trump's room did not lure him out; Trump said he was not available.

On Thursday night, ahead of the Bush acceptance speech, Stone asked Laurence Gay, an associate at his firm who was volunteering at the convention, to escort Trump on the floor. The covered turf of the Louisiana Superdome was congested with delegates and alternates organized by state and territory, chanting and holding placards; party bigwigs presiding over the most important event on their calendar; and one of the largest collections of media ever assembled in a single room. Overhead, nets contained hundreds of balloons ready to drop at the moment the speech ended.

"You need to stay close," Gay told Trump as they started to navigate the organized chaos of the convention floor. Trump was mesmerized, enraptured by the display around him. It was like a giant sporting event, except in honor of one man. "This is what I want," Trump said.

A few months later, the results of Schoen's polling research reached Trump. The subsequent report did not include standard items such as how the poll was conducted, the size of the samples, and over how many days, suggesting it was written more as a document for Trump's consumption than as a scientific compilation. It was broken into categories, including one on the impact Trump's book was having on his profile. "While less than one-third of American voters are familiar with **The Art of the Deal,** among those who are familiar nearly half say it presents a picture of an effective leader," the study said. "Increased familiarity with the book, particularly in regions outside of the northeast where it is less well-known, promise to boost Trump's favorability and image as a leader."

Then there was a section about Trump's own finances. "It was explained to the sample that Donald Trump pays little or no income tax," the survey said. "The majority, 51%, said this fact had no effect on their opinion in the election for President."

And still more: "Those same voters who said Trump not paying taxes made them less likely to support him for President were told the following, 'Donald Trump will say that as a businessman, he has taken advantage of the tax laws that provides [sic] incentives and tax breaks for those who create new housing and jobs.' 27% said this made them <u>less</u> concerned about Trump not paying taxes. 66% said it had no impact on their opinion."

The report said that Trump polled well among Black and Latino voters. "Significantly, minority voters are extremely favorable to Trump, his background and message on issues. The results of our poll show that for blacks and Hispanics he represent [sic] the American Dream and the potential for betterment and upward mobility," the report said. "Of course, mainstream Republican voters also find Trump and his message appealing and many of these voters are quick to support him when they learn about the ideals and issues he represents."

The poll questions presupposed voters would see Trump as operating from a level of knowledge similar to George H. W. Bush and Michael Dukakis, but the reality was different. He had a keen knowledge of power dynamics in New York, but when it came to a political worldview, he often just grasped around for things that sounded right to him. He had experienced such a moment that summer when, in his later telling, he heard two people whom he respected cite a "feeling of supremacy" as though it were a geopolitical doctrine. He and Ivana had gone to dinner to see Abe Rosenthal, who had just left his post as **The New York Times**'s executive editor to become a columnist at the paper, and his wife, Shirley Lord. Rosenthal, whose wife was friendly with Ivana, did not take Trump seriously, but was somewhat entertained by the boisterous up-and-comer. At dinner, writer Gay Talese, who happened to have covered the dedication of the Verrazano-Narrows Bridge as a reporter for the **Times** and who had mingled with Trump in George Steinbrenner's box at Yankees games, joined the party.

The dinner at an Upper East Side Italian restaurant might not have left as long-lasting an impact on Trump as the bridge's dedication ceremony, but he did find himself describing one takeaway from it days later. "They used a—an expression, which I thought was fantastic," Trump recounted. "It was the feeling of supremacy that this country had in the 1950s, it was a feeling of supremacy, it really was. And I had—I didn't know it well, I was very young at that point and I didn't know the feeling of supremacy. I've known that since the Vietnam War and even a little bit before, this country hasn't had the feeling of supremacy, and what's happening is Japan and Saudi Arabia and Kuwait and so many countries are just ripping off America left and right and down the middle, like nobody."

Those who knew Rosenthal told me they couldn't imagine him using the term "supremacy" in such a way—it sounded much more like something Trump would say—and that if he actually did, it would likely have been in the context of the United States emerging a superpower unrivaled in its military and economic might after World War II. It may have been an example of Trump crediting someone with a thought of his own. (If he used any word, Rosenthal friends suggested to me, it was far likelier he used "primacy.") Either way, Trump used it to mean something very specific, less about geopolitical clout than about national self-esteem. The writer Adam Davidson would later trace Trump's ambition for raw dominance to the economics of Manhattan real estate, in which wealth comes from grabbing one's share of scarce land and extracting income from others as its value grows. The "rentier economy," Davidson explained, enshrined a zero-sum mentality in which the person (or country) with power gets to set the terms of exchange. Trump assumed—or wanted to assume—that the entire world worked that way.

CHAPTER 6

On the Way Down

Of everything Donald Trump bought during the 1980s consumption binge that ultimately nearly destroyed him financially, he spoke of one acquisition as meaningful beyond all others. "I tore myself up to get the Plaza," he said of the iconic Fifth Avenue hotel after taking ownership of it in early 1988 after a yearlong pursuit. "This isn't just a building. It's the ultimate work of art. I was in love with it."

The Plaza was barely two blocks from Trump Tower. If one stood for the owner's ability to demolish obstacles in his path and coax grandeur from the rubble, the other could attest to his ability to be a guardian of a hometown landmark. Trump decided he wanted the Plaza even before he knew what it might cost him or whether it would be worth the money. "When I was buying in Brooklyn and Queens," Trump explained, "I'd know every screw and bolt before I bought. But that's an income investment, not an art investment. If you have to check each room in the Plaza, you shouldn't be buying it."

There was interest in buying the iconic hotel on the southeastern corner of Central Park from more than

150 investors, including the Sultan of Brunei, reportedly the wealthiest person on earth. Trump chafed at the idea of having to bid against them in a structured sale. "I don't like auctions," Trump explained. "I negotiate with my personality, one to one." Instead, he attempted to buy the massive holding company known as Allegis, which owned the Plaza as part of its Westin hotel chain alongside United Airlines and the car renter Hertz, with the intent of selling off all the company's other assets to keep just the Plaza. Trump never saw that plan through and, after a complex process, outbid two other prospective buyers to claim the hotel for $407.5 million. The news made the front page of the next day's **New York Times,** albeit laced with a face-saving lie by Trump: he said the purchase price was just $390 million. Trump's interlocutor with the property's former owner was an executive named Thomas Barrack, who coaxed him into the high price. Yet Trump did not put up the money for the hotel himself. Rather he personally guaranteed a portion of a loan from Citibank and a consortium of others, a decision that would soon prove fateful.

Trump told the paper that he bought the Plaza as a "toy" for Ivana, whom he appointed to manage the hotel for a salary of "$1 a year plus all the dresses she can buy." This was not the first time Trump had put his wife in charge of a major property; she had previously served as the president and chief executive officer of Trump Castle, one of his two already-functioning Atlantic City casinos. There she worked tirelessly, and became knowledgeable about aspects of the casino business about which she had previously known nothing. Trump enjoyed pitting her against Trump Plaza executive Steve Hyde, which led Ivana to try to prove herself by working to take business from his other casino, Trump Plaza. But her tenure was not seen as a success by other executives, who were unimpressed by her approach to the casino's finances (it had poor profit margins, former casino officials recalled). She also was known as a difficult manager, at various points belittling cocktail waitresses—including one episode in which she expressed horror that a server's uniform was modified to accommodate her pregnancy. She dug into the new job and claimed she was excited about it. "The Donald gave me my chance. I love to work and would be lost without it," she said.

Trump seized the promotional opportunities that his new property provided him. When the director Chris Columbus was filming a sequel to **Home Alone** and wanted to use the Plaza's lobby, Trump forced his way into the film. "The only way you can use the Plaza is if I'm in the movie," he said. Columbus thought of cutting the cameo, but Trump's appearance drew applause from the test audience.

If Trump had indeed overpaid for the Plaza, some around him suspected he might have had a motive beyond "art." By moving Ivana back to New York City to run the hotel, he could keep her away from Atlantic City, where he was increasingly spending time with another woman. The artifices Trump had

spent years lacing through both his business and personal lives were about to be tested.

Trump spent part of 1988 weighing an offer that
would finally give him a way out of the West Side
rail yards. Even as Trump had maintained his desire
to develop the massive plot of land just a mile west
of the Plaza, he had never come close to breaking
ground. Just talking about his grandiose plans for the
area had rallied intense and forceful grassroots opposition. All the superlatives about what he envisioned
going up there were almost perfectly scripted to prey
on the fears of those already living nearby. A new
neighborhood organization, People for Westpride,
emerged to channel the anti-Trump energy, and
many Manhattan politicians saw more to gain standing with the activists than with the developer. (Trump
took to dismissing one of them, a City Council member named Ruth Messinger, who would soon become
the Manhattan borough president, as "Ruthie" and,
in private with aides, using misogynistic terms and
caricatures about the way Jewish people look.) Their
efforts kept Trump from securing the zoning changes
and land-use approvals he needed to begin construction. Unlike when he got the Commodore deal,
Trump had had few of the same prized guides through
city government helping him. Beame was long out of
City Hall, Trump could no longer count on a diminished Fred Trump or Roy Cohn to grease the wheels

of city government for him, and he had destroyed his relationship with Mayor Ed Koch through their ongoing feud.

Trump was offered $550 million for the land by William Zeckendorf Jr., the scion of another New York real estate dynasty who was as low-key as Trump was flamboyant. "I am torn between two worlds," Trump told the **Times** in October. "I love the idea of building this wonderful city at the same time that it is close to fruition in terms of zoning. But I am being offered sums of money . . . that are staggering." Even as reporters wrote that he had other, higher offers, the Zeckendorf bid itself represented a massive cash return on a stagnant property whose borrowing costs were draining Trump: he would get a more than fourfold return over what he had paid just four years earlier. Zeckendorf even acquiesced to the seller's demand that "the most prominent thoroughfare" there would be "prominently named Donald J. Trump Boulevard." But with the down payment sitting in a bank account, Trump pulled out of the negotiations. He always hated to sell his properties, and despite how much money the sale could have provided him, he wasn't ready to give up on his dreams for the rail yards.

It was hard to tell from the way Trump acted during the months and years following the October 1987 stock market crash—continuing to spend recklessly for new assets while passing on major paydays for others—how much economic conditions had changed in the areas where his business interests were concentrated. The New York real estate market, whose gains had helped fund Trump's acquisitions over the course of the decade, immediately cooled. Atlantic City's casino business, too, slowed, even as Las Vegas continued to thrive. These trends helped to transform Trump's balance sheet: the value of his assets was in decline, even as he had to pay debts serviced at high interest rates to hold on to them.

Trump never slowed down. He developed a reputation for making advances on large publicly traded companies, only to pull back the offer once the stock rose and he had the chance to sell off his holdings at a gain, a practice known as greenmail. When he saw others aiming leveraged buyouts at Northwest and United, Trump made an unsolicited offer to acquire the company that ran American Airlines, for more than $7 billion. He claimed he would put up $1 billion for the purchase, and proposed a stock buyout at $120 per share. News of Trump's bid helped coax the stocks up well above their previous price. The offer was viewed with either excitement or skepticism, depending on which analyst was assessing Trump's ability to pull off the deal, and the company he sought to acquire did not take it seriously. Still, Trump made headlines and boosted the stock for a short period of time, before it crashed spectacularly during a dark day on Wall Street. Some believed Trump's manipulations helped precipitate the crash.

But not all of Trump's offers were feints or stunts.

Over the course of several years in the 1980s, he acquired a sports team, an airline, a megayacht, and scads of property and ownership stakes in a variety of companies, along with media attention related to them. On one hand, Trump was known for being personally cheap; one practice he learned from Cohn was a simple refusal to pay invoices submitted to him. ("Do you know how much publicity these people get for having me as a client?" Trump told underlings.) On the other hand, he was increasingly profligate, using borrowed money to pay exorbitant prices for new assets and financing the purchases at high interest rates. He was often using his personal wealth to guarantee his company's bank debt.

Trump was on the verge of taking over his third casino in Atlantic City, envisioned as a replica of India's Taj Mahal, after a protracted and costly fight with the entertainment mogul Merv Griffin. Trump emerged with the casino, and he crowed about his victory, even as Griffin walked away with the rest of its parent company, Resorts International. In Trump's telling, everything was going fabulously for him.

Trump's limousine rolled to a stop outside McFadden's bar on Second Avenue in Manhattan on a December evening. Inside, Andrew Cuomo, the son of New York's governor, was celebrating his birthday. Andrew Cuomo and Trump did not have a deep relationship, but it had been established over years. As Trump continued to pursue the West Side rail yards, he retained the law firm where Andrew Cuomo worked to handle the negotiations. By the decade's end, Trump was among Mario Cuomo's most generous donors.

When Trump arrived at the bar, he beckoned Cuomo outside to take a peek inside the limousine idling at the curb. Trump opened the door, revealing a young blond woman sitting in the back seat. She seemed anxious and fragile as the men standing outside the car stared in. "You see that?" Trump said to a startled Cuomo. "A perfect ten."

It was Marla Maples. One story had it that they were introduced through Tom Fitzsimmons, a former cop Maples had dated who became one of Trump's bodyguards. Another had them meeting somewhere in New York City. Another is that a different mutual friend introduced them. A beautiful blond former beauty queen and aspiring actress from Georgia who was seventeen years Trump's junior and had a pronounced Southern drawl, Marla could not have been more different from wife number one. Donald had grown bored and frustrated with Ivana. He concluded it had been a poor decision to give her serious work to do at the casino, because it turned her into a business competitor rather than a homemaker. And he did not share her interest in endless evenings on the social circuit. Often in the afternoons, Donald would get a call from Ivana delegating him a seating assignment for that night's dinner. "I'd suddenly feel like a low-level employee who'd just been handed some meaningless, mind-numbing assignment," he later reflected in his sequel to **The Art of the Deal,** a book called **Surviving at the Top,** which was much more authentically Trump. He would oblige Ivana but upon hanging up the phone would declare loudly enough to be heard outside his office door, "My life is shit."

Marla offered Trump a departure from it all. For the most part, Trump holed up with her in a hotel room in Atlantic City. But she appeared to be like a drug he couldn't get enough of, a contrast to the stale life of society dinners that his wife favored. By 1988, she was being secreted into Atlantic City and kept in a suite at the Trump Plaza, cloistered from view and there for Trump to visit as he wanted. Trump, known by his executives for his strange habits, such as appearing to have slept in his clothes upstairs at his casinos when he came down the next morning, had started disappearing from view more regularly.

The relationship with Marla particularly mortified some of Trump's employees; even if they didn't particularly like Ivana, they were appalled by the brazenness of his conduct. Trump insisted on making his advisers and executives share in the details of his personal life. Some did so willingly, while others did so only because they felt worn out by Trump and found relenting to be easier. He often solicited opinions from others about how they perceived Maples, repeatedly asking, "Do people know how smart she is?" And he did little to keep her at a remove from his family or

business. When in October 1989, as Trump's stunt
with American Airlines was playing out, a helicopter
carrying three Trump casino executives crashed into
a Garden State Parkway median, killing them as
well as the pilot and copilot, Trump—hardly known
for displays of emotion about anyone other than
himself—seemed unusually shaken by what had happened. "I'm sick, just sick; it's unbelievable," he said.
"I can't find the words." Ivana accompanied him to
two of the funerals, but Marla was there, too, standing in the back of the room.

Rather than trying to avoid an encounter between
the two women in his life, Trump made decisions that
led to one happening. After planning a Christmas vacation to Aspen with his wife and children, Trump
made arrangements for Maples to be in the Colorado
ski resort town at the same time. Ivana Trump later
recalled in her memoir that while waiting to be seated
for lunch at a restaurant there, a young blond woman
approached her and said, "I'm Marla and I love your
husband. Do you?" In Marla's telling, it was Ivana who
caught sight of her dining with a friend and stormed
over, bent on confrontation. Regardless, Donald was
present for the entire encounter, watching the show,
avoiding being drawn in directly and only slowly intervening to tell Marla she should leave the restaurant.

The Trump Taj Mahal Casino and Resort was called
the "eighth wonder of the world" by its owner. Trump

tried to convey that scale of grandeur the week the casino opened in April 1990. To cap the opening, Trump strolled through the casino lobby with singer Michael Jackson, surrounded by onlookers and trailed by cameras for **Lifestyles of the Rich and Famous.**

But the appearance of one of the world's biggest pop stars, who had become a bona-fide friend to the Trump family, was a balm on an otherwise abysmal first week. Few celebrities whose names had been floated to attend actually showed up. Despite Trump's hopes of capturing an Indian aesthetic, the Taj Mahal featured onion-shaped domes that observers noted were less evocative of India than of Russia. Hotel guests reported getting lost inside the absurdly large building, and having room keys that would not fit their locks. Cash machines did not work. Worse was the chaos in the casino that was supposed to be the facility's financial engine. Employees had not followed state protocols for tracking how much cash associated with the slot machines came onto and left the floor, leaving the casino's president scrambling to figure out how much money there was. Trump bluffed his way through an interview with a group of reporters—"The only problem that we had was we made so much money we couldn't count it fast enough"—but he looked broken, hollow, as he drifted through the hotel to the back offices, where he demanded to know who was to blame.

His fits of anger had his staff on edge. He blamed employees hired by one of the executives who had perished in the previous fall's helicopter crash, and berated his brother Robert, whom he had years earlier put in a position of responsibility for the new property. "I listened to you and you got me into this!" Trump vented at Robert. "You think you're clean on this one?"

Donald had often scorned his brother in discussions with employees, making clear he thought Robert did not work hard while mocking his marriage to a prominent socialite named Blaine Beard. To associates of Donald, it seemed she represented what he had wanted his own wife to be—already accepted on her own terms, rather than seen as a social climber. The blowup over the botched opening led to Robert quitting his job.

Donald's stress about the opening-weekend debacle traced to the fact that they had spent so much to build the Taj that they needed extraordinary cash flow to sustain it. The casino needed to take in $1.3 million a day in revenue just to stay afloat. Just weeks earlier, when a casino-industry analyst named Marvin Roffman had been quoted in **The Wall Street Journal** saying he thought the Taj would have trouble generating that revenue, Trump called Roffman's bosses at the investment firm Janney Montgomery Scott threatening to sue the company if Roffman did not either apologize and say publicly that the Taj would be a massive success or lose his job. Roffman refused to recant and was fired shortly after, a situation that led Representative John Dingell, a Michigan Democrat who chaired the House Energy and Commerce Committee, to call for a Securities and Exchange Commission investigation.

Trump might have succeeded in delivering vengeance, but he could not keep scrutiny of his finances at bay. A pair of journalists at **Forbes** received a leaked copy of a financial-disclosure report that Trump was required to file with New Jersey's Casino Control Commission. Most notably, the filing made clear how dire the day-to-day cash flow was for the Taj's owner: his businesses were already in the red, stretched by debt from all his purchases. When he learned **Forbes** was going to write the story, Trump applied pressure.

In one telling, Trump dangled the threat of a lawsuit against the magazine. In another, according to a journalist who worked for the magazine, Trump made clear to the **Forbes** leadership that he was ready to embarrass the family of the magazine's recently deceased owner, Malcolm Forbes, a gay man who had worked hard to keep his sexuality secret. The journalist said that Trump warned that shortly before his death Forbes had attempted to enter the Plaza Hotel's bar with two male friends below the legal drinking age. Trump claimed he blocked their entry, prompting Forbes to call the next day and threaten him. The hit piece about his net worth, Trump alleged, was that retribution. (In **Surviving at the Top,** Trump recounted that story and twisted the knife into Forbes's corpse. "I also saw a double standard in the way he lived openly as a homosexual—which he had every right to do—but expected the media and his famous friends to cover for him.") There were reasons to question Trump's account—the two reporters behind the article said they did not begin work on it until after Forbes's death—but Trump's threats, whether it was about Malcolm Forbes or simply the possibility of a lawsuit, succeeded: the story was changed before publication.

Even with a sudden change of his net worth from below zero to $500 million, the article was devastating to Trump on its publication in May 1990. To keep financing new acquisitions, and likely to save face, **Forbes** concluded, Trump assigned "unrealistically optimistic" values to his properties in his financial disclosures. In contrast with the earlier glossy covers that emphasized the photogenic subject's playful qualities, **Forbes** used a picture of Trump looking evasively off to the side, his lips pursed as though in devious calculation. The cover asked: "How Much Is Donald Really Worth Now?"

It was by no means Trump's only encounter with bad press. The satirical magazine **Spy,** which had been launched specifically to mock the elite culture of 1980s New York, repeatedly skewered Trump and Ivana because, as its cofounder Kurt Andersen would explain, they "epitomized so much of the sudden ostentation" of the era. The magazine mocked the "great temptation of objets de Trump" arrayed in the Trump Tower gift shop, mailed checks to his office upstairs to see if he would cash their increasingly infinitesimal sums (he did, down to thirteen cents), and identified him relentlessly with the epithet "short-fingered vulgarian." Most other people who claimed to see all press as good press probably would have found a way to laugh it off, but Trump reacted with fury and the usual threat of lawsuits.

But the media coverage he would soon face expanded beyond personal ridicule to cut straight to the core of Trump's preferred image as a juggernaut, raising questions about whether he understood the business world with any depth beyond the construction industry and whether he could afford his holdings. After so many media organizations published Trump's financial claims without even a note of skepticism, some outlets were now throwing reporting resources at the same question that **Forbes** had posed on its cover.

Shortly after the **Forbes** article appeared, a financial analyst named Abe Wallach, of the real estate development firm First Capital Advisors, was invited on PBS's **MacNeil/Lehrer NewsHour** to discuss the topic. Wallach, who had never met Trump, made the relatively innocuous observation that Trump both thought very highly of himself and may have overextended his finances. "If your ego is as large as his is and you just buy everything in sight, part of the blame has to squarely rest in your own lap," he remarked.

Trump responded with a $250 million lawsuit for defamation of character. Learning that the almost comically enormous amount of the suit had succeeded in rattling Wallach, Trump sent word through an attorney, who also happened to represent Wallach's firm, that he wanted to meet him. Thus began an unlikely courtship, in which Trump tried to get Wallach, who had expertise in handling properties with problematic loans, to work for him. He eventually succeeded; in 1990, Wallach joined the Trump Organization as its head of acquisitions.

There were some journalists who could not be silenced with either carrot or stick. For years, the media had played an unwitting role in developing the aura of a successful business empire built on wealth, savvy, and self-made success. But there were red warning lights that it was not what it appeared, including the news that Trump was in discussions with bank lenders about restructuring an estimated $2 billion in debt.

In the face of having the reality of his situation unmasked, Trump's employees saw him as emotionally vulnerable in a way he had not been before, and eruptions of his temper became more frequent. One day after his forty-fourth birthday, Trump missed a payment of more than $42 million due to bondholders. That Saturday night, he had planned a birthday party, and to further boost his spirits, Taj executives organized a surprise minirally to welcome him to Atlantic City. Hundreds of hotel and casino employees massed on the boardwalk alongside the Taj Mahal, where an eight-foot inflatable Godzilla doll sporting a Trump Plaza cap swayed in the oceanfront breeze. "Let's stand behind our Donald because he's the father of our babies," the facility's catering manager told them.

Low fog prevented Trump's arrival by helicopter and nearly foiled the surprise, but when Trump learned of the gathering he rushed down by limousine. Addressing the crowd, Trump could not bring himself to talk about much beyond the news coverage. "We're setting every record" for revenues at the Taj, Trump told the crowd. "Nobody wants to write about the positive. They just want to write about the negatives." One journalist in attendance noted "that the unflappable Donald's voice quavered" as he alluded to his current predicament. "I've given you a lot of surprises before," he said. "I'm going to give you more surprises in the future."

His party that night, inside a Trump Plaza ballroom, showcased a roster of comedians, singers, and video messages from celebrities paying tribute to Trump's birthday. ("When Donald was eight, his father gave him his first set of blocks—Thirty-Ninth Street, Forty-Eighth Street, Park Avenue," joked Robin Leach.) Entertainment media were permitted to cover the party, but Trump attempted to keep out reporters who would cast a more skeptical eye on the festivities.

Among those blacklisted was Wayne Barrett, the **Village Voice** reporter who had remained Trump's most aggressive journalistic foil, and was finally seeing others in the media catch up with him. He sent a young colleague, Tim O'Brien, who was allowed into the ballroom after being mistaken by a casino employee for an invitee. Barrett himself was turned back, and then when he tried to question Trump upon his entrance, he was muscled away by a security guard. When Barrett tried to gain entry via a back stairway he was apprehended and arrested by a police sergeant. As Trump was serenaded by Joe Piscopo singing "Happy Birthday" in an impersonation of Frank Sinatra, Barrett was handcuffed to a wall at a nearby jail.

On February 11, 1990, the **New York Daily News** reported something long whispered about in New York elite circles, but only hinted at in print: Donald Trump was having an affair, and it was about to end his marriage. When word of the holiday melee in Aspen reached Manhattan newsrooms, both the Trumps and Maples declined for weeks to confirm it had happened. But when Donald left for Japan alone a few months later—supposedly the first time she did not accompany him on a major business trip—Ivana took the chance to break the news on her terms.

She met with **Daily News** columnist Liz Smith, who had questioned Trump about his relationship with Maples both before and after Aspen. He refused to address the rumors, but now Smith had Ivana's full side of the story. The column described an attentive mother of three young children and "her husband's full-time business partner" blindsided by the news "that Donald was betraying her." (Smith was vague about the infidelity, and did not name Maples, but she would not remain anonymous for long.) "While friends hope for a reconciliation," Smith wrote, "many sources tell this columnist that attorneys have already been engaged to divide the spoils."

That front-page scoop launched an epic war between the city's primary tabloids, each effectively picking sides in the household conflict. In his corner, Donald had the **New York Post**, whose gossip columnist Cindy Adams had been a guest at his wedding to Ivana. (Adams grew so close to Trump that when she and her ailing husband moved into a new apartment, Trump had a security system installed.) Ivana's side was taken up by the **Daily News** and Smith, who reportedly became the country's most highly paid print journalist in large part due to her Trump scoops. At one point, their teetering marriage occupied the **Daily News**'s front page for twelve days straight.

Throughout 1990, the three parties leaked and gave interviews to the papers in an effort to frame themselves as sympathetic victims and others as aggressors, in an unending tit for tat. (Maples to the **Daily News**: "I hear she really wants to go back to him. But that could be a game she's playing." Ivana via press statement: "I won't dignify anything Marla Maples has to say. She sounds just like Donald.") News consumers were equally fascinated and horrified, like watching a car wreck where the victims repeatedly tried to hurt themselves more instead of accepting medical help.

There was little real news in it, and at the same time everything was news. One veteran **New York Post** reporter, Bill Hoffmann, was handed a name and phone number that had been passed on by a new advertising executive at the paper. The contact information belonged to someone who had taken an acting class with Marla Maples. When Hoffmann called her, she told him that Maples "often boasted of a great 'romance' with Trump."

"Uh, 'romance'—you mean, sex?" Hoffmann asked.

"Well, yeah, sex too," she replied.

"The best sex she ever had, I bet," Hoffmann offered up.

"Yeah," the friend said.

From that, Hoffman typed up a story built around a thought only he had ever spoken. MARLA BOASTS TO HER PALS ABOUT DONALD: "BEST SEX I'VE EVER HAD," a designer wrote for the **Post**'s front page. **Post** editors debated whether they would face any blowback for the scoop dubiously confected through a mix of tabloid factual elasticity and a reporter's instinct for a headline. "What's Trump going to do?" one asked. "Call a press conference and say, 'It's a lie, I stink in bed'?"

Trump, naturally, did the opposite. He prized the "Best Sex I've Ever Had" cover as an advertisement of his virility. He delighted in coverage that others might find invasive and prurient, especially when it flattered him, as did every story about the fact that two women were fighting over him. At the same time, he would also rail about the publicity that his personal life generated. "Donald complained bitterly that the coverage had been excessive and called it 'sick.' He, of course, wanted it both ways—megacoverage when he was on one of his ego trips but press discretion and restraint when he found himself in distress," wrote the columnist Sydney Schanberg. (Trump's interest in beating back media he did not like had already become apparent. When a real estate developer named Leonard Stern backed a documentary project investigating him, Trump leaped into action, sending letters to Stern's lawyers and claiming that Stern's wife had called him to ask for a date, which she denied. The resulting film never made it to broadcast after the back and forth between the moguls.)

Trump's personal antics had begun to wear on the few society friends he had, many of whom liked his wife. Estée Lauder, a fellow Roy Cohn associate, had taken Trump under her wing and introduced him to elements of elite society that had eluded him. Fond of Ivana, she urged Trump to save his marriage and, over the years, watched as he carried on publicly with one woman after another. "This may be the last thing I say to you—grow up," she said years later, after encountering him at a social event. "You're probably right," Trump replied, kissing her. Donald Trump's mother was fond of Ivana, and made a public show of attending a party for her as the marital strife broke out into the open. Mary Trump disapproved of the public relationship with Marla, and would later disapprove of their having a baby without being married.

That fall, Ivana formally filed for divorce, claiming that Donald's affair subjected her to "cruel and inhuman treatment." Trump agreed to settle, looking to take the best possible deal at a time when his own finances were teetering. Ivana got nothing more than what was in the couple's final prenuptial agreement.

Trump, forever compartmentalizing when it came to major events in his life, was handling the fallout from his split with Ivana at the same time that the reality of his dire financial situation, and just how close he was to ruin, was becoming apparent. **The Wall Street Journal** reported in August 1990 that Casino Control Commission documents revealed that Trump had a negative net worth of as much as $294 million. His chief financial officer, a well-respected executive named Steve Bollenbach, negotiated with the banks to keep Trump afloat; Trump was put on an allowance. He refused to concede publicly that his future was anything less than bright.

The Taj was struggling just as the analysts had said it would, and banks were once again discussing how to restructure Donald's debt. He gave notice that he would put the Taj into bankruptcy unless his debt load was slashed. Yet that December, it was Fred who once again solved one of his son's massive problems. On December 17, Fred sent a lawyer, escorted by police, to the Trump Castle with more than $3 million in cash, which he exchanged for gaming chips just like anyone who had come to play blackjack might. It was a way for Fred to give his son money out of the banks' view, through a means by which he could have it instantly returned any time he wanted to cash the chips, without having to compete with Donald's other creditors.

Hours later, Trump announced to great fanfare that he had met his scheduled debt obligations on the Trump Castle and the Trump Plaza. "We made the payment on time—in fact ahead of time if you look at the grace periods," he said. It was, he insisted, a sign of strength.

A month later, the world learned the full story of how Trump had pulled off that escape, how it was a family safety net rather than business acumen that had saved him. Gambling regulators had noted Fred's transaction and demanded answers about the propriety of what appeared to be an interest-free loan, unreported by the casino, in violation of state requirements. (The chips, which regulators intended solely for use in casinos, were essentially collateral that guaranteed Fred would get his money back. Regulators, concerned about the unreported loan, ordered the chips secured at the casino. When one went missing, it raised questions about whether Donald may have been involved in the chip's disappearance.) Some regulators were livid; Trump was slapped with a fine. The Casino Control Commission held hearings in 1991 to debate his financial viability. They could have declined to renew his licenses, but didn't. It was in their broader interests—given the jobs that Trump provided and the tax revenue that his casinos gave the city and the state—to let him remain on, just as they had overlooked so many of his transgressions in the past. Trump denied the story.

Fred's role in helping Donald's business was first reported in **The Wall Street Journal** by Neil Barsky, a reporter who over time became a nuisance as he wrote about Trump's business dealings, doing more than any other journalist to bring to light his financial circumstances. Over the course of 1990, Barsky had gained accolades as he doggedly documented Trump's overextended state in one story after another. Barsky had been the one who quoted the pessimistic outlook of Marvin Roffman, the industry analyst Trump had succeeded in getting fired, and a few months later reported bluntly that "Trump's cash shortage has become critical." In June 1990, Barsky revealed that Trump had personally guaranteed $500 million of his bank debt, a crushing load that he couldn't possibly meet.

In May 1991, two weeks before Trump faced another debt payment, Barsky reported that he "once again" might need to borrow money from Fred Trump to meet the looming $46 million obligation. Low down in the article was a reference to the fact that borrowing from his father would be cutting into his own "long-term wealth," because "any funds borrowed from his father will come out of Mr. Trump's share of his father's estate, according to people familiar with the situation." If the **Post**'s "Best Sex I've Ever Had" cover helped to relieve Trump's insecurities, **The Wall Street Journal**'s choice of headline went right at them: TRUMP MAY HAVE TO BORROW FUNDS FROM HIS FATHER.

The danger for Trump from the story was his father feeling squeezed, as well as having the public think Donald was relying on him, something he'd quietly done in one way or another for years. (Just months earlier, Trump had attempted to get his father to sign a codicil to his will that would strengthen Donald's position as the sole executor of the estate and protect his inheritance from creditors. "This doesn't pass the smell test," Fred would tell his lawyer daughter, Maryanne, according to her testimony in an affidavit. He found new lawyers who drafted a version of his will that removed Trump as sole executor.)

So Donald Trump got to work on trying to take out Barsky. In early April, Barsky had accepted an invitation from Trump casinos executive Nick Ribis to attend a heavyweight championship boxing match in Atlantic City. Barsky's editors knew he was attending the fight courtesy of Trump, but didn't know that the reporter had accepted two additional tickets so that family members could join him. Trump told Ribis, "The next time he writes anything I'm going to blast him like he never got blasted before."

After the "Borrow Funds from His Father" piece hit print, a public relations agent for Trump called a journalist at the **New York Post**'s flagship gossip column, Page Six, offering an exclusive that, the agent said, would be damaging to a **Wall Street Journal** reporter. Trump told the **Post** that Barsky's article was "evil, vicious, false and misleading." On top of the truth about the three tickets, Trump shared wild and false claims about Barsky, including that he had sought (and didn't receive) other freebies. Amid the attention, **Journal** editors removed Barsky from its Trump coverage; media watchers took note that the new executive editor, Norman Pearlstine, had taken a free ticket and a ride on Trump's helicopter himself. It all was a favorite model for Trump: an ostensible offer of generosity would also potentially taint the recipient, kept in reserve as future ammunition. It seemed less the instinct of a "counterpuncher," as Trump would try to characterize himself, than of someone intent on silencing those who might present facts that appeared to contradict his preferred narrative. (Despite Trump's efforts, his attack had a fleeting impact on Barsky's career. He continued to thrive at the **Journal,** and went on to become a successful hedge fund manager, documentary filmmaker, and founder of the Marshall Project, an award-winning nonprofit news site covering criminal justice.)

The negotiations with the banks went on; several floated Trump a bridge loan after an agreement was reached. The banks were forced to stare into the abyss and choose which would have been worse for them—letting Trump sink, or letting him survive. Collectively, they ultimately decided on the latter.

Besides, a number of the bankers over time appeared to have been seduced by the magic of Trump's personal salesmanship. One financial journalist who covered Trump's successful efforts to persuade lenders to stay with him called it "his finest hour," a virtuoso performance. One lender became ill with hepatitis, and Trump, the germaphobe, went to the hospital to see him. The lender, moved by Trump's gesture, took him to the next room to introduce him to an AIDS patient. Trump later raced to a janitor's sink to wash his hands.

Trump would later take loans from his share of his father's estate, which required sign-off from his siblings, biographer Tim O'Brien later reported. In 1995, reporting $916 million in personal losses cleared the way for Trump to write off more than $50 million in taxes each year over the following two decades.

Senior and experienced Trump executives departed, including both Heilbron and Gliedman in 1990. Trump was furious when he learned that Gliedman was leaving to join the Amrep Corporation, a housing-development firm. "If it's a matter of money, why didn't you come to me?" Trump asked. He was not satisfied by Gliedman's explanation that this represented an opportunity to fulfill a dream of becoming a top executive at a publicly traded company. During Gliedman's exit interview, Trump threw something at him. One friend recalled it was a shoe.

O'Donnell left too. Within days of the deadly helicopter crash, Trump had intimated that he had been close to taking that flight himself, a notion that was farcical to employees, who said he had never been scheduled to be part of the fateful trip aboard a leased helicopter. (Roger Stone insisted that Trump was not showboating and was indeed supposed to make the trip and only rescheduled at Stone's insistence for a meeting on other business.) The insinuation that he just escaped death was offensive to the widows and the fiancée of the three men who had died. Within months, Trump began to blame one of them for the troubles his casinos faced. O'Donnell pushed back at criticism of a friend. "Jack," Trump shot back, "he's dead. What difference does it make what I say about him now?"

Trump spent 1991 watching much of what he had acquired and built over the previous decade slip from his grasp. In late March, he and Ivana reached a final divorce settlement. She got their Connecticut house, but he kept the Trump Tower apartment and Mar-a-Lago. In July, Trump filed for corporate bankruptcy for the first time. Ultimately all his casinos were placed in structured bankruptcies, and he was forced to turn over half of the Plaza Hotel as part of a deal to restructure its debt. He had to pare back his grand plans for Manhattan's West Side, and the Trump Shuttle, the airline he'd bought and renamed, was gone. Equally stinging were the headlines about his fall, which were almost giddy. STRIP POKER: TRUMP IS RUNNING OUT OF CHIPS read one.

Still, in an era when Trump was seen as synonymous

with wealth and bankers were crashing, he kept his place at the head of his company. Trump seemed to have learned a lesson from his travails: his personal brand mattered more than what was on his balance sheet, the projection of strength and success was more significant than any actual fact set underneath. It was important to tell the world that he was on his way back.

CHAPTER 7

Nice and Complicated

On the night of August 3, 1992, Marla Maples strode onto the stage of Broadway's Palace Theatre in a tiny cowboy outfit that barely covered her body. It was her opening night in **The Will Rogers Follies**, a song-and-dance revue about the life of the famous humorist, in which she played a girlfriend of theater producer Florenz Ziegfeld. It was an exceptionally high-profile debut for a model and minor beauty-pageant winner who had barely acted before meeting Trump. "It takes a lot of guts," he said, "but I think she's going to be great."

The Palace was the same Broadway playhouse where a little more than two decades earlier Trump had entered a producer's office to inquire what it would take to be in the theater business himself. His foray with **Paris Is Out!** had been relatively brief, but the acting aspirations of his wife-to-be presented a new opportunity to play impresario. "I create stars. I love creating stars. And, to a certain extent, I've done that with Ivana. To a certain extent, I've done that with Marla," he told ABC News. He leaned on Richard Fields, a California entertainment executive he had befriended, to launch a stage career for Maples. Fields helped to place her in **The Will Rogers Follies,** which had opened on Broadway in the spring of 1991 and had won the Tony for Best Musical before seeing its ticket sales flag. Trump worked to make Maples's debut an event, giving out two hundred tickets to famous friends and acquaintances, including LaToya Jackson, former New York City comptroller Harrison Goldin, and Regis Philbin and Kathie Lee Gifford. (Not everyone was impressed by what they saw. "Go look for a drama critic" was all that one of them, **60 Minutes** interviewer Mike Wallace, could muster to a reporter when asked about Maples's performance.) Many of those who weren't personally invited by Trump were still there because of him. "I wanted to see the woman who stole Ivana Trump's husband," a woman who had seen the show with its original cast told one of the many journalists who came out to file stories on Maples's opening night.

It was not the only flagging cultural commodity whose comeback Trump was working to stage. Trump, the business mogul, financial sage, and symbol of American success, was trying to show himself as an unstoppable force. Yet there were significant changes to his lifestyle and his empire. As a consequence of his divorce and four separate corporate bankruptcies, he had been forced to give up many of the trophies—the Greenwich mansion went to Ivana, the **Trump Princess** yacht was repossessed by one of Trump's lenders and then sold to a Saudi prince—that he had accumulated over the course of the 1980s. Prevented from selling off his historic Palm Beach compound in chunks, Trump was forced to convert Mar-a-Lago into a private club and hawk memberships to his part-time home. Banks were newly cautious about lending to him.

He finally had to abandon his pitch to build a new neighborhood centered around the world's tallest skyscraper on Manhattan's West Side. Local officials rebuffed his entreaties to move the elevated West Side Highway to make way for the project, and then pressured him to accept a more modest design. Trump had little choice but to accede to their demands, although he still lashed out at the local congressman who did more than anyone to thwart his ambitions, mocking him as "Fat Jerry Nadler." Ultimately, Trump was effectively bailed out by a group of Hong Kong–based investors, who provided cash while letting him keep operational control of the project. The deal likely helped Trump avoid personal bankruptcy and save face in the process. But he nonetheless struggled to make anything work on the site.

The adventurous forays into unfamiliar new sectors, such as aviation and professional sports, stopped. His property portfolio grew more slowly and modestly; he bought a golf course in suburban Westchester and a historic seventy-two-story building across the street from the New York Stock Exchange in downtown Manhattan, heralding the latter as a key acquisition in a new market. Even as he retrenched, Trump remained an isolated presence in the world of New York real estate, desiring elite approval while rejecting the idea that he had any peers. When the president of the Real Estate Board of New York, Steven Spinola, asked Trump to join the trade group, Trump replied, "I'm not a joiner."

The currency he valued on a cellular level—laudatory media coverage—was harder for Trump to acquire, as the end of the dramas around parallel paths to divorce and bankruptcy left him a damaged presence in the press. (In one more example of Trump blaming staff for problems of his own making, he responded to the run of bad headlines about his divorce by firing his publicist Howard Rubenstein, although he would work with him again.) He continued to boast of his ability to spin reporters—he liked to say he had the capacity to put them "under the ether"—but instead of baiting them into covering business maneuvers that showed him (however dubiously) as a predator, now Trump stoked stories that presented him as a victim of outside forces. Attempting to explain his financial struggles, Trump told **The Washington Times** that "I see myself as a very honest guy stationed in a very corrupt world."

As Trump tried to regain his footing, his father was diminishing. In the 1990s, Fred had begun a slow disappearance into Alzheimer's. Donald, firmly in charge of the family business, further shaped it according to his style and preferences. Figures who had helped Trump navigate the New York City bureaucracy and power culture, notably Louise Sunshine and Tony Gliedman, were gone. In their place were a group of advisers who helped Trump as he tried to make a return to both solvency and relevance.

Their chosen path ran through the New York Stock Exchange. Trump had had mixed emotions about selling shares in some of his holdings, but in the wake of his bankruptcies he became convinced that a public offering gave him the best chance of reassembling his casino empire. In 1993, he won back Trump Plaza (by issuing $325 million in junk bonds) and the Trump Castle (by refinancing its debt)—both steps toward an eventual public offering in early 1995. For a time the Trump Organization became oriented around the arduous federal compliance process necessary to list shares for trading.

A key figure in the business at this point was Ribis. Since the 1970s, according to Alan Marcus and others, Trump had often used Ribis—who was deeply wired in New Jersey's business circles—as an enforcer and as a resource, including to avoid the type of interpersonal confrontation he dreaded. When he wanted to fire Ivana from her Trump Castle post, Trump instructed Ribis to do it, then denied to her that he had sent him on such a mission. After his sister Maryanne complained that her husband, John Barry, was not getting enough legal work from the company, Trump told her Ribis was the one blocking it.

Ribis joined a hodgepodge of official and informal advisers at Trump Tower, still the center of gravity. The low-key Allen Weisselberg, Trump's decades-long chief financial officer, had started as a bookkeeper for Fred Trump and, in the minds of other Trump officials, was a form of supervision over the son. Abe Wallach, the industry analyst Trump had sued for $250 million before deciding to hire him, worked to find financing and refinancing for properties that would help rebuild Trump's portfolio. Marcus was brought on to handle various issues including press. Dino Bradlee, the son of famed **Washington Post** editor Ben Bradlee, negotiated real estate projects including a historic estate north of New York City called Seven Springs, which had been owned by the family of the **Post**'s publisher, that Trump bought in 1995. Trump's former bodyguard Matt Calamari continued to handle various assignments for the business. Trump began to rely on Fields, the entertainment executive who helped place Maples in **The Will Rogers Follies** and began managing her career, as an adviser and confidant. (Her previous manager, Chuck Jones, had been convicted of taking seventy pairs of Maples's shoes into his possession as part of a sexual fetish.) Roger Stone had never left Trump's orbit.

He still could not let go of his bitterness toward those who he believed had abandoned him at his lowest point. When **The New York Times Magazine** ran a special issue devoted to "The Rich" in 1995, Trump decided to reflect on the theme of loyalty. "It is almost impossible to figure out without truly being tested," Trump wrote. "During my three-year crisis period, there were those whose loyalty and devotion I would literally have 'bet the ranch' on. Some let me down. But in practice you are either loyal or disloyal, there is no middle ground. I also learned that loyalty is not necessarily returned."

Much of the two-page essay was dedicated to itemizing grievances with dubious details against two former employees, whom he did not name but whose descriptions were familiar to those who knew the Trump Organization's inner workings. One, he boasted, he "took from a relatively low-paying job and moved into a much higher-paying executive position," Trump wrote. "I hired her because she seemed smart and unusually competent. Above all she seemed devoted to me," he wrote. "She was one of those individuals, I thought, who would run through a concrete wall to help accomplish the goals of Donald Trump."

In fact, he claimed, he had welcomed a leaker into his circle. "These are the most dangerous people, however, because when the flaw of disloyalty surfaces they are the ones you least suspect. In this case I was getting a tremendous amount of bad coverage from a particular newspaper and could not find out how and by whom this information was being disseminated. I viewed some of my people with great doubt, but this person was, in my foolish opinion, beyond reproach," Trump wrote. "When I sternly confronted her about leaking misinformation to a reporter, she spent 15 minutes swearing on her life that she could never do such a thing to 'the man who has been the greatest force in my life,'" he recounted, until "she broke down and admitted it was true."

Then he turned to the second unidentified employee, who was unmistakably Gliedman, who had quit for a better job during Trump's difficult period and by then had died of a stroke. "Then there was the man who unjustly, perhaps unethically, fought me many years before (I won) and whom I later stupidly hired. He was another who I felt would be loyal, but when the chips were down, he was gone in a flash, leaving a segment of my company without leadership."

It was the headline that left the most durable impression: I'M BACK by Donald J. Trump. The piece did little to explain how Trump had come back from his very public crash a few years earlier, only that he was keeping score.

What's that on your face?" Trump was asked.

The question came from Ribis, who sometimes worked out of an office next door to Trump's on the twenty-sixth floor of Trump Tower, convenient for winning the boss's attention on a particular matter. Ribis was in the middle of a phone call, with Marcus on the line, when Trump wandered by his open office door and poked his head in.

"Makeup," Trump replied.

"Why?" asked Marcus, inserting himself into

the conversation over speakerphone. In later years, Trump would routinely put orange-hued foundation over his rosacea-afflicted skin, but at forty-nine, this was a striking sight.

"Oh, stage makeup," Trump replied. "I did a commercial."

Marcus was alarmed. Among its rules for companies preparing to list their stock for public trading, the Securities and Exchange Commission required what was known as a "quiet period," which would likely be violated by Trump's appearance in an advertisement.

"You did what?" Marcus asked.

"Oh, this has nothing to do with the casinos," Trump said.

Even after all this time, Trump did not seem interested in how one part of his business could affect another part. Marcus explained that he was selling an entire lifestyle: Come to the casinos and be like Trump. Anything you do could tie into that, Marcus tried to explain, or at least federal regulators could see it that way.

The ad, Trump disclosed, was for Pizza Hut. "It's really cute. It's me and Ivana. And we're sharing a pizza," he said. "I'm in black tie, she's in a gown, and we're fighting over the last piece."

Marcus was confused. "You mean Marla?" he asked, referring to the woman to whom Trump was now married, with a two-year-old daughter.

"No," Donald replied. "Ivana."

"What the hell did you do that for?!" Marcus asked.

"Five hundred thousand dollars," Trump shot back.

Marcus asked Trump whether he had told Marla about the commercial. Trump said that he had not. Marcus suggested he tell his wife what happened.

Trump returned to Ribis's office a few minutes later, having followed Marcus's push to immediately call Marla. "The poor kid," Trump recounted. "I started to tell her and she got sick. She said she had to go," Trump said, turning his voice higher to a nasal falsetto, "and 'puke her fucking guts out.'"

Marcus's instinct that Marla would be put off by the commercial content was right. The ad for Pizza Hut's new "stuffed crust" line, filmed in the Trump Tower triplex apartment while Marla was at Mar-a-Lago, cheekily showed Trump and Ivana moving close to each other. "It's wrong, isn't it?" Trump says, before a smiling Ivana replies, "But it feels so right." "Then it's a deal?" Trump says. "Yes, we eat our pizza the wrong way," Ivana says, whipping open a box. Donald grabs a piece and bites into it crust first.

Trump's desire for cash and attention may have persuaded him to briefly poke fun at himself, but he still could not permit himself to become the butt of a joke. A year after the Pizza Hut episode, Trump called Marcus at home in New Jersey. "You know what today is?" Trump asked giddily. Marcus said he did not. "Today is 'Liberation Day,'" Trump explained. To him, the term had a very specific meaning: it was the first warm spring day, when women stopped wearing coats and "liberated" their upper bodies. As they later walked to the Plaza Hotel for lunch—Trump gawking at the many jacketless women along the way—Marcus told him that the weekend the ad first aired he and Ribis had briefly toyed with having a hundred boxes of Pizza Hut delivered to Mar-a-Lago. They had dropped the plan, Marcus said, after Ribis cautioned that Trump had no sense of humor. Trump paused. "Ribis was right."

On June 7, 1995, shares of Trump Hotels and Casino Resorts stock representing about 60 percent of the company's total value began trading on Wall Street, under the trading symbol DJT. It sold modestly but not overwhelmingly, but generated enough revenue to solve dire cash-flow problems for Trump. The stock offering generated cash as Trump was exploring new projects in Atlantic City and beyond, including a riverboat casino in Indiana.

The stock pitch related to the riverboat casino began to get attention, Marcus recalled, because Trump had asked one of the people involved in preparing the slides for investors to doctor a map to suggest that Buffington Harbor, Indiana, where the casino was docked, was adjacent to Chicago. In reality, it was a roughly forty-minute drive. Reminded that he was dealing with an SEC-monitored public offering, Trump told an aide that the map could be used outside Chicago, because no one would realize it was misleading. As Trump's casino business stabilized, executives at other companies began to praise Ribis's abilities. Instead of taking pride, Trump seemed to stew that someone else in the company was receiving accolades for his business acumen. Trump began to ask other executives a pointed question. "What do you think of Ribis?" he would say, coaxing a negative answer whenever he could get one.

Keeping his own staff on edge had become part of Trump's management approach. Former employees said he followed unusual business practices, such as accepting cash for lease payments and maintenance services, recalling that one parking garage leaseholder for the General Motors building sent over the cash portion of the lease in dozens of gold bars, wheeled up by one of his associates and given to Calamari. Trump told aides he didn't know what to do with it when the cardboard Hewlett-Packard box arrived. Trump ordered Calamari to take them to his penthouse apartment. (A lawyer for Calamari declined to comment on the gold bricks incident; Trump called it "a fantasy question!") In another instance, he was said to have borrowed several million dollars from one of his executives, George H. Ross, an investor and longtime friend who came to work at the Trump Organization in the mid-1990s. Some employees were told the loan was given to meet payroll. Ross confirmed to me that he had at some point extended Trump a "short-term" loan to "cover a situation that was disposed of very quickly," although he and Trump denied it was for payroll or any of Trump's expenses.

Trump siloed executives off from one another, so that even those working on related matters did not always know what the other was working on. In this environment, minor events, such as an employee spending hours with Trump behind closed doors, blossomed into subjects of office-wide paranoia. Trump not only wanted his people in silos—his executives and advisers always said he enjoyed being the only person who knew exactly what was happening around him—but enjoyed the chaos of their fighting with one another and sought to prevent people from forming alliances. When Trump passed along a piece of information related to the casino company to Marcus that Marcus then shared with Ribis, the holding company's president, Trump was angry. He questioned why Marcus would have shared something he had told him. Marcus did not like being lectured, and replied that he didn't want to know something about the casino company that he couldn't share with the person leading it. This sort of thing was why, he recalled telling Trump, no one would confuse the Trump Organization's corporate governance with IBM's.

Trump was especially bothered to see people creating paper records in meetings. "Don't take notes when you meet with him," Trump's brother-in-law and lawyer, John Barry, warned Marcus and his associate Tom O'Neil before a meeting. Once, with a dozen people around a Trump Tower conference table, Trump came up behind a junior associate at a law firm employed by him, swooped over the young man's shoulder, and crumpled up papers on which the lawyer had been diligently scribbling down notes.

In October 1996, Trump announced that he had acquired the Miss Universe, Miss USA, and Miss Teen USA franchises. It was clear why he wanted the beauty pageants: his ownership would needle the rival Miss America corporation, which was based in Atlantic City. The events would help indelibly associate Trump with women aspiring to a certain beauty aesthetic. This was a running theme—Trump had grown fixated on turning his older daughter, Ivanka, into a model. At one point, Trump had flashed photos of his young daughter at building officials who came into his office, boasting about her legs. Ivanka would cohost the Miss Teen USA pageant the following year, and Maples cohosted Miss Universe. Perhaps most important, the acquisition would keep Trump's name in the papers and enforce the impression that he was expanding once again. But some senior Trump Organization officials did not know about the deal itself before it was announced.

As part of his effort to promote hundred-thousand-dollars-a-person memberships at Mar-a-Lago, Trump spent roughly a year appealing to **Official Preppy Handbook** author Lisa Birnbach to come and spend a weekend there for a cover story he hoped to see run in **New York** magazine, calling her monthly even before it was clear the magazine was interested in such a piece. He appeared oblivious to the fact that Birnbach had been a deputy editor of **Spy,** the source of endless torment for Trump. (She was also close friends with advice columnist E. Jean Carroll, who later accused him of a rape that allegedly took place in the fall of 1995 or early 1996.)

He gave Birnbach a tour of the property, demonstrating the endless salesmanship for which he had become known, and posed for a photo with his fourteen-year-old daughter, Ivanka, sitting on Trump's lap, holding his cheek with her hand. "Look at these doors. Look at the quality in these doors. Nobody has ever seen stuff like this." And then: "This is a good room. This is the French Room. This is rated like No. 18 or something like that." Birnbach interrupted, asking whether the rooms were actually rated. "**I** rate the rooms," Trump replied. "This room . . . but this is a . . . You know, it's very hard . . . I rate the rooms in terms of levels of, you know, what **you** think is the best." Birnbach pointed out he had used the phrase "the best" quite a bit during their tour. Trump replied, "**The best** is a very important expression to me." (Trump ended up complaining bitterly to Birnbach's editor about how the story, almost entirely a transcript of his own quotes, made him look.)

At night, he invited Birnbach to join him on the club's patio for dinner along with Marla, her mother, and Marcus. Trump seemed done with his wife; at one point, Trump turned to Marcus and said Marla "looks terrible. She's lost too much weight." He pointed to his own chest as he said it.

The marriage was another relationship that for Trump just ran its course, although he would maintain a connection to Maples for decades afterward. Trump complained to associates that he thought he was marrying a homebody, and instead, not unlike his first wife, Maples wanted to go out constantly. Before they married, Maples was said to have traveled with a wedding dress in tow, in case he proposed, so the wedding could happen immediately. But Trump had dragged things out, at one point breaking up with her by FedEx as she stayed at the home of an entertainment executive in California. At another point, when word swept through the Trump Organization that Maples was having a relationship with the singer Michael Bolton, it created tumult; associates recalled that after he won Marla back, Trump took her to one of the performer's concerts as a show of dominance over Bolton. Trump and Maples had finally wed in December 1993, two months after the birth of their daughter, Tiffany. Trump had been pushed to let a friendly gossip columnist, who was under pressure from her boss, crash the delivery room for an exclusive, at first saying no but then relenting when she said she would get fired if she did not deliver the story. "What is she doing here?" the columnist, Linda Stasi, recalled Maples asking. "I'm here because I want to see the baby," Stasi said. "It's okay. Her boss would have fired her," Trump told his wife. When Maples protested having a photo taken, Trump took Stasi into the hallway, picked up a handful of receiving blankets, crafted them into a semblance of a covered child that he held in the crook of his arm, and told her photographer to take the picture. "Nobody will know," he said of the faked baby. Stasi let the photo be taken, but declined to publish it.

Associates recalled Donald and Marla parenting Tiffany in different ways. Marla had a breast pump brought to her on a silver platter while sitting poolside at Mar-a-Lago. Former company officials recalled Marla having concerns about vaccines and chemicals, while Trump, according to Marcus, favored them for his child.

In the spring of 1996, a few months after Birnbach's article appeared, a police officer patrolling a beach near Mar-a-Lago in the predawn hours found Maples and a Trump bodyguard together under a lifeguard station. When the supermarket tabloid **National Enquirer** publicized the incident, both denied there had been an affair; she had simply needed to pee, they explained, and could not locate a bathroom nearby.

In May 1997, Jeane MacIntosh, who as deputy editor of the **New York Post**'s Page Six gossip column had been writing items on the Trumps for years, received a strange tip. Maples, she was told, had purchased two gold Lexus cars from a Manhattan dealership, and Trump had forced her to return them. She reached out to the Trump Organization to ask about it, and Trump himself quickly took MacIntosh's call. An item about him forcing Marla to return cars could make him look like he was broke. "I have something better for you," Trump told MacIntosh, proposing to trade one piece of news for another. "I'm divorcing Marla," he said. MacIntosh pressed him on why.

"Are you old enough to remember the show **The Beverly Hillbillies**?" he asked. Of course, MacIntosh said. Trump laughed and referenced the Clampetts, the fish-out-of-water sitcom's fictional hayseeds. "That's exactly her family, except they came to New York City instead of Beverly Hills." MacIntosh asked what he meant. "She was always surrounded by an entourage of dumb Southerners," Trump said, putting on a Southern accent to imitate Marla's mother. But, he added, he still planned to have Maples host the upcoming Miss Universe pageant, as it had received strong ratings when she did it the previous year.

For Trump, however, the timing was essential. The prenuptial agreement he had negotiated set a horizon of five years, after which Marla would be entitled to more money in a divorce. Separating before then would leave her with a paltry fraction of what she would get if he let another year pass. Through anonymously placed quotes in news stories about the split, Trump and his lawyers made plain his primary motivation: leaving his marriage when he did was simply smart money.

Trump seemed to spend as much time packaging the narrative of his return to greatness as he did trying to steady the business itself. With the help of the financial journalist Kate Bohner, he wrote **The Art of the Comeback,** which made **The New York Times** bestseller list upon publication in 1997. Ultimately the book's message was less about comeback than about payback, against those who left his side at his lowest. In an interview promoting the book with the British **Daily Mirror** tabloid, Trump gloated about sending notes reading "Fuck off" to people who had rejected him but sought his help once he was again doing well.

Perhaps the most expansive work in the comeback-publicity genre was a profile that ran in **The New Yorker** in 1997. Writer Mark Singer, given an assignment he didn't particularly want, got hours of time to follow Trump over months, including aboard his newly reacquired private jet on a trip to Florida. (Among those present on the flight was Ghislaine Maxwell, the daughter of media baron Robert Maxwell and by then a close confidante of Trump's friend Jeffrey Epstein.) Trump loved watching movies to relax, but the one he'd chosen for the flight with Singer, the John Travolta rom-com about an angel on earth named Michael, quickly bored him. He switched to **Bloodsport** with Jean-Claude Van Damme, and had his thirteen-year-old son, Eric, fast-forward through much of the dialogue to get to the fight scenes. During one part, "when a beefy bad guy who was about to squish a normal-sized good guy received a crippling blow to the scrotum, I laughed," Singer said. Trump immediately picked up on it and pressed on the vulnerability that Singer had just exposed. "Admit it, you're laughing!" Trump bellowed. "You want to write that Donald Trump was loving this ridiculous Jean-Claude Van Damme movie, but are you willing to put in there that you were loving it, too?" (Singer did.)

Singer was also present in New York as Trump hosted Aleksandr Lebed, a former Soviet military commander seeking the presidency of a newly independent Russia. While Lebed relished a chance to demonstrate to voters that he was at ease among the world's billionaires, Trump had his own agenda. As his business refound its footing, he had revived his interest in forging a real estate deal in Russia, particularly for a Trump Tower in Moscow. He traveled there in 1996 with fellow real estate investor Howard Lorber, who had business in Russia and was helping to pave the way, as well as Lorber's partner, Bennett LeBow, and a Moscow-based businessman, David Geovanis. "I hope I'm not offending by saying this, but I think you are a litmus testing paper. You are at the end of the edge," Lebed told Trump of his ambitions. "If Trump goes to Moscow, I think America will follow. So I consider these projects of yours to be very important. And I'd like to help you as best I can in putting your projects into life." After sending Lebed off with **The Art of the Deal,** Trump confided in Singer that he thought he had won over his visitor. "When we went out to the elevator, he was grabbing me, holding me, he felt very good. And he liked what

I do," Trump boasted. "You know what? I think I did a good job for the country today."

Singer's time investment yielded him a relatively unguarded version of Trump. "One day, when I was in Trump's office, he took a phone call from an investment banker, an opaque conversation that, after he hung up, I asked him to elucidate," Singer wrote. Trump replied, "Whatever complicates the world more, I do." When Singer asked him to elaborate, Trump explained, "It's always good to do things nice and complicated so that nobody can figure it out."

CHAPTER 8

The America We Deserve

For a real estate developer attempting to rebound, a golf course presented a unique opportunity. It was straightforward to design, drew cash up front in the form of club memberships, and put the owner in the presence of celebrities and major media events. In 1996, as part of a settlement after Trump sued Palm Beach County over jet noise at the local airport, he won the right to develop a parcel of nearby land, and the next year broke ground on his first course. He then began aiming to place one in New York too. He had hoped to do so on the Seven Springs property he owned in a bucolic patch of suburban Westchester County. But as it had in so many other places, local opposition to a project that could significantly impact the area helped stall the development. Trump ultimately abandoned it.

Things looked more promising in nearby Briarcliff Manor. Trump had acquired the Briar Hall Country Club in late 1996 through a foreclosure process, along with several acres of property around it. He spent the next few years refurbishing it into a course magnificent enough to one day host a PGA Tour event. But residents did not share those ambitions, fearing that tournament crowds could swamp the town with traffic. Others were bothered by the general demeanor of Trump's local lobbyist, Al Pirro, whose wife, Jeanine, served as the county's district attorney. They were social friends, and Trump used their home to host a themed surprise birthday party for Trump's adviser Richard Fields; guests recalled Jeanine greeting them wearing a bustier, stockings, holsters that carried tequila bottles, and bandoliers with shot glasses. Al Pirro was indicted for tax fraud while Trump was trying to win approvals from Briarcliff officials. Trump waved away those planning difficulties as a by-product of a famous name. "I think being Trump is a huge asset and it's a huge liability," Trump told **The New York Observer.** "I think that if I were a developer up in Westchester, I think probably [the golf club plan] would have been a little less controversial, probably a lot less controversial. But it wouldn't have been the quality that it is."

Trump scaled back his plans from their original iteration. Still, the course opened to strong reviews of its rolling scenery and a stunning waterfall that had been constructed next to the thirteenth hole, the "signature hole." It was modeled on Augusta National Golf Club, site of the Masters Tournament, but with distinctly Trump touches, such as the 101-foot granite cliff from which the waterfall tumbled.

When **Golf** magazine editor George Peper requested permission to play the course so he could write a review, Trump personally returned his call. "Come on up—you and I will play it together," Trump said. Peper asked to bring his teenage son, Scott, himself an avid golfer. It was Scott who dominated the game, outhitting his father and the others playing in the group. Trump took notice. "Scott, you're hitting the shit out of the ball," he told the teenager. Near the signature hole, Trump looked for a review of what he had built. "What do you think of my golf course?" he asked Peper, who did not hold back. "It's spectacular," Peper said.

"Well, do you think I could get a PGA Tour event?" Trump asked. After a pause, Peper answered, "No." Trump sighed. "You know, being Donald Trump is a double-edged sword," he said. "People love me because I bring quality to everything. But people hate me because I love to fuck supermodels." The group was silent. Peper glanced at his son. **What could you even say to that,** Peper thought.

Peper was right. Trump did not get a PGA Tour event for the course. Trump had never asked why Peper had been so certain of that outcome. But to Peper, the explanation was simple: Trump's reputation had fallen so far over the previous decade's bankruptcies and personal scandal that such a prestigious event would prefer to keep its distance.

Trump continued to try to revive his casino holdings, despite growing competition in Atlantic City from

Steve Wynn, who had done what Trump had not: ventured into Las Vegas and built successful casinos. Wynn had been in Atlantic City years earlier and agreed to return only after securing a deal with the governor that involved a series of incentives and benefits. The project divided the city's casino owners, with Trump squarely in the opposition. In the midst of a public conflict that had become unusually personal, Alan Marcus suggested to Trump that he change his efforts from a negative political strategy to a positive marketing effort about Trump. Trump replied in a resigned tone, "I can't compete with Steve Wynn."

Against smaller targets in Atlantic City, however, Trump savored the chance to dominate. After spotting homes near his casino that he considered eyesores, he ordered them painted without even seeking permission from the owners. When an elderly widow refused to give up the home she had occupied for more than three decades—Trump wanted the site for a casino parking lot—he prodded city officials to seize the property through eminent domain. The widow, Vera Coking, fought in court and ultimately won, keeping Trump at bay. He mocked her as playing for sympathy in the press. "Did she put on her old clothing for you?" Trump asked one reporter. Trump developed a habit of using money from one property to advance another, and to draw large fees for himself.

Instead of giving in to the layers of oversight required of the casino holdings, Trump's pattern of drawing unwanted scrutiny from the entities overseeing his interests began anew in 1999, driven by the desire to paint a rosy picture at all times.

According to Marcus, that October, he sent Trump a draft of a press release describing the Trump Hotels and Casino Resorts' earnings for the third quarter of the year. Marcus said he planned to put the release out, with his own name listed as a contact, but Trump sent the draft back to Marcus marked up, with far rosier descriptions of the quarter in the narrative than was the reality. Marcus said he would not put his name on it. The release went out with the version that Trump had written, without Marcus's name.

There was an earnings call held the same day that painted a similarly rosy picture. The narrative relied partly on a onetime cash infusion that was misidentified as part of operating income. The day the release went out, according to an SEC document, the stock rose five times the previous day's volume. A few days later, when a report from a Deutsche Bank analysis was published that poked holes in the earnings release, the stock dropped dramatically.

The SEC began looking into what had happened. Trump, who loved to boast about not settling, did exactly that three years later, in a deal in 2002 with the SEC that allowed the resorts company to move on. By then, Marcus and Ribis had left the company. During the investigation, Marcus said, he warned Trump's lawyer, Jay Goldberg, that a draft of the press release existed with Trump's markups on it. Nonetheless, Goldberg implicated Ribis as responsible for what had happened when the settlement was struck in 2002. The fact that Ribis left Trump's employ nearly two years before the settlement, and the fact that Ribis never received a complaint from the SEC, according to Marcus, did not deter Goldberg. Goldberg told me that he did not recall the phone conversation with Marcus but acknowledged, "I put the blame for the circumstances at the feet of Ribis and absolved Trump," and insisted Trump had little involvement with the running of the casino company bearing his name. Trump denied Marcus's account.

Despite the settlement, there was no acknowledgment by the company that anything amiss had happened. There was also no fine, so shareholders who didn't know what had taken place wouldn't be involved. "This type of accounting is something that many, many companies do," Trump said at the time.

Marcus said it was unlikely that anyone held the earnings call without Trump's knowledge. Other than Trump, Marcus said, the casino company's officers "understood and respected the limits imposed" by the NYSE and the SEC. "Donald never really saw the difference between the tightly regulated casino company and his real estate interests, where his ability to exaggerate was a key component of the marketing strategy," he told me.

"Trump was an intimidating figure who wore people down," Marcus said. "He was as overbearing with his own executives as he was with reporters, always pressing a fanciful narrative which exaggerated his worth, his ability as a manager, his relationships with women, etc. The narrative was more important than reality. What he never appreciated was that the S.E.C. has higher standards than 'Page Six.'"

Trump was being forced to navigate politics beyond the urban land-use questions he had faced in New York and its outlying areas. This included interacting with the federal government in the most visible way since the family business had been targeted by the Justice Department two decades earlier for discriminatory rental practices.

His frequent guide through political thickets was still Roger Stone, who had represented his lobbying interests since the mid-1980s and had remained a consultant to him even as other top advisers had been driven away. Stone's primary geographic interest was the Northeast. In addition to advice about media, his key role was trying to tamp down emerging threats from other potential casino operators. Trump's main rivals were Native American tribes, whose ability to run gambling establishments on their own lands had been affirmed by the U.S. Supreme Court in the late 1980s as a matter of tribal sovereignty. Congress then created a law to regulate them.

The biggest threat to Trump was the Connecticut-based Mashantucket Pequot tribe, whose Foxwoods Casino and High Stakes Bingo competed with his Atlantic City properties for gambling traffic from the New York City area. When he received an invitation to testify at a House Native American Affairs

Subcommittee hearing on tribal casino pacts, Trump happily made the appearance at a high-profile platform from which he could attack a business rival for receiving preferential treatment from the government. En route to Capitol Hill, Trump and Stone chatted about what Trump would tell the legislators. Trump said that he wanted to call the Connecticut casino a "scam." "These people sure don't look like Indians to me," he explained. Stone warned against making such an observation; Trump was not quite wrong, he said, but it would be too charged a thing to say at a congressional hearing.

But Trump leaned in to his natural impulses. At the hearing he insisted that tribal-run casinos were rife with organized crime even though an FBI official testifying at the same hearing said it was not an issue. "I think that people have got paper bags over their faces and nobody's looking," said Trump, before expounding upon the caustic observation he had auditioned for Stone earlier in the day.

"I'll tell you what. If you look, if you look at some of the reservations that you've approved, that you, sir, in your great wisdom have approved, I will tell you right now—they don't look like Indians to me. And they don't look like the Indians," Trump told the committee. "Now, maybe we say politically correct or not politically correct, they don't look like Indians to me, and they don't look like Indians to Indians. And a lot of people are laughing at it. And you're telling me how tough it is and how rough it is to get approved.

Well, you go up to Connecticut and you look. Now, they don't look like Indians to me, sir." When a reporter asked him to explain exactly what an Indian looked like, Trump replied, "You know. You know."

It did not stop Trump from seeking to partner with Native American tribes for casinos elsewhere, including with the Seminole tribe in Florida, and a separate tribe in California. He did not seem bothered by the inconsistency that he had spent years trying to beat back gaming in New York and Connecticut as an inappropriate use of public resources.

The Seminoles' push was led primarily by Trump's friend Fields. They began courting the chairman of the Seminoles tribe, and hired a lobbyist with ties to the state's governor, Democrat Lawton Chiles. Fields and Trump traveled to Florida to watch the tribe's chairman, Chief Jim Billie, wrestle an alligator, and later invited Seminole leaders to a concert at Mar-a-Lago to try to forge a deal.

Chiles was notably queasy about Trump's proposal, but some of those involved in pushing on Trump's behalf believed there was a glimmer of hope. Stone was not among them, and he told Trump as much. After Chiles passed away suddenly, the Republican who wanted to succeed him, Jeb Bush, told Trump's advisers at the funeral that a Trump gaming casino, with the specific license Trump sought in order to preserve his Atlantic City holdings, would happen "over my dead body." (Bush told me he doesn't recall the details around the Trump casino effort or making that statement.) Throwing a five-hundred-dollar-a-head campaign fundraiser for Bush did not get the incoming governor to budge on his opposition. Concluding the casino was too much trouble and wasn't going to happen, Trump withdrew from the project; according to the lobbyist whom Trump had hired, Mallory Horne, Trump told Fields that if he wanted to proceed without him, he could, but that Trump was done with the effort. But when the casino opened nearly a decade later after years in development, without Trump's involvement and with Fields having partnered with a Maryland developer named David Cordish, Trump sued Cordish and Fields, claiming they had misrepresented to the Seminoles that Trump was still involved. Even for the litigious Trump, the suit was unusual: it was one of the rare instances of him going to court not against the government or a media organization or a business associate, but a onetime friend.

Trump found that the heavy-handed tactics that had sometimes helped him get his way during land-use battles with the New York government did not have the same effect elsewhere. Trump accepted the cash infusion from investors to salvage his plans for Manhattan's West Side shortly after he sought federal support to pursue his more modest plans for the site, now known as Riverside South. He applied for $350 million in loans intended to subsidize low- and moderate-income housing. In this effort, Trump secured a boost from Giuliani, whose mayoral administration sent a letter to the Department of Housing and Urban Development supporting the loans on the dubious basis that they were needed to save a "blighted neighborhood."

Some New York elected officials did not take Trump's side. Jerry Nadler, who as a liberal state assemblyman had channeled neighborhood resistance to the rail yards project before being elected to Congress in 1992, pressed HUD not to extend the loans. Nadler found an ally in Senator John McCain, an Arizona Republican. "I certainly have nothing against luxury apartments nor do I have anything against very successful project developers, including Mr. Trump," McCain said on the Senate floor in 1996. "I do object, however, to asking the taxpayer to bear the risk of a development for one of the wealthiest entrepreneurs in the country, to help finance a project that will predominantly benefit upper-income Americans."

After Andrew Cuomo was appointed by President Bill Clinton to lead HUD, Trump wanted to make his case directly to the cabinet secretary. Trump turned to one of the many firms he employed to handle his seemingly unlimited legal work: Willkie Farr & Gallagher, which Mario Cuomo had joined as a partner following the end of his third term as governor. What exactly happened next changes depending on the narrator.

Trump told me that he personally called Mario Cuomo and asked him to arrange a meeting for Trump with his son. "I'm sorry, I can't do that,"

Mario replied. "He's your son," Trump replied. "He's the secretary of HUD," Cuomo replied. "It wouldn't be appropriate." Trump has bragged over the years that he then told Cuomo to "go fuck himself." It was, Trump insisted, the last time he spoke to Mario, who he complained had been disloyal after getting Trump's financial support for his gubernatorial campaigns.

Cuomo recalled the exchange quite differently, according to an ally. Trump had avoided direct conflict throughout the process. He attempted to reach Andrew Cuomo directly about his business matter, but the secretary would not take the calls. Trump then spoke to Jack Nusbaum, the chairman of Willkie Farr, and told him he wanted Mario to make the call to his son. Trump included an ultimatum: if Mario Cuomo refused, either the firm would have to fire its partner or Trump would take his business elsewhere. "I'm not going to have that conversation with my son," Mario Cuomo told Nusbaum when he relayed the request. When Nusbaum informed him of Trump's ultimatum, Cuomo said, "You won't have to fire me, I'll leave." Nusbaum retreated, and ultimately Trump dropped the matter.

I asked Trump in one of our post-presidential conversations if he had threatened the Cuomos. "No. I don't say that," Trump told me. "After years of never asking him for even the slightest thing, which wouldn't have been wrong if I did," he said about Mario, "I asked him if he would set up a meeting with the head of HUD, who happens to be his son.

"In retrospect, I could have just called up myself and set it up. But I thought it would be nice if his father set it up. His father was out of government, he was at a law firm and he said he couldn't do that or wouldn't do that," Trump went on. "And I blasted him and that was the last time I ever spoke to him."

As he sat there with his arms folded and his hands jammed into his armpits, Trump did not betray any recognition as to how differently his tactics sounded two decades later.

Trump's divorce from his second wife was finalized in 1999. By then he was already deep into a relationship with a woman who would become his third. He reportedly met a Slovenian-born model named Melania Knauss at a September 1998 party hosted by Paolo Zampolli, the manager and agent who had been responsible for helping to secure Knauss's visa to work in the United States. Tall, with striking looks and Eastern European ancestry, she harkened back to some of the same elements Trump had found attractive in Ivana.

Knauss was not Trump's first serious relationship after splitting with Marla. On and off over roughly two years he had dated another beautiful model nearly two decades his junior. Kara Young was seen by his employees as fun, interesting, and down to earth. She was also the daughter of a Black mother and white father. "Do you think she looks Black?" Trump asked Marcus.

Young has said very little about the relationship over the years. In one of her few interviews on the topic, she described a boyfriend who exhibited a cultural ignorance about Black people and appeared to rely on stereotypes to process unfamiliar activities. When they attended a tennis match featuring the sisters Venus and Serena Williams, Trump expressed surprise at the racially diverse crowd because he appeared to believe that Black people were not interested in tennis. "He was impressed that a lot of black people came to the U.S. Open because they were playing," Young recalled to **The New York Times** in 2017. Yet she also helped Trump ingratiate himself into a new world of Black celebrities, such as the rap artist Sean Combs and the influential music producer Russell Simmons. Trump would later point to those associations as examples of why he couldn't be a racist, because he knew Black people, and, more significantly they had engaged with him without taking issue. (Weeks after meeting Young's parents, Trump told her that she had gotten her beauty from her mother and her intelligence "from her dad, the white side." He laughed as he said it; Young told him that wasn't something to joke about.)

The relationships with Young and Knauss overlapped. (Knauss reportedly broke up with him several times.) Despite how Trump dismissively talked about Young with some of his associates, others said he seemed to be genuinely infatuated with her and capable of kindness in their interactions; he found a specialist for her mother when the mother had an illness and helped coordinate her care. On their first date, Young, forgetting that Trump wasn't a drinker, ordered them both a glass of wine. Trump put the glass to his mouth, pretending to drink, apparently not wanting to say that he abstained. Realizing her error, she picked up his glass and dumped the contents into her own. Another time, when Young had trouble getting a car service to the airport, Trump surprised her by driving his limousine himself to pick her up, wearing the driver's cap. They attended a James Brown concert together, where Sharpton was in the audience, and Trump went onstage at the end with the singer. Yet Trump clearly understood he would have to choose between the two women, and he sought out opinions from others on the decision. Regardless of what they told him, he appeared to have already made up his mind. He liked to characterize Knauss as coming from a distinguished family; to some, he said she was half German. He also told associates that she did not criticize him or tell him to change his behavior, something he considered a positive attribute. Knauss was, he would say to associates, "out of central casting."

When Fred Trump passed away, eleven days after his second son's fifty- third birthday, it was Melania who showed up to mourn him. In private, with family members, Donald teared up over his father's death, one of the few if only times people could remember him doing so. But in public, he projected a very different image, one almost entirely about himself. "My father taught me everything I know. And he would understand what I'm about to say," Donald said at the wake, which was attended by many of Fred's old political allies, including Mario Cuomo. "I'm developing a great building on Riverside Boulevard called Trump Place. It's a wonderful project."

At the funeral, Donald spoke after the mayor had paid tribute to Fred's place in the city, and his other surviving children to his meaning in their lives. Donald began by recounting that when his brother informed him of their father's passing, he was reading the newspaper, which was covering a great year for Donald Trump. And suddenly it was over. "This is by far the toughest day of my life," he said from the dais of Marble Collegiate Church, above a coffin covered in white roses. "My father was a great builder. I learned everything from him. He was a master builder, but also a very hard worker." He joked that his father would be "very upset" to know his kids were taking the day off from work for a funeral.

It had been such poor timing for him personally, to have learned of his father's death just after a big story in **The New York Times** about his own successes, Trump went on. He described his own financial struggles in the earlier part of the decade, and praised his father for standing by him. "Whether I was building Trump Tower, the Taj Mahal," he said, "or the Wollman Rink, he was always there for me. But more important, he was a great husband for sixty-three years to my equally incredible mother." After saluting the longevity of his parents' marriage, he brought it back to himself: "something I'll never be able to catch him on, and he knew that."

Trump's self-referential speech was met with a confused silence by his fellow mourners. From a pew, Giuliani was heard to whisper, "What the fuck?"

With Fred's death came the eventual carving up of his estate by his children and the squeezing out of Freddie's kids, Mary and Fred III, by Fred Trump's surviving children. When Freddie's own children went to court to argue for a greater share of the estate, Donald and his siblings cut off medical funding for Fred III's son, William, who had cerebral palsy. Donald Trump and his siblings would later be accused of misrepresenting how much the estate was worth during that court fight, which had paved the way for a toxic family dispute that haunted Trump nearly two decades later.

By the late 1990s, Trump was getting a morning clips package from a service featuring mentions of his name in the national press. The pile had grown thicker by the day.

The success of the comeback narrative helped inspire Stone in late 1998 to renew his ruminations about a Trump presidential campaign. Stone was optimistic that he could persuade an unenthusiastic Trump to see the opportunity, and began to build a foundation for a real campaign if he did. In order to lay out a more clearly defined Trump Doctrine distinct from his previous, largely nonpolitical books, Stone found a writer named Dave Shiflett to work as Trump's coauthor. They spent a mere one hour and forty-five minutes together before Shiflett began writing a book. He found Trump to be not particularly deep, but affable and charming, with humor evocative of a frat house. While together in Trump's office, Trump answered a call from New Jersey senator Robert Torricelli, who had once dated Bianca Jagger, the ex-wife of Mick Jagger, the lead singer of the Rolling Stones. Trump had appeared to befriend Torricelli in part to get closer to his famous girlfriend. "Does she rake the leaves?" Trump asked Torricelli, showing off for his audience. Afterward, Shiflett had to look up the sexual euphemism.

Trump came to the book project with just a few broadstroke ideas. He remained fixated on foreign threats, including from North Korea, and the threat of local terrorist attacks using a "bomb the size of a suitcase," the same idea he had credited his nuclear scientist uncle with putting in his head twelve years earlier. He also had instincts about the types of proposals he thought would appeal broadly: a government-run universal health-care system and increased taxes on the wealthy. But that left Stone to fill in the bulk of the details on policy. He was always more libertarian than Trump, particularly on issues of morality and personal behavior. In the book, called **The America We Deserve,** Trump presented himself as concerned with gay rights. He made a point of calling out the murder of Matthew Shepard, a gay Wyoming college student who was tied to a fence, beaten with the butt of a pistol, and left to die, in perhaps the most famous anti-LGBT hate crime in American history.

In December 1998, Stone was looking at data points for a potential Trump campaign. He called on Tony Fabrizio, a Republican pollster who had worked for years on corporate projects for Trump, typically to measure public opinion on gambling in areas where Trump saw a business opportunity. (When Trump first received an invoice for one of his polls years earlier, he sent it back after scrawling on it that Fabrizio had to be out of his mind charging those prices.) As soon as Fabrizio started his research, he saw how rich a subject Trump was nationally: just 17.3 percent of voters had no opinion of Trump, and just 2 percent of those questioned had never heard of him.

Fabrizio's full survey revealed the extent of the damage that had been done by headlines about Trump's financial and marital struggles since Stone had first asked a pollster to explore attitudes toward him. Only 22 percent now viewed Trump favorably, and few voters volunteered clearly positive associations upon hearing his name. (The top four: his wealth, that he was a businessman, "affairs/women/soc life," and his involvement with casinos and gambling.)

Seventy-eight percent said that they would never consider voting for him; just 14 percent said they would. And yet there were also clear openings for Trump. The data showed that he was fairly well branded as a businessman, a "visionary," a "rags to riches American success story" and a "no nonsense, get it done guy." And there was an opening for him to define himself on issues: nearly half of those surveyed didn't know how to characterize his ideology, but just over a quarter described him as "liberal" while only 16 percent called him "conservative."

The fact that Trump had no natural constituency was not seen as a major obstacle. In 1987, Stone had defaulted to the idea that a get-rich-at-all-costs businessman with a tough-talking foreign policy would have to run in the Republican primaries. Twelve years later, he was arguing it might be possible for Trump to bypass the two-party system altogether. Stone's preferred vehicle was the Reform Party, an early harbinger of the antiglobalization backlash and populist fury that would realign American politics along lines Trump would define.

The Reform Party had been established by Ross Perot, the billionaire founder of a computer data-processing company who in 1992 had mounted one of the most successful third-party presidential candidacies in modern history on a platform of deficit reduction and trade protectionism. But nearly as soon as Perot had done the difficult and costly work of building an alternative party on the ballot in fifty states, others who did not necessarily share his priorities started vying for control of it. In 1996, Perot had to beat back a challenge from an idiosyncratic former Democratic governor of Colorado, Dick Lamm, to be his party's nominee. Two years later, a former professional wrestler named Jesse "The Body" Ventura shook up the political system when he was elected governor of Minnesota on the Reform ticket.

Perot had been eclipsed within his own party, setting up a wide-open contest for the Reform nomination in 2000. Among the potential candidates were Pat Buchanan, the isolationist, anti-immigrant commentator who had won New Hampshire's Republican primary in 1996, a quantum physicist named John Hagelin who ran as a champion of transcendental meditation, and Lowell Weicker, a centrist former Connecticut governor and senator who had clashed with Stone when Stone was rising in national politics in the mid-1980s and whom Stone was happy to take on.

Memory of the press he had received by merely flirting with presidential politics once before ultimately made Trump receptive to trying it again. On October 8, 1999, he announced he would be forming an exploratory committee, a step further than he had gone in 1987 but still not a full-fledged candidacy. Disclosing his plans in an interview with CNN host Larry King, Trump said that he was motivated to consider a run because the existing options—at this point likely to be Democrat Al Gore and Republican

George W. Bush—were too extreme. "I don't think anybody's hitting the chord, not the chord that I want to hear, and not the chord that other people want to hear," Trump said.

It was impossible to separate out Trump: The Potential Political Candidacy from Trump: The Established Brand, a fact that Stone acknowledged upon launching the exploratory effort. He told **Daily News** reporter Joel Siegel that Trump was not running merely for publicity, even if it "probably enhances the brand name." "But if he didn't have one to start with," Stone said, "this effort wouldn't be where it is today. What other New York real estate developer is a national figure with 97% name identification? People are not running around the country talking about Lew Rudin."

Trump, who talked openly about how he would be the first person to make money running for president, began to behave nominally like a potential candidate. He held a reception at Mar-a-Lago for Reform Party officials, where he worked the room, talking about the future of the country. He agreed to speak with a local group in Palm Beach, saying he would devote the question-and-answer session to a potential campaign (but devoting his actual speech to the golf club he had recently opened). He traveled to Minnesota for a press conference with Ventura, the party's biggest star. Trump made clear in their private meeting that he was far from sure he would run, and spoke publicly about one source of his ambivalence. "I'm a registered Republican. I'm a pretty conservative guy," he said. "I'm somewhat liberal on social issues, especially health care, et cetera, but I'd be leaving another party, and I've been close to that party."

When pressed in interviews, Trump often struggled to articulate his position on those issues as clearly as he did in the pages of a ghostwritten book. "I'm very pro-choice. I hate the concept of abortion," he told NBC's Tim Russert. "I hate it. I hate everything it stands for. I cringe when I listen to people debating the subject. But you still—I just believe in choice. And, again, it may be a little bit of a New York background, because there is some different attitude in different parts of the country." When King asked Trump if he thought universal health care was "an entitlement of birth," Trump didn't appear to understand the question. "I think it is," Trump said. "It's an entitlement to this country, and too bad the world can't be, you know, in this country. But the fact is, it's an entitlement to this country if we're going to have a great country."

He found a more natural groove attacking Buchanan, the most prominent announced contender for the Reform nomination. "He doesn't like the Blacks," Trump said. "He doesn't like the gays." He zeroed in on Buchanan's past observation that Adolf Hitler had never posed a real threat to the United States. Trump, roasted in some corners of the press a decade earlier for keeping a copy of Hitler's speeches by his bedside, saw a chance to flip the script. "Look, he's a Hitler lover," Trump said of Buchanan. "I guess he's an anti-Semite."

And then, after a few months, Trump suddenly decided he did not want to go through the motions anymore. Nothing he had done or seen convinced him he could actually win, and he told Stone he did not want to splinter the conservative vote in a way that could elect Gore. In an essay that was published in February 2000 under his byline, Trump dismissed Buchanan along with David Duke, the former Ku Klux Klansman, and said he was leaving the Reform Party to them. (He was also unsatisfied with the voluminous media coverage. When a **Fortune** magazine reporter tagged along with him on the Minnesota trip—who delivered the mocking assessment that "Trump is to business what professional wrestling is to sports: part of it, certainly, but also a cartoonish parody of it"—Trump was unhappy that the cover story focused on his presidential campaign and not his company.) Despite never actually declaring his campaign, Trump won two Reform Party primaries, in California and Michigan. Trump's second quasi-campaign over; all that was left behind was a trail of policy positions he would be pressed on again and again in years to come.

Before the 2000 election season was out, Stone would return to the Republican Party fold. The race between Bush and Gore was exceedingly close, coming down to just a few hundred votes in the pivotal state of Florida. As a local Miami-Dade County election board canvassed disputed votes two weeks after Election Day, a mob of protesters—many of them conservative lawyers and political staffers in well-tailored suits—attacked the building, successfully shutting down the count. The incident became known as the Brooks Brothers Riot, a bare-knuckle tactic celebrated among Republican operatives for helping pave the way for an eventual Bush victory at the Supreme Court. For years, despite competing claims from others, Stone would boast that he had helped lead the fateful protest in Miami.

When two planes flown by Al Qaeda hijackers hit the Twin Towers of the World Trade Center, Trump was ensconced in his own tower, watching television like almost everyone else. Unlike many Americans, however, Trump was ostensibly not just learning from news coverage who Osama bin Laden was.

His book **The America We Deserve,** written by Shiflett with extensive input from Stone, had included a notable reference to bin Laden, minimizing him to make a point about American foreign policy's fecklessness. "One day we're told that a shadowy figure with no fixed address named Osama bin Laden is public enemy number one, and U.S. jet fighters lay waste to his camp in Afghanistan," the book declared. "He escapes back under some rock, and a few news cycles later it's on to a new enemy and new crisis. Dealing with many different countries at once may require many different strategies. But there isn't any excuse for the haphazard nature of our foreign policy. We don't have to reinvent the wheel for every new conflict."

Yet when he appeared on a local TV news broadcast on September 11 to discuss the day's news, Trump did not express much interest in the geopolitical consequences of the attack. He talked about what "my people" saw from nearby Forty Wall Street, the historic skyscraper he owned near the New York Stock Exchange, one that had become a cash cow for his company. (A few years earlier, Trump drew attention to the building by giving the Reverend Jesse Jackson free office space there for his Rainbow/PUSH coalition). "I mean, Forty Wall Street actually was the second-tallest building in downtown Manhattan, and it was actually before the World Trade Center was the tallest, and then when they built the World Trade Center it became known as the second tallest, and now it's the tallest," Trump told the interviewer, his voice passing tinnily through the telephone. It wasn't even true—Forty Wall Street was not the neighborhood's second-tallest building—but Trump's mind was clearly on his own interests as New York City reeled.

Two days later, Trump was spotted in the area now known as Ground Zero, high-fiving police and firefighters as they headed to join search-and-rescue operations at the site of the collapsed towers. "I have a lot of men working down here," Trump told one journalist. "I want to make sure they're okay." He didn't say who these "men" were, how many were present, or where they were working. To another interviewer, he claimed to have "hundreds" of men helping work at the site, and he gave an elaborate description of finding survivors in the rubble. "The great thing is when they find somebody that's alive like the five firemen that they just found a little while ago," he said. In reality, six firefighters had been found alive two days prior, but there is no record that construction workers connected to Trump were involved in the rescue or that he had sent hundreds of people to the site at all.

Giuliani, in the closing months of his second and final term as mayor, was elevated to a global icon for his authoritative and empathetic leadership in the first days after the attacks. When he and New York's governor, George Pataki, needed to travel to Washington to listen to Bush's speech before a joint session of Congress nine days after the attack, a mayoral aide called Trump to ask if they could borrow his private jet. Trump's plane was grounded at LaGuardia Airport, part of a broader suspension of air travel as federal authorities first cleared U.S.-registered aircraft to resume flight. Trump, whose Boeing 727 had a tail number registered in Bermuda, offered a deal: he would lend the plane if the mayor's administration could help him win authorization to fly it overseas afterward. Giuliani's aide accepted the deal, without ever learning why Trump was in a rush to take his plane out of the country or where it was headed. The short flight to Washington aboard Trump's plane was a release valve for Giuliani and Pataki, who had been mired in death and destruction. The tackiness of the plane's gold fixtures, carpeting along the cabin's walls, and the presence of a bedroom despite the jet's relatively small size was startling; one person in the entourage said that it resembled a "Moroccan whorehouse." It was the first time any of them had laughed in days. (When a Giuliani friend, Jim Simpson, asked a few months later if the mayor could again use the plane, this time for an official visit to Israel, Trump quoted him a high number to rent it. No other option seemed feasible, so Simpson went back and negotiated a lower figure, which was paid by two other businessmen.)

Bush promised vengeance against those behind the attacks while urging gentleness with Muslims in the United States. His call was not heeded in some corners of the conservative media. In the pages of the **New York Post,** the instant anti-Muslim bias was on display. Twelve days after the World Trade Center collapsed, Victoria Gotti, a daughter of the convicted mobster John Gotti who was a **Post** columnist for several years, described her return to air travel for the first time after the terrorist attacks. She believed she was entirely alone on her flight, Gotti recalled, until a flight attendant informed her there was one other passenger on board. "I looked up, then nearly passed out. My cabinmate, as I later learned from speaking to him, was a middle-aged Arab, well dressed, well groomed, and clutching a briefcase," she wrote. "Someone's idea of a joke I thought. I was not amused." A new era of mistrust had been born in the United States, threading through the periphery of its politics, waiting for someone who could help shove it into the spotlight, where it couldn't be ignored.

As so often happened in Trump's life, when the world seemed to be falling apart, he managed to find his own good luck. About six months after the September 11 attacks, Trump welcomed a visitor to the Wollman Rink, which he was still managing under a contract with New York City (and which was described as "Donald Trump's Wollman Rink" in press clips). Mark Burnett had just produced a hit prime-time television show called **Survivor,** in which normal people were stranded in remote locations—the Australian outback, the Amazon rainforest—and over thirty-nine days forced to compete for primacy through a gauntlet of staged competitions and psychosocial gamesmanship. "I have an idea to do a show," Burnett told him, as Trump later recalled to me. "It's **Survivor,** but it's with asphalt instead of a jungle."

Burnett was a fan of **The Art of the Deal,** the book that introduced those outside New York to Donald Trump as a wise businessman. He was a natural to play the same version of himself on television. But Burnett had spun the conceit of the show as being about a fortunate billionaire repaying a public debt, with a cast of tycoons rotating through each season.

Unscripted "reality" competition shows had become the hottest thing in network television, and NBC lagged behind its competition in developing them. The president of the network's entertainment division, Jeff Zucker, badly wanted the rights to **The Apprentice.** Part of the appeal to Zucker was that Trump would not only be the show's star but its top publicist. When Burnett and his business partner, Conrad Riggs, showed up to pitch the show, Zucker and his colleagues wouldn't let them leave the lot until they agreed to sign with NBC. They agreed to a one-season contract, in which Trump would be paid in the mid-five figures per episode for his performance.

The Apprentice was built around a competition among sixteen contestants to win a job at the Trump Organization. Trump began each episode delivering them a soliloquy about the rules of business, supposedly drawn from Trump's own experience. Then he would assign them a "task" often tied to an existing Trump enterprise—renting out a luxury penthouse at Trump World Tower, registering gamblers at the Trump Taj Mahal, or settling bottles of Trump Ice Natural Spring Water—to test their acumen. Contestants were split into two competing "corporations," initially along gender lines, with the members of the winning team surviving until the next episode. At the outset, three low-performing members of the losing team, however, were forced to report to Trump,

who from a red-leather throne selected one for elimination in a "boardroom" showdown.

Once they started filming, producers realized that
the closing scenes that were originally something of
an afterthought were really the most riveting part of
the hour. He ad-libbed the "You're fired" line used
to dispatch each week's loser as an apparent, and un-
acknowledged, homage to George Steinbrenner, the
Yankees owner whose revolving door of managers was
one of New York's great ongoing tragicomedies. The
two men had first crossed paths in the early 1980s,
when both served on the New York State Sportsplex
Corporation board as it explored the prospect of
building new stadiums, including one in Queens that
Trump hoped would house his New Jersey Generals.
At a press conference following the board's first meeting, in 1984, Steinbrenner complained that Trump
was hogging the microphone. "This isn't going to be
a one-man show or I'm not going to stick around,"
he said, raising his arms to obscure Trump so that
photographers could not capture them together. That
show of ego, and willingness to set the terms of debate, did not stop the men from becoming friends,
and Trump was a constant presence in the owner's
box at Yankee Stadium. As he was still trying to
figure out how to be a boss of a company, Trump
looked upon Steinbrenner—and the ease, even glee,
with which he fired people—and other members of
Steinbrenner's social circle as examples. When he had
to play an executive on television, Trump adopted

Steinbrenner's voice and recast **The Apprentice**'s spirit as gleefully punitive.

The Apprentice debuted in January 2004 and quickly dominated television. Trump's performance was so central to its success that the idea of rotating hosts was abandoned, and the show was reordered to make it a Trump franchise. He expanded the board-room set piece and found supporting roles for Trump's adult children, who started flanking him at the dark wood table. Trump knew that he was performing well with audiences, and let executives know that he knew, sending them weekly ratings reports marked up with a black Sharpie. Outside of the television bubble, Trump's casinos later that year faced a fourth bank-ruptcy amid a massive weight of debt; Trump referred to the prepackaged bankruptcies as "pre-packs" and repeatedly pointed out he didn't personally go bank-rupt. He said he didn't like "the b-word."

When it was time to negotiate a new contract for **The Apprentice** after the first year, Trump went to lunch with Zucker and another NBC executive, Marc Graboff, at Jean-Georges, the restaurant at the Trump International Hotel in Columbus Circle, to discuss the next season. Trump arrived with a leather folder, which after pleasantries and a look at the menu, he pulled open to reveal papers inside. "I brought with me my financial statement that shows my net worth," Trump said. It was not in fact a lengthy statement, but a certified summary of his wealth, listed in a range of up to $4 billion. It was an odd prop to bring to a negotiation for more money. But the aim appeared to be to demonstrate that NBC was lucky to have him.

He demanded an increase of more than tenfold over his current pay, citing the combined wages of the six stars of NBC's hit sitcom **Friends.** "You're paying six million dollars for them for a half hour show," Trump said. All he wanted, he explained, was one million per episode. Graboff and Zucker broke in. Your brand has been enhanced by being on the show, they told him. "Oh, absolutely," Trump said. "What would you say it was enhanced by, five percent or ten percent?" Zucker asked. "Absolutely," Trump said. "All right," Zucker replied. "Then you should be paying us." Trump did not have a response.

While Trump did not receive his $1 million per episode, NBC decided to bump his salary by a relatively small amount. Through an aide, Trump passed on the offer, but when Graboff responded that NBC would then move on with a new host, the aide quickly backtracked. And so Trump reupped for another season at a job that not only gave him, at age fifty-seven, the first consistent paycheck he ever received outside of his father or real estate, but additional benefits that were hard to measure—more than $400 million in eventual residuals, salaries, and licensing deals, a tremendous boost to his recognizability, and a televised affirmation each week that he really was a major player in the world. "There's something very seductive about being a television star," Trump said to a reporter at the time.

Trump almost instantly regretted the price he had negotiated to keep going with the show. During one phone call, he told Graboff he had fired his William Morris–based agent because "he writes a bad deal," as he put it. "He didn't make the deal, you made the deal," Graboff reminded him. Trump then asked, "Don't you think it'd be good for me to hire a Jewish agent?" Graboff advised him to hire an expert in the field, regardless of religion. "Well, I'm gonna hire a Jewish agent," Trump insisted. He ended up with Steve Smooke at Creative Artists Agency, and later Ari Emanuel.

Trump said no to various options for office space for filming, then volunteered that he had an empty floor that he could rent the producers. The disparity between the world created on the show—a commanding businessman flying from one site of luxury to another—and Trump's reality was jarring for those who worked on the show. The boardroom scenes were shot on a stage set erected only after producers had struggled to make the threadbare parts of the Trump executive floors look camera ready. The same was true for the episode filmed at the Taj Mahal, which greeted the contestants with a thick miasma of smoke and well-worn carpets. Beneath the surface, things were not what they appeared. "We walked through the offices and saw chipped furniture," an **Apprentice** producer, Bill Pruitt, said years later. "We saw a crumbling empire at every turn. Our job was to make it seem otherwise." One time Graboff allotted one hour for a meeting in Trump's corner office, where he typically held court behind a large desk piled high with magazines and newspapers. Trump talked right through the hour, mostly about the show's ratings, with no apparent regard for the time. The phone never rang once.

But the show helped create a new reality for Trump. I didn't fully realize it myself until I was in Dubuque, Iowa, at a half-open airport hangar, on a cold January day a year and a half after Trump had concluded his fourteenth season as host of **The Apprentice.** It was the final week before Iowa's Republican caucuses, and as I waited for his campaign rally to begin, I approached people in the crowd to ask them why they were there. I presupposed it was to witness a spectacle that would soon come to an end, as Trump's other flirtations with electoral politics always had.

One middle-aged man gave me a strange look when I asked and assured me he would be casting a ballot for Trump at the caucuses. I asked him why he planned to do that. Without missing a beat, he looked at me and said, his voice earnest, "I watched him run his business."

CHAPTER 9

Asphalt Survivor

In 2000, as the St. Regis Mohawk tribe neared a deal to bring a casino to New York's Catskill Mountains, ads opposing the arrangement began appearing all over media statewide, from local radio stations to the pages of **The New York Times.** "Ask Governor George Pataki Why?" they read. "Why would Governor George Pataki give millions of dollars to a group accused of drug smuggling, money laundering, trafficking in illegal immigrants and violence?" There was a disclaimer stating who had placed them: something called the Institute for Law and Society, located in Rome, New York, a small city three hours from the site of the proposed casino.

Ultimately $1 million was spent on the ads, without any of the required disclosures to state authorities. When the head of the lobbying commission, David Grandeau, investigated the source of the money, he found a front group created by Roger Stone. Despite its august name, the New York Institute for Law and Society had a narrow mission: opposing new tribal casinos that would present a threat to Trump's Atlantic City interests. "Only reason it existed was so you could hide the actions of Trump?" Grandeau asked when he got the chance to depose Stone. "From the public?" Stone said yes to both questions, explaining that he believed the anti-casino message had more credibility coming from an apparent third party. He also insisted he did not think the activities met the legal definition of lobbying.

The commission's report on its investigation disclosed that the ads were just one part of a broader effort by Stone and Trump to mobilize political power against commercial competition. They had met with the State Senate majority leader, Joe Bruno, earlier in 2000 to discuss a bill that would require the state legislature to approve new casinos; Bruno introduced it shortly thereafter. Stone had also hired a Washington-based private investigator to look into the financial dealings of a top Pataki aide, Charles Gargano, who oversaw a state development corporation that regulated projects around New York. Pataki claimed that by failing to disclose the activity, Trump had violated the state lobbying law. Stone was unrepentant. "I found what I believe to be corruption," he said of his look into Gargano, against whom he held a two-decade-old grievance dating to Ronald Reagan's campaign. (Gargano denied any impropriety and said all his financial holdings were properly disclosed.) Stone maintained afterward that the ads were all fact based. Nonetheless, Stone, Trump, and the institute itself were required to issue a public apology and in late 2000 were fined $250,000. It was the largest lobbying-related fine levied in the state's history at the time.

Trump had no relationship with Grandeau, an unelected official. But prosecutors were elected, and therefore subject to different pressures. Trump spent decades building a personal rapport with the one responsible for the place where he lived and conducted most of his work. When Robert Morgenthau announced he would be seeking a ninth, and ultimately final, term as Manhattan's district attorney in 2005, Trump went to great lengths to show his support. At one Trump Tower fundraiser, donors to Morgenthau were whisked upstairs to the massive living room in the heart of Trump's living space. The furniture was white, the walls and ceilings adorned with gold and mirrors. Trump introduced Morgenthau with his usual list of affirmations and superlatives, and then Morgenthau gave his own speech thanking Trump.

It wasn't solely a transaction by this point. According to people who knew Morgenthau, he liked Trump, even if he joked that the Police Athletic League was the only charity to which Trump actually honored commitments. Morgenthau rarely if ever had self-doubt about his own motives; he always believed he was on the side of right. His office had received complaints from contractors claiming that Trump—by then notorious for stiffing people who worked for him—had failed to pay their invoices. The district attorney's attitude was that his office wasn't in the collections business;

complaining contractors were a civil matter, not a criminal one. Prosecutors in various jurisdictions had also heard rumors about links from organized crime to Trump properties, but nothing substantial ever materialized that connected wrongdoing to Trump, other than the tip that Giuliani, as federal prosecutor, had received years earlier.

Morgenthau was not the only prosecutor whom Trump worked to cultivate. In late 2001, President George W. Bush appointed Chris Christie, a lawyer and onetime elected county official who had been active in statewide Republican politics, as the U.S. attorney for New Jersey. Not long thereafter, Trump asked his sister Maryanne Trump Barry, a federal appeals court judge, to introduce him to the new federal prosecutor working in her circuit. Trump and Christie met for dinner, and the businessman made an early impression when he fended off a photograph seeker by telling her that they would get together another time.

It was the start of what would become one of the most consequential relationships of Trump's life, and over the next few years, Christie would discover what it was like to be in Trump's circle. One day in the summer of 2004, Christie was in a conference room with staff when Trump called him. Earlier that day, New Jersey governor Jim McGreevey, who was married to a woman but facing threats from a male ex-lover, had called an extraordinary press conference in which he came out as "a gay American" while announcing his plans to quit office. "Can you believe what's going on?" Trump bellowed through the phone to Christie. "I'd always heard the guy was gay, but I didn't know he was going to resign over it."

They talked about what would happen in the race to succeed McGreevey—Trump had called because he wanted to see if Christie was going to run—but Trump returned to the titillating private details. "You know, Chris, he's different than me and you, right? We may have all kinds of problems ourselves, but not this one. Me and you, just chicks—right, buddy? Just chicks." As his aides stared in wonder, Christie replied merely, "Yeah, that would be right, Donald."

On January 22, 2005, Trump married his third wife, Melania Knauss, at the Episcopal Church of Bethesda-by-the-Sea in Palm Beach. The bride had two different dresses, one worn at the ceremony and one at the reception. She was photographed in a wedding gown for the cover of **Vogue.** She walked down the aisle carrying a diamond cross and rosary. A news story ahead of the ceremony suggested that members of the royal family might appear and then, a beat later, made clear that some had merely been invited. Yet there were enough famous people and elected officials under the palm trees dotting the grounds of the church to give it all the feel of a major society event.

Among those under the palm trees were Bill and Hillary Clinton. Trump had been largely positive about Clinton's presidency, calling him "terrific" and a "victim" of women who accused him of sexual impropriety, but also criticizing his judgment for not taking the Fifth Amendment in legal interviews related to the investigations. Hillary was in her first term as a senator from New York, and the two had settled into their new life in Westchester County, in a home just fifteen minutes from Trump's Briarcliff golf course. Always looking to collect powerful people, Trump invited Bill Clinton to join, issuing the invitation and then leaking it to reporters before Clinton had accepted.

"I'm proud to have him," Trump said upon announcing his new member in 2003. "He's a great gentleman, a good golfer and a wonderful guy." Trump frequently showed up at the club when he heard Clinton was there, once trying to follow him around the green with a recording crew in tow that appeared to be for **The Apprentice.** Around the same time, Trump made a small donation to Hillary. When Trump announced his wedding the following year, the senator made clear to aides that she considered the occasion interesting and important enough to add to her schedule; aides tried telling her that Trump had never held a major fundraiser for her, but she didn't budge.

The wedding marked a new phase for Trump's public life. **The Apprentice** had been an instant success. "The Donald Trump I saw the day before **The Apprentice** premiered was very different from the guy I walked to nine national interviews the first day after the show aired," NBC publicity director Jim Dowd later told **The Washington Post.** "People on the street embraced him. He was mobbed. All of a sudden, there was none of the old mocking, the old **New York Post** image of him with the wives and the parties. He was a hero, and he had not been one before." His relentless personal promotion of **The Apprentice** had solidified his place as a regular guest on television and radio nationwide, to talk about matters well beyond finance and business.

Trump rarely sounded as comfortable as he did in the New York studio of bawdy shock jock Howard Stern, sometimes bringing along his children Ivanka and Don Jr. to join him on air as they became more active on **The Apprentice.** In one exchange, Trump raised no objections when Stern referred to Ivanka Trump as a "piece of ass."

To Stern, Trump talked about how much he loved sex, the number of partners he had at a single time, the way he liked to wander backstage at his beauty pageants while the contestants were getting dressed. "You see these incredible looking women, and so, I sort of get away with things like that," he said of his behavior at the pageants. When news broke that golfer Tiger Woods was splitting from his wife due to his affairs, Trump said, "One thing we've learned about Tiger Woods, definite: He is not gay. Do you agree with that?" Stern agreed: "He is absolutely not gay." Trump and Stern laughed, then quickly moved to Stern teasing Trump. Stern pressed Trump on whether he had ever been with a man, or had sexual thoughts about one. "I've never had a thought, there's never been like a big thought process," he said of his own sexual encounters, chuckling as he spoke while Stern laughed, about "Jimmy or Ronald or any of that."

Stern's show was grounded in the kind of proudly sexist banter that Trump used as a bonding ritual with other men. As the two went back and forth, Stern's audience heard Trump as an idealized version of a high-testosterone alpha male, unapologetic and refusing to bend to what he would call "political correctness." When Trump had pitched a season of **The Apprentice** in which the two teams would be divided by race, NBC executives were taken aback by the idea. But he gleefully recounted the pitch for Stern and his audience. He wanted nine Black contestants, with "an assortment" of skin tones, against nine white people, who would all be blondes. "Do you like it?" Trump asked Stern. "Yes," Stern said. Trump turned to Stern's cohost, Robin Quivers, who is Black. "I think you're going to have a riot," she said.

Trump had always created alternate realities for himself, but the addition of his own prime-time parallel universe meant that he was suddenly everywhere. He was seeping himself deeper into the country's pop culture fabric. In 2006, one of Trump's made-for-the-tabloids feuds with Hollywood celebrities—a name-calling tit for tat with the actress and talk-show host Rosie O'Donnell—prompted an invitation from World Wrestling Entertainment chairman Vince McMahon. In the late 1980s, Trump had twice hosted the company's marquee Wrestlemania tournament in Atlantic City, but this time he was being asked to star himself in the scripted event. At the 2006 installment, a fake Trump wrestled a fake O'Donnell, and Trump came back the next year for a storyline called the Battle of the Billionaires, in which he and McMahon had proxies fight for them, with the loser getting his head shaved. Trump first body-slammed McMahon outside the ring in a choreographed move, then wielded an electric clipper as his foe was strapped to a chair inside the ring. McMahon, playing to the audience, yelled for help. The crowd loved it. Trump looked ecstatic.

As part of an ongoing effort to narrate his comeback, Trump had eagerly cooperated with a book about him by Tim O'Brien. O'Brien had been a researcher for Wayne Barrett when he was working on his 1991 biography, and afterward had gone to work for **The New York Times** as a business reporter. A decade later, O'Brien returned to the subject. Unlike Barrett's book, which came out when

Trump was at his lowest, O'Brien's—published in the fall of 2005—captured him at a very different stage. The cover of **TrumpNation: The Art of Being The Donald** featured Trump rendered in action-figure plastic, ironically given the way that inside O'Brien cut Trump down to size.

Nothing rankled Trump more than O'Brien's estimate that he was worth no more than $250 million, and possibly as little as $150 million, just a year after Trump had published his own book titled **Think Like a Billionaire.** Insisting O'Brien was wrong, Trump in January 2006 filed a $5-billion libel lawsuit against both the author and his publisher, Warner Books, claiming the author had knowingly made false and malicious statements about a variety of topics, including his net worth. Years later, Trump described the goal of the suit—one of many he filed or threatened to file over decades—as inflicting pain on the author and the publisher. "I spent a couple of bucks on legal fees, and they spent a whole lot more. I did it to make his life miserable, which I'm happy about," he reflected on his motivations. Once the suit was allowed to go forward in state court, O'Brien's lawyers reviewed Trump's tax returns and deposed Trump as well.

At points in the sworn interview, Trump was clearly less than truthful, claiming that he had never done business with people identified as organized crime members, even though his own previous statements showed he was aware of their reputations.

The lawyers who had prepared him for the deposition, from the same Kasowitz Benson Torres firm that handled his bankruptcy cases, learned that Trump simply could not be coached out of saying whatever he wanted to, writing his own script as he went along.

Trump undercut the premise of his central claim—that his net worth was a demonstrable fact, and that O'Brien had vastly understated it—by riffing on how he arrived at that figure. "My net worth fluctuates, and it goes up and down with the markets and with attitudes and with feelings, even my own feelings," Trump said. O'Brien's lawyer pressed on that point. "You said that the net worth goes up and down based upon your own feelings?" the lawyer said. "Yes, even my own feelings, as to where the world is, where the world is going, and that can change rapidly from day to day." Pressed again, Trump said, "I would say it's my general attitude at the time that the question may be asked. And as I say, it varies." When asked whether he had calculated projections of future profits from his golf course, Trump said that he had done so. "Mental projections," he said.

Years later, Trump would be investigated by prosecutors for whether he was inflating when trying to convince both lenders and magazine editors that he was one of the country's wealthiest people, and deflating when tax assessors came around. But his explanation of the intangible nature of his value ironically captured a truth about how the success of **The Apprentice** had built on his branding efforts, and transformed him into something else entirely. He was no longer seen primarily as a builder whose economic activity could be measured in square feet or acres, or sized up in steel, glass, and concrete. He was now firmly in the business of selling his name.

Most banks had stopped lending to Trump after his run of bankruptcies, in a way that effectively made it impossible for him to build on the scale he had in the 1970s and '80s. There was one major exception: Deutsche Bank, a lesser player on Wall Street that was willing to take on heightened risk in order to build up its presence in the United States. In order to borrow, Trump agreed, once again, to personally guarantee his loans, which put him on the hook once they came due years later. When Trump in 2006 suddenly paid more than $10 million in cash to buy a huge patch of land in northeast Scotland, his mother's native country, with the goal of building a golf resort, it wasn't clear where he had come up with the money to do so.

The Trump SoHo, on which ground was broken that same year in Lower Manhattan, was more typical of his new projects. Trump did not invest any of his own money in the 391-room condominium and hotel, instead offering his name and deploying his eldest son and daughter to serve as liaisons to a new demographic to which Trump wanted to appeal, in exchange for an 18 percent equity stake. The majority partner was the Bayrock Group, a New York real estate firm known to be led by the Soviet-born investors Tevfik Arif and Felix Sater. The latter had an especially notable background: Sater had been convicted for both first-degree assault (shoving a broken margarita glass into a man's face) and fraud (a pump-and-dump penny-stock scheme involving the Genovese crime family) before becoming a government informant. He maintained an office at Trump Tower and a business relationship with its namesake that he said was more than cordial. The building they erected together would be the final one constructed in New York with Trump's name.

Over the course of his career, Trump had been a pioneer in the business of marketing brand-name condos, discovering the value of his own name in the process. Soon, that name was not landing only on buildings, hotels, and golf courses, but on Trump Vodka, **Trump Magazine,** Trump Ice bottled water, Trump Steaks, Trump Office desk chairs, Donald Trump: The Fragrance, **Donald Trump's Real Estate Tycoon** video game, Trump Home mattresses, the GoTrump.com travel booking website, and the Trump Network, which lent its name to a dubious line of vitamin sales. Still, it was a surprise when he called a Trump Tower press conference to announce that he would be creating Trump University, a real estate training "school." (Roger Schank, whom Trump tapped to act as "chief learning officer," said the school would try to teach students the concept of "learning by doing.")

It was during this period that the long saga of the West Side rail yards finally came to an end. In 2005, construction was complete on a series of three apartment buildings, and Trump's Hong Kong partners decided to sell the 77-acre site—now known as Trump Place—for $1.76 billion. Trump claimed that he was blindsided by the sale, and he sued to stop the transaction and to try to win $1 billion in damages. One partner, who claimed that Trump had been informed in advance, called the lawsuit a "shock," while Trump hurled back all kinds of accusations, ranging from fraud to kickbacks. His obsession with being ripped off by foreign actors had acquired a new villain: instead of Japan, he would soon talk about China.

Trump kept attacking his partners in court, but he lost his fight. However, as part of the eventual sale, Trump ended up with a 30 percent stake in the profits from two buildings owned by the large real estate trust Vornado—one on Sixth Avenue in Manhattan, the other a skyscraper in San Francisco's Financial District. After decades of trying to avoid sale of his properties, even when it would help him, Trump had reflexively fought tooth and nail against the deal but, by dint of luck, ended up benefiting from it. The two Vornado holdings would bring him more than $176 million over the course of nearly twenty years, providing much-needed cash at times when he appeared to have few other sources of it.

For years after the Mohawk casino controversy, New York Republicans who distrusted Trump and Stone for the lobbying attacks on Pataki beat their chests about how the lobbying commission's judgment had put the two in their place. Indeed, Trump and Stone had been hit with a monumentally large fine, but Trump's share was against Trump Hotels and Casino Resorts, not him personally, making it just another business expense for the company. They had been compelled to make a public apology, but admitted no legal wrongdoing and dodged a criminal referral. And while the two had not managed to kill the casino project, it encouraged other problems that hobbled it. Rather than chastening Stone, the experience appeared to embolden him.

In 2006, as Pataki's third term came to an end, New Yorkers replaced him with Democrat Eliot Spitzer, the son of a Manhattan real estate scion who rode to an easy victory as a crusading attorney general known as the "Sheriff of Wall Street." Within days of taking office as governor, he was reported to have told a legislative leader, "I am a fucking steamroller and I'll roll over you or anybody else." That took the form of threats and muscle flexing when he did not get his way, and reports of improperly using state resources for political ends. Among the allegations was that Spitzer had deployed the State Police to investigate Bruno, who as Senate majority leader was the most powerful Republican in the state and a patron of Stone's.

Eight months into Spitzer's term, his eighty-three-year-old father, Bernard, filed a complaint with a State Senate committee over an obscenity-laced, threatening voice mail left on his office answering machine. His lawyer identified Stone as the voice on the recording and said it led back to Stone's phone number. Stone insisted it was not him, and claimed as an alibi that when the call had been placed he was at a showing of the play **Frost/Nixon.** A reporter pointed out that the play was not staged that night. Stone maintained that the Spitzers had somehow accessed his phone, calling it the "ultimate dirty trick."

The controversy cost Stone his role with Bruno and the Senate Republicans. He resigned from his consultancy with the Republican caucus. Trump, who ostensibly traveled in similar circles as Bernie Spitzer, was described as angry over the fiasco, and separated himself from Stone publicly and privately at least in part because of it. "He always tries taking credit for things he never did," Trump said, calling his adviser of a quarter century a "stone-cold loser."

For a few years, the two men kept their distance. During that period, Stone became attached to a different New York businessman he could help launch as a guided missile against the political establishment. In so doing he would find that a theme he had been road-testing for years—a resentment politics that saw Republican and Democratic elites as part of the problem—was ready for a broader audience.

By the late 2000s, books by Donald Trump were coming out so frequently that it was not always clear how to tell one from the other. The books, some thirteen since **The Apprentice**'s debut, repackaged similar business advice under interchangeable titles and subtitles such as **Trump: How to Get Rich, How to Build a Fortune: Your Plan for Success from the World's Most Famous Businessman,** and **Way to the Top: The Best Business Advice I Ever Received.** (The closest thing to an outlier was **The Best Golf Advice I Ever Received.**) As Trump prepared for the release of his fifteenth book in April 2009—**Think Like a Champion,** a follow-up to 2004's **Think Like a Billionaire: Everything You Need to Know About Success, Real Estate, and Life**—publisher Vanguard Press sent its online-marketing director, Peter Costanzo, to brainstorm new promotional possibilities with the author.

Costanzo visited Trump Tower several times to meet with Trump and the aides who worked on his book projects, including his steady ghostwriter, a former ballerina named Meredith McIver. In one meeting, Costanzo volunteered that there was a relatively new social media site attracting attention. It was called Twitter, he explained. People could post bite-size thoughts that could be easily disseminated to others. Trump could use it to communicate directly with his fans and customers at no cost. Trump was intrigued. When Costanzo took out his laptop to show how the site worked he found that there was already a Twitter user impersonating Trump under the handle @donaldtrump. Costanzo created a new account, @realDonaldTrump.

Trump glanced at his aides, telegraphing his surprise that he hadn't been aware of this new media option before. There was one catch, Costanzo pointed out: celebrity accounts where the namesake did not engage personally did not catch on with users. To succeed on Twitter, some degree of participation from Trump himself would be necessary. That did not give him any pause. "Okay," Trump said, slapping his hand on his desk, "let's do it."

His first tweet, on May 4, was uninspired self-promotion: "Be sure to tune in and watch Donald Trump on Late Night with David Letterman as he presents the Top Ten List tonight!" But with time he found a voice: sharp, funny, mean, conversational, irreverent. The site was clearly a perfect match for Trump, given that it was quick and simple and gave his followers the impression he spoke directly to them. Unlike in broadcast interviews, he could say whatever he wanted on almost any topic, not be directly challenged, and then walk away without having to take ownership of whatever he had just whipped up. Even after he was done using the site for book promotion, Trump wanted to continue with Twitter. In late 2009, Costanzo learned why. Aides confided to him that Trump was once again considering a run for president. Trump came to see that Twitter could be useful for far more than promoting talk-show appearances and selling books.

Licensing agreements that put Trump's name on everything from a cologne to a menswear collection were bringing in a flood of cash in a way he had rarely experienced, but his more traditional businesses were struggling. Some thirteen years after a public offering allowed investors to buy a piece of his casino business, the value of TRMP stock had plummeted to just 31 cents a share by November 2008. The collapse of the subprime mortgage market in 2008 impacted Trump's shrunken real estate portfolio, most notably in Chicago at his eponymous tower. The broader global financial crisis it triggered hit tourism-heavy locations like Atlantic City especially hard.

With Trump facing down his fifth casino bankruptcy, and with his one-time semi-protégé Richard Fields finding success with the Hollywood, Florida, casino that Trump was said to have walked away from, Fields made a move to acquire the Trump Marina, as the Trump Castle had been renamed as part of a larger rebranding effort, offering more than $300 million for the property. (He planned to rebrand it Margaritaville, in partnership with the singer Jimmy Buffett.)

As the ongoing litigation between Trump and Fields over the Seminoles casino was going to trial—the Seminoles had said in 2007 that Cordish and Fields never said they were working with Trump—a settlement was abruptly agreed to. Under the deal, Fields's group would be able to acquire the Marina. (Even after the two settled, the casino sale fell apart, and Trump ended up selling it for a mere $38 million in 2011.) Yet few fallings-out were permanent with Trump. Years later, Trump and Fields had a rapprochement over dinner with their wives. Trump laughed about the lawsuit he had filed that had cost Fields millions of dollars over the course of several years. He had to do it, Trump made clear over dinner, because he had not received proper credit for Fields's success after leaving the Trump Organization.

The entire episode was a reminder of how much Trump's world turned over in the first decade of the new century. An executive who had helped Trump navigate his escape from bankruptcy in the 1990s— Nick Ribis—had departed, as had his consultant Alan Marcus. Trump fell out with Fields. Roger Stone was kept at a distance for a time. Only a few people who had known him in the 1980s—notably an assistant of nearly two decades, Rhona Graff, security chief Matt Calamari, and chief financial officer Allen Weisselberg—endured.

Trump had grown more reliant on his older children, Don Jr. and Ivanka. Like the younger Eric, they had joined the Trump Organization as executive vice presidents. In 2009, Ivanka, with whom Trump was closest and whom he told friends was the smartest of his children, married Jared Kushner, who as the son of a well-known and politically wired New Jersey developer had also entered his family's real estate business. Ivanka converted to Judaism in order to marry the devout Kushner. "Can you believe I have a Jewish daughter?" Trump said to friends at the time. Kushner tried to help his new father-in-law reestablish a relationship with his own lenders at Citi Private Bank, one of the institutions that no longer wanted to extend money to Trump after previously being burned in the early 1990s. Officials at Citi agreed to meet with Trump and Ivanka; she appeared to be Kushner's main target for help, as she was venturing her own real estate deals. But when the officials reviewed what providing a loan for the Trump Organization would look like, they shut down the discussions.

As always, Trump continued to collect new additions to his world, and one was a lawyer he first noticed when the man defended his name in a contentious co-op board meeting in a Manhattan building where he was a tenant. Michael Cohen was a failed Republican City Council candidate and taxi medallion investor, but the credential that may have mattered most to Trump was the fact that he was an unabashed Trump fan whose family had bought several apartment units in Trump buildings. Cohen was quickly subjected to the type of abusive behavior that had become almost inevitable upon entry into Trump's inner circle. Cohen joined the Trump Organization in 2006 technically as a lawyer but mostly as a general fixer for Trump to rely on, but within a few years, Trump cut Cohen's salary and began questioning his abilities around others, purely to humiliate him. When I noted to Cohen years later that Trump was abusive to him, he replied, adding Trump's children into the mix, "He's abusive to everybody." Some of Trump's friends found Cohen's presence—with his thick Long Island accent and sometimes abrasive personality—unwelcome and unnecessary. Andrew Stein, the former New York City elected official with whom Trump remained close, once asked Trump why he trusted Cohen enough to keep him so close. "He has his purpose," Trump replied.

On September 27, 2010, Trump opened his Trump Tower offices to help raise money for Republicans seeking office from coast to coast. There were barely five weeks before Election Day, and the party was expected to deliver an epic rebuke of Barack Obama in the first midterm vote of his presidency. The leaders of the Republican Governors Association, Mississippi governor Haley Barbour, and the group's young executive director, Nick Ayers, were traveling the country to raise money for candidates in races across thirty-seven states, and Trump had volunteered to host a fundraiser.

Since flirting with a Republican candidacy in 1988, Trump had drifted away from the party. After his Reform Party feint, he had updated his voter registration to Democrat in 2001 and started to pursue his very public friendship with Bill and Hillary Clinton, who was expected to be her party's standard-bearer in 2008. But she lost the nomination to Obama, and Trump pulled away from the Democrats. He eventually threw his support behind the presumptive Republican nominee, John McCain, despite the fact that the Arizona senator had been one of the loudest congressional critics of extending low-interest federal loans for Trump to build the Riverside South project. (Trump had praised Obama early in the campaign, calling him "a very capable guy and a great speaker," but then the candidate cited Trump's use of the bankruptcy process to renegotiate mortgages on his homes in a way less-wealthy people never could.) He called one of his former lobbyists, Charlie Black, who was then advising McCain, and offered to host a "big event" to raise money for the campaign. After Black told him that he would be expected to raise a half million dollars, Trump was quiet for a moment before asking, "Can't we do something less?" Ultimately he agreed to cohost a New York event already being planned. An aide later called Black to check on how Trump would get credit for what he had raised.

Trump formally changed his voter registration to

rejoin the Republican Party just as it began a radical transformation away from both the free-market absolutism of the Ronald Reagan era that spoke to Trump as a young businessman and the George W. Bush–era aggressive neoconservatism that had ultimately repelled him. Within the first months of Obama's term, activists—likening themselves to the colonial-era revolutionaries who rose up against British rule—began to organize protests, nominally against federal bailouts of banks and automakers and Obama's proposal to remake the American health-care system. Their ferocity came in part from backlash to the country's first Black president. The self-identified Tea Party protesters had twin targets: the Democrats who controlled Washington and a Republican political establishment they saw as insufficiently confrontational.

Trump was quickly shown to be out of sync with a party increasingly in thrall to its activist base. He had Rex Elsass, an Ohio consultant then working with a number of Tea Party–style outsider candidates running nationwide, commission a survey of voters in Iowa and New Hampshire. The results were terrible for Trump, demonstrating that he would need to do an about-face on a number of issues he had laid out a liberal position on—from health care to abortion—if he had any hope of competing for a Republican presidential nomination. (Nonetheless, weeks later, in a telephone interview with MSNBC's **Morning Joe,** Trump brought up the private poll and lied that the results were "very positive.")

Trump had been introduced to Elsass through a Republican operative named David Bossie, one of Trump's guides to his new party's changing political terrain. (Trump had discovered Bossie through casino mogul Steve Wynn, the rival turned friend, and grew closer to him during his separation from Stone.) In the 1990s, Bossie had worked as a congressional investigator as the Republican majority probed Clinton's administration on various charges. In 2000, Bossie took charge of the advocacy group Citizens United, which became known (including through a landmark Supreme Court decision that bore its name) for advancing conservative arguments through feature-length documentary films, including one about Hillary Clinton that was released during her 2008 campaign. When Stone created an outfit called Citizens United Not Timid (CUNT) during the 2008 presidential campaign, Bossie's group sued him. Stone, maintaining it was a gag, settled the lawsuit.

In 2010, Citizens United Productions released a film about the financial crisis directed by Steve Bannon, the former Goldman Sachs executive turned right-wing media entrepreneur. Bossie thought Trump would benefit from knowing him. The unkempt Bannon was not the kind of person Trump instantly took to. But his Wall Street credentials got him a second look. The two men met at Trump Tower and had an open-ended conversation about politics. Trump talked extensively about China and said that the country—which was on a trajectory to soon have the world's largest economy—was ripping off the United States through its trade practices. Bannon talked positively about populism, and suddenly Trump piped up. "That's exactly what I am—a popularist," Trump said. Bannon corrected him. "No, it's populist," he said. "Yeah, popularist," Trump responded.

If Trump was looking for an example of how a first-time outsider candidate with an unconventional résumé could channel this Tea Party anger, there was one emerging in his midst. A Buffalo real estate developer with no political experience named Carl Paladino began preparing for a long-shot candidacy for governor that he promised to fund with $10 million of his own money. Stone informally advised Paladino even as he managed the campaign of another gubernatorial candidate running on a third-party line, Kristin Davis, a former madam who had recently emerged after four months in prison stemming from her involvement in the prostitution ring that would take down Eliot Spitzer in March 2008. (Davis ran on the Anti-Prohibition Party line, and her platform emphasized legalizing prostitution and marijuana.) Paladino surrounded himself with other advisers linked to Stone's extended orbit. Paladino's campaign manager, Buffalo native Michael Caputo, had once been Stone's aide and drove Trump to his Capitol Hill testimony in 1993. Caputo brought on Tony Fabrizio, who had known Stone since the late 1970s and who had conducted survey research on both business and political topics for Trump, to be the pollster. "This is a campaign of junkyard dogs, not pedigreed poodles," Caputo told **The New York Times.**

The front-runner for governor was Andrew Cuomo, Mario's son, who had bided his time as the state's attorney general as fellow Democrat Spitzer was caught in the prostitution investigation that ended his career and his successor, David Paterson, sank under press coverage of his own scandals. (Stone claimed a role in the Spitzer scandal; the **Miami Herald** reported that Stone had written a letter to the FBI four months before Spitzer resigned, claiming he frequented prostitutes and wore black socks to bed. Spitzer denied it, but the image was indelible.) To face Cuomo in a general election, Paladino would have to beat Rick Lazio, a moderate Long Islander who had moved up from the county legislature to Congress and was well liked by other elected officials in the state.

Paladino's campaign got off to a rough start. On the day he formally announced his candidacy, newspapers were filled with reports about a child he had fathered through an extramarital affair. A few days later, a local news site published racist and explicit emails that Paladino had sent to people he knew, including those targeting Barack and Michelle Obama. One message, titled "Obama Inauguration Rehearsal," included a clip of African tribesmen dancing. Yet Paladino did not give a full-throated apology for it. If anything, the mainstream press coverage and his defiant response—"To me it's just humor," he said, invoking other slurs—helped to introduce him to the base voters he needed to win a Republican primary, a fact that was not apparent at the time.

As a matter of both personality and political strategy, Paladino was drawn to controversy, and an irresistible one was emerging in Lower Manhattan. The first public reports of a plan to build a Muslim cultural center a few blocks from the World Trade Center site had come out in December 2009. Media outlets latched on to the story, stoking community resistance. By the following summer, the proposed development—inaccurately dubbed the "Ground Zero mosque" in headlines, including by me—had become a flash point in the post–September 11 culture wars. While Obama welcomed the development as an example of American pluralism, as did New York's mayor and governor, conservative politicians including Lazio speculated about nefarious sources of foreign money funding it.

Paladino went further, making the mosque and the embrace of it by elected officials in both parties a focal point of his campaign. In radio ads, he vowed to use eminent domain to block the development if necessary. "The Islamic fundamentalists are fascists—women have limited rights, there is no free speech or freedom of expression, and citizens are subject to the often barbaric Sharia Law. I oppose a mosque near the site of ground zero, not because of race, but because of the ideology of the Islamic fundamentalists," Paladino said in one ad.

"I say it is disrespectful to the thousands who died on September 11 and their families, insulting to the thousands of troops who've been killed or injured in the ensuing wars, and an affront to American people. And it must be stopped."

When the issue began to draw national media attention over the summer, Trump jumped in, using a familiar playbook of inserting himself into a controversy that didn't relate to him at all. He sent a letter to one of the major investors in the project—and quickly leaked it to **The Wall Street Journal**—offering to buy the investor's shares for $6 million, so he could then force the project to move. "I am making this offer as a resident of New York and citizen of the United States, not because I think the location is a spectacular one (because it is not), but because it will end a very serious, inflammatory, and highly divisive situation that is destined, in my opinion, to only get worse," Trump wrote.

Establishment Republicans went into primary day expecting Lazio to win easily. But thanks in part to the emergence of the "Ground Zero mosque" issue, and the way it mobilized the rage nascent in New York's state politics, Paladino upset Lazio by a nearly two-to-one margin. About two weeks after his victory, one of the country's biggest upsets that year, I went to interview Paladino in a Midtown hotel lobby. He vented about the coverage of his affair—and the ten-year-old child he had fathered through it—telling me, "My daughter is off-limits." About ten minutes later, he asked, "Has anybody asked Andrew Cuomo about his paramours?" Caputo, his campaign manager, quickly added, "When he was married." Cuomo's marriage to a Kennedy scion had ended years earlier, with competing reports in the tabloids about an affair she had had with a Westchester polo player. But Paladino was talking about something else.

I had never witnessed such a thing before: a politician who made deeply personal claims against a rival, on the record from his own mouth, without even pretending to offer evidence in the moment (Caputo later claimed he'd chased down evidence trails to no avail). It was so foreign to me that I didn't initially realize that it was a newsworthy moment, and only did when I discussed it with others. But since this was the Republican nominee for governor, there was no way for the media to ignore it entirely, the way we likely would if he had outsourced the allegations to allies whose names were not on the ballot. I published a story in **Politico,** which I had recently joined as a New York–based reporter, headlined "Paladino Alleges Cuomo Affair."

A Cuomo spokesman told me that "we have not and will not descend into the gutter with Paladino, Caputo, and Stone." Yet Cuomo had his aide Joe Percoco reach out to Paladino through Stone as Paladino's attacks became nastier, hoping to defuse them to some extent.

Neither of Stone's two candidates for governor were elected—Paladino received about one third of the total vote share, and Davis won less than half a percent. But Stone, who had been immersing himself in the power of the internet to spread information and ideas without relying solely on the mainstream media, discovered that the merging of celebrity and conflict could now be an even more powerful force in politics.

A month after Paladino's defeat, Stone published a column on his website, the Stone Zone, a venue for his scattered opinions on political and fashion topics, arguing that conditions were right for Trump to run for president in 2012. "The Donald Trump of 2010 is not the Donald Trump of the '90s. Gone is the single playboy with dozens of model girlfriends," he wrote. "Today the Donald is happily married to a wonderful wife and has a son in his formative years. Today Donald is a stable and wiser figure who could be the only person who could save this country."

Stone's phone rang shortly after it was published. It was Trump. He had seen the column and was both charmed by Stone's flattery and convinced by his logic. He was ready to resume the relationship.

CHAPTER 11

Rising on a Lie

Donald Trump had changed his party on a New York voter-registration form in the late summer of 2009, but his baptism as a born-again Republican took place a year and a half later in Washington. The 2011 installment of the Conservative Political Action Conference arrived at a particularly auspicious moment for the American Right. Republicans had just reclaimed control of the House of Representatives while winning back six Senate seats, six governorships, and nearly seven hundred seats in state legislatures nationwide. The results were viewed as a large-scale repudiation of Barack Obama's ambitious agenda and a validation that the Tea Party movement could be not merely a noisy opposition but an electoral force as well.

Yet Republicans had no obvious national candidate who could harness those forces. The front-runner, Mitt Romney, had worked assiduously to win over major donors and party elites since a failed 2008 campaign. But the former Massachusetts governor, whose health-care reforms had helped serve as a partial template for Obama's, was viewed as too politically

moderate for the Republican base. His Wall Street ties
and proper, demure personality left him out of sync
with the party's populist drift. Those who spoke to
the rebellious mood—such as the Tea Party congresswoman Michele Bachmann or Ron Paul, a onetime
Libertarian presidential candidate making his second
bid for the Republican nomination—were unimpres-
sive as potential general-election candidates. Those
who were treated as plausible, such as Governors Tim
Pawlenty of Minnesota and Jon Huntsman of Utah,
could not keep up with Romney's fundraising. The
CPAC event scheduled for February 2011 would be
one of the first high-profile opportunities for candidates to make their case to a broad cross section of
Republican activists.

Shortly before the event, Roger Stone began discussing a way for Trump to crash the party. He
worked with GOProud, an insurgent organization of
Republican gays and lesbians who were cosponsor-
ing the conference, to secure a prime speaking slot
for him. It was not a huge stretch: amid his paranoia
about AIDS, Trump had donated to the Gay Men's
Health Crisis two decades earlier while married to
Ivana. Despite his private disparagement, his public
commentary on gay people had become far more accepting, particularly when either someone who might
be a customer of his, or someone who was a celebrity,
was involved. When the singer Elton John was joined
in a civil union with his longtime partner, David
Furnish, Trump wrote on a Trump University blog,

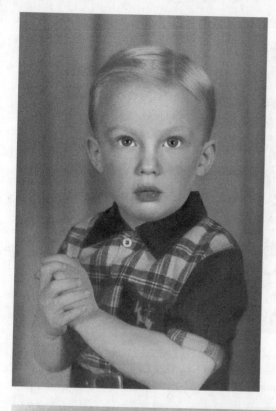

Donald Trump was born in Queens in 1946, the second youngest of Fred and Mary Trump's five children.

Trump's relationships with his siblings evolved over time, but none was more significant than his relationship with his older brother, Freddie, with whom he had a rivalry encouraged by their father.

The house on Midland Parkway in Jamaica Estates where Donald Trump grew up. Trump later described the neighborhood as an "oasis" in New York City, aware that he was set apart in class and in lifestyle from much of the urban landscape surrounding him.

When Trump was a young teenager, he was sent to the New York Military Academy, where he faced slaps and punches from leadership. His sudden disappearance from his previous school startled his close friend Peter Brant, who struggled to understand what had happened.

Those who encountered the Trumps in New York City were often struck that the family appeared to travel as a unit. Here, Donald and his four siblings sit for a portrait, the three sons dominating what one of Trump's sisters would later call "a man's family."

By 1973, Donald Trump was a visible presence at his father's company. He and his father were often described in the same sentence in media coverage of the real estate firm's activities. That year, they would be sued by the federal government for allegedly discriminatory rental practices.

A young Donald Trump, wearing a three-piece suit, stands next to the proposed redesign of the decrepit Commodore Hotel on Manhattan's East Side. The project would give Trump a foothold in Manhattan.

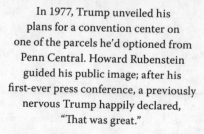

In 1977, Trump unveiled his plans for a convention center on one of the parcels he'd optioned from Penn Central. Howard Rubenstein guided his public image; after his first-ever press conference, a previously nervous Trump happily declared, "That was great."

Trump and his eventual nemesis, Mayor Ed Koch, discussing Trump's redevelopment plans in Manhattan. After having a direct line to Koch's predecessor, Abe Beame, Trump would struggle to gain influence in the Koch era.

The Mod Squad, Trump edition. Trump and his first wife, Ivana, pose for a photographer in their home, before moving to their triplex in Trump Tower.

In 1982, Trump stood on the unfinished roof of Trump Tower, holding an American flag. The staging foreshadowed how Trump would infuse himself with a brand of patriotism he urged his followers to support, one that revolved around Trump's own name and image.

Other than his father, there was no greater influence on Trump than Roy Cohn. Cohn became Trump's mentor and interlocutor into the elite worlds of Manhattan that had little interest in him without Cohn's power behind him.

Donald Trump and two of his siblings, his wife Ivana, and his parents appear with Roy Cohn, just over a year before Cohn's death from AIDS. As Cohn battled the disease, maintaining publicly that it was liver cancer, Trump began distancing himself. "I can't believe he's doing this to me," Cohn said at the time, according to Trump chronicler Wayne Barrett.

The ceremony to open Wollman Rink, after Trump's renovation, was emblematic of his uninterest in sharing credit with others. Instead of spreading around the thanks and kudos, Trump turned it into an event about himself.

Trump's flying palace was one of his prized possessions. Here, he looks out at the twin World Trade Center towers. A few years after they were destroyed, Trump, who was not involved with the site, proposed rebuilding them similar to how they had been.

Rarely has so much been made from relatively little. Trump, standing with his father, Fred, at the site of the ice rink that Trump had finished rehabilitating, which he then used to puff his image as a master builder.

In the 1980s, Trump developed relationships with Al Sharpton and Don King, two prominent Black figures who were often tabloid fodder. The relationships were largely transactional and masked Trump's otherwise limited interactions with Black people outside the realm of sports or celebrity.

The Reverend Jesse Jackson was another Black leader with whom Trump sought a mutually beneficial relationship. In the late 1990s, Trump donated office space in Lower Manhattan to Jackson's Rainbow/PUSH Coalition.

Trump sitting with New York Yankees owner George Steinbrenner, one of the key influences on Trump's blustery style and attempts to appear to be an authoritative boss. In the 1980s, Steinbrenner represented a type of hypermasculinity that Trump seemed to study.

Trump looks bored, staring off into the distance, as he sits in Atlantic City in 1988 with his wife Ivana and his father, Fred.

Trump with his mother, his wife Ivana, and his brother Robert and Robert's first wife, Blaine, in 1988. Over the years, Trump talked about his mother far less frequently than he did his father. His relationship with Robert soured for many years after Trump blamed him for problems opening the Trump Taj Mahal casino in Atlantic City. They reestablished their relationship before Trump became president.

Trump posing for a 1989 cover issue of **Savvy Woman** magazine with three executive vice presidents at his company: Susan Heilbron, Barbara Res, and Blanche Sprague. The Trump Organization was a stand-out among New York companies for having so many women in senior positions, but everyone around him got used as a set piece in one way or another—the magazine article became something campaign aides pointed to approvingly years later.

Shortly after their relationship became headline news, Trump and Marla Maples posed over golf balls at Mar-a-Lago, Trump's oceanfront estate in West Palm Beach, Florida.

Trump with Marla Maples and the outgoing mayor of New York City, David Dinkins, who signed the couple's marriage license for their 1993 wedding. After his struggles earlier in the decade, Trump was thrilled when **The New York Times** wrote a large front-page story about him picking up the license.

Despite his germaphobia, Trump samples a piece of food from a buffet-style plate during a 1996 trip to Russia, as he pressed on with his yearslong dream of building a project in Moscow.

Trump and his adviser Roger Stone—who would spend years helping shape Trump for political office—outside the federal courthouse in New Jersey.

Trump and his then-girlfriend, Melania Knauss, pose with Jeffrey Epstein and Ghislaine Maxwell in 2000. Trump associates said that he was once fascinated by Epstein but ultimately had a falling out with the convicted sex offender.

At the White House Correspondents' Association annual dinner, Trump, accompanied by his then-girlfriend, Melania Knauss, shakes hands with Michael R. Bloomberg, who was soon to be a New York City mayoral candidate. Nearly twenty years later, the two men would run for president the same year.

Trump with Mark Burnett, producer of **The Apprentice**, in 2003. For many Americans, the show created an indelible image of Trump as a successful businessman.

With Central Park visible behind him, Trump sits in his corner office at
Trump Tower, his desk cluttered as always with newspapers and magazines.

Trump in his gold, glass, and
marble fortress in the sky in
2005, a decade before he became
a declared presidential candidate.
Trump loved giving photographers
glimpses of the space over the years.

Trump's affection for wrestling was a natural fit for the
developer, who liked to fight. His relationship with WWE's
Vince McMahon became a durable one over the years. In 2007,
Trump helped shave McMahon's head in front of a crowd.

Trump was the ultimate attempted insider until he decided he liked being on the outside more. In 2008, Trump played golf with Bill Clinton, Rudy Giuliani, sitting New York City mayor Mike Bloomberg, former Yankees manager Joe Torre, and the actor Billy Crystal.

It was the dinner that helped make history. At the White House Correspondents' Association annual dinner in 2011, President Barack Obama mocked Donald Trump for his so-called "birther" crusade, which had tried to challenge the legitimacy of the first Black president. Trump, humiliated, mustered a small smile and then, four years later, a campaign of his own.

Trump went to New Hampshire with lawyer Michael Cohen in tow during his explorations of a campaign against President Barack Obama, visiting a diner and meeting with local leaders.

In 2014, Trump made feints at running for governor in New York, but it never really captured his interest. Still, he made a few trips around the state to test the waters, including appearing at an event condemning Governor Andrew Cuomo—with whom he'd had a complicated relationship over the decades—for Cuomo's desired restrictions on guns.

"In any event I'm very happy for them. If two people dig each other, they dig each other. Good luck, Elton. Good luck, David. Have a great life."

On February 10, 2011, Trump set out for Washington accompanied by Michael Cohen. Trump's appearance was not announced until the last minute, creating a sense of excitement. Upon his arrival at the Washington Marriott Wardman Park Hotel, Cohen tried to create a buffer between Trump and the reporters who trailed him from the lobby to the ballroom. When he took the stage, with **Apprentice** theme song "For the Love of Money" blaring overhead, the room was packed, a mix of religious activists, libertarian-minded college students, and corporate lobbyists unlikely ever to assemble anywhere else.

Stone had helped arm Trump with a few points to make in the speech in order to make any inroads with the crowd. Having called himself "very pro-choice" while floating a presidential campaign twelve years earlier, Trump now reversed himself. "Just very briefly," Trump said, "I'm pro-life. I'm against gun control, and I will fight to end Obamacare and replace it." Then he returned to the issues he cared most about. He decried, as he had for decades, other countries he said were ripping off the United States, proposing new tariffs on China as a solution.

Trump laid out what was perhaps the most salient case he could make for himself, or any other celebrity businessman without the accumulated baggage of having spent a life running for and serving in elected office. "By the way, Ron Paul cannot get elected, I'm sorry," Trump said with first a smirk and then a smile. He was booed by Paul fans, applauded by the rest of the hall. He smiled more. "I like Ron Paul," he said. "I think he is a good guy. But honestly, he has just zero chance of getting elected." The line got enormous cheers. Three years into Obama's term Republicans wanted someone who believed in winning. Trump had struck a nerve.

Matt Strawn, the chairman of the Iowa Republican Party, watched the speech on television from his living room. He was riveted by the crowd's reaction. He reached out to a party official and suggested inviting Trump to keynote the party's Lincoln Day Dinner. Within two weeks, Strawn and the official, Casey Mills, traveled to New York to meet with Trump and Cohen. Once the conversation turned away from golf, and an Iowa course Trump had once considered buying, Trump delivered a startling statement about Obama. "I'm not even sure he was born here," he said, holding up paper from his desk. The theory that Obama, born in Honolulu to a Kenyan father, was not a natural-born American had floated through the right-wing information ecosystem since before he was elected. It was first promoted by a small group of ardent but anonymous Hillary Clinton supporters grasping at anything they could to derail Obama's nomination. It was later adopted by fringe Republicans trying to push it into the mainstream conversation.

Trump was measuring how Strawn would respond,

part of the testing of reactions he often did with people around him. But he got little in response, and quickly moved on. The discussion turned to when Trump would come to Iowa. They agreed on early June. The meeting, which Strawn and Mills anticipated would be relatively short, had dragged on for more than forty-five minutes. Trump's interest in the presidency seemed sincere.

A few days after Trump's CPAC speech, my editor at **Politico** told me to interview Stone about what a Trump candidacy in 2012 might look like. I knew Stone from covering New York politics and had heard from Republican sources that he had been involved in arranging the CPAC speech. Stone was insistent to me that he was not formally working for Trump, characterizing himself as an "observer" of the process. Nonetheless, over lunch Stone laid out a well-considered vision for a campaign. Trump would run as a critic of the decade-long war in Afghanistan and a supporter of a harder line in American policy toward China. He didn't like to travel, Stone warned, and he typically didn't like to work that hard. But he could self-fund a campaign and take advantage of social media's growing reach. "I think even people who don't like him have a certain fascination with him," Stone told me. "He's Donald Trump. There's a public fascination. So I don't think he has to go shake hands among the pig farmers."

After my story appeared online, I received an email from Trump's office with an unsolicited statement. "Roger Stone has appeared in the news making very favorable statements about me and my potential candidacy for president. While I greatly appreciate his flattering comments, Roger does not represent me and is not an adviser to my potential campaign," the statement quoted Trump. I had just started to read the email when my phone rang. It was Rhona Graff, Trump's assistant, saying he was on the line. "Maggie," he began, "Roger Stone doesn't speak for me." He went on to basically recite the statement I had open before me.

I was confused. In our conversations Stone had never said he was speaking for Trump, and I had not written that he was. Trump was denying something that no one had ever claimed. While Stone never described himself as Trump's brain—and always said the opposite in interviews and in his own writing—Trump was, I would learn, particularly sensitive to the notion that he was anyone's puppet. Competing with Stone for primacy with Trump in relation to politics, Cohen, a comparative novice, set out to manufacture his own effort to "draft" Trump into the 2012 race, much as Stone had first done a quarter century earlier. Trump encouraged the competing efforts, caring only that he would have possession of the eventual list of names that was developed.

The media responded by pursuing Trump as a potential candidate. In March, he was interviewed aboard his plane by ABC News's Ashleigh Banfield, who asked him about the speculation regarding Obama's origins. Trump said that he had "a little doubt, just a little" about Obama's birthplace because he "grew up and nobody knew him." Anyone who "even gives any hint of being a birther," he lamented, would be labeled "as an idiot."

When the interview aired on **Good Morning America,** Trump's remarks on "birtherism"—the lie that Obama may not have been born in the United States—made news. Unlike some of his other provocative comments over the years in interviews, this one was not at all improvised. In the month since his CPAC speech, Trump had been exploring this new conspiratorially minded subculture. He sought out a conversation with **WorldNetDaily** founder Joseph Farah and later the writer Jerome Corsi, who was planning to publish a book called **Where's the Birth Certificate? The Case That Barack Obama Is Not Eligible to Be President.** Stone insisted he did not give Trump the idea and told Trump he would be called a racist. But publicly, he said it was "brilliant" in its appeal to the right-wing base.

Republicans had complained for nearly three years that Obama had received a relatively free pass for saying that rural white voters clung "to guns or religion or antipathy toward people who aren't like them," and they thought McCain had failed to fight Obama hard enough. But most conservative commentators, even otherwise caustic voices such as Andrew Breitbart and

Ann Coulter, nevertheless derided Trump for questioning Obama's legitimacy as president. Trump kept with it, delighted by the headlines. "We've studied it very closely. His family doesn't even know what hospital he was born in. You know that, right? Do you know that? This is all fact. This is all in the records," Trump told the **Daily Caller** website, launched over a year earlier by conservative journalist Tucker Carlson. He escalated with each interview, claiming in one that he was dispatching investigators to Hawaii to search for the birth certificate and "they cannot believe what they're finding." Even as they mocked Trump's shamelessness, the mainstream press could not turn away from the story, believing itself a fact-checker responsible for educating the public that it was false. (Obama had in fact released a version of his birth certificate in 2008.) All that did was further spread the lie, which was itself a barely coded way of suggesting that the first Black president illegitimately held the office.

On March 23, six days after Trump went public about his birther thoughts, Strawn announced that Trump would headline the Iowa GOP Lincoln Day Dinner that June, as politicking in the first caucus state would be heating up. Trump was suddenly interested in the idea of expanding his political operation. He tried to persuade Fabrizio to say he would work on a potential Trump candidacy, but Fabrizio politely declined. (He would end up working for another candidate.) An old Trump family friend, the political strategist Dick Morris, suggested he talk to a Republican pollster named John McLaughlin and his brother, Jim. The two had worked previously for Frank Rizzo, the Philadelphia mayor who had been an avatar of white-grievance politics under a law-and-order banner and who was the police commissioner in Philadelphia when Trump lived there as a college student.

John McLaughlin tried to impress upon Trump the reality that if he decided to seek office he would have to leave **Celebrity Apprentice**, a spinoff of **The Apprentice** that pitted largely B-list or over-the-hill stars against one another. Trump insisted McLaughlin was wrong, but it was the only thing that seemed to give him pause in those conversations, at least momentarily. But he still told the brothers to go ahead and draw up a campaign plan he could use if he decided to proceed. To some around him, Trump seemed to be engaging in yet another stunt. But the face he presented to the McLaughlins was one of a serious potential candidate.

And yet, even as he went through the motions toward running, few if any consultants were paid for their work; most were working for free to prepare him for a possible race.

They probed where he stood on issues. He said the economy was flat and the budget deficit too high. He disagreed with Obama's pursuit of new free-trade deals. He barely mentioned immigration as a concern. When Jim McLaughlin asked where Trump was on social issues like abortion, Trump explained his conversion to a pro-life position with a story about a couple he and Melania knew who had almost aborted a pregnancy and then decided not to.

Never content to have just one person doing a task, Trump started calling the Republican pollster Kellyanne Conway for advice. He knew Conway through her husband, George, an attorney active in conservative legal circles. The Conways owned an apartment in a tower Trump had built near the United Nations headquarters, and when other residents sought to remove Trump's name from the building, George defended him. When Trump asked George to sit on the board of the building, he declined, but suggested his wife. Her client list tended toward more evangelical candidates and socially conservative causes, and she offered to connect him with evangelical leaders.

Trump worked to build relationships elsewhere within Republican politics. Despite being notoriously cheap in his charitable giving, and, by then, his fundraising, Trump gave vague assurances to the Republican National Committee's newly minted chairman, Reince Priebus, that he would help the cash-strapped committee with a six-figure fundraiser at his golf club in Virginia. The assurance seemed to quell the risk of Priebus publicly rebuking Trump over the birther claims at a time when Priebus privately asked Trump to stop. The promised Trump-led fundraiser never came to pass.

After a month of work, the McLaughlins returned

with a plan by which Trump could get into the race by May 25. They recommended a former Rudy Giuliani aide named Jason Miller to serve as the campaign manager, and a New Hampshire operative named Corey Lewandowski as the state director there. Already the lack of a professional political infrastructure was becoming clear: Trump's narrow sphere of advisers were completely unprepared when reporters did the routine work of digging into his personal voting history and record of party switching.

The national media were deeply skeptical that Trump would actually run, let alone do well, and yet could not get enough of the story he was creating. He worked to feed the growing interest in his potential candidacy, leaking items about his finances, including the unverifiable—and hard to fathom—claim his aides made to me that he was worth more than $7 billion (one that editors nonetheless wanted a story on). In one interview after another, he described what he would do as president in terms that were completely disconnected from the actual powers of the office. Yet few interviewers were able, or tried very hard, to pin Trump down on how exactly he intended to accomplish what he claimed he could.

Polls began to show him moving to the top of the field on the back of his birther claims. At a Tea Party rally in Boca Raton in mid-April 2011, where Stone joined him, he gave a speech promoting his demand that Obama release his long-form birth certificate, which Trump insinuated would contain material different from the shorter version already public. The crowd ate it up, and as he entered his limousine afterward Trump exclaimed, "Wow! That was unbelievable." Over the course of just a few weeks, Trump proved so successful at bringing birtherism into the mainstream that Obama decided he could ignore it no longer. After days of answering questions about his birth certificate, the White House released a copy of the long-form document provided by Hawaii's secretary of state. Obama told the press he did so to settle the question and avoid continued distraction by "carnival barkers" who had elevated the issue.

That same day, Trump was on his way to New Hampshire, home of the first nominating primary. He deboarded his helicopter in Portsmouth, where a huge throng of reporters waited inside the airport hangar, reminiscent of the scene when Trump visited the state in 1987. But this time, instead of talking about America's global standing or the economy, Trump, appearing surprised, congratulated himself about Obama's decision to release the birth certificate. "I've accomplished something nobody else was able to accomplish," Trump said. Then he tossed out a new question for the media to chase: where was the president's college transcript? If Obama was angry about having to engage with Trump in this way, he didn't express it to most of his aides. Instead, he talked about his frustration that the distraction was happening at all.

I followed Trump around New Hampshire during

that trip, and was struck that after his victory lap at the hangar, he did not seem especially invested in what he was doing in the state. He ducked out of a meeting with local activists, intended to be a critical piece of the one-day visit, to take a call related to Trump Organization business. On one of his final stops, at a Portsmouth diner, I watched him stop greeting voters when he spotted a large television screen on which NBC was covering the birth-certificate news. He stalled in the middle of an aisle, and stared at the screen. He remained there so long that it didn't seem to be a performance for the press, but that he was really captivated by himself. "I know what I think, he only did it because of Trump!" he said of Obama.

Then he was done, and headed back out to the black limousine that had ferried him around. He rolled down the passenger window, stuck his face through it, and opened his mouth in that familiar Cheshire smile, signaling that he was thrilled with how the day had gone.

A few days after the New Hampshire trip, Trump was in Washington to attend the White House Correspondents' Association annual black-tie dinner as guest of **The Washington Post.** Upon his arrival, Trump told reporters he knew he could expect some ribbing from **Saturday Night Live** star Seth Meyers, hired to provide the night's entertainment.

But the sitting president had his own speaking slot,

typically used to deliver a comic routine, and Obama set out to roast Trump. First, the birth certificate was put on large screens overhead, the image pulsing to loud music that filled the cavernous ballroom. "Now, I know that he's taken some flak lately, but no one is happier, no one is prouder to put this birth certificate matter to rest than the Donald," Obama said to laughter. "And that's because he can finally get back to focusing on the issues that matter—like, did we fake the moon landing? What really happened in Roswell? And where are Biggie and Tupac?"

Then Obama's sarcasm grew even more scathing. "All kidding aside, obviously, we all know about your credentials and breadth of experience." More laughs. "For example—no, seriously, just recently, in an episode of **Celebrity Apprentice,** at the steakhouse, the men's cooking team did not impress the judges from Omaha Steaks. And there was a lot of blame to go around. But you, Mr. Trump, recognized that the real problem was a lack of leadership. And so ultimately, you didn't blame Lil Jon or Meatloaf. You fired Gary Busey. And these are the kind of decisions that would keep me up at night. Well handled, sir."

Trump's face was frozen, eyebrows slightly furrowed, like a face carved into an apple. People craned their necks to see him. He managed a tight smile and a little wave, but that was all. He left quickly once the dinner ended, skipping the parties afterward. Trump and his aides insisted at the time that he loved the experience, because he was the center of attention.

In the years that followed, one adviser after another finally, privately, acknowledged that he was miserable as three thousand people laughed in his face and he had to sit and take it. A humiliated Trump insisted to an associate that the whole mess was actually Obama's fault for not just releasing the long-form certificate sooner. "I never did anything to him," Trump railed. "He created the problem himself."

By the time Sweeps Week rolled around during the second week of May, the period when national television audiences are measured for size in order to set advertising rates, executives at NBC had tired of Trump's birther fixation. **The Apprentice** had been unusually popular with African American audiences, and its star's gleeful attack on the legitimacy of the first Black president put that in peril. Trump was not ready to let go of the television franchise that had provided his return to relevance. He also was not prepared to find a new trick after seeing the birth-certificate issue defused by Obama. Trump had Cohen send out a statement that finally ended the speculation they had stoked for months. "After considerable deliberation and reflection, I have decided not to pursue the office of the presidency. This decision does not come easily or without regret, especially when my potential candidacy continues to be validated by ranking at the top of the Republican contenders in polls across the country."

The collective reaction from New York politicians and most national journalists was: **We knew it.** I was mostly aggravated by the whole experience, after treating his efforts as a somewhat serious proposition. So much time had been invested in what was, predictably, to people who knew him best in New York, a balloon that popped.

But even as Trump foreclosed on running as a Republican that year, Stone returned to the prospect of doing so outside the two-party system. In a memo to Trump titled "Trump Hostile Takeover of 2012," he argued that "third-party candidates have failed for three reasons: poor candidate performance, regional candidates (Strom Thurmond, George Wallace), or ideological, protest candidates (Teddy Roosevelt, John Anderson, Ralph Nader). All these candidacies were before the internet and cable TV age. Trump's ability to connect with average voters through electronic media is unparalleled."

By January 2012, Trump decided he did not want to begin the process of qualifying for individual state ballots—"It's not the money," he insisted—and instead wanted to endorse the likely nominee. Even after his win in the New Hampshire primary, Romney was stuck at around 25 percent support among Republican voters nationwide. Former House speaker Newt Gingrich, reinventing himself as something of an insurgent, surged as an alternative. A boost from Trump could prove helpful to Romney, whose strategists also had an interest in keeping a potential rival from drifting toward an independent run.

In negotiations with Romney aides, Cohen

demanded that an endorsement event take place at a Trump-branded property in Florida. But Romney's team was worried that he might lose the primary being held in that state and didn't want outsize attention drawn to it. They countered with Nevada, a caucus state where a large Mormon electorate pointed to a strong Romney performance, and where Trump polled relatively well. The two sides agreed on the Trump International Hotel on the Las Vegas Strip, where a blue backdrop and flags were put up to cover the gaudy lobby designs. Romney seemed uncertain what to say. "There are some things that you just can't imagine happening in your life. This is one of them," he remarked. He credited his endorser with being "one of the few people who stood up and said, 'You know what, China has been cheating. They've taken jobs from Americans. They haven't played fair.'"

The appearance was intoxicating to Trump, who wanted to become more involved in Romney's candidacy. The campaign rejected Trump's request to participate in live events, and offered instead to have him record automated calls targeted in a few states. When he wanted to be featured at the Republican National Convention, Romney aides working on the event agreed to let him appear only in a video. Trump decided he would hire a Black actor portraying Obama and "fire" him, as on **The Apprentice.** But when a hurricane bearing down on Tampa forced the cancellation of the first night's program, when the video was set to air, Romney aides were quietly relieved.

Weeks before Election Day, **Mother Jones** published a video of Romney at a private fundraiser. "There are forty-seven percent of the people who will vote for the president no matter what," Romney told donors. "There are forty-seven percent who are with him, who are dependent upon government, who believe that they are victims, who believe the government has a responsibility to care for them, who believe that they are entitled to health care, to food, to housing, to you-name-it."

Observers across the political spectrum cited the video as an illustration of Romney's weakness, a wealthy businessman out of touch with the working-class voters necessary for a winning majority coalition. "Why would you insult half the country?" Trump asked people in his office. Within days of the 2012 election, he had filed a trademark on a familiar phrase in politics, used most notably by Ronald Reagan and Bill Clinton: "Make America Great Again." The following January, Trump was visited in Las Vegas by Aras Agalarov, an Azerbaijani-Russian oligarch, and his son, Emin, a pop star active in the family's real estate company. Later that year the Miss Universe contest Trump co-owned with NBC would be hosted for the first time in Russia, and he had sought out the Agalarovs to help stage it at one of their Moscow properties. The elder Agalarov had ties to President Vladimir Putin, and Trump hoped his appearance at the pageant would help to facilitate his long-held dream of developing a project in the Russian capital. "Will he become my new best friend?" Trump asked on Twitter. Putin never met with Trump, but that did not dampen Trump's ambitions. "I had a great weekend with you and your family," he tweeted afterward at Aras Agalarov. "TRUMP TOWER-MOSCOW is next."

Years later, federal officials would scrutinize Trump's trip to Moscow, and his political opponents would compile a document filled with lurid, and unsubstantiated, claims. But for now the more threatening investigations were coming from state and local probes into fraud across a range of Trump businesses.

In New York, longtime district attorney Robert Morgenthau, Trump's friend for decades, had retired in 2009, and shortly thereafter his successor, Cy Vance, opened an investigation into the Trump SoHo hotel-condo project that had opened in 2010. Tenants had filed suit against the Trump Organization, claiming "deceptive sales practices." Trump's lawyer, Marc Kasowitz, directly lobbied Vance not to bring a case and made two donations to Vance's campaign, both of which Vance ultimately returned.

Vance decided not to convene a grand jury. Vance associates ultimately believed he saw it as a complicated case—the Trumps and their partners had settled the lawsuit related to the condos, with plaintiffs agreeing not to cooperate with prosecutors unless subpoenaed—and he had already had a recent high-profile loss in a different case. Nonetheless, it was another Trump-related investigation that ultimately went nowhere.

At the same time, Trump faced the threat of independent probes by attorneys general in some of the country's largest states. All were looking into whether Trump University, the glorified real estate training seminar launched in 2005, had defrauded students by portraying itself as an academic institution despite its inability to confer academic degrees or award credits. In 2010, Greg Abbott, the Texas attorney general, opened a civil investigation into "possibly deceptive trade practices," but after Trump University abruptly pulled out of the state, Abbott dropped the matter. Trump gave thirty-five thousand dollars to Abbott's gubernatorial campaign that year.

In New York, Attorney General Eric Schneiderman was more persistent, even after Trump University fully ceased operations there in 2011. To try to make the potential civil action go away, Trump hired Avi Schick, who had been involved in Schneiderman's transition, to represent him in the case. Schick floated a potential settlement. Around five hundred thousand dollars was discussed, but Trump wanted his attorney to move faster. He replaced Schick, an overweight Orthodox Jew whose physical appearance Trump made clear repelled him, with Kasowitz in the negotiations with the attorney general.

But no deal was forthcoming, and in August 2013, Schneiderman filed a suit against Trump University, alleging fraud and deceit. Trump was done trying to settle and ready to fight back. In December, he countered with a pair of ethics complaints against Schneiderman alleging, in a convoluted way, that the official had used the investigation as a mechanism to coerce campaign contributions from Trump and his family and then punish them for failing to give. It was a telling indication of Trump's view of all public officials, including prosecutors and investigators. Trump's foundation donated twenty-five thousand dollars to one of Florida attorney general Pam Bondi's campaign committees. She had considered joining Schneiderman's suit, but ultimately declined to. (During the same period, Trump also sent four-figure donations to California attorney general Kamala Harris, a Democrat. Her office ultimately took no action against Trump University even as it went after other for-profit educational entities.) "As a businessman and a very substantial donor to very important people, when you give, they do whatever the hell you want them to do," he later said. "As a businessman, I need that."

Unlike his previous near campaigns for president, after which Trump drifted away from politics, after 2012 he sustained and if anything deepened his interest. He appeared bored by a business that had several years earlier moved away from building and more heavily into branding the Trump name.

He began using advisers to help expand his footprint online. A Stone protégé named Sam Nunberg worked to develop a rapport with conservative outlets that did not have a natural affinity for him, such as **Breitbart** and the **Daily Caller.** Trump, however, remained dismissive of anything that was not the type of media outlet—a big-city newspaper, glossy magazine, or television station—that existed when he had first emerged as a public figure. When Nunberg would show him printouts of articles about him that he had helped to place on websites, Trump would reply, "Did you get me anything real?"

Even as he was disdainful of newer digital media outlets, Trump eagerly experimented with social media. Justin McConney, the young son of Trump's company controller, saw how relatable to others Trump had been during the free-flowing, anything-goes conversations he had had on Howard Stern's radio show, and thought he could replicate that online—only now with complete control. McConney began having Trump record videos, speaking directly to camera, to be posted on a company YouTube channel. But Twitter's easily quantifiable measures of success and failure especially appealed to Trump. He closely tracked his number of followers and retweets, and relentlessly toyed with his voice and subject matter to discover what gained traction on the site. He started with tweets that pushed fake controversies—weighing in on the split between young actors Robert Pattinson and Kristen Stewart, taking the man's side—when the real goal was to promote the Miss Universe pageant. When McConney suggested that Trump live-tweet a debate between Obama and Romney, Trump eagerly jumped in. With time, Trump saw the opportunity to respond to those he felt had attacked him. (His first-ever tweet about me came just before Election Day 2012, responding to my reporting at **Politico** on a Chrysler executive calling him "full of shit" for attacking Obama as a "terrible negotiator." It was a straightforward story; he wrote that I was "an unprofessional hack who belongs @politico with all the other Obama hacks.")

A few months later, Trump—who didn't like to use email and was not particularly tech savvy—sent out the first tweet he had typed out for himself on an Android smartphone, thanking an actress for her warm words about him. McConney later compared the moment to the scene in the movie **Jurassic Park,** when dinosaurs realize they can open doors themselves. In Trump's case, no longer having to rely on staff meant there was no one to mediate his worst impulses, such as when he targeted the 1950s actress Kim Novak for her plastic surgery, sending her into a deep depression. (After Novak released a statement that accused him of bullying, he apologized privately.)

One morning in December 2013, Meredith McIver sent Nunberg an email. "DJT was wondering if there was any reason he gained 6,000 followers yesterday," she wrote. "I noticed the Pete Rose and Mandela tweets did well. His quotes usually do well too," she wrote. "When he mentions NY-centric issues or people (Graydon Carter, AG etc) there is not as much pick up. A lot of people worldwide don't know who they are and don't care. That's one explanation but are there other reasons (not urgent, just to let you know he is wondering)."

Yet Trump was keeping his options open in New York. That fall he had received a memo from an upstate state assemblyman, Bill Nojay, who like many Republicans agonized about his party's inability to find a strong candidate to challenge Governor Andrew Cuomo's reelection in 2014. Trump, he argued, would fit the bill. "Trump must transition from being entertainment to convincing voters he can help them get a job, pay their taxes, educate their children, stay safe," Nojay wrote. But even if, as Stone insisted to him, Trump should keep his eye on the presidency, winning the governor's mansion would set him up for it. "No one in U.S. history has won the White House without first holding high public office (Grant & Eisenhower had never been elected to anything, but were Generals of the Army during wartime; all the rest had been state or national elected figures before going to the WH)," Nojay argued. "He is the right age; it's show time; now or likely never."

Especially after the Nojay memo was provided to the **New York Post,** which published excerpts, Trump considered entering the race, but it never received his full focus. He made a few trips upstate and to western New York, where he delivered meandering speeches.

Conversations with New York State Republican Party chairman Ed Cox revealed that Trump did not understand the party's process for selecting a candidate, presuming falsely that Cox could clear the field for him ahead of a nominating convention, which was the only way Trump really wanted to run. Even as he claimed he was ready to fund a campaign, Trump would not commit to a consistent amount of money. When he first contacted Cox to express Trump's interest in the race, Cohen said he had budgeted $30 million. A few weeks later, Cohen told Cox that Trump was prepared to relinquish control of his company to his children but to spend only $5 million on a race. When Trump himself met with county Republican chairs, he talked about a willingness to spend $15 million, but wanted to be able to recover it if necessary.

Even as Trump's advisers worked to explore a potential run, many had reason to be skeptical of his prospects against Cuomo, a formidable campaigner in an overwhelmingly Democratic state. When Kellyanne Conway polled the race for the group Citizens United, the report found a mixed reaction to Trump. "NY loves its celebrity politicians and families: the Kennedys, Moynihans, Buckleys, Clintons, and even the Cuomos," she wrote. "Donald Trump fits that (loose) bill, and he has the money and moxie to compete if he chooses to enter the race. He may need to convince a skeptical electorate of his candidacy, given his very public consideration of running for POTUS before. When offered a choice between offices, New Yorkers are more than twice as likely to urge Trump to run for Governor of New York (27%) than President of the United States (12%). A plurality [sic] a third option: run for neither.”

After months of observing him, Cox became convinced Trump lacked the commitment necessary to run and the kind of political discipline required to win statewide. He traveled to Mar-a-Lago in March 2014 to tell him that it might not work out. Trump reacted angrily; they didn't finish their dinner. The next day, Trump made public that he would not seek the governorship.

He refocused his interest on the presidency. Later that spring, Trump was alerted by Bill Palatucci, a top adviser to newly reelected New Jersey governor Chris Christie, that Christie would be using Trump's golf club in Bedminster, New Jersey, to raise money for Iowa governor Terry Branstad. As a Washington outsider, Christie had developed a reputation for tangling with New Jersey public employee unions and in name-calling showdowns with citizens at town-hall meetings, a style of confrontation that a strain of Republicans craved after the 2012 race. Christie had passed on a presidential run then, but was looking ahead to 2016 and was using a new post as chairman of the Republican Governors Association to build relationships nationwide. Unlike past occasions, this time when Trump learned the fundraiser was for Iowa's governor, he asked, “Can I come?” “Of course,” Palatucci said.

Unbeknownst to Palatucci, Nunberg had repeatedly attempted to undermine Christie in conservative media. The governor was almost certain to seek the presidency in 2016, and as a pugnacious northeasterner with a history of moderate politics on some key issues would occupy a similar space to Trump in a primary field. Trump was aware that Nunberg pushed research to outlets such as **Breitbart** that raised questions about Christie's conservative bona fides, especially on immigration.

During the fundraiser, Christie sat on one side of Branstad, and Trump on the other. Trump listened quietly through Branstad's remarks and the question-and-answer session that followed. When it was over, Trump approached Palatucci. "Bill, great event," he said. "Do you mind if I have five minutes alone with Terry Branstad?" Palatucci acquiesced, and Trump and Branstad slipped outside to talk. It was the first of many instances of Trump attempting to exploit Christie in the service of his own ambitions.

That fall, Branstad was easily reelected, ensuring that when Iowans became the first voters to cast ballots in the 2016 election cycle he would be the state's most important figure.

It proved to be a triumphant November for Republicans, who took back control of the Senate, solidified their advantage in the House, and claimed new majorities in ten state legislative chambers. And the way they did was a dramatic reversal from the vision for a comeback laid out by the Republican

National Committee just a year earlier. After Romney's defeat, the committee's chairman, Reince Priebus, had commissioned an "autopsy" report to learn from the experience. The principal strategic recommendation returned by the Growth and Opportunity Project was for Republicans to better appeal to the country's fast-growing Latino population, notably by moderating hard-line attitudes toward immigration.

But in place of the upbeat outreach the RNC prescribed, some of the party's most successful candidates in 2014, such as newly elected senator Tom Cotton of Arkansas, ran on dark warnings about foreign threats and border security. Summertime gains by the Islamic State against the Iraqi government helped to stoke fears of Middle Eastern terrorists, while an Ebola outbreak in West Africa in the months before the election led Republicans to demand that border authorities turn away travelers from that part of the world. Many of the candidates who ran on those themes succeeded, and the sense of menace they described matched where voters' emotions were. Pollsters told me they could not remember another time so many candidates in statewide and local races had won their elections with voters viewing them more negatively than they did positively. An electorate made restless by misguided wars and a financial crisis—marked by few prosecutions of bankers responsible but massive bailouts of their companies—didn't punish candidates for engaging in slashing attacks on their rivals. They expected it was going to happen.

It was an environment primed to reward Trump, who in his previous forays in electoral politics had always done a better job of articulating what he was against than what he was for. As 2015 began, Trump took steps well beyond anything he had done any of the three previous times he publicly entertained a run for the White House. He located a campaign manager, Lewandowski, the New Hampshire operative and former congressional aide who had worked for the Koch brothers–funded Americans for Prosperity, who came recommended by Citizens United president David Bossie. One of Lewandowski's first acts after being hired was to call John McLaughlin, the pollster whose campaign plan four years earlier stayed on the shelf, and tell him it was time to start polling Iowa.

Yet few people took Trump's ambition to run for president as seriously as he took himself. When I later asked a longtime acquaintance why Trump had finally decided to run after so many prior feints, the person responded without hesitation, "He's gotten crazier."

CHAPTER 12

Make or Break

T rump is going to announce on June 16 and we want you to break it," Sam Nunberg told me in the spring of 2015.

I had joined **The New York Times** three months earlier, uncertain as to whether I would spend more of the next two years reporting on Democratic front-runner Hillary Clinton, whom I had covered since her first run for office in 2000 and who was of special interest to the **Times** as a hometown candidate, or the burgeoning Republican field. I had remained in regular contact with Trump's advisers, including Nunberg and his mentor Roger Stone, who would periodically email me about items in the news or their thoughts on candidates seeking office.

Despite the specificity of the announcement date, I thought what Nunberg told me was almost certainly bullshit. Trump had floated this so many times previously when there was media coverage to be had and pulled back before he had to do any of the really difficult work of being a candidate, such as filing personal financial-disclosure reports. Despite my inherent skepticism, I had taken Trump fairly seriously as a political force in 2011 because of the reception I saw him get from voters as he visited New Hampshire. Friends and sources in New York had mocked me as gullible for that coverage. After that experience, I came to think that Trump had not ever really entertained a run even as he put on a performance of doing so, and I rued the thought that I may have been manipulated into helping elevate his profile. In the fall of 2014, working with a **Politico** colleague on the large Republican presidential field beginning to assemble, I advised to leave Trump out lest we fall for another bluff of his.

I expressed my thoughts to Nunberg, telling him, "I'm not writing anything until he announces" his candidacy. He asked if I would meet with Trump to hear the campaign plans from him directly; I agreed. I first went up to Trump's office for the standard tour of his display of collectibles. Trump lingered on Shaquille O'Neal's gargantuan sneaker and a photo of him alongside Wisconsin governor Scott Walker, then seen as one of the most formidable Republican presidential contenders, which Walker had sent him. Then he led me to the area outside his office, pausing with instructions for an assistant—known as one of "the girls" at Trump Tower—to "pull up the rap videos." She obliged: on her computer screen was a YouTube video of a rap artist I didn't recognize. Trump's name was mentioned in the song. "See?" he said. "The Blacks" liked him.

We headed downstairs to the Trump Grille, near the large orange marble waterfall that my grade school class had once trekked to see. Servers pushed two-tops together to make our table, placed in such a way as to ensure that tourists passing through the atrium could gawk at Trump. We were joined by his enforcer Michael Cohen; Corey Lewandowski, the manager of his campaign-in-waiting; and his new spokesperson, Hope Hicks. All seemed in thrall to Trump, most laughing dutifully whenever he cracked a joke and nodding as he described his plans.

Trump ordered a Diet Coke, and almost immediately started selling me on why this time he was serious about running. Moving through the Republican nominating calendar, he and Lewandowski tossed off eight-figure amounts—$25 million here, $30 million there—that he planned to spend in states like South Carolina. I looked back and forth between them, like at a tennis match. I did not even bother taking notes on everything that was said; it seemed like another performance, and nothing I heard dislodged my cynicism about the whole enterprise. I could tell Trump was growing frustrated that I did not believe any of it, furrowing his brow and throwing his hands up in exasperation.

What I didn't realize then was how far along a Trump candidacy already was. Few outside of a small circle

did. Other Republican candidates had been making
their own trips to Trump Tower to flatter him in the
hopes of winning him over, or at least to keep him
out of their way. Even Bill Clinton continued to treat
Trump as something passing for a friend. When the
two men spoke that May, Clinton—ever the pleaser
himself and needing to see his own inherent abilities
reflected in others—told Trump that he had tapped
into a real current of dissatisfaction among a segment
of Republicans.

Much of Trump's appeal as a candidate, his advisers knew, would come from his wealth, celebrity, and charisma. Stone believed that Trump's
views were generally right of center and able to be
pitched successfully to Republican primary voters.
Trump had already had his about-face on abortion, which would have been the main impedi-
ment. Nunberg realized early on that Trump had
little emotional investment in most issues, but that
proposing tweets for Trump to send was a way to
get the prospective candidate engaged. They both
suggested Trump speak with conservative talk-radio
hosts. Nunberg sold both Trump and the radio host
Mark Levin on each other, facilitating an interview,
which gave Levin the sense that Trump was at least
passingly serious.

Perhaps most important, Stone and Nunberg had
attempted to draw Trump's attention to immigration,
a point of friction between grassroots activists and
the party's pro-business establishment since McCain

had promoted a 2005 bipartisan bill pairing increased border enforcement with a path to citizenship that conservative media called "amnesty." But Trump had little organic interest in the topic; he was far more interested in the concept of other nations' "ripping us off" through trade practices and international institutions. In 2014, Stone and Nunberg came to a new way of approaching the issue: he should propose a physical barrier along the border. They initially imagined the pitch as a mnemonic device that would remind the often unfocused potential candidate to remember to touch on immigration in speeches and interviews. But for a lifelong builder, the concept of a "wall" clicked in a way that visa-overstay enforcement never could. It became a political cause unto itself. And when he delivered that promise in Iowa in January—"We have to build a fence," he said, "and it's got to be a beauty"—the audience took to it immediately.

As Trump toured prospective-candidate forums in the early-voting states, one staple of his 2011 near campaign had disappeared from speeches. His lie about the birthplace of the first Black president, Trump was told by advisers, would ultimately cap his support in a Republican primary and have further consequences in a general election. But it was the negative response from NBC executives in 2011 about the topic that ultimately seemed to prove persuasive to him. He had been warned that memories of his birther crusade still hurt him in the African

American community, and that upon launching a campaign he would benefit from visible Black supporters willing to vouch for him. Trump told Cohen that he wanted him to film a testimonial video with "that black guy," referring to a man named Clyde Frazier, to whom the Trump Foundation had given twenty-five thousand dollars for a basketball charity he ran in Harlem in honor of a son killed in the terrorist attack on the World Trade Center. Trump, Cohen recalled, pressed him to extract from Frazier a testimonial that "no white man has ever done" as much for me "as Donald Trump." (Frazier recorded a video, without using that formulation. Trump never used the video for anything, because, according to Cohen, Frazier's praise for Trump wasn't strongly worded enough.)

Birtherism was not the only part of his past Trump allies sought to neutralize ahead of a presidential campaign. In early 2015, Trump met with David Pecker, the owner of the **National Enquirer.** Unlike traditional news outlets, the **Enquirer** freely paid for stories, a source not only of print exclusives but of influence for Pecker. He practiced what were known as "catch and kill" operations—buying material that would damage a friend, and then burying it on their behalf—and had deployed the method to quash stories about allegations of Trump's extramarital affairs. Pecker arrived at Trump Tower with a copy of the tabloid featuring Prince Andrew, the Duke of York, and Jeffrey Epstein, the investor and convicted sex offender and onetime friend of Trump, with whom Trump had fallen out years earlier. The two men talked about Epstein's private island, where he was rumored to bring powerful men to have sexual encounters with young women. Trump called it "whore island" and told aides he had never been there.

Once, in the Trump Tower office, Nunberg asked Trump what his biggest worry was about running. Trump had a simple reply: "The women." Not business, not being violent with anyone, Nunberg recalled, but women. Trump pointed up toward his penthouse. "I'll get in trouble upstairs."

The official campaign kickoff began with Trump descending an escalator into the same Trump Tower atrium where we had lunched a few weeks earlier, now decked out for the occasion with a certain odd-ball sense of pageantry and people hired through an outside firm to build out a crowd.

Almost immediately after reaching the podium Trump put aside the speech his advisers had written for him. He went on for nearly an hour, a blizzard of unverifiable boasts about his financial situation and borderline-paranoid warnings about foreign threats, laced with his decades-old anger about trade and enough of a sense of grievance and a promise to restore what he described as America's dulled luster to appeal to a segment of voters. "The

U.S. has become a dumping ground for everybody else's problems," he ranted at one point. It was a moment of demagoguery a few beats later—"when Mexico sends its people," he said, "they're rapists"—that captured a number of the headlines, although his trade position resonated with core Republican voters. Trump managed to overshadow the previous day's campaign announcement by former Florida governor Jeb Bush, whose father and brother had served as president.

Trump had done exactly what he set out to do: make the contest about himself, at least for that day. He returned to the embrace of his advisers, except for one. For thirty years, Stone had tended to the dream of a Trump presidential campaign, but missed the announcement speech due to eye surgery. "Well, this is what you always wanted," Trump told Stone of the kickoff.

Trump went upstairs to tape his first interview as a candidate, with Fox News host Bill O'Reilly. Trump insisted on having the backdrop out the window behind him be the Plaza Hotel that he no longer owned. O'Reilly probed Trump about his views toward Russia, whose leader Vladimir Putin had sent troops into the Ukraine-held peninsula of Crimea less than two years earlier, to international condemnation. "I was over in Moscow two years ago and I will tell you—you can get along with those people and get along with them well," Trump said. "You can make deals with those people. Obama can't."

"So you could make a deal with Putin to stop his expansion?" O'Reilly said, referring specifically to Crimea. Trump did not give any sense that he was aware of what had happened in Crimea. "I would be willing to bet I would have a great relationship with Putin. It's about leadership," he said.

"Based on what?" O'Reilly protested. "You're two macho guys?"

"No, no, no, I mean based on a feel," Trump said. "I would be able to get along, in my opinion, with Putin."

Republican leaders responded to Trump's candidacy with instant alarm. Shortly after the kickoff speech, a colleague got word of a private meeting at the Hay-Adams Hotel where several prominent Washington-based Republicans commiserated about the predicament in which he was putting their party. What struck me about this conversation, and others like it, was how powerless some of the most powerful people in American politics felt when up against Trump.

The Republican National Committee's chairman, Reince Priebus, decided to try. A diminutive Wisconsinite with a thick midwestern accent and a mild demeanor, Priebus called Trump in early July. The call started out pleasantly: they talked about Trump's performance in the campaign. But Priebus quickly shifted to a warning: Trump's rhetoric about

Mexicans created a problem for the entire party, he said. **The Washington Post** soon reported on the exchange, and I called Trump to try to get the same story. Trump denied the **Post** story at first. "It was more of a congratulatory call," he insisted. When I pressed whether Priebus had chastised him, Trump did not say the story was false. Instead, he said, Priebus "knows better than to lecture me." There was a pause, and he added, "We're not dealing with a five-star army general." I chuckled reflexively at the line. The conversation with Priebus had been tougher than Trump portrayed to me, and it did little but embolden him. Trump loved to do the opposite of what he was asked by someone trying to control him, a quality that had only gotten more intense as he got older.

Barely a month after formally entering politics for the first time, Trump found himself at the top of the Republican primary polls—ahead of senators and governors, candidates with dozens of years of combined government experience. Trump approached campaigning for president much as he did everything else in his life—intimidating, threatening, and humiliating anyone he saw in his path. Trump's public pronouncements got progressively meaner, steadily more shocking, and almost always in response to criticism. The attacks garnered condemnation from other Republicans, which drove even more news coverage to Trump before yielding to his next outrage.

In mid-July, Trump gleefully attacked John

McCain, who had spent five years in captivity during the Vietnam War before eventually becoming his party's standard-bearer, as a "loser" and "not a war hero" in response to relatively mild criticism that Trump was bringing out "the crazies." When South Carolina senator Lindsey Graham, a McCain friend and presidential candidate himself, responded in an interview that Trump should "stop being a jackass," Trump read Graham's cell-phone number aloud from a rally in his home state and encouraged people to call it. Graham chose to play it off as a joke rather than confronting the egregious violation of his privacy, the kind that Trump aides complained about privately when a mobile number that had belonged to Trump was made public a short time later by the website **Gawker.**

I remember growing queasy as I watched the cell-phone stunt in real time. I was in the **Times** newsroom, with the rally airing on a nearby television as I spoke on the phone with a source, who I hung up on so I could focus on what Trump was doing. I assumed there would be extensive backlash. I was wrong. "It was so funny," one colleague in the news business remembered thinking about the Graham stunt years later. And there, in a nutshell, was the essence of how Trump was being interpreted. It seemed as though there was both a menacing psychological-thriller score and a sitcom laugh track playing behind him at all times.

●　●　●

A defining feature of anything Trump has run has been the active disdain that people working for him have for one another. It was true with his business executives and consultants in the 1990s and among his political advisers in the 2000s. Trump fostered their conflict, pitting them against one another, telling one not to do something and then ordering a colleague to carry out the same order, gossiping about them to one another constantly and deflecting the attention they might put on his own actions. But even as Trump's office split into warring camps, there was usually a larger sense of purpose. When he became a political figure, that spirit largely evaporated.

He had become a top-tier presidential candidate without ever building out a traditional campaign staff, which remained unusually lean due to Trump's stinginess about paying consultants and skepticism about political professionals. (The campaign was based at Trump Tower, and paid Trump to rent the space.) His digital strategist was Brad Parscale, a Texas web developer who had managed sites for the Trump Winery and Eric Trump Foundation and had worked only on one political race, for county tax assessor. But he was familiar to the Trumps and, initially, he came cheap: he charged only fifteen hundred dollars to build the campaign's website.

But that small inner circle was riven even before Trump announced his candidacy. Nunberg and Lewandowski, both sharp-edged and impatient personalities, hated each other almost upon meeting.

When the website **Business Insider** reported on years-old Facebook posts by Nunberg in which he referred to civil rights activist Al Sharpton's daughter using a racist slur, Lewandowski and Cohen pushed Trump to banish their rival. Nunberg blamed his co-workers for the posts' becoming public and insisted he didn't recall writing them, although he wrote Sharpton a letter of apology. Trump told Cohen that he didn't want Sharpton thinking he was a racist and agreed to have Nunberg fired. Stone left shortly thereafter, while Trump was in the midst of a week of attacks on the Fox News host Megyn Kelly. Stone had given me a copy of a resignation letter days before he ultimately submitted it. When he presented it to Trump, I reported that Stone had resigned. Trump spoke to a reporter at **The Washington Post** and insisted Stone had been fired, issuing a press statement that alleged the consultant was using the campaign for his own publicity purposes.

That left Lewandowski, who enthralled Trump with close attention to his needs and an irrepressible desire to troll the establishment, with an unchallenged role running the day-to-day campaign. To Trump's three oldest children, Lewandowski over time would seem to be going even further—acting like a member of the family, a sixth child. Lewandowski was not always in Trump's good graces; he was screamed at like all the rest at various points. But in him, Trump saw a like-minded man who appealed to his impulses. A former campaign adviser once told me that he believed that when Trump looked in the mirror, he saw Lewandowski's image reflected back.

Trump, who could accept being told "no" only in measured doses, always needed at least one sycophant in his orbit. Those in his circle willing to go along with that were the ones who survived. By autumn 2015, those who remained around Trump were rarely constraints on his behavior, and sometimes served to abet his worst instincts. In late August, Trump was challenged at an Iowa press conference by Jorge Ramos, an anchor for the Spanish-language network Univision and the country's most prominent Latino journalist. "Excuse me, sit down, you weren't called," Trump told Ramos before looking in the direction of Keith Schiller, a former New York Police Department detective who had started working for Trump as a part-time bodyguard and eventually became security chief for both his company and campaign. As Ramos continued trying to ask his question, Schiller approached him and then escorted the newsman out of the room. A week later, on the sidewalk in front of Trump Tower, facing a pack of activists protesting Trump's immigration views, Schiller was captured on video taking away one of their signs. In a lawsuit filed later, protesters alleged that when one ran after Schiller and wrapped his arms around him to grab the sign back, Schiller whirled around and slammed him in the face. ("I love the Hispanics,"

Trump insisted in response to questions about the activists. "I have thousands of Hispanics right now working for me.")

The protesters had gathered outside Trump Tower as Priebus was inside, trying to mitigate a lingering threat to the Republican Party that Trump had left open. On a debate stage the previous month Trump had been the only candidate who refused to say he would support the party's nominee if he failed to win the nomination himself, something he'd dangled as a possibility earlier in the campaign, depending on how he felt he was treated. Indeed, in the absence of such a commitment, it was hard to imagine him endorsing many of his rivals, whom he had systematically attacked in devastating terms. He called Bush "low energy." He attacked Senator Rand Paul and businesswoman Carly Fiorina as physically unattractive. ("Look at that face. Would anyone vote for that?" Trump asked about Fiorina in a private moment with a reporter.) Only one candidate would truly threaten Trump's early standing in the race: acclaimed pediatric neurosurgeon Ben Carson, who was also seeking office for the first time and was the only African American candidate in the large field. When Carson rose in the polls, Trump drew attention to a passage in his memoir in which Carson described his "pathological temper" as a young man. "That's a big problem because you don't cure that," Trump told CNN. "As an example:

child molesting. You don't cure these people. You don't cure a child molester. There's no cure for it. Pathological, there's no cure for that."

Priebus had arrived that early September day with a written pledge that committed Trump not to launch a third-party bid, which would almost certainly sink whoever ended up the Republican nominee. The two men met privately, and then Trump tried to coerce Priebus to join him before the cameras. Priebus declined. Trump went downstairs alone, and waved around the piece of paper Priebus had brought, now featuring his signature. "I will be totally pledging my allegiance to the Republican Party and the conservative principles for which it stands," Trump said, echoing the patriotic recitation that children are taught in school. As he almost always did, though, Trump left himself a trap door. "I have no intention of changing my mind," Trump said, before another hesitation. "I see no circumstances under which I would tear up that pledge."

Even as Trump sat atop the Republican field, there was no guarantee he would stay there, especially as the contest became more serious in the fall. Trump was aware of that. Early on, he discussed with advisers what he would do if his fortunes reversed. One idea was that Trump would quit the race when his numbers began to sink, blaming a Republican Party out of step with him on a number of issues, among them marriage equality. He had already declared himself opposed to gay marriage, but to make an excuse as he left the race he was open to saying the opposite.

In a conversation with his friend Christie, who got into the race two weeks after Trump did, Trump was blunt, confiding that he wasn't sure he would make it past October. Throughout his life, Trump was forever trying to keep his options open, and he made no exception as he embarked on his first political race.

CHAPTER 13

Many People Are Saying

Donald Trump began his campaign for the presidency in the summer of 2015 by demagoguing Mexican migrants. Events that fall provided him with an even more urgent appeal to fear. On November 13, a coordinated attack in Paris, France—on a concert hall, restaurants, and outside a full soccer stadium—killed 130 people and injured more than 600 more. The Islamic State, which had come to displace Al Qaeda as the primary overseas terror threat, claimed responsibility for the attack. Trump's response was to warn America that Syrian refugees "could be the great Trojan horse" (while offering up a wildly inflated number that he claimed the Obama administration was planning to admit) and said that as president he would consider shutting down mosques. Within a Republican Party that was divided on matters of foreign and domestic policy, Trump had located a strain of thought uniting different factions of conservatives: anti-Muslim sentiment.

In an interview shortly thereafter, Trump pined for the days after September 11 when the New York Police Department surveilled mosques as an antiterror measure. More surveillance, Trump insisted, was necessary. "We're going to have to do certain things that were frankly unthinkable a year ago," he said. But Trump was not at all specific about what that might entail, so the reporter began offering up a menu of hypotheticals. What about warrantless searches? Or some kind of registry of Muslims? "We're going to have to look very, very carefully," Trump said, seeming open to endorsing a policy proposal no officials had actually introduced.

It was a common Trump rhetorical device, a vague pronouncement loaded with ambiguous language and logical stretches, offering just enough to leave the impression he was agreeing with the idea in question, either to get out of the situation without revealing his actual knowledge about it or to please the interviewer. "Many people are saying" or "and other things" were Trump's often-used filler descriptors. He had done a version of this for decades, but as a presidential candidate his words carried much more weight, so journalists pressed for details that Trump was inevitably unable or unwilling to provide. "There should be a lot of systems, beyond databases," Trump told an NBC reporter, who approached him at a campaign event to follow up on his earlier comments and asked whether a database should track Muslims in the country, before veering to talk about a border wall. The reporter pressed about a database. "I would certainly implement that. Absolutely," Trump said. When the reporter asked what that would accomplish, Trump said that "it would stop people from coming in illegally." But how would they get registered in the database? "It would be just good management," Trump said. Would you go to mosques? "Different places. You sign them up at different places." When Trump was pressed on how such a registry was distinct from German policies under Nazi rule, his only response was, "You tell me. You tell me. Why don't you tell me?"

Trump had every opportunity to set the record straight with a quick sentence that he did not favor registering Muslims. But he didn't seem to want to stop people from reading that possibility into his remarks or to admit he had said more than he'd intended to say. The next day, writing a story about the controversy surrounding them, I called his campaign manager to understand what exactly he was saying. Trump got on the phone, but he would not give me a statement about what he had meant. He was about to speak onstage at a candidate forum in South Carolina, he told me, and he would probably address it there. I should watch it, he said. He ended the call.

I watched the event, held at Wofford College in Spartanburg, South Carolina. Trump answered preselected questions, including one from a student about Obama's statement on Syrian refugees that the "idea that somehow they pose a more significant threat than all the tourists that pour into the United States, every single day, just doesn't jibe with reality." The host of the town hall asked Trump, "Your thoughts?"

"I mean do we really even need to answer that

question?" Trump said, to applause. No one asked about the Muslim registry comments, and he didn't raise the topic. I asked to speak to Trump again, and was told no.

Left with no choice but to quote what he'd said publicly, I went ahead and, working with a colleague, prepared a story about Trump's apparent embrace of a system to track the country's Muslims. The issue had by then roiled the political race, with Jeb Bush taking the lead in condemning the proposal. Our story addressed the "smear" Trump had perpetuated against Muslims by labeling them a threat based solely on their faith. But I made an imprecise word choice in how I described what Trump was doing. We wrote that he had made "calls" for a registry, in part based on what he had said to the television reporter who caught him on the rope line; a better description was that he expressed openness to one. The story ran on A1.

The conservative website **Breitbart,** run by Trump ally Steve Bannon, went to work. One of their reporters produced a supposed "fact check" of our story, repeating Trump's statement that someone in the media had first raised the idea of a Muslim registry without taking note that Trump had not said yes or no to it. A separate piece, by one of the site's columnists, attacked me personally, with an unflattering picture and a false claim that I was somehow supporting Hillary Clinton. Trump sent out a tweet that read "So nice when media properly polices media. Thank you @BreitbartNews." It was the 1990s Trump play-book, using one media outlet against another to sow doubt about a story.

I suddenly found myself in the middle of a Twitter swarm, while colleagues at other outlets strained to give Trump the benefit of the doubt and his sup-porters eagerly retweeted him. For his part, Trump held a rally in Alabama that day, and had a new example to cite for one of his favorite claims: that he was being treated unfairly. In his rally speech, he suggested he wanted a "database" of Syrian refugees entering the country and surveillance of "certain" mosques, similar to the defunct NYPD program after September 11, 2001.

I wrote a short article on the rally that focused on two other developments that struck me as newswor-thy. During Trump's speech, a man wearing a Black Lives Matter T-shirt began to boo loudly. "Get him the hell out of here," Trump directed his security guards. When the man refused to leave, a half dozen people in the crowd began to punch and hit him with no evident disapproval from Trump. The piece also described how Trump, in defending his interest in more aggressive surveillance of Muslims, delivered a detailed recollection of the September 11 attacks that had no basis in reality. "I watched when the World Trade Center came tumbling down," Trump said. "And I watched in Jersey City, New Jersey, where thousands and thousands of people were cheering as that building was coming down." It was not at all clear what Trump was talking about. Among other things, he had been miles away from the Trade Center site, and miles away from New Jersey for that matter, when it all took place. An internet rumor had circulated claiming that people in Paterson, another city in northern New Jersey with an expansive Muslim population, had celebrated the attacks from their rooftops, but police had investigated and found nothing to substantiate it.

Trump refused to concede that his account was concocted. ("I know it might be not politically correct for you to talk about it," Trump told ABC News's George Stephanopoulos. "It was well covered at the time, George.") Right-leaning outlets backed Trump by surfacing a fifteen-year-old **Washington Post** report from after the 2001 attacks that law enforcement had questioned "a number of" people in Jersey City shortly after the attacks. Asked about that news clip, the article's two authors said they did not recall "thousands" of people cheering and had never been able to verify the rumors.

At another South Carolina rally that week, Trump mocked the two **Post** journalists for walking away from their original reporting, which they hadn't in fact done. At one point, he turned to impersonation, standing ramrod straight behind the lectern, then waved his arms around while dangling his hands. "Uhhh, I don't remember!" he hammed to laughs from the crowd.

It was not likely a random impression: one of the

authors, Serge Kovaleski, was born with restricted movement in his right hand. This was easy to see when one encountered him in person, as Trump had extensively when Serge covered his businesses for the **Daily News** in the 1980s. Serge had since become a dear colleague of mine at **The New York Times,** and when I saw Trump's depiction of him it struck me as disturbingly precise. When others made the connection, Trump claimed it was just a generic impression. He insisted he did not remember Kovaleski, which others who had observed them together—as well as those of us familiar with Trump's steel-trap memory for past media coverage of him, especially in the publications he most closely followed—found implausible.

The entire chain of events that had started with the Paris attack would prove to be a perfect encapsulation of Trump's candidacy. It began with provocative but deliberately imprecise language that drew people in, then the refusal to claim ownership of his own words while never quite clarifying his views, and then the taking advantage of a relatively small media error—in this case, my imprecise choice of words—to portray himself as the victim of the feeding frenzy he had unleashed. Much as he had during his divorces, bankruptcies, and public feuds, Trump drove days of news based only on his reactions to people reacting to him, with one controversy rolling frictionlessly into the next, so that the controversies clouded the media's line of sight.

A few weeks later, on December 2, 2015, another

terrorist attack made the issue even more immediate for Republicans preparing to cast votes in the statewide contests about two months later. In San Bernardino, California, a married couple opened fire at a nonprofit social-service provider, killing fourteen people at an office Christmas party. Both of the perpetrators were of Pakistani descent (one was born in the U.S.). Trump immediately remarked that it "looks like another Islamic disaster, I mean, frankly." This time he had a policy proposal at the ready, announced on Pearl Harbor Day: a "total and complete shutdown of Muslims entering the United States." It was accompanied by a white paper that relied heavily on a poll conducted for a group run by Frank Gaffney, a notorious Islamophobe who had once accused a governor of treason for appointing a Muslim to serve as a state judge.

Here Trump was proposing to banish an entire religious faith from entering the country (a proposal even Trump's eventual running mate, Indiana governor Mike Pence, saw as blatantly unconstitutional) not long after he had spent days arguing over whether he had "called for" creating a database of Muslims or had been merely "open" to one, and the media had scrambled to make more sense of his views than he had been willing to. Many who looked closely at the substance of those controversies in November 2015 criticized Trump as a conspiracy-minded fabulist with a flimsy grasp of policy questions. But still that episode had served him well in the context of an election where he was competing with others for a limited amount of attention and a central place in the news of the day. Even if much of what he was saying was unfounded or hard to follow or unclear, voters heard Trump talking about terrorism as it rose among their concerns. His leading rival at the time, the novice candidate Ben Carson, by contrast, began to face harsh scrutiny of his depth of knowledge around foreign-policy issues. In fairness, Trump, who had previously stumbled explaining the nuclear triad, and Carson were more or less equally matched on the topic. But voters came away with the perception that Trump was better prepared.

Every few weeks, the demise of the Trump candidacy was predicted over some new outrage, from declaring Iraq War combat deaths pointless ("it's not like we had victory") to the misogynistic attack on Fox News host Megyn Kelly because she asked him questions he didn't like during a Republican debate (she had "blood coming out of her wherever," he claimed). Even though he'd publicly abandoned birtherism, Trump frequently passed along conspiracy theories, from the debunked claim that vaccines caused autism to whether Supreme Court Justice Antonin Scalia may have been murdered instead of dying naturally. (Trump deferred to the idea "that there's an invisible hand at work that you can't see," the Republican writer Erick Erickson told me at the time.) But then

Trump would wait out the controversy and bounce back. It was a phenomenon completely antithetical to anything observed before in modern political history, entirely because voters either did not judge Trump as a politician or because they felt unusually bonded to him from his time as a celebrity businessman. Whatever he did, his base was meeting him there. "I've never seen a situation before where someone fucks up and their numbers go up," a Trump political adviser told me at the time.

The most surprising part of that appeal was the apparently durable connection he was making with evangelicals, many of whom were Protestants. When Trump appeared in mid-January at Liberty University, the college founded by the politically influential televangelist Jerry Falwell, both sides of his peculiar rapport with religious conservatives were immediately visible. He spoke clunkily about matters of faith—attempting to read from the book Second Corinthians, Trump remarked, "Two Corinthians, 3:17, that's the whole ballgame"—but that stuck with the more than ten thousand attendees less than the eagerness with which he appeared to relish conflict with their common foes. "Christianity, it's under siege," he began the speech.

Accompanying Trump that day was a young former ballerina named Ashley Byers who had attended one of his campaign events and interacted briefly with him there. She was suddenly invited to visit him at Mar-a-Lago. She then traveled with the Trump team to Liberty aboard the Trump plane, wearing a skirt that Trump aides saw as too short for the event, so one of them insisted on lending her a coat. Byers went largely unnoticed by the crowd. She later took an official role on the Trump campaign in Florida. (She met her husband during the 2016 campaign, and was later accused of shooting him to death over a custody dispute, which she claimed was in self-defense.)

Byers did not appear to be anything more to Trump than a hanger-on who fit his ideal of beauty. It was, however, another reminder that Trump's traveling road show was different from most candidates seeking the support of religious voters. It did little to scare away people of faith; in fact, many evangelicals appeared willing to grade him on a curve. "His personal life is saintlike compared to Bill Clinton's," a self-described evangelical voter in North Carolina told a **Times** colleague; another said, "He is the only one who can pull us back from the abyss."

Trump until then had eschewed small-scale campaigning and local electioneering rituals, but reluctantly consented to a few such appearances as the caucuses and primaries drew near. In Iowa, he attended church with Melania and, despite mistaking the communion plate for the collection plate, sat through the sermon and appeared reasonably engaged. He preferred to fly back to New York whenever possible to sleep in his own bed, but on one trip he surprised observers by staying overnight at a Holiday Inn Express.

Over the first six months of his candidacy, Trump's adult children monitored much of this activity at a remove while working at their jobs as Trump Organization executives. But as the first primaries approached, they traveled to Iowa to drum up support for him. None of them knew anything about the political dynamics of the state or the mechanics of elections. When son-in-law Jared Kushner arrived in Iowa with Ivanka, then pregnant with their third child, he learned about the state's caucuses procedures via Google search. The children told associates they were stunned by the disarray they found. As they participated in local photo ops, the thirtysomething son Don Jr., who already spoke the language of the Republican activist base more fluently than anyone else in his family, and his quieter brother, Eric, traded text messages expressing worry about how little campaign organization seemed to have been developed. Kushner went to an event featuring staff from several campaigns, only to discover there was no one representing the Trump team; he moved around a table himself to plant a flag. That threadbare Iowa operation fed the children's shared distrust of campaign manager Corey Lewandowski.

Trump swaggered through Iowa, bolstered by an endorsement from Sarah Palin, whose attack on the "lamestream media" during her 2008 vice-presidential campaign made clear there was an appetite for such displays. He was oblivious to the possibility that he might lose the caucuses. During an appearance at a Christian college in Sioux Center, Trump talked about the bond between him and his supporters, marveling at his inability to offend them regardless of what he did. It had all become a show of just how much he could get away with. "I could stand in the middle of Fifth Avenue and shoot somebody, and I wouldn't lose any voters, okay?" Trump said. "It's, like, incredible."

Trump seemed so unconcerned about his standing that he showily announced he would skip a Fox News–hosted debate in Iowa because Megyn Kelly would be one of the moderators. (Fox disclosed that Lewandowski had previously levied threats against the anchor in a call with a Fox News executive. "Lewandowski stated that Megyn had a 'rough couple of days after that last debate' and he 'would hate to have her go through that again,'" a spokesperson said.) Trump's team scrambled to put together a simultaneous event three miles away at Drake University, which they said would raise funds for groups aiding veterans. But before the money would reach designated charities, it would have to go through Trump's personal foundation, officials said.

Trump announced to great fanfare that he had raised $6 million in an hour, including from reliable sources of support, such as his Las Vegas hotel business partner, Phil Ruffin, and a pharmaceutical billionaire named Stewart Rahr, who had paid for Trump Tower office space just to be near Trump, former Trump aides recalled, and helped fund Michael

Cohen's explorations into a Trump candidacy in 2011. Trump said he gave $1 million personally to the veterans' fundraiser.

A few months later, **The Washington Post**'s David Fahrenthold uncovered that Trump had raised about half, or roughly $3 million, of the claimed sum, and he only gave the million dollars he promised after Fahrenthold began asking questions. The coverage drew interest from the New York attorney general Eric Schneiderman, who had first tangled with Trump over alleged fraud at Trump University, and who was now investigating whether Trump used his charitable foundation for his personal benefit.

On February 1, Donald Trump's name appeared on a ballot for the first time as an active candidate. He should have been riding high, having led polls for his party's nomination almost continually since entering the race and having set the terms of engagement for his rivals throughout. But there was little recognizable joy in Trump's language on the campaign trail—mostly a sense of indignation, and anger. "A lot of people have laughed at me over the years, now they're not laughing so much, I'll tell you," he said during a speech in New Hampshire, where he made a detour that weekend to hedge his bet on Iowa. At a rally there on the day of the caucuses, he primed his audience for violence against imaginary agitators. "So if you see somebody getting ready to throw a tomato,

knock the crap out of 'em, would you? Seriously.
Okay? Just knock the hell—I promise you, I will pay
for the legal fees. I promise. I promise."

That night, he visited a caucus site with Melania.
The couple sat in the front row at St. Francis of Assisi
Church in West Des Moines, watching as local results
were tallied. Lewandowski crept up to them, bending
down to whisper to Trump that the results around the
state looked positive. Kushner attempted to focus on
the data coming in, but he had little ability to inter-
pret it. "You should really be calling every precinct
chairman and asking if the data is real," Kushner told
Michael Glassner, an experienced campaign operative
who had joined the Trump team earlier in 2015, apparently unaware that the state had 1,681 precincts.

When all the results were in, Trump ended up with
24 percent of the vote, just over three points behind
Texas senator Ted Cruz and edging out Florida senator Marco Rubio for second place. When Trump
took the stage that night at an election-night party
in West Des Moines, he was somewhat subdued, but
startlingly gracious. "We finished second, and I want
to tell you something, I am just honored," Trump
said before leaving for New Hampshire. He declined
to speak to his Iowa-based staff, viewing them as
failing him.

Within hours, it was clear that Trump had accepted
nothing about the result. His equanimity about defeat had dissolved into fury. "It was stolen from me,"
Trump told his advisers. For days thereafter, he called

Iowa's Republican chairman daily with an order to redo the vote, threatening to sue over what he called "fraud." Trump fixated on a few perceived infractions by the winner, including a supposed dirty trick in which Cruz's campaign disseminated a rumor at caucus locations that Carson was leaving the race. "One of the most disgusting things I've ever seen," Trump told a radio host. He ultimately spent much of the week before the New Hampshire primary complaining to the state's voters that "Ted Cruz didn't win Iowa, he stole it."

Trump ultimately carried New Hampshire, a state where Lewandowski had lived and understood far better, in a landslide, winning twice as many votes as the runner-up, former Ohio governor John Kasich. He won big in the subsequent South Carolina primary and Nevada caucuses as well. Those victories forced many of Trump's once-formidable opponents from the race, nearly all attacking Trump as they did so. The remaining contenders and other party leaders slowly awakened to the reality that if they stood any chance of stopping Trump from accumulating the delegates necessary to win the nomination they would have to look beyond their differences and work together.

New Jersey governor Chris Christie, who dropped out of the race after garnering less than 10 percent of the vote in New Hampshire, made a different calculation in the face of Trump's seemingly unstoppable momentum. He endorsed his friend's candidacy on February 25, becoming the first major Republican establishment figure to do so. "I will lend my support between now and November in any way for Donald," Christie told stunned reporters, who were kept in the dark about the endorsement, before appearing with Trump at a rally in Fort Worth, Texas.

Christie quickly learned what it meant to be a Trump adviser as opposed to a friend. At the press conference, a journalist asked Trump about a new crisis surrounding his campaign: a gathering storm of support arriving from white supremacists. Racists who had largely operated at the fringes of party politics saw kinship in Trump's anti-immigrant policies, condemnation of Black Lives Matter protesters, and proposed ban on Muslims entering the country. Shortly after the South Carolina primary, the country's most famous former Ku Klux Klan official, David Duke, expressed his own enthusiasm. "Go in there, you're gonna meet people who are going to have the same kind of mind-set that you have," Duke told listeners of his radio show about the Trump campaign. "I hope he does everything we hope he will do."

Trump did little to repudiate these new supporters, even retweeting a post from an account calling itself WhiteGenocideTM. In Fort Worth, he mustered only a muted "I disavow" when asked how he felt about Duke's support. He was pressed on the subject that weekend by CNN anchor Jake Tapper and dodged entirely. "I don't know anything about David Duke. Okay? I don't know what you're even talking about with white supremacy or white supremacist. I don't know. I don't know, did he endorse me, or what's going on?" he said. Trump advisers fretted about Trump's refusal to be more forceful; Stone was among them, telling Trump staff with whom he was still in contact that there were no votes to be had with what Trump was doing.

Trump never had a problem forcefully condemning someone when he wanted to, as he specifically had with Duke in 2000, when he mentioned the Klansman as part of his exit strategy from a potential Reform Party candidacy. And yet Trump aides pointed to his "I disavow," a statement in which he did not in any way acknowledge Duke, as if it was a clear and forceful denunciation. It was similar to what had happened with Trump's answer about a possible database of Muslims a few months earlier: he gave a weak answer, waited until he was described as taking a position he appeared to be taking without actually definitely doing so, and then claimed outrage that the media was taking him out of context.

Beseeched by other Republicans, Christie called Trump to tell him he had to be more forceful in distancing himself from his white-supremacist backers. Reaching him on a golf course, Christie implored Trump to quickly issue a strong statement. The model, Christie suggested, was Ronald Reagan's rejection of the John Birch Society's backing during his first gubernatorial campaign, when he called the conspiracy-minded anticommunist group a "lunatic fringe." Trump was heard assuring Christie that he would get to it, but that it didn't have to happen too quickly. "A lot of these people vote," Trump said, and ended the call.

CHAPTER 14

Stop the Steal

On March 5, 2016, Donald Trump and Ted Cruz both found themselves in Wichita, Kansas, where some of the state's Republicans were gathering at a caucus site, so they could come together in an arena to hear directly from the campaigns and then vote. (A third contender, Marco Rubio, was represented by the local congressman, Mike Pompeo, who said Trump would be "an authoritarian President who ignored our Constitution.") The day before, Trump aides told party chair Kelly Arnold three times that Trump had to speak first. But the next day, the program had Cruz speaking last, just before ballots were cast, and Trump decided he wanted the spot for himself. Arnold told Cruz's team that Trump was refusing to come out unless he got the speaking slot. Cruz's team decided it didn't matter to them, and agreed to let Trump have their spot, but by then Arnold didn't want to go back to the basement area where Trump was waiting, furious. Cruz's team would have to share the news with Trump. A group of Cruz's aides took the elevator down and found Trump standing right outside the doors, glaring at them. They did not even bother getting out. "You can go last," they blurted out, then closed the doors quickly. A few minutes later, Trump came upstairs; once he had what he wanted, he was all smiles, as if nothing had happened. "You guys are running a great race," he said genially.

That day, Trump and Cruz split four contests; Cruz won caucuses in Kansas and Maine, while Trump won the Kentucky caucuses and Louisiana primary. (Trump would ultimately carry every state in the Deep South.) It was the last of the four that had the most lasting impact. In Louisiana, he beat his three competitors and claimed victory. But media estimates soon concluded he was likely to lose most of the delegates due to the arcane rules by which they were awarded.

The outcome left Trump gobsmacked. Much as he had after the Iowa caucuses, Trump depicted himself as a victim of an unjust process. "Just to show you how unfair Republican primary politics can be, I won the State of Louisiana and get less delegates than Cruz," he wrote on Twitter. He threatened to file a challenge with the Republican National Committee, as well as a lawsuit against the state party demanding a retroactive change in rules that had been in place well before he decided to run for president. Trump never pursued either remedy as his campaign moved from one controversy to another. The fact was simply that Cruz's far more sophisticated campaign had figured out how to game a complex system that Trump's small circle of advisers, some without presidential election experience, never bothered to learn.

Trump had set his own rules for seeking the presidency, treating the perceived obligations of a candidate as a menu from which he could choose. He had skipped a candidate debate and generally avoided the retail politicking of touring small businesses and marching in parades. (The New Hampshire diner visit I had witnessed in 2011 turned out to be a rarity over the course of Trump's political career.) He was slow to build out traditional campaign functions, such as a research department, and for most of the campaign, infrequently attended fundraising events. He ultimately relied on the Republican National Committee for such infrastructure. Where other candidates upended their schedules to make it to studios for television interviews, Trump persuaded producers to allow him to call in by phone.

Trump had managed to do most of this without any evident cost or damage. But as the press increasingly gave Trump the attention reserved for party nominees, he could no longer fully evade some of the typical scrutiny that faced candidates seeking public office. The biggest source of tension was around his tax returns, which presidential candidates (including nearly every major-party nominee starting with Richard Nixon) had routinely released voluntarily. Republicans who knew Trump in New York had always predicted privately that he would never come around to doing it, speculating that he was more worried that people would see the actual amount of money he made than he was about scrutiny into his sources of income.

Aboard his plane between campaign events ahead of Super Tuesday, Trump tried to relax, but his advisers prodded him to deal with the growing crisis.

Seated around one of the gold-adorned tables in the main cabin, Corey Lewandowski told Trump that his tax returns were becoming an issue they needed a plan for. The press secretary, Hope Hicks, pointed out that every other Republican and Democratic candidate had put out their taxes and that the pressure would increase after a strong Super Tuesday performance. Trump reclined in his leather seat, then looked across the aisle at his former rival Chris Christie. "Romney made a huge mistake, releasing his taxes," Trump observed, referring to the decision of the previous election's Republican nominee, whose returns showed him paying a lower effective tax rate than many working-class Americans.

Trump thought for a second about how to "get myself out of this," as he said. He leaned back, before snapping up to a sudden thought. "Well, you know, my taxes are under audit, I always get audited," Trump said. Christie looked puzzled. "So what I mean is, well I could just say, 'I'll release them when I'm no longer under audit,'" Trump said. "'Cause I'll never not be under audit." There was no legal prohibition keeping Trump from putting them out, even if they were under audit, Christie pointed out.

"But my lawyers," Trump said. "I'm sure my lawyers and my counsel will tell me not to." He told his bodyguard, Keith Schiller, to reach out to his assistant, Rhona Graff, once they landed. Almost immediately, he began citing the claim that he couldn't possibly release his under-audit taxes.

A week and a half after Super Tuesday, Trump scheduled a Friday night rally at the University of Illinois at Chicago Pavilion. Chicago was always likely to be unfriendly territory—a large, overwhelmingly Democratic city whose population was half nonwhite and proudly claimed Barack Obama as a native son. Protesters arrived at the arena twenty-four hours before Trump's scheduled start time, leading to fights with his rally attendees inside. Trump made it to Chicago before he abruptly announced he was canceling the event, a decision that came after a security assessment. All that remained were the images on cable television of Trump supporters fighting with his detractors, one scuffle after another.

The episode did nothing to quell Trump's momentum: he won four out of five state contests the following Tuesday, including Illinois and across the deep South. The results made it all but certain that he would enter the party's convention that July with more delegates than any of his opponents. Some Cruz supporters began laying a plot to wrest the nomination from Trump there by persuading his delegates to defect. Trump dealt with Cruz throughout the course of the primaries by nicknaming his opponent "Lyin' Ted," highlighting increasingly personal stories about Cruz run by Trump's friend David Pecker in the **National Enquirer,** ranging from allegations of affairs to insinuating that Cruz's father was somehow proximate to the assassination of John F. Kennedy. He also made Cruz's wife, Heidi, a target, threatening to "spill the beans" about her and retweeting a less than flattering snapshot of her alongside a glamorous photo of Melania with the caption "A picture is worth a thousand words."

The Louisiana debacle convinced Trump that his current campaign leadership was ill-equipped to mount the broader defense necessary to hold off the Cruz forces. He was directed by his friend Tom Barrack to Paul Manafort, a longtime Republican operative whose experience in the peculiar game of hunting and counting delegates stretched back four decades. He and Trump had first crossed paths in 1988, when Manafort's business partner Roger Stone had arranged for the businessman to visit the Republican convention that Manafort helped to stage. After a meeting at Mar-a-Lago in 2016, Trump decided to hire Manafort to oversee a delegate-counting operation ahead of the convention to be held that July.

Manafort's lobbying work had mostly been outside the United States of late, notably in Ukraine, where he advised Viktor Yanukovych, a pro-Russia politician who served as both his country's prime minister and president. That work was not a wild departure for Manafort, who had built his Washington lobbying business in part on work for some of the world's most brutal and antidemocratic leaders, including Philippines president Ferdinand Marcos and the Angolan rebel commander Jonas Savimbi. The overt ties to Yanukovych had scared off John McCain's 2008 presidential campaign—where Manafort's then–business partner, Rick Davis, and a former Manafort business partner maintained top posts—from granting Manafort any role. But some on Trump's campaign team appeared oblivious to the potential baggage being brought aboard by Manafort.

Manafort and Trump had little personal chemistry; they were close in age, but Manafort seemed unaware of what was important to his new client. This became immediately apparent when in a CNN appearance after joining the campaign he referred to Trump as "Donald," which by then Trump aides almost never called him publicly. Manafort had a grand demeanor that suggested that he saw himself as something of a peer to the candidate—a presentation that ensured that Trump would have to find a way to dominate him.

Manafort joined the campaign just as the Republican field was whittled down to three candidates. As the likely Republican nominee, Trump was automatically the center of attention, and for the first time in his life did not have to perpetually scheme ways to get media coverage. Yet Trump did little to adjust to this new situation.

Even as he attacked **The New York Times,** Trump was fixated on the paper, particularly the legendary columnist Maureen Dowd. Unlike Trump's inter-actions with some of the columnists at the tabloids, he and Dowd were not friends. But he also knew that she was revered in media circles, and so when he was on the cusp of securing the nomination, he agreed to be interviewed by her for several columns and a piece for the **Times Magazine.** In an interview for one col-umn, Trump made the rare concession something he had done was unwise, in this case the Heidi Cruz tweet. "Yeah, it was a mistake," he said. "If I had to do it again, I wouldn't have sent it." He tried to sell Dowd that he hadn't viewed the tweet "necessarily as negative," and she cut him off. The interview hop-scotched from one topic that had been in the news to another, including whether Trump had ever paid for abortions while he was in the club scene, a question he declined to answer.

Trump was well aware that the magazine interview was on the record. But when one adviser asked about the Maureen Dowd interview, Trump conflated it with the lunch, and falsely implied he hadn't realized what he was getting into. "She took out her tape re-corder, and I didn't want to be rude. She's my friend," he said, apparently unwilling to admit he had volun-tarily sat with the paper for an extensive interview. The adviser was stunned to hear how concerned Trump claimed to be about offending a reporter. "She's not your friend," the adviser said.

In a large primary field, Trump's ability to generate press coverage out of nothing—by perpetually talking about everything, issuing provocations, and creating conflict, then making a story out of the coverage itself by turning on the media—had served him well: every time Trump was in the spotlight it meant no other candidate was. Any opponent who wanted to share that spotlight would have to do so on Trump's terms, which were almost always those that most career politicians would consider beneath them.

Typically a candidate moving toward the nomination would use that period to move away from his more controversial statements to make themselves more palatable to centrist voters in both parties. But facing a newly large built-in audience, Trump treated the campaign as an opportunity to settle old scores and promote old products. At his press event after winning the Michigan and Mississippi primaries, Trump came out before a table at his Trump National Golf Club in Florida piled high with what he claimed were Trump products, including some—like raw beef still in a local butcher's packaging—that he had not actually marketed in years. "So you have the water, you have the steaks, you have the airline that I sold. I mean, what's wrong with selling?" he asked reporters. "Trump University, we're going to start it up as soon as I win the lawsuit."

The campaign gave Trump a platform he could weaponize against the legal case that had bedeviled him long before his presidential run. In May, Trump made a stop in San Diego, where at the federal courthouse a district judge named Gonzalo Curiel was presiding over a pair of consolidated class action lawsuits against the defunct Trump University. The matter loomed over Trump, scheduled for trial shortly after Election Day in November. "I have a judge who is a hater of Donald Trump, a hater. He's a hater. His name is Gonzalo Curiel," he said to boos that kept him going. Ultimately Trump spent more than ten minutes of his rally talking about the judge, demanding he recuse himself and also be investigated for unspecified improprieties. The implication of Trump's rant was clear: the Indiana-born Curiel—whom Trump alternately described as "Mexican," "Hispanic," and "Spanish"—could not be trusted to do his job because Trump was campaigning on a tougher border policy. "Look, he's proud of his heritage, okay? I'm building a wall," Trump said later on CNN. He told CBS "it's possible" that Muslim judges, too, could be biased against him. "I'm talking about common sense," he explained. "You know, we have to stop being so politically correct in this country."

As with the proposed Muslim ban, prominent Republicans publicly condemned Trump's language and advisers such as Christie and Trump's daughter Ivanka persuaded him in private to issue a statement declaring that he did not believe that "one's heritage makes them incapable of being impartial" and that his comments about Curiel had been "misconstrued." Trump insisted he should not be seen as backing down. "You think I'm going to change?" he asked when the issue came up during a press conference. "I'm not changing."

Throughout the spring, the campaign expanded to prepare for the general election beyond the small retinue of advisers who had guided Trump through the primaries. After spending little on opinion research during those contests, Trump hired Tony Fabrizio, the well-respected pollster who had done corporate work for Trump. Trump brought on Rick Reed, an ad maker with extensive political experience, who had crafted the "Swift Boat Veterans for Truth" spots against the Democratic presidential nominee Senator John Kerry in 2004. The campaign they joined was marked by incessant fighting and pervasive distrust on all sides. Some aides were afraid that the headquarters was bugged by Trump, who had a reputation for taping calls on his office lines and, at Mar-a-Lago, listening in on them live. Distractions were constant, not least from the candidate himself, who interrupted planning meetings with his senior campaign aides to fume at his children about business deals that had gone awry. Reed struggled with Trump's penchant for trying to write advertising scripts and for quashing spots his aides thought were effective, including one about Hillary Clinton and the attack on a U.S. consulate in Benghazi while she was the secretary of state. Reed quietly left the campaign in the fall.

Staff and consultants largely split along pro-Manafort and pro-Lewandowski lines. After Iowa, Trump's three oldest children became more directly involved in the campaign, joining meetings with Manafort and his right hand, Rick Gates. As their front man in dealing with Trump, paid staff noticed that the children often deferred to Ivanka's husband, Jared Kushner, whose soft voice and generally neutral demeanor appeared to soothe their father, and as a nonblood relative was better positioned to confront him directly. When Trump railed about wanting to fire his entire campaign staff, Kushner told him, "Donald, four of us you can't fire."

On June 20, the children finally succeeded in orchestrating Lewandowski's ouster. With Trump recused somewhere else in Trump Tower, Don Jr. and Michael Cohen took Lewandowski aside and told him he was fired. Trump closely monitored Lewandowski's appearance on CNN shortly after the firing to see if he would say anything bad about him or his family. Lewandowski did neither; he had learned enough about Trump to understand that doing so would be one of the few ways to ensure the rupture was permanent.

Lewandowski's departure elevated Manafort to an unchallenged position as the campaign's top strategist. He tried to get Trump to focus on running a traditional campaign of policy speeches read off a teleprompter; it became a modest news story when Trump relied on one for an economic speech. His daughter Ivanka assured people outside the campaign that it marked a new phase for the campaign, suggesting that Trump would sustain discipline. Trump's advisers, inside and outside his family, urged him to use the change of guard as a reset, to run a more strategic campaign. Trump seemed to be listening.

There would be two big summertime tests of his willingness to do so. On July 18, the Republican convention would begin in Cleveland. Responsibility for staging it fell to Manafort and Gates. Trump was excited about the weeklong balloons-and-bunting festival in his honor, but not at all focused on the acceptance speech he would give that Thursday night. It was in large part outsourced to professional speechwriters who used aspects of Richard Nixon's 1968 address as their guide. Trump fixated instead on the visuals of the convention—the type of lighting that would guide him onstage, the speaking order of family members.

Before the convention began, Trump would have to pick a running mate. Realistically, Trump had few options. Most Republicans wanted nothing to do with serving on a ticket with him after the way he'd conducted his campaign. The feeling was more or less mutual. Trump had spent his business career within the confines of a family business and was naturally inclined to distrust everyone, especially outsiders.

He could imagine a relationship primarily in terms of domination. Even though his power over a running mate would be undisputed, in a vice president he would be nominating a constitutional officer who, unlike members of the cabinet or White House staff, he could not fire or drive away through insult or neglect. As opposed to many tough choices, which Trump let drift out of a refusal to commit, he faced a hard deadline to choose a running mate.

Generally presidential nominees systematically whittle down lists that begin with dozens of potential candidates. Trump only ever really had three. There was Christie, an experienced executive who had delighted Trump with his early endorsement but who had faced a scandal involving allegations of political retribution by his aides, which some of Trump's children and Trump's political advisers cited as a concern. Former House speaker Newt Gingrich was the choice of some of the party's most influential figures, including talk-show host Sean Hannity and casino magnate Sheldon Adelson, but while his pugnaciousness with the press appealed to Trump, the candidate's aides worried Gingrich and Trump would end up in competition. Indiana governor Mike Pence, a former congressman and one of the country's most prominent evangelical politicians, had disappointed Trump by endorsing Cruz ahead of the Indiana primary in May. Trump had also briefly floated Michael Flynn, a retired army general who had been one of his earliest foreign policy advisers, but dropped the idea after a media interview in which Flynn discussed his own support for abortion rights.

The Flynn episode highlighted a concern about Trump's own record on social issues and inability to speak the language of evangelicals. In particular, Trump's advisers knew there were lingering concerns among some religious conservatives on that issue and his marital history. Trump did not know Pence at all as well as he did the other two finalists, but Pence could do the most to validate Trump's claim to have changed.

Trump let his selection process play out in public. At a fundraiser, he turned the question of who he should choose into a game with attendees. Ultimately Kushner and Manafort helped persuade him to go with Pence, who had the advantage in Trump's mind of looking perfect for the part. "He's right out of central casting, isn't he?" Trump said of the former radio host. Trump also liked that he could be sure his cautious and conflict-averse number two would never upstage him.

Trump spent the night of Wednesday, July 13, in San Diego for a fundraiser. Its presence on the calendar was both a sign of acquiescence by major GOP donors, who had previously viewed Trump's campaign with distaste, and Trump's newfound willingness to cater to them. He called the Indiana governor's residence, where Pence had been primed to expect his call. Pence let Trump know he was in his study alongside his wife, Karen.

"I just want to give you a little advance notice," Trump said. "I'm going to be giving you some real big news, okay?" he went on. "Nobody knows." Trump told Pence that choosing him had been the subject of recent conversations with Jeff Sessions, the immigration restrictionist from Alabama who was the first senator to endorse Trump's campaign. "He was so strong about you. I want to congratulate you," Trump said. "Perhaps," he went on, "you won't tell, other than Karen, you won't tell anybody." Trump told Pence of plans to bring him into New York for a news conference on Friday morning—"We have a massive press, like, crazy," he promised—and talked about their common future. "We'll get this ship turned around properly," Trump said of the campaign.

Trump was obviously talking about making Pence the vice-presidential nominee, but he never came out and said as much. The language danced around the edges; it was all about secrecy and surprises. Despite the celebratory tone that suffused the entire conversation, Trump had not offered the job to Pence, who was not given the chance to say whether or not he would accept.

About twelve hours later, on Thursday morning, Trump spoke with Christie. The New Jersey governor had already been put in charge of planning Trump's presidential transition, even as the candidate was so superstitious he did not want to discuss what life in the White House might look like until after the election. Trump's interest in transition planning focused mostly on whether the funds being raised to support the work were being misspent, money that Trump kept referring to as "mine." Christie still craved the vice-presidential nomination, as he made clear to Trump, and some Christie allies were still lobbying Trump to choose him.

"Are you really sure you want this?" Trump asked Christie. Christie thought Trump was asking to find "an easy way out," as he would later recall, and did not want to give it to him. "Yes, I really want it," Christie responded. "I'm in."

"All right," Trump told him. "I'm definitely making the decision today. I just want to make sure that you two are ready for this." Trump warned Christie that he and his wife would face "a lot of scrutiny."

Even as Trump professed uncertainty to Christie, his campaign was finalizing plans to quietly bring the Pences to New York for the next day's press conference. Word that the Pence family would be landing at a private airport in his state reached Christie. He called Trump. "The least you could do, when you made a final decision, is to let me know," Christie told Trump. "I haven't made any final decision," Trump protested. "You haven't made any final decision? You haven't offered the vice presidency to anybody?" Christie asked. "Absolutely not," Trump said.

"Well, then, explain to me why Mike Pence is landing at Teterboro in half an hour," Christie said. "I have no fucking idea," Trump claimed, before issuing an instruction: "Turn on Fox News."

A few minutes later, Trump appeared on the network's air. "I haven't made my final, final decision," he maintained. "I've got three people that are fantastic." He called Christie right after, insisting this proved that he hadn't settled on Pence. "Do you believe me now?" Trump said to a skeptical Christie.

Trump posted a tweet saying that he had postponed the news conference because of a terrorist attack in Nice, France. That delay presented an opening to opponents of a Pence pick—and supporters of Christie—to press harder. On Friday morning, despite the delayed press conference, someone leaked word to a Washington news outlet that Trump was indeed going with Pence. Trump had started complaining that he was being lobbied to pick Christie; if Trump had actually been having misgivings, he was now locked in. He called Christie at the New Jersey State House a few hours later. "Chris, I'm about to send out a tweet that I'm picking Mike Pence as vice president," Trump said.

In the span of a few days, Trump had simultaneously led Pence to take a job he never formally offered him while pleading with him to keep quiet and then telling one of his old friends, Christie, that he hadn't made up his mind, concocting an elaborate display on live television to bolster that claim in order to avoid the direct confrontation with Christie as long as possible. After leaving himself wiggle room to get out of the decision, and after forcing others to expend mental and emotional energy on his choice, Trump ultimately did exactly what he indicated he was going to do in the first place. Trump chose someone who filled a hole he couldn't fill himself with evangelical voters, and who, most important, would never be a threat to step out of Trump's shadow down the road.

The effort to build a more traditional campaign around Trump did not mean an end to the more cynical approach to politics that had accompanied his rise. Roger Stone was outside the formal campaign apparatus after his exit, but he still retained ties through associates working there (Trump also still spoke with him periodically and had consulted Stone when he hired Manafort). Stone was ubiquitous during the convention in Cleveland, as usual seeking out angles few others were interested in to play in Trump's favor. Stone had formed a group, which he called Stop the Steal, to counter the last-ditch efforts of Cruz supporters to strip away Trump delegates. "We will disclose the hotels and the room numbers of those delegates who are directly involved in the steal," he warned. He and the conspiracy-theorizing radio host Alex Jones marketed T-shirts accusing Bill Clinton of rape. (Another effort under way proceeded more discreetly: Trump aides were blunt in private discussions that they planned to try to elevate the campaign of Green Party nominee Jill Stein, who had quiet backing from the Home Depot cofounder Bernie Marcus, with the goal of strengthening her as a competitor on Clinton's left flank to draw votes away from the Democrat.) Even if Stone kept official distance from Trump, he made clear he was still in touch with the campaign. "I had some meetings that I had to conclude over at the Westin with members of the Trump staff," he apologized to a crowd on his late arrival at an America First Unity Rally on the convention's opening day.

Two days later, I went to Trump's suite at the Westin in Cleveland with my colleague David Sanger. Trump sat in a large living-room area, with giant windows looking out on downtown Cleveland to one side and a giant television set to one of the cable news channels to his right. Trump's head tended to turn toward the television as we spoke.

Sanger, a onetime foreign correspondent who remained the paper's premier international-affairs specialist, and I had interviewed Trump together in March by phone. We had gone into that interview hoping to distill Trump's worldview and came away with a grab bag of statements about foreign countries. Trump seemed into the conversation—he called Sanger's cell phone a few hours after we thought we had concluded to resume the chat, for reasons not entirely clear—even if there was never much in the way of thematic coherence. At times Trump sounded like a dovish isolationist, at others a hawkish interventionist. He indicated he wanted Japan and South Korea to pay for the U.S. to defend them, and appeared open to both obtaining nuclear weapons.

Stylistically, a durable aspect of the exchanges was seeing Sanger invoke the term "America First," the name of a discredited movement to keep the country out of World War II that seemed unfamiliar to Trump when Sanger said it during the first phone call (Trump claimed in the second phone call to be aware of its historical significance), then watching Trump begin to appropriate it constantly to characterize his ideology.

Ahead of the convention, Sanger and I approached Hicks to request another interview with the now certain nominee. We wanted to press him on a variety of foreign-policy issues, including in the areas that had dominated our March interview: China, North Korea, the Middle East. But Manafort's emergence as Trump's top strategist intensified questions about how the candidate saw Russia, and the post–World War II order.

Over a forty-five-minute interview, for which Manafort was not present, Trump repeatedly took stances that aligned with Moscow's view of the world. He explicitly questioned whether as president he would honor American commitments to defend other members of the NATO alliance, depending on whether they hit their defense spending targets. Sanger asked what that would mean for the Baltic nations, which faced the ongoing threat of both military attack and cyberattack from Russia with little ability to defend themselves. Trump shrugged away concern at their plight. The United States, he said, had no standing to judge Russian conduct. "I don't know that we have a right to lecture," he explained. "Just look about what's happening in our country. How are we going to lecture when people are shooting our policemen in cold blood?"

Trump's words drifting toward a more Russia-friendly foreign policy were matched that week by the actions of some of his political aides. During the meetings of the Republican platform committee, often a pro forma affirmation of uncontroversial principles, one committee member proposed a resolution to supply lethal weapons to Ukraine. Before the committee could adopt it, a Trump foreign-policy adviser stepped in to soften the resolution.

That night featured a rarity in a modern presidential campaign: actual drama on the convention floor. Cruz, in one of the prime speaking slots, tried to walk a fine line by not endorsing Trump—"History isn't kind to the man who holds Mussolini's jacket," Cruz told an associate—without antagonizing the crowd who had gathered to nominate him. But when he instructed those listening to "vote your conscience," it was met with one thing Cruz had said he hoped to avoid: boos. Trump watched in delight as the delegates who once seemed at risk of abandoning him now rallied behind him.

I heard from Trump later that night. He did not want to discuss the Cruz speech and the reaction of the delegates, or his son Eric's own well-received address. Instead top of mind was an article in that week's

New Yorker about Tony Schwartz, Trump's **Art of the Deal** ghostwriter, in which he expressed a "deep sense of remorse that I contributed to presenting Trump in a way that brought him wider attention and made him more appealing than he is." Trump responded by sending a cease-and-desist letter demanding (with no apparent legal basis) that Schwartz repay all the royalties he had earned from his work on the book. Trump had seen our coverage in the **Times** and wanted to discuss that instead of his political future.

The Democrats held their convention the following week. It was quickly disrupted when the group WikiLeaks released tens of thousands of stolen emails from the Democratic National Committee's servers. Republicans had been hoping to make the opposition's information-security practices a major election-year issue ever since the **Times** first reported in July 2015 that Clinton was being investigated by the FBI for using a private email server and deleting messages from it in apparent violation of federal record-keeping rules. After a year, the bureau closed the probe, but did so in a way that defied its typical practice of refusing to comment on closed cases. In early July, just weeks before the party's conventions were to begin, FBI director James Comey held an extraordinary press conference to discuss the matter. Despite giving Clinton a clean bill of legal health, Comey's observation that she had been "extremely careless" in using a personal server for State Department business proved to be a gift to Trump.

To the extent Republicans landed on a line of attack against Clinton, it was less about ideology or policy record and more about what the investigation revealed about her personal ethics. In Cleveland, mentions of Clinton's emails elicited chants of "Lock her up!" among delegates. The WikiLeaks release days later proved embarrassing enough to force the Democratic Party's chair to step down from her post. Federal officials determined that Russia was behind the apparent hack; Vladimir Putin had long made clear his antipathy to Clinton. Instead of expressing concern, however, Trump appeared to goad a foreign government in its quest to humiliate his domestic opposition. "I will tell you this, Russia: If you're listening, I hope you're able to find the thirty thousand emails that are missing," Trump said from a press conference at his Florida golf resort. "I think you will probably be rewarded mightily by our press."

Trump would later say it was a joke, but initially his campaign attempted to explain Trump's remarks away, although advisers could not settle on how. A statement from new communications adviser Jason Miller claimed Trump simply wanted Russia to turn the emails over to the FBI. Pence attempted to inject a note of normalcy, saying that if Russia was involved in the hack, "I can assure you both parties and the United States government will ensure there are serious consequences." Gingrich, still an informal adviser, said Trump had been joking at the press conference. Miller tamped that down, saying only Trump could speak for Trump.

That Friday, while in Colorado for an event, Trump sat down with George Stephanopoulos to tape an interview that would air Sunday morning on **This Week.** Trump started out on a high, boasting how much higher television ratings had been for the Republicans' convention than the Democrats'. He had a feisty response when asked about the criticism he had received from Khizr Khan, whose son, a U.S. soldier, was killed in Iraq in 2004; Trump insinuated that the young man's mother had not been permitted to speak because the family was Muslim. (In reality, she was just too overwhelmed by grief.) But his mood darkened fast once Stephanopoulos asked, "What exactly is your relationship with Vladimir Putin?"

When Trump said he had "no relationship with him," Stephanopoulos responded by citing instances, including around the 2013 Miss Universe pageant, in which Trump had claimed otherwise. "Because he has said nice things about me over the years. I remember years ago, he said something—many years ago, he said something very nice about me," Trump said. Stephanopoulos pushed on the inconsistency. "Well, I don't know what it means by having a relationship," he said. "I mean he was saying very good things about me, but I don't have a relationship with him. I didn't meet him. I haven't spent time with him. I didn't have dinner with him. I didn't go hiking with him. I don't know—and I wouldn't know him from Adam except I see his picture and I would know what he looks like," Trump said.

Stephanopoulos then turned to Trump's finances. "You said you have no investments in Russia. But do you owe any money to Russian individuals and institutions?" he asked. No, Trump said definitively, maintaining—despite the significant outstanding loans on some of his properties—that he owed little to anyone of any nationality. The interview amounted to the most extensive and focused questioning Trump had faced on the topic of Russia after a campaign season in which he praised Putin and seemed to invite further cyberattacks during the election.

Once the cameras turned off, storm clouds came over Trump's face. Trump summoned an ABC producer into a small area away from the cameras, where Trump was surrounded by Secret Service agents, and snarled, "That was bullshit." The producer, John Santucci, asked which part of the interview he meant. "Russia," Trump replied. "Eight fucking follow-ups—are you fucking kidding me?" he thundered. "It's like asking me if I beat my wife. You ask me once, I say 'Fuck no,' and we move on. You don't then ask if I hit her with a fucking baseball bat or a fucking golf club! That was bullshit and you better fucking fix it in the edit."

Then Trump called for Stephanopoulos to join them. When Trump mentioned Russia, Stephanopoulos chuckled, saying, "I know, my team says I didn't ask you enough about it." Trump exploded. "Are you fucking kidding me! Eighteen fucking follow-ups—how many different ways do I have to say I don't know the guy?" he said, before eventually stalking off.

On Saturday, the **New York Post** website published photos of an entirely nude Melania Knauss, wearing only high heels, taken in the 1990s. YOU'VE NEVER SEEN A POTENTIAL FIRST LADY LIKE THIS! read the front of the Sunday edition, alongside a full-page photo of Melania, hands covering her crotch and a newspaper-generated graphic obscuring her nipples. Trump, asked about the photos for the **Post** story accompanying them, had none of his typical bluster. "This was a picture taken for a European magazine prior to my knowing Melania. In Europe, pictures like this are very fashionable and common," he said. Inside the tabloid's newsroom, the understanding was the photos had been obtained directly from the photographer.

Around the same time the Stephanopoulos interview would air across the country, Miller was scheduled to appear live on CNN's **Reliable Sources,** a press-criticism show that Trump's team routinely used as a vehicle to attack those they saw as enemies in the media. (When Senate Republican leader Mitch McConnell asked why he responded to everything, Trump replied, "I have to defend myself.") Trump called Miller early that day, asking if he had gotten many inquiries about the pictures. "Not really," Miller said. Most reporters would ignore them, he told Trump, treating them as tabloid material unfit for serious coverage. "Well, if you get asked about the photos, I want you to say this," Trump said, beginning to dictate a statement. "Say, 'It was a different time, sensibilities in Europe are different, they're artistic.'" Trump also directed Miller to call the shots "tasteful" and to point out that they were taken before the candidate had met his wife.

Only with one of his last questions did the CNN host, Brian Stelter, address the photos. "The **New York Post,** a Murdoch paper, typically conservative, but this morning, the front page here, Donald Trump's wife, these are nude photos from the 1990s, which I guess the **Post** has newly unearthed," Stelter said. "Do you think it's inappropriate for the **Post** to be putting this on the cover?"

Stelter may have been hoping to bait Miller into an unlikely feud between Trump and Murdoch, and if so likely came away disappointed. For once, a Trump representative invited to weigh in on a media controversy defended coverage of the candidate as opposed to condemning it. "Look, these are photos that are twenty years old, before Mrs. Trump met Mr. Trump. They're a celebration of the human body as art. Nothing to be embarrassed about with the photos, she's a beautiful woman," Miller said.

Stelter tried again, asking if Trump gets "furious when he sees something like that." Instead of a diatribe about the unfair media, Miller said, "I think Mr. Trump is more focused on the direction of the country and what we need to do to get it turned around." It was not a bluff, or misdirection. In their phone call, Trump had not sounded at all as if he were upset that the newspaper had acquired them or angry that they were now public.

CHAPTER 15

The Sci-Fi Campaign

Paul Manafort spent less than three months serving as Donald Trump's campaign chairman before Trump grew tired of him. Among his other complaints, Trump did not consider Manafort a particularly hard worker. Steve Bannon, who would take over as the campaign chief executive officer, noted that Manafort sometimes dressed like Thurston Howell III, the wealthy boater on **Gilligan's Island.** (Manafort often spent weekends in the Hamptons, a locale frequented by the elites at whom Trump had repeatedly sneered over the years, even as he happily traveled to that part of Long Island to attend events and tried to build there.) When Trump held an early work session at his New Jersey golf club to prepare for the fall debates against Hillary Clinton, Manafort was not invited, and only drove out to attend when he learned from another aide that it was taking place.

On August 13, Alex Burns and I published a story about the latest stage of dysfunction in the Trump campaign. Those who had tried over the spring and early summer to focus the candidate—including getting him to read prepared speeches and avoid the off-the-cuff musings that caused so much trouble—had effectively given up. "Advisers who once hoped a Pygmalion-like transformation would refashion a crudely effective political showman into a plausible American president now increasingly concede that Mr. Trump may be beyond coaching," we wrote.

Trump was infuriated by the article, tearing into Manafort after reading it. "You treat me like a baby," Trump screamed at him. "Am I a fucking baby, Paul?"

It was the beginning of the end for Manafort. Trump had continued to miss Corey Lewandowski, calling to check in with him on the night Trump became the official Republican nominee while his former campaign manager sat on a television set as a CNN commentator. By August, Manafort's Ukraine ties had become a growing subject of media scrutiny and Democratic attacks, even as he insisted the reports were inaccurate. When two of the country's most generous donors to conservative causes, the elusive father-and-daughter team of Robert and Rebekah Mercer, approached Trump to say they thought he should replace his campaign chairman, Trump was ready.

Despite his **Apprentice** catchphrase, Trump hated firing anyone directly himself. He tasked Kushner—who had by then become a key figure in the campaign, writing some speeches for his father-in-law and advising on staff hires—with dismissing Manafort. When Kushner called to check in with Trump as the candidate traveled to an event in Louisiana, Trump asked if it was done yet. Kushner explained he had plans to take Manafort to breakfast and break the news there. "We don't need to buy him eggs," Trump replied. "Let him go." Trump demanded Manafort be fired by the time his plane landed. (Manafort continued to assist the campaign even after he was ousted, sending a memo about the Midwest to Fabrizio and working a backchannel with a major labor union to boost Trump's standing in the Midwest.)

At the Mercers' urging, Trump elevated pollster Kellyanne Conway, who had been hired weeks earlier as an adviser, to the role of campaign manager, appealing to her repeatedly to take on the new role before she said yes, and Bannon. Trump had an existing relationship with Conway, who had lengthy political experience as well as a gift for reading the emotions of the people she worked with, and came to deeply understand Trump.

Trump barely knew Bannon but took quickly to his bawdiness and authoritative demeanor if not his disheveled physical appearance. (After taking the job, Bannon got a haircut and started wearing dress shirts to work.) Bannon, who had no political campaign experience to speak of, helped to bring in Cambridge Analytica, a London-based analytics firm in which the Mercers had invested. The campaign's digital director, Brad Parscale, assumed more responsibility as the campaign dramatically ramped up its online spending on Facebook. Soon Citizens United president David Bossie joined as a deputy campaign manager; he was generally the person delivering news to Trump that he did not want to hear during that period, and he paid a price for it with Trump's anger. The Trump campaign had melded uncomfortably with the Republican National Committee, which had money and a voter-turnout operation that Trump's campaign relied on heavily. Priebus was the main contact point with the campaign, while the party committee's chief of staff, Katie Walsh, and its spokesman, Sean Spicer, handled day-to-day matters dealing with both entities.

Trump was almost instantly more at ease with his new team. Conway mostly stayed back at the Trump Tower campaign headquarters, while others traveled with the candidate. The entourage increasingly included Rudy Giuliani, who just a few months earlier had told associates he couldn't endorse Trump because of his Heidi Cruz tweet. Now Giuliani embraced the party's nominee wholeheartedly, becoming one of his most vocal defenders.

Hillary Clinton's campaign had made a strategic decision to focus on Trump's ties to the so-called "alt-right" movement, whose members she once characterized as "deplorables." At the same time, Trump's campaign was making an effort to peel off Black voters from Clinton—"What the hell do you have to lose?" he said over and over—largely by pointing to her husband's signing of the 1994 Violent Crime Control and Law

Enforcement Act and her own twenty-year-old characterization of young criminals as "superpredators."
It was an effort that Stone encouraged. But any effort to gain support among Black voters would likely
be vexed by continued media questions about
whether he still endorsed the falsehood that Obama
may have been born in Kenya, as he'd suggested in
2011. So with the candidates' first debate looming
in late September, Trump's advisers persuaded him to
finally put to bed the fiction that had vaulted him
to political prominence.

Trump agreed to hold a news conference on the
topic at the newly opened Trump International Hotel,
constructed in the historic Old Post Office building
leased from the federal government just blocks from
the White House. Trump read a statement that was
absent an apology. "President Barack Obama was
born in the United States. Period," Trump said. Instead of acknowledging his role in promoting the fiction, he decided to pin the blame on Clinton. "Her
campaign of 2008 started the birther controversy.
I finished it," he said. "You know what I mean."
It had been a group of rabid Clinton supporters who
had begun the rumor, not her campaign, but that
was irrelevant to Trump. He left the podium without
taking questions.

He was well into the groove of asserting things
about Clinton that plainly were not true, often when
his back was against the wall or when he simply
wanted to diminish her. Some claims about Clinton's

campaign were to make his own look good by comparison, such as when he unveiled a family leave plan and made the false claim she did not have one and "she never will." Other times it was simply to raise questions about her fitness and her character, as when a pneumonia-stricken Clinton was caught on video badly stumbling; Trump and his team said it showed weakness and accused her of covering up an even worse medical condition. Trump called her "Crooked Hillary" on nearly every reference, a moniker that stuck and that fed into long-held voter perceptions about the Clintons' honesty that dated back decades, before her candidacy and before her private email server use.

The media writ large was unprepared to cover a political candidate who lied as freely as Trump did, on matters big and small. Even those of us who had covered Trump for years struggled with how to handle the gush of falsehoods that dotted his sentences. The word "lie" was infrequently used by mainstream outlets, which tended not to write more than they felt they could glean about a politician's motivations. And few large media institutions had truly accepted what was clear since February—that Trump would likely be the nominee—leaving many people scrambling to deal with the reality.

Stone, working from outside the campaign, had begun a few weeks after the D.N.C. email hacks were made public to talk in speeches about "communicating" with WikiLeaks, saying the site's founder had an "October surprise" for the fall related to Clinton and damaging documents. Stone had written a book published in late 2015 focusing on the various accusations of sexual misconduct made against Bill Clinton while he was the governor of Arkansas and when he was in the White House. Stone spent several weeks promoting the book, titled **The Clintons' War on Women,** an ironic play on a phrase used by Democrats to describe Republican policies. Stone and Bannon were working on separate tracks to bring questions related to the Clintons and women out publicly. Soon, they would have an opportunity to deploy them.

Trump had settled in for dinner at his Miami golf resort. It was a Friday night in the fall, and he could not stop thinking about a poll he had been given showing him further behind Clinton in the state than he had ever been. The poll left Trump livid; someone needed to be held responsible. He told his body man to fetch Susie Wiles, whom he had installed as his state director not long before in place of an underperforming loyalist. "Sit down," he said when she arrived. Wiles took a place across from him, at a table filled with his corps of traveling advisers. Trump was hacking at a large steak, devouring the pieces as quickly as he could free them.

He immediately began complaining that she was not any good, no better than the woman she had replaced. How could he be down that many points? He demanded to know.

"Well, sir," Wiles tried. "I told you in the beginning you'd be down—" Trump screamed, cutting her off. "Don't give me a lecture about fucking polling," Trump said.

Others at the table sat silent, avoiding Trump's gaze as he berated her, hoping not to become targets themselves. She did not get up, and did not punch back, but listened.

"Why am I losing?" Trump kept asking. "Why do you think?" Then he turned to the others. "Do you think she's doing a good job?" he asked them of Wiles. He did not wait for an answer. He moved on to a new complaint, an ad against Clinton referencing "terrorists and dangerous criminals," and asked for Wiles's opinion.

"I think it's a bad ad, sir, I wouldn't have it on the air," she replied. "Why the fuck do you have it on the air here?!" he demanded. "Sir, I don't have any control over the ad buys," Wiles explained. "Well, why not?" Trump demanded.

In the span of minutes, he had gone from calling her incompetent to demanding to know why she was not fully in charge. Trump started hunting for other aides to complain to about why the situation was bad for him. Kushner, who usually didn't answer his phone on the sabbath, was unresponsive. "Fucking Shabbat," Trump groused, asking no one in particular if his Jewish son-in-law was really religious or just avoiding work.

Trump turned to Wiles and said, "I don't think you can do this job." To the group, he said, "Find me somebody else." Wiles told him that if he wanted someone to set their "hair on fire," she was not the right person. But "if you want someone to win the state, I can do it," she said.

Even after Trump paused and said he wanted to "make sure you get everything you need," he did not stop berating Wiles. She finally got up from the table and walked back toward her room. She was one of the only people who withstood an emotional cannon blast from Trump without withering. She remained with the campaign, filling operational holes in the Florida organization.

A few weeks later, feeling better about his prospects in Florida, Trump told Wiles, "I'm sorry we had to have that little motivational talk." Wiles objected quickly. "That was nothing short of abuse, and we can't do that again," she replied. "We won't have to," Trump assured her.

Trump kept up a steady pace of rallies at which he repeatedly said the word "jobs," which Democratic pollsters told me was resonating with voters, while Clinton maintained a comparatively light schedule during the summer; some of her aides still had trouble imagining a world in which the country could elect Trump. Trump's advisers had begun preparing him for the debates early, recognizing that while he had fared well in the primary face-offs, their structure had played to arguably his greatest strength: standing out in a large group and keeping himself the center of attention. The fall debates would be a one-on-one, ninety-minute-long encounter with a famously well-prepared opponent, its length a test of Trump's attention span, and the sustained scrutiny a challenge to his temper. Kushner had made calming people concerned about his father-in-law's regular eruptions one of his special projects, intimating the rhetoric was an act that would change if he came to office.

The prep sessions had been difficult for Trump, who grew bored with the format. At his New Jersey golf club, he invited in guests, including the Fox News founder Roger Ailes and his anchor Laura Ingraham, who brought with her a lawyer friend named Pat Cipollone. Trump welcomed them as a distraction, although many like Cipollone had no role other than observing. As the debates grew nearer, Priebus and Christie moved the preparations to Trump Tower, where others could join the group to watch, but only they were allowed to speak.

At the first debate, in late September, Clinton was well prepared with attack lines, and Trump was on defense. To reporters watching, it seemed as if Clinton had the edge. Yet Trump got his points across, highlighting the reality that he had been outworking Clinton on the campaign trail, something that became painfully clear to her supporters after Election

Day. "I've been all over the place. You decided to stay home," he said at one point. At another point, he said, "She doesn't have the look. She doesn't have the stamina."

The second debate, two weeks later, would feature a town hall–style format, in which the candidates were questioned by regular citizens selected by the organizers. Since he would be interacting with people often recounting their own struggles, it would require Trump, who had held almost no retail events or town hall forums during the campaign, to be more empathetic than in his often belligerent encounters with journalists or other politicians.

In one practice session at Trump Tower during the first week of October, Priebus tried to broach the topic of how single-sex school bathrooms should accommodate transgender students. He played a character, the young head of the transgender student association, who identifies as female. Priebus asked Trump his position on whether someone like her could use the girls' bathroom. Earlier in the campaign, Trump got tangled up when he criticized a controversial North Carolina bill banning transgender bathrooms, and walked it back a day later after Republican blowback. The hope at the session was that Trump would respond with an empathetic opening, acknowledging the student's personal experience before addressing the underlying policy issue.

Instead, Trump replied, "I have a question." The rest of the room, filled with people, waited and glanced at one another. Then he went ahead with it. "Cocked or decocked?" he asked.

The group looked back blankly. **Decocked?** Trump started making a chopping gesture with his right hand. "With cock or without cock?" he said. Slowly it dawned on his coaches that he was asking if the student had gone through a surgical procedure. What difference does that make? someone asked.

Trump looked around the room. "Well, I think it matters a lot," he said. He wasn't done. What if a girl was in the bathroom and someone came in, lifted up a skirt, and "a schlong" was hanging out, he said.

A few days later, Trump's penchant for such comments burst into the open and would threaten his political campaign in a way little else had. That Friday, Hicks interrupted another debate session with news that **The Washington Post** was about to report on a decade-old television outtake of Trump making brutal, bawdy statements about women. "When you're a star, they let you do it. You can do anything," he had told Billy Bush, host of the television show **Access Hollywood,** after boasting that upon encountering women he would "grab 'em by the pussy." The **Post** claimed to have the original recording. Its reporter, David Fahrenthold, at first sent over only a transcript in an email seeking Trump's response. When the quotes were read, Trump told the group that they did not sound like things he would say, backed up by some of the people present who had known him longest. But a short time later, Fahrenthold sent the video, and Hicks played it for the room. "It's me," Trump acknowledged without hesitation. Kushner nevertheless posited that the fallout might not be that bad, a comment that stunned others. "This is as bad as it gets," Priebus said. Clinton's team agreed; in the coming hours, I would receive calls from two of her advisers, cackling about the tape.

Their joy came after a nearly debilitating night before. Hours after the **Access Hollywood** tape was made public, WikiLeaks began to release a cache of documents it claimed were from the email account of John Podesta, Clinton's campaign chairman. Like most in-boxes, the contents of Podesta's messages were mostly banal, but there were also messages detailing paid speeches that Clinton had given to private groups that had never before been made public. It was an unprecedented moment in an American election—a huge dump of apparently stolen confidential material, provenance unknown, some of its accuracy difficult to independently verify.

The next day, my editors sent me to Trump Tower, where Trump had holed up with his most trusted advisers as they tried to assess and manage the fallout from the **Access Hollywood** tape. In his first public acknowledgment of it, on Friday afternoon, Trump had said, "I apologize if anyone was offended." ("This was locker room banter, a private conversation that took place many years ago," he asserted in the written statement. "Bill Clinton has said far worse to me on the golf course—not even close.") After midnight

Saturday, the campaign, under siege from people saying he needed to go further, released a videotaped
statement from Trump, this time apologizing but
also promising to discuss allegations against Bill and
Hillary Clinton. Priebus fielded calls from Republican
candidates and officeholders who had long been
skeptical of Trump and said that his display of vul-
gar chauvinism constituted a breaking point. Many
issued scolding statements, some withdrew their endorsements, others said Trump should be replaced on
the ticket. (It was not clear if or how this could legally
be accomplished just a month before the election and
after voters in some states had already begun casting
ballots with his name on them.) His instinctual refusal to express remorse merely intensified the anger.

Cable networks had begun tallying the defections,
but there was a source of solace for Trump: dozens of
supporters had begun to gather outside Trump Tower
in a show of solidarity, with its namesake cloistered
inside. For every senator who had left his side, it
seemed at least one person had come to stand outside to replace them. And from where Trump sat, the
people were louder.

It would be an early look at a future in which
Republican leaders discovered the deep disconnect
between what they found beyond the pale and what
many of their voters did. Among the most vivid il-
lustrations of this new dynamic took place that day
in Wisconsin, where Trump had been scheduled
to appear alongside House Speaker Paul Ryan at a

campaign stop in his home state. On Friday, Ryan had announced himself "sickened" by the tape. He said he wouldn't appear with the candidate, so the campaign announced that Pence would replace Trump there. Then Pence, for whom such behavior was the most likely to be a bridge too far, decided not to show up either. Ryan began by addressing the "elephant in the room," reiterating his distress at the language on the **Access Hollywood** tape. But he was quickly drowned out by boos and chants of Trump's name, a scene that played out with other local candidates that weekend.

I waited most of the day in the Trump Tower lobby, which remained open to the public, watching the elevator banks to see who came and went. At the same time, I was talking to campaign aides upstairs, some in tears, uncertain what would happen next. Trump's team concluded that there needed to be some kind of presentation to voters beyond the previous day's wan statement. Advisers persuaded him to sit with Melania for a joint interview by ABC News's David Muir in which the couple could address the remarks together. But even as the ABC crew was loading into a freight elevator at Trump Tower, the Trumps pulled the plug on the idea: the media-leery Melania, who was angry about the tape but, according to aides, always mindful of avoiding situations where she looked like a victim of her husband, changed her mind.

There had been no movement by Trump from his fortress in the sky. Then, late in the afternoon, I was surprised to see the elevator doors open and Trump walk through them. With Conway and Don Jr., flanking him, Trump strode through the lobby and out to the sidewalk. Trump immersed himself in the crowd, who drew him close, reaching out to touch his arms, his back, his shoulder. He raised a fist in the air and pumped it. The energy in the air was menacing, despite Trump behaving as if he were celebrating. Trump turned back into the building, looking revived. He clapped his hands, almost as if cheering himself on. "Hundred percent," he told a reporter who asked if he would stay in the race.

But he was not ready to move on. Don Jr. was furious on his father's behalf and looking toward the payback. "They're all out to get us," he told an associate, referring to the media writ large. "You watch what happens now."

That weekend's events would acquire a kind of lore in Trump's world, a near-death experience that focused the collective mind. Long afterward, Trump would reminisce to aides and associates about it all: how stricken Priebus looked, how Trump had defied people who said he should drop out, even how he had dealt with his wife. The moment created a new hierarchy of loyalties among Trump intimates: Christie, as the counterattack came together, made himself unavailable for the rest of the weekend, while Giuliani volunteered to represent the campaign on the Sunday talk shows. (Even that act by Giuliani didn't exempt him from Trump's gratuitous humiliations. Flying on Trump's private plane in the final weeks, Trump loudly complained about the odor after Giuliani had used one of the plane's bathrooms, so that other aides could hear. "Rudy! That's fucking disgusting!" he bellowed.)

Instead of causing him to retreat from a discussion about misogyny, the controversy over the tape propelled Trump toward one. Trump arrived at the town hall debate in St. Louis with four surprise guests: three women who over decades had accused Bill Clinton of sexual misconduct, along with a rape victim whose alleged attacker had been represented by Hillary Clinton, who had been running a legal aid clinic at the University of Arkansas in the 1970s. Trump's team tried to seat the women with the candidate's family, so that the Clintons would have to walk by them as they entered the hall. Debate officials blocked the move.

At their third and final debate, after Trump had insisted that Russian president Vladimir Putin did not respect her, Clinton said, "Well, that's because he'd rather have a puppet as president of the United States." He interrupted her. "No puppet," he said. "You're the puppet. No, you're the puppet."

The **Access Hollywood** experience would eventually only harden Trump's sense that Republicans well beyond his initial base would reward him for standing up to people they resented—the mainstream media and censorious political elites who saw themselves as guardians of order and responsible conduct—and that, regardless of the underlying issue, he could always reject criticism of his speech as "political correctness." After Trump said repeatedly on visits to Pennsylvania that he could lose the state due only to a successful scheme to steal the election, prominent Republicans led by Ryan countered that fraud was rare and voters should have confidence in the results. Trump quickly made their refusal to back his conspiracy theories the focus of his ire and the proof of the conspiracy itself, writing on Twitter, "Of course there is large scale voter fraud happening on and before election day. Why do Republican leaders deny what is going on? So naive!"

Democrats found themselves almost perpetually disoriented by autumn. During preparations for the third debate, Clinton's team was disrupted by a warning from the husband of Senator Dianne Feinstein, who said he had been told that Russians might try to poison Clinton through a handshake with Trump, to inflict a dramatic health episode during the debate. Clinton did not take it seriously, and Ron Klain, a former adviser to Al Gore and Joe Biden who was aiding with debate prep, wondered how Trump would poison Clinton but not himself. Her communications director, Jennifer Palmieri, took the prospect seriously enough to check it out; the warning turned out to be mere speculation from a historian with no knowledge of Russian plans.

Clinton and her team felt wronged—by Comey

and the FBI, by the email hacks, and by the media coverage, which they believed was stacked against them. The campaign and prominent Democrats were frantic to get people to pay more attention to possible connections between Trump's world and Russia, which the FBI had been investigating for months. A lawyer for the Clinton campaign helped seed funding for in-progress research led by a former British spy that resulted in a dossier filled with unconfirmed salacious allegations about Trump. They also focused on research into computer servers used by his company; people connected to the campaign then gave the information, claiming the Trump Organization was communicating with a Russian state bank, to the FBI. A campaign lawyer pitched my **New York Times** colleagues on a story about the server activity and an FBI investigation into it. But after several discussions with the reporters, the evidence did not support the incendiary claim.

In the span of days after the WikiLeaks email dumps, the entire campaign seemed to have entered an alternate universe. Anything was possible, because the seemingly impossible had already happened.

In the final stretch, after advisers had worked in vain to discipline Trump over the months of the general election—conditioning him to give teleprompter speeches only to watch him upend them with rally addresses or early-morning tweets—his new team

achieved a major success, getting him to agree in late
October not to use Twitter on his phone, his sec-
ondary method of contemporaneous speaking during the campaign, for the duration of the race. That
kept the news, for once, on his opponent, who was
suffering from her second October surprise: an announcement from FBI director James Comey that
the bureau was reopening the email investigation after
finding messages on a computer belonging to adviser
Huma Abedin's husband, Anthony Weiner, who was
being prosecuted for using it to send obscene material to a minor. For the last ten days, the only digital communications going out under Trump's name
were messages sent by his social media director, Dan
Scavino, that made the candidate sound, however
briefly, like a conventional politician.

Heading into election night, Trump did not expect to win. The part he had most enjoyed was seeing
how close he could get, in a campaign that had been
built around making him feel good, often headlining
more than one large rally a day. On his plane between
stops, Trump would watch news coverage of himself
until he couldn't take it anymore—"I've ODed on
Trump!" he would say—and then switch to something else. To help him relax, aides played him movies, particularly classic Hollywood films in black
and white.

On election night, Trump seemed overwhelmed by
his victory, stepping away from his aides to collect
himself. Trump had no speech prepared. The one he

read after being proclaimed the winner, just before 3:00 a.m., was written hastily by Christie, Ivanka Trump, Pence, and Stephen Miller. It was distinctly not Trump's voice honed on the campaign trail. "For those who have chosen not to support me in the past, of which there were a few people, I'm reaching out to you for your guidance and your help so that we can work together and unify our great country," he said. It was one of the few moments of reaching out to people who did not already like him. It did not last long.

CHAPTER 16

No One Smarter

On November 10, two days after winning the presidency, Donald Trump visited the Oval Office to meet with the man he would replace there. Trump and Barack Obama were scheduled to spend an hour together but ended up speaking for ninety minutes. Trump told Obama that they were both great politicians—unlike Hillary Clinton, able to draw large crowds—and approached the meeting as if it were an opportunity for two maestros to exchange notes on the craft. How did Obama keep his approval ratings so high? Trump wanted to know. Had Obama noticed the way Trump could make the media do whatever he wanted?

Obama repeatedly had to guide Trump back to the substance of the role he was about to assume. He was intent on passing on a warning that North Korea was likely to emerge as a primary foreign-policy concern. Obama also advised that the personnel choices Trump made would prove crucial for managing matters a president could not tend to directly. Obama also had a list of his administration's initiatives he appealed to Trump to keep, including the international pact to curb Iran's nuclear capability and an immigration policy that differentiated those who had been illegally brought to the United States as children from those who chose to come as adults. He told Trump that the health-insurance regime known as Obamacare was finally working as intended and that people would be upset if it was taken away; if he wanted, Obama suggested, just add Medicaid subsidies and call it Trumpcare. Trump had run against nearly everything Obama was recommending but did not seem inclined to argue about any of it. Rather he seemed simply overwhelmed, appearing slackjawed once the meeting ended.

To the extent anyone in Donald Trump's orbit had given serious thought to what would happen once he was declared the election's victor, it was Chris Christie. In his role as the director of Trump's transition planning, the New Jersey governor had overseen a team that prepared several binders mapping out the first decisions facing a president-elect: a day-by-day schedule for the period leading up to inauguration, and names of potential appointees for administration posts that reflected an early weeding-out of undesirable candidates. He and his aides came up with a series of suggestions.

But as soon as it became clear that Trump was being elected, those who had largely ignored Christie's planning were suddenly eager to assert themselves. As early as election night, Pence allies had discussions about dumping Christie as the head of the transition. That week, Trump's oldest children joined transition meetings with Christie to impose themselves on the personnel process. A campaign adviser, Michael Flynn, joined too. Bannon and Kushner had the binders that Christie's team produced tossed into the trash, and Kushner seemed deeply satisfied about the entire thing when he talked to associates. In a matter of hours, months of work had been undone.

Crucial jobs were filled not based on qualifications or informed by vetting, but because of perceived loyalty and sheer proximity. It had long been anticipated that the campaign's counsel, Donald McGahn II, would become the White House counsel, but Trump's daughter had other suggestions. "Pam Bondi can be the White House lawyer," Ivanka Trump said in one transition meeting, waving her hands as though dispatching a simple decision. (McGahn, not Bondi, ended up serving in that role.) At another point, Ivanka asked Flynn, who Trump was certain to want to reward with a job but whom Christie had recommended only for an intelligence post outside the White House, what job he wanted. He was given a prominent role: the president's national security adviser, despite Obama's warnings about Flynn's tenure in his own administration.

When Kushner brought in Goldman Sachs executive Gary Cohn to deliver an economic-policy briefing later that month, it took only a few minutes for Trump to conclude that he wanted to hire Cohn on the spot. It was the type of impulsive personnel acquisition he had used to staff his business over the years. "You're gonna work for me," Trump told Cohn, who demurred. "No, no, no, you're not listening," Trump pushed back. "You should be the deputy defense secretary." Cohn, who had no military experience, made clear the Pentagon post would be a bad match for him. Trump then grabbed a list of cabinet positions and began offering various ones to Cohn. Steve Mnuchin, an old friend of Trump's who had raised money for the campaign and who wanted to be the treasury secretary (and who was warned by McGahn and Bossie that Kushner was holding separate meetings with possible candidates for the job), hovered during the meeting. It was only well after that meeting that Cohn agreed to be an economic adviser and director of the National Economic Council.

Trump's wanton approach to hiring, and his willingness to offer jobs to people without thinking or particularly caring about how their roles would overlap and conflict, ensured that life would never be easy for his chief of staff. When former New York City mayor Mike Bloomberg called to congratulate Trump shortly after Election Day, he cautioned the president-elect to hire smart people. "Mike," Trump said, "there is no one smarter than me."

Trump refused to move the transition entirely to Washington, as was typical practice, and instead ran it from the Trump Tower offices as though an extension

of his existing business. He did so with little regard for
the rituals of international affairs. He publicly recommended, via Twitter, that the United Kingdom select
his friend, the nationalist politician Nigel Farage, as its
ambassador to the United States, in a clear violation of
diplomatic protocol. Trump took phone calls, including on his cell phone, with foreign leaders depending
on who managed to get through to him; one, with
the president of Taiwan, violated nearly forty years
of American policy toward China. (An exasperated
Obama told his aides after it happened that Trump
was "fucking clueless," with no interest in learning
what he did not already know.) Around the same time,
Kushner was meeting with the Chinese bank Anbang
to secure its investment in the signature building in
his family's real estate portfolio.

Foreign heads of state were interested in reaching
out to the new president more directly. A few days
after Trump was elected, the Japanese prime minister,
Shinzo Abe, requested a meeting with Trump. Trump
and his team were almost completely unfamiliar with
what issues Abe would care about, or what Trump
would need to discuss with him. An associate passed
along some talking points.

The Trump Tower lobby was transformed into
something of a circus. At one point, Trump descended
to appear, for no apparent reason, alongside the rapper
Kanye West. At another, Trump welcomed Robert F.
Kennedy Jr., a nephew of President John F. Kennedy
who had been transformed into one of the country's

most vocal proponents of the discredited theory that childhood vaccines promote autism. After their meeting, Kennedy told reporters that the president-elect wanted him to "chair a commission on vaccine safety and scientific integrity." Trump aides, trying to fix a needless distraction, quietly told reporters it was not going to happen.

Just under two weeks after Election Day, a group of television executives and anchors gathered around a conference room table on the building's twenty-fifth floor. Representatives of all the broadcast and cable networks were there, including CNN, whose journalists had been frequent targets of Trump during the campaign. The contingent from Fox News appeared cheerier than the rest; their frequent morning-show visitor over the years, who had often favored their network during the campaign, was about to become president.

Any pretense of a cordial meeting was tossed aside as soon as Trump entered the room. One by one, he complained about the coverage from the various networks, berating people in front of their peers. Trump attacked nearly every network, singling out CNN for what he insisted was the unfairly negative tone of its reporting on him. (Kushner had inserted himself into the relationship between Trump and CNN's president, Jeff Zucker, calling the network president directly to complain about "fairness.") Then the executives confronted Trump about his decision six days earlier to slip away from the pool reporters assigned to monitor his every move and head for dinner at the "21" Club, his old haunt. He was unmoved by their complaints about the need to document a president's movements.

After the meeting ended, Trump, scheduled to take part in a photo shoot for a CNN coffee-table book, shifted to trying to charm Zucker, inviting him and a top Time Warner executive, Gary Ginsberg, to his twenty-sixth floor office. Trump stood in one corner of the office, chatting amiably with Zucker as if the meeting beforehand hadn't happened. Standing nearby, Kushner railed to Ginsberg about Zucker loudly, seeming to hope Zucker would hear as he said, "He's a psychopath!" If they heard him, Trump and Zucker didn't react.

In early December, Trump received a visit from House Speaker Paul Ryan. Ryan and his aides had arrived intending to offer Trump a tutorial on how the federal government works; they had prepared charts detailing the federal budget process, assuming as a builder he would take to a visual rendering of the system. But regardless of how the information was presented, Trump seemed unable or unwilling to focus on it. He wanted to discuss how he had already inserted himself into the Air Force's negotiations with Boeing for a new Air Force One plane, to note how much fun he had watching people react angrily to his tweets, and to inquire, out of nowhere, "Why don't we tax Amazon?" Trump interrupted the meeting to take a call from a cable news host. "You'll never guess who's here, it's Paul Ryan, want to talk to him?" Trump said before handing the phone over to his surprised guest.

Trump continued to gauge personnel decisions based on potential press coverage. He favored keeping Preet Bharara as the U.S. attorney for New York's Manhattan-based Southern District, despite the fact that he had been appointed by Obama and was known to be an aggressive prosecutor against public officials. The onetime New York City politician Andrew Stein, who had been successfully prosecuted by Bharara six years earlier for his alleged role in a Ponzi scheme, told Trump "he would indict you in two minutes if it satisfied his own ambitions." Stein said keeping Bharara was "the craziest idea I've ever heard." Trump countered, "The press would love it." After selecting Rex Tillerson, an ExxonMobil executive with extensive international experience, to be secretary of state, Trump roamed the patio at Mar-a-Lago, boasting to his paying club guests about the country's top diplomat having "the look." "He's just got that," Trump said, pinching his fingers together in a chef's kiss, and wagging his hand.

And Trump never fully moved on from the campaign. He was still interested in appeasing fringe figures who he believed represented part of his political base. (At the prodding of Roger Stone, Trump had been interviewed by Alex Jones in late 2015, and Jones said on his radio show that Trump placed a postelection thank-you call to him to acknowledge his role in the win.) He also began rewriting the history of the most painful moment he faced as a candidate. In early January, he told a senator that there were questions about whether the **Access Hollywood** tape—for which he had apologized immediately after it became public—was in fact authentic. "We're investigating it," Trump said, "but we don't think that was my voice."

On the morning of January 6, the day prescribed by law for Congress to certify the states' electoral college votes, Trump was visited by the country's top intelligence officials. They had just briefed congressional leaders on the intelligence community's assessment of Russian interference in the 2016 election, and flew up to New York immediately afterward to share the findings with Trump.

Trump was joined by the core of the national security team forming to join him in the White House. His advisers were already straining from internal divisions and had varying attitudes toward the arriving delegation from Washington. The incoming deputy national security adviser K. T. McFarland, a onetime Senate candidate from New York and a Fox News commentator, had been warning that the intelligence they would be shown was likely to be exaggerated. Tom Bossert, a Bush administration veteran Trump had picked as his homeland security adviser, recommended the president-elect conduct himself carefully

in the meeting. "In terms of your ability to have a
trusted relationship with the intelligence community, these are the future witnesses for the prosecution against you if you mistreat the situation or the
sensitive intel they give you," Bossert said. He meant
a political prosecution, not a criminal one, a warning about what could be used against Trump down
the road.

The heads of the FBI, the CIA, the National
Security Agency, as well as the director of national intelligence addressed Trump once they were all seated.
Their presentation outlined the intelligence assessment that Russians had interfered in the election on
Trump's behalf. Trump did not ask many questions
in response; when he did, he indicated he viewed the
interest in the hackings as attempting to diminish from
his victory by suggesting it was obtained nefariously.
("It could have been the Chinese," Trump speculated
at one point.) Toward the end of the session, Trump
raised questions about the different types of information that informed the CIA's assessment—which
came from both intercepted communications and
human intelligence—and he expressed skepticism
about what could come from live sources, whom
Trump called "sleazeballs." As the then-CIA director
John Brennan recalled later, Trump was essentially asserting that human intelligence can never be trusted.
"Anyone will say anything if you pay them enough. I
know that, and you know that," he said.

As the meeting ended, FBI director James Comey

said he needed to speak to Trump privately. (Even before the room cleared, Trump's advisers began discussing drafting a press release dismissing the role of Russian interference in the election, national intelligence director James Clapper would recall.) When the two men were alone, Comey informed Trump about a dossier assembled by a former British spy about Trump's ties to Russia, which had been circulating for months among news media. The most salacious part, Comey detailed for Trump, involved his 2013 trip to Moscow, and an allegation involving tapes of him and prostitutes at the Ritz-Carlton presidential suite. (A part of the dossier also claimed that Trump had paid the prostitutes to urinate upon a bed, and that he wanted to defile the room because the Obamas had stayed there on a trip as president.) Trump said there were no prostitutes and that he always assumed his hotel rooms were being monitored. Comey assured Trump that he was not under investigation.

When they were done, Trump strode toward a bank of elevators, with Comey heading toward a different one. Bossert caught up to Trump and grabbed him. "You did well," he told Trump, who did not reveal anything in his expression. "You've done this before," Trump replied, the rare acknowledgment that he had something to learn from the people coaching him. The intelligence officials left the building and Trump returned to his office with aides to finalize the press release they would put out about the briefing. Trump sat calmly behind his desk, no emotion visible on his face, without mention of what had transpired between him and Comey.

Later that day, Trump spoke with Hope Hicks, his spokesperson; by then, the fact of the intelligence briefing had become public. He was livid about all of it—the briefing, the implication that his victory was not in fact his. Bannon later told Trump that he could not trust the intelligence community. Any intended distinction between the intelligence agencies and the FBI, part of the Justice Department, would be forever lost on Trump.

A few days later, those private conversations broke out into the open, when CNN reported on the Comey meeting and the existence of the dossier, without specifics about its contents. Trump was furious again at Zucker's network, insisting a broader conspiracy was at work between intelligence officials and the media. On Twitter, Trump compared the leaks to Nazi Germany. Clapper called Trump; on the call, Trump asked that he issue a press statement declaring that the dossier contained false information. Clapper said it was not something the intelligence community could do.

The dossier's contents did not remain secret for long, as **BuzzFeed** published the document almost in its entirety on January 10. It went online the evening before Trump was about to announce plans for handling his business assets while in office. Folders brimming with sheets of white paper were stacked high on a long table near a podium in the Trump Tower library for his press conference; aides said they were to illustrate the complexity of the Trump Organization businesses its chief executive was about to turn over to his older sons. "They're not going to discuss it with me," he said of business matters. But journalists' focus at the press conference was on the dossier and the broader issue of Russian interference in American politics. "It's all fake news. It's phony stuff. It didn't happen," Trump said. "And it was gotten by opponents of ours, as you know, because you reported it and so did many other people. It was a group of opponents that got together—sick people—and they put that crap together." He closed with fury toward CNN's reporter in attendance, Jim Acosta, after having attacked the network for reporting on his briefing from Comey. "You are fake news," he said, appropriating an emerging term, used to describe online misinformation campaigns, for his own use as an all-purpose epithet. Trump aides complained the entire mess felt like a leak designed to inflict maximum damage.

Trump's advisers, some of whom had yet to read through the dossier that was posted online, tried to grapple with what it might contain. There was also the matter of the larger intelligence assessment and its details. Trump advisers agreed that Trump's incoming CIA director, Mike Pompeo, would be the one to read the complete intelligence community assessment, in a secure room set up in Trump Tower, and report back on what it said. Trump later turned to Pence. "Mike, can you believe this?" he asked, citing the "golden

showers" episode in which he allegedly watched prostitutes urinate on the bed in a Moscow hotel. Trump
became obsessed with that detail, mentioning it over
and over in the middle of unrelated meetings.

Trump had never before interacted with Comey, and
neither man knew the other well enough to anticipate
how he would respond to their first encounter. Comey
was blind to the depths of Trump's paranoia and to
his long history of gamesmanship with government officials. Trump had seen how Comey had handled his
bureau's investigation of Hillary Clinton's email practices, and how much his disclosures of it had impacted
her campaign. Trump could not help but conclude
that Comey had essentially threatened him, letting
him know there was something out there that could
be used against him for leverage if necessary.

The brief interaction between the two men turned
out to set the terms for Trump's interactions with his
intelligence and law-enforcement chiefs for his entire
time in office. Two weeks before he would be sworn
in, the presidency had begun.

CHAPTER 17

Why It's Presidential

Three days after his inauguration, Donald Trump hosted a reception in the White House's State Dining Room with the congressional leadership from both parties. Trump had arrived in Washington knowing almost no one there who was not a fellow New Yorker, and so now, surrounded by Capitol Hill's senior figures, he was naturally drawn to the Senate's minority leader, Brooklyn Democrat Chuck Schumer. Schumer's grandfather had worked in the real estate business alongside Fred Trump, and Donald had donated to his political campaigns, as he had with nearly everyone who held power in his hometown.

In greeting Schumer, Trump loudly remarked that he was the senator's biggest donor, which was not true. (Trump had donated to the Democratic Congressional Campaign Committee in the 2006 election cycle when the party was likely to retake the House. Once those efforts were successful, he sent new House Speaker Nancy Pelosi **The New York Times** front page from the day she was sworn in, with his signature and the inscription "Nancy, you're the best!") To leaders of Trump's party, seeking to maximize their productivity during the coming two years in which they would have total control of government, the fact that the new president gravitated toward the opposition was disturbing. Already Schumer and Jared Kushner had both appeared at a postelection event hosted by the Partnership for New York City, where, at adjacent panels, the two had acknowledged that Trump was closer to the Democratic leadership on a possible infrastructure plan than he was to the Republicans.

The Republican Senate majority leader Mitch McConnell told colleagues that they hadn't needed the new president to be a modern-day Abraham Lincoln, but just a normal, right-of-center president who could help them achieve their goals. He was blunt that all the qualities he would want to see in a president—conviction, temperament, intellectual curiosity, honesty— simply were not there in Trump, and after meeting with the president-elect, he observed that Trump had no idea what he believed in.

For all of the unpreparedness he brought to his first stint in public service, Trump quickly took to serving as host at the country's most famous home, bringing a hotelier's sense of hospitality to the presidency. Trump told Schumer that the kitchen had specially prepared canapés that would appeal to him—"Have the meatballs, they're kosher"—and turned toward the row of unfamiliar, racially diverse faces against the wall. "Why don't you get" the food, he asked. Reince Priebus, his face blanching in embarrassment, told the president that those were top officials working for the Democratic leaders; Priebus went to get the servers himself.

As the little meatballs and pigs in blankets emerged—finger food that would soon become a White House staple at the president's request—Trump turned the conversation to a topic he had been raising in the days since he had assumed the presidency. His three-million-vote deficit in the national popular vote could be attributed only to the ballots cast by "illegals," he asserted. House Minority Leader Nancy Pelosi broke the silence that followed. "I don't believe so, Mr. President," she said.

Trump insisted that his evidence came from Bernhard Langer, a professional golfer he called a friend. In Trump's telling, when Langer went to vote in Florida, there were people in line near him who did not appear to be citizens but were nevertheless handed provisional ballots. Later Langer's daughter tried to correct the record, noting that her father and Trump were not friends, and White House officials conceded that Langer, a German citizen who could not vote in American elections himself, had been relating a story told to him by someone else.

It was in many ways a quintessential Trump tale: beginning with a small fragment of something that had occurred, shrouded in other basic details that were completely wrong, distorted to make a larger point. (Around this time, Trump also repeated a similarly baseless story that Massachusetts voters had been bused across the border to cast ballots in New Hampshire, a state Clinton won narrowly.) But as president, this fabulism had consequences. Within months, Trump had launched a Presidential Advisory Commission on Election Integrity to investigate supposed instances of fraud, featuring state administrators and chaired by the vice president. Pence, who over time also came to prefer giving Trump positive news when he had to deliver "negative" information, took the assignment without complaining, and others in the building were relieved to avoid being the ones tasked with it.

Trump was the only modern president who had never met most of his senior advisers and cabinet appointees before he won the presidency; his three top White House aides—Priebus, Bannon, and Kushner—had never served in government either. He approached the new bureaucracy in much the same way he had a family-run business, demanding that employees sign agreements that would prevent them from ever speaking publicly about the experience. The White House counsel made clear to some staff that the contracts were not enforceable.

It didn't take long for Trump's group of new aides to pick up on the fact that he was effective at raising an idea without revealing his motive for why he was doing so. He was equally effective at suggesting someone ought to handle a task without openly giving them a directive. On Trump's first day in office, his new press secretary, Sean Spicer, went to the briefing room and delivered falsehoods about the unprecedented size of the inaugural crowd. Spicer told people that it was not at Trump's direction; nonetheless, his colleagues said, being validated was indisputably what the president wanted.

The seemingly impossible task of directing Trump's attention and energy fell on his chief of staff, the top White House administrator responsible for managing workflow and personnel. There had been few obvious options for the job. Trump knew he could not get away with appointing a relative like Kushner. Ever looking for people who could speak for him in public, Trump repeatedly said he wanted his campaign manager, Kellyanne Conway, available to serve as a representative on television. Both of his party's congressional leaders helped to persuade Trump to select Priebus, whom Trump had come to rely on as a source of staff and financial support, even as his campaign and the party had interacted under conditions of mutual suspicion.

Bannon, who claimed not to have been interested in the chief of staff role for which he'd been passed over, was named the White House's chief strategist. Bannon seized the chance at unprecedented access to power in the White House. Bannon asserted himself as the guardian of the Trump policy agenda that appealed to the president's base of supporters, as detailed on four large whiteboards arrayed under a "Make

America Great Again" headline on his office wall. They were filled with objectives—from "hire 5,000 more border control agents" to "repeal and replace Obamacare"—marked with a red X when completed. There were plenty of unmarked objectives ultimately. In his first week in office, Trump signed an executive order granting Bannon a permanent seat on the National Security Council's Principals Committee, elevating him above the chairman of the Joint Chiefs of Staff and director of national intelligence, an unprecedented elevation of someone appointed to a political post. "His primary role is to control or guide the president's conscience based on his campaign promises," former White House chief of staff and CIA director Leon Panetta told my colleague at the time. "That's not what the National Security Council is supposed to be about." The executive order also downgraded the CIA seat, and the uproar and bad headlines the whole mess created infuriated Trump, who insisted he hadn't realized the potential fallout from the details of what he was signing.

Regardless of titles, Kushner sought to establish himself as the most consequential gatekeeper of the presidency. He had an outsize view of his ability to solve problems by changing their nature, as he liked to say during the campaign. After the election, he gave a rare on-the-record interview to **Forbes** about his role, and his soft-spoken boasts led to the cover-line "This Guy Got Trump Elected," a headline his father-in-law resented. Kushner entered the White

House with an unformed portfolio; at a meeting during the transition, he told corporate executives that "everything" would run through him.

He was often described as a shadow chief of staff, holding his own meetings with prospective cabinet members. Yet it was more accurate to call him a shadow president. Trump tasked Kusher with working on Israeli–Palestinian relations, to the astonishment of foreign policy experts. Kushner—who had a fleeting family relationship with Israel's prime minister, Benjamin Netanyahu— soon began to look beyond the Middle East, establishing his own foreign-policy ties, to the frustration of State Department officials. He worked on Trump's ultimately successful effort to revise the quarter-century-old North American Free Trade Agreement with Canada and Mexico; Secretary of State Rex Tillerson once bumped into Mexico's foreign minister at a restaurant in a surprise encounter, only to discover that he was in Washington to meet the president's son-in-law.

Kushner mixed know-it-all confidence with a stunning lack of preparation on some issues. He told aides to the House Speaker that the committee system defining how bills move through Congress sounded "inefficient," and that the system may need to be rethought. He seemed genuinely surprised when warned by White House officials that his family's plan to buy the Miami Marlins baseball team was a conflict of interest, because the team's owner was under consideration for an ambassadorship.

Though they went to Washington as allies, Kushner and Bannon soon found themselves in conflict. Bannon came to describe Kushner as "the air," for entering meetings without leaving an impression, and he would insist Kushner was spreading unfavorable stories about him to the press. Some of it was internal bureaucratic politics as they built up rival power centers, jockeying for staff, visibility, and internal allies as a way of asserting influence on presidential decisions. Nowhere were the stakes of that personal conflict higher than over the issue of immigration.

During the final months of the campaign and throughout the transition, Kushner had indicated to a steady stream of pro-immigration-reform advocates, tech executives, and longtime party strategists that Trump's invective against Latinos was not going to dictate policy. It was similar to how he and Ivanka tried to engage with other progressive activists, suggesting that there were deals to be made on various policies. The most urgent immediate issue was the fate of Obama's program halting deportations for undocumented immigrants who had come to the United States as children. Like much of his party's pro-business establishment, House Speaker Paul Ryan was interested in finding a permanent legislative solution, and Kushner signaled that the White House was at least willing to discuss it. Trump insisted he was open to a broader immigration-reform deal in a luncheon with television anchors at the White House on the day of his first address to Congress, a predecessors' tradition to which he adhered. "The time is right for an immigration bill as long as there is compromise on both sides," Trump said. But when the cameras were on him that evening, he offered a mixed bag of positions, calling for his border wall while also saying "real and positive immigration reform is possible." He appeared not to understand that these concepts were not seen as compatible in Congress.

Kushner continued to engage with liberal groups who had hopes for a version of Trump that ultimately did not exist. One such overture was to David Plouffe, a former top adviser to Obama now working with Mark Zuckerberg–funded groups. Arriving in the West Wing to meet with Kushner, Plouffe looked around the room at what had once been his own work space and said to Kushner, "I love what you've done with the office." Kushner looked blankly at Plouffe and said, "Oh, have you been here before?" Plouffe's eyes traveled to the small television sets that had been embedded into the wall since he worked there. Why were they there? he asked. Kushner replied that his father-in-law was watching throughout the day, and he needed to know what Trump was seeing.

When it came to immigration policy, it was the hard-line Bannon and the policy adviser Stephen Miller, previously a Sessions staffer in the Senate, who ultimately had the most impact. Miller had been a significant force in the presidency before it began. During transition, he was a proponent of a legal theory by which Trump could declare members of drug cartels "unlawful combatants" and send active duty troops to the border. "Can we do that?" Trump asked advisers. They said no, repeatedly.

Miller, at the time seen as a Bannon ally, had more success with his anti-immigrant agenda. His first accomplishment was a policy restricting visitors, refugees, and people with immigrant visas from seven Muslim-majority countries, a more targeted version of the blanket ban on Muslims that Trump had proposed as a candidate. Miller discussed the planned policy with personal contacts at the Customs and Border Protection agency, but Secretary John Kelly, whose Department of Homeland Security would be tasked with enforcing it, had little time to give input before Trump signed the executive order. Overly broad, the final version did not account for, among other things, people already in airplanes at the time it was signed, ensuring a mess upon their arrival at American border checkpoints. Proponents of the order later insisted it was not simply incompetence at work, that the chaos was by design. Miller told border control officials that they were performing their jobs well.

Isn't this place great?" Trump said to his first major visitor from overseas, British prime minister Theresa May. But, he added quickly, "I've been to Buckingham Palace and that's even greater."

Trump had traveled to the United Kingdom during his presidential campaign—the occasion was the opening of his Turnberry golf resort on the Scottish coast—and spoke in reliably familiar terms about the "special relationship" between the country and the United States. May came to the White House with a clear plan to extract some kind of clarity on issues where the two allies had historically seen eye to eye but Trump's campaign statements had hinted at conflict: international trade, a posture toward Vladimir Putin's Russia, and the North Atlantic Treaty Organization and its mutual-defense commitments. But for May, getting Trump to focus on any issue was impossible.

He talked about the crowds at the inauguration—he spent his first full day as president obsessing over its coverage, even fuming about it in front of a CIA wall honoring agents killed—and the Women's March that had drawn millions of Americans to the streets in protest. "Abortion is such a tough issue," Trump said, unprompted, according to extensive notes of the discussion. "Some people are pro-life, some people are pro-choice. Imagine if some animals with tattoos raped your daughter and she got pregnant?" He pointed to Pence, who was in the room. "He's the really tough one on abortion," Trump said, before asking May whether she was pro-life. From there, Trump brought up that his mother came from Scotland, then asked whether May's predecessor had mishandled things. "Why isn't Boris Johnson the prime minister, didn't he want the job?" Trump asked about the former London mayor then serving as May's foreign minister. "Sounds like you have a team of rivals," Trump told her. "I couldn't do that. John Kasich wanted to work for me after the election but I couldn't do that."

When the discussion turned to Northern Ireland, Trump appeared to get bored and turned the conversation to an offshore wind project he wanted to block near his Scottish golf course. Trump asked whether immigration was a factor in the previous year's vote to remove the United Kingdom from the European Union. May said that it had been, but in the context of a broader issue about borders and sovereignty. "We're going to get tough on immigration," Trump said. "The Europeans have opened the doors to bad people." The United States would not have a situation like the terrorist attack in Paris, he said. He moved on to criticizing Angela Merkel, the German chancellor. "Crime is way up in Germany, women are getting raped all over the place," Trump said, predicting Merkel would lose her election that fall. May contradicted him, saying that Merkel in fact was Europe's best politician.

May went to one of her primary interests for the conversation—sanctions against Russia, and whether Trump planned to discuss them with Putin. Trump turned to his national security adviser and asked if a call had been scheduled with Putin. "Tomorrow," replied Michael Flynn. Trump looked flustered, and he returned to the topic a few times, clearly unhappy, and indicated he was unaware that Putin had called previously. "Vladimir Putin tries to call me, and they didn't even tell me!" May warned Trump that while he had to engage with Putin, that Putin only respects strength, and he needed to be tough with him. "I have to talk to this guy," Trump replied, noting that Putin had a thousand nuclear warheads that could be deployed. "This isn't the Congo."

Upon leaving the Oval Office, Trump and May walked down the steps onto the famous White House colonnade. As they were descending, Trump grabbed May's right hand with his left, appearing to need it to steady himself. As they arrived at the bottom of the short staircase, he tapped the underside of their clasped hands with his other hand. Trump's preference for dress shoes with leather soles may have made it harder for him to navigate slopes, but May came away with the impression that he had a separate phobia about steps. The moment prompted May to call her husband to explain why she was holding another man's hand, so that he would hear it from her before seeing it on television. To staff, she conveyed bewilderment. "He just grabbed it," May told her aides. "What can I do?"

In the first weeks of his presidency, Trump's attention was dominated by the project of generating a plan to repeal Obama's health-care reforms and by his ongoing encounters with foreign leaders. While Japan's prime minister Shinzo Abe was at Mar-a-Lago, which Trump now called the Winter White House, his country came under threat from a North Korean missile launch. Trump and Abe examined sensitive documents, as dinner guests—many of whom paid a club membership fee that Trump had doubled to two hundred thousand dollars when he became president—looked on, posting snapshots of the de facto open-air war room on social media.

He also moved to fill a Supreme Court vacancy that had remained open for much of the previous election year. Trump was as interested in Neil Gorsuch's silver hair and tall, slim build—"central casting," he liked to say—as the judge's judicial philosophy or approach to the law. The search and announcement, overseen by counsel Don McGahn, was executed as a well-choreographed reveal: a prime-time introduction that went off without a leak. Afterward, Trump groused that his nominee had not been appreciative enough because of mild criticism over Trump's personal attacks on jurists; an aide had to track down a thank-you note from Gorsuch to placate him.

Even as Bannon focused on the items on his whiteboard, Trump's advisers had difficulty getting the president to ignore slights, as they tried to push forward with the more complicated items he professed to be interested in, such as an overhaul of the tax code and a new health-care plan. Trump had a vague, high-level understanding of what the various agencies did—the State Department handled international diplomacy, for instance—but he knew little more about how they worked or interacted with one another. A lack of awareness about basic economics revealed itself when Trump talked about having the U.S. Treasury simply print more money, at one point suggesting the federal government could issue debt and buy it back easily with the new cash. His attention over time repeatedly gravitated instead toward things that related to construction projects, such as a new Air Force One and FBI headquarters, or his promise to build a wall along the country's southern border.

Trump's lack of discipline was frustrating to his new staff, including Gary Cohn. ("This guy Gary used to pay $175 million in taxes, and now he only makes $175,000 a year," Trump marveled in introducing his staff to a visiting dignitary.) In one Oval Office meeting while leading a process to rewrite the tax code, Cohn was interrupted by Trump voicing an unrelated grievance. "You see the kind of shit I have to deal with?" Cohn said to his deputy, Jeremy Katz, gesturing with his thumb across the Resolute Desk. Trump, reclining in his high-backed chair, did not appear to hear Cohn, and kept talking.

Trump, already wrapped tightly around the axle of the Russia investigation, finally had his chosen director of national intelligence in place. A career elected official and former ambassador, Dan Coats was hawkish toward Russia, having urged Obama to take punitive action after the country's 2014 incursion into Crimea. Many top intelligence officials were offended when, on the first full day of his presidency, Trump delivered a political diatribe in front of a wall memorializing CIA officers at the agency's Langley headquarters. Coats discovered during their briefings that Trump was almost impossible to pin down. In one of their first encounters, he warned Trump gently, "There are going to be times I'm going to tell you things you don't want to hear." Trump just stared at him and didn't respond. It was very hard for Coats and others involved in the briefings to get points across. It required scaling down the main points as much as possible. Often there were other things Trump wanted to talk about, and he would hijack the briefings. Sensitive to the perception that the briefers found him uninformed, he would sometimes cut them off and say, "I know all about that, you don't have to tell me about that."

Kelly, the secretary of the Department of Homeland Security, had been watching the situation in the West Wing from afar for months, periodically fielding calls from Trump. "This guy calls me all the time and asks me all sorts of questions on things I know nothing about," Kelly told an associate in the spring. Kelly firmly believed the problem was that Trump was being poorly served by his staff.

Most of Trump's new cadre of advisers believed that his behavior was not normal. But some either rationalized that it was not as bad as the press made it out to be, or that he behaved the way he did only because he felt under siege. For those in the administration confronting their own negative headlines, most notably Priebus and Spicer, constantly battling with the press had the effect of drawing them closer to Trump; after all, he had been elected to the office, and he had the same enemies. When he received pushback that something he wanted to do, from attending relatively small-bore events to sending a tweet, was not presidential, Trump had a ready response. "You know why it's presidential?" he would say. "'Cause I'm the president!"

CHAPTER 18

Out Like Flynn

Donald Trump had been warned about Michael Flynn. The transition planning documents developed by Chris Christie and his aides had recommended only placing him as the director of national intelligence. Barack Obama, too, had a specific piece of personnel advice for the president-elect when Trump came to visit him after the election: don't hire Flynn.

But Flynn navigated the disarray of the transition period to his own benefit. The retired army lieutenant general had joined Trump's campaign when not many people with significant foreign-policy or national security experience were willing to, and had earned the appreciation of Trump's children by vocally defending Trump on television. Flynn had been appointed director of the Defense Intelligence Agency by Obama in 2012; during his tenure, he claimed to have become the first DIA director physically allowed into the headquarters of a branch of Russian intelligence during a trip approved by the Obama administration (he was not in fact the first). He got to know the Russian ambassador to the U.S. during that trip.

He was also heavily focused on Iran as a threat. He was eventually forced from his post in 2014 for what officials considered erratic behavior. He also was vocal about Muslims and terrorism, and had echoed back to the crowd its chants of "Lock her up!" about Hillary Clinton during the Republican National Convention. On Election Day, he had written an op-ed for **The Hill** on behalf of Turkey's government, which, it later emerged, was paying him as a consultant, raising questions among Justice Department officials about whether he had violated foreign lobbying registration requirements.

Within weeks of being invited to serve as national security director, Flynn began to grate on Trump's nerves. Flynn had his son work on the transition as an aide and was planning on bringing him into the National Security Council to work with him; the younger Flynn made the news himself when he promoted a conspiracy theory fabricated from fragments contained in the hacked emails from Clinton's campaign that claimed she and a top aide were involved in child trafficking through a Washington pizzeria. Trump wanted the son gone, and he was, but the flap stayed with Trump. (Senior aides said they elevated the role of homeland security adviser to be Flynn's equal, in an effort to provide structure around him). During a trip to the Army–Navy football game that month, Trump brought the Fox News anchor Chris Wallace down with him for an interview. While they traveled on Trump's plane, Trump disparaged

Flynn for his son's focus on the so-called Pizzagate conspiracy.

Just days after Trump took office, Flynn was visited at the White House by FBI agents seeking to question him about conversations he had had in late December with Russia's ambassador. One of those calls was said to have come at the request of Kushner, who was busy trying to rally members of the United Nations Security Council to oppose a resolution condemning Israel. But one of Flynn's phone calls with the ambassador, Sergey Kislyak, also came just as the outgoing Obama administration was imposing sanctions on Russia and expelling its diplomats in retaliation for its interference in the 2016 election. Following that call, Russian officials had a muted public reaction to the new sanctions, and Trump took to Twitter to praise Putin's reaction. The FBI was monitoring Kislyak's phone as part of routine surveillance conducted on some foreign officials; they did not tell Flynn they had a transcript of the call. At the direction of Comey, who later said in another administration he would have alerted the White House, FBI agents did not inform the White House counsel's office before they went to speak with Flynn. It was "something we, I probably wouldn't have done or maybe gotten away with in a . . . more organized administration," Comey said later. Flynn initially indicated that he and the ambassador spoke to share holiday greetings and denied that the sanctions the Obama administration was imposing had come up. Or that he had spoken to Kislyak about anything meaningful. The FBI used language from the call to jog Flynn's memory, but it did not appear to.

The fact of an exchange between Flynn and Kislyak leaked to **The Washington Post** during the transition, and Flynn told Trump's team the same thing he later told the FBI. When Pence and Priebus were asked in television interviews about the Kislyak call, they repeated what they had heard from Flynn.

Sally Yates, the acting attorney general, met with McGahn on January 26. She was vague at points, leaving wiggle room as to whether the FBI believed that Flynn had been lying to them, and White House officials, particularly McGahn, protested the propriety of Justice Department officials caring about them lying to one another. But Justice Department officials believed that the call—and Flynn's lack of specific disclosures about it—turned Flynn into a counterintelligence risk, as another government knew the truth and they could use it as a source of leverage over him. Trump was subsequently briefed by McGahn about what Yates had said. As it happened, Yates, who was only there until there was a new attorney general was confirmed, was about to be pushed from her job. Four days later, Trump fired her for refusing to mount a legal defense of his ban targeting a range of people from seven majority-Muslim countries. (She questioned whether the policy was "wise or just.")

• • •

At Mar-a-Lago the next weekend, Trump drifted by a television in a bar area where some of his aides were watching **Meet the Press.** Trump leaned on the bar, and looked up at the screen, and saw an image of Flynn. "Lotta problems with this guy," he said, pausing. "Think he's gonna make it?"

Trump's inclination to watch the Flynn controversy as a passive observer, devoid of responsibility, would not last long. Officials got word that **The Washington Post** was working on another story about the Kislyak call, and Flynn again insisted he had not discussed sanctions with him. After the story was published, on February 9, saying that Flynn had indeed discussed sanctions with Kislyak, Priebus, McGahn, one of his deputies, Uttam Dhillon, and others immediately confronted Flynn about the report. "You said you didn't discuss sanctions!" Priebus told him. Flynn replied that he didn't believe that he had. He later blamed a blip in his memory for the oversight. Someone volunteered that a transcript of the call existed; when officials reviewed it, the details were there.

Pence's team was angry, saying they believed that Flynn had misled the vice president. Trump was less interested in the battle, but he was open to replacing his national security adviser for other reasons, such as the stilted way Flynn conducted his briefings, along with Trump's lingering aggravation about the negative press coverage Flynn's son had drawn. A few senior White House aides were already questioning whether Flynn was up to the job, and the FBI inquiry only intensified those concerns. The following Monday, Trump agreed that Flynn had to go; Priebus told Trump he would take care of it. Within hours, Flynn submitted his resignation. In announcing his departure, the White House attempted to leave the story there—Flynn had left on his own.

The next day, Trump and his advisers were in the Oval Office discussing what Spicer should tell the press about Flynn's dismissal. Priebus told Trump that Paul Ryan, who had just spoken to reporters on Capitol Hill about the Flynn situation, said he was "really happy you asked for his resignation." Trump looked at Spicer. "That sounds better," Trump said. "Say that."

"Well, which is it?" Spicer asked. **Which set of facts was the correct one?** "Say that I asked for his resignation," Trump said. Spicer went to brief reporters, while Trump had lunch with Kushner and Christie. Trump, alternately happy to be rid of Flynn and angry at the FBI, insisted to Christie that the bureau's investigation would now be put to bed. "This Russia thing is all over now, because I fired Flynn," he said. "Sir, this Russia thing is far from over," Christie responded. "What do you mean? Flynn met with the Russians. That was the problem. I fired Flynn. It's over," Trump said, to Kushner's agreement.

They misread how it would impact the investigation, in part because Trump would not let go of the anger that stemmed from that January 6 meeting when Comey had told him about the dossier, in what Trump viewed as a predicate to blackmail. Just days after taking office, Trump asked a small group of aides, as he was receiving his first presidential daily brief, the regular summary of state secrets available to the chief executive, if they thought he should fire Comey. Shortly thereafter, Trump hosted Comey for a private dinner in the White House, where he raised the possibility of having the FBI investigate the dossier's salacious allegations, to prove they were false. Comey cautioned against that, because the FBI wasn't investigating Trump at the time, but if that changed, it could require updating the public. Trump had a broader request. "I need loyalty," he said. In a later meeting, in the Oval Office, Trump asked Comey if he could find his way to "let this go," referring to the Flynn investigation.

Trump had been told by some of his advisers that he needed someone loyal overseeing the Justice Department, and he often insisted that previous attorneys general had served as gatekeepers. Without many options for the role, Trump—having decided against Christie and seeing Giuliani refuse any role other than secretary of state—had gone with Jeff Sessions. But in early March, **The Washington Post** reported that Sessions had the previous year held discussions of his own with Kislyak that he failed to disclose to the Senate when nominated to serve as attorney general. Sessions saw no choice but to recuse himself from his department's Russia investigation, but Trump was livid at this turn of affairs, and at finding himself blindsided by the news. "What the fuck?" he asked Spicer on Air Force One, throwing his hands up in the air. White House officials outside the counsel's office scurried to reach Sessions's aides in the hopes of getting their boss to undo the recusal. Sessions flew to Mar-a-Lago to discuss the travel ban, as the president refused to take his calls; once there, Trump pressed him to reverse his decision on the recusal. Sessions declined.

Fury gave way, as it often did with Trump, to a search for the hidden hand controlling a situation. Under the Foreign Intelligence Surveillance Act, which became law in 1978, the government has a much freer hand to monitor foreign powers than it does U.S. citizens or permanent residents. If intelligence services listened in on the Russian ambassador's phone, the identities of any Americans with whom he spoke would have to be obscured in government records of his calls. Trump's conservative media allies had begun to focus on how details of the conversation between Kislyak and Flynn had leaked to **The Washington Post,** with some speculating that the Trump adviser may have been the original target of the surveillance, not the foreign diplomat. The printout of a **Breitbart** story summarizing these theories made its way to Trump.

The next morning, from Mar-a-Lago, Trump sent out a series of four tweets. "Terrible! Just found out that Obama had my 'wires tapped' in Trump Tower just before the victory. Nothing found. This is

McCarthyism!" Trump wrote in the first tweet. "How low has President Obama gone to tapp my phones during the very sacred election process. This is Nixon/Watergate. Bad (or sick) guy!" he wrote in the last. Spicer later that day released a statement imploring Congress to investigate "whether executive branch investigative powers were abused in 2016"; White House officials said McGahn was trying to obtain the surveillance warrant that may have targeted some Trump associates; he directed people to see what was legally permissible, but nothing came of it. After posting the tweets, Trump called outside advisers to ask their opinions of what he had said, revealing that he had put little thought into learning ahead of his public statements how the procedures surrounding government wiretapping actually worked.

On Capitol Hill, members of Trump's party reacted either with alarm that he was right or concern that he could be wrong. California congressman Devin Nunes was the top Republican on the GOP-led House Intelligence Committee, which in January 2017 had launched its own investigation into the Trump campaign's interactions with Russia. Legislators' probes lacked the same teeth as prosecutors', but the Democrats on the House intelligence committee were pressing for disclosures from current and former government officials. Nearly three weeks after Trump's "wiretap" tweet and the frantic search to explain what he had meant by it, Nunes held a press conference at the Capitol and announced he had to head to the White House to brief Trump on information he said he had obtained showing that Flynn's name had been "unmasked" after it was initially obscured in incidental intelligence collection.

Nunes's ardent defense of Trump impressed the former president for years to come. But he was rushing to inform the president about material Trump could have learned of from his own government. Trump began to call Ryan repeatedly, urging the House Speaker to subpoena the Justice Department for documents related to the Russia probe. A dumbfounded Ryan replied, "Mr. President, they work for you. If you want documents released to the public, release them to the public." Trump never did. But his request of Ryan helped establish a practice of Trump outsourcing functions he could have performed as president so that someone else appeared as the frontperson or source, often blurring the separation of powers between the House Republican conference and the Trump White House.

At the beginning of May, while at Bedminster, Trump set to work on a plan to rid himself of Comey. To justify removing the FBI director before the end of his ten-year term, Trump enlisted his chief speechwriter, Stephen Miller, to help draft a letter outlining his reasons. The letter claimed, offering no evidence, that Comey had essentially lost the support of rank-and-file FBI agents. Much of the letter targeted his handling of the Clinton email investigation, which Comey had defended in a congressional hearing that month, even as he said it made him "mildly nauseous" to think his actions affected the election outcome. "Your conduct has grown unpredictable and even erratic—including rambling and self-indulgent public performances that have baffled experts, citizens and law enforcement professionals alike—making it impossible for you to effectively lead this agency," the letter said. The testimony was "another media circus full of unprofessional conjecture, bizarre legal theories, and irresponsible speculation," it read. An aide later described the letter as Trump's "primal scream" about the investigation bearing down on his presidency.

When the letter made its way to the counsel's office, McGahn believed it should not see the "light of day." Instead, when Trump moved ahead with Comey's firing on May 9, he would explain it with different rationales provided in letters from Sessions and one of his deputies, Rod Rosenstein. Late that afternoon, Trump called Spicer into the Oval Office, where he had been talking with Priebus. "Get it out!" Trump directed his press secretary. Spicer told the president that they needed to alert the congressional leaders before putting out a press statement. "I don't give a fuck," Trump said, then offered up the vice president. "Mike can call." Priebus and others in the room objected to how Trump was going about the dismissal. "There's a right way to do this and a wrong way to do this," Priebus told Trump. This, he said, was the wrong way.

Trump and Kushner were convinced that Democrats, who had criticized Comey throughout 2016 for letting his Clinton investigation play out at least partly in public view, would applaud the move. Kushner told several people that it was going to be an effective move. "The Democrats have said nothing but awful things about Comey. They hate him," Kushner explained to Christie after the firing. "So they're going to be vapor-locked from criticizing the president for firing him. It would be inconsistent with what they've said before." Trump was taken aback by the adamant response he heard from the Democratic leader in the Senate. "This is a horrible idea," Chuck Schumer told Trump when he eventually called. Firing the head of an agency investigating his campaign was, for veterans of Washington, as alarming an act as a president could take, conjuring memories of the Saturday Night Massacre, which accelerated Richard Nixon's impeachment during Watergate.

Even as Trump continued to denounce Comey— "He was so fucked up!" he told advisers, sitting with his arms folded across his chest the following day—his focus scattered. He made a show for a guest of keeping his office television turned off, part of his lingering sensitivity to my remark to Charlie Rose about his viewing habits, and was delighted as an aide unveiled a poster-size map showing areas of the country he won, telling him that ten of them would be framed and hung around the West Wing.

Trump offered different explanations for Comey's

removal throughout the week. Initially the White House tried to paint the firing as coming at the recommendation of Rosenstein. In a private meeting with Russia's foreign minister and ambassador, Trump volunteered that he had removed the "nut job" Comey and that doing so relieved "great pressure." Then Trump gave an interview to NBC News anchor Lester Holt, during which he seemed to connect the firing to the Russia investigation. "In fact when I decided to just do it, I said to myself, I said, 'You know, this Russia thing with Trump and Russia is a made-up story, it's an excuse by the Democrats for having lost an election that they should have won,'" he said. But Trump's answer was so clunky and at times incoherent that it wasn't entirely clear that he was intending to say the investigation was the reason for the dismissal.

Comey's firing set in motion a series of events that overwhelmed Trump's presidency for the next two years. A week later, my colleague Michael Schmidt revealed that Comey had drafted a slew of secret memos about his encounters with the president, including the one in which Trump had indicated that Comey should end the Flynn investigation. It swiftly changed the view of Trump's intentions among Democrats, media, and some Justice Department officials. With that pressure bearing down, in place of the recused Sessions, Rosenstein—who was not a Trump loyalist—named a special counsel to investigate not only the possibility of conspiracy between

Russians and the Trump campaign, but whether Trump had attempted to obstruct the investigation by firing Comey.

A former FBI director now in a private law practice, Robert S. Mueller III, was named as that special counsel. Mueller had just been in the West Wing, conferring with Trump about what to look for in the FBI director role, which some White House aides had considered Mueller for before he withdrew himself from consideration. Trump ultimately selected Christopher Wray, a former federal prosecutor and Justice Department official who had also served as Chris Christie's personal lawyer, after a fitful search that included junior White House aides using Google to find names of possible candidates and Trump asking John Kelly to take it on and offer "loyalty." Kelly declined. It was a matter of months before Trump began to complain about Wray not moving fast enough to rid the FBI of people who Trump believed were aligned against him.

Trump's aides tried to argue that the meeting with Mueller, along with the fact that Mueller was a former member of one of Trump's golf courses, created a conflict of interest for the special counsel, a claim that made little sense. When that effort to disqualify him failed, Trump tried to grab control of the investigation by directing McGahn to tell officials to remove Mueller, which McGahn refused to go along with, and prepared to resign. Trump, still uncertain about how the White House functioned, did not go any further. Trump had already touched one hot stove and, with his hands burned, seemed unsure how to proceed. Bannon, watching the chaos, predicted privately to his colleagues that this was the beginning of the end of the Trump presidency. Trump berated Sessions over the recusal with such savagery that it appeared designed to drive him away. (Trump would enlist others to exert pressure on Sessions, including junior aides and people outside the government. At least twice Trump asked his former campaign manager, Corey Lewandowski, to do so.) After one Oval Office meeting at the time Mueller was appointed, in which Sessions said he would resign, Priebus learned what had happened and chased after Sessions in the parking lot to prevent what he believed would be a disaster for the president. Sessions went so far as to write and submit a letter of resignation, which Trump declined to accept, though he didn't immediately return the letter either.

"Jeff Sessions takes the job, gets into the job, recuses himself, which frankly I think is very unfair to the president," Trump told me and my colleagues Peter Baker and Michael Schmidt when we visited him in the Oval Office that month. "How do you take a job and then recuse yourself? If he would have recused himself before the job, I would have said, 'Thanks, Jeff, but I'm not going to take you.' It's extremely unfair—and that's a mild word—to the president."

Despite his anger, Trump was a calm and solicitous host to us in a way that was difficult to reconcile with his Twitter persona and what I was hearing daily from sources about his interactions with his staff and cabinet. The next day, I asked a senior White House aide: why is Trump attacking Sessions this way?

The response I received stayed with me for a long time: "Because he can."

For the first year of his presidency, nearly every conversation Trump had would at some point drift toward the various Russia probes being conducted by the special counsel and congressional committees. Trump could not compartmentalize the investigation from his duties as president. Among other things, he appeared to believe the probe of Russian hacking of email servers was an attempt to deny him his due in victory. But the ceaseless fury he showed about the investigations—combined with his public warmth toward Vladimir Putin—left some of his own staff wondering what else, if anything, might be factoring into his behavior.

That summer, the investigations moved closer to home for Trump. In July, the **Times** reported that the president's eldest son had held a meeting the previous summer with a Kremlin-linked lawyer who arrived with the promise of "dirt" on Clinton. (The meeting had been arranged by a man named Rob Goldstone on behalf of the son of the oligarch who had cohosted the 2013 Miss Universe pageant in Moscow. Don Jr. later said it was a "bait-and-switch" that turned out to be about a Russian retaliatory effort against a U.S. measure in response to a human-rights abuse.) Most of Trump's advisers believed that Don Jr. did not pause to consider what he might be walking into and simply rushed ahead. But Don Jr.'s impulses to respond to the **Times**'s reporting in his own way, and more candidly, were overtaken by his father, who cut his own lawyers out of the process and directed how to respond as he flew home from a foreign trip aboard Air Force One.

Also that month, Mueller's recently established office executed a search warrant on the home of Paul Manafort, Trump's ousted campaign chief. Kushner, meanwhile, agreed to speak to congressional investigators in a closed-door session. For weeks, he had been the subject of news stories that drew him more deeply into the Russia intrigue. First was a report about a private meeting he had had during the transition with an official from a Russian state bank. Then there was one about his proposal to the Russian ambassador, made through Flynn, that Trump's team use the embassy's secure communications equipment to relay messages to the Kremlin, which would have likely shielded any exchanges from American intelligence services. (The covert channel appears never to have been used, and Kushner said he suggested it solely as a mechanism for closer cooperation between the U.S. and Russian militaries in efforts to end the civil war in Syria.) Kushner and Ivanka Trump also drew negative scrutiny when it was discovered that they were using a private email server for government work, something White House lawyers cautioned against and which Trump ran an entire campaign attacking Hillary Clinton for doing. Trump asked Kushner how he could be so "stupid."

Amid the crush of attention, Kushner and his wife brought two of Trump's personal lawyers, Marc Kasowitz and Michael Bowe, to meet them at the Trump-owned golf course in New Jersey, where they were staying at a cottage on the grounds. Ivanka Trump had joined her husband in the White House in late March as a special assistant to the president, and the attorneys arrived expecting to have a conversation about the investigation itself. But she and Kushner were more interested in discussing White House palace intrigue, especially the perception that Kushner's rival, Bannon, was using the Russia stories to undercut them. The legal dynamics seemed like an afterthought to public relations. The quartet flew to Washington immediately so that the attorneys could validate to the president that his daughter and son-in-law were under internal attack. Trump was at times frustrated but also sympathetic to his daughter, quizzing her in front of other aides, "Why do you want to do this? I don't know why you want to be here."

After his congressional testimony in late July, Kushner addressed the press outside the White House, the first time most of the country had heard him speak. He said he "did not collude" with Russia and had had no improper contacts with the country;

any problematic meetings he took during the transition were the result of being a political novice scrambling to respond to his side's earthshaking win. Trump watched the live coverage on television in the small room off the Oval Office. As he listened to his son-in-law's soft, high-pitched voice, his face contorted into disgust. "He sounds like a child," Trump said.

CHAPTER 19

Executive Time

"People aren't allowed in here, but I'll bring you in," Trump would say to visitors he had guided up from the function rooms on the White House State Floor, just before leading them into the Lincoln Bedroom. It was a version of the tour he had given for years at Trump Tower, pointing out prized sports memorabilia and his own image on framed magazine covers, only this time bolstered with whatever bits of knowledge of American history he had retained from the building's permanent staff.

I had always anticipated he would start to drift back to his familiar surroundings after his swearing-in. Melania decided to remain at Trump Tower after the inauguration, so that their son could complete the school year at his Manhattan private school, leaving the new president to move into the White House alone. On the rare occasions he went back to the city for events, he didn't stay for long, concerned about the protests he would attract that would tie up the city. Still, even as the city had rejected him, Trump was thrilled to be home from time to time. Driving up the West Side Highway, with traffic cleared and the lights and sirens of his motorcade whisking him along, Trump turned to an aide. "Can you believe this?" he asked.

He brought the same sense of exuberance to the perks of the presidency. Friends said he loved Air Force One, and Marine One, and the button staff had put on his desk that enabled him to call for a Diet Coke from the valet. I had believed he would find ways back to New York City, and its emotional resonance, more frequently than he did. Instead, he spent most weekends at one of the private clubs he owned, choosing Florida or New Jersey depending on the season, where he was able to bill the federal government for the cost of protecting him, including rooms and meals for Secret Service agents.

Trump also remade the White House to suit his tastes. He placed an extra television in his bedroom, so that one sat atop a piece of furniture at the foot of his bed and the other in a corner. He had carpet installed in his bathroom, similar to the look of the lavatory on his private jet; he also brought a television there. In later years, bathrooms in the residence were stocked with Trump-branded toiletries; staff repeatedly stopped him when he tried to press cash into the hands of military aides serving as valets. In the Oval Office downstairs, he brought small touches from home, including a photograph of Fred Trump looming over the credenza behind his desk (after many weeks, when people took note that there were no other family photos, he added some). To the small room just off the Oval Office, Trump added a large television; the cream-colored room became dotted with presidential-related knickknacks, all tossed together without much thought, save for a wrestling belt gifted by the promoter Vince McMahon, which was eventually displayed as though it were a museum exhibit. Trump called the space "the Monica room," because it was said to have been where Bill Clinton had the sexual encounters with intern Monica Lewinsky that led to his impeachment.

When Trump showed visitors his workplace, he invited some to peer into what he periodically described as his "secret bathroom," which he occasionally presented with the claim he had renovated the entire space, down to the toilet. "You understand what I'm talking about," Trump said to one guest. The statement was strange and vague and open to interpretation as to why he emphasized the changes, but the guest interpreted it to mean Trump did not want to use the same bathroom as his Black predecessor. (Trump's claim of a full remodeling happened to be untrue, officials said at the time: only the toilet seat was replaced, which was customary during a change in officeholder. The most significant addition he made might have been the collection of hairsprays that some visitors took note of.)

For Trump, unlike many of his predecessors in the White House, there was nothing new about sleeping above his office. A fitful sleeper, Trump was often awake and calling friends and political allies as early as 5:00 a.m. He spent the morning with the television on—he seemed to view television stars as his peers—and he would save cable-news shows throughout the day on a recording system he called his "SuperTivo." He would weigh in on what he was seeing via Twitter, as if he were still monitoring the news from Trump Tower instead of the center of government, whether it was superficial observations about news anchors or remarks about global affairs that risked setting off international crises.

For Priebus, the periods where Trump lived in a liminal space between work and leisure were a source of anxiety. Priebus's staff started trying to schedule meetings for around 9:00 a.m. in the Oval Office. Over the course of the year, the first meeting of the day began to slide back, later and later, until Trump's day was starting closer to 10:30 a.m., as it had at Trump Tower. By around 6:30 p.m., he would typically return upstairs. There, he would have dinner, sometimes with invited guests, before ultimately heading to his bedroom to catch up on television shows that he recorded and make phone calls. During those long mornings and evenings at the beginning, when Trump was out of the business suit he wore nearly everywhere other than the golf course, he sometimes donned a robe. He was far from the first president to choose comfort while in private, but his team was enraged by a story in which a colleague and I mentioned him wearing a robe in an account of the White House's nocturnal chaos. The White House press secretary was dispatched by a colleague to tell reporters on Air Force One that the story was false, and that Trump did not even own a bathrobe. A short time later, years-old photos of Trump in such a robe surfaced online, even as the press secretary denied the detail, and staff began speculating about who had leaked it.

His new aides were struck that Trump refused to recognize that reporters assigned to his White House would cover him more skeptically than the gossip pages or entertainment media. When the coverage did not turn out the way he wanted it to, Trump labeled the press "the enemy of the American people." (It went well beyond Bannon's habit of calling journalists "the opposition party.") It was a refrain often used by despots around the globe, and Trump would repeat it dozens of times over the years. Much as Trump remained willing to speak to reporters out of his own interest in attention, his staff did so, too, out of concern for their own survival or to impact policy outcomes or to damage colleagues. This created a cycle of endless "leak hunts" and a culture of paranoia that some officials learned to weaponize against internal rivals.

For his part, after the bathrobe incident, Trump seemed to withdraw further into perpetual suspicion about the loyalty of the people surrounding him. He had aides carry stacks of paper in cardboard boxes, trailing him when he went from the Oval Office to the residence and back again or traveled on a trip. He developed a habit of tearing up documents, scattering their pieces in a trash bin or on the floor, leaving presidential record keepers in a scramble to tape them back together to preserve the documents in accordance with the Presidential Records Act. Trump would periodically throw print paper into the toilet, which would clog the pipes and require engineers to clear them; staff sometimes found clumped-up paper themselves, with his handwriting on it, and recalled it happening on some foreign trips. White House staff discussed whether to try to find ways to make him stop; they were unsure of why he was doing it, whether it was his inherent paranoia or simply one of his behavioral tics, but they speculated the papers involved some material that he did not want to be seen. (Trump called this reporting "fake" and said I had no way of knowing if this was happening.)

Other habits of Trump's were so clearly beyond his control that even the aides who disliked his public behavior, such as his name-calling of critics, or aspects of his policy positions, could not help but feel some sympathy for him. Ubiquitous hand sanitizer attested to his well-known germaphobia, even though the fear appeared situational. At Mar-a-Lago, disinfectant wipes were placed out in display bowls. The White House doctor or a traveling aide kept them available when Trump hit the road, despite packaging that said they were only to be used on nonporous surfaces and not skin. His hands often appeared red, rubbed raw by the chemicals.

• • •

Melania's absence from Washington had a striking impact on Trump. Chronically afraid of being alone, Trump often seemed to friends to be concerned about Melania's reactions to events, and White House aides noted that he appeared particularly anxious when she wasn't around. (After the ugly election, Melania renegotiated her prenuptial agreement.) When Melania and Barron did resettle in Washington, more than four months into Trump's term, in June, they remained a bunkered unit in the residence. While the president ultimately developed a personal rapport with some of the military aides who served them, the first lady kept at more of a remove.

The president had lots of people who had attached themselves to him, but few actual friends. One, New England Patriots owner Robert Kraft, attempted to convey that Trump had a softer side, giving an interview in which he recalled how attentive Donald and Melania had been after his wife's death, calling once a week for a year. Tom Barrack tried to become the equivalent of a life coach for some of the cabinet members encountering Trump for the first time and trying to understand him.

Trump tried to outsource government functions to friends, at times because he saw a public-policy problem as a construction project he could manage himself and avoid the government bureaucracy, a high-level version of the Wollman Rink. In his first weeks in office, Trump asked Richard LeFrak, the developer whose family's prowess in New York real estate had always overshadowed the Trumps', about construction of the wall along the southern border. The Department of Homeland Security's estimates were tens of billions of dollars—too high, in Trump's view. "Would you do it?" Trump proposed to LeFrak, who made clear that he was not a government contractor.

Other times, wealthy acquaintances pitched him directly. At Mar-a-Lago, Trump spoke with Ike Perlmutter, a club member and chairman of Marvel Entertainment, who said he wanted to help run the Veterans Affairs Department. Trump accepted the offer, as Kushner recounted the episode to someone outside government, empowering Perlmutter and two associates—none of whom had any experience in government or the military—to begin engaging with, and influencing, the department's appointed leadership on personnel and policy matters. (House Democrats would accuse the "Mar-a-Lago crowd," as department officials referred to them, of violating federal transparency laws in their unofficial roles.)

For every Kraft or LeFrak or Perlmutter, there were dozens of New York business and finance leaders who had never given Trump much thought—or had worked to defeat him as a candidate—who would now at least take his calls. Trump marveled at how many people were newly eager to engage with him. "I can invite anyone for dinner," he boasted, and they would show up.

Hedge-fund manager Paul Singer, a philanthropist who over the previous decade had emerged as one of the country's largest donors to conservative candidates and causes, had opposed Trump during the 2016 election, but some of the president's advisers thought it would be worthwhile for them to meet. When Singer arrived in the Oval Office one midday, Trump's team was preparing him for a press conference that afternoon. Trump invited Singer to sit at the Resolute Desk alongside Pence and a half dozen Trump aides as they batted around potential questions and answers. As staff drifted to the East Room for the press conference, Trump made idle chat with Singer, asking "How conservative are you?" Singer responded that he was quite conservative on economic issues but more moderate on other issues, such as gay rights, and that he had been involved in efforts to legalize same-sex marriage. (After winning office as an opponent of marriage equality, Trump gave some gay-rights activists hope when he said he accepted the Supreme Court's 2015 ruling ordering states to let gays and lesbians marry. "It's irrelevant because it was already settled," he told CBS's Lesley Stahl. "It's law.") Apparently unbeknownst to Trump, Singer was a backer of GOProud, the gay Republicans' group that had helped to bring Trump to the Conservative Political Action Conference six years earlier.

"Are you gay?" Trump asked Singer. No, Singer replied, but my son is. Pence began to leave. Trump gestured toward the vice president, and said, "You're not like those guys, that kind of conservative?" Then he added, "The gays, they love me," noting that the line in his convention speech that received the most applause was a vow to "protect our LGBTQ citizens from the violence and oppression of a hateful foreign ideology."

Trump asked Singer to join him at the press conference. Singer explained that he was a low-profile person and was heading back to New York City. Trump was undeterred in using Singer's name and, before taking any questions, told reporters about his visitor. "Paul Singer just left," he said. "As you know, Paul was very much involved with the anti-Trump or, as they say, 'Never Trump.' And Paul just left, and he's given us his total support."

For a while, Trump called Paul Ryan every morning, often in predawn hours when Ryan had yet to wake. (It took several weeks for Ryan to condition Trump not to ring before he had completed his morning workout.) Ryan had been openly critical of Trump during the 2016 election, but the two men were suddenly forced to work together. Trump often acted as though Ryan were yet another source of information or a subordinate.

Ryan's priority for the first months of Trump's presidency was delivering on a long-standing Republican promise to unwind the health-insurance law known as Obamacare. Despite his party's majorities in both houses of Congress, Trump had trouble uniting his party around a single approach, with the right wing preferring immediate full repeal of Obama's reforms and moderates expressing concern that such an approach would cause too much disruption. With a vote looming on a partial repeal bill, in late March Trump made the trek to Capitol Hill to force holdouts to fall in line. He told legislators that this was their one opportunity to deliver on their pledge to repeal Obamacare, and that they would be inviting a primary challenge if they did not act on it.

Trump aimed particular attention at the holdouts to the right who believed federal spending on health-care subsidies should be cut further, many of them part of the House Freedom Caucus, a splinter faction of hard-line conservatives who had been antagonizing party leadership for years. They were working in concert with some of the most conservative Senate voices. Trump looked at the caucus's chairman, a North Carolinian with a gentle voice and thick Southern accent who was slow to support Trump in 2016. "Mark Meadows. I'm coming after you," Trump said. Meadows's eyes opened larger. If there was truth to Meadows's later insistence that he did not take Trump's words as a threat, it was because few people, if any, in the room had experienced a president speaking that way to lawmakers, especially of his own party.

A number of the Freedom Caucus members, still learning to navigate dealing with the new president and how seriously to weigh his words, did not budge from their resistance. Senator Ted Cruz, who since his stand against Trump at the Republican convention the previous summer had worked to repair their relationship, met with the Freedom Caucus and then called Trump with a warning. "You do not have the votes," he said. "Don't put this on the floor." It was at odds with what Trump was hearing from Ryan, who was intent on bringing the bill to the House floor in short order. Trump decided to trust the House Speaker over the junior senator.

Just before the vote, Ryan abruptly pulled the bill; Cruz had been right. Trump was angry, embarrassed, having expended capital—corralling votes himself—and fallen short. He laid fault on Ryan and regretted having given in to the congressional leadership's judgment on how to organize their shared agenda. "I should have done tax cuts first," he said that night.

Trump began listening more to the band of conservative lawmakers whose defiance doomed his first major legislative initiative. He was always most attentive to people who were in the process of turning their backs on him, and to that end his constant fear of losing his own supporters was visible for everyone to see. Meadows and another Freedom Caucus leader, Ohio representative Jim Jordan, became key guides for Trump to what their shared political base would favor and what it could not tolerate. Meadows helped tune Trump into a new issue: ending taxpayer-funded gender-reassignment surgeries for military personnel. But retired general James Mattis, the defense secretary, was opposed to it, as were some business leaders. With the White House and Pentagon in a standoff over the issue, Meadows and his allies ratcheted up the pressure, threatening to block all military funding until they got their way. Inside the White House, advisers such as Bannon encouraged Trump.

Just past 9:00 a.m. on a Wednesday morning in late July, as aides were preparing to discuss options with Trump for how to move forward after months of discussion, Trump wrote on Twitter, "After consultation with my Generals and military experts, please be advised that the United States Government will not accept or allow transgender individuals to serve in any capacity in the US Military." That went much further than Meadows and his allies had asked, a sweeping policy change that caught some of the Pentagon leadership that would be charged with it by complete surprise.

The fact that Trump was often influenced by the last person to speak to him, and that he often treated input from people outside the administration as better and more valuable than what he heard from his actual staff, put a new focus on how he spent his long nights and mornings in the residence. Typically the flow of information to and from a president is controlled by the chief of staff, but Trump did not

always place his calls through a White House operator, a practice which would have logged them in such
a way that the chief of staff's office could track them,
instead using his own cell phone and sometimes that
of an aide.

Aides noticed that Keith Schiller, his former bodyguard and then head of Oval Office Operations, was
an owner of one of the phones that Trump often used.
When officials tried to tell him that foreign governments were likely listening in on the unsecured de-
vices, Trump scoffed, saying that was not possible.
On more than one occasion when Trump agreed to
relinquish his personal phone, he managed to acquire
another; advisers believed he had sent a staffer who
had worked for him prior to the presidency to buy
one at a store without any of the standard security
precautions. At one point, Trump left his phone in
a golf cart at his New Jersey club. A senior White
House lawyer's notes documenting the frantic search
for "misplaced phone for six hours" specify that it
was "not our phone," apparently meaning it was not
a government-issued device.

Trump accepted reading material from a variety of
people, regardless of whether it had been vetted by
staff or experts, and he continued to stay in contact
with people he'd fired. (When the lost phone was
examined afterward for any evidence of tampering,
a White House lawyer noted, curiously, "found message from Flynn. May never have been opened.")
Officials seeking his attention would attempt to stroll,

unannounced, into the residence, in defiance of the chief usher or Secret Service agents tasked with controlling access. What Trump heard or read often became grist for a tweet, which could itself become the catalyst for an eventual policy or personnel change.

Those who wanted to shape the president's thinking learned how to exploit this situation, raising the pressure on the chief of staff's office to manage his interactions—or at least reconstruct them just to understand his thinking. Trump found ways, as always, to avoid those trying to handle him. Over time, he began holding meetings more frequently in the residence, including those related to electoral politics, and was dismissive of ethics concerns about conducting partisan business in the White House. At one point, a group of advisers persuaded him to accept a process of committee approval over his Twitter posts. That process did not stick. Over time, social media director Dan Scavino, who closely monitored the internet on Trump's behalf, printed out a list of tweets from which Trump could choose. He joked that he would someday create a Twitter account featuring all the unsent tweets. Trump devoted enormous energy into maintaining his Twitter presence, keeping the @realDonaldTrump handle active while the official handle of the presidency became vestigial. One tweet, posted shortly after midnight in the spring, trailed off midsentence. "Despite the negative press covfefe," the tweet said. Scavino told colleagues that Trump had simply fallen asleep midtweet.

People used Trump's paranoia to turn him against a chief of staff who was always concerned with his own standing, and against those who worked for him. They discovered how easy it was to manipulate Trump's uncertainty about who could be undermining him, and they used reporters, including me, as cudgels. A fringe-right website posted a piece falsely claiming that a Priebus deputy, Katie Walsh, had been feeding me stories. I was told later that a printout of the article was given to someone close to Trump, who raised it with him. It had the effect hoped for by those behind the story: the combination of the word "leak" and my name set him off. The confected incident complicated Walsh's remaining time in the White House and was used by other advisers to damage Priebus, heightening Trump's suspicion of the group of former RNC officials who were awkwardly grafted onto Trump loyalists in the White House.

That episode was a relatively minor ding on Priebus's standing, which was already more heavily dented by the internal rivalry between Kushner and Bannon, whose competition for influence often came at Priebus's expense. Priebus was weakened by the fact that Kushner repeatedly told people in private that Priebus was in over his head, as well as the fact that in Trump's White House traditional job titles and hierarchy meant little; the chief of staff was, on a good day, just another adviser among equals. Trump made managing the White House staff and systems nearly impossible. His people pleasing resulted in him agreeing to events being put on his calendar, then yelling at aides for loading up his schedule. His aversion to hearing bad news led to people tiptoeing around him or trying to avoid telling him certain things. Efforts to keep meetings productive usually required limiting attendance to a compact group. Anything above a handful of people inspired Trump to play to the room; a smaller number left a chance that work would get done.

Significantly, Priebus took the hit for Ryan's management of the health-care bill; the chief of staff owed his job in part to his fellow Wisconsinite's recommendation, and Trump knew they were close. It took six weeks after Ryan pulled the vote on the repeal bill for House Republicans to reach a compromise that did enough to satisfy both wings of the party. When the Senate voted in late July, the Republican leadership was unable to hold its members together, with decisive resistance from Trump's longtime opponent John McCain, who returned to Washington shortly after having a blood clot removed and being diagnosed with brain cancer, to kill the bill with a dramatic late-night thumbs-down gesture on the Senate floor. Priebus would not last much longer.

Trump had begun putting out feelers for a new chief of staff months earlier, warning Lewandowski and Bossie that he was making changes before the summer began as explanation as to why he didn't want them coming to work there; Trump told them that he was about to blow everything up, suggesting they should remain outside the White House, as though protecting them while they worked for him was beyond his control. Just before ousting Priebus, he even asked his chief of staff if Priebus should be replaced by the Homeland Security secretary, John Kelly, the only one of the retired or active military generals he had appointed to political posts on whom he had yet to sour. (Trump had also considered two of the former Goldman Sachs executives serving in his White House, economic adviser Gary Cohn and the deputy national security adviser, Dina Powell.) Nevertheless, Trump enjoyed speculating about such job moves instead of overseeing a search or a coherent hiring process. At one point, Rupert Murdoch brought John F. W. Rogers, a veteran of the Ford and Reagan White Houses who later served as a chief of staff to several Goldman Sachs executives, to meet Trump as a prospective successor to Priebus. Trump barely asked Rogers a question, spending the first thirty minutes hectoring Murdoch about the supposed leftward drift of Fox News. "It's going to become too liberal when James takes over," Trump said, referring to the Murdoch son expected to follow his father as the parent company's chairman. "No," Murdoch interrupted. "It's going to be Lachlan." That was one of the first times the succession plan for News Corp—a subject of immense ongoing speculation in media and political circles worldwide—had ever been made public, and Trump only managed to elicit it because he was so uninterested in dealing with his own staffing issues.

The internal disarray, caused in no small part by the Kushner and Bannon factions trying to destroy each other, constantly leaked into public view, prompting fury from Trump, who wanted everything to appear in control. Amid weeks of news coverage of in-fighting and the president's own indecisiveness, Trump couldn't figure out how to contain the fallout. He railed to his staff, "Where does this shit come from?"

CHAPTER 20

In the Tank

The National Military Command Center, a cavernous, auditorium-like room known as "the Tank," is among the most revered spaces in the Pentagon, a place that signifies a larger sense of duty and purpose to those who wear the uniform everywhere. When Trump entered on July 20, 2017, his aides hoped the new surroundings would humble him and force a focus often absent from the briefings they delivered him in familiar White House spaces. Everything that took place in the Oval Office, a bustling environment in which people freely came and went throughout the day, risked devolving into distractions. Even without the flow of human traffic, Trump had little interest in what he perceived as lectures from his staff. There were a few issues he either had been talking about for decades, such as trade and, loosely, other countries ripping off the United States, or which he had campaigned on and succeeded at drawing support for. He believed that he had proven he knew better than others merely by winning an election he was told he would lose, despite the fact that he, too, had not expected to win.

A Situation Room meeting about Afghanistan a short time earlier with the generals he'd filled the administration with had resulted in Trump feeling frustrated, as he had for months. He felt he was being talked down to by the generals, whom he mocked for not understanding "money," and was being told to follow policies that had been tried and with which he didn't agree. "Why am I wasting my time?" he asked aides afterward.

Two of his administration's top officials thought it was time for a new approach. James Mattis and Gary Cohn came from wildly different backgrounds. One was a four-star Marine general sometimes called a "warrior monk" for his quiet, determined intellectualism, the other a former Goldman Sachs executive at home amid the clubby culture of Wall Street. When they met for an introductory lunch in February, both tried to hint, however gingerly, at their new shared situation. Both served a president who knew little about policy, or the world more broadly, but liked to talk about a range of topics and fire off tweets without any sort of process beforehand. Even as they met in the earliest weeks of the administration, there was already a vivid illustration of the consequences of his management style: the ban on travelers from seven majority-Muslim countries had proved to be a fiasco, creating chaos at airports and prompting broad-scale demonstrations nationwide, criticism from congressional Republicans, and a number of court challenges. There were occasional moments when Trump's

White House functioned as a normal one might. When Syrian president Bashar al-Assad deployed a chemical agent on his own citizens in April, the haunting images of children dying slowly, motionless, helped move Trump to order a missile strike against one of Assad's air bases. "Years of previous attempts at changing Assad's behavior have all failed and failed very dramatically," Trump said as he announced the operation, before a blue-curtained backdrop and surrounded by flags. His aides worked so that everything was handled according to standard procedures, including briefing the press. Trump received widespread positive media coverage for one of the few times since taking office. An adviser told me that week that the episode was what Trump had always believed the job was going to be: decision, action, praise.

But such moments were rare. Trump remained impervious to most coaching. He fixated on North Korea and its nuclear capabilities, having his National Security Council draw up a menu of options, from the equivalent of annihilation to total appeasement, and a series of possibilities in between. One high-level option involved personal contact with the country's reclusive leader, Kim Jong-un, but months passed before that option was visited. In the meantime, his desire to end the war in Afghanistan ran up against a lack of internal consensus within his cabinet about how to approach the region and blowback from the generals and national security officials he'd appointed. Trump cared about fulfilling a campaign promise, but aides were struck that he seemed rattled by the number of deaths involved; over time, he came to resent every "Killed in Action" letter he was forced to sign after a servicemember died, not wanting to attach his name to a war he disliked and its needless deaths.

Uncertain about how his new environment worked, Trump sometimes seemed open to taking a course of action that ran counter to his instincts. Yet there was far more evidence through the first half of 2017 that Trump was not interested in modulating his views in office. On calls with global counterparts, he tried to manipulate them, highlighting for one leader criticism that another leader had made about them, trying to play them off one another much as he did his own staff. On his first foreign trip, to the Middle East and Europe, Trump had turned to Bannon after arriving in the Saudi capital of Riyadh to a display of pageantry and said, "Lawrence of Arabia," the most accessible frame of reference even after preparation for the trip. He seemed to care most about a luncheon with the region's leaders and some of the United States' top financiers at which he was the main attraction, as well as a state dinner there; it was during that trip that Middle East officials realized how susceptible Trump was to flattery. During a visit to the North Atlantic Treaty Organization headquarters in Brussels, he did not adhere to a written speech text calling for a commitment to the principle of mutual self-defense. Trump had enjoyed a subsequent trip to France, but largely because the centerpiece was a Bastille Day

The two major party nominees on the 2016 debate stage for the first time, sparring over Trump's "birther" crusade and his refusal to release his tax returns.

Hillary Clinton in the center of the hall at the second debate. Trump and his aides brought women who'd accused Bill Clinton of sexual misconduct to sit in the audience, as well as a rape victim whose alleged attacker had been represented in court by Hillary Clinton. Trump's aides seized on the chance to deploy the women against Hillary Clinton.

Trump and Clinton on either side of Cardinal Timothy Dolan, the archbishop of the New York archdiocese. As is tradition in presidential campaigns, the two major party nominees attended the annual Alfred E. Smith Memorial Foundation Dinner benefiting Catholic charities.

Trump at a rally in the final days of the 2016 campaign, one of many he held throughout the contest. The rallies replaced typical retail campaigning and town halls for the candidate and drove an intensity among his fan base.

Every president has a family member whom staff find themselves working with or around, but Trump enmeshed four of his adult children and his son-in-law in his political operation to various degrees.

Trump hugs his final 2016 campaign manager, Kellyanne Conway, on election night in 2016. Conway went to work for Trump in the White House and became a close associate of First Lady Melania Trump.

President-elect Trump meeting with Senate Majority Leader Mitch McConnell two days after Election Day 2016. McConnell would be forever aghast at Trump's behavior, but he took advantage of total Republican control of the government to push through key agenda items.

During the presidential transition, Trump's fixer Michael Cohen speaks with Lieutenant General Michael Flynn (retired) and former Texas governor Rick Perry at Trump Tower. Flynn would become Trump's national security adviser and Perry would serve as energy secretary.

The incoming president strides to the podium, preparing to deliver a speech describing a ravaged America. The size of the inauguration crowd he spoke to became the first of many angry fights with the media during his presidency.

Trump on the phone with Russian president Vladimir Putin during his first year in office, surrounded by aides who, save for Vice President Mike Pence, would all be gone by the end of the year.

It became noticeable within the first weeks of the Trump presidency that he had one photo on the credenza behind him in the Oval Office: his father, Fred, watching over him, omnipresent in almost everything Trump did. Eventually the president would add other photos, but one always stood out.

Trump welcomes Jeff Sessions as his attorney general, a job with parameters that the incoming president little understood. Within one month of Sessions's swearing-in, he would recuse himself from the investigation into ties between Russia and the Trump campaign, forever infuriating Trump.

Former New Jersey governor Chris Christie was one of Trump's earliest endorsements in 2016. He went on to be fired from leading Trump's transition team, but he was later tasked with helping lead a presidential panel on opioids.

No one tended to the fantasy of a Donald Trump presidency more consistently than Roger Stone, despite a sometimes tempestuous relationship with him. Stone has an extensive collection of memorabilia of both Trump and Richard Nixon.

Trump's relationship to Puerto Rico was always fraught; he described it to aides as a place with "absolutely no hope." His behavior on a trip there after Hurricane Maria in 2017 became infamous after he tossed paper towels into a crowd of people who were grappling with the aftermath of a natural disaster.

After the debacle around efforts to repeal the Affordable Care Act, the passage of Trump's tax bill was a significant moment for the unified Republican government.

Trump shaking hands with Scott Pruitt, the head of the Environmental Protection Agency, at an event announcing the U.S. withdrawal from the Paris Climate Accords. Pruitt had been among those pushing for the move.

John Kelly, the one-time White House chief of staff, stands near Trump's daughter Ivanka and her husband, Jared Kushner. After welcoming Kelly to the West Wing, the two would engage in open warfare against the retired Marine, who, at Trump's direction, tried to curtail their influence.

A New York native and former protégé of Roger Stone, Sam Nunberg helped Trump devise aspects of the platform he ran on in 2016, including his focus on building "the wall" along the southern border of the United States.

Few were closer to Trump during his White House years than Hope Hicks, pictured here on her last day at the White House as communications director. She would later return as an adviser when the coronavirus was beginning to swamp the United States in 2020, a particularly fraught period of Trump's tenure.

Reporters, including the author, sitting in the president's cabin on Air Force One in 2018. Trump liked to bring reporters up to the front of the plane periodically.

Trump's soft tone toward Vladimir Putin confused his staff and stoked endless questions about why an American president would adopt such a verbal posture. Trump always seemed intrigued by his one-on-one meetings with Putin.

Trump became enamored of the right-wing radio host Rush Limbaugh, even granting him the Presidential Medal of Freedom late in his presidency. Limbaugh's proud misogyny and the racist comments on his radio show drew a fan base that overlapped with Trump supporters.

Michael Cohen, Trump's fixer, raises his right hand ahead of his sworn congressional testimony about his work for Trump. Cohen's testimony was key to the New York attorney general's investigation of Trump's valuations of his properties.

Trump, obsessed with the number of border crossings, visits with the border patrol in Calexico, California, in 2019. It was on that trip that he suggested his incoming acting secretary of Homeland Security should close the border and that he'd pardon the man if he was accused of crimes. The secretary told people that he believed Trump was joking; others were less sure.

David Bossie and Corey Lewandowski, Trump's former deputy campaign manager and campaign manager. Bossie was known in 2016 for delivering news that Trump didn't want to hear—and paying a price for it. Lewandowski, despite being fired, remained close to Trump.

Trump with Ukrainian president Volodymyr Zelensky. A month before this meeting, Trump had called Zelensky asking for investigations related to Joe Biden's son Hunter soon after Trump's government put a hold on congressionally approved military aid to Ukraine. The call helped spark Trump's first impeachment by the House.

One of the rituals that presidents engage in is the dignified transfer of the remains of soldiers killed in action. Trump, who once invited the actor Jon Voight to join him for such an event, stands with the first lady for the ceremony.

Trump hosted Brazilian president Jair Bolsonaro at Mar-a-Lago in March 2020. The weekend meeting was one of several to occur at the club just as the coronavirus was taking hold across the country. A Bolsonaro aide was among those who tested positive for the virus after the weekend.

Trump takes part in a coronavirus task force briefing at the White House with Attorney General William Barr looking on. Their most contentious months began as the pandemic accelerated.

On June 1, 2020, Trump tried to display dominance over protesters outside the White House by walking to the historic St. John's Church, the basement of which had been set on fire the previous night. Aides suggested that he carry a Bible, wanting him to read scripture. Instead, Trump held it aloft like a prop.

Trump was delighted to unveil his third Supreme Court pick, Judge Amy Coney Barrett, in late September. But the announcement became known as a superspreader event, as mostly maskless attendees swamped the Rose Garden and the West Wing. Trump would test positive for the coronavirus shortly afterward.

Trump, determined to show that he was unbowed by COVID-19, marches up the steps at the White House after returning from his hospitalization at Walter Reed National Military Medical Center. At the top, he would rip off his mask, appearing to gasp for breath.

Trump's longest-serving friend and adviser, Roger Stone, poses for pictures in Washington, D.C., a day before the riot at the Capitol.

Former New York City mayor Rudy Giuliani addressing the "Stop the Steal" rally crowd on January 6, 2021. He called for a "trial by combat" shortly before rioters disrupted congressional certification of the electoral college results. Giuliani's agitated allegations that the election had been stolen from Trump helped contribute to Trump's second impeachment by the House.

MAGGIE HABBERMAN BOOK QUESTIONS (VIA ▮▮▮▮

- DJT is said to have sent money to Stanley Friedman's wife when Friedman was in prison. Does he have any comment on this?

STANLEY WAS A GOOD MAN WITH GREAT COURAGE -

- DJT attended Roy Cohn's funeral but stood in the back; he told people who knew them both long prior to Cohn's death that he hadn't believed Cohn was gay. Does he have any comment on this?

FALSE

FALSE

- DJT had an intense concern about AIDS that he talked about a lot in the 1980s as it was spreading around the country, a topic he talked about frequently. Reporters he dealt with often recall him worrying that people he'd shaken hands with might be gay and transmitting the virus. Does he have any comment on this?

FALSE

WHO DIDN'T?

- DJT threw a surprise birthday party for Richard Fields in the 1990s at the Pirros' house. Does he recall why he threw it?

A NICE GUY - DON'T REMEMBER PARTY

- When Neil Barsky wrote the story in 1991 about how DJT may have to borrow money from his father, associates of DJT said he worried about the story leaving the impression that he was strong-arming his father publicly, or waiting to collect his inheritance. Is there additional context around what happened with Barsky that he wants to provide?

BARSKY WAS A SLEEZELBAG - MY FATHER AND I HAD A GREAT RELATIONSHIP - STORY WAS FAKE NEWS

- When DJT's father bought more than $3 million worth of casino chips, they were ordered by regulators to be preserved because they were an unreported loan. One of the chips, worth many thousands of dollars, went missing from the lockbox where it was kept; ▮▮▮▮ ▮▮▮▮ Did he take it or was it someone else?

FANTASYLAND!

- When DJT took a loan from his share of the estate and his brother objected, he wrote a letter to family members criticizing him, according to a friend of the family. Does he have a comment on this?

MY BROTHER AND I WERE VERY CLOSE RIGHT UP UNTIL HIS PASSING - CALL ANN MARIE (WIFE)

- In the 1990s, former employees recall DJT taking percentages of leasing agreements on amenities like parking garages in cash (treated as a brokerage fee). One case involved having dozens of gold bricks wheeled to DJT's office on the 26th floor by Matt Calamari; it was said to be attached to a lease held for the GM building ▮▮▮▮ Was this kind of "brokerage fee" common for the Trump Organization? And

A FANTASY QUESTION!

was the gold related to the gold investment DJT declared on his personal financial disclosure form?

- DJT took a loan from George Ross, a wealthy man in his own right who for years worked for the Trump Organization; former employees were told it was to cover the Trump Organization's payroll. Does DJT recall have a comment on this?

FALSE

- Former employees recall him describing gay people as "queer" or "faggot;" Alan Marcus, a former DJT employee, recalls DJT referring to Abe Wallach as a queer who he didn't have to pay as much because of ithat fact. Does DJT have a comment on this?

TOTALLY FALSE

- Marcus recalls DJT using Nick Ribis to solve interpersonal fights in the office. He also recalls DJT marking up a draft earnings release for the casino holding company and sending it to Marcus for ultimate release. The issue was investigated by the SEC and Nick Ribis was blamed by Jay Goldberg. Marcus recalls calling Goldberg and telling him the release existed, and believes DJT was aware that the earnings statement was inflated. Does DJT have a comment either on the call or marking up the earnings release?

FAKE NEWS

- Associates recalled Trump saying that Roy Cohn would tell him that he should hope for a Black judge on cases; the implication, the associates said, was that Black judges could be manipulated in some way. "Let's hope the judge is Black," Trump periodically said about a legal case, they recalled. Does he have a comment?

NOT TRUE

- The former POTUS directed Pence to stay at his hotel in Doonbeg. Does DJT have a comment?

NOT TRUE - HIS RELATIVES LIVED OR HAD A BUSINESS IN DOONBEG -

- The former POTUS was unhappy with Flynn even before the reporting in the Washington Post about his discussion with Kislyak involving sanctions, but started expressing regret after firing him. Does he have a comment on that, and can he say why they began talking again?

FALSE - HE WAS, AND IS, A GREAT PATRIOT.

- Former POTUS wanted John Kelly to move the president's daughter and son-in-law out of the White House. Why did he ultimately decided not to?

FALSE STORY - KELLY WAS TOO DUMB TO PROPERLY HANDLE SUCH AN EVENT IF TRUE, WHICH IT WAS NOT.

- Officials say the former POTUS directed White House officials to hold the G-7 at the Doral. Does DJT have a comment on this?

WOULD HAVE BEEN A GREAT LOCATION AND BEAUTIFUL PLACE. MIDDLE OF MIAMI, NEAR AIRPORT ETC. TOO POLITICAL

- When DJT talked to Erdogan in 2019 just before the incursion into Syria, officials said that on their call, Erdogan swayed him by promising to take care of terrorists. Does DJT have a comment on this?

FALSE. I TOOK CARE OF THE TERRORISTS, GOT OUT OF SYRIA, SAVED BILLIONS OF $'s, GOT ALONG WELL WITH ERDOGAN.

- DJT repeatedly expressed regret over criminal justice reform. Does he have a comment on that? *DID IT FOR AFRICAN AMERICANS. NOBODY ELSE COULD HAVE GOTTEN IT DONE. GOT ZERO credit -*

- Former employees recall DJT keeping salacious photos of women he said he'd been involved with and showing them to employees. Does he have a comment on this? *FAKE NEWS - NOT MY STYLE*

- DJT, talking to NBC executive Marc Graboff, said he thought he needed a Jewish agent. DJT had sought a hefty contract increase after the first season of the Apprentice, ultimately agreeing to a minor bump. Does he have a comment on this?

FAKE STORY *I MADE A FORTUNE MAJOR ON THE APPRENTICE - BIG HIT*

- DJT spoke in the early 1990s about a relationship Marla Maples had with Michael Bolton, the singer, and how he won her over from Bolton despite an intense wooing effort. Associates said he wanted to attend a Michael Bolton concert with Maples shortly after they traveled to Hawaii, a trip he also talked about. Does he have comment on this/memory of this? *I DID WELL WITH SUCH THINGS - NEVER FAILED - Another DAY IN THE LIFE OF. WHO CARES?*

- Alan Marcus recalls DJT asking someone involved in preparing slides for investors for the stock pitch for the Trump casino holdings to doctor a slide related to the pitch for the Buffington Harbor, Indiana casino, showing the location as adjacent to Chicago, as opposed to a 40-minute drive away. When an aide reminded DJT that he was dealing with an

- DJT is said to have been encouraged on troop withdrawals from Germany by Ric Grenell. Why did he think this was an important move and has DJT's perspective changed in light of the Russia attack on <u>Ukraine?</u>

THEY DON'T PAY FAIR SHARE (LIKE MOST OTHERS) WOULD NEVER HAVE HAPPENED TAKE ADVANTAGE OF USA. WITH "TRUMP"

- There was a plastic surgeon whose office has photos of the former first family in his office and a piece about DJT sending him clientele - his name is ████████ who treated several female staffers with outpatient treatments inside the White House medical unit. Why was he there? *HE WAS THE DOCTOR FOR MISS U - WHICH I HAD SUCCESSFULLY SOLD PRIOR TO W.H.*

- Meadows told Pence folks that POTUS wanted to delay his transition funding after election day. Does DJT have a comment about why? *KNOW NOTHING ABOUT IT.*

- DJT has told people if Roy Cohn was still alive, he would still be president. Does he recall saying this and can he explain what Cohn could have done that others didn't? *I GOT FAR MORE VOTES THAN ANY SITTING PRESIDENT. ELECTION WAS RIGGED & STOLEN.*

SEC-monitored public offering, DJT told the aide the map could be used outside Chicago, because no one would realize what the actual distance was. Does he have a comment on this? *HE MUST HAVE A BAD MEMORY (OR BAD/ PRETTY EASY TO FIND OUT. BRAIN).*

- Associates recall DJT describing then-Melania Knauss as, for what he wanted for his life, "out of central casting."

ACTUALLY, THERE IS SOME TRUTH IN THAT!

- Throughout the campaign and the presidency, DJT complained about Kushner taking time off for <u>Shabbat.</u> Does he have a comment on this?

FAKE NEWS -

GOOD NIGHT!

Trump answered questions about some of the reporting in this book two weeks after the deadline had passed, replying with handwritten notes to each.

President Trump addresses the rally crowd at the Ellipse on January 6.
Trump told his supporters that he would join them in marching to the
Capitol before he left the event and went back to the White House.

A grim Trump climbs the steps of Marine One for the last time of his term on January 20, 2021.

parade, a grand affair with multiple jet flyovers and tanks rolling down Paris's boulevards. Trump did not appear to emerge from the visit with a greater appreciation of the American relationship with its oldest ally, as French president Emmanuel Macron had hoped in extending Trump a welcome fit for royalty. Rather, Trump, who was awestruck by the jet formations flying overhead, returned to Washington eager to see a military parade of his own on the streets of the capital, although he told aides he did not like the sight of wounded veterans at such events.

Cohn believed that Trump's problems with foreign policy stemmed from a lack of understanding about the globe's interconnectedness and the importance of the post–World War II international order to it. In the Tank, one large map showed where the United States has active military bases, an oversize visual aid that generals and cabinet officials could use to guide Trump through the world, demonstrating where American military presence and national security concerns overlapped with economic interests, and the importance of alliances throughout.

Trump sat and listened, his arms folded. The tour of the world began in Europe, where the question of whether Trump would try to impose tariffs had loomed for months. Trump complained that the U.S. was spending too much money on NATO. Next up was the Middle East. Trump seemed not to grasp the use of the Air Force base in Saudi Arabia, or why there was a naval base in Bahrain. He told the military leaders that they were overly cautious by having so much high-priced equipment, even as he repeatedly demanded that they buy more. The generals were "dopes" and "you're losers and you're babies," he told them, and he would not go to war with any of them. (Elsewhere Trump would repeat that he wanted them "more like German generals," a desire befuddling to anyone familiar with modern European history.)

But it was the discussion of American bases in South Korea that set Trump off. "Mr. President," one official said, "the South Koreans are important to protect South Korea, but they also have a much broader strategic function." To illustrate the point, one aide noted that intelligence related to military movements in China could be picked up quickly, in fewer than six seconds; if Americans had to monitor from facilities in Alaska, the next closest system, it would take two minutes. "That's nice," Trump chirped sarcastically. "I don't really give a shit," he said in response to another data point. He insisted that the United States had overextended itself around the world. "We'll be fine" without those bases, he said.

Trump was plainly furious at nearly everyone in the world. He did not want to shoulder costs for defenses overseas. He was willing to slap tariffs on various countries. All the effort the group had put into trying to make him understand the connections between national security, military security, and economic security—that instead of seeing them as three separate pillars, it was just one—proved pointless.

Cohn tried again, reframing it for Trump as a cost-benefit proposition. What would it take to bring enough stability to the Pacific for him to sleep well at night? "I sleep like a fucking baby at night," Trump responded. "I don't need anything out there!"

After the ninety-minute meeting, Trump's advisers tried to make sense of it. ("He's a fucking moron," Tillerson concluded.) Some thought Trump was trying to give a motivational speech to the generals. But Trump demonstrated once again that he simply didn't believe that the post–World War II order benefited the U.S. He treated foreign countries as one-off entities, with which to engage primarily through bilateral trade deficits, a data point he often sought before speaking with their leaders. That was how he could tell which one was "up" and which was "down." Those who did not know Trump well and who sat through that meeting in the Tank with him failed to consider something that people who had dealt with him over years had experienced: Trump knew that he was being told something he did not fully comprehend, and instead of acknowledging that, he shouted down the teachers.

Under Trump, even the routine duties of governance— relief for areas hit by natural disasters, or aspects of Trump's official budget—were subject to the president's whims and moods, his ideas about friends and enemies. When wildfires struck California later in his presidency, he threatened to hold up federal aid; only when the new Republican House minority leader, Californian Kevin McCarthy, got involved did Trump relent. After Hurricane Maria struck Puerto Rico, Trump was reluctant to dispense aid, due in part to his refusal, in conversations with aides, to accept that the island was a part of the United States; he seemed to view it as a distressed property, referring to it as a place with "absolutely no hope" when an aide described its potential. Trump's staff learned that to get him to act, they often had to explain an issue or event from a perspective he might experience on a personal level. Trump's new staff notched minor victories by steering him away from his impulses to ignore established processes altogether or to reward supporters in ways that would be difficult to explain away.

When word reached the National Economic Council that Trump's schedule included a meeting with an Ohio coal executive named Bob Murray, a significant donor to political groups supporting Trump, staffers raised an alarm. Officials at FirstEnergy Solutions, a coal-powered energy provider, argued it faced a dire situation as coal plants were shutting down due to market dynamics. Insisting it was the only way to continue reliably delivering power to its customers, FirstEnergy's CEO Chuck Jones pushed the administration to invoke a legal provision whereby the Department of Energy could force plants to stay open. Jones warned White House aides that, if necessary, energy executives would go around them to make their case directly to the president. Murray, whose company provided FirstEnergy with coal, was said to have had a relationship with Trump's former campaign manager, Corey Lewandowski. (Lewandowski's exact relationship with both wasn't clear—he told a reporter he wasn't working for either Murray's company or FirstEnergy—but White House aides maintained that he was involved in setting up meetings between the two sides.)

The powers that FirstEnergy was demanding Trump exercise were usually reserved for emergencies, and independent assessors of the region's energy grid delivered assurances that the situation was not the frightening one the company depicted. In this instance, exercising its executive authority to keep plants open would amount to little more than a federal bailout for a single company. The National Economic Council's deputy director, Jeremy Katz, warned colleagues that the White House could not be seen to be advocating for the move and needed to be emphatic about its reasons why. Before Murray led a group of energy executives to make their case to Trump, Katz and the main energy adviser, Mike Catanzaro, went to brief the president.

In the little dining room off the Oval Office, they warned him that the executives were coming to ask for a bailout that could ultimately benefit Murray, and that there were three reasons not to agree. For starters, they said, what the coal executives wanted was beyond his legal authority.

"Whoa, whoa," Trump said, stopping them. "Do we really need to hear two or three" of the reasons, he asked, if one was illegal? They explained the remainder to him, and told him it wasn't breaking a criminal law, it was exceeding the bounds of his authority. Trump held up his hands. "I got this, I got this, we're not doing it," he said. He told them to follow his lead in the meeting.

In the Oval Office, Trump assumed his position behind the desk and Katz and Catanzaro sat on one of the couches, along with lawyers and others familiar with energy policy. Moments later, Murray and two other people came into the room. Murray had an oxygen tank hooked up to an apparatus that made a loud wheezing sound every few seconds. "What's that machine?" Trump asked. "What does it do for you?"

"The machine helps me breathe," Murray replied.

"Is it black lung?" Trump asked.

"No, Mr. President," said Murray, who told people at the time that he suffered from idiopathic pulmonary fibrosis. "This is keeping me alive."

"What would happen if they unplug the machine?" Trump said.

"I need this to breathe," Murray explained. "I probably wouldn't survive."

Trump raised a fist and pumped it. "Keep up the good fight, Bob," he said.

Then the discussion turned to business. Trump, ever concerned to avoid direct interpersonal conflict, tried to push the blame on others. "Bob, I hear you," Trump said, before pointing to Katz and Catanzaro. "Those guys," Trump said, "they're telling me I can't do it. And I need to look into it more, because I really think we need to help you guys."

After Murray left, Trump asked his advisers again why they could not simply help. His advisers refused to waver. If you do this, they told him, you will get destroyed in a messy court fight. Unsaid was that it could also be politically disastrous to do what amounted to a favor beyond the bounds of his legal authority for a large donor to his super PAC. Trump dropped it, and the crisis was averted. Murray later claimed that Trump had told them he was on their side and they should get what they needed.

It was around that time that, after rising frustration at press coverage for which he never faulted his own behavior, Trump finally took action by announcing he had hired a new communications director. Trump had already been through three appointees to the post; the first of them, his old campaign hand Jason Miller, had to step away from it even before Trump took office, after reports he had had an extramarital affair with a female campaign transition aide. (In a meeting with Pence, Jason Miller, and other aides when Miller visited the White House early in the administration, Trump turned to Pence and said that Miller "likes the ladies" and added, "You know how sometimes someone turns out to be gay later and you knew? This guy, he isn't even like one percent gay.")

Trump's unlikely pick, financier and long-time Republican donor and fundraiser Anthony Scaramucci, had no formal background in political communications. He had been promoted for the post by Jared Kushner and Ivanka Trump, whose allies said they hoped the appointment would help drive out two internal rivals—Priebus and Spicer—likely to feel threatened by Scaramucci's arrival. When Scaramucci addressed the media in the briefing room, and it was perceived as going well, Kushner sounded a boastful note to colleagues about whose idea it was. The gambit appeared to have a welcome effect when Priebus complained to Trump after reading in the press release announcing the new hire, for which the chief of staff had not been consulted, that Scaramucci would report directly to Trump. "You worry too much about things like that," Trump responded. But Priebus got the message, and the next week told Trump he was ready to leave; Spicer, too, announced plans to depart.

The next day, a Friday, Trump asked John Kelly to become chief of staff. Kelly requested time to think it over; Trump agreed and told Kelly to come in and see him the following week. Priebus, who was preparing to finalize his departure, was making what was to be a final trip on Air Force One that day. The destination was Long Island, for an event trumpeting arrests of members of the brutal MS-13 gang, formed decades earlier by Salvadoran immigrants. But the event was part of Trump's ongoing demagoguery of immigrants as dangerous. In a community-college auditorium surrounded by law-enforcement officials, Trump talked about "liberating" towns from the "thug" gang members who had preyed on them. ("When you guys put somebody in the car and you're protecting their head, you know, the way you put their hand over?" Trump told the law-enforcement officers, pretending to protect a suspect's head as they were being loaded into a police car. "You can take the hand away, okay?" he said to laughter from the officers.) When Air Force One landed back in Washington, Trump tweeted out that Kelly would be his new chief of staff just as Priebus had departed the plane.

Scaramucci did not survive the Kelly era, fired ten days after he was hired for the communication director job. The catalyst was the publication of an interview in which Scaramucci spoke disparagingly of his new colleagues in a tirade filled with expletives, and threatened to fire the entire communications staff. Trump often engaged in his own bawdy private commentary yet complained about his aide having done so to a reporter who quoted him. But Scaramucci had already served a purpose: once he helped end the tenure of Priebus and Spicer, Trump's family and their allies no longer saw a value in fighting for him.

The West Wing was about to receive some overdue maintenance, forcing aides to scatter because
they couldn't work in the building. While the work
was completed, Trump decamped to his golf club in
Bedminster, New Jersey, where he expected to spend
most of August with only a skeleton crew of White
House advisers by his side. A week into his stay
there, national attention turned to Charlottesville,
Virginia, where a far-right organizer describing himself as "pro-white" had brought together strands of the
white-nationalist and white-supremacist movements
emboldened by Trump's ascendance to the presidency for a large gathering called Unite the Right.
On Friday night, attendees gathered for a prerally
march to defend a monument to Confederate general
Robert E. Lee against efforts to remove it. The next
day, amid clashes with counterprotesters, a demon-
strator drove his car into a young progressive activist
named Heather Heyer, killing her.

Trump was scheduled to speak to the press a short
time later, for an unrelated bill signing about the
Department of Veterans Affairs, and aides wrote a
statement acknowledging the events that had overtaken the news. "We're closely following the terrible
events unfolding in Charlottesville, Virginia. We condemn in the strongest possible terms this egregious
display of hatred, bigotry, and violence on many sides,
on many sides," he said. "It's been going on for a long
time in our country. Not Donald Trump, not Barack

Obama, this has been going on for a long, long time. It has no place in America."

The statement was instantly viewed as insufficient, including by members of Trump's own team, some of whom were Jews. Almost immediately upon landing at the White House that Monday, Trump went to the Diplomatic Room and read a new statement that staff had written for him. "Racism is evil, and those who cause violence in its name are criminals and thugs, including the KKK, neo-Nazis, white supremacists, and other hate groups that are repugnant to everything we hold dear as Americans," he said. This time, there was no reference to "both sides." After he was done, his economic advisers filed into the room for a scheduled meeting on possible steel tariffs. "What do you think of that statement?" Trump asked them. "Mr. President, it was great," said Cohn, who is Jewish.

But Trump wanted to hear from those he believed spoke for his "base." Peter Navarro, a former academic who had entered Trump's orbit as a China critic and, in that room, the most vocal defender of Trump's hard-core supporters, said he wasn't sure why Trump did it. Commerce Secretary Wilbur Ross backed up Navarro. Already casting about for some form of do-over, Trump complained later that the counterprotesters in Charlottesville had been trying to destroy "history," as he put it, by taking down Confederate monuments. "This is just wrong," he said. "Robert E. Lee was like the greatest general."

Staff secretary Rob Porter suggested that Trump speak publicly more about history, and how there are ways to progress without erasing the past. When Porter said "heritage," Trump's ears perked up. He liked that word. He wanted to try using it.

The following day, Trump's aides planned an announcement of an executive order simplifying the approval process for public-works projects, the first initiative in a long-floated turn toward infrastructure policy. The plan was for Trump to make a three-minute statement about the executive order, and then turn the microphone over to Cohn and two cabinet members who had joined him in the Trump Tower lobby. Trump had been warned that if he took questions, whatever he said would overwhelm any news on infrastructure; the elevator operator was instructed to hold the doors so he could immediately reenter after reading his statement. But after reading from the piece of paper he removed from his pocket, Trump looked up at the cameras and those of us who had assembled behind a velvet rope. "How about a couple of infrastructure questions?" Trump suggested.

Reporters were more interested in the events in Charlottesville and the criticism of Trump's initial response. I also had something else I wanted to ask. "Two questions," I said when I got the chance. "Was this terrorism? And can you tell us how you are feeling about your chief strategist Steve Bannon?"

I had been hearing from sources for many weeks that Bannon's job security was precarious, especially with a new chief of staff. Trump was rankled by characterizations that he was a mere puppet of Bannon's; "The Great Manipulator" read the February 2017 cover of **Time,** for a profile headlined IS STEVE BANNON THE SECOND MOST POWERFUL MAN IN THE WORLD? I had seen these same sensitivities at work six years earlier, when Trump called me, clearly upset at any perception that Roger Stone was puppeteering Trump. I knew Trump was getting pressure from his children and a range of outside interests to oust his chief strategist, whose internal antagonists were now legion. They included Kushner and Ivanka, with whom domestic-policy adviser Stephen Miller had cannily aligned himself and shared their view of Bannon as a "leaker," and H. R. McMaster, the retired army general whom Trump had appointed to replace Mike Flynn as national security adviser and whom Bannon allies were believed to have been undermining for months. Bannon had treated his role partly as an emissary between Trump and his hard-right base, but Trump's critics were focusing on the relationship after Trump's initial response to Charlottesville. Trump offered a defense of Bannon, before turning to the weekend's rally and counter-protest. Discussing the effort to take down Confederate statues, he asked if George Washington or Thomas Jefferson would be next. "I watched those very closely, much more closely than you people watched it," he said. "And you had a group on one side that was bad and you had a group on the other side that was also very violent. And nobody wants to say that. But I'll say it right now."

He said that he was "not talking about the neo-Nazis and the white nationalists—because they should be condemned totally. But you had many people in that group other than neo-Nazis and white nationalists." There were, he said, "some very bad people in that group, but you also had people that were very fine people, on both sides." He got angry as he spoke, interrupting reporters and waving his hands.

After the press conference, Trump wandered over to those of us behind the roped-off press line. Trump had rebounded and was suddenly cheery again, having blown off steam by yelling at us a few minutes earlier. He chatted with us about his winery in Charlottesville. But the rest of Trump's team seemed defeated as they returned back upstairs to the Trump penthouse. The Trump aides were mostly silent, save for personal aide John McEntee, who pumped his fist in the air. "That kicked ass!" he said. "That was awesome!"

Cohn, however, had seen enough. He left to play golf, and over the next several days decided he had to resign. He went to Bedminster that weekend with a resignation letter in hand, although he did not give it to Trump, whom he found in the clubhouse, piling a plate high with food. Cohn asked if Trump had seen video of the Charlottesville march. "You have to understand that there's no good people on that side," Cohn said, referring to the part of Trump's earlier statement that most offended him. "No, no, no, that's not what happened," Trump countered, insisting he had been taken out of context. Trump told Cohn to think about it and they would talk at the beginning of the week. Ivanka Trump reached out to Cohn privately, telling him that her father wasn't a racist and echoing his claim that he'd been taken out of context.

On Monday, Trump returned to work at the White House, and Cohn went to the Oval Office with his resignation letter. With Pence and Kelly looking on, along with his daughter, Trump appealed to Cohn not to quit his job over the issue. "I've got one major legislative agenda," said Trump, sitting on the arm of a couch. "Without you, I'm not going to get tax reform." And then, the hammer: "If you leave, you're committing treason."

Trump, who plainly did not want to lose his top economic adviser, told Cohn he should feel free to publicly voice his disagreement, and encouraged him to go to the briefing-room podium and say whatever he needed to. "You'll do the right thing," Pence said, putting an arm around Cohn. Cohn said he would complete his efforts to pass a tax bill, which had been his passion throughout the year, and not stay much longer. "But you should assume I'm done," Cohn said. He still had his resignation letter in hand, undelivered and unaccepted. As Cohn left the Oval Office, Kelly whispered to him, "If I were you I'd have shoved that paper up his fucking ass."

Trump was visited shortly thereafter by Ronald

Lauder, a major philanthropist to Jewish causes whose friendship linked Trump to his prior life in New York. (The two men first met through Lauder's mother, Estée, who had served as Trump's social interlocutor for years.) Lauder urged Trump to take a different tone in speaking about the events in Charlottesville. Say you misspoke, he advised. **Don't go there,** Trump replied angrily.

John Kelly may as well have been constructed in a lab as Trump's polar opposite: a sober figure with a thick Boston accent, a wisp of silver hair, and a career of public service. In November 2010, Kelly's son, a twenty-nine-year-old second lieutenant, died during combat in Afghanistan, an excruciating loss that hollowed the father for the next decade. Trump, who years earlier had dismissed Priebus as not being a "five-star army general" in an interview with me, was enamored of Kelly and initially acquiesced to Kelly's efforts to impose order on the White House. There were new restrictions on who could enter the Oval Office and give the president information, which Trump would later tell me took it "from Grand Central Terminal to an empty railroad flat. And I like the Grand Central."

Kelly's limits were most significant on the free-wheeling access and influence that his daughter Ivanka, who had arrived in the spring and was developing her portfolio, and her husband had enjoyed as superstaffers. They initially were supportive of the selection of Kelly, primarily because they wanted Priebus gone and they believed Kelly would expedite Bannon's departure. When they encountered Kelly's restrictions, that changed. They convinced themselves and their allies that Kelly was targeting them out of spite, and there was certainly antipathy between them over time. Yet allies of Kelly believed they simply didn't like being told "no," which the chief of staff said repeatedly. Trump frequently told Kelly and other aides that he was eager to see Jared and Ivanka depart the White House, although whether he consistently felt that way—rather than calibrating his language based on audience—was hard to gauge. In fact, he saw his chief of staff as a means to do what he himself did not want to. In meetings with Kelly and McGahn, Trump gave instructions to essentially fire the pair. Kelly and McGahn resisted, expressing their fear that he would not back them once his daughter and son-in-law pushed back. At one point, Trump was about to write on Twitter that his daughter and son-in-law were leaving the White House. Kelly stopped him, saying Trump had to talk to them directly before doing so. Trump agreed, then never followed up with the conversation.

Even as Trump avoided direct one-on-one confrontation, he created a world in which those working for him felt compelled to fight for primacy. His relatives were not exempted from those fights. Both his daughter and son-in-law had been hired despite existing, porous anti-nepotism laws and the counsel from some Trump aides that hiring family members for the government was unwise. Kushner never fully divested from his company, raising questions about specific aspects of policy that he was involved in.

The couple was viewed by officials elsewhere in Washington—by legislators and by some cabinet officials—as helpful guides to navigating the Trump presidency. But within the West Wing, and atop the State Department, the view was more jaundiced. Kushner was actively involved in some of Trump's notable legacy successes on policy, even if they did not particularly interest Trump (a bill revamping aspects of the criminal justice system in particular he viewed from a distance). But having both spent their professional lives cosseted in family businesses, neither Kushner nor Ivanka Trump had much experience with situations and people they could not control. As a result, they were often seen as meddling and overbearing inside the White House. It became clear that even they had a limited effect in moving Trump on policy matters when Trump was playing to his voting base, and they often focused on trying to influence personnel issues and how the president viewed his own team; senior aides were struck that Kushner did not like people developing independent relationships with the president. They tried to turn Trump against specific staffers by calling them "leakers," which was not always true. A few likened the two to Tom and Daisy Buchanan, the fictional couple described in **The Great Gatsby** as "careless people" who "smashed up things and creatures . . . and let other people clean up the mess they had made." Kelly and others called them "the royal couple" to colleagues, while in the East Wing they were known as "the interns."

And yet it did not matter. Trump trusted few if any people who did not have the last name Trump or were married to someone who did. When Ronald Lauder, who had a relationship with the Palestinian president Mahmoud Abbas, tried early on in 2017 to pitch Trump on a specific two-state plan for resolving the conflict between Palestinians and Israelis, Trump sounded enthusiastic. But Kushner canceled a planned meeting between Trump and Lauder scheduled for a few months later to discuss it. "You cannot tell the president things like you told him without going through me first, particularly when it deals with the Israelis and Palestinians," Kushner told Lauder. Kushner was in charge of that account, he told Lauder, and Lauder could not go around him.

Over time, Kushner and Ivanka Trump managed to change the conversation about whether they belonged in the White House at all to whether they were being treated "fairly" and were being given credit they insisted they were due for policy work, similar to the way in which Trump tried to reframe substantive criticism about himself. They also both eventually switched their voter registration to Republican. When Bannon was pushed out of his role in the middle of August after the caustic war with Kushner and Ivanka Trump, Kushner believed he had regained his footing and gloated about his rival's departure. "Which of us is happier that Steve Bannon's not here?" he said to Steven Law, a political ally of Mitch McConnell's, during a West Wing meeting. To another White House visitor, Kushner smirked, "Did you see I cut Bannon's balls off?"

CHAPTER 21

The Greatest Showman

From the outset of his presidency, Trump began to undo every trace of the Obama presidency that he could. No hand-me-down items from his predecessor's term divided Donald Trump's White House over the course of its first year—and seemed to stymie the man himself—as much as how to handle his predecessor's program suspending deportations of undocumented immigrants who had arrived in the United States as children. Despite his campaign rhetoric, Trump had seemed unsure of his own position upon reaching office, and the battle to sway him had been a factor in some of the most toxic staff fights across the administration. To Trump's right, a faction that visibly included Stephen Miller, pushed him to end the program as part of a broader tightening against what they called "open borders" policies. To Trump's left, Kushner, a developer who favored work-visa programs, was pushed by a mix of activists, Democratic politicians, and business leaders. He emphasized that the people whose status was in question had been brought to the country by their parents and had grown up to become valuable members of American society.

Trump sided with people in each faction on different occasions, uninterested in the policy details and willing to be supportive of two ends of a debate depending on who was speaking to him at any moment. (To lobby Trump on the issue, Pelosi recruited Apple chief executive Tim Cook, knowing the president's responsiveness to major business titans and the need to send many people as reinforcements on an issue. When Cook called to lobby him on the issue, Trump assured Cook they agreed the country needed more high-skilled immigrants, then made no meaningful move to increase their numbers.) That kept the status quo in place until a coalition of attorneys general in Republican-leaning states, led by Texas, together threatened a lawsuit if the Trump administration did not end the childhood-arrivals program by a set date. Advocates hoping to keep the policy in place believed that Miller had played a role getting the attorneys general to file their suit; a Justice Department lawyer aligned with Miller stated in a deposition that he had been in touch with the Texas attorney general's staff about it. Attorney General Jeff Sessions, who shared his former aide Miller's hard-line views, was eager to end the program. Trump's lack of certainty about what to do hung over him as a deadline drew close for the threatened lawsuit. Trump asked an aide, "How do I get out of this?"

Ultimately he had Sessions deliver the news that the program would be winding down, emphasizing that the administration believed it would not survive a court challenge. In his public statements Trump revealed how conflicted he remained on the issue. He told reporters at the White House that he had "a great heart for the folks we're talking about, a great love for them," and later wrote on Twitter, "Does anybody really want to throw out good, educated and accomplished young people who have jobs, some serving in the military? Really!" Amid national protest, Democratic leaders denounced the decision; when Trump called Pelosi, she asked him to make clear that people did not have to fear immediate deportation. "This is what I asked the president to do and, boom boom boom, the tweet appeared," she said afterward. Instead, Trump set a six-month deadline for the program's protections to disappear—time in which he said he wanted Congress to deliver a permanent legislative solution. Pelosi and Schumer tried to pin Trump down during a Chinese-food dinner at the White House in mid-September, after Trump's initial DACA announcement, rushing out to reporters to declare that a deal had been struck that excluded border wall funding. Trump aides who opposed the move prodded him to shoot it down publicly.

It threw one more big issue to Capitol Hill, where Republicans sought a legislative achievement they could deliver ahead of the November 2018 midterm elections. After failing to repeal the Affordable Care Act, Republicans never did follow through on a promise to present their own plan; for Trump's part, his staff believed he plainly did not understand how the health-care system worked and was hearing from conflicting voices just as he was on immigration. He agreed to back a lawsuit that would gut existing regulations in the name of the free market while praising nationalized health-care systems. "Why don't we do that here?" he asked after recalling an experience he'd had in Scotland, where he had golf courses; he recounted to aides the physical appearance of the male ambulance drivers he had seen there as part of his endorsement of that nation's approach.

Party leaders prioritized a tax bill, which began as an effort to simplify the federal code and ultimately ended up doing more to reduce individual and corporate rates. Trump was barely involved in the details—"twenty is a pretty number," he suggested during a negotiation over the new corporate tax rate—but he was deeply focused on the branding, savvily insisting that his side refer to it as a tax "cut" rather than "reform." He described it as the biggest tax cut in history, and he pushed for a low corporate rate; negotiations ultimately settled at a 21 percent corporate rate. Trump told me later that the mess around the health-care bill was key to the tax bill's passage, as Republicans "became desperate to get it because we couldn't have had two big failures." (Even after four years in office, Trump failed to grasp basics about Senate vote counting, insisting to me that the minority could block any legislation by skipping votes. "If the Republicans don't show up and don't vote, you know that, right? The vice president's vote doesn't count. It doesn't count. You might want to check this.")

Trump's efforts to win over the opposing party were halting and not especially effective. In June 2017, he hosted a dinner for a group of moderate House Democrats who pitched him on linking his tax bill to an infrastructure spending package, with the promise they could pass them together on a bipartisan basis. Trump greeted his guests around the table by boasting of his successes, not always accurately; he told Florida's Stephanie Murphy that he was popular in her Orlando-area district, which he had actually lost to Hillary Clinton. The discussion barely touched on legislation, as Trump was more interested in resurrecting nicknames for some of the Democrats who could challenge him for reelection. "Crooked Hillary" would not run again, he said. He asked about "Pocahontas," a reference to Senator Elizabeth Warren, whose Native American heritage had become a subject of recurring ridicule in conservative media. "Is he going to run in a wheelchair?" Trump asked about Bernie Sanders, the Vermont senator less than five years his senior, pretending with hand motions to wheel himself around. Trump seemed particularly interested in winning over New Jersey's Josh Gottheimer, who was seated next to him. At one point, Trump could be heard taunting Gottheimer by pointing out that if the congressman was defeated at the polls, he would lose his title while "I get to keep my title for life." For dessert, Trump made sure to receive one more scoop of ice cream than his guests were served.

Outreach to his own party was more traditional. A number of Republican lawmakers had formed their own relationships with Trump, but aides to the party's congressional leaders and to the president were trying to forge common ground. A few months after the Democrats' dinner, he invited the Republican congressional leadership for a weekend visit to Camp David; Trump never really took to the retreat in the Maryland hills—its rustic nature was less appealing to him than his own properties—but aides saw it as an opportunity to have a less formal setting to meet with Republicans to try to set their upcoming legislative agenda. After a day of meetings, Trump arranged for a screening. Of the five films available to be viewed, Trump chose **The Greatest Showman,** about P. T. Barnum, the promoter and entertainer who constantly craved more attention and respectability. When it ended, an elated Trump stood up, turned to his guests, and said, "Wasn't that great?"

In the White House, Trump continued to consume media in much the same way he had as a private citizen: hours upon hours of television, mostly cable news; a handful of daily newspapers, including the **New York Post,** the tabloid in which he had been a fixture for years; and a steady stream of clips. He continued to respond to some of the coverage the way he used to, expressing his approval or disapproval on social media and marker-scrawled notes, some of which made their way back to the reporter.

But he also had a newly opened direct channel to offer feedback about the media organization central to modern Republican politics. Rupert Murdoch had previously considered Trump something of a fool from their interactions in New York, but it had been a long-standing dream to be close to an American president; now, for a time, he and Trump spoke three to four times a week. Murdoch was satisfied to have the president's ear, and Trump believed that meant he should have Murdoch's, no matter what. At one point, Trump complained to Murdoch about the Fox News Channel not being helpful enough to him. "We need 100 percent support," Trump said. Murdoch replied, "We don't work for you." Nonetheless, Fox News was host to a slew of Trump-friendly anchors, including informal advisers such as Sean Hannity and longtime friends such as Jeanine Pirro. The ongoing Trump Show was appealing to their viewers, and Fox covered it that way.

As Trump spent more time in office, the allure of being celebrated by fans only grew. Crossing from the Florida mainland to the slender oceanfront strip where Mar-a-Lago is located, Trump was thrilled to see people lining the bridge to cheer his motorcade and directed his surprised aides to invite several of them to come to his club, which White House aides interpreted as less about entertaining the fans than using them to put on a show for club members.

Visitors to the White House were struck by how much more easily Trump could recount who and what he'd seen on television than he could details of policy, and how much more interested he was in gossiping with people, some of whom he barely knew. He remained singularly interested in who was representing him and what they looked like. He complained to aides that he did not like the way his ambassador to the United Nations, former South Carolina governor Nikki Haley, whom he named to the post so that a political ally could fill her seat—looked on television. "Can't we do better lighting or give her better makeup?" he asked. The woman who temporarily replaced Kelly at the Department of Homeland Security, Elaine Duke, looked "like a housewife. Can't someone tell her she needs to dress better?" The director of the Secret Service resembled "Dumbo" because his ears were too big.

In Trump's discussions of everyone's looks, few people were as perfect as his older daughter. Yet White House staff came to see the resemblance between Ivanka and Donald Trump when it came to their approach to the media, with heightened sensitivity about any perceived slight and an interest in trying to control what was said about them. She was initially reluctant about working in government and felt burned by a barrage of negative headlines during her first months. Still, staff saw her as competitive with the first lady—when Melania Trump announced a trip to Africa, Ivanka Trump's aides told Melania Trump's aides that Ivanka was planning her own trip there, approved by the West Wing, but hadn't announced it yet—and at times with her husband in terms of media coverage, praising him but seeking her own headlines when he was in the spotlight.

Both she and Kushner dipped in and out of different policy areas, which her allies insisted in her case was only because she was responding to requests for help. While her husband worked on a criminal justice reform bill and reworking the NAFTA trade deal, she got involved in the tax proposal. She worked with Republican lawmakers who backed a child tax credit as part of the package—some of them appeared starstruck by her presence—and traveled to promote the bill. By late 2017, Trump indicated to White House officials that he believed Kushner was pursuing his own agenda. Within the West Wing, some stopped reflexively treating the couple known as "Javanka," a name Bannon had favored, as a unit forged of equals. Their colleagues believed that Kushner's power clearly derived from his wife.

The Tax Cuts and Jobs Act eventually passed both houses, uniting Trump's party in a way the health-care bills had never been able to. (Republican opposition came mostly from California, New Jersey, and New

York representatives angry about the elimination of a deduction for state and local taxes.) Trump signed it into law on December 22, rushing to host a signing ceremony just before leaving to spend Christmas at Mar-a-Lago. He said he believed his next major legislative push could be bipartisan. "Infrastructure is the easiest of all," he said. "People want it, Republicans and Democrats."

The most urgent question for Capitol Hill concerned immigration, especially after pro-immigration advocates filed their own lawsuit alleging the administration had wound down the childhood-arrivals program in an "arbitrary and capricious" fashion. With Trump having set a six-month deadline to act, Republican and Democratic lawmakers were forced into negotiations with the president over some sort of broader immigration deal, possibly one where he secured funding for his wall along the southern border. Speaker Paul Ryan's staff later tried to explain to Kushner how intractable such negotiations had been in the past. "I am unburdened by your history," Kushner interjected, briefly summarizing a persistent view of everything that preceded the Trump presidency. The staffers blinked in stunned silence.

It was hard for some of the negotiators to keep track of Trump's whipsaw of views—sympathy for young people brought to the country as innocent children on one hand, and on the other, angry castigation of some of the places from which they hailed. "Why are we having all these people from shithole countries come here?" he barked in a White House meeting with lawmakers, specifically singling out Haitian, El Salvadorian, and African immigrants among those he did not want entering the country, according to people briefed on the meeting. Two Republican senators in attendance, Arkansas's Tom Cotton and Georgia's David Perdue, both of whom had become close allies, said that Trump had used the word "shithouse," referring to nations with poor plumbing systems; Cotton insisted later that Trump's focus was enforcing immigration laws, and not on what country immigrants came from. Regardless of the distinction in word choice, the incident cemented for many Trump's view of the developing world.

That stalemate over immigration left Congress unable to agree to a funding bill. For three days, the federal government shut down, forcing furloughs of civil-service and military workers. It was an unnecessary crisis whose origins were in Trump's proposed deadline for ending the childhood-arrivals program because he was uninterested in doing it immediately himself.

As Trump completed his first year in office, the public learned what many in Trump's circle had suspected: the story of his presidency was being narrated more visibly and more successfully by Bannon than by almost anyone else. Administration officials had long believed Bannon was behind unflattering news stories about his internal rivals, especially when those stories landed in right-wing news outlets, regardless of whether he actually was. But long after he left the White House it became clear that he had undercut Trump himself. A producer at CBS News's **60 Minutes,** Ira Rosen, later revealed that, while at the White House, Bannon had said to him he worried the president suffered from some sort of dementia and privately floated the idea of invoking the Twenty-fifth Amendment's mechanism for removing the president as "unable to discharge the powers and duties of his office." (A handful of other administration officials periodically mused about the Twenty-fifth Amendment among themselves, including Deputy Attorney General Rod Rosenstein and a member of the Joint Chiefs of Staff over time, but for most it was more of a tool for coping with Trump's behavior than a serious constitutional proposal.) When Bannon left the White House, he was furious, and reportedly told people he refused to answer Trump's phone calls. "I'm sick of being a wet nurse to a 71-year-old man," he reportedly said.

In January 2018, writer Michael Wolff published **Fire and Fury,** the first book-length account inside Trump's presidency, depicting a chaotic atmosphere in which everyone was in perpetual conflict and people wondered about the president's stability. While trying to win the favor of Trump officials, Wolff had publicly criticized White House reporters' media coverage of Trump, singling me out during a panel with

Kellyanne Conway as having the beat of the "aberrant president." "I know the president's views of Maggie Haberman, and yet, why does he speak to her?" Wolff asked. Conway chastised Wolff in response. "I just have to push back, that's just not true," she said of his comment about Trump's views. His book ultimately affirmed much of what I had reported about the White House, and in an interview shortly after it was published, he declared, "This is an aberrant president, an aberrant presidency."

It would not be the only book-length account that would emerge during Trump's term with promises of exposing the truth about the president and drive him toward retaliation. One would arrive from Omarosa Manigault Newman, an original **Apprentice** cast member who went on to serve in the public liaison office; when Trump aides called her dishonest, Newman released secret audio recordings she had made in the White House. Mary Trump, the daughter of the president's late brother Freddie, laid bare the internal dysfunction of the Trump family, including from surreptitious recordings of Maryanne Trump speaking disparagingly about her brother. The Trump campaign sued Newman (and lost, ordered to pay $1.3 million in legal fees) and his niece over their books. But secretly taping Trump, and one another, to have proof that conversations had happened became a recurring practice for people in his extended orbit.

But Wolff's arrived first, with an account providing

an extensive view through the eyes of Bannon, who was quoted throughout describing the messes that Trump had gotten himself into and how out of step his family members turned staffers were with his political base. Most significantly, his onetime chief strategist appeared to validate the idea that the special counsel probe playing out in the close background of the presidency was not a baseless "witch hunt," blown out of proportion by unfair media, as Trump often said. Rather, the meeting that Trump's son and son-in-law had had during the campaign with a Russian lawyer promising "dirt" on Clinton was "treasonous" and "unpatriotic," Bannon said in Wolff's book, predicting that members of Congress were going to "crack Don Junior like an egg on national TV." (No such public testimony ever happened. Don Jr. spent hours before both the House and Senate committees, and neither ever pursued legal action.) Bannon was relaying a sentiment shared by some of the president's most senior advisers, who thought that Trump's elder son had been reckless in having that meeting, but no one other than Bannon, by then pushed outside the Trump circle, said it publicly. He told Wolff that he knew where the special counsel's investigation was headed. "This," he said, "is all about money laundering."

CHAPTER 22

Taking a Bullet

Donald Trump spent the afternoon of Tuesday, January 30, preparing for that night's State of the Union address, his first. After a year in office, Trump had some real achievements he could boast about; some companies had responded to the tax cut taking effect at the start of the year by extending cash bonuses and stock grants to workers. He had ideas to discuss for the year ahead: once again, he was focused on a potentially bipartisan infrastructure-spending package, on his wished-for construction of his wall along the southern border, and on continuing to appoint conservative judges to the federal appellate courts at a record pace, nominated through a process steered by McGahn and McConnell, but one that cemented Trump's standing with conservatives.

The night combined just about everything about the presidency that appealed to Trump—a prime-time television event to one of the largest audiences he was likely to claim between his inauguration and reelection, filled with pomp and pageantry, with him as the focal point. But as he retreated upstairs to the residence before the speech, his focus was elsewhere.

Trump was still fixated on removing his attorney general, Jeff Sessions, over the decision to recuse himself from the Russia investigation months earlier. Yet Sessions, who had resigned a safe Senate seat for the role, refused to budge, despite Trump's public and private abuse. (When officials wanted to redirect Trump from a tirade directed at them, they would mention the Justice Department; Trump would rant that he should get credit for nominating "the first mentally retarded attorney general" in history.) Trump was considering two of his cabinet members as replacements, Labor Secretary Alex Acosta and Environmental Protection Agency administrator Scott Pruitt. Holed up in the hours before his address to Congress, Trump spoke with Pruitt, who administration officials believed had been effectively campaigning for the job over weeks of private interactions.

As he prepared to depart for the Capitol, Trump caught sight of his staff secretary, Rob Porter, amid a pack of staff waiting at the bottom of the stairs for the brief motorcade ride to the Capitol. "Why the fuck haven't you talked to Scott? I thought you said you were going to do it," Trump asked him. "I just talked to him on the phone, and he said that the two of you hadn't connected."

Just over eight months into the special counsel's probe, as the president's lawyers expressed public and private skepticism that the investigation would touch Trump, he was letting it subsume his presidency. When Robert Mueller was first appointed to

investigate Russia's role in the 2016 election and possible conspiracy with the Trump campaign, Trump
believed he could treat him as he had the prosecutors
he had encountered over several decades in the private sector. He had told his legal team shortly after
Mueller was appointed that he wanted to go speak
with Mueller directly as soon as possible, an idea that
they instantly moved to stop. Trump's team believed
the appointment of Mueller was an unnecessary escalation by the Justice Department, but they recognized they needed to attempt a strategy to handle the
investigation. The one they chose was cooperating.
Trump signaled to McGahn, who was being sought
by Mueller's team as a witness, that he should speak
with them. Yet the other lawyers hired to work at
the White House as official representatives to inter-
act with Mueller set no limit on what McGahn could
be asked. Over thirty hours of voluntary testimony,
McGahn revealed the president's continued efforts
to control the investigation, from his demand that
McGahn tell Justice Department officials to fire
Mueller to his comments about Comey during his
firing. Parts of Mueller's probe were marked by cau-
tion, but his decision to turn the White House counsel into a real-time central witness was extraordinary.
When my colleague Michael Schmidt and I reported
on the amount of time that Mueller had spent speaking to McGahn, Trump was stunned—and rattled.
McGahn had taken copious notes, a practice Trump
railed against, as he did with several aides over the

years, even though sometimes McGahn took notes at Trump's direction; when Trump demanded to know why he was scribbling things down, McGahn replied it was because he was a "real lawyer."

The rest of the staff had become weary of the investigations too. They were deeply disruptive, requiring hours not just with Mueller's investigators but with congressional committees, distracting them from their jobs, costing hundreds of thousands of dollars in legal fees, and generating seemingly endless news stories that crowded out the work they were trying to do.

For all the dark moments in the investigation, such as when Flynn pleaded guilty to charges of lying to the FBI and withdrew from a joint defense agreement with Trump's team, there were some that heartened the president's advisers. The revelation in the fall of 2017 that the law firm of the Clinton campaign's top lawyer and the Democratic National Committee helped fund research that led to the dossier about Trump and Russia was seized on by Republicans as evidence affirming their claim that the entire investigation was a plot hatched by Democrats. Their campaign, Trump officials often said, had been too inept and disorganized to have conspired with a foreign government.

Trump wanted to contain the investigation, but any hope he had of doing so required help from the leadership atop the Justice Department. Sessions refused to yield. Trump had already raised the specter of having aides get involved in other Justice Department matters, venting to advisers in the Oval Office about the fact that the merger of Time Warner and AT&T was proceeding. Trump's primary concern appeared to be that the merger would positively impact CNN. Sitting in the little dining room off the Oval Office, Trump railed at Gary Cohn, who as chairman of the National Economic Council had no authority whatsoever to litigate on the federal government's behalf. "I've been telling Cohn to get this lawsuit filed and nothing's happened! I've mentioned it fifty times. And nothing's happened," Trump said to his chief of staff, John Kelly. "I want to make sure it's filed. I want that deal blocked!" When Trump tried to hand Kelly a piece of paper, Cohn told him not to touch it and not to make the call Trump wanted.

Trump had now fired two major department officials—the FBI director and the federal prosecutor responsible for Manhattan, Preet Bharara, in early March 2017, a move Trump's personal lawyer, Marc Kasowitz, claimed credit for engineering by suggesting that Trump fire dozens of prosecutors—and, having seen the months of blowback after dismissing Comey, he was willing to hold off on firing Sessions. Instead, he tried sending others to encourage Sessions to resign, to no avail.

Feeling under siege by the various investigations into his campaign's dealings—the special counsel, House, and Senate were conducting parallel inquiries—Trump was beginning to realize the limits of the powers of the presidency, and felt stymied.

As Mueller's inquiry expanded, to cover not just Russian election interference but potential obstruction of justice afterward, Trump struggled to find white-collar defense lawyers willing to take on a client notorious for not listening to advice and refusing to pay his bills. Marc Kasowitz continued to represent him, but few others wanted to. Trump's lawyers wanted to set up a model similar to how Bill Clinton's White House compartmentalized the response to the 1998 impeachment inquiry separate from official work of the presidency; Trump wasn't interested in following it. The spokesman hired for the legal response was quickly under attack from Trump's loyalists. In June 2017, Trump hired veteran Washington attorney John Dowd. At their initial meeting, aides later said, Dowd told Trump that a resolution to the Mueller inquiry could be reached very quickly. Trump's existing attorneys knew that was not possible; one of his lawyers, Michael Bowe, who'd brought Dowd into the White House, was said to be furious at hearing the claim, knowing it wasn't realistic. Dowd denied making the statement, but others said he seemed happy to deliver news that his prospective new client clearly wanted to hear.

As his frustrations about his limitations grew, Trump did discover one power that did not require any sign-off from others and was immune from judicial or legislative pushback. He deployed his first presidential pardon on behalf of Joseph Arpaio, the nativist former sheriff of Arizona's Maricopa County whose raids in search of undocumented aliens made him a national poster boy for aggressive immigration enforcement. After violating a court order telling him to stop targeting Latinos for arrest, Arpaio was held in criminal contempt of court, a misdemeanor. Early in his time in office, Trump began to consider the idea of pardoning Arpaio. He beckoned Porter into the dining room one day, where he joined Pence and lawyers from the Justice Department and White House counsel's office. "I want to pardon Sheriff Joe. What do you think?" Trump asked. Porter told him that in addition to the concern about whether he wanted to use his power for something that would be seen as political, the larger issue was that it was an inappropriate time. Arpaio had yet to be sentenced by the court that convicted him, Porter pointed out. "Oh, okay. All right," Trump said.

They were words that became familiar to Trump advisers as a form of deferral of action; Trump would sound agreeable to deciding against a controversial action, but the "okay" usually indicated he was merely putting it on hold. With Arpaio, that was exactly what happened. With a stroke of a pen on August 25, 2017, Arpaio was granted clemency before he had been sentenced to any penalty.

His would not be the last grant of clemency that year. Kushner's father's conviction had inspired a personal interest in reforming federal prisons and sentencing rules, an effort often at odds with Trump's unempathetic view of those on the wrong end of the "law and order" he valorized. (Trump would often praise the Philippines' president Rodrigo Duterte for his violent crackdowns on drug dealers and addicts, which had resulted in thousands of deaths.) But when it came to Sholom Rubashkin, the former CEO of a major kosher meat-processing plant serving prison time on fraud charges after a raid on his plant led to the arrest of hundreds of undocumented immigrants—and whose plight had become a cause across the Orthodox Jewish community to which both Rubashkin and Kushner belonged—Kushner went directly to his father-in-law to lobby for Rubashkin's release. He bypassed the Justice Department pardon attorney whose recommendations have typically guided White House decision making in this area. Kushner thought Porter was among those slowing it down. In late December, Trump obliged.

For Trump, who never fully accepted the fact that Congress was a separate and equal branch of government, the ability to deliver justice on a case-by-case basis hit like a revelation. By year's end, Trump's lawyers would discuss the possibility of pardons for people ensnared in the Russia investigation.

In January 2018, **The Wall Street Journal** reported that Michael Cohen, the New York–based fixer who had left the Trump Organization but retained financial ties to it, had made a payment to a porn star named Stephanie Clifford in October 2016, weeks before Election Day. The good-government group Common Cause had filed a complaint with the Federal Elections Commission about it, alleging it counted as an illegal contribution to Trump's campaign.

Facing a deadline to respond to the commission's complaint, Cohen in February gave me a statement declaring that he had personally made the payment to Clifford. He said that neither the Trump Organization nor the campaign was involved, but would not answer whether Trump himself played a role. In April, the FBI raided Cohen's office, his apartment in Trump Park Avenue, and the hotel room where he was temporarily staying, in search of evidence. Trump called Cohen personally after the raid. "Stay strong" was the message he gave.

The probe into Cohen was led by the Southern District of New York federal prosecutor's office, where a former Trump campaign volunteer lawyer named Geoff Berman was serving as the U.S. attorney. The investigation had been an offshoot of the Mueller probe and was kept quiet until the raid. Most of the New York investigation ultimately concerned Cohen's personal finances, which were at one point used to threaten an indictment against his wife and eventually used to indict Cohen, but there was one bit of alleged wrongdoing that potentially related to Trump: the $130,000 payment to Clifford, who performed under the name Stormy Daniels, first revealed by

The Wall Street Journal. Clifford had alleged she had had a sexual relationship with Trump beginning in 2006, shortly after the birth of his youngest son.

Michael Bowe, Trump's lawyer, was among those who perceptively realized that the New York investigation could prove a real threat to Trump in a way that Trump's team did not believe the special counsel's probe would, because all of the Trump Organization's business sat in its jurisdiction. Federal prosecutors could take any large entity in New York and "unzip" it to find something to make a case out of, he warned.

A little more than a week after the raid, I coauthored a story about what had become plainly obvious to Trump's circle. Despite once claiming he would "take a bullet" for his boss, Cohen might have reason to cooperate with prosecutors if forced to choose between defending Trump and his own self-preservation to avoid jail. "Donald goes out of his way to treat him like garbage," Trump's longest-surviving adviser, Roger Stone, who had worked with both men, told me for the story.

The morning after it appeared, I awoke to a text from my **New York Times** colleague Michael Schmidt. Don't worry about the tweets, he said. I went directly to Trump's Twitter feed and found three posts about the story. There had been three names in the byline, but I was the only one he attacked, with a now-standard claim that I was defending Hillary Clinton and a strange caveat about his contact with me. "The New York Times and a third rate reporter named

Maggie Haberman, known as a Crooked H flunkie who I don't speak to and have nothing to do with," he identified me. Cohen, Trump added in a subsequent post, would never flip on him. Mueller's investigators took note of those tweets, which could be seen as an effort to pressure a potential witness against him, as a possible act of obstruction of justice.

Nonetheless, Trump decided it was time to heed his own instincts. He had mostly listened to lawyers and aides who'd urged him to avoid attacking Mueller on Twitter. But Cohen had been one of Trump's personal lawyers, and the FBI actions alarmed Trump's legal advisers. Trump had pushed out John Dowd, the lawyer who'd assured him the ongoing Mueller probe was nearing a conclusion several months earlier, and he had moved Kasowitz to the sidelines. That basically left one of his remaining lawyers, Jay Sekulow, to rebuild the team.

Trump announced he was adding Rudy Giuliani, along with two other former federal prosecutors. Trump was seeking a more aggressive approach, which Giuliani happily obliged. He went on Fox News immediately after being brought on board and told a surprised Sean Hannity that Trump had repaid Cohen for the $130,000 payment. Most of Trump's political advisers were apoplectic about the disclosure, but Giuliani privately made clear he had intentionally done so to keep Trump from being accused of a campaign finance violation. Unlike some of the other attorneys he had managing his interactions with the special counsel, Giuliani was willing to deliver—and often seemed to relish—relentless attacks on the investigators and those who emerged as witnesses against Trump. Either way, Trump's advisers were aware that Trump was almost certainly protected from indictment by existing Justice Department policy and of the fact that Mueller was not going to test it. And Trump's lawyers argued he was simply expressing his First Amendment rights when he railed against the investigation, separating himself from the presidency even as he held the job. Yet soon the cache of evidence taken by the FBI became known to Trump's lawyers through a joint defense agreement with Cohen; it included a recording Cohen had secretly made of himself talking to Trump about a past payment by the **National Enquirer** to a different woman who'd claimed a past affair with Trump, Karen McDougal. Just two months into the investigation, Trump's family decided to stop paying Cohen's legal bills; an irrevocable break followed.

Clifford had already begun to speak out after the original **Journal** story, giving a detailed account of being threatened by a Trump associate to keep her from telling her story. (Trump called her account a "con job.") Trump became consumed with attacking her, interrupting meetings to talk about her, including to ask aides whether he should call her "horseface." While he denied the affair, his concern, as he raised the subject during unrelated White House discussions, seemed to be that anyone would think the then thirty-nine-year-old mother looked the same way twelve years earlier, when she claimed to have been sleeping with him.

Eventually, inevitably, it was Mueller who sought a meeting to question Trump. At one point, the chief of staff considered possible locations for such an encounter, with Camp David the leading choice. But when the list of questions Mueller wanted to ask—from his relationship with Sessions to interactions with his short-lived national security adviser, Michael Flynn—got to Trump's lawyers, they balked; they were concerned about the topics but were also concerned that Trump would perjure himself under oath.

Others in the campaign circle, and beyond, found themselves at risk. Mueller had already charged two of Trump's top 2016 campaign officials, chairman Paul Manafort and his deputy Rick Gates, initially on charges of conspiring to launder money, and later on bank and tax fraud charges. Gates pleaded guilty in 2018 and began cooperating with prosecutors, while over the course of the spring Mueller returned further charges against Manafort and Konstantin Kilimnik, a Russian-Ukrainian political consultant who would later be identified by a bipartisan Senate intelligence report as a Russian intelligence agent, on charges related to work the two had done in Ukraine. A foreign-policy adviser to the campaign, George Papadopolous, had pleaded guilty to charges related

to lying to the FBI (officials later said the initial counterintelligence investigation began in mid-2016 with
Papadopolous, two months after an alcohol-infused
conversation he had with Australia's top diplomat in
the UK). Kushner continued to feature in negative
headlines. Yet so far, while there had been a string of
charges, Trump's advisers often pointed out that none
were specific to a conspiracy involving the election.

Trump's prodding that Kelly and McGahn find a
way to move his daughter and her husband out of the
White House had heightened the permanent sense
of tension between Kushner and Ivanka Trump and
the chief of staff. When my colleague Mark Landler
and I reported in March 2018 that Trump had been
pushing Kelly to force their departure, officials said,
Trump called Ivanka and suggested she had put the
information out because she was the one who wanted
to leave her job. Trump almost certainly knew that
was not the case, but his actions became wrapped
with a film of confusion.

Kushner had become hooked on the influence he
had. He was trying to impact policy on a few fronts,
and he was tending to his relationships in the Middle
East. He wanted to be present for his father-in-law's
discussions with Ronald Lauder after that first year,
telling associates that Lauder was making assurances
of delivering Palestinian cooperation that he couldn't
carry off. And the fact that Kushner was seen in some
quarters as a version of a U.S. prince helped him establish what became a warm relationship with the

Saudi crown prince, Mohammed bin Salman, which some senior White House aides suspected was motivated by Kushner's desire to develop personal business ties. He had access to many of the government secrets available to presidents, which some West Wing staff believed he had become hooked on seeing as well. Upon entering the White House, Kushner had been unable to secure a top secret/SCI security clearance to review top-secret material, which required not only an internal White House review but sign-off from the Central Intelligence Agency. Kushner insisted to people that he had no idea what the issue was and that no one ever told him; it was believed among Trump aides that Kushner's overseas business entanglements and foreign contacts—some of which he had failed to accurately or completely report as part of the background-check process, prompting repeated revisions—stood in the way of receiving a clearance.

The number of people working in the administration with temporary security clearances became public in early 2018, when allegations against the staff secretary, who also had a temporary clearance, by two ex-wives of abuse prompted Kelly to tighten access across the White House (the staff secretary denied the allegations). After that, presidential aide and Trump favorite John McEntee was walked out of the West Wing after his security clearance was revoked over gambling debts, which arguably could make him susceptible to blackmail. Still, the decision to forcibly remove him struck Trump's loyalists in the West

Wing as an excessive affront to Trump. Kushner saw
his clearance downgraded from the highest-level "top
secret" to the less restricted "secret."

The president had the ability to issue security clearances, but Trump sought for as long as possible to
keep his own stamp off granting Kushner's request.
Trying to cajole his chief of staff into facilitating it,
Trump told Kelly that the downgrade had caused social embarrassment for Kushner and his wife. Eventually, in the face of resistance from his chief of staff,
who made clear to people there was a larger issue
related to the lack of a clearance, but declined to
gossip about what it was, Trump made the decision
to grant Kushner a permanent top-secret clearance
after official agencies had ruled against it. One piece
of the clearance, which Kushner had not received,
was typically granted through a separate CIA process. Trump could have interfered with it, but White
House officials believed he did not because he knew
that directing the agency would be a bridge too far
and could lead to leaks. Nonetheless, the circumstances around the clearance grant were so outside
what Kelly considered normal or appropriate that he
and McGahn documented them in memos. In an unusual move, Kushner's lawyer rushed to tell reporters that the clearance had been granted through a
normal process.

At the same time, Kushner had integrated himself
completely as the steward of Trump's political operation. He installed Brad Parscale, a digital marketer

who had led Trump's online efforts in 2016 and was a close friend of Trump's son Eric, as manager of a 2020 campaign that had officially begun earlier than any in history. Trump filed notice he'd met the threshold to start raising money as a candidate the day of his inauguration. Parscale built out a massive online fundraising operation, and the feverish fundraising benefited not only Trump's political prospects but his private businesses. Republican organizations hosted events at Trump properties, helping to establish the Trump International Hotel on Pennsylvania Avenue as a repository for political allies and hangers-on. (Foreign officials, too, often chose it on trips to Washington, believing their stays could predispose Trump to view their policy requests favorably.) The super PAC supporting Trump also became a place for people who various members of the Trump family or extended orbit wanted to keep paid. With Parscale in place, Kushner believed he could prevent Corey Lewandowski, ever one of Trump's favorites, from returning as campaign manager, and ensured that Trump's political efforts, including the swelling pile of money raised for the campaign, which Trump referred to as "my money," would be overseen by someone the family trusted.

CHAPTER 23

Extreme Action

On May 14, 2018, the United States officially moved its embassy in Israel from Tel Aviv to Jerusalem. American presidents had for decades run for office saying they recognized Jerusalem as Israel's capital, but each time one came to office he did not act on it. National security and diplomatic officials could recount a parade of geopolitical horrors that would follow any move to formally acknowledge Jerusalem's status: diplomatic protest that the matter should be left to the peace process, anti-Israel protests across Arab capitals, violence toward Israel from the occupied territories, all with the risk of triggering a regional conflict.

Donald Trump received all the same warnings. But he also heard from other voices, some inside his government and some outside it, telling him the risk was worth it. Among them was Sheldon Adelson, the billionaire Las Vegas casino magnate and Republican Jewish Coalition benefactor who had become one of his party's leading donors. Adelson's singular focus was Israel; in Trump he saw a chance at enacting change in American policy toward the country, and gave $20 million to a super PAC working to elect him. As a candidate, Trump promised that he would open an embassy in Jerusalem "fairly quickly," and after his victory, Adelson pushed him to act on it. Over meetings during the transition and first year of the administration, Adelson assured Trump that the nightmare scenarios that he would be warned about in briefings as a possibility following such a move were overblown.

Trump had already bypassed the typical approach to appointing his ambassador to Israel. For a sensitive posting to which every predecessor for a half century had sent someone with high-level diplomatic or foreign-policy experience, Trump picked his former bankruptcy lawyer, David Friedman; Trump dispatched spokesman Sean Spicer to inform his secretary of state about the appointment. It was just one example of the way Trump tested the limits of a bipartisan tradition of stacking the ambassadorial corps with donors and friends. (At Trump's suggestion, his ambassador to the United Kingdom—the New York Jets owner Woody Johnson, a friend and fellow billionaire—tried to steer the British Open tournament to the Trump Turnberry golf course in Scotland, asking an embassy colleague how to approach the matter and then raising it with a Scottish official.)

Friedman, with extraordinary backing from and access to his boss, helped shift the U.S. approach to the region. He and Kushner, ignoring concerns about treating Palestinians as if they were on equal footing with Israel in pursuing peace, pushed through a string of measures, such as slashing financial aid to Palestinians, forcing the Palestine Liberation Organization from its Washington offices, and the embassy relocation. Trump did not attend the ceremony to mark the opening, held to coincide with the seventieth anniversary of Israel's creation, instead recording a video message while his daughter and son-in-law represented the White House. Friedman, with an obsequiousness that had become standard for Trump's underlings, said that "today's historic event is attributed to the vision, the courage, and the moral clarity of one person to whom we owe an enormous and eternal debt of gratitude, President Donald J. Trump." A confidant to Israel's prime minister credited "David Friedman's brains, Sheldon Adelson's money, and Trump's balls."

The world braced for the possibility of violence. At least 58 Palestinians were killed in protests and 2,700 injured the day the embassy opened. But a major terror attack or a massive uprising in response did not come to pass. It was a turning point for Trump, who had taken from it a crucial lesson about governance: the experts and intelligence officials did not necessarily know any better than he did, and his advisers needed to bear that in mind.

Over the course of his first year in office, Trump, unsure of where the levers of power were or what he didn't know, often felt obliged to at least listen to the counsel of those who had experience or expertise he lacked. He had previously decried the presence of U.S. forces in Afghanistan, but over six months, concluding in a Camp David meeting with his national security team, Trump succumbed to their arguments for how to win in the conflict. His new strategy, as he announced in a televised address from a military base in Virginia, combined a troop increase with measures to train local forces and exert diplomatic leverage on neighboring Pakistan for greater cooperation fighting terrorism. It was not far from plans proposed during his predecessor's administration that Trump had challenged as a candidate. "My original instinct was to pull out, and historically I like following my instincts," Trump said during the announcement. "But all my life, I've heard that decisions are much different when you sit behind the desk in the Oval Office."

But that began to change. Trump had promised during the campaign to impose tariffs on all Mexican and Chinese imports, saying China could not be permitted to "rape" the U.S. But there was no interest in the Republican-controlled Congress to enact them. Trump, acting on advice from McGahn and the administration's trade representative, nevertheless sought to use an obscure provision of a half-century-old trade law that allowed him to impose tariffs to respond to a national security threat. As Trump prepared to invoke the provision so he could impose tariffs on steel and aluminum imports regardless of origin, some senior figures in his administration—including Defense Secretary James Mattis and National Economic Council director Gary Cohn—discouraged him from doing so. After a first year in which he gave dissenting voices a hearing, Trump developed the confidence to heed those telling him what he wanted to hear: Commerce Secretary Wilbur Ross, Trade Representative Robert Lighthizer, and the free-floating adviser Peter Navarro. After he announced the tariffs in March 2018, he expressed a controversial view that "trade wars are good, and easy to win." Tom Barrack and others told him he was undoing the gains he'd made with the tax bill, but while the stock market faltered, it ultimately stabilized. Trump again believed he had shown that his impulses were superior to his advisers' experience, and his decisions on trade proved durable.

Still, those who wanted to manipulate Trump learned to exploit his frequent uninterest in assessing the motives of whoever was providing him information. **The Washington Post** had reported in late March that prior to a recent phone call with Vladimir Putin, Trump had been given briefing materials warning him not to fall into praise over the autocrat's recent reelection; "DO NOT CONGRATULATE" read one piece of advice, but Trump went ahead and did so and complimented Putin anyway. It was an apparent leak from inside the White House, one that seemed designed to humiliate Trump. The perceived pro-Trump-above-all-else leanings of the staff at the

National Security Council had become a constant source of tension, with Trump loyalists targeting people to be pushed out, often for specious reasons, and institutionalists who hoped to tamp down some of the growing aura of suspicion inside the NSC resisting doing so. Trump was receptive when Sean Hannity, the Fox News host who served as an informal adviser, called to share a rumor spreading online, initially promoted by the far-right media personality Mike Cernovich shortly after the **Post** story published. Hannity told Trump that the Putin vignette had been leaked by Fernando Cutz, an Obama administration national security official who had become a senior adviser to national security adviser H. R. McMaster. The claim, which Cutz's allies believed was being fanned by antagonists within the administration, was easily disproved. Cutz had not been present for Trump's exchange with Putin and officials could see logs of those who had access to the transcript; Cutz was not among them.

McMaster went to see Trump in the Oval Office. "You've got three hours to find the leaker," Trump told him. McMaster said that he would do his best. "You've got three hours," Trump repeated. McMaster later returned to Trump to say he would be unable to identify the person responsible in that time frame. "The leaker is Fernando Cutz," Trump said. "I have a very trusted source telling me that."

The entire episode appeared to have been partly if not entirely orchestrated by people who had been trying to oust McMaster for months, due to differences over policies like Afghanistan, and anger at some of McMaster's personnel moves. Someone else simply got smeared in the process for something he had not done. Ultimately McMaster and Cutz left their jobs that April. If Trump was actually worked up about the false allegation, he did not show it during their final few weeks in the White House. Trump was friendly and gracious to Cutz during a trip to Mar-a-Lago during that time, and as a farewell presented him a bottle of wine from the Trump vineyard and signed a photo of Cutz standing in the Oval Office. "Fernando—great job!" he wrote.

Trump sometimes made clear to aides he knew when people were trying to manipulate him, but if their ends matched his own, or if he worried about them turning against him, he did not object. Other times, what mattered was less the credibility of the person trying to persuade him than simply who got to him last. In January, an offer that Schumer made to Trump for $25 billion for funding for his proposed border wall in exchange for a plan to deal with DACA recipients, in an effort to avert a government shutdown, was eventually rebuffed by Trump after Republicans balked. In March, White House negotiators reached a deal on an omnibus spending bill with congressional leaders, with Mattis and Senator McCain working to increase military spending to a fifteen-year high. Speaker Paul Ryan went on the Fox News morning program **Fox & Friends** to promote the agreement; knowing that Trump was almost certainly watching, he stressed aspects of the deal that would appeal to the president. He called it "the Trump–Jim Mattis budget for the military." Knowing that Trump had been incensed that some funding might go to a tunnel linking New York and New Jersey—Trump had turned against it because he was angry at Schumer's lack of support for Trump's nominees and agenda—Ryan emphasized that there was no money specifically for New York for the so-called Gateway project.

Trump signed off on the deal, boasting on Twitter of an increase in military spending to the "most ever." But the next day on **Fox & Friends,** Trump supporter Pete Hegseth condemned the bill as a "swamp budget," a betrayal of Trump's base because it failed to fund a wall along the southern border. So Trump began to condemn it, too, threatening—again on Twitter—to veto his own budget deal. Eventually Trump acquiesced, signing the omnibus budget into law while continuing to attack it.

During the campaign, "the wall" was little more than an idea, a mental cue that Trump realized was a powerful tool to whip up his crowds. But in the White House, it became the centerpiece of his vow to engage in action on immigration and border policy whose complexities did not interest him. He viewed the wall as a construction project, and he knew his supporters could visualize his success or failure. It became a focal point of Trump's perpetual fear of losing his political base.

As Congress refused to meet Trump's funding requests, he pushed his cabinet officials to focus on border crossings, issuing instructions that generally were vague, including the idea of using the Insurrection Act to dispatch troops to the border. Much of the pressure to deliver on Trump's unreasonable demands fell on Kirstjen Nielsen, a former deputy to Kelly whom he recommended for his old Senate-confirmed job atop the Department of Homeland Security. Trump berated her behind her back and in front of other cabinet members over the high number of border crossings. Trump appeared not to realize that Nielsen's department handled a number of issues beyond immigration, including cybersecurity and disaster relief, and that the wall construction itself fell beyond her direct purview.

Kushner nevertheless egged on Trump's anger at Nielsen, whom Trump routinely pushed to consider new, violent extremes to reduce immigration; domestic-policy adviser Stephen Miller—who saw Trump as a vehicle to enact restrictionist immigration policies he had favored for years—told people he liked Nielsen personally but also believed she should be going further. Over time, Trump wanted the wall to be painted black so that the skin of immigrants trying to scale it would burn when they touched it, with spikes on top, and a moat dug along it. He asked whether border agents could shoot migrants attempting to cross. Some agents, responding to Trump's demand for "extreme action," suggested using a machine capable of emitting heat, or loud noises that would damage migrants' ears. Nielsen resisted these proposals, some of which violated the law.

But midway through the term, some Trump officials saw another way forward. In 2017, officials within the Department of Homeland Security had quietly implemented a pilot program to refer adults for prosecution, resulting in the children they traveled with being held by Health and Human Services officials. It was an imagined deterrent against future border crossings. It received relatively little attention that first year. By the spring of 2018, Trump was demanding prosecutions of people detained at the border, and Sessions and the Justice Department, with Miller at the White House encouraging action, pushed for a "zero tolerance" policy on border crossings. "We need to take away children," Sessions told U.S. attorneys charged with the future prosecutions, although Justice Department officials were aware that whatever happened to the children, who would be treated as if they had entered the U.S. as unaccompanied minors, was the responsibility of another department. Nielsen's agency was required to make the referrals of adults for prosecution. She resisted the concept repeatedly, while other cabinet officials signaled approval to move ahead with it. Despite warning flags, officials at agencies that would handle the prosecutions and that would be responsible for the children insisted that it could be legally done, and that there were proper resources to reunite families. Eventually, Nielsen signed a memo to refer all adults detained for unauthorized border crossings for criminal prosecution. When the separations became the subject of national attention, administration officials, including Sessions, repeatedly deflected blame, and Nielsen bore the brunt of criticism.

Soon, one story after another appeared showing the human impact. In one instance, a Honduran man died by suicide after being separated from his wife and child; in another, a breastfeeding infant was pulled from her mother while being fed in captivity. The conditions under which children separated from their guardians were kept became known as "kids in cages" and led to weeks of media coverage about children weeping in their holding cells. Laura Bush, the former first lady, publicly derided the practice as "cruel."

The voice of a Bush family member did little to sway Trump, but when his own wife and child joined the chorus, they eventually did; he told a meeting of Republican lawmakers that Ivanka (who by then, after critical press coverage in 2017, was trying to minimize the attention she was receiving publicly for engaging with her father on policy) requested the change; his wife had too. He signed an executive order ending the practice, something he'd previously insisted he couldn't do by executive order. His daughter—who was among the many officials who tried to use public praise, from themselves or from others from whom they could muster it, as a tool to reinforce a move Trump had made—took to Twitter to applaud him for ending something he had shown no problem with until television coverage became too overwhelming for him to ignore.

Ultimately, thousands of children were separated from adults in the span of a month between May and June, typically one of the higher months for border crossings. Hundreds would remain separated from their parents for years, incurring incalculable psychological damage.

In July, Trump went to Helsinki, Finland, to meet with Putin. It was not their first encounter; one, a side meeting during a G20 summit in the summer of 2017, had included a Russian interpreter but no American officials in a break with typical practice for meetings between heads of state. Afterward, Trump tweeted that he and Putin discussed establishing a joint cyber unit, which would effectively let the Russians into the U.S. investigations into hacking. A furious Bossert confronted him. "Let me guess, you're mad at my tweet," Trump said, laughing. Hours later, Trump tweeted a course correction: "The fact that President Putin and I discussed a Cyber Security unit doesn't mean I think it can happen." The 2018 meeting was different, an official summit between Russian and American leaders less than two years after the

United States imposed sanctions for interfering in the 2016 election.

Trump continued to chafe while dealing with foreign counterparts, most notably Angela Merkel, the German chancellor, with whom he had no personal chemistry (several Trump cabinet officials believed he had issues with women leaders). But he enjoyed moments when he carried out his impulses over the objections of experts in his cabinet and White House staff. Already in 2018, he had finally followed through on his threats to withdraw the United States from the global deal to limit Iran's nuclear program, a signature Obama achievement that some of Trump's advisers nevertheless believed should remain intact. He had also conducted a meeting with North Korean leader Kim Jong-un, an unprecedented gesture between two countries without diplomatic relations. The meeting alarmed foreign-policy experts in Washington but met with less blowback from his own staff, some of whom had been concerned about the rise in tensions with North Korea at the end of 2017 and Trump's love of Twitter taunts that could escalate the situation. Amid the anxiety about Kim's intentions, Trump repeatedly pressed his aides to withdraw the families of U.S. personnel stationed in South Korea. Mattis ignored his desires, and Trump, who could never differentiate between his "generals," blamed the national security adviser H. R. McMaster. Still, aides favoring a meeting with Kim felt that everything else had been explored and hadn't worked. Among them was Kelly, who was aware that such a grand event played to Trump's ego. "I do better with the strong ones. I don't know why that is," Trump would say.

After nearly two hours behind closed doors in Helsinki, Trump and Putin held a press conference at which Trump said the special counsel's "probe is a disaster for our country" because it had interfered with U.S.-Russian relations. Jonathan Lemire, of the Associated Press, asked Trump about the assessment of U.S. intelligence that Russia conducted the email hackings, and asked, "Would you now with the whole world watching tell President Putin—would you denounce what happened in 2016 and would you warn him to never do it again?" Trump responded with a rambling answer about wanting to see the server from the Democratic National Committee and Clinton's deleted emails, before saying, "President Putin—he just said it's not Russia. I will say this. I don't see any reason why it would be." Putin chimed in that the matter needed to be settled in a court of law, not by an investigation. Some aides speculated that Trump was simply being contrary or trying to please the person standing next to him. Regardless of his motivations, by taking Putin's denial at face value, Trump was publicly siding with the leader of a foreign adversary over his own intelligence officials. Most of Trump's advisers and cabinet officials were uncertain how to process what had just taken place. Some Trump senior aides said they felt physically ill watching it happen.

That December, Trump announced the United

States military had defeated the Islamic State—something his own military advisers repeatedly informed him was not yet the case—and that it was time to withdraw troops from Syria. Mattis spent an hour in the Oval Office trying to get Trump to change his mind, to no avail, and decided he would have to resign. He released a resignation letter that amounted largely to a list of areas where Mattis thought Trump's foreign-policy views were wrongheaded. "My views on treating allies with respect and also being clear-eyed about both malign actors and strategic competitors are strongly held and informed by over four decades of immersion in these issues," he wrote.

Trump had not read the letter when, in an effort to beat Mattis to the announcement, he wrote on Twitter that his defense secretary would be leaving the Pentagon. The initial plan was to have Mattis remain in place for two months, a period that included a NATO summit where Mattis hoped to enshrine commitments against Russian aggression. But after days of media coverage praising Mattis for his stand on principle, Trump tweeted announcing a new acting defense secretary. One by one, Trump was confronting people leading institutions that had existed long before he took any interest in politics and bending them to his will, either by winning concessions from them or driving them away while he refused to move.

One month prior, Attorney General Jeff Sessions had finally been fired from his position too. Even with the departure of the official who Trump blamed above all others for the existence of a special counsel investigation that had cascaded into a number of indictments and spinoff investigations, Trump's belief that he was being undermined by his own government had not subsided. If anything, it had intensified, increasingly focused on the idea that those working against him included people who had served under his Republican predecessor, George W. Bush, the brother of his primary challenger in 2016. "The Bushies are out to get me," Trump told one associate. "I don't know who they are."

Sessions's replacement, Acting Attorney General Matt Whitaker, did not give Trump quite what he wanted over his brief tenure either. On his watch, Trump's lawyer and fixer, Michael Cohen, worried his wife might be indicted for charges related to taxes, pleaded guilty to charges related to the hush-money payments he had made to women "at the direction" of Trump, as he told a federal court. Whitaker told Justice Department colleagues that the prosecutors had been out of control in their pursuit of Cohen. Justice Department officials had long complained about the Southern District of New York as a rogue office, but in this instance, the U.S. attorney, Geoff Berman, had recused himself from the Cohen investigation because, like Sessions, he had been active in the Trump campaign under investigation. Trump suggested that Whitaker try to get Berman to reverse his decision, but that did not happen.

But it didn't matter. Trump believed he was about

to get the defender he had been seeking in vain throughout his presidency. William P. Barr had served as attorney general under President George H. W. Bush, and had demonstrated an expansive view of the powers granted to presidents under the Constitution. As a private citizen working "of counsel" at the Kirkland & Ellis law firm, Barr had remained vocal on the legal issue that mattered most to Trump: Special Counsel Robert Mueller's investigation. Barr took issue with the probe in terms both political (many of Mueller's investigators had personally contributed to Democratic candidates) and constitutional (a president cannot obstruct justice while doing his job). He had sent an unsolicited memo to the Justice Department and the Trump legal team in 2018 about the propriety of the investigation. Some aides to Trump believed that Barr could be an "adult" who would stand in contrast to Sessions. When Trump invited Barr to return to the Justice Department, he seemed hopeful that, at last, he had found his Roy Cohn.

CHAPTER 24

Party Man

The flags had been lowered long enough.

That was the message a White House deputy chief of staff, Zach Fuentes, delivered to a top aide at the Department of Homeland Security, Miles Taylor, as he traveled in Australia with the secretary for a meeting of the "Five Eyes" alliance, the national security agencies of Australia, Canada, New Zealand, the U.S., and the U.K. Flags had been lowered to half-staff at all federal buildings upon the death of McCain, from brain cancer, in August 2018. The president wanted the flags "raised back up," Fuentes said.

The Arizona senator had been a source of ire throughout Trump's emergence as a national political figure. In the 1990s, the two men argued about Native Americans and had tangled over federal tax benefits for Trump's massive West Side development. When McCain became the Republican nominee for president in 2008, Trump volunteered to raise money for him late in the race, but they never developed a relationship. When Trump ran himself, McCain said that he stirred up "crazies"; Trump used the remark as pretext to ceaselessly attack the senator, including the jibe that he was "not a war hero," which early on helped to set the terms of Trump's unapologetic insult candidacy. McCain then played a small but crucial role in catalyzing the fateful first encounter between Trump and Comey by bringing the later largely discredited Russia dossier to the bureau's attention. After Trump's election, McCain became the standard-bearer of a Republican Party—aggressively internationalist, favoring immigration and global trade, committed to at least the rhetoric of bipartisanship—that Trump had sent into exile. McCain's vote dooming the healthcare bill had dramatically derailed Trump's first-year legislative agenda. Throughout it all, McCain received the type of reverent press coverage afforded few politicians. Trump hated watching it.

On his order, the flags at the White House alone went back up, even as they remained at half-staff everywhere else. Trump came under a crush of criticism; he ultimately acquiesced as the White House staff urged him to undo the decision. A short time later, flags were restored to half-staff. The next morning, the Homeland Security aide who had passed along Fuentes's order began work on an essay inspired by the contrast between the man about to be buried and the one who refused to praise him. "We may no longer have Senator McCain," wrote Miles Taylor, the Homeland Security Department's chief of staff, in a draft that didn't bear his name. "Mr. Trump may fear such honorable men, but we should revere them."

The New York Times published Taylor's op-ed

anonymously under the headline I AM PART OF THE RESISTANCE INSIDE THE TRUMP ADMINISTRATION. With a few well-chosen if vague observations of Trump at work, the essay depicted the commander in chief as so reckless, unfocused, and indecisive that "many of the senior officials in his own administration are working diligently from within to frustrate parts of his agenda and his worst inclinations." Taylor, who'd worked in the Bush administration, called this internal resistance the "steady state," a characterization that could have been drawn from Trump's own assessments about forces in his own government arraying to undermine him.

Trump responded to the op-ed's publication with anger; some of his aides and allies went on a hunt for the author of the piece that lasted months. It intensified when, more than a year later, "Anonymous" published a book building on the op-ed's observations. It was among the first of what would become many insider accounts about Trump's presidency from those who had worked for him, most of them quite damning. Taylor would not be identified as the op-ed's author for two years, by which time he was involved with a small group of Republicans trying to defeat Trump's reelection; his stark warnings ultimately were categorized as urgent flares by Trump's critics, and dismissed as opportunistic by Trump loyalists.

The entire cycle of events had begun with Trump's visceral need to engage in what he called "counterpunching," in this case against McCain, a man whose positive reception in death Trump seemed to take as an affront. McCain had made sure before he passed away that Trump would not receive an invitation to the funeral; Trump later complained that he had not been recognized for facilitating aspects of the memorial. Kushner and Ivanka Trump showed up to the service at the Washington National Cathedral, infuriating McCain's daughter Meghan, who later said they had "no business" attending.

The moment came a little more than two months before the midterm elections, when Republican dominance of Congress would be on the ballot. Trump delighted in political fights, and as the party's figurehead he enjoyed the sports-like competition, the ability to try to pick favorites and perform before large crowds in candidates' states. He would become obsessed with his record of successful primary endorsements, working with his party's leadership on whom to support in fields that were not always competitive; in general election contests, his record was decidedly mixed. Nonetheless, he told his political aides he thought Republicans overall were "weak," asking several times, "Would it be the worst thing if we lost the House?" After years of finding homes in different political parties, Trump maintained an ambivalent attitude toward the coalition he inherited and was expected to lead. He often found himself more animated by conflicts with fellow Republicans than with Democrats, because the divides were over interpersonal dynamics such as loyalty and respect rather than policy differences or ideology.

As a candidate, Trump had seen his initial success come at the expense of the party establishment; now, in at least some respects, he was the party establishment. He brought the Republican National Committee's leadership into the White House—chairman Reince Priebus, and two of his top deputies, Katie Walsh and Sean Spicer—but all were gone within the first year. Trump had replaced Priebus at the committee with a state-party chair who, unlike some of her peers, had enthusiastically taken to his candidacy and seized control of the organization. It became a source of technical capacity that his political operation lacked, and a wealth of opportunity for people who Trump aides or family members wanted to see receive consulting contracts.

In Trump's earliest interactions with the party's new chair, Ronna Romney McDaniel, he spoke admiringly of her grandfather, the former Michigan governor and cabinet secretary George Romney, as the kind of political patriarch whom Trump himself hoped to become. But antipathy for her uncle, Mitt Romney, complicated Trump's view of her family heritage. In a familiar style of Trump commentary—a sincere statement that he could also pass off as playing for laughs—he suggested she should drop the Romney name and go by McDaniel instead. "It's so beautiful," he said of her married name. (She later said she made the name change on her own.)

Over time, Trump used McDaniel as everything from political sounding board to intermediary, even to deliver messages to his children. (He once called her to ask her to call his eldest son to complain about one of his tweets.) Trump's interest in her put her on the radar of John Kelly, as Trump reached out to her without going through channels Kelly was trying to establish. Aides recalled a meeting involving Kelly and McDaniel, at which Kelly was angry that she and Trump were in direct contact and him saying he would put her meetings on weekends when it was personally inconvenient for the mother of two if it continued. (They later forged a peace, and McDaniel found Kelly helpful in trying to sway Trump away from some of his more problematic impulses, such as backing some lost-cause candidates.)

Kelly tried to stop some of Trump's more erratic impulses and did not see submitting to the president's whims as part of his job. And his efforts to impose an orderly process on what was often described as the Oval Office's rolling cocktail party before he got there worked for a time. But it produced a list of enemies who preferred the way things had been, including the man who'd hired Kelly. Trump had told Kelly to fix the place and then bristled at what he did and tried to undermine it. Kelly had a military brusqueness, and could be stern when he saw something as an affront. But many in the White House thought that Kelly, almost Trump's peer in age, had done as well as possible in the situation he was working with. His colleagues believed he suffered when his efficient deputy, Kirstjen Nielsen, was nominated to head the Department of Homeland Security and was replaced by the less experienced and controversial Zach Fuentes, who became known by the nickname ZOTUS, "Zach of the United States." Kelly eventually made clear to his subordinates at various points how much he hated the job; when he wanted to quit at various points, various cabinet officials including Nielsen worked to keep him from doing so.

His detractors, primarily Jared Kushner and Ivanka Trump, argued for a change in chief of staff as the midterm elections approached, using Kelly's lack of political background as one pretext. Trump was already interested in Nick Ayers, a young political strategist who'd had his own business working with several other Republicans, and who was serving as Vice President Mike Pence's chief of staff (Trump first met Ayers when he hosted the Republican Governors Association at Trump Tower nearly a decade earlier). Ayers was often aligned with Kushner in the West Wing, but Trump liked him personally and liked how Pence's office functioned (seeming not to realize that some of it was because the vice president was an easier person to manage). Trump attempted early on to keep secret his courtship dance with Ayers over the summer of 2018, arranging for a job interview in the residence to keep it off his official calendar. "Do you want to do this?" Trump asked. Ayers told Trump he would do the job, but that he had a plan he wanted agreed to for staffing and process changes; Trump did not commit to them. Several conversations followed, turning at times to dealing with the man currently in the job. Trump told Ayers that he should be the one to tell Kelly that he was being replaced. The chatter about Trump talking to Ayers for Kelly's job soon spread in the White House. But Ayers told Trump he was not going to do what Trump wanted—fire Kelly for him—and without someone willing to carry out his efforts, Trump did not make a change before the midterms.

Trump's name was not on the ballot, but Republicans recognized that he could be a powerful force in primaries, particularly if he was critical of a candidate. In an Alabama special election to fill the Senate seat left by Jeff Sessions when he was made attorney general, Trump took Majority Leader Mitch McConnell's recommendation and endorsed the establishment favorite, Luther Strange, over his rival Roy Moore, a favorite of the Republican activist base that supported Trump, who became the nominee and was accused of sexual misconduct with teenage girls. "I might have made a mistake. I'll be honest, I might have made a mistake," Trump conceded when he went to Alabama to stump for Strange. Strange lost, which further soured Trump on McConnell. But such campaign stops nevertheless served a purpose for Trump, who that night added a riff to his speech criticizing football players, led by the biracial Colin Kaepernick, who had taken to kneeling during the national anthem as a protest against police brutality. ("Wouldn't you love to see one of these NFL owners, when somebody disrespects our flag, to say, 'Get that son of a bitch off the field right now, out, he's fired,'" Trump said in Alabama.) "You know, I tried to use monuments—that didn't work," Trump acknowledged to a group of conservatives at the White House the next night. "But the flag thing, this kneeling flag thing, we're going to test that and I think it's gonna work."

Trump expected that in exchange for such an endorsement he would win the limitless fealty of the recipient. Before a 2018 gubernatorial primary in Florida, Trump went the opposite direction from what he had done in Alabama, bypassing the perceived establishment favorite to endorse Representative Ron DeSantis, a combative conservative who as a member of the House Freedom Caucus had been among Trump's most committed congressional defenders. Trump extended DeSantis his endorsement, while the head of his own successful Florida campaign, veteran strategist Susie Wiles, joined DeSantis's. After his come-from-behind primary victory, DeSantis—trying to win a general election in a state with the country's largest population of transplants from Puerto Rico—found himself stuck in the middle of Trump's ongoing quest to minimize Hurricane Maria's damage to the island. When

Trump wrote, falsely, on Twitter that Democrats had falsified the numbers of deaths to "make me look as bad as possible," a DeSantis spokeswoman countered that "Ron DeSantis is committed to standing with the Puerto Rican community, especially after such a tragic loss of life. He doesn't believe any loss of life has been inflated." Trump complained that, after the support he had offered, DeSantis should never have contradicted him publicly.

As much as Trump was partial to bending members of his party to his will, the fear of losing his political base often led him to defer to the power centers he most associated with it, such as evangelical Protestants and gun owners. Despite having had his own concealed-carry permit, Trump was so unfamiliar with the language of the national gun rights debates that during the campaign he spoke about "Second Amendment people" taking matters into their own hands to stop undesirable Supreme Court appointments. But nevertheless the National Rifle Association had broken its own spending records on his behalf to become the country's most profligate outside group during the 2016 election cycle, and a top official had become close with Don Jr.

When, in early 2018, a nineteen-year-old gunman killed seventeen people at a Florida high school, there was a recognition that the moment demanded Trump's involvement, and for a time, he met that moment. He agreed to host a forum for students and parents from the school as well as other people impacted by gun violence, who shared divergent views on gun rights and gun control, offering up disparate ideas such as increasing background checks and abolishing gun-free zones around schools. Trump, who spent most of the hour listening and serving as something of an emcee, promised action. "It's not going to be talk like it has been in the past," he said. "It's been going on too long, too many instances, and we're going to get it done." For Washington veterans, it felt like an uncommonly traditional response to a political crisis; the show of basic empathy amounted to its own victory, and Trump's staff was relieved.

Trump acknowledged that any new gun measures would put him at odds with his backers, a fact he initially seemed unconcerned about. He told Republican lawmakers that they were "scared" of the NRA, observing separately that "we have to fight them every once in a while," in comments that, for a moment, offered hope to people looking for a more tempered version of Trump, and for a change in gun laws. But Trump backed off his statements after conversations with NRA officials. A year later, after two horrific mass shootings in Texas and Ohio, Trump's daughter was among those encouraging him to back a law requiring universal background checks for gun purchases, hoping the draw of a bipartisan bill-signing ceremony in the Rose Garden might motivate him. Again, he did not act. (After a different, earlier mass shooting, at the Tree of Life synagogue in Pittsburgh, Trump did not focus on guns but did condemn the perpetrator's motive in a full-throated way, saying "antisemitism and the widespread persecution of Jews represents one of the ugliest and darkest features of human history." The moment was among those that his Jewish supporters pointed to for months afterward to explain why they backed him in spite of remarks he'd made playing into anti-Semitic stereotypes.)

Trump had produced few legislative accomplishments he could boast about to voters, but his opponents provided him with the type of issue on which he preferred to campaign. That summer, Trump was handed his second Supreme Court vacancy, upon the retirement of Justice Anthony Kennedy. Trump chose one of Kennedy's former clerks, a young federal appeals court judge, Brett Kavanaugh. As his nomination was making its way through Capitol Hill, Kavanaugh was accused by someone who was in high school at the same time he was of sexual assault, prompting senators to reopen his confirmation hearings so they could hear her testimony. The claims, and Kavanaugh's angry denial of them in his own testimony, did not change Trump's view of his pick. Trump generally saw himself in men accused of sexual impropriety, and he dismissed the allegations as essentially "bullshit" from nearly forty years earlier, just as he'd stood by Roy Moore, despite most senior Republicans urging Moore to drop out. Trump also was convinced of the political risks to himself and other Republicans in withdrawing a nomination. Instead of backing away—as he had with other nominees overcome by scandal—he bore down on backing Kavanaugh. Trump dismissed the allegations as the story dominated news coverage, and he mocked Kavanaugh's accuser, Christine Blasey Ford, for her testimony, suggesting she was a weak witness.

With McConnell keeping Republican senators together behind Kavanaugh and telling Trump no one was wavering, his confirmation was ensured. Trump pointed to the allegations against Kavanaugh—there were additional ones following Blasey Ford, which were also met with extensive questions about veracity—to appeal to his supporters. "Think of your husbands," Trump warned his rally attendees. "Think of your sons." (Trump yoked Kavanaugh's plight to that of a Saudi government challenged over its role in the kidnapping and dismemberment of dissident journalist Jamal Khashoggi inside a Saudi consulate in Turkey in October 2018. "Here we go again with you're guilty until proven innocent," Trump responded to a reporter who asked about the case, which haunted the administration for months. Trump downplayed the killing, which the CIA concluded was ordered by the Saudi crown prince, soon after it happened, telling associates that it simply "seemed like" the situation in the consulate "got out of hand"; he later bragged to Khashoggi's **Washington Post** colleague Bob Woodward that he'd "saved" Prince Mohammed bin Salman's "ass" in the U.S. amid the outcry.)

In his efforts to engage Republican voters ahead of the midterms, Trump turned back to the immigration playbook that he had often used. He called attention to a northern-bound caravan, which began with 160 Hondurans and snowballed to a few thousand as they moved north into Mexico, warning of the danger that loomed once they tried to enter the United States. After nearly two years of demanding more force at the border, Trump finally had a pretext for sending 5,000 active-duty troops just before the election. But then Election Day passed, Republicans lost their majority in the House, and Trump's intense focus on the caravan faded.

On November 6, Trump gathered his staff, along with outside friends and political allies, for an election-night party in the White House. Some of his biggest financial backers, including the casino magnate Sheldon Adelson—whose health, and therefore his ability to remain a fundraiser, Trump often focused on—and Wall Street executive Steve Schwartzman, circulated through the East Room as results came in.

As had been long expected, they were decidedly mixed for Republicans: while the GOP picked up seats in the Senate, Trump had become toxic to moderate, college-educated voters, particularly women, and his party suffered losses in suburbs nationwide. Democrats picked up governorships in both Michigan and Wisconsin, states crucial to Trump's own winning map. In the House, districts from coast to coast flipped, ensuring that Nancy Pelosi would return to the speakership.

Even as Republicans lost power in Washington, the party moved in Trump's direction. House Speaker Paul Ryan had decided not to seek reelection; he would be replaced as the Republican's House leader by Kevin McCarthy, a malleable Californian who worked hard to ingratiate himself with Trump as a way to consolidate his own power. Two senators with whom Trump had clashed had given up their seats instead of fighting to keep them.

It all gave Trump reason to be chipper despite the broader results for his party. At a press conference the next morning, he would refuse to acknowledge that any of the results should be read as a referendum on his presidency, mocking Republicans who had distanced themselves from him and were nevertheless defeated. "Mia Love gave me no love. And she lost," he said, referring to a Utah congresswoman. "Too bad," he added sarcastically, visibly enjoying himself.

At the election-night party, Trump kept his eye on Ayers, the Pence chief of staff Trump was still hoping to make his own. The Democrats' takeover of the House shrank the Republicans' influence, and the Democrats would shortly begin the process of selecting their nominee to challenge Trump in 2020. The Trump-Kelly relationship had curdled, and there was ostensibly a renewed urgency to having a more politically savvy chief of staff in place before the reelection campaign began in earnest. Trump, with Melania by his side, brought over Ayers to sit with them in full view of the rest of the room, seeming aware that the sight was spurring chatter and speculation. Later, as Ayers left the party, Trump walked behind him, calling out to Ayers's wife, with the clear intention of having his hints and nudges heard by others: "He's gonna be great."

A few days after the election, Trump left Washington for France, where he would commemorate the hundredth anniversary of the armistice that ended World War I. The emotional centerpiece of the trip was a ceremony at an American military cemetery in Belleau, along with Kelly and the country's senior military officer, Joseph Dunford, both four-star Marine generals. But Trump never made it to Belleau.

He had been in a sour mood from the time he boarded Air Force One at Andrews Air Force Base. Over the Atlantic, he had erupted by phone at British prime minister Theresa May with a litany of perceived grievances after she tried to play to his vanity by congratulating him on his party's midterm successes. After arriving in Europe, Trump praised Adolf Hitler, saying that he had accomplished some good things. Some who were told of the remark in real time suspected—and perhaps hoped—that it was intended purely to provoke Kelly. Even when Trump didn't intend to tweak Kelly, he managed to offend him: at one point during Kelly's tenure, Trump questioned in Kelly's presence why people would choose to go into the military. At that moment, he and Kelly were standing together at the Arlington National Cemetery gravesite where the retired general's son was buried.

Kelly and Dunford ended up heading to Belleau alone, as Trump remained in his Paris hotel room. A few explanations went around for the last-minute cancellation. The weather was bad, and traveling by car instead of helicopter would take too long or force the closure of too many Paris roads. However, Kelly deputy Zach Fuentes alerted other officials to the decision not to travel about fifteen minutes before the Secret Service made its determination about the safety of flying. Media coverage of Trump traveling all the way to France only to skip the ceremony honoring American war dead was predictably critical (and included several accounts from staff saying anonymously that Fuentes had been responsible). When he saw how his trip was being covered, Trump screamed at staff, complaining that the decision not to attend had been made for him and that he could have gone after all. It was reported much later, by **The Atlantic**'s Jeffrey Goldberg, based on several sources, that Trump had derided the war dead and told Kelly that he did not want his hair to get wet in the rain.

Trump was regularly speaking with Ayers, the man he wanted to have replace Kelly. (At one point a photo of Ayers appeared on the **Drudge Report** website, which over the years had driven coverage not just among conservative media but the broader press corps, as part of speculation about the chief of staff post.) By then, Ayers's openness to taking the job had diminished; Trump would not commit to the changes Ayers wanted to make. When Trump observed to Ayers that he was getting "a lot of good press," Ayers said he did not know what was driving it. Trump, who by then was known among his own staff as the "leaker-in-chief," replied, "It was me."

Over a weekend late in the year, Ayers, tired of the public pressure, asked Kushner if the intense drama around his name could be paused for twenty-four hours so he could celebrate his triplets' birthday. Trump had other ideas. Walking to Marine One, Trump stopped to speak to reporters and abruptly said Kelly would be leaving the White House at year's end. Ayers had seen too many instances where people were steamrolled in the press by Trump; he decided he was not going to let himself become one of them.

Ayers went to see Trump after the Kelly announcement and was guided to the residence. The president and first lady came out to meet him. "I don't have a great feeling about you today," Trump told his visitor. Ayers responded that Trump would not like what he had to say; Ayers had tried repeatedly to get Trump to commit to what he needed, and they remained far apart. Trump looked sheepish. "This is why I always broke up with them first," he said, chuckling. "I'd be dating someone, and I'd know they were about to dump me, and the day before, I'd break up with them and I'd leak it to the press. I should have broken up first." The visit between Ayers and Trump was cordial, but Kushner, who was at the White House and seemed to believe Ayers would ultimately bend, looked stricken.

There was a discussion about having Kelly remain for at least a time, but that was never likely. Kelly suggested a few names to Trump of people to hire—he warned him to avoid a yes-man or he would be impeached—but none of them wanted the role. (Trump also attempted to lure Chris Christie, whose term as governor of New Jersey had ended, into his administration by leaking that the two had met to discuss the chief of staff job. "It was good for you and good for me. It was good," Trump said of the subsequent press coverage. Christie, mindful of Trump's habit of tweeting whatever reality he wanted to see exist, publicly withdrew his name from consideration a short time later.) Ultimately, Trump chose Mick Mulvaney, a conservative former congressman, who led two agencies, including the Office of Management and Budget. Kelly shared with Mulvaney his view that Trump was the most flawed person he had ever met. Mulvaney had watched some Democrats talk about impeaching Trump for two years; he believed Trump's enemies would try it, regardless of what he did.

Kelly had begun his stint in the job believing that the main problem with the Trump White House was one of staffing. By the time he left, his distant view of Trump had been replaced by a fuller picture. A

Marine to the end, Kelly declined for years after he left to be openly critical of the commander in chief except for occasional remarks amid extreme circumstances. But several people who spoke with him said he described Trump as a "fascist," uninterested in history or geography, and uniquely unfit for the job of leading a constitutional democracy.

On the eve of Trump's second State of the Union address, in early 2019, Homeland Security officials received word that another caravan of immigrants from Central America and Mexico was moving toward the United States. "We can't let them in," Trump told Nielsen, before suggesting something clearly beyond the bounds of the law. "You have my permission to close the border, you need to send them all back." He wanted to include a version of that sentiment in his State of the Union address, but ultimately didn't. Trump had been obsessed with the number of border crossings for most of his presidency, insisting Nielsen hadn't done enough by merely enforcing the existing laws. He had often pressed Nielsen to turn "family separation back on," but she refused, along with an eventual push Trump made to target migrant families in the U.S.

Nielsen had been working for many months with Central American governments to slow the flow of migrants, including minimizing violence they faced along the way and discussing increasing asylum capacity in Mexico and elsewhere in the region. In January 2019, the administration began implementing, through DHS, the Migrant Protection Protocols (informally known as "Remain in Mexico"), after months of discussions between Nielsen and Mexican officials. MPP was intended to keep people seeking asylum at the southern border, in Mexico, as their cases worked through the courts. It was a major, and controversial, shift in how the asylum system had functioned up until then, leading to legal challenges.

Yet Trump still wasn't satisfied. Months later, while Nielsen was visiting a border patrol station in Yuma with her aide, Miles Taylor, the "Anonymous" author, Trump demanded to speak to the secretary. Taylor joined their conversation midway through, hearing Trump renewing his directive to Nielsen that the border be closed, even to trade. "We are full, and no one should be able to claim asylum," he said, proposing another legal impossibility. "You're making me look bad!" he said. "Why won't you just not let them in?"

Nielsen replied that she was doing her job; working with Central American governments to limit the flow of immigrants, she was doing everything in her power to respond. He wanted to see Congress eliminate the judges who adjudicated asylum claims. "Get the bill sent. I just need you to do your fucking job," Trump said.

"Sir, as we have discussed, that is not my job and not within my purview," she said. "Perhaps the White

House counsel or Department of Justice can draft a bill on judges?"

He told her that he wanted her to tell the Defense Department, where the Army Corps of Engineers was responsible for building the border wall, to get moving.

"I cannot order the Defense Department what to do," she said, pointing out that she was not the secretary of defense and that Trump was the commander in chief. "So now it's my fault?" Trump snapped back. "I have one hundred and thirty fucking things that I'm supposed to do." Trump slammed the phone down in the middle of the conversation, ending the call. Nielsen tossed her own away in frustration.

A short time later, Trump elevated the head of Customs and Border Patrol, an Obama administration holdover named Kevin McAleenan whom Stephen Miller often contacted and whom Kushner liked, to replace Nielsen as acting secretary. Both men approved of the replacement. As Nielsen was about to resign and hand over her duties to McAleenan, the two traveled with Trump to southern California for a visit to the Calexico border station. To television cameras there, Trump said, "We're full, our system's full, our country's full—can't come in! Our country is full, what can you do? We can't handle any more, our country is full. Can't come in, I'm sorry. It's very simple." Privately, he said he wanted border agents to deny admission to migrants, in defiance of the law, and told McAleenan he would pardon him if

he was ever prosecuted for the crime. Those who encountered McAleenan at the time described him as
stunned; McAleenan later told people he believed
Trump was joking. Others were less certain. It did
not much matter.

CHAPTER 25

Tougher Than the Rest

Almost immediately after joining Donald Trump's legal team handling the special counsel investigation in the spring of 2018, Rudy Giuliani found ways to impress his client. The former mayor, who had spent the prior three decades practicing politics more than law, took an aggressive approach. He attacked the probe at every turn, sparring with investigators and trying to diminish and undermine witnesses, partly to shift public opinion around the issue.

But for most of those who worked in Trump's administration, Giuliani was often a source of annoyance at best, and alarm at worst. In 2017, Giuliani had advocated for a prisoner swap in which a gold trader accused of money laundering and violating sanctions would be sent to his native Turkey in exchange for a pastor being held captive there. The man charged in the U.S., Reza Zarrab, was a client of Giuliani's, and his status was a source of interest for Turkish government officials. Trump had business ties to Turkey, where a pair of towers in Istanbul licensed the use of his name; he was also fascinated by the way Turkey had been presented in films. Trump was a

fan of **Midnight Express,** the gruesome 1978 movie
about an American brutalized for years in a Turkish
prison. ("My father loves that movie. He used to make
us watch it all the time when we were kids," Ivanka
Trump recalled of his frequent viewings during a senior staff meeting when **Midnight Express** was proposed for a White House "movie night.") Trump told
Secretary of State Rex Tillerson to work with Giuliani
on the Zarrab case, but Tillerson said he could not,
because of the ongoing Justice Department investigation, and because it could set a bad precedent.

Other efforts to limit Giuliani's engagements with
Trump were not so successful. In early 2019, Giuliani
started talking to Trump about what he said were
corrupt schemes involving Vice President Joe Biden,
his son Hunter, an energy company, and a corrupt
prosecutor in Ukraine. Biden was the most familiar candidate in a historically large field seeking the
Democratic presidential nomination for a chance to
challenge Trump's reelection. As two candidates from
the party's progressive wing, Vermont senator Bernie
Sanders and Massachusetts senator Elizabeth Warren,
surged in polls on proposals of free college tuition
and universal Medicare coverage, Trump grumbled
to aides that he would need to match giveaways of
"free stuff" to blunt their appeal, telling aides to come
up with such plans for him. But at certain moments
early in the campaign cycle, Trump seemed to recognize that Biden, who connected with working-class
white voters as well as the Black Democratic base,

might be the most formidable general-election challenger.

So Trump listened to Giuliani when he repeatedly unspooled stories about a Ukrainian gas company that had paid Biden's younger son, Hunter, up to fifty thousand dollars a month in fees despite having little if any relevant experience. While Hunter Biden was doing this work, the Obama administration was pushing Ukraine's prosecutor general, Viktor Shokin, to be more aggressive about corruption, leading to his dismissal. As Joe Biden ran for president, Shokin began offering up the claim that he was pushed away from investigating the firm connected to Hunter Biden, and that the American ambassador had given his successor a list of people not to prosecute. Giuliani began to champion the claim. The State Department said this was an outright fabrication, but Giuliani succeeded in creating a new target for Trump's most aggressive henchmen outside the White House: Marie Yovanovitch, a career diplomat still posted in Kyiv. Donald Trump Jr. tweeted disparagingly about her. So did his father.

Throughout the first half of 2019, Giuliani, surrounded by two Ukrainians and working with two lawyers who were briefly part of Trump's legal team, met with officials in Warsaw, Paris, and Madrid. They shared information about their quest with an opinion writer at **The Hill** named John Solomon, who wrote stories based on Giuliani's investigation, which were amplified by Trump and his media allies.

That year, it became clear that officials at the budget office that Mulvaney previously ran had put a hold on hundreds of millions of dollars in military aid approved by Congress and signed into law by Trump the previous year to help Ukraine defend itself against its neighbor Russia. Administration officials gave different explanations as to why, but a central one was Trump's concerns about foreign aid, including military assistance. His ambassador to Germany, a California Republican named Richard Grenell who had once called Trump's foreign-policy views "dangerous," channeled Trump's views in Europe; Trump voiced interest in pulling American troops from a country where they had been stationed since the end of World War II. Administration officials for years said Trump distrusted and disliked German chancellor Angela Merkel, whom Trump referred to in a meeting later in his term as "that bitch." Defense Secretary Mark Esper, who believed Trump was acting purely out of personal spite toward Merkel, reminded the president that Esper was already reviewing American force positions and would make adjustments in line with global priorities. Robert O'Brien, who became the final national security adviser, advocated moving some of the troops to Poland to guard that border against Russia. That the troops in Europe were essential to NATO's strategy toward Russia did not mean much to Trump, who frequently told cabinet secretaries "we should just get out" of the alliance. Some cabinet officials dealt with his statements by saying that should be a second-term priority, and Trump agreed. The top ranks of his administration were split between those who shared his MAGA foreign-policy goals and more alliance-minded Republicans; Trump had become deeply frustrated by those he believed were stymieing his agenda.

Still, Giuliani's pressure campaign went beyond merely advancing Trump's well-established foreign-policy views and alarmed various figures in the White House and State Department as they learned of it. John Bolton, a hawkish veteran of George W. Bush's administration who had replaced H. R. McMaster as national security adviser, described the president's lawyer as a "hand grenade" who would blow everyone up.

On March 22, 2019, Mueller submitted his "Report On The Investigation Into Russian Interference In The 2016 Presidential Election" to the Justice Department. The liberal activists who called themselves the anti-Trump "resistance" had vested in the special counsel's probe many of their hopes for ending Trump's presidency, developing a cult of expectations around the special counsel and hoping that he would find evidence tying Trump directly to Russian interference. The fervor did not appear to be based on available evidence—many of us reported on the most explosive developments in real time, even as House Democrats dangled the never-substantiated idea that there was even worse information that wasn't yet public—but on a desire for the two-year investigation to end with Trump being prosecuted. In April 2018, **The New Yorker** published a story by Adam Davidson with a headline forecasting THE END STAGE OF THE TRUMP PRESIDENCY. Mueller was the hero of this morality tale, his image placed on votive candles and his name on the **Mueller, She Wrote** podcast. One comic strip featured him flying through the air with a red cape.

Mueller's report went to Attorney General Barr, who had been confirmed for his new role weeks earlier. As a private citizen, Barr had written an unsolicited memo to Justice Department officials arguing there was no legitimate obstruction of justice case against the president. In his Senate confirmation hearings, he validated Trump's use of the phrase "witch hunt" to describe the investigation that had dominated his time in office, although he said that he didn't think Mueller would be involved in one. Taking all this in, Trump thought he knew what he could expect from the new attorney general: a loyal defender who would look out for his personal interests from within the government. In two parts, Mueller's 448-page report established definitively that the Russian government had interfered in the 2016 election with the goal of helping Trump win. And it described a number of Trump advisers or aides happy to take that help, through a series of meetings that Trump had insisted never took place.

After Mueller submitted his report, Barr issued a

four-page letter summarizing the findings. He established that the Russian government had two primary avenues for interfering in the 2016 election, the hack-and-dump operation of Democratic emails and a project to spread online disinformation through social media trolls. But, Barr wrote, the investigation "did not find that the Trump campaign, or anyone associated with it, conspired or coordinated with the Russian government in these efforts, despite multiple offers from Russian-affiliated individuals to assist the Trump campaign." Barr would later hold a press briefing saying there had not been "collusion," a term without legal significance that Trump's team had taken to using in the press to describe the central question of the investigation.

Barr said the Justice Department would move quickly to make the report public, but there were necessary redactions. The process took weeks. In the meantime, Barr's description began to take hold in the public consciousness, despite Mueller's private protestations. Mueller's request for a more detailed offering from Barr was not granted. The Mueller report was more complicated and detailed than the summary. There were several instances of Trump trying to control the Mueller investigation, to use the government to tamp it down, or to tell people to say things that weren't true. Mueller's investigators found that Russian hackers first tried to enter Clinton's personal office servers the same day in 2016 that Trump publicly said, "Russia, if you're listening, I hope you're able to find the thirty thousand emails that are missing." They also found that Russians had paid to stage pro-Trump rallies in the United States.

Of the various potential acts of obstruction of justice that Mueller's team considered, one was most damning for Trump. According to Don McGahn's testimony, Trump told McGahn to deny a story that Michael Schmidt and I broke in 2018, that Trump had told McGahn to dismiss Mueller. McGahn said he would not do that because the story was correct. "Did I say the word 'fire'?" Trump asked. McGahn responded, referring to the deputy attorney general, "What you said is, 'Call Rod, tell Rod that Mueller has conflicts and can't be the Special Counsel.'" Trump said he'd never used the word "fire" and simply wanted McGahn to raise it with Rosenstein, who could make the decision. McGahn made clear to investigators that he understood it as a directive. The report also showed Trump's conflicting statements to and about his aides. Trump told his aide Hope Hicks that Kelly had said that McGahn denied **The New York Times** story and would put out a statement saying so. But Kelly himself said he hadn't discussed the story with McGahn. Trump also tried to have Porter, the staff secretary, get a letter from McGahn "for our records" disputing our story; McGahn refused, saying the story was true. (McGahn, who had been constantly wearied by Trump's eruptions, left toward the end of 2018.)

Yet the report offered something for everyone to

claim that it validated their preexisting suspicions. It did not establish a legal conspiracy between the Trump campaign and Russians. And while the report did not exonerate Trump, the takeaway—which relied on investigators' interviews and notes from witnesses including McGahn—never made a clear case about the intent behind any activity between Trump's associates and Russians. Mueller early on had to remove a senior FBI official who was working on the case who was having an affair with an FBI lawyer involved in the investigation. They'd traded texts that appeared to show bias against Trump winning the election in 2016 (Trump took to calling them the "lovers," and, when the texts were declassified, conducting dramatic readings of them to friends). The most salacious allegations contained in the so-called Steele dossier of information about Trump funded by a Clinton ally, which served as a piece of surveillance warrant applications for a Trump campaign adviser who'd visited Russia, were ultimately discredited.

The main offshoots of the Mueller probe were indictments that didn't specifically allege a conspiracy between the campaign and Russia. Mueller spent months probing whether Roger Stone was a conduit to WikiLeaks and its founder, Julian Assange, something the House Permanent Select Committee on Intelligence also interviewed him about. When he was ultimately indicted in January 2019—and arrested during a predawn raid by a phalanx of FBI agents—Stone faced seven charges, five for false statements, including lying to Congress, along with one count of obstructing an official proceeding and one count of witness tampering. The witness in question was a comedian and impressionist named Randy Credico, a well-known political gadfly in New York. Stone had for years declared Credico dead in his Twitter posts in a running gag, at one point having a notice of the alleged death printed. Prosecutors said Stone was trying to threaten Credico so that he wouldn't cooperate with investigators; Stone and his lawyer downplayed it.

Mueller's investigators were equally interested in Stone's former partner, Paul Manafort. Manafort's former deputy, Rick Gates, pleaded guilty to conspiracy and lying to the FBI, and began cooperating with Mueller against Manafort and Stone; among the information that emerged about Manafort was that he allegedly passed campaign polling data to a business associate who a bipartisan Senate intelligence report later identified as a Russian intelligence agent. Stone maintained his innocence and denied the specific allegations, but was convicted of all charges after Bannon and Gates testified that Stone had essentially been a point man with regard to the WikiLeaks email dumps. (Transcripts showed a portion of Bannon's House testimony on the question of Stone and Assange appearing to contradict his own trial testimony, but Stone's lawyer never raised that issue at the time.) Documents later showed that Mueller believed he could not prove "beyond a reasonable doubt that

Stone knew or believed that the computer intrusions were ongoing at the time he ostensibly encouraged or coordinated the publication of" the emails. By the time it was over, most of Trump's allies brushed off the charges as "process crimes."

Michael Cohen, Trump's former fixer, also cooperated with criminal and congressional investigations into his onetime boss. Before the House Oversight Committee, Cohen described discussions within the Trump Organization about a Trump Tower project in Moscow, conversations that he claimed continued well into 2016, and the lengths to which he said Trump went in efforts to inflate his net worth (the New York attorney general, Letitia James, said Cohen's testimony helped spur her to investigate the matter). Since taking office, Cohen said, Trump had "become the worst version of himself." While later under home confinement in connection with his guilty plea, Cohen found himself returned to prison as part of what he said was an effort to silence him from expanding on these observations in a tell-all memoir, which would come out two months before Election Day 2020. (A judge ordered Cohen released, and ruled that the Bureau of Prisons behaved improperly; the book, entitled **Disloyal,** was published on schedule.)

While many of the Democrats running for president argued that Mueller's report was sufficient basis for impeaching and removing Trump from office, the Democratic congressional leaders who would

have to bless such a process were not interested.
"Impeachment is so divisive to the country that unless there's something so compelling and overwhelming and bipartisan, I don't think we should go down
that path, because it divides the country," House
Speaker Nancy Pelosi explained. "And he's just not
worth it."

A few weeks after the report's release, amid an
outcry from Republicans in Congress and in conservative media, Barr asked a U.S. attorney named
John Durham to investigate the origins of the Russia
investigation in 2016. Any satisfaction that gave
Trump dissipated when the Justice Department's
inspector general, Michael Horowitz, returned with
the results of a separate investigation into James
Comey's actions while trying to force a special counsel appointment. Horowitz concluded that Comey
had violated the department's information-handling
policies by sharing memos about his conversations
with Trump. But the inspector general ruled that
Comey had not released any classified information, and department officials declined to file criminal charges. "You have him dead to rights!" Trump
shouted at Barr. "How could you have done that?
I read that report!" Barr explained that Horowitz
had not made any criminal referral, and as inspector
general, it was not his job to do so. Trump—who
often wanted prosecutors and lawyers to target his
political rivals and critics, entreaties most aides
ignored—was beginning to see that even if he and

Barr saw eye to eye on the special-counsel probe it did not mean he would do what Trump wanted at all times.

In July, well after Mueller wound down his investigation, he was called to testify about his findings before consecutive sessions of the House Judiciary and House Intelligence Committees. It represented a significant moment, one in which Americans would hear extensively from the special counsel. Mueller stuck rigidly to the facts of the report. Republicans attacked him intensely, a fact that stood out as Mueller—who seemed frail and faltering at times—would not deviate from the investigative material. Trump and his aides were thrilled as they watched: Mueller's threat had passed, and he could move on.

The next day, Trump held a call with Ukraine's president, Volodymyr Zelensky, who had come to office that spring. The call had been previously arranged by the National Security Council. For Zelensky, a pressing matter was establishing a rapport with the U.S. president; Trump had other things on his mind. He asked Zelensky to "do us a favor" by investigating the hacks of the Democratic National Committee email servers (which Mueller had said were committed by Russia) and initiating investigations into the Bidens. Whether those items and the withheld aid were connected was at the heart of the new controversy about to swamp Trump's presidency.

◆ ◆ ◆

Three days later, Dan Coats was at Trump's golf course in Virginia when he learned by tweet that Trump was dismissing him as director of national intelligence. The question of how people quit or were fired had become a constant standoff between Trump and his own aides; after spending their tenures hoping to avoid him attacking them, several of his aides found themselves jerryrigging a resignation to try to avoid Trump beating them to the punch by tweeting. In Coats's case, he had tried submitting his resignation several months earlier, in part over lingering frustration about the Helsinki summit, where Trump had chosen President Vladimir Putin's account of the 2016 election over his own intelligence services'. That summit, and Trump's behavior, had led several officials—Coats among them—to wonder if there was something behind Trump's appeasing Putin in public. He told the president that he could not do his job without the president's support; Trump asked Coats to stay on, concerned how it might appear if his director of national intelligence departed while the special counsel investigation was ongoing. Trump had not been entirely ready to get rid of Coats, but was pushed into it by outside allies who floated the name of another candidate, trying to lock Trump in. Coats argued to Pence that he be replaced by Joseph Maguire, a New York native and thirty-six-year military veteran who was the head of the government's counterterrorism center; he believed there was no one else who could do the job who better understood what was at stake. (Maguire was not seeking the job; he had hoped the number two official at DNI, Sue Gordon, would take the role, but Trump did not like her.)

Trump viewed the national security apparatus within his government—the military leaders, diplomats, and intelligence officers who implemented his policy—with suspicion and distrust. In some cases the feeling was mutual, due in part to concern over his loose behavior regarding the nation's secrets. He tweeted a sensitive picture of damage at an Iranian space facility without waiting for officials to ink out classified details, because he liked how the image looked. "If you take out the classification, that's the sexy part," he protested as they tried to make changes.

John Kelly tried to prevent intelligence from being taken upstairs to the president or left in Trump's possession after briefings. Trump's behavior illustrated why Kelly was concerned: Trump waved items such as his letters with Kim Jong-un, which he appeared to believe the North Korean leader had written himself, at visitors to the Oval Office, including reporters. Some saw nefarious ends in this behavior while others believed he was operating with the emotional development of a twelve-year-old, using the intelligence data to get attention for himself.

Yet his frequent attacks on the "deep state" did not preclude him from engaging jovially with some of the people briefing him each week on curated intelligence. His aversion to direct one-on-one interpersonal

conflict meant that he was at times funny and solicitous with his briefers, making small talk and being
genial in his interruptions and musings as the discussions went on. Often he signed things, like a stack of
photographs handed to him by aides, or presidential
appointment commissions, using his black Sharpie as
the briefers spoke.

While his initial lead briefer, Ted Gistaro, a veteran
of the CIA, never quite grew accustomed to Trump's
style, Gistaro's successor, Beth Sanner, also a CIA veteran, fared better, striking up a rapport with Trump
and finding a way to get through to him. Trump appeared not to know her name for some time, which
she raised with another official; someone said something about it to Trump, because he made a point of
greeting her after that with "Beth!" (Trump had similar difficulty with a national security adviser's name,
repeatedly calling him "Mike" in apparent confusion
with the singer Michael Bolton.)

Sanner engaged with Trump without being fearful of him, an attribute that not many who worked
in his government possessed. The effect was of having a conversation, as opposed to Trump feeling he
was being lectured to. But Trump was sometimes dismissive of her in briefings, mostly as a reflection of
his uninterest in expertise. "You talk too much," he
would sometimes say. Topics that could derail a briefing by sending Trump off on a tangent—such as matters related to Russia—were often saved for the end if
possible. Sometimes, the briefings turned dark, and

quickly. Dismissing what he was told about activity in Europe during one briefing in the second half of his presidency, Trump declared, "Everything they do is to hurt us."

Throughout his presidency, Trump vacillated between bellicose language—about striking Iran and bombing North Korea—while also worrying about being held responsible for casualties. After Iran shot down an unmanned American surveillance drone in June 2019, Trump authorized a retaliatory strike on a string of Iranian targets. Several top officials favored such a response, and Trump did not appear conflicted about it, but there was last-minute interference. Once planes were already flying toward the target, National Security Council lawyer John Eisenberg abruptly ran into the Oval Office without informing his superiors to tell Trump the strike could kill 150 people. Trump called Bolton, who was on his way to the White House, and informed him that he did not want to see body bags on television as a result of his actions. "You don't think I'm tough—I'm tough," Trump told Bolton when he arrived in the Oval Office. "I'm tougher than you think, tougher than you. Maybe someday you'll find out."

Trump's decision to pull back fighter jets as an attack was about to happen was highly unusual, an instance of Trump wrestling in real time with his competing impulses—and of his desire to avoid blame winning out. Trump took to Twitter to tell a version of what had happened. "We were cocked & loaded to retaliate last night on 3 different sights [sic] when I asked, how many will die," he wrote.

Throughout the summer of 2019, Trump's foreign policy was otherwise dominated by pursuit of grand, even cinematic, gestures. In June, after months of waving around letters from the country's leader to impress Oval Office visitors, Trump became the first sitting U.S. president to visit North Korea. That year, Bolton had pushed an idea that was gaining traction in various circles outside the White House, and was advocated by Trump's friend Ron Lauder—acquiring Greenland, which had strategic importance and natural resources. The concept gained some traction inside the White House—until becoming public, instantly killing it amid a sea of criticism. Still, Trump had other ambitious ideas for the year, including an audacious finale to one of the country's most intractable national security challenges.

To facilitate a permanent withdrawal of American troops from Afghanistan, Trump's secretary of state, Mike Pompeo, had pursued a peace agreement with the country's Taliban insurgency. Bolton was forcefully opposed to such an agreement, worried it would lead to a resurgence of terrorist activity in the absence of the U.S. and its NATO allies. Trump then became intrigued with the idea of a signing ceremony in Washington shifting into an even more historically resonant venue: hosting the Taliban at Camp David. Trump did not seem concerned that his would-be guests had given harbor to the mastermind of a terrorist assault on United States soil that killed more than three thousand people, including a strike on the Pentagon, or about the fact that the proposed September date fell around the anniversary of the attacks. Beth Sanner questioned such a summit—"Is Ivanka going to wear a burka?" she asked sarcastically—and a wide range of officials were horrified that Trump took it so seriously.

When Bolton's opposition to the ceremony was reported by the media, it brought to light months of tension between him and his boss over policy. In a familiar back and forth between the president and an aide, Trump wrote on Twitter that he was forcing out his national security adviser; Bolton said he had already resigned. Ultimately, a U.S. servicemember was killed in Afghanistan during the discussions, and the Taliban never came to Camp David. A deal would be signed the following year, paving the way for American troops to leave Afghanistan for good.

A few weeks after Trump spoke with Zelensky, an "urgent" complaint reached the intelligence community's inspector general; a CIA employee, who wanted to remain anonymous, was alarmed by what he had heard was said on the call between the two leaders and a "series of events" that preceded it. The complaint, which the inspector general deemed credible, was the first ever filed by a whistleblower against a president of the United States. It arrived just before

Joseph Maguire's first day as the acting director of national intelligence. Maguire realized the allegations were explosive. Before the complaint could be sent to the House, there were issues of executive privilege to consider. White House officials seemed to believe Maguire could have done something to stop the complaint, which his allies said was not possible, and it was given to House Democrats, who used their newfound majority to initiate an investigation into the matter.

The military aid was finally released to Ukraine in September, but there would be ceaseless interest in what Trump had said to Zelensky (administration officials maintained that the aid was delayed over Trump's disdain for foreign aid, and his concerns about "corruption" in Ukraine). Around the time the two leaders met in person for the first time, on the sidelines of the United Nations General Assembly meeting, the White House declassified a transcript, notes put together by U.S. officials listening simultaneously, of the call. Barr and White House counsel Pat Cipollone—who sent letters to House investigators describing their effort as politically motivated—believed that releasing it would end the matter. (Mick Mulvaney, the chief of staff who had replaced Kelly, objected to the decision, but it was done while he was traveling with Trump.)

The transcript showed a familiar, decades-old version of Trump: pushing for what he wanted to see happen, steering a conversation toward his personal interests. "The United States has been very, very good to Ukraine" came the prompt. "There is a lot of talk about Biden's son, that Biden stopped the prosecution, and a lot of people want to find out about that" came the vague float of an idea. The U.S. ambassador to Ukraine, Marie Yovanovitch, was "going to go through some things." When the details emerged, Trump would maintain that the call was "perfect."

Three times in the past, a congressional Democrat in Texas, acting without support from leadership, had introduced articles of impeachment against Trump for "sowing discord," as the first bill filed in 2017 put it, with his response to the violence in Charlottesville, with his remarks about "shithole countries," and with other inflammatory rhetoric. In early 2019, hours after a freshman Democrat from Michigan, Rashida Tlaib, was sworn in, she vowed to stop "bullies" from winning, and issued a call to "impeach the motherfucker." As with the push for impeachment hearings based on Mueller's findings, none of it ever went anywhere.

But the Ukraine scandal was different from any other during Trump's presidency. The whistleblower's allegation was, for Democrats, Trump crossing a line. And it was simple and self-contained—alleging a sitting president had withheld military aid from a besieged ally in exchange for an act that could harm a political opponent—in a way that Mueller's complex report was not.

Efforts to get Trump to engage with congressional Democrats were increasingly fruitless.

In 2019, Trump was initially receptive to encouragement from his legislative affairs director, Eric Ueland, a stately veteran of Senate Republican politics, to develop a more productive relationship with Pelosi and Schumer (Trump had hired Ueland after three meetings, one in which the president said graphology was one of his hobbies and that he'd studied a thank-you note that Ueland had written after their initial sit-down). But once Democrats started to speak more seriously about impeaching him, Trump balked at interacting with Pelosi in particular, developing a habit of referring to her in private conversations as "that woman." "This is just not going to be successful, Eric," Trump told Ueland. "What are we going to get out of this?"

That included whatever fleeting interest Trump had in working with Congress on new gun restrictions after two deadly shootings in Ohio and Texas, where Trump traveled to meet with hospitalized victims, delivering a jarring performance. Trump, who was never interested in context around whatever he wanted to do, posed with a smile and a thumbs-up, and talked about his crowds. He expressed interest in reviving a ban on assault weapons, but he quickly fretted about losing support from conservatives and, as he almost always did, leaned toward the place he thought would make his political base happy.

Trump abruptly decided not to travel to Poland, where he was to see Zelensky again at a World War II commemoration; Trump blamed his cancellation on the preparations for an upcoming hurricane. Trump sent his vice president as a stand-in, drawing him into the Ukraine scandal too. It would not be the only uncomfortable situation Trump created for Mike Pence on the trip.

CHAPTER 26

One Strike and You're Out

Donald Trump had a weekly standing lunch with his vice president, in which he and Mike Pence would sit off the Oval Office and discuss politics, policy, and various goings-on. The meetings had been initiated by Pence during the transition, after one of his predecessors suggested it. At some point, their chiefs of staff began attending the lunches too. The vice president and Trump chief of staff Mick Mulvaney usually munched on grilled chicken or turkey-avocado salads; Trump and Pence's chief of staff Marc Short ate cheeseburgers with french fries. Pence used the lunches to make himself a frequent source of counsel and patient listening, running interference for the president in the House, where Pence had served. When they met in the summer of 2019, Pence was set to depart for Europe in place of Trump and he briefed the president on his itinerary and plans. He would go to Warsaw to meet with Poland's leaders and Ukraine's president, Zelensky, a meeting that would eventually take on new significance after congressional investigators had begun examining the circumstances around Trump's call with Zelensky a month earlier. Then he would visit Ireland and Iceland for less-fraught encounters, then stop in London for a night on the way back to the United States.

Ireland was where Pence's family had roots, and he had included a visit to the village of Doonbeg, on the western coast, from which his family hailed and where he still had cousins. When Trump heard Doonbeg, he volunteered that Pence should stay at his hotel there. Pence demurred, saying the optics might be problematic; his team had already arranged to have him spend the night an hour away specifically to avoid questions of propriety. "The optics would be worse if you didn't," Trump said, instructing Short to arrange it through his son Eric.

Testing Pence's loyalty had become something of an ongoing parlor game for Trump. Rupert Murdoch had suggested to allies that Nikki Haley, Trump's former ambassador to the United Nations and the former South Carolina governor, could be a strong vice president. In June 2019, Murdoch's top American newspaper, **The Wall Street Journal,** published an op-ed with an unsubtle headline: TRUMP-HALEY IN 2020. "It's too late for Mr. Trump to revamp his political personality," wrote former New York City politician and Trump friend Andrew Stein. "But with the 2016 election in the past, Nikki Haley on the ticket could tamp down the antipathy for Mr. Trump that seems to afflict so many moderate and Republican-leaning women." Within the West Wing, some aides believed that Kushner was fueling interest in replacing Pence (something he denied to allies), and that Stein may have been acting on his behalf. Kushner complimented Stein on the piece after it ran.

Trump never appeared to really be considering swapping out Pence for Haley, but he enjoyed putting others on the spot about it. Trump interrupted one White House meeting with the board of the Club for Growth, a conservative interest group, and some of its larger donors to ask its president, David McIntosh, "David, what do you think of Mike Pence?"

McIntosh, a former Indiana congressman who had a close relationship with Pence, replied, "I like Mike, he's a great guy."

Trump shook his head. "No, no," he said, trying again. "What do you think about Mike Pence?"

It dawned on McIntosh that, without directly raising the question, Trump was really asking if he should keep Pence on the ticket. "There are a lot of conservatives that support you because you picked him," McIntosh said. "And he's done a great job of defending you."

Trump quickly agreed. "Yeah, I think it would probably be disloyal of me to take him off the ticket," Trump said, before turning to stare directly at Kushner.

When McIntosh saw Pence later that day at the White House, he relayed the exchange. "Oh yeah, I know," Pence said. "He does that to a lot of people." (Kushner, working with McIntosh on a separate matter months later, explained that Trump often asks "placebo questions" when he's testing an idea or a message.)

Reporters traveling to Europe with Pence asked questions once they saw the Trump International Golf Links & Hotel on his itinerary; Short said Trump had "suggested" Pence stay there and that every aspect had been approved by the State Department. By the time Pence completed his two-night stay at the Irish resort, American media attention was focused on Hurricane Dorian, a rapidly intensifying storm in the Atlantic Ocean when it made landfall in the Bahamas, headed toward the American coast.

Aboard Marine One at the beginning of September, Trump was briefed by a National Security Council official, who on a map demonstrated the storm cone tracking northwesterly onto the mainland United States deep into the inland South. Repeating what he was told, Trump wrote on Twitter shortly thereafter that "South Carolina, North Carolina, Georgia, and Alabama will most likely be hit (much) harder than anticipated." By the time he did, however, the hurricane was already switching direction and it would stay far from Alabama. In a hurricane briefing, Trump fumed about the criticism he had received for sharing misleading, inaccurate information in an emergency. "This is fake news. Fake news is coming after me," Trump murmured to himself, reaching for one of the black Sharpie markers he kept on his desk. On an official storm map before him he drew an elongated cone, a bubble reaching past Georgia and into Alabama. "Do not show this to the press," Mulvaney said before journalists were brought into the Oval Office to hear about storm preparations. Once cameras were present, Trump beckoned to his Homeland Security secretary for the map; there was no choice but to hand it over.

There was at least some basis for Trump's behavior—he told people the map he had been presented showing the storm's track projected to Alabama could not be located by staff—but when meteorological reality changed, Trump stuck with the old one and tried to draw his version of it. The rest of Trump's government was compelled to respond to that, with top officials at the National Oceanic and Atmospheric Administration threatened with firing by the commerce secretary, Wilbur Ross; decades earlier, Ross had represented bondholders in a Trump casino bankruptcy.

Nevertheless, amid an uproar that became known as Sharpiegate, Trump took time to rewrite the truth about Pence's itinerary as well. "I had nothing to do with the decision of our great @VP Mike Pence to stay overnight at one of the Trump owned resorts in Doonbeg, Ireland," he wrote on Twitter. "Mike's family has lived in Doonbeg for many years, and he thought that during his very busy European visit, he would stop and see his family!"

• • •

The summer had begun on a rosier note for Trump. For weeks ahead of June 18, Trump and his aides had hyped the rally he would hold in Orlando, Florida, as the official kickoff of his reelection campaign. As a legal matter, Trump had been running since he was sworn in, and those around him had been scheming about their place in the campaign organization for nearly as long.

Trump entrusted leadership of the campaign to Kushner, who remained in government while overseeing the operation, with a role similar to that played by other White House political strategists, such as Karl Rove (for George W. Bush) and David Plouffe (for Barack Obama). Trump would speak glowingly of Kushner in public, appearing to cast him as worthy of his daughter, a type of performance Trump's own father had done with him. And he considered Kushner to be an effective negotiator. But in private, Trump often diminished Kushner, mocking him as effete, and seemed to delight in needling him in front of others. At one New Jersey fundraising event that summer attended by both Kushner and Chris Christie, the former governor and prosecutor who had helped to send Kushner's father to prison, Trump remarked in front of guests, "We've got to get Christie back into the government." Then he turned to his son-in-law, asking, "What do you think, Jared?"

In February 2018, Kushner had helped to install Brad Parscale, the family loyalist with whom he had worked closely on Trump's digital operation in 2016, as manager of the reelection campaign. But after failing in December 2018 to place Nick Ayers in the chief of staff role, Kushner posited on one conference call with political aides that month that Ayers could take over as campaign manager. Parscale, he suggested, could be moved to the outside group supporting Trump, a treatment of aides as chess pieces that was stunning to those who learned of it.

Trump showed that his gratitude toward those who had helped him win the presidency only went so far. Florida operative Susie Wiles, whom Trump credited with his comeback win in the state, was informally part of his operation throughout the presidency. But Ron DeSantis, who was sworn in as Florida's governor in 2019 after Wiles helped him win his general election and who was believed to have national ambitions of his own, turned on her, demanding that Trump expel her from his circle. (She was close to another Florida politician DeSantis saw as a potential rival, Senator Rick Scott.) Many, including Trump's deputy campaign manager, Bill Stepien, thought it was a mistake, and they were angry that Parscale did not do more to protect her. Parscale maintained to his own allies that he'd done all he could. A Trump friend and Mar-a-Lago club member, Ike Perlmutter, had echoed negative thoughts about Wiles to Trump, who was fully aware of what was happening but invisible as the drama played out. It once again left his aides speculating that maybe he didn't know what was taking place. When it became clear that he had been aware, Trump advisers were struck at how pliant Trump seemed to be with DeSantis.

To formally launch the campaign, Kushner floated the idea of having the candidate again descend the Trump Tower escalator, but it was quickly shot down as sending the wrong message—that Trump was looking back, not forward. When the kickoff rally finally arrived, Trump tried to rouse his supporters, many of whom waited for hours through sporadic downpours in sticky Florida weather outside the Amway Center for the chance to see him. Standing onstage after emerging to Lee Greenwood's "God Bless the USA," Trump kicked off by saying that Democrats "want to destroy you and they want to destroy our country as we know it, not acceptable. It's not going to happen." He attacked the news media and the political establishment that he didn't acknowledge he was now a part of.

The Orlando rally and others he would hold around the country were envisioned as moments when Trump would recapture some of his favorite parts of running in 2016: appearing before crowds constantly, flying on a plane surrounded by people to chat with, dominating media coverage nearly every time he appeared. And they provided an emotional balm to all that pained him in Washington; instead of being told "no" or seeing a raft of investigations, he got to speak to a crowd that told him all he did was right.

Trump had notched accomplishments during his tenure, and he spoke about them to his crowds. Yet Orlando revealed that essentially Donald Trump had nothing new to sell. In place of a campaign message or a forward-looking plan for a second term, he spent much of his time relitigating his perceived injustices about the last election.

The vicious internal politics within Trump's White House, his shiny-object impatience with employees and constant desire to find someone new who enticed him, and an ongoing series of ethical scandals or controversies throughout the executive branch caused unprecedented turnover within the administration. By the middle of 2019, Trump had seen more of his original cabinet depart than any of the five presidents who had immediately preceded him. He was on his third press secretary, third chief of staff, and sixth communications director.

Trump had set the rhythms of his White House, but he had little interest in certain specifics. He did not particularly care about most of the government, he had little use for most of his cabinet secretaries unless their department interested him personally, and whoever was in his line of sight was usually the one he tasked with a job, even if it was the valet tending to him or a Secret Service agent, which was why there were often two simultaneous efforts for any one task. In early 2019, during a discussion in the Oval Office that included two of his aides, assistant to the president Johnny DeStefano, and the head of presidential personnel Sean Doocey, the conversation turned to someone whose confirmation in the Senate was stalled.

"Johnny, you're a nice guy, but you suck at legislative affairs," Trump said. "I'm giving it to Sean. Sean's going to be in charge of legislative affairs now." DeStefano had nothing to do with the Office of Legislative Affairs; by then, it was run by Shahira Knight, a former National Economic Council deputy director under Gary Cohn. Nonetheless, both agreed, until they left the room and carried on as if nothing had been said.

Much of the government became reoriented to moving Trump off what one former cabinet official called "nutty" ideas, and managing him throughout the day as he popped off about various topics and chased fragments of conversations with outside advisers or things he'd heard on television. Traveling aboard Air Force One to the Army-Navy football game in 2019, Trump grew enraged when he learned he had already signed an executive order on professional

sports eligibility that he thought he would be signing while flanked by flags and service secretaries at
the game. Aides had to scramble to craft a statement
essentially reaffirming the already signed policy, and
still Trump complained that their last-minute effort
wasn't good enough. But he moved on after the game.

Other times, ideas that lodged in Trump's head
stayed with him for months. Trump met with public health officials and drug enforcement officials
in the Oval Office about stemming the tide of fen-
tanyl across the southern border, where there was
shared frustration that the Mexican government
wasn't doing more to curtail drug labs. One of the
officials, Assistant Secretary for Health Brett Giroir,
was also an admiral in the U.S. Public Health Service
Commissioned Corp, part of the uniformed services but not the armed forces; Giroir would wear
his dress uniform to the Oval Office, which former
officials said confused Trump, who thought Giroir
was a member of the military. So when, in that
meeting, Giroir volunteered that the drug labs
should be dealt with by bombing—put "lead to target," he suggested—Trump was enchanted by the
idea. He raised it several times, eventually asking a
stunned Defense Secretary Mark Esper whether the
United States could indeed bomb the labs; Trump
described all missiles as "Patriot missiles," not realizing it was a specific type of weapons system. The
response from White House aides was not to try to

change Trump's view, but to consider asking Giroir not to wear his uniform to the Oval Office anymore.

One of the few people working closely with Trump who had remained with him since the inauguration was Madeleine Westerhout. Among the group of Trump skeptics to follow him from the Republican National Committee into the White House—she was seen crying on election night in 2016—she had endured where others had not. As his personal secretary and later director of Oval Office operations, Westerhout sat just outside his office. She used the perch to alert others in the West Wing when Trump was on a potentially troublesome phone call, or had a visitor proposing problematic ideas, so they could try to step in. Her colleagues thought she came to enjoy the proximity she had to the seat of power a bit too much, and she made enemies in the West Wing because of it.

In the late summer of 2019, while they were accompanying Trump on a trip to his New Jersey golf club, a top press aide invited Westerhout to join him at an off-the-record dinner with a group of reporters. At one point, he left to make a television appearance. Westerhout, after drinking heavily, began to speak about how Trump felt about various family members, sharing a pejorative description of his younger daughter, Tiffany. Word of that exchange spread around the West Wing. Yet instead of acknowledging the errors committed by their colleague or by Trump, White House officials tried to blame reporters. Westerhout's internal enemies were happy to draw Trump's attention to the act of impropriety. After dithering about getting rid of Westerhout—Trump had come to rely on her and was reluctant to see her go, but was under pressure from his family—he ultimately directed his chief of staff to fire her.

The day the firing took place, Trump learned that Barr's department was not charging Comey, infuriating Trump. He met that day with McDaniel in the dining room off the Oval Office for a prescheduled meeting, during which a foul-humored Trump called one person after another demanding to know if they agreed with him that Comey should have been charged. Mulvaney arrived in the room to let Trump know Westerhout was gone, saying, "I took care of that." Other staff drifted through the Oval Office. Trump paused for a moment. Then he reached for a remote control sitting on the table before him, picked it up, and threw it at the credenza along the wall. Flying with Trump and others later aboard Marine One, Mulvaney lamented that it was unfortunate that Westerhout had to be let go. Trump agreed, but seemed indifferent. "Sometimes you get three strikes," he said. "Sometimes you only get one."

If his chiefs of staff had all been unable to get Trump to see the value of a traditional gatekeeper, Westerhout had for two and a half years succeeded in fashioning herself as something of an alarm system to the chiefs and to Trump's political advisers, when certain people or information were getting to the president, or in his vicinity. With her gone, so were the sharpest warnings about who was seeking to influence Trump.

By his third year in office, Trump was no stranger to steering resources toward his commercial properties. What had begun with staying weekends and vacations only at his clubs in New Jersey and Florida, where records showed the Secret Service would sometimes pay high rates for rooms and food and even use of golf carts, grew more expansive. Trump properties, including his Washington hotel, became the default venue for all his campaign and Republican National Committee events, and much else in the conservative ecosystem. Republicans often said that in a polarized era where businesses were reluctant to associate with the Trump name or were refusing to serve his aides, holding events at Trump's properties was easier. As the United States prepared to host the annual meeting of the Group of Seven largest developed economies in 2020, Trump told Mulvaney that he wanted to see the summit at his Doral golf resort outside Miami. (At different points, Trump suggested Russia should be allowed to rejoin the meeting, from which it was ousted for annexing Crimea in 2014, and just before the 2019 event, he mocked Obama as having been "outsmarted" by Putin.)

Mulvaney directed a deputy, Dan Walsh, to find any reason why the event, which typically drew hundreds of government officials and media, could not be held at Doral and to generate a list of alternative venues. Doral, Walsh concluded, was the best fit. Top aides knew they would pay a price in press coverage for its being held at a Trump property. Trump clearly had decided to use Mulvaney as something of a crash-test dummy to measure just how angry the reaction would be.

When Mulvaney went out to the briefing room to answer questions in mid-October, reporters were less interested in the G7 than the whistleblower complaint about Trump's dealing with Ukraine. For weeks, the White House had steadfastly denied there was any linkage between the withheld military aid to Ukraine and Trump's desire for investigation into the Bidens, as well as the debunked theory that Ukraine had hacked the Democratic National Committee servers. "The look back to what happened in 2016 certainly was part of the thing that he was worried about in corruption with that nation, and that is absolutely appropriate," Mulvaney explained. When a reporter pointed out that what Mulvaney had described was a quid pro quo, he responded, "We do that all the time with foreign policy. We were holding up money at the same time for, what was it, the Northern Triangle countries. We were holding up aid at the Northern Triangle countries so that they—so that they would change their policies on immigration." Mulvaney, who often seemed to be thinking about a previous question when he gave an answer to a later one, added, "I have news for everybody: Get over it. There is going to be political influence in foreign policy."

At first, Trump praised Mulvaney's performance. But he changed his mind after hearing from both his personal lawyers and those within the White House counsel's office, all of whom were frequently at odds with Mulvaney, that his chief of staff had damaged their case in the recently launched impeachment inquiry.

In October, Trump called Turkey's president, Recep Tayyip Erdogan, to ward off a potential crisis along his country's border with Syria, where Turkish troops had massed in preparation for an attack on Kurdish-led rebels. For several weeks beforehand, the chairman of the Joint Chiefs of Staff and top Pentagon officials had been speaking to counterparts in Turkey about the looming crisis. General Mark Milley, an avuncular combat veteran who had testified during his Senate confirmation that he would not be "intimidated into making stupid decisions," came in at the end of September; Milley saw no other option than a Trump call with Erdogan, which few had high hopes for as a solution. Trump had declared late the previous year that U.S. forces had defeated the Islamic State, and he did not relish the idea of leaving forces in Syria.

Trump's degree of pushback with Erdogan on the call depended on the telling, with one version painting

Trump as defiant and another painting him as pliant, doing more listening than talking as Erdogan tried to sell him on the idea that Erdogan's forces would combat the remains of ISIS. We will take responsibility for it, was Erdogan's message, promising to "return" terrorists to the countries they came from, along with promising to preserve democratic structures that had been put in place. From there, Milley, the newly named national security adviser Robert O'Brien, Esper, and Pompeo discussed how to handle the remaining U.S. forces in Syria; they discussed a plan for a smaller number to protect key areas, which Trump ultimately signed off on. A statement went out that night from the press secretary, saying the U.S. would "not support or be involved" in Turkey's operation.

Trump's Republican allies in the Senate were deeply alarmed and privately said Trump simply hadn't been strong enough in pushing back. Administration officials credited Senator Lindsey Graham with devising the notion that Trump could claim that the U.S. "kept the oil," a reference to oil fields on the southeast border that were guarded (the U.S. had nothing to do with the oil, but it was strategically necessary to keep hostile forces from taking it).

Trump wrote a letter to Erdogan, with O'Brien by his side, from the White House residence. "You don't want to be responsible for slaughtering thousands of people, and I don't want to be responsible for destroying the Turkish economy—and I will," Trump wrote to Erdogan. "History will look upon you favorably if you get this done the right and humane way. It will look upon you forever as the devil if good things don't happen."

"Don't be a tough guy. Don't be a fool!" Trump said, and then, as if he was still a private business-man, concluded with, "I will call you later." The entire episode needlessly frustrated some of Trump's Senate Republican allies at a time when he depended on their votes in the upcoming impeachment trial. The letter seemed to work, however, and senators he met with were given copies of it as souvenirs.

For many of his advisers, the episode underscored Trump's strange relationships with, and preference for dealing with, strongmen. At one point in his term, Trump startled aides by declaring, "I know more about Vladimir Putin than you'll ever know!" as a discussion about Russia was taking place. He was much the same when it came to Erdogan or other leaders, always insisting he knew more than the officials briefing him.

When the articles of impeachment were introduced, Trump reacted at different points with a familiar refrain. "I'll just sue Congress," he told his top advisers in the Oval Office. "They can't do this to me." He believed, he said, that if Pelosi didn't send the articles to the Senate after he was impeached—she held on to them for no clear reason for several days—he could "go straight to the Supreme Court." "They'll dismiss the case," he said. White House aides explained to him that this wasn't an actual trial, and that it was beyond his control. He was forced to wait.

Before the vote took place, Trump pushed Republican lawmakers to "get tougher and fight," and they did just that, with roughly two dozen storming a secured room where Democrats were interviewing a witness. Trump reciprocated with lavish attention, one time tossing branded candy bars at visiting lawmakers who scrambled to collect them. Trump's advisers, meanwhile, looked for ways to appeal to Democrats to vote against the articles of impeachment. Bill Stepien, Trump's deputy campaign manager and a New Jersey native, and Kellyanne Conway worked to convert a Democratic congressman, Jeff Van Drew, to the Republican Party. But Trump remained incensed that New York Democrats would not side with him. He couldn't fathom that Carolyn Maloney, of Manhattan's Upper East Side, was averse to supporting him after he had donated to her years earlier. He also believed that Debbie Dingell, a Democrat from Michigan who took the seat held by her late husband, John, should vote against impeachment. Decades earlier, John Dingell sought an SEC investigation into Trump's efforts to get the stock analyst Marvin Roffman fired after he raised questions about the Taj Mahal casino's finances. But Trump believed he deserved credit for being gracious when Dingell died in February 2019.

The second week of December 2019, Dingell,

appearing on Fox News, criticized the White House approach to the impeachment inquiry. Trump responded with a tweet and an attack, calling her "Really pathetic!" Three days later, Dingell wrote an op-ed saying that Trump's actions with Zelensky rose "to the level of a threat to our democracy."

Trump was livid. The next day, he happened to fly to Battle Creek, Michigan, for a rally that was billed as a "Merry Christmas" event. At the rally, he quickly took aim at Dingell. He described giving her husband "the A+ treatment" for his funeral. He recalled Dingell calling him to thank him, changing his voice as he imitated her. " 'It's the nicest thing that's ever happened. Thank you so much. John would be so thrilled. He's looking down. He'd be so thrilled. Thank you so much, sir.' I said, 'That's okay, don't worry about it,'" Trump said, performing for the crowd. And then, the dagger. "Maybe he's looking up? I don't know," Trump said, to groans from the crowd. Dingell replied on Twitter that Trump was attacking her during her "first holiday season without the man I love."

The next day, hours after an appearance on CNN, Dingell's cell phone rang from what popped up as an unknown number. When she answered, the man on the other end identified himself as a **Washington Post** reporter, and said he knew her husband from his investigations in Congress. The name he gave was not one she recognized. The man asked Dingell if she was looking for an apology from Trump. No, she replied, merely that people could be civil to one another. As the man talked, Dingell couldn't shake the idea that his voice sounded like that of the forty-fifth president. Dingell never got a clear answer as to who it was. She never saw a story in the **Post** using her comments from that call.

CHAPTER 27

Acquitted

Donald Trump made his way through the dining room at Mar-a-Lago, the postholiday crowd boisterous in part due to the presence of another 1980s New York celebrity enjoying his life's second act: retired Mets first baseman Keith Hernandez was in a private room near the bar. Trump had his dinner at a table in a dining room indoors, but he popped up to greet diners on the patio, prompting applause by reminding them of his latest overseas success and then peering into their faces for a reaction.

Three days earlier, he had given an order to kill Qassim Suleimani, an Iranian general who headed the country's fearsome Quds Force, roughly two months after the death of Abu Bakr al-Baghdadi, a top leader of the Islamic State, during a raid by U.S. forces. Over the prior three years, Trump was most consistently caustic about Iran, albeit without a consistent strategy. The Suleimani strike had in the past been among a list of options presented to Trump, with Bolton's team setting up the process for its approval months before; this time, Trump raised it. It came after a week of exchanging taunts on Twitter with the country's supreme leader over a series of Iran-directed attacks on American interests in Iraq. "They will pay a very BIG PRICE!" Trump had written. "You can't do anything," responded Ayatollah Ali Khamenei. Other presidents had weighed targeting Suleimani, who was responsible for foiling American objectives across the Middle East, but had decided against taking the risk. Some of Trump's top advisers worried about the potential consequences of reactions by Iran to such an attack. But there was compelling intelligence about Suleimani's upcoming plans to attack Americans around the region, and Trump had no second thoughts. A drone-fired missile killed Suleimani as he departed the Baghdad airport in a convoy.

In response to the killing, Iran fired at U.S. bases in Iraq, injuring roughly one hundred troops. (One White House aide later said Trump directed aides to downplay the severity of the injuries, writing off concussions as headaches.) Many national security experts girded for an even worse reaction from Iran, and a threat of escalation with the United States, which ultimately never came to pass. For the White House, the Suleimani strike provided a framework for what advisers believed the year of his reelection could look like: strength, dominance, action.

Trump had seen a dismal end to 2019, becoming only the third president to be impeached by the House of Representatives, accused of withholding military aid to Ukraine in exchange for political favors. But he was certain to prevail after an impeachment trial in the Senate, where Mitch McConnell remained the Republican majority leader and a reluctant Trump partner. Democrats were unlikely to get the super-majority necessary to remove a president from office. The week the Senate trial began, Trump was scheduled to celebrate another foreign-policy victory, a signing ceremony for "phase one" of a deal with China to resolve the eighteen-month trade war that Trump initiated with tariffs. His political advisers believed such achievements, against the backdrop of a strong economy, were going to matter more than whatever concerns the various investigations might have lodged in voters' brains about Trump's behavior. And after years of compromising to bring aboard party officials, decorated military officers, and veterans of past administrations whose experience he was told would help him govern, Trump was finally going to get the team he had always wanted.

Among those waiting at Mar-a-Lago for an audience with Trump just after New Year's Eve was Texas congressman Louie Gohmert. He had brought with him a few aides and allies, including Rich Higgins, a former National Security Council staffer who had been fired in 2017 after writing a conspiratorial memo alleging a vast network of people within Trump's government and outside it, working to undermine him. Gohmert would later describe Trump listening intently as Higgins described the array of people harming him. Upon emerging from the meeting with Gohmert and Higgins, Trump recounted the unfairness of the firing ("I guess McMaster fired him or something," Trump said) and told an aide he wanted Higgins now hired as a deputy chief of staff. "We hired a lot of Never Trumpers," Trump lamented. It was time to change that.

Ever since the former college athlete Johnny McEntee had been forced out of the White House over questions about gambling debts in relation to his security clearance, a pervasive mythology had developed around him as being the consummate support staffer who knew intuitively what Trump wanted. By early 2020, Trump decided that McEntee's unique loyalty could be channeled into presidential personnel appointments. The suggestion did not go over well with other staff, who liked the person already serving in that role, former Bush White House aide Sean Doocey. "Why don't you want to work with him?" Trump asked deputy chief of staff Emma Doyle when she registered her objection to McEntee. "He's so handsome." (Such running commentary about looks was directed toward both men and women, including occasionally asking a female staffer to twirl around and telling an openly gay male staffer that Trump's "very fit" golf partner for the day "would throw you around a room and make you forget your husband.") McEntee got the job.

When he took charge of the presidential personnel office, McEntee was charged not just with coordinating new hiring in key agencies such as the defense and justice departments, but a review of existing employees—both political appointees and civil-service employees—to vet fidelity to Trump and his goals. He prepared loyalty questionnaires that asked staff to report any times they had remarked on Trump to media alongside questions such as "What political commentator, thinker or politician best reflects your views?"

The same week, Trump announced he was naming Richard Grenell, his ambassador to Germany, to serve simultaneously as the acting director of national intelligence. (Trump aides often touted that he had named the first openly gay cabinet-level official in history, despite Grenell's temporary status in the role; Trump would sometimes describe Grenell as a "proud gay American.") Grenell left officials at DNI believing, in multiple discussions, that Trump wanted to move out of the agency the anonymous whistleblower whose complaint to the House set in motion Trump's impeachment. The whistleblower had specific legal protections, raising concerns for officials about how to handle the matter. There were other specific requests from Grenell as well. Amid a frequent complaint from some Republicans that intelligence was being skewed through analysis, officials recalled Grenell insisting that any intelligence material related to Russia needed to be "fact-based"; he wanted the raw reporting to speak for itself, apparently with minimal interpretation. Some intelligence community officials shared the view that analysts did not always use common standards to evaluate the actions of foreign powers, and that individual perspectives on Russia or China could color assessments. But some officials suspected that Grenell was less interested in creating common standards than in stripping out analytic points that might be contrary to Trump's perspective.

Trump believed the U.S. intelligence services were arrayed against him as he came to office, and he was making adjustments there too. Just a few days before he was removed to make room for Grenell, Joseph Maguire led a small group from the FBI and the intelligence services, including his deputy, Beth Sanner, who had been Trump's main briefer for many months, to see Trump. They were informing Trump, Vice President Mike Pence, and a group of senior officials, including the two mens' national security advisers, about measures to ensure election security. Trump was impressed by what he was told about the steps being taken to secure the election, even wanting to schedule a press conference to promote the findings.

But toward the end of the briefing, Trump abruptly interrupted. Intelligence officials had recently briefed members of the House Intelligence Committee that Russians were interfering in the 2020 election, including the Democratic primaries. The committee's chairman, Rep. Adam Schiff, helped lead the impeachment inquiry and the House investigation into ties between the Trump campaign and Russia. "Hey Joe, what's this I hear about you going to Schiff and saying that Russia is interfering for me in the election?" Trump asked Maguire. "That's not how it was," a junior briefer from the FBI volunteered, adding, "I was there." Trump, undeterred, continued to yell. Maguire protested, saying that officials went to both the House and Senate committees, the latter headed by Republicans, and that no one had had a problem. What's more, Maguire said, they had already briefed the president on the same information.

There was silence elsewhere in the room. Pence and the White House's national security advisers averted their gazes as Trump again bellowed at Maguire, "Why is my DNI briefing Adam Schiff on Russian interference!" Maguire asked the junior briefers to leave, realizing nothing else would get accomplished that day. As they departed the room, Sanner approached the Resolute Desk to offer up a defense of both Maguire and the intelligence community. "Mr. President, we are not against you," she said.

Trump, generally uninterested in face-to-face, one-on-one confrontation without a crowd backing him up, replied quietly, "I know."

It never should have fucking happened," the president growled, his jaw jutting out. "Never should have fucking happened."

On February 5, 2020, Trump sat at the head of a table in the dining room next to the Oval Office, intently watching the television as one hundred senators voted on the two impeachment articles that would determine the fate of his presidency. The final result was almost entirely predetermined by party-line politics. Throughout the process, Trump had worked, cajoled, threatened, and lavished praise on Republican lawmakers in the House and the Senate who dutifully, and sometimes out of fear of reprisals, echoed his claims that he was being persecuted for simply performing the duties of his office.

But there had been wrenching drama in the final days of the Senate trial about whether the Republicans who controlled the proceedings would allow Democrats to summon witnesses who could testify firsthand to Trump's conduct. Along with my **New York Times** colleague Michael Schmidt, I reported on an upcoming book by his former national security adviser, John Bolton, that was not scheduled to be out for several weeks. The information in the book validated some of the most damning allegations against Trump; Bolton said Trump had directly tied the investigations he sought into the Bidens to withholding the aid to Ukraine. We broke the story just before the case was concluding and heading to a vote, prompting days of questions about whether there would be witnesses.

Ultimately McConnell, a recurring Trump skeptic and temperamental opposite who in a marriage of convenience had become one of his biggest protectors on Capitol Hill, blocked Democrats from calling any witnesses. (That meant that Bolton, who had said he would only cooperate with a subpoena from the

Senate but not the House, never appeared.) Without any new testimony during the trial, McConnell succeeded in corralling all but one Republican to stand uniformly against Trump's removal. There was one exception: a first-term senator who had become in many ways the embodiment of Republican discomfort in the era of Trump, Mitt Romney. He accepted Trump's endorsement in 2012 at Trump's insistence, only to call him a "con man" in 2016 before auditioning to be Trump's secretary of state, then accepting his endorsement for a Senate race in Utah and criticizing him after he had won. Romney became the first senator in the history of the United States to vote in favor of convicting a president from his own political party.

But Democrats still fell short of a majority, let alone the two-thirds supermajority necessary for removal. "The Senate adjudges that the respondent, President Donald John Trump, president of the United States, is not guilty as charged," the chief justice of the United States, John Roberts, repeated for each charge.

Trump was, in that moment, handed as smooth a path as he could have hoped for to a second term. The end to the impeachment saga came just under a year after the end of the first existential threat to his presidency, the special counsel probe into whether his campaign had conspired with Russia to impact the 2016 presidential race. He beat back both threats by using the same set of tools: browbeating members of his party and other allies into fealty, refusing to accept anyone else's perspective or version of reality but his own, and taking any missteps by his opponents and using them to undermine their entire argument. Now the U.S. Senate had presented him the type of clear exoneration rarely offered to politicians facing scandal, one easy to communicate to voters. He would be able to reclaim the agenda and dedicate the final year of the term to laying out the case for his own reelection and focusing on a thriving economy.

And so the moment was joyous. The advisers who had squeezed into the small room cheered. Some rose to slap palms in high-fives, a wave of relief rolling through the room. Everyone was thrilled, except for one person.

Trump's impulse was not for celebration, but for vengeance. And he began seeking it the next morning, when he was scheduled to speak at an annual National Prayer Breakfast, where the theme happened to be "Love your enemy." In the past he had used his turn on this dais to read staid remarks about the role of religion in America. This time he waved the front page of **USA Today** at the crowd to showcase its banner headline: ACQUITTED.

"As everybody knows, my family, our great country, and your president have been put through a terrible ordeal by some very dishonest and corrupt people," Trump told an audience mixed with clergy and politicians. The president had no interest in moving on, and he turned his attention toward his next phase—retribution—almost immediately. A day later, Trump dismissed two key impeachment witnesses—European

Union ambassador Gordon Sondland and Lieutenant Colonel Alexander Vindman—and also targeted Vindman's brother, Yevgeny, a lieutenant colonel and the national security council's ethics counsel, in retaliation for reporting concerns about the Zelensky call.

Shortly after the acquittal vote, a group of aides sat with Trump to plan out his first presidential trip to India, scheduled for later in February. In the middle of the impeachment trial, Trump became the first sitting president to speak in person to the anti-abortion "March for Life," solidifying his standing with a group of conservative voters who once viewed him warily, but who saw him evolve from tortured answers on how to criminalize abortion early in the 2016 primaries and relying on Pence to articulate the administration's position to now giving a clear statement that he would appoint Supreme Court justices who would overturn **Roe v. Wade,** and back changes to the federal funding formula for groups that provided abortion.

Yet January and February were fraught months beyond the impeachment trial. A novel coronavirus had begun to spread beyond China, and Melania Trump was concerned about cases she had seen popping up in South Asia ahead of their trip. She shared her husband's fear of germs and did not want to get sick. The federal government's top infectious-disease expert, Dr. Anthony Fauci, told the group there were only a few cases of COVID-19, as the novel coronavirus was designated, in India. The trip could go on.

• • •

On February 20, Roger Stone was sentenced to more than three years in prison in connection with the charges stemming from the Mueller investigation. Barr had suggested less than the nine years career prosecutors sought for Stone, a decision the judge ultimately agreed with. When Paul Manafort was indicted, Trump tried to minimize his campaign chairman's involvement in his campaign. But despite the highs and lows their relationship had seen, that was not possible for Trump to do with Stone; among other things, Trump, who sometimes tried to avoid too pointed a separation with people, gave his aides the impression that he was afraid of entirely icing Stone out and making him an enemy.

As Stone was sentenced, Kushner received a visit from Tucker Carlson, host of a popular Fox News show and someone who seemed to intimidate Trump, who wanted to talk about Stone's case. Carlson and Stone had known each other for many years; in the documentary **Get Me Roger Stone,** Carlson had lauded Stone's penchant for writing his own role in events as larger than it was. "Is it more brilliant and impressive to influence world events or to stand on the periphery of world events and yet get recorded as having influenced world events?" he asked. "Maybe the latter."

Just two days before Stone's sentencing, Trump had commuted the sentence of former Illinois governor

Rod Blagojevich, a Democrat who had been convicted nearly a decade earlier on corruption charges, including trying to sell Obama's Senate seat when it became available and extorting an official at a children's hospital. Blagojevich had appeared on Trump's **Celebrity Apprentice,** but the stronger bond between the two men derived from a common nemesis, or at least the appearance of one; the federal prosecutor responsible for Blagojevich's conviction was close friends with Comey. "It's the same guys who were going after me," Trump told aides. At other times, he said Blagojevich was prosecuted for doing what many other politicians had done (Mulvaney had tried telling Trump that clemency for Blagojevich should be a second-term item, and had House Republicans explain to the president how severe Blagojevich's crimes were, but Trump was unmoved).

Carlson came to Kushner to demand clemency for Stone, which Blagojevich and ten others—including former New York police chief Bernard Kerik and junk-bond dealer Michael Milken—were about to receive, to prevent him from going to prison. If Trump failed to deliver, Carlson made clear, he would press the issue publicly. Kushner was nevertheless noncommittal, and a few days later Carlson launched what became a monthslong campaign on his friend's behalf. "Democrats will become unhinged if Trump pardons Roger Stone, but they're unhinged anyway," he said. "What has happened to Roger Stone should never happen to anyone in this country of any political party." Trump shared the Carlson segment on Twitter, where he had already lamented Stone's sentence as a "miscarriage of justice." As it all played out, Barr told an ABC News reporter that Trump's social media posts were making it "impossible for me to do my job." Despite the appearance of being personally outraged, Trump commuted Stone's sentence many months later, just before he was scheduled to submit to authorities.

Trump's public show of solidarity with an ally who'd been prosecuted was a reminder to his supporters of the powers he still held. And he made clear he was weighing clemencies for several people connected to the Mueller probe. Manafort, who'd originally cooperated with the Mueller investigation, had been accused by prosecutors of lying to them; his lawyers, who repeatedly said he had no information about Trump to offer, denied that. After new information was made public about the FBI handling of Michael Flynn, the former national security adviser had withdrawn a 2017 guilty plea that he had reiterated at his December 2018 sentencing. In so doing, Flynn, who Mueller had said provided useful information, accused the government of bad-faith practices in its investigation. Flynn's accusation was part of a strategy developed by a Southern lawyer named Sidney Powell. A few months later, the Justice Department dropped the charges entirely, a move to which no career prosecutors involved in the case were willing to sign their names. Powell, to whom Trump had started speaking by phone after being impressed by her appearances on the Fox Business show **Lou Dobbs Tonight,** became a hero to Trump's followers; Flynn was free of the legal system, and he was newly committed to the Trump political movement.

Air Force One departed Washington for Ahmedabad on February 23, and throughout the thirteen-hour flight Trump watched cable-news channels. Their coverage was all focused on the coronavirus, which had since spread from China to Europe. Trump had already begun to try to wish away the topic, as he had convinced himself he had so many other difficult moments he'd faced. The first lady, traveling despite staff having been told she disliked flying, warned him that he needed to take it more seriously as a potentially dangerous situation. Campaign polling showed that the coronavirus was becoming a worry for voters, but Kushner's strategic advice appeared oblivious to it: he was encouraging a "Get Healthy America" tour that would show Trump was serious about developing a new health-care plan.

Other than the moments cheering his presidency, Trump was focused during the trip on the food put in front of him—he claimed to have known someone who got gravely sick eating food while traveling in India. At every meal, even a state dinner hosted by Prime Minister Narendra Modi at the official presidential palace in Delhi, Trump said later, he pushed items around his plate, moving them from side to side as a form of avoidance, and drank only from special glassware that he said Melania had the White House staff pack for the trip, primarily for fear of contracting the coronavirus.

The trip had mostly appealed to Trump because he had been promised a large public event in his honor, and Modi delivered 110,000 people to a Gujarat stadium for a "Namaste Trump" rally. Despite few substantive advances from the trip, Trump left India relatively happy. On the flight home, most of the senior staff crammed into the Air Force One conference room, trying desperately to rest after being awake for more than twenty-four hours. Some were sprawled on the floor, some curled in chairs. All felt relatively pleased after visiting three cities in two days, without any incidents. The feeling of success was often elusive in the Trump White House, and so they reveled in it as they drifted off to sleep.

A troubled sleeper during international flights, Trump usually entertained himself by calling one staff member after another up to his quarters and forcing conversation to stave off the loneliness that always seemed to be stalking him. But on this flight, everyone was sleeping. So he watched television. And the news coverage was grim, focusing on a public warning from a leading Centers for Disease Control official, Nancy Messonnier, that community spread of the coronavirus in the United States was inevitable.

Her words left the president livid, and he hunted for a staff member from whom to demand answers.

He banged open the door to the conference room, his hulking figure filling the doorway as he yelled at staffers, who kept their heads down, pretending to remain asleep. "Who is this woman!" he asked. "Who is she!? She's going to scare people!"

By the time Air Force One had landed in the United States, Trump had decided to give a newly launched coronavirus task force the imprimatur of presidential significance by placing Pence in charge. In reality, the task force was relocated within the White House, giving the president's staff, who had been rattled by Messonnier's unexpected remarks, greater control over what information the administration released.

Even in his zeal for payback against Democrats for the impeachment saga, Trump had been singularly focused on two things. He wanted to avoid offending China, the site of the virus's initial discovery, with whose leader he had forged a trade deal that he considered a major accomplishment. He also worried that acknowledging the new crisis would undermine plans to campaign on his record of job creation; Trump had always appeared to believe that things only existed if they were discussed openly, and he set about minimizing the virus in public, despite private warnings from his National Security Council team that it was significant and from aides such as Kellyanne Conway and Brad Parscale to treat it seriously.

But by early March, Trump sensed political danger for himself in the health crisis, even if he couldn't figure out how to address it beyond venting his frustrations. Meeting with political aides in the Oval Office at the beginning of that month, Trump was handed a sheaf of polling data that showed how strongly voters supported his handling of economic issues.

Trump, who had spent four years treating daily stock-market fluctuations as though they were polling data reflecting on him personally, flung the papers onto the Resolute Desk. They didn't mean anything now. Everyone in the room knew the numbers were terrific, but with what was coming with COVID, Trump said, they would be worthless. The economy he had presided over was about to be wiped out. He queried aides on what he should do about possible shutdown measures around the country, and their potential impact on the economy.

He knew, and his aides knew, that the landscape for his reelection had changed. But it was not in Donald Trump to adapt for very long, if at all, to rules that were not his own.

CHAPTER 28

Get Healthy America

When the World Health Organization's first warning about the coronavirus arrived in early January, the public-health issue that had recently received attention within the Trump administration had been vaping. Health and Human Services Secretary Alex Azar, bolstered by Kellyanne Conway and the first lady, who was concerned about the easy availability of e-cigarettes to children, had been in favor of more aggressively regulating the burgeoning industry. In early January, Trump, told by some advisers that the issue could help him with suburban mothers, endorsed narrow limits on flavored vaping products marketed particularly to youth. But he quickly had buyer's remorse after hearing from his campaign manager, Brad Parscale, who argued that such new regulation would alienate his political base. Aides pointed to data from his pollster, John McLaughlin, conducted for the vaping industry, to argue his point. "I never should have done that fucking vaping thing!" Trump told Azar, looking for someone to blame for his own decision.

The next week, the first case of the novel coronavirus

arrived on the West Coast, in a local man who had returned home from travel to China. The spread across continents prompted comparisons to the 2003 virus that spread the Severe Acute Respiratory System (SARS) from China and killed 774 people worldwide. From the World Economic Forum in Davos, Switzerland—the kind of elite-status event Trump mocked but relished attending—Trump told an American interviewer that the United States had the virus under control, and that he trusted Chinese president Xi Jinping to be up front about the extent of the threat. "I have a great relationship with President Xi," Trump said.

On January 23, Trump received his first intelligence briefing related to the virus. Many of the China hawks and national security officials in Trump's orbit thought he needed to recognize the danger. Matt Pottinger, a deputy national security adviser who had been shaped by the experience of covering SARS contagion as a Hong Kong–based newspaper reporter, was strenuous in his warnings. The national security adviser, Robert O'Brien, warned Trump it was the biggest national security threat to his presidency.

Trade adviser Peter Navarro wrote two pointed memos describing a looming and potentially devastating pandemic, one that required significant resources and protective medical equipment such as masks. An invisible menace from overseas lent itself to Navarro's natural paranoia. In an effort to satisfy Trump's desire to identify the anonymous author of the book

A Warning, Navarro had falsely accused a National Security Council aide, Victoria Coates, with rumors swirling inside and outside the White House to the point that she volunteered to take a lie-detector test to prove her innocence, and Trump accepted the offer (officials couldn't figure out who would administer the test, and it never happened). Later, he became convinced that a woman with an Eastern European last name who toured his house as a potential buyer might be a Russian spy and demanded the Secret Service investigate. On coronavirus he was prescient, but also annoying to Trump, who was not happy that Navarro had committed the predictions to paper he circulated among White House advisers. Navarro's warnings were easy for his colleagues to dismiss, because they didn't consider the messenger credible.

Trump initially shrugged off those who wanted him to be more confrontational. When Azar said he wanted to go on television to criticize China in relation to the virus, Trump believed he was trying to use the moment to promote himself. "Stop panicking," he told Azar. "They have enough to worry about without you doing that." Trump's initial reaction to urging from Arkansas senator Tom Cotton that he limit entry to travelers from China was that such a sweeping move was fraught. "They were just here!" Trump told White House advisers, referring to the Chinese delegation that had just attended the signing ceremony. His public-health advisers initially questioned the likely effectiveness of such a ban.

But on January 31, after the public-health experts reconsidered their own initial hesitancy and recommended the measure, Trump issued a partial ban on travel from China. (American citizens were exempted, as were others who routed their trips through points outside the Chinese mainland, such as Hong Kong.) The same week, he established the White House Coronavirus Task Force, which included Azar and Dr. Anthony Fauci. Trump gave little indication he thought many other preparations were necessary. In an interview a few weeks later with Bob Woodward, for the legendary reporter's second book about the Trump White House, the president said the coronavirus was "more deadly than even your strenuous flu," but that he was intentionally downplaying it so as not to cause a "panic."

Generally, Trump wanted to treat the virus as a short-term inconvenience, and he wanted people around him to do the same. "It's going to disappear. One day—it's like a miracle—it will disappear," he insisted. Another time in February, Trump said publicly, "This is a flu. This is like a flu." Nine days later, Trump scheduled, then canceled, then abruptly rescheduled a visit to the Centers for Disease Control in Atlanta, where he wore a red campaign hat and lied about the availability of coronavirus tests. "Don't talk about it on TV," he told McDaniel, who wanted to blame China for the outbreak.

Trump had told aides to continue scheduling rallies. But by the second week in March, those commands were no longer tenable. The World Health Organization officially designated the coronavirus a pandemic, and it affected nearly every corner of American life. With cases popping up all over the country, school districts began to switch to distance learning, the national basketball and hockey leagues suspended their seasons, and college tournaments were canceled. Robert O'Brien argued for a ban on travel from Europe, meeting with fierce opposition from the treasury secretary, Steve Mnuchin, who had since 2017 maneuvered to be a significant economic adviser. Trump realized the various measures would almost certainly grind economic activity to a halt, but he ultimately took the recommendation. Aides pushed for him to explain the policy—as well as to encourage people to take interpersonal precautions—in an Oval Office address.

Trump's speech on the night of March 11 underscored why he gave few such addresses during his tenure. His delivery was halting—just before the program began he was caught on a hot mic exasperatedly saying "Fuck!" about a visible spot on his white shirt—and, more significantly, there were a series of basic factual errors about what the ban entailed, such as which European countries were covered and whether it applied to freight as well as people. "Okayyyy," Trump said uncertainly to no one in particular after the speech ended, unbuttoning his suit jacket.

The unfavorable coverage Trump received for the speech and the confusion it caused left a mark on his willingness to speak publicly about the virus. He already resented Fauci's ubiquitous media presence as the government's primary narrator of the pandemic, calling him a "showboat" to aides. As the coronavirus dominated media attention, chairing the task force provided a vice president who had long harbored presidential ambitions the chance to look like a leader. He had traveled to Washington State, where the first case in the United States was discovered, and offered the type of visual reassurance during a crisis that normally comes from presidents. Pence joined Fauci and other government doctors for their daily Coronavirus Task Force press briefings, held in the White House briefing room, where the vice president presented limited detailed information but displayed not just a seriousness and sobriety, but conveyed empathy, winning approving marks in the media.

Local officials, especially in the coastal states where the disease was spreading most quickly, had begun to command the national stage too. When the navy made available two hospital ships to support local medical efforts, Trump was able to help choose in which ports they would be docked. California governor Gavin Newsom was a Democrat who nonetheless had developed a working relationship with the president. Trump seemed to temper his instinctive criticism of a Democrat in part because Newsom's ex-wife, Kimberly Guilfoyle, was dating Trump's eldest son. When Newsom signed a measure requiring presidential candidates appearing on his state's ballot to release their tax returns, Trump angrily called him, claiming he had made more than $400 million the previous year (Trump never made his taxes public as president).

Newsom "helped us much more, is much better to us than the governor of Washington," Trump observed to advisers during an Oval Office meeting with several attendees, including Pence. "Let's give it to Newsom." (Trump had separately discouraged kindness toward Washington governor Jay Inslee, who had criticized the administration's pandemic response. "I told Mike not to be complimentary to the governor because that governor is a snake," Trump said during his visit to the CDC headquarters.) "Newsom said nice things about me, Inslee said bad things about me," Trump said from behind the Resolute Desk. Pence replied that the decision could not be made that way and had to be based on data showing local need. Trump nevertheless decided to call Newsom, putting him on speakerphone without alerting him that others were in the room, as he often did. "I'm having to make a decision here about this ship," Trump told the governor. "You've been so good to me that I want to give it to you. But we've got to figure it out." Newsom carefully replied that he would love to have the ship in California, but that Trump should send it wherever it was most needed. Trump made a dumbfounded expression to everyone in the room, shocked that Newsom was not simply grasping for whatever he could get. (One of the ships ended up in Los Angeles.)

Envious of the televised media spotlight shining on Pence, and with no outlet available to him with his rallies and fundraisers on hold, Trump agreed to an aide's suggestion that he attend one of the task-force briefings for the press, which were broadcast live without interruption by all the cable-news networks. Initially, Trump said he would sit off to the side, but he ended up saying some words from the podium, and then he was hooked. The briefings were marked by first Pence, and later Trump, surrounded by doctors who were ostensibly giving public-health updates. Trump overtook them with his own messaging, answering questions from the reporters assembled in seats in front of him.

At first, there were glimmers of what would pass for traditional leadership at the daily events. After a "Fifteen Days to Slow the Spread" campaign encouraging Americans to stay at home if sick or whenever possible proved insufficient to end the pandemic, Trump succumbed to pressure from public-health experts to encourage continued closure measures even as members of his own party opposed them. "I want every American to be prepared for the hard days that lie ahead," Trump said on March 31 with uncommon seriousness. "We're going to go through a very tough two weeks. . . . This is going to be a very painful, very, very painful two weeks."

The last day of March was the first at work for Mark Meadows as Trump's fourth chief of staff, more than any other president had had in a single term. Meadows, as a leader of the conservative House Freedom Caucus, had been one of Trump's most committed champions on Capitol Hill. As chief of staff, Meadows was intent on pleasing Trump in a way none of his predecessors had been, hoping to establish himself not only as the White House's internal manager but Trump's most important adviser. Meadows became the latest chief to try to show Trump he could root out press leaks just as Trump wanted, going at it with distinct vigor. I later learned that Trump, angry about my published stories, would bellow that he wanted administration officials to obtain my phone records and identify my sources. It did not appear that anyone ever acted on it.

Meadows told associates that he was deliberately telling some aides bad information to see if it became public, and he berated those who questioned the gambit. He eagerly made plays for Trump's favor while complaining to associates outside the White House that it was more dysfunctional than he had previously understood. Most significant was his blocking of Pence, piping up "I've got it" when Trump mentioned something that needed to be done. By adopting those tasks, such as calls to Capitol Hill lawmakers that Trump had previously assigned to the vice president, Meadows managed to drive a wedge between Pence and Trump just as they were preparing to campaign for reelection together.

Within days, I began to hear from sources, including those who wanted him to succeed, about another aspect of Meadows's leadership revealing itself to colleagues. Meadows passed through a range of moods and appeared not in control of his emotions, veering from screaming in one instance to tearing up in another. One example, in a story spreading quickly through the staff, involved Alexa Henning, who as broadcast-media director was responsible for booking White House figures for interviews and had been for years an object of anger among administration officials who did not receive the television time they wanted, usually because television networks decided against putting them on. Meadows summoned Henning to his office, where she defended herself and her job. Many people had tried to get rid of her over time, Henning explained, and she was loyal to one person in the building—the president. Meadows's eyes welled with tears in response. "I care about this man so much," he said. Henning left the meeting with her job intact, but she appeared shaken by what had happened. She told two other staff members, who were put off, and from there, eventually, the story reached me. I filed it away for an article I was writing about Meadows's early tenure.

In early April, **The New York Times** published a long story I had worked on with five colleagues that held Trump accountable for his handling of the pandemic. He and his advisers did not like the article, which appeared under the online headline HE COULD HAVE SEEN WHAT WAS COMING: BEHIND TRUMP'S FAILURE ON THE VIRUS, and, instead of rebutting it on the merits, set out to retaliate in a unique way. The next day, at the coronavirus task force's briefing, Trump played a video assembled by social media director Dan Scavino's team showing pundits downplaying the virus's threat and then others praising the administration's response to it. At one point, the video featured my voice, from an appearance on a **Times** podcast, **The Daily,** in which I discussed the decision to limit travel from China. In the clip, I said that the partial travel ban was probably effective. But someone had edited out my observation that Trump had treated it as his "Mission Accomplished" moment and chose not to do much else. Trump was pleased with himself as he aired the clip in the briefing room, the Cheshire Cat grin reappearing as it played.

Five days later, my article on Meadows came out. I included the crying anecdote; a chief of staff tearing up in front of aides was objectively worth reporting. Meadows tormented Henning over it, blaming her for the publication of a story she had played no role in putting out. She was cut from communications staff meetings and blocked from moving into new positions within the West Wing.

Trump, meanwhile, was embarrassed by what he saw as a revelation of vulnerability, one that could reflect badly on his own choices. Trump complained about me in Oval Office meetings regularly over the following week. In the briefing room a short time later, Trump devoted two minutes to attacking me, seemingly out of nowhere, during remarks that were ostensibly about the coronavirus. He transitioned from complaints that he was not getting enough credit for expediting medical equipment to excoriating me as a "terrible, dishonest reporter."

"Because we exposed her as being a bad reporter, what happened is she came out and said Mark Meadows was crying," he said. "And they made it sound—I said, 'Mark'—and it's okay if he did. I wouldn't—you know, look. But I think he was crying probably—really, for the wrong reason they had it down. But he's not a crier. And if he was—I know criers. I could tell you people that you know that are very famous. They cry, and that's okay too."

Trump was by then turning the briefings, which sometimes lasted more than two hours, into small versions of his rallies, with free-flowing attacks and stream of consciousness venting that often had little to do with the virus. Aides who had suggested he participate in the briefings now encouraged him to pull back, or at least to defer to the doctors at the start of the event. It worked for a time. "That was so much easier!" Trump said after a briefing where he only spoke for a few minutes. "It's hard to be up there for ninety minutes—go onstage for ninety minutes, that's like Broadway!"

Trump had given up on the medical and science experts with whom he shared the daily stage. Despite initially praising Dr. Deborah Birx's "elegance"—he was captivated by her collection of silk neck scarves, and some noticed that, from certain angles, she resembled

Trump's mother later in life—he stopped heeding her advice. Trump had never entirely trusted Fauci, but after Fauci changed his guidance on wearing face masks, Trump complained about him too. Once conservatives made the infectious-disease specialist into an avatar of what they saw as a heavy-handed government response, Trump followed his political base, even promoting a social media post with the hashtag "fire Fauci" as if he were a bystander to it all. (As director of the National Institute of Allergy and Infectious Diseases, Fauci was a civil-service employee theoretically insulated from politically motivated removal.)

Trump's aides tried to buffer him from criticism that he had been downplaying the virus, shifting blame to those who'd briefed him about it. When news reports began zeroing in on exactly when Trump was first briefed about the coronavirus, and the fact that he'd known of its threat for weeks before his address to the nation, and had described it as "like the flu," officials suggested to reporters that it had been others who'd given Trump less-than-dramatic warnings. The implication was that Sanner, his intelligence briefer, had downplayed the virus. Sanner had told Trump the virus was deadly among older people and the immunocompromised, and she confronted Trump, reminding him she'd told him there were ways in which it would be acute. "I would have remembered if you said elderly," Trump replied curtly. Sanner reminded him she took notes of what she told him and that what she'd said was in them.

Behind the scenes, Kushner, who told friends he was now in charge of most aspects of the pandemic response, set up what was essentially a shadow task force. Staffed largely by private-sector employees operating outside traditional government channels, Kushner's team started emailing political appointees at various agencies, directing them to look for ways to "unfuck" the supply chain on specific alternative therapeutics Trump was touting. Some officials elsewhere within the government credited Kushner with helping to expedite medical ventilators in some cases. For the most part, however, his group of outsiders had no experience with federal procurement rules and relied on personal relationships in a way that created an unnecessary muddle in the government's operations.

On camera, Trump could not resist trying to one-up and undermine his own specialists. After a top Homeland Security science adviser presented research revealing the virus to be vulnerable to higher temperatures, Trump mused aloud about potential applications of this finding. "So supposing we hit the body with a tremendous—whether it's ultraviolet or just a very powerful light—and I think you said that hasn't been checked because of the testing," Trump said, before looking off to the side of the room where his doctors typically sat while he spoke, apparently in search of affirmation. "And then I said, supposing you brought the light inside the body, which you can do either through the skin or some other way, and I think you said you're going to test that too." And then,

"I see the disinfectant that knocks it out in a minute, one minute. And is there a way we can do something like that by injection inside or almost a cleaning? Because you see, it gets in the lungs, and it does a tremendous number on the lungs, so it would be interesting to check that."

Trump searched for a quick virus remedy, from anyone who could get through to him. After billionaire tech entrepreneur Larry Ellison and the Fox News host Laura Ingraham evangelized to him about the supposed efficacy of the malaria drug hydroxychloroquine as an alternative therapeutic to prevent the virus, Trump began to endorse its use. "Look, it may work and it may not work," Trump told reporters, relying on Norman Vincent Peale's power-of-positive-thinking method to combat the novel virus. "And I agree with the doctor, what he said: It may work, it may not work. I feel good about it. That's all it is. Just a feeling. You know, I'm a smart guy. I feel good about it."

Members of Trump's party watched these daily performances with apprehension. Polling conducted by the Republican National Committee showed the coronavirus was voters' top concern, and that they did not believe Trump was leading on it. Republicans believed he was hurting not only himself, but potentially all the party's other candidates and officeholders as well. Yet Trump seemed to view the virus as a different kind of threat. Over and over again he asked visitors and callers to the Oval Office and White

House residence the same rhetorical question: "Can you believe this is happening to me?"

Unlike other human tragedies he observed only from a distant remove, the early stages of the pandemic became real for Trump because they struck the place he knew best. From late March through most of the spring, New York was the epicenter of the American outbreak, streets filled with ambulances and overrun hospitals short on beds and ventilators, a precursor of what would eventually touch nearly every corner of the country. The particular sights relayed by television and newspaper images in the city where he was born were painfully recognizable: bodies piled up in a refrigerated truck outside the Elmhurst Hospital Center, a fifteen-minute drive from where he had grown up in Queens. One of Trump's peers in the local real estate industry, an investor named Stanley Chera, fell ill from the virus and was hospitalized in New York; Trump checked in with his family repeatedly.

The attention on New York cast a spotlight on the state's third-term governor, Andrew Cuomo, with whom Trump had first crossed paths decades earlier as scions of emerging Queens-based dynasties who learned how to be useful to the other's ambitions. Now as they navigated the same crisis as executives, and as Cuomo sat in one of the country's media capitals, their leadership was being regularly compared. Cuomo's daily briefings, also carried live on national television, were praised in part because of their contrast with Trump's; they were empathetic, data rich, grave, warning of thousands of deaths to come. "Don't make such a big deal out of this," Trump said of the pandemic in one March conversation with Cuomo. "You're gonna make it a problem." "You don't understand. I'm not making it a problem," Cuomo replied, saying there were sirens all night long. Trump told him, "That's just you. It's just New York, it's not the rest of the country."

Nevertheless, the two men began speaking somewhat regularly, Trump seeming drawn to Cuomo, a familiar presence from his past as much as someone who was in the news himself. At times, Trump could be solicitous, as when he called Cuomo to laud the television ratings that his briefings received. "Everybody's watching it. Melania's watching it!" Trump said, calling out to his wife nearby: "It's your boyfriend, come say hello, he's on the phone." Trump appeared to envision their briefings as dueling versions of **The Apprentice**—Cuomo would go in the morning, and then Trump would go at night.

But as Cuomo got more attention and fawning coverage, Trump began to see the governor as a potential threat. Friends such as Fox News anchor Sean Hannity were whispering in his ear that a famous name like Michelle Obama would become the Democratic nominee for president; some Republicans were convinced that the presumptive nominee, Joe Biden, was too addled to survive the year and that Democrats would come to see they had to replace him. (Biden and Trump spoke briefly at the beginning of April, at Biden's initiation, to discuss the pandemic. Despite mocking Biden's mental acuity for months, Trump told advisers he did not detect anything odd during the phone call.) Trump and Hannity, who followed Democratic Party politics only through news coverage and understood little about its internal dynamics, treated the scenario of Biden being replaced as a certainty. Trump was so convinced that Biden would be dumped from the ticket that he made aides delay advertising spending attacking him.

Trump asked Cuomo about these rumors and claimed Hannity had mentioned the governor as a possible substitute for Biden. Cuomo, who had a long relationship with the presumptive nominee, told Trump that Biden was not "weak," as Trump claimed, and regardless did not plan on running for president himself. When the **New York Post** published a poll, conducted by Trump's close allies at the Club for Growth, showing Democratic voters preferred Cuomo to Biden, Trump called the governor about it. "I told you that they were gonna move Biden aside and run you and you denied it," Trump said. "I denied it because it's not true," Cuomo responded. "That's bullshit," Trump said. "You're going to say, 'The Democrats made me do it.'" Trump went on, "Hannity says he knows it for a fact."

Trump had been in Washington for more than three years. But he had never really left New York.

• • •

To the extent that Trump was interested in dramatic, high-profile moves to confront the pandemic, they all seemed tied up with the challenge of winning reelection against what appeared to be increasingly steep odds.

One idea came from his new chief of staff, who otherwise had been a coronavirus skeptic, in both medical and political terms. Meadows eschewed mask wearing inside the White House and considered Purell hand sanitizer the only necessary protection. He held meetings related to the virus that Pence was not part of, mocked the public health experts as clueless, and endorsed a view taking hold in the West Wing that it was primarily spreading in large cities in Democratic-leaning states, with an implicit suggestion that it was less urgent for Republican governors and a Republican administration. But Kushner's shadow task force took on increased responsibility.

Kushner was also forging ahead with an ambitious plan to normalize relations between Israel and the UAE and Bahrain, known as the "Abraham Accords." Efforts to move forward with a broader peace deal had not succeeded, so Kushner pushed on other fronts. Advocates eventually viewed the accords as a significant achievement, bringing change to the Middle East and refocusing alliances against the threat presented by Iran. (Kushner was aided on the effort by some of O'Brien's National Security Council staff; Kushner would spend the final year of Trump's term enlisting various aides, including Meadows, to press people at the CIA about his lack of a security clearance from them, asking some colleagues to write letters to the CIA director on his behalf.)

As Kushner flexed muscle and found success, Meadows found himself in competition to show that he, too, could put together deals to please the president. The White House and drug manufacturers were coming close to a deal to lower drug prices, when Meadows pushed to include millions of cash cards for prescription drugs to American households. It helped sink the drug-pricing deal; the entire pitch seemed, to pharmaceutical executives who were approached about it, like a mechanism to send a Trump-branded card to voters' homes before Election Day.

In May, Trump announced his own audacious plan, called Operation Warp Speed, in which the administration would spend heavily to back private efforts to develop a coronavirus vaccine. Trump had long been disdainful of the pharmaceutical industry, a target of negativity among older voters in his political base. (Drug companies were "getting away with murder," he said in 2017.) And much of his response to the pandemic had relied on shifting responsibility elsewhere, especially onto state and local governments. But Operation Warp Speed placed money directly into the hands of pharmaceutical companies and plainly put the White House on the line for their ability to help deliver a vaccine. "We're looking to get it by the end of the year if we can, maybe be-fore," Trump said when the project was unveiled in May. Administration officials were later blunt that the timeframe was tethered to Trump's campaign calendar. Kushner helped clear logistical obstacles at the White House—declaring grandly that he was in charge of developing the vaccine—and the effort was more impactful in terms of distribution than devel-opment. Nonetheless, despite criticism that it was an unrealistic timeframe, it turned out to be one of the most consequential decisions of his presidency.

CHAPTER 29

Divide and Conquer

Bill Barr went to see Donald Trump to tell the president he was harming himself. He was not the only one in the top echelons of Trump's government to believe so. By the spring of 2020, it had become clear to many of his top advisers that Trump's impulse to undermine existing systems and bend institutions to suit his purposes was accompanied by erratic behavior and levels of anger requiring others to try to keep him on track nearly every hour of the day.

Unlike many in the administration, Trump's attorney general was willing to confront, even argue with him. Unimaginable human and economic pain had arrived on Trump's watch, but instead of accepting the crisis as an opportunity to look authoritative and in control—a cold political calculation that any number of politicians had made over the years—he had been unwilling to modulate his own conduct. Barr warned Trump that he was now on course to lose the election. "Look, in 2016, the electorate was more fluid," Barr explained. "So there were people who were going to break for you at the end. That's not going to happen this time." Barr warned Trump that he could still affect the outcome, but he could not wait to do so. "Because you could change the last three weeks and people would listen to you, but now everyone knows who you are," Barr said. "And it's going to take a longer time to persuade people that you're not an asshole."

Unlike other times when he didn't want to hear what someone had to say and he simply talked through the meeting, Trump sat quietly and listened. When he replied, it was to emphasize the importance of his bedrock supporters to him. "They want a fighter," Trump said. Barr pointed out the irony that by listening to Washington players who told him they understood what his base wanted, Trump had become captive to the type of establishment thinking he abhorred. The base didn't care about the wrongs that have been done to you, said Barr, who told Trump that he often encountered die-hard Trump supporters and that without fail they asked him if he could get the president to dial down his behavior. Instead of constant "counterpunching," Barr said, Trump should turn on the charm of which he was capable. "People are tired of the fucking drama," Barr said.

In the final week of May, a forty-six-year-old Black man named George Floyd was arrested after an employee at a Minneapolis convenience store called police to say he had paid for cigarettes with a counterfeit twenty-dollar bill. Within minutes, officers had pinned Floyd to the ground, one kneeling on his neck. A young woman standing nearby recorded the encounter on her phone. Her footage captured the moment when Floyd fell lifeless, contradicting the official, sanitized police report about the incident.

When the video was broadcast on cable-news channels, Trump told his aides that what had happened was horrible. He appeared genuinely outraged, and told Barr to do everything he could to bring justice in the case. As was often the case with Trump, he found sympathy for individuals, such as Floyd, whom he otherwise categorized by general and often unflattering stereotypes. But that would have no bearing on how he saw the protesters loosely affiliated with the Black Lives Matter movement who gathered in Minneapolis, and eventually cities nationwide.

Early on the morning of May 29, the street protests had days earlier turned violent outside, and fires had started burning through the police station that was home to the officers responsible for Floyd's death. Trump was watching television in the residence, and his immediate impulse was to respond on Twitter. "These THUGS are dishonoring the memory of George Floyd, and I won't let that happen," he wrote. "Just spoke to Governor Tim Walz and told him that the Military is with him all the way. Any difficulty and we will assume control but, when the looting starts, the shooting starts. Thank you!"

The startling line about the looting and the shooting had a racist history. It was first spoken in 1967 by

Miami police chief Walter Headley at a press conference after a crime wave. (Headley said that his department did not "mind" being accused of brutality.) Alabama's segregationist governor George Wallace, running for president the next year, told an interviewer he would echo Headley's guidance on "shooting." The phrase was so blatant in its racist roots and live provocation to reckless cruelty that it was difficult for White House staff to spin it away. Meadows, the first person to speak to Trump about it that morning when the workday began, tried to explain why his post was so inflammatory, and thus unhelpful in an already combustible moment. Trump protested that there was nothing wrong with a phrase he told aides he had heard first from Frank Rizzo.

The tweet was a test for Twitter executives who had struggled for years with what to do with a presidential account that often violated the rules on extreme speech enforced on other users. They finally settled on affixing a warning label on the tweet, saying that it was glorifying violence. Trump initially wanted to fight against the Twitter label, but advisers convinced him that such conflict was more likely to draw unhelpful attention to the controversy. Rather, Trump aides suggested he call Floyd's family. Trump, with a handful of aides and advisers in the room, told Philonise Floyd that what had happened to his brother should never have occurred. "Mr. President, Black lives matter," Floyd responded. They absolutely do, Trump replied; his brother's life had mattered. In an interview that weekend Philonise Floyd compared that exchange unfavorably to one he had had with Trump's opponent, Vice President Joe Biden. "The vice president, I loved his conversation. He talked to me for like ten, fifteen minutes. And I was trying to talk his ear off because he was talking to me constantly. Great conversation. But Trump, it lasted probably two minutes," Floyd told CNN. "It was very brief. The conversation was okay with him. I was just respecting him, you know, listening to what he had to say."

Hours later, Black Lives Matter protesters pierced a barricade outside the Treasury Department, next door to the White House on Pennsylvania Avenue. Screens around the West Wing turned red, with the security code WHINRED indicating the president needed to be moved to safety. Secret Service agents hustled Trump downstairs to the Presidential Emergency Operations Center below the East Wing, where he was met by the first lady and their son, Barron. Eventually that evening, the threat passed, and the First Family returned upstairs. But it portended a stormy few days to come.

The next day, Trump traveled to Florida for the launch of a privately owned spacecraft at Cape Canaveral. The grandiosity of space travel captivated Trump's imagination, and the development of Space Force as the sixth service branch of the American military was among his proudest achievements, but the president—still cranky after the protests in Washington—was not in the mood for the trip. Aides, still worried about the repercussions of the "shooting" post, encouraged him to read a public statement disclosing that he had spoken with Floyd's family to express his "horror, anger and grief." Trump resisted any statement he thought would glorify George Floyd, who press reports disclosed had a criminal record. "I don't want to praise him as a good guy," he said. "This guy was a crook."

He settled with aides on a statement that described Floyd's death as a "grave tragedy" while also condemning the protests that had grown violent. Trump was angry when the statement he read at the Kennedy Space Center received little attention from the media. "They're all still saying I didn't say something," he complained afterward. "I said it, I'm not saying it again." Floyd's death had opened up a broader national conversation about racial discrimination, and White House staff discussed other possibilities for showing Trump was engaged in it. Jared Kushner floated having Kanye West lead a healing church service on the South Lawn; Meadows retorted that Trump's own supporters did not like the rapper. So nothing happened. Trump reverted to his initial position toward those protesting police brutality. Much as he had done after events in Charlottesville nearly three years earlier, he dug in.

That Sunday, cities nationwide were filled with protests, in many cases the first mass gatherings of any kind since the start of the pandemic. In Washington, crowds surged into areas surrounding Lafayette Square in front of the White House, their peaceful daytime protests turning menacing at night. Late on Sunday, rioters set fire to a basement area of St. John's Episcopal Church, the historic congregation where incoming presidents had traditionally prayed on the morning of their inauguration. No one was hurt by the fire, and the property damage was minimal, but Trump was incensed by the imagery he saw on television of Lafayette Square and beyond. Violent protests had left dozens of officers injured, but "you wouldn't know to turn on the television," Trump said to Barr, complaining about the lack of coverage. U.S. Park Police began working on a plan to expand the White House's security perimeter, to keep protesters farther away.

Trump began the next morning, June 1, with a call with Vladimir Putin, then met in the Oval Office with Pence alongside Barr, Esper, and staff sitting on the couches in the center of the room. Trump had, for years, talked about sending active-duty troops to the southern border. But this time, he wanted to deploy active-duty troops into the streets of his own country, using the Insurrection Act to make it happen. As he talked, Trump's anger escalated. The country looked "weak," Trump said. "How do you think this makes us look to other countries?"

It was not the only outrage on his mind. The previous afternoon, my colleague Peter Baker and I had reported on the incident a few nights earlier when Trump was taken to the White House's underground security bunker. Trump felt humiliated by a disclosure that he thought made him appear incapacitated by street protests. (In other meetings with aides, Trump demanded to know, "Who leaked that story?" He proposed that the person responsible be "executed," a statement in line with his repeated calls for critics and the media to be investigated or declarations they were guilty of "treason." His visit to the bunker was "really a tour" rather than a trip made out of fear, he tried to convince people he spoke with in the days after our story. Yet he was so angry about our story that when, weeks later, Secret Service agents hustled him away from the briefing room podium because of an active shooter near the White House, he told aides, "If you put a gun to my head, I'm not going back to that fucking bunker.")

Trump channeled that fury back at the protests, wanting to see ten thousand active-duty troops on the streets. Pence was mostly silent as Trump's cabinet members worked in tandem to talk an increasingly irrational president down. Trump wanted a show of force, and was refusing to move off it. Barr suggested that he could move in enough law enforcement to manage the situation, while Defense Secretary Mark Esper talked about the capabilities of the District of Columbia National Guard, in which he had once served. But Trump was only growing angrier, rising out of his chair and falling back into it. "You are all fucking losers!" Trump screamed, including Pence in his deliberative diatribe, peering at the vice president at one point as he yelled. Trump's bursts of anger were familiar, but this time, his fury and irrationality were beyond what most in the room had seen, Esper later recalled. He asked about the protesters, "Can't you just shoot them? Just shoot them in the legs or something?"

Trump turned to Mark Milley, the chairman of the Joint Chiefs of Staff. "I want you to be in charge of this, General," Trump said. Milley, sounding taken aback, said, "I don't command troops." Esper offered up an alternative, trying to appear to give something up without submitting to Trump's demands: he would bring in active-duty military police. Barr, less concerned than the other cabinet officials that Trump was on the verge of issuing a directive to deploy active-duty troops into the streets, volunteered that from various parts of the federal government, including U.S. Marshals and Park Police, he could muster five thousand more law-enforcement officers. Trump told Barr that he was putting him in charge.

Trump then brought Esper, Milley, and Barr with him as he went to the Situation Room to join a weekly call about the coronavirus response with the nation's governors, on which Pence typically represented the administration. Trump declared, incorrectly, that he had just put Milley in charge of efforts to contain the protesters and told the governors of protests in their states, "You have to dominate. If you don't dominate, you're wasting your time. They're going to run over you. You're going to look like a bunch of jerks. You have to dominate." Esper described the nation as a "battle space" in need of being controlled, a phrase that was common at the Pentagon; Esper realized a short time later it was an error to use it in that moment, but he and Milley had been deeply alarmed by how Trump was behaving. It colored much that followed.

Illinois governor J. B. Pritzker, a Democrat, told Trump that he needed to change the way he spoke about the protests. "It's been inflammatory, and it's not okay for that officer to choke George Floyd to death but we have to call for calm. We have to have police reform called for. We've called out our National Guard and our State Police, but the rhetoric that's coming out of the White House is making it worse," Pritzker said. Trump shot back, "Okay, well thank you very much, J.B. I don't like your rhetoric very much either because I watched your response to coronavirus, and I don't like your rhetoric, either. I think you could have done a much better job, frankly."

Back in the Oval Office, Trump heard a range of ideas from formal and informal advisers. He discussed options with Jenna Ellis, a lawyer whom Trump had sought out after seeing her television commentary, including whether to federalize the National Guard. It was an idea that some of the other lawyers he spoke with considered unwise. Still, aides to the White House counsel and staff secretary worked on a draft of an order applying the Insurrection Act in Washington alone, in case the city's mayor did not take additional actions.

Ivanka Trump had her own suggestion: Trump should visit the church whose basement was set on fire a day earlier. A plan began to form for Trump to give a speech in the Rose Garden about what had taken place there, before walking through Lafayette Park to St. John's. Hope Hicks, a Trump adviser, arrived at the White House later in the day; Trump told others to fill Hicks in on Ivanka's idea about the church. Hicks suggested that Trump bring a Bible with him and read from it outside the church; a few passages of scripture were printed out and given to him so he could choose one. Someone recommended finding a "pretty Bible" for the occasion, and Ivanka picked out one from a batch brought to the Oval Office.

"We cannot allow the righteous prize and peaceful protesters to be drowned out by an angry mob," Trump said in the Rose Garden, where the sounds of those protests being broken up nearby could be heard. "I am your president of law and order and an ally of all peaceful protesters." What was happening, he went on, were "not acts of peaceful protest. These are acts of domestic terror."

Suddenly, cabinet officials and White House staff were being lined up to walk out the north side entrance of the White House; they were told Trump wanted them to join him looking at the damage outside. It was a motley group, including both the country's highest-ranking military officer in combat fatigues and the young aide who helped Trump set the playlist of songs for his campaign rallies. It was notable for who was missing: Pence did not join the president. His aides had concluded that whatever was being planned for the church was likely not well thought out. Milley and Esper walked out of the White House alongside Trump, but Esper quickly realized that they had been "duped" into something. Milley pulled away en route, telling an aide "this is fucked up" as he did. When Trump arrived at the yellow church with its boarded-up doors, Ivanka Trump took a Bible from her purse and handed it to him. Rather than opening it and reading scripture, as Hicks had imagined, Trump took the book in his right hand and thrust it aloft, his face grimly closed.

As he led his retinue back to the White House, Trump left an even bigger mess behind. A short-handed Park Police had not attempted to move back the perimeter earlier in the day, as discussed Sunday night, and law enforcement had initiated a belated and belligerent effort to shove protesters away just before Trump arrived. Journalists were caught up in the melee. Trump's most slavish acolytes, who had initially celebrated the church photo op—a few called it "iconic"—were oblivious to how it looked on television, as unarmed protesters were shoved by police in riot gear. It became clear by the next morning that Trump's photo op had gone awry.

Esper and Milley were incensed to have been used

as props in what was clearly a political portrayal of Trump against the protesters. Both drafted memos the following day, on June 2, choreographed for when they'd be released; together, they underscored an oath to the Constitution, the military remaining apolitical, and the right to freedom of speech. Esper scheduled a press conference for June 3, aimed at quelling concerns that the White House was politicizing the military and trying to calm a storm that he feared Trump was stirring across the country; he said that he did not believe that troops should be used against Americans. Trump was furious at Esper's remarks and called him to the Oval Office a short time after the press conference to berate him; he and Milley walked in to find a room filled with people averting their gazes. "You betrayed me," Trump screamed at Esper. "I'm the president, not you!" He told Esper that he'd taken away "my authority," somehow suggesting that it was Esper's doing that he couldn't invoke the Insurrection Act. He accused Esper of making statements the secretary had never made; Esper plopped his remarks down on the Resolute Desk in front of Trump in response.

Esper had not directly criticized the commander in chief, but his predecessor, Jim Mattis, finally delivered the rebuke of Trump he had held in for years. "Donald Trump is the first president in my lifetime who does not try to unite the American people—does not even pretend to try. Instead, he tries to divide us," Mattis told the **Atlantic**'s Jeffrey Goldberg, before invoking "the Nazi slogan for destroying us . . . 'Divide and Conquer.'

"We are witnessing the consequences of three years of this deliberate effort," Mattis went on. "We are witnessing the consequences of three years without mature leadership. We can unite without him, drawing on the strengths inherent in our civil society."

The Black Lives Matter protests continued through the summer in major cities such as New York and Chicago, at times devolving into violence that evoked the image of "American carnage" Trump had spoken of during his inaugural address. In some cases, fires were set and storefront windows smashed, with the most sustained chaos in Portland, Oregon. There, a specific group of agitators targeted the federal courthouse day after day in a rolling protest that began as activism against police brutality during daylight hours and was overtaken by people smashing windows and hurling objects at night. Trump was enraged by all of it, and by Portland in particular, where he spent the summer exhorting his cabinet to mobilize a military response. "To do what?" Barr would ask Trump, envisioning a scenario like the worst of the Vietnam War–era protests where military police stood as objects were hurled at them. (Trump's frustrations with the Justice Department would deepen when it became clear that the review by prosecutor

John Durham into the origins of the Russia investigation would not arrive before the election.)

Aide Stephen Miller continued to goad Trump toward using military force, declaring, "Mr. President, they're burning the country down." And so nearly a dozen times that summer, Barr was called over to the White House, sometimes with Esper and Milley joining him, to discuss Trump's demand for a military presence. To Trump's cabinet officials, Miller was an agitator who was making a fraught situation worse. "You don't know what the fuck you're talking about," Barr snapped at Miller during one of those exchanges. Milley and Esper shared the frustration with Miller; after one meeting, Milley expressed regret to Esper about not pushing back more forcefully. "I should have told him to shut the fuck up," Milley said, a person close to Esper recalled later.

Trump had been critical of Black Lives Matter protests since his first presidential campaign, but now, facing a more challenging opponent given his preference for polarizing politics—Biden, an older white man who'd spent a career as a centrist in the Senate, was harder to caricature as a puppet of the far left—Trump saw new value in protesters as an election-year foil. Over the course of three months, he posted dozens of times to social media about unrest in Portland and elsewhere. "The Radical Left Democrats, who totally control Biden, will destroy our Country as we know it," he wrote in one. "Unimaginably bad things would happen to America. Look at Portland, where the pols are just fine with 50 days of anarchy. We sent in help. Look at New York, Chicago, Philadelphia. NO!"

The fallout from Floyd's killing helped inspire Trump to bring back to the fore the type of racial politics he had learned in 1970s and '80s New York. Trump, who repeatedly worried to aides that his criminal justice reform bill would hurt him with his white working-class base, became vocal in defending people who believed in the Confederate flag. In late July, Trump's aides became convinced it would be useful to make an aggressive effort to dismantle a rule implemented by his predecessor requiring communities to demonstrate they were providing equal access to housing as a condition for receiving certain federal funds. Conservatives had been critical of the measure as needless bureaucracy, but few if any treated it as the urgent threat that Trump did.

The Department of Housing and Urban Development, led by Trump's former campaign nemesis Ben Carson, had already suspended the rule. Trump's lone Black cabinet official, Carson had been embroiled in controversy from the start of the term over expensive furniture that had been ordered for his government office. "I can't fire him," Trump explained to one conservative ally at the time, adding, "You know why." (When he was introduced to a Mitch McConnell favorite, Daniel Cameron, running to be the first Black attorney general of Kentucky, one of Trump's first questions concerned a rapper whose release from a Swedish jail the White House had just helped to secure. "Daniel, **you've** obviously heard what we've been doing with A$AP Rocky," he began.) As he campaigned for reelection, Trump ended the HUD rule entirely.

Depiction of suburbs under siege became a staple of Trump's campaign stump speeches. Some of his advisers in the White House were open in conversations that they were in search of a wedge issue to try to rescue Trump's standing in the suburbs, and that they believed this could be it. "You know the suburbs, people fight all of their lives to get into the suburbs and have a beautiful home," Trump said in Midland, Texas. "There will be no more low-income housing forced into the suburbs." On Twitter, Trump had warned the "Suburban Housewives of America" that Biden "will destroy your neighborhood" and the "American Dream."

The rule in question had been based on the Fair Housing Act, the landmark civil rights law under which Trump and his father had been sued by the Justice Department in 1973. Back then, Trump told reporters that signing a consent decree would force him to accept welfare recipients in his buildings. The specifics had changed, but, nearly a half century later in America, many of Trump's views had not.

CHAPTER 30

Tulsa

G uests voluntarily assume all risks."
That was the disclaimer issued to people who signed up for a free ticket to see Donald Trump at a rally in Tulsa, Oklahoma, a warning that had not been necessary when he held a similar rally almost exactly a year earlier in Orlando to kick off his re-election campaign. Even without a serious primary challenger (Trump's deputy campaign manager, Bill Stepien, had worked for months to stave one off), Trump began to maintain a regular schedule of rallies, up to three in a single week in late February. But the start of the pandemic the following month put an end to the large-scale events that had been Trump's favorite part of being a candidate.

Democrats had taken an even harder line, canceling not only big public gatherings such as rallies but nearly all in-person campaigning. At first Kellyanne Conway reassured Trump that these conditions would help him, because his opponent, Joe Biden—who did not make a campaign stop outside his Delaware home for two and a half months—was largely invisible while the president could dominate news from the White House. But with time, Conway reversed her view. She told Trump that the dynamics were in fact hurting him. Without having to be in public all the time, Biden was able to control his message and keep the spotlight trained on Trump's disjointed coronavirus briefings.

As the pandemic wore on, Trump consistently lagged Biden, only briefly rising above 45 percent in poll averages during the early pandemic weeks before he began participating in daily coronavirus task-force briefings. (At no point during Trump's presidency did a majority of Americans approve of the job he was doing, although he came closest in March 2020, when the pandemic was in its early stages, according to Gallup.) When Trump saw internal campaign surveys that showed him trailing his Democratic challenger, he erupted at campaign manager Brad Parscale. "I'm not fucking losing to Joe Biden!" he screamed, threatening to sue Parscale, although for exactly what was unclear.

Trump was an avid consumer of public and private polling, although he was not a straightforward believer in its findings and searched for the data set that would back his preexisting view. Instead of having a consistent message or strategy, Trump and some of his outside advisers perpetually searched for the kind of single-note issue that Trump believed helped him win in 2016. Always hunting for someone who would tell him what he wanted to hear and questioning what his actual staff said, Trump quietly had polling data

shared with Dick Morris, a veteran political consultant to members of both parties who was a longtime
Trump family acquaintance; Morris began recommending questions to test for the elusive issue Trump
sought to use in the campaign. It was not immediately clear to others on the campaign who was recommending the questions or where they were coming
from. Sean Hannity, who told the president not only
that Biden could be replaced on the Democratic ticket
with Andrew Cuomo, but former first lady Michelle
Obama as well, told Trump aides he did not trust
the polling he was seeing and would commission his
own. Kushner, who oversaw reelection strategy from
his post as a White House senior adviser, advised a
different campaign pollster, Tony Fabrizio, to inflate
Trump's standing in surveys that would be shown to
the candidate by adding percentage points to his position in the horse race. The ostensible reason was his
claim that the scientific polls always missed Trump
voters, but campaign officials suspected the real reason was to avoid upsetting Trump (when I reported
on internal campaign polling that showed Trump
struggling and that Parscale had talked about to a
number of people in 2019, Trump was livid. Parscale
responded by tightening the circle of who received
the data, keeping top campaign aides in the dark).

By the summer, much of Trump's blame for the
state of his campaign fell not on his own behavior, but on Parscale, who had built a campaign that
raised unprecedented sums from both large and small

donors early in the election calendar but had spent
it at nearly as rapid a clip. Much of that spending
was routed through a limited-liability company that
Parscale and members of the Trump family, among
others, had created, a mechanism for ad spending that obscured where some of the other dollars
ended up. (Lara Trump was not the only one of his
sons' partners being paid. Don Jr.'s girlfriend, Kim
Guilfoyle, had been hired to work on fundraising.
Some donors liked her but others were turned off by
frequent banter during remarks at events about her
private life with Don Jr. At one fundraiser, she offered
a lap dance to whoever gave the most money, and at
congressman Kevin McCarthy's annual donor retreat
in Wyoming, her boyfriend raised eyebrows when he
joked about donors paying to get in a hot tub with
her.) As a result, it was impossible to determine from
public data just how much Parscale was making, but
a British tabloid documented his lifestyle, including a
Ferrari and waterfront Florida home. That story was
handed to Trump by one of Parscale's many detractors. Parscale insisted he was being wrongly maligned
by the implication that he was exploiting his position, that his money had come from other business,
and that members of the Trump family signed off
on all spending decisions. But as the pandemic wore
on, and as Trump blamed everyone else for his problems, Parscale traveled far less frequently to northern Virginia, where the campaign was based, a fact
that angered aides who continued to work out of the

headquarters and added to a sense of dysfunction. Trump did not stop complaining about Parscale personally; the tabloid article offended his anger at the notion anyone was making money on his name without his permission, as Parscale's detractors who gave it to the president hoped it would.

The Republican National Committee decided in July 2018 to place its next convention in North Carolina, a state Trump won comfortably after Barack Obama had succeeded in making it a battleground for the first time in a generation. "Charlotte's booming economy is a prime example of how President Trump's agenda is improving lives," Parscale said in a statement applauding the decision. But by the summer of 2020, Charlotte had become an example of something Trump's team was not inclined to celebrate. City and county governments had been early to declare a state of emergency due to the coronavirus, and North Carolina governor Roy Cooper had implemented statewide restrictions that limited capacity and required face masks be worn in public spaces. Trump insisted that he be renominated before a full, unmasked crowd, and in the late spring, Trump called Cooper to urge that he relax the rules for the convention, dangling a reminder to the governor that the Trump administration had sent the state equipment to fight the pandemic as part of his pitch to get his way. "We can't do social distancing," Trump said.

When Cooper, a Democrat, asked if Trump was not worried that his own supporters could get sick, Trump coldly stated, "No, I'm not because we've learned a lot about" the virus. Shortly thereafter, Trump announced the convention would no longer be held in North Carolina, writing on Twitter that "we are now forced" to look elsewhere.

It was just a day after the Lafayette Square debacle, and Trump was angry about what he considered a double standard: Black Lives Matter protesters were regularly coming together in massive crowds with little interpersonal distancing, with little public criticism, but Republicans were forbidden from doing so. Trump, who saw the disruptions to daily life as a threat to his reelection and who would soon call for schools shuttered during the pandemic to be reopened, wanted to start holding rallies again. Parscale at one point told Trump that he could just hold a rally and call it a "protest." They looked at states with relaxed public-health precautions and politically friendly local leaders. After Florida governor Ron DeSantis quietly waved Republican officials away, because viral case counts were rising in the state, the campaign decided to hold the rally in Tulsa, Oklahoma, a geographically central location that could pull a large crowd of supporters from surrounding red states. They chose the date of June 19.

It was a fateful combination of time and place. Tulsa was the site of a 1921 massacre of Black citizens, an event that, while only sporadically taught in schools, stood as one of the country's bloodiest acts of racist violence. June 19 is the annual holiday of Juneteenth, which commemorates the anniversary of the day in 1865 that slaves in Texas learned they were free after the end of the Civil War and maintains particular salience to African Americans in that state bordering Oklahoma. "I think that's a really bad idea," Ronna McDaniel warned of the scheduling decision, sending articles about the Tulsa massacre to campaign officials. "We're not going to let them control the narrative," said one White House official, among many who vowed they would not be intimidated by "political correctness." Trump began to ask people he encountered if they had ever heard of Juneteenth, including a Black Secret Service agent who said holding the event on that day offended him. Only after the controversy had already made headlines did Trump switch course and agree to push it back by a day.

Parscale was dedicated to making Trump's return to the campaign trail more than just another rally in a sports arena. Spurred on by Trump, Parscale plotted for something akin to a second campaign kickoff, telling Republican National Committee officials that it would take the pressure off them ahead of a full-fledged convention. Parscale made arrangements to build a second, outdoor stage to accommodate overflow attendees, and told colleagues he was working to secure a camera that could shoot an image of the gigantic crowd from space. In social media posts,

Parscale boasted of the number of attendees who had signed up—each clicking the "guests voluntarily assume all risks" disclaimer—as it grew astronomically, hundreds of thousands at a time. The crowd stood to be so large that public-health experts worried it would serve as a "superspreader" event, drawing in participants from far and wide who would bring the virus back to their communities. Privately, some Trump aides voiced worry that the president's expectations for the crowds at his triumphant return were too high.

However, by the time Trump departed for Tulsa, his actions had driven media attention elsewhere. The day before, Justice Department officials had attempted to force the resignation of Geoff Berman, the Manhattan-based federal prosecutor who was believed to be investigating issues that could touch on Trump, including the two Ukrainians whom Rudy Giuliani had leaned on for "dirt" about Hunter Biden. When Berman did not oblige and leave, Bill Barr sent a letter informing Berman that Trump had fired him. ("We're getting rid of him," Trump told one adviser, without specifying why or what the rush was. "It's gotta happen now.") Berman resisted leaving until a temporary replacement he approved of was tapped for the role. On his way out of the White House, Trump faced reporter questions about the second federal prosecutor he had fired from that very office in just over three years. He claimed that he was "not involved" in Berman's removal, and officials insisted that Trump focused on appointing the SEC chair, Jay Clayton, simply because Clayton wanted to return to New York.

But Trump boarded Air Force One with grand ambitions. So many campaign aides and surrogates wanted to be in Tulsa that the campaign had to charter an extra plane to bring them all there. (After seeing a news report that some advance staff at the rally had tested positive for the virus, Trump told aides that the campaign should stop testing staff, lest it reveal more cases.)

And even the excited predictions about attendance didn't alleviate Trump's anxiety. "Why the hell would you go and say one million?" Trump had complained, despite Trump pushing his campaign manager to fan the flames publicly. "You set the expectations way too high."

On board, Trump watched television coverage marveling at how sparse turnout in Tulsa seemed to be. Parscale told others that attendees were delayed because left-wing protesters—who, too, had gathered in Tulsa, to confront Trump—blocked checkpoints at the security perimeter. Parscale told Trump by phone that it "looks like Beirut." But as the presidential motorcade passed through empty streets from the airport it became clear that could not be the only explanation. After surveying the arena, aides delivered the news to Trump: it was mostly empty. Thousands of online tricksters had faked signups to dupe the campaign. And it seemed to have worked. "What do you mean, it's fucking empty?" Trump asked, cursing about Parscale, who was by then telling colleagues he was told to stay away from Trump after being informed he was a close contact of someone who had tested positive. During his speech, Trump complained about testing for the coronavirus, saying that he told his team to "slow down" testing so that there would be fewer cases, a comment his team later wrote off as a joke, but which Trump maintained was serious.

On the way back to Washington, Trump tried to handle the situation gamely, keeping his calm as he joked with staff. To those who knew him, he appeared sad and defeated, able to demonstrate only so much fight. Late that night he stepped off Marine One and walked alone into his borrowed house, a crumpled-up red campaign hat in one hand.

Trump had another campaign stop scheduled in Phoenix a few days later, but beyond that stopped scheduling rallies until just before the Republican convention in late August. In place of rallies Trump insisted on presiding over a major July 4 fireworks show at Mount Rushmore, where such displays had been halted for a decade due to concerns they could set off wildfires in the surrounding Black Hills. As in Oklahoma, South Dakota was led by a friendly Republican governor, Kristi Noem, who enforced no pandemic restrictions on the thousands of attendees, saying they could rely instead on "personal responsibility."

All of Trump's adult children decided to attend; staff thought the extended Trump family seemed struck with the apparent realization that their opportunities to be part of such pageantry, such as the U.K. state visit they all wanted to be part of in 2019, could be gone in a few months. Guilfoyle felt under the weather after arriving in South Dakota. Once she tested positive, she and Don Jr. told people they were going to drive back to the East Coast (and then took a charter plane). They were not the only Trumps whose summer plans were grounded by the pandemic. "Ivanka wants to rent one of those big RVs," Trump mentioned in one meeting about campaign strategy. "This skinny guy wants to do it," he said, gesturing to Kushner. "Can you imagine Jared and his skinny ass camping? It'd be like something out of **Deliverance.**" Trump made noises mimicking the banjo theme song from the 1972 movie about four men vacationing in rural Georgia who are attacked, pursued, and in one case brutally raped by a local resident.

Trump barely mentioned the pandemic in his July 4 speech, sitting on a dais with his wife and advisers, all of whom were without masks. Instead, his speech focused on "cancel culture"—a catchall term for various expressions of moral disapproval, from loud criticism to boycotts and revoked job offers against a range of Trump supporters or critics of aspects of the political left—as examples of a "new far-left fascism" that he maintained was sweeping the country. (He ignored his own repeated calls for people to be fired or jailed, or companies to be boycotted.) Trump had one solution to offer, predictably a new building project that duplicated previous efforts: a National Garden of American Heroes featuring statues of 244 famous historical figures who embodied American greatness. "We will not be tyrannized, we will not be demeaned, and we will not be intimidated by bad, evil people," Trump said, standing beneath the faces of four of his predecessors, including one whose farewell address was filled with warnings against the dangers of partisanship.

Noem sent him home with a bronze sculpture showing Trump's face as the fifth carved onto the mountain, but Trump left disappointed by both the fireworks and his appearance in pictures from the event. He threatened, as he had previously, to fire his lead photographer, whom he often criticized in part because the first lady told him that he looked better in the photos that her official photographer had taken. (A similar overflow of the East Wing's aesthetic priorities was visible when a plastic surgeon treated some White House staffers in the building's medical unit; officials said he had a long-standing relationship with the First Family.)

It was easy, however, for Trump to move on to other worries. On July 5, the **New York Post** ran an article headlined GHISLAINE WILL "NAME NAMES." Days earlier, the socialite-heiress Ghislaine Maxwell had been arrested for her role in a sex-trafficking scandal that had already sent her longtime companion Jeffrey Epstein to federal jail, where he had died nearly a year earlier while awaiting trial. The story, by Page Six editor Emily Smith, quoted an Epstein business associate named Steve Hoffenberg: "Ghislaine thought she was untouchable—that she'd be protected by the intelligence communities she and Jeffrey helped with information: the Israeli intelligence services, and Les Wexner, who has given millions to Israel; by Prince Andrew, President Clinton and even by President Trump, who was well-known to be an acquaintance of her and Epstein's."

Sitting in the Oval Office with his campaign advisers shortly afterward, Trump asked, "You see that article in the **Post** today that mentioned me?" He kept going, to silence. "She say anything about me?"

In an early July meeting with campaign staff, Trump again heard the advice he had dismissed since the coronavirus emerged: change his public behavior, or at least use the crisis in a way that demonstrated some concern for its human impact. He remained unmoved. "I'd rather lose my way than win your way," Trump told aides.

Trump saw himself as a victim of a specific political change prompted by the pandemic. Many states had changed their voting processes to accommodate voters wary of voting in person as the virus continued to spread, adopting policies that would dramatically expand the use of mail ballots (various changes had been enacted beginning in 2019, but they were more aggressive during the coronavirus fallout). Senior Republicans begged Trump to insert some nuance into his statements, given how reliant they were on by-mail voting in certain districts and states. But Trump made no change in his language; a veteran conservative lawyer, Cleta Mitchell, called him at Meadows's suggestion to tell him that his team needed to be doing more to get ready for Election Day. "If they say I lose," Trump said, "it's gonna be because they cheated." At various points, Trump floated the idea of delaying the election, which is held on a date set by statute and would require at least an act of Congress to reschedule. "What? You can't do that," informal adviser Chris Christie challenged him. "Well, we might need to," Trump said. "They stole the first couple years of my administration from me, we might need to delay it. It's not fair what they're doing."

By the end of the summer, Trump was back in touch with Steve Bannon, the former chief strategist who'd left the White House in 2017. Bernie Marcus, the cofounder of Home Depot and an ally of both Trump and Bannon, urged Trump in early summer to move Kushner aside and bring in Bannon. Trump demurred, but it provided another opening for Trump to diminish Parscale, and he struck up a relationship with Bannon again even after Bannon was indicted on allegations he defrauded Trump supporters with an effort to build the border wall. Bannon, who denied the charges, did not come into the campaign, and Kushner remained.

It was Parscale who was pushed out in mid-July and replaced by Bill Stepien, the deputy campaign manager who had worked on the 2016 race and who served as White House political director. (Trump had initially asked Jason Miller to take the job, but he declined.) Trump, at Stepien's urging, brought the Florida strategist Susie Wiles, who had been ousted at DeSantis's behest, back into his political operation. Trump called DeSantis to alert him to the move, and by then did not seem to care that it made the governor livid. Trump made changes to his team after he'd started hearing complaints from his former campaign manager and deputy campaign manager, Corey Lewandowski and David Bossie, that Trump 2020 was, in essence, the Hillary Clinton campaign of 2016 in its sprawl and its difficulty making strategic shifts. Trump told Stepien to reevaluate the campaign's spending, and raised two specific concerns: he did not like that his daughter-in-law and son's girlfriend were being paid by the campaign. Stepien was inheriting a system that had been built over years with Parscale and Ronna McDaniel working closely together. Stepien, whom Trump sought to dominate, and McDaniel did not like or trust each other, and the relationship was toxic. Stepien minimized pollster Tony Fabrizio and brought in a new pollster, and he slashed the campaign's ad spending in the fall based on how online fundraising was performing. McDaniel believed the cuts were too deep and argued that case to Trump directly. Kushner brought in Katie Walsh, the departed Priebus deputy, to help direct the ad spending. Within the campaign, those who had benefited from Parscale's leadership were distrustful of Stepien; those aides said Stepien, often brusque, repeatedly described himself as having to "land the plane," a remark that struck them as premature defeatism.

There had been no shortage of controversies during Parscale's tenure, but ultimately it was the Tulsa rally—an event that Trump had demanded holding—that helped ensure his downfall. "That was the worst goddamn thing I ever saw," Trump interrupted himself to tell Parscale in a meeting before his firing. "I can't believe you did that to me. You should be embarrassed."

Ultimately Donald Trump decided to bring the convention to him. After pulling out of North Carolina, party officials had looked at Florida, another Sun Belt battleground state Trump had carried in 2016 and one that was under Republican leadership and relatively relaxed about public-health restrictions. Trump put out word he was interested in Jacksonville, but encountered resistance from DeSantis, for reasons that Trump advisers came to believe were related to fear of inviting viral spread. Trump eventually conceded that finding a city willing to host anything approaching a traditional, weeklong convention was impossible. Instead, they settled on staging it in Washington, with the bulk of the program at the neoclassical Mellon Auditorium blocks from the White House and showcase speeches on the South Lawn itself. Nine months after being impeached for using the powers of the presidency to advance his reelection, Trump finally dropped any pretense of attempting to separate the two. (Pompeo made arrangements to record a campaign speech from Jerusalem, where he was traveling on government business, a breach of long-standing diplomatic protocol and ethical norms.)

Democrats had their convention the week before, but Trump was distracted by family matters. His remaining brother, Robert, with whom he'd reconciled from their feud during the disastrous Taj Mahal opening before Trump became president, died in a New York hospital following complications after falling; the president visited him in his final days and called into the hospital room as the end was near. Trump, seeming withdrawn and subdued in ways his staff had never observed before, held the funeral at the White House. But he nevertheless saw enough of the Democrats' convention—which they had pulled out of Milwaukee and replaced with a diffuse broadcast production featuring little in-person interaction—to conclude with aides that they could deliver a more elaborate, visually pleasing, and high-octane event. It would highlight what had become, over the course of the pandemic, a core campaign message: that Biden was essentially hiding from the virus and Trump had the endurance to remain president.

Over the course of the week, Trump presided over a surprise naturalization ceremony for five immigrants in the White House's Great Hall and from the Oval Office announced a pardon of Alice Johnson, a sixty-five-year-old woman whose federal drug charges he had previously commuted at the urging of reality-show star turned criminal justice activist Kim Kardashian, who worked through Kushner outside of normal pardon channels, as Kushner was trying to take over a piece of that process, and whose celebrity delighted Trump. On the night Trump accepted the nomination by his party for a second term, hundreds of folding chairs were placed on the White House lawn. Invitees roamed without masks, joyously celebrating and acting as if life were functioning normally, in a way that felt disjointed from one of the most traumatic years in American history. But it reflected the view of a White House that believed its supporters wanted to move on from the pandemic restrictions. Viewers heard from officials who rarely spoke publicly, such as social media director Dan Scavino, in personal video tributes.

The objective was to humanize a politician who resisted being humanized, to project a sense of empathy onto a man notoriously devoid of it. Trump had sought his first term on promises to "drain the swamp." Now he was holding fast to Washington's most visible icons in an increasingly desperate effort to win a second.

CHAPTER 31

Not One of the Diers

On September 22, 2020, one week before Donald Trump and Joe Biden were set to face off in their first presidential debate, the United States surpassed two hundred thousand deaths from the coronavirus. The occasion was marked by somber tributes around the country, but the White House did not join them.

Trump had returned to a regular schedule of rallies, including, by mid-September, indoor venues. Trump was appalled at the sight of masks, snapping at one aide in the middle of a meeting, "Get that fucking thing off." Staff rarely wore them, despite the fact that the White House's own medical experts recommended it and the District of Columbia required it in other surrounding workplaces. When pollster Tony Fabrizio told Trump that public opinion overwhelmingly favored such mandates, he listened. But once chief of staff Mark Meadows joined the conversation in the Oval Office and said that the "base" would revolt against a mask mandate, Trump said he would not support it. He relented to wear a mask in public just a handful of times, and each time it was an ordeal for aides, who later recounted their victorious struggle in the face of Trump's uninterest.

Within Trump, who required a staffer to carry hand sanitizer near him at all times, a deep fear of germs found company with an irrepressible self-destructive streak, eschewing masks and discouraging more extensive social distancing. When in May the aide who served Trump his meals fell ill with the coronavirus, Trump was shocked that someone sick had been so close to the food he ate. But it did not force Trump to rethink his approach to the virus, as a matter of either policy or personal behavior.

Nor did testing positive himself. At some point over the last weekend in September, Trump received a positive result on one of the rapid antigen tests the White House had been using to test staff, according to Mark Meadows. (Trump had initially been receiving such tests daily, but at some point decided he was tired of doing it so frequently and simply stopped with the regular schedule.) Trump proceeded to a campaign rally in Pennsylvania. Meadows claims by the time Trump arrived there, he had turned up negative on a different testing brand, although Meadows's description of the process used ran counter to testing recommendations by Trump's own government. Trump, Meadows later wrote, took that result as "full permission to press on as if nothing had happened." He appeared to believe that germs were something he could catch from someone else, but was oblivious to the notion that he could pass them along to others.

Even at his most carefree when it came to the disease ravaging the country, mortality was not far from Trump's mind. That Saturday, just before what Meadows described as his first positive test, Trump had filled the Rose Garden with senators and other political allies, a jubilant, largely maskless crowd that flowed through the West Wing after, without any real medical safeguards. The occasion was the nomination of Trump's third appointee to the Supreme Court, the young federal appeals judge Amy Coney Barrett. She replaced liberal Ruth Bader Ginsburg, an eighty-seven-year-old who had been in and out of hospitals for much of Trump's term before succumbing to cancer. For weeks, when the subject of Supreme Court justices came up in meetings, Trump would clasp his hands together and look skyward, "Please God. Please watch over her. Every life is precious." Then, almost winking, he would quickly look at his aides and say, "How's she doing?" When another visitor came to the Oval Office, Trump asked, "She gonna make it? How much longer you think she has?"

As soon as they found their seats in the debate hall that Tuesday, members of the Trump family all removed their face masks, in violation of health rules that had been set by physicians at the hosting Cleveland Clinic and Case Western Reserve University, and agreed to by both parties in advance. Standing onstage at a lectern opposite Biden, with twelve feet and eight inches between them to address the threat of transmission, Trump looked sweaty and agitated from the outset. When Biden delivered a criticism of the administration's response to the pandemic, Trump replied, "Did you use the word 'smart'? So you said you went to Delaware State, but you forgot the name of your college. You didn't go to Delaware State. You graduated either the lowest or almost the lowest in your class. Don't ever use the word 'smart' with me. Don't ever use that word. . . . Because you know what? There's nothing smart about you, Joe."

Trump, who believed his performance in the 2016 campaign debates was what led him to victory, had been nominally preparing for this encounter for nearly three months. Chris Christie, after removing his name from consideration to be the chief of staff, had again assumed responsibility for overseeing the practice sessions. Getting Trump to focus was close to impossible. As many sitting presidents have, Trump believed he didn't need the preparations; his day-to-day work was enough. Christie tried to disabuse him of that idea. Standing in as Biden, just as he had for Hillary Clinton four years earlier, he tried to prepare Trump for aggressive questions about everything from the coronavirus to his children. For as long as he could manage, Meadows worked to keep Rudy Giuliani away from the sessions. But Meadows failed to entirely block Giuliani, who worked to shift Trump's attention onto the Biden family's overseas business dealings. Despite the fact that his overzeal-ousness on the matter had already helped lead to the president's impeachment, Giuliani's obsession with the topic had not abated. By the time the first debate was taking place, Giuliani was working with Bannon to find a media outlet willing to publish the contents of a laptop belonging to Hunter Biden that Giuliani would later say Hunter dropped off at a computer store in Delaware and abandoned. When he finally made his way into the debate practice sessions, Giu-liani spun through names of people and business arrangements in which he claimed Biden's son was involved, alongside references to Hunter's drug use.

Giuliani's influence on Trump's inherent dislike of the Bidens became clear onstage. When Biden invoked his deceased son Beau's military service in Iraq, Trump interrupted. "Are you talking Hunter? Are you talking about Hunter?" he heckled Biden. "I don't know Beau. I know Hunter. Hunter got thrown out of the military." It was a twist of the knife about Hunter's history of addiction, delivered with more clarity on the topic than on any of his allegedly cor-rupt business deals. If Trump's decision to focus on opioid addiction early in his term was politically wise, attacking someone's drug habits was not.

Trump badgered Biden, interrupting and insulting him for ninety minutes. Most observers treated the evening as a train wreck for Trump, especially in an exchange after Biden attacked him as welcoming of support from white supremacists. Trump demanded that Biden actually name a group, and Biden volunteered the Proud Boys, a violent right-wing group that had been unabashed in its support for Trump. "Proud Boys, stand back and stand by," Trump replied. "But I'll tell you what, I'll tell you what: somebody's got to do something about Antifa and the left because this is not a right-wing problem. This is a left-wing, this is a left-wing problem." When Biden pointed out that the administration's own FBI director had said the loose cadre of antifascist agitators who embraced the label "Antifa" were not a single organization, Trump said the FBI director was "wrong."

On the flight home, Trump insisted he had done well. It was hard to find many other people aboard Air Force One who agreed with his assessment.

The next night, returning home from a rally in Minnesota, staff were startled by a rare sight. Trump did not spend the flight immersed in television or banter with staff. Instead his aides could see Trump through the partially open door of his cabin, asleep in his chair. Upon arrival back in Washington, Trump had to be roused awake.

The following day, Trump traveled to his New Jersey golf club for a fundraiser, where he walked along a rope line shaking hands, and participated by phone in a so-called "tele-rally" for a congressional candidate with a noticeably congested voice. That night, Bloomberg News reported that Hope Hicks, the notoriously private communications director frequently in physical proximity to Trump, had tested positive for coronavirus. (She had first shown symptoms on the flight from Minnesota, and had isolated from other travelers.) Trump called into Sean Hannity's Fox News show and appeared to suggest that Hicks had become sick from hugging military veterans at a White House event that weekend. He offhandedly mentioned to Hannity that he was now awaiting a result from his own test, and left the impression he believed that if it came back positive it was because he had acquired the virus from Hicks, rather than the other way around. Several hours later, before daybreak on October 2, Trump announced on Twitter that he and the first lady had both tested positive.

The elderly president of the United States was sick with a potentially deadly disease, and few people knew much more than that. A typically chatty White House had gone silent. Kushner, fielding concerned outreach, told people, "We need prayers." But even some in Trump's extended family were not initially told of the severity of Trump's condition.

I eventually learned, while Trump was receiving care, that he'd been put on oxygen, and I reported it, as officials were declining to provide nearly any information. But it took months to piece together some of the basics of what was happening there. Meadows, responding to concern from the White House doctor, called the head of the Food and Drug Administration to ask for permission to use as-yet unapproved monoclonal-antibody treatments for the Trumps. (The first lady, who had gone to Walter Reed two years earlier for a kidney-related issue, declined to take the experimental procedure.) Trump was deeply phobic of hospitals and all things related to illness—it fell into the bucket of "weakness" for him—and his own illness was no exception. While still in the second-floor residence, according to Meadows, Trump was administered the antibodies; when his blood-oxygen levels dropped, Meadows confirmed that Trump was given supplemental oxygen as well. Trump was getting sicker, his breathing increasingly labored. But he rebuffed plans to go to Walter Reed National Military Medical Center, telling one associate who called him, "This is going to be bad imagery going to Walter Reed."

Sean Conley, the Navy doctor who served as Trump's personal physician, made clear there was more medical care he could offer from the military's premier medical campus. Deputy chief of staff of operations Tony Ornato warned the president that if he fell into a more dire situation, procedures to ensure the continuity of government would have to be set into motion. It would be best, staff explained, if Trump walked out to Marine One on his own. Trump eventually relented to the pressure. He got up from his bed, where, according to Meadows, his hair was disheveled and his eyes streaked red, put on a suit, and around 6:15 p.m., went downstairs. He was holding a briefcase, which he dropped by the door, telling

Meadows he couldn't carry it outside. He walked out of the White House for the short helicopter trip to Walter Reed.

Upon his arrival, Trump managed to walk to get treated once in the complex; a battery of tests revealed infiltrates consistent with so-called "Covid pneumonia." Then he took up residence in the facility's presidential suite, where over the weekend he had a meal from McDonald's—a signal to his family and close aides that he was feeling better—and spoke by phone with friends and political allies, much as he would have been happy doing anywhere. But he was processing the reality of his circumstances. "They say I could be one of the diers," he relayed to one associate about what doctors had told him. (Trump had explained to people over the years that he liked fast-food restaurants because they would not know he was coming, something they attributed to his fear of being poisoned.) Meadows, who refused to leave Trump's side, spent the night in another room.

At both the White House and campaign headquarters, aides realized that on Saturday someone would have to address the public about a president who was now not only seriously ill but on a heavy-duty steroid known to cause mood swings. But they also knew that none of the people who had communicated on his behalf on other issues had much credibility with the public. Hicks and Miller, speaking to Conley by phone, urged him not to take questions. Along with the nine other doctors who comprised

Trump's medical team, Conley stood before the Walter Reed complex for the small group of print and television media known as the press pool. Conley seemed slightly nervous. Trump was, as always, watching. Despite the warning, Conley responded to the reporters who engaged with him (Trump aides believed Meadows had contradicted his colleagues and told Conley he should provide answers). "This morning, the president is doing very well," Conley said with a slight smile. Minutes later, he added, "He's got plenty of work to get done from the chief of staff, and he's doing it."

After the doctors had returned inside, Meadows crept over to the gathered reporters and asked to speak anonymously, apparently unaware a camera was capturing the exchange. He set out to correct the overly rosy picture that Conley had painted of the president's health, but he did not want his own name attached to the clarification. A note shortly thereafter went out summarizing Meadows's remarks, identified only as from a "senior administration official," that Trump was not yet out of the woods and that the next twenty-four to forty-eight hours would be critical. Finally someone was talking about how sick he actually was. "Who the fuck said that?" Trump asked when he saw the quote reported. To counteract the dire prognosis from Meadows, Trump decided he needed to be seen, and—despite the fact that he may still have been contagious—arranged for the Secret Service to drive him in an SUV past fans who had gathered outside the hospital complex.

Trump appeared to bounce back quickly on the antibodies treatment, aided by the steroid regimen, and began to focus on his discharge from the hospital. He came up with a plan he told associates was inspired by the singer James Brown, whom he loved watching toss off his cape while onstage, but it was in line with his love of professional wrestling as well: he would be wheeled out of Walter Reed in a chair and, once outdoors, he would dramatically stand up, then open his button-down dress shirt to reveal the Superman logo beneath it. (Trump was so serious about it that he called the campaign headquarters to instruct an aide, Max Miller, to procure the Superman shirts; Miller was sent to a Virginia big-box store.) Trump was talked out of that idea, but upon returning to the White House he insisted on walking up the stairs to the second-floor portico. "They need to see that I'm fully back, I beat this," Trump told aides who discouraged him. When he reached the top of the long, curving stairway, he ripped off his face mask and looked out as cameras captured the moment. He appeared to be gasping for breath.

Once he had recovered, campaign advisers proposed having him record an ad in which he talked about the coronavirus in personal terms. Trump rejected the script; it was too intimate, especially for a man who had a phobia of hospitals and illness. Still, the weekend after he was released, Trump hosted the White House medical team to thank them for their work. The doctors knew exactly how sick Trump had been; without the monoclonal antibody treatment, the administration's health officials believed, Trump may not have survived.

The following week, Trump refused to participate in the second scheduled debate after organizers—responding to his positive diagnosis and uncertainty about how long he would remain contagious—announced plans to conduct it remotely. By the time of the final debate, on October 22, Trump's campaign had shifted almost entirely to a focus on Biden's son. "Where's Hunter?" he asked at rallies. Trump had never laid out an agenda for a second term and struggled to focus on what he had actually accomplished. He still hoped to have a vaccine developed before Election Day, but time was running out.

Despite the chaos that others felt emanating from the White House, Trump operated as if his reelection was not in doubt. Throughout the year, he had amplified social media posts from accounts connected to a conspiracy theory known as QAnon that was popular among his backers, and in the final days of the campaign wrote what read like praise for supporters accused of trying to run a Biden campaign bus off the road in Texas. He was preparing to shape Election Day his way, telling aides weeks beforehand that he would go to the podium that night and say he won even if votes were still being counted. Traveling on Air Force One, Trump seemed relaxed, as if he was enjoying himself for the first time in many months. On one flight, his attention turned to the small group keeping him company: Kushner, Stephen Miller, and Jason Miller. "Who would have thought my top guys are Jews," Trump said. This after months of Trump telling Jason Miller that he has a "sweet, understanding Jewish wife." Except Jason Miller's wife was not Jewish, and neither was he. He told Trump he was not, in fact, Jewish. "Wow," Trump said, appearing surprised. "So only your wife is."

Trump continued to complain that the material that Giuliani provided to the **New York Post** (and few other media outlets) was being ignored or effectively banned from circulation on social media, which Trump counted as another force conspiring against him. Priebus warned Trump's team that he believed they had insufficient absentee and early-vote ballots and might come up short on Election Day. Trump had spent months insisting publicly that the election was going to be stolen from him and refusing to say he would concede if defeated. It was such an extraordinary set of remarks from a sitting elected official—and created such uncertainty about what might happen after the votes were counted—that Milley and other national security officials, including the head of the U.S. Cyber Command, spent the weekend beforehand on a call with television anchors. Before they took to the air on election night, officials wanted them to be aware of the security of the election, and General Milley wanted them to hear from him that the military had no role to play in what might happen after the polls closed.

• • •

Ever superstitious, Trump ensured his final stop before the 2020 election would be in Grand Rapids, Michigan, the same place where he had ended his 2016 campaign. That year, Trump had not believed he would win, and few people were as surprised by the outcome as he was. Yet four years later, Trump had no doubts that he was going to win. It was close, but Kushner had insisted the campaign's internal data showed they would win. On the flight back from Michigan, Trump's son Eric encouraged aides to bet on how large the electoral-college victory would be. "We're just trying to get to two hundred seventy," adviser David Bossie cautioned.

The next night, Trump hosted an election-night party in the East Room, while he watched returns with a smaller group in the residence. For the first part of the evening, as guests mingled, it appeared as if 2020 was going to follow the exact path that 2016 had. Trump was declared the victor in Florida, just as he had been four years earlier, and staff started texting allies about what they assumed was a domino effect starting to fall into place. "Congratulations! You won Texas," the state's governor, Greg Abbott, told Trump an hour later, as things were tightening in a number of battleground states. Joking as questions remained about Trump's standing in other states, Abbott went on, "You go out there and declare victory before it's too late!"

When Giuliani tried to make the same recommendation a few hours later, he was not joking. The evening was about to turn for good. At around 11:20 p.m., Fox News became the first network to announce that Biden had won Arizona, the first Democrat to do so in nearly a generation. Trump directed his aides to get the call changed, and they set about contacting Fox officials and the Murdoch family who owned the network, to convince them. Trump's eldest sons appeared stricken by the news, with Eric seeming especially defensive as he loudly protested, hovering over data analyst Matt Oczkowski as they looked at the campaign's statistical modeling.

Around 2:00 a.m., Trump began to make his way to a stage in the East Room that had been set up for him to deliver a victory or concession speech. Trump stopped at a wall of televisions that had been set up. He looked at each one. The coverage was all the same. Aides told him it was time to go. "I'll go onstage when I'm ready to go onstage," Trump barked. "They'll wait for me."

CHAPTER 32

Trial by Combat

In the immediate aftermath of November 3, Donald Trump shifted back and forth on whether he won or lost his bid for a second term. In a fiery, non-concession speech while votes were still being tallied, he insisted, "Frankly, we did win this election." In the days that followed, however, he told one adviser, "We did our best," as a form of comfort. "I thought we had it," he told junior press aides, seeming almost embarrassed by the outcome. To another, he vented about the fact that he had, in his words, been winning up until the point when he wasn't; the campaign's data guru had told Trump for two days after Election Day that he would win, until a meeting days later, when he abruptly said there weren't enough votes. Trump asked others to tell him what had gone wrong.

The far-flung network that Trump had built over the course of his adult life lit up with different responses in the days that followed. Rudy Giuliani, eager to jump into the fray, on election night told other Trump advisers that Trump should simply declare he'd won. The next night, Giuliani told his own advisers that Trump had designated him to work on changing results through legal challenges, although Trump aides insisted that Trump had done no such thing. The president continued to rely on his campaign counselor, Justin Clark. They began to raise money with email and text-message blasts alleging "voter fraud," but it became clear to campaign officials that chances were slim that legal challenges on that basis would be productive. At a meeting with an array of Trump aides at the Virginia campaign headquarters, Stepien and Clark described extremely steep odds. Hicks believed Trump needed to concede. Trump's son-in-law Jared Kushner encouraged a group of aides to go to the White House to brief the president. When asked why he was making no move to join them himself, Kushner likened it to a deathbed scene. "The priest comes later," he said. Off they went, hired help, to deliver the bad news. They drove through traffic-halting celebrations throughout the city, as the networks had just called the race for Biden. When Stepien and Clark arrived at the White House, joined by Dave Bossie, Jason Miller, and a White House adviser named Eric Herschmann, they found Trump in casual clothes; aides brought out little meatballs and pigs in blankets for the guests to eat. Trump listened to Clark and Stepien paint a grim case, laying out a 5 to 10 percent chance of success if they pressed ahead. Trump did not yell or scream. He listened and said, "Okay."

Most people would have heard those odds and taken them as a sign to curb their expectations. Instead,

Trump took it as an opening. "I think it's more like forty or fifty percent," he said of his chances. By the coming week's end, aides had been dispatched to states where Trump would need to reverse the results to win an electoral-college majority. In some, the current margins were narrow enough that he might be able to plausibly do so through recounts and other challenges. The same day that Trump met with his aides in the White House, Giuliani and Lewandowski hosted a press conference in Philadelphia to object to the results there. (Promoting the press conference on Twitter, Trump left the mistaken impression it would be at a downtown luxury hotel rather than a streetfront yard servicer in an out-of-the-way corner of northeast Philadelphia with which it partially shared a name: Four Seasons Total Landscaping.) Kushner tried reaching Giuliani by phone to get him not to forge ahead, but to no avail. Yet Giuliani's claims wilted under scrutiny; an allegation that Trump poll watchers in the state had not been allowed to get close enough to the ballot-counting process was rejected by a court. Hicks was among the few who told Trump in a meeting she had seen no proof of widespread fraud. "You're wrong," Trump replied coldly, hoping to scare others out of agreeing with her.

Trump's supporters began exploring the possibility that Republican-controlled state legislatures could bypass the decision of voters and give the states' electors to the sitting president. "I love it," Meadows replied to a message from a member of Congress shortly after Election Day, reportedly discussing an idea in which state legislatures would send alternate slates of electors. (Just days earlier Meadows had discouraged Trump from saying he had won before the votes were all in.) The scheme to throw the election to Congress was ultimately embraced by Bannon, who by then was speaking regularly to Trump. Bannon's main political clubhouse was a conspiracy-minded online television show and podcast called **The War Room** that he had launched at the start of the impeachment proceedings, repurposed to fight the public-health establishment during the pandemic, and then shifted to push back on the outcome of an election he had long speculated would be "stolen." After several years of estrangement, Bannon was once again useful to Trump.

Roger Stone, who in April 2016 had begun promoting a "Stop the Steal" effort in connection with efforts at the Republican National Convention to deprive Trump of the delegates needed to clinch the nomination, also began to vocally protest the results on social media and in interviews. Far-right activists began using the "Stop the Steal" hashtag on social media, and promoted events using the name protesting the election outcome.

Michael Flynn, the former national security adviser, returned to Trump's orbit too. His lawyer, Sidney Powell, soon connected with Giuliani on efforts to reverse the outcomes in states. Speaking to a Pentagon official after Election Day, Flynn described a scenario he appeared to believe could become reality: the election machinery and ballots would be taken into custody; within weeks, Flynn would bring a version of that scenario directly to the Oval Office for Trump to hear.

Trump was willing to speak with almost anyone whom he thought could offer him a solution to the worst predicament he could imagine: being turned into a loser by the entire country. (With so many people attempting to see Trump the weekend after Election Day, Kushner asked Bossie to monitor some of the meetings, which he started to do, until he was sidelined by a positive coronavirus test.) As Trump's allies sprang into action on his behalf, their challenge grew even steeper. News organizations had begun covering Biden as president-elect. ("We should throw this guy over," Rupert Murdoch said of Trump, exhausted by Trump's refusal to concede and his almost manic speech on election night.) As more voters were counted in states he was still fighting over, such as Georgia, and as votes were tallied sluggishly in New York and California, the popular vote margin for Biden grew bigger, further infuriating Trump and adding to his insistence that something nefarious was taking place. His own portion of the popular vote grew by more than 11 million beyond what he received in 2016, but he never questioned that number, only the Democrats'. Just as he had done nearly three decades earlier when trying to claw his way back from dire financial straits, Trump was keeping open as many options as possible for as long as he could.

But he couldn't decide exactly which one to follow, quizzing nearly everyone, even the valet who brought him Diet Cokes after he pressed a red button on the Resolute Desk, about which different options would lead to success.

Trump's sanguinity had worn off by the second week after the election. He informed aides he had no intention of departing the White House for Biden. "I'm just not going to leave," he told one. "We're never leaving," he told another. "How can you leave when you won an election?" To the chair of the Republican National Committee, he was overheard asking, "Why should I leave if they stole it from me?" Never before in history had a president refused to vacate the White House—the closest parallel might have been Mary Todd Lincoln, who stayed in the mansion for nearly a month after her husband was assassinated—and Trump's cold declaration left aides uncertain as to what he might do next. They ignored his comments, hoping he would move on, but his defiance soon took other forms.

He was not willing to hear from anyone about a concession to Biden. On November 12, Trump had planned to meet with campaign officials to discuss a plan for what to do with the massive sums—ultimately more than $200 million over three weeks—raised since the election, on the pretense of combating voter fraud. That conversation was delayed, as the campaign leadership was overtaken by what became an hours-long session about contesting election results in the six states where Trump's allies were trying to change the results. As Clark, the top lawyer on the campaign, presented an update on the situation in Georgia, delving into arcana about the state's statutes to explain the so-called hand recount under way, he was interrupted by a voice on the phone. "No, it's all wrong," said Giuliani, to whom Trump had been criticizing Clark in private. White House counsel Pat Cipollone, who would become Clark's closest ally in the weeks ahead, said Trump's lawyers should let the hand recount finish before pursuing other legal remedies in Trump's name. "We should stop the recount immediately," Giuliani protested. Clark replied that the process was part of the secretary of state's authority. "It is what it is," he said resignedly. "You're lying to the president," Giuliani yelled back, claiming that Clark was minimizing Trump's chances of success. Clark yelled back, "You're a fucking asshole." Trump hung up the phone and turned to Clark. "Will you go call him and make up?" Trump said. Clark agreed and, after the meeting had concluded, apologized to Pence for swearing in front of him. "There's no reason to apologize when it's the truth," Pence replied.

But the next day, after a dismissal in a case in Arizona, Trump decided to give Giuliani full responsibility for his legal efforts. "Okay, Rudy, you're in charge. Go wild, do anything you want. I don't care," Trump said over the phone. "My lawyers are terrible."

Afterward, Trump turned to Kushner, who had stood silent through the call, and said, "I know you don't like him. But just don't say anything." Giuliani brought on Kerik, the former New York City police commissioner, to help him; Trump mocked his own White House counsel in front of Giuliani and Kerik. Pointing to Kerik, he told Giuliani, "You've got him." Then, of Pat Cipollone, who stood there, Trump said, "That's what I've got." Giuliani was never paid for his work beyond some expenses, at Trump's insistence; the former mayor's associate and radio cohost, Maria Ryan, tried unsuccessfully to set up a large daily fee for Giuliani, who Trump said shouldn't be paid "a dime" unless there was success, and later sought a consulting fee for herself, as well as for Trump to grant the Presidential Medal of Freedom to Giuliani.

On November 16, nearly two weeks after the election, Tom Barrack, one of Trump's few real friends, came to visit the West Wing. Barrack was in Washington on other matters, but thought he might be able to reason with the president. Kushner told him Trump was not listening to anyone. (Kushner offered up his own reason for not being able to press harder for Trump to concede the election: "He's the grandfather of my children.") "Don't bother, I'm not going to concede," Trump said to his visitor as soon as he entered the Oval Office.

Barrack told him that if he continued on this path he would create problems for a post–White House life, in which he was going to face existing investigations without the institution of the presidency behind him. Barrack asked him to think about his business, about everything he had built over the decades and the support he still needed. Trump mentioned the total number of people who had voted for him. "They're there for me," he told his friend, seeming insistent that he had really won the election. You are losing your stature, Barrack went on, urging him to try to take Biden's hand and welcome him into the White House as a more "elegant" approach to leaving. "You're elegant, and I'm president of the United States, so get out of my office," Trump said.

Trump was not only moving away from all norms or conventions, but any rational calculus about self-interest. He preferred losing his way than losing anyone else's way.

After the election, Meadows began to regularly speak with Ron Klain, who had been tapped to become Biden's chief of staff. The two men were in contact to plan the handover of the White House on January 20, a routine but complicated milestone in democratic governance that Trump's public remarks indicated he did not believe would occur. "I know the president's saying these things," Meadows told Klain. "We will get it worked out." As Meadows was reassuring Klain and telling Senate Republican leadership that there would be a peaceful transition, he was trading texts with Ginni Thomas, the wife of Supreme Court justice Clarence Thomas, who was urging him to elevate Sidney Powell and to continue contesting the election. "This is a fight of good versus evil," Meadows wrote to Thomas.

Kushner and Ivanka began operating on two tracks, planning for a post-presidential life in Florida while attending White House meetings and leaving it to the self-described "pack mules" staff to contend with Trump. "What have we got to lose?" one Trump family member asked a paid aide, who was waiting for Kushner to do more to intervene. Ivanka soon began to write transition memos, as presidential personnel officials threatened anyone who looked for a new job with being fired. A more formal transition-planning effort had already been under way for months, led by Chris Liddell, a former Microsoft executive who had served as a deputy chief of staff to Trump. The president expressed little interest in Liddell's work and was told little of it in return, which meant he did not disrupt it. Biden's transition staffers still faced problems, from delays receiving information from the Pentagon or a holdup in arranging vaccinations for incoming White House staff so they could safely show up for work on Biden's first day. "I told them to fix it," Meadows would tell Klain, and then nothing would get moving. Elsewhere, Meadows turned intransigence into a matter of principle; upon refusing Biden's team access to a specialized computer system necessary to begin work planning the next president's budget, Meadows said, "You just can't expect us to endorse your spending plans."

In one mid-November call, Klain told Meadows that it was time for Biden to start receiving the president's daily intelligence briefing. "How many days a week is Vice President Biden gonna want this daily brief?" Meadows asked. Klain, dumbstruck by the question, said that Biden would want to be briefed every day. It was how he did it as vice president, he said. "No president ever does that. That's never happened," Meadows said. It seemed so beyond Meadows's own experience that he could not comprehend it.

But increasingly the government that Trump controlled was being used to attempt to back up his efforts to fight the election results. Meadows passed along unsubstantiated tips, sometimes no more than wild conspiracy theories, to various departments and agencies; he explained to the director of national intelligence, John Ratcliffe, after asking him to check out a conspiracy theory, that special thermostats had been used to hack into Georgia voting machines. Ratcliffe, telling Meadows that the security of voting machines was a domestic law-enforcement issue, passed the matter along to the FBI.

Across the administration, the yearlong project to use the presidential-personnel office to place Trump loyalists throughout cabinet agencies, under the leadership of Johnny McEntee, had succeeded. McEntee had helped to craft a list of dubious reasons for removing Defense Secretary Mark Esper, including Esper calling himself "apolitical" and consulting with transgender people for input on issues affecting them. Trump fired Esper the Monday after the election, saying "the press expects Esper," by way of explaining to an aide how he picked which disliked member of his national security team would go. (He backed off other desired changes, with Pence and Cipollone talking him out of essentially forcing the CIA director, Gina Haspel, to quit by installing a Trump loyalist as her deputy, and would soon call the FBI director, Christopher Wray, whom he'd repeatedly wanted to fire, to assure him his job was safe.)

At the Justice Department, a White House liaison named Heidi Stirrup complained to senior officials that Attorney General Bill Barr should be doing more to investigate the claims of election fraud. She was banned from the building after she tried to collect information about the investigations, which officials presumed she was trying to pass on to the White House. (Separately, the White House installed a communications lawyer named Adam Candeub to oversee the department's antitrust division. Barr had earlier blocked his appointment. It came months after McEntee aides reached out directly to Justice Department officials to learn about a possible lawsuit against Google ahead of Election Day. Justice Department officials believed White House aides were bent on conflict with tech companies and did not understand the difference between century-old antitrust regulations and the 1996 telecom law, a section of which afforded online platforms immunity from certain types of litigation and on whose abolition Trump had campaigned.)

Within weeks of the election, Barr, who was in frequent contact with Senate Majority Leader Mitch McConnell, became the first major figure in the administration to publicly break with Trump's postelection obsession, with a statement that asserted that there was no widespread election fraud that would have impacted the November race. His statement infuriated Trump, who informed Barr that he "must hate Trump" to say such a thing. Barr disagreed. "Look, you have five to six weeks before the electoral college, you need a crackerjack team to go and get the courts to order the states to do certain kinds of auditing in certain key districts," Barr told Trump in person. "Instead," he went on, "you've wasted five weeks on this bullshit about the machines. There's nothing wrong with the machines." Trump gestured to the television and told Barr he should watch Newsmax, one of several upstart conservative broadcast networks that had been aggressively covering his fraud allegations. Barr offered to resign, prompting Trump to slam his hand down on the table in front of him in the small study off the Oval Office. "Accepted!" Trump screamed. Barr left and went to his car in the parking lot. Just as Priebus had prevented another attorney general, Jeff Sessions, from resigning three and a half years earlier, Cipollone, the White House counsel, rushed to follow Barr and banged on the window of his car, telling him Trump had changed his mind.

In late November, a pack of lawyers gathered for a press conference at the Republican National Committee's headquarters on Capitol Hill. They were there, as attorney Jenna Ellis said, to unveil "an elite strike force team that is working on behalf of the president and the campaign to make sure that our Constitution is protected."

Trump did not see much to instill confidence. He was repulsed by the sight of Giuliani as rivulets of sweat blackened by his hair dye ran down the sides of his face. But it was claims made by fellow lawyer Sidney Powell—including that all tabulations from Dominion voting machines were flawed because of manipulation somehow connected to deceased Venezuelan leader Hugo Chavez—that left the enduring mark. Trump advisers who disliked Powell, who became something of a hero to die-hard Trump supporters for her work contesting the criminal case against Flynn, used the bizarre Venezuela conspiracy theory as a basis to expel her. Just three days after they had participated together in a nationally televised press conference as members of the Trump legal team, Giuliani issued a statement saying that Powell was not, in fact, a part of the Trump legal team.

Ultimately, Trump's legal team filed sixty-five

different postelection lawsuits in state and federal courts and lost sixty-four of them, according to one analysis. As their litigation hit dead end after dead end, Giuliani and Ellis began touring state capitals to implore legislators there to effectively overrule local election administrators on Trump's behalf. Part of Giuliani's traveling entourage was a man named Phil Waldron, a retired army colonel and Texas bar owner who helped to seed the notion that the federal government could seize locally administered voting machines so they could be examined for traces of hacking. Giuliani became fixated on the idea that the machines had been manipulated, and that there was a mechanism inside them for erasing data, at one point focusing on a conspiracy theory that Italy had somehow used satellites to switch votes in machines from Trump to Biden. Giuliani asked Clark to authorize the campaign to rent a plane to take the engineer alleged to be behind the scheme into custody in Italy; Clark balked. At another point, Giuliani insisted that the man was actually in custody in Maryland, and he wanted Trump to have the government allow him to be questioned. Meadows asked the Justice Department to look into the satellite conspiracy theory; it, too, had no basis in fact.

In mid-December, economic adviser Peter Navarro publicly released a report about the election, filled with claims that had been debunked by courts, state administrators, and media. The next day, someone from Navarro's office helped bring into the West Wing

Flynn, Sidney Powell, and Patrick Byrne, the founder of online retailer Overstock.com, who had become something of a clearinghouse for Trump-era conspiracy theories about the deep state. Trump saw them loitering outside the Oval Office and waved them in. They had gotten entry to the building, and hoped to tell Trump that his political advisers and even Giuliani's legal team were not fighting hard enough for him.

Trump had a week earlier told Powell he was planning to appoint her as a special counsel to investigate election fraud, and told her he wanted her to have a security clearance that granted access to government intelligence. He also mused about returning Flynn, who had been fired ostensibly for lying to the vice president, to the White House as its chief of staff. Powell and Flynn were said to favor plans for having the government seize voting machines to produce irrefutable evidence the election was stolen from him; Giuliani had also been intrigued by the idea the voting machines were compromised, but he did not favor using the military to take control of them. One idea would have Homeland Security do the work, the other would leave it with the Pentagon; executive orders decreeing the seizure had been drafted so that Trump would sign them, but the paperwork was not crafted by the White House counsel's office or the staff secretary, and it was unclear who did craft it.

The White House counsel, Pat Cipollone, alerted to the visitors' presence by Herschmann, who happened upon the meeting, rushed to the Oval Office in the hopes of blocking Trump's most extreme impulses. What ensued was an hours-long meeting; Herschmann called Giuliani in, knowing his antipathy for Powell would make him a useful ally. In tandem, Herschmann, the staff secretary Derek Lyons, Cipollone, Giuliani, and ultimately Meadows argued against Flynn and his group. (At some point around the time of the meeting, after Giuliani suggested inquiring about the Homeland Security option, Trump told him to call the acting deputy secretary of the Department of Homeland Security, Ken Cuccinelli; Cuccinelli said it was not within the law, but Trump still asked him about it in the coming days.) When the meeting disbanded, Trump invited the visitors to resume it upstairs in the residence; the White House officials followed once they realized that the meeting had continued. Through it all, Trump acted as both a passive observer and an orchestrator of events, and a collaborator to those treating his administration as an adversary. Shortly after the meeting, from which some participants departed in tears, Trump turned his focus to a new date: January 6, 2021, when the electoral college tallies would be certified by Congress.

Trump went to Mar-a-Lago for the holidays, but he was consumed with talking about the election, debating whether he would attend Biden's inauguration even as he maintained he was still going to be sworn in for another term. Bannon called Trump and told him he needed to return to Washington. While

Pence spent the Christmas holiday in Vail, Colorado, with his family, his office received a request via an intermediary for him to meet for coffee with Powell, supposedly also on vacation there. Powell would eventually get involved in a lawsuit filed against Pence on behalf of Texas congressman Louie Gohmert. The congressman was seeking a court ruling that, in his capacity presiding over the Senate's certification of electoral votes, Pence was free to accept and reject states' elector slates at will (the theory that Pence had such power had begun bubbling up to Trump aides and some Pence aides in early December). Pence's aides suspected that Powell, who they believed was working on the suit even though she hadn't said so publicly, was looking for an opportunity to serve him with legal papers face-to-face; the intermediary, Arizona Republican Party chair Kelli Ward, had recently joined Gohmert's suit with a slate of would-be Trump electors. When Pence's chief of staff objected, Ward said that they wouldn't be doing this if the president wasn't okay with it. Some Pence aides began to see the vice president as akin to a political prisoner whom Trump was trying to break.

While Trump had spent November and December dwelling on the election he had lost, most Republican leaders were looking ahead to one they felt they needed to win. On January 5, Georgia voters would participate in two separate runoff elections for the

U.S. Senate, made necessary after no candidate in the race for either of the state's two seats had won a majority in November. Control of the Senate hung in the balance, and Republican strategists thought the most straightforward campaign message would focus on letting voters know that by retaining Republican senators they could impose a check on Biden's presidency. (The Democrats' Senate leader had made this argument for them shortly after Election Day, telling an elated crowd in Brooklyn, "Now we take Georgia, then we change America!") But that would require the implicit admission that the White House had lost.

Trump reluctantly attended a rally with the Republican candidates in rural Valdosta in early December. He appeared less interested in helping the two Republicans on the ballot win their races than in persuading them all to help him win the one he had just lost. "We just need somebody with courage to do what they have to do because everyone knows it's wrong. We need somebody with courage, somebody that makes decisions, then we'll be going up to the Supreme Court very shortly," Trump said.

He was particularly incensed by the interim senator Kelly Loeffler, whom Trump had tried to dissuade the state's governor, Brian Kemp, from appointing to an open seat in 2019. The state's senior senator, David Perdue, was among the few in the chamber who had developed an unwaveringly strong relationship with Trump. When they finally shared a ballot, each running for reelection, they were so close that

it was impossible for Perdue's associates to imagine
Trump venting the kind of anger at him that he had
at others. It was different with them, Perdue assured
associates—Trump wouldn't leave him hanging out
to dry. But after November 3, their interests began to
diverge. All Trump wanted out of Georgia was to see
Biden's sixteen electoral votes handed over to him.
"David? What's Georgia doing?" Trump would ask
him. "What's the governor doing? What's the legislature doing?"

Shortly after his trip to Valdosta, Trump reached
Perdue on his campaign bus and began complaining about the decision of Georgia's attorney general,
Chris Carr, not to join a lawsuit organized by Texas's
attorney general to challenge the results in other
states. "This is absolutely crazy," Trump said. Trump
wanted both Perdue and Loeffler to intervene on his
behalf. Perdue said he was a federal official, without
any direct responsibility for state issues, but that he
was doing what he could.

Republican officials heard from activists knocking
on doors in Georgia that Trump's claims of widespread fraud in the election had trickled down to
individual voters, who were angry that more wasn't
being done to rescue the president as he claimed
to be a victim of an egregious abuse of the system.
Only Trump could let his voters know that it was
still important to turn out, they believed, and they
tiptoed around Trump in the hopes he would be less
destructive. Trump might not have had the same

canvassing infrastructure reporting back to him, but he appeared to understand the leverage he now had over Republicans in the state. "You know, David, I wish I could stop it, but people are pissed off. They're not going to turn out to vote. I'm gonna come down there. I'm gonna tell them they need to vote," he told Perdue, before warning once more, "They're not gonna vote." Perdue got the message and connected Trump and Carr and Giuliani's team to Republican leaders in the state legislature. Giuliani made claims that he could not prove. A Perdue aide declared that Giuliani was "fucking crazy."

Trump considered ways to use the Justice Department to intervene. He mused about appointing a special counsel, asking Cuccinelli about it (Cuccinelli said it was unwise), while another official in the government contacted the U.S. attorney in Washington, D.C., Michael Sherwin, to see if he'd be interested; ultimately Trump never went ahead. Then, with Barr having resigned and an acting attorney general named Jeff Rosen in his place, Trump pressed Rosen to call the election "illegal." "Just say the election was corrupt and leave the rest to me" and my House allies, Trump said on one call. Trump wanted the Justice Department to file a brief directly with the Supreme Court challenging the results, and considered appointing an eager assistant attorney general named Jeffrey Clark to the top job. Cipollone and others warned Trump against the move, with Cipollone calling it a "murder-suicide" and top

Justice Department officials threatening to resign if it happened.

After two recounts were completed in Georgia, Trump still trailed Biden by 11,779 votes. Governor Brian Kemp told legislators under pressure from Trump and his attorneys to call a special session, that they lacked the authority to certify any other result; secretary of state Brad Raffensperger, a Republican who oversaw Georgia's elections, said that to do so would be "nullifying the will of the people." Raffensperger avoided repeated efforts by Trump to reach him directly, but when the two men eventually spoke by phone, on a call set up by Meadows, Raffensperger had his staff record it. "So look. All I want to do is this," Trump told Raffensperger. "I just want to find 11,780 votes, which is one more than we have. Because we won the state."

After failing in their various coast-to-coast efforts to overturn the election results by filing legal appeals, lobbying state legislatures, and bullying election administrators, the nodes of Trump's political network collapsed on one point where they believed they could bend the system to save him: the certification of electoral-college votes by a joint session of Congress.

All fifty states had awarded electors on December 14 to the winners of their state's popular vote, as ordered by federal statute. Some Republicans who had quietly humored Trump's various challenges had been waiting for that mid-December day to acknowledge what was now abundantly clear: that Biden was going to be the next president. When, as expected, Biden won that electoral-vote count by 306 to 232, Senate Republican leader Mitch McConnell, who had become a frequent contact for senior administration officials worried about Trump's refusal to acknowledge the results, finally called the president-elect to congratulate him. But some of Trump's team did not treat that as the end of the process. "As we speak, an alternate slate of electors in the contested states is going to vote," Stephen Miller told a television interviewer. When it was pointed out that the Trump lawyers had repeatedly lost in court, Miller said the judges were falling under pressure from the media and that Trump needed "heroes to step up and do the right thing."

The Electoral Count Act and the Twelfth Amendment of the Constitution suggest the vice president's role in the events of January 6 were purely ceremonial. Certificates sent in by the states identifying their electors were to be opened and read, tallied, and the winner affirmed. If a dispute couldn't be resolved, the election would be sent to the House of Representatives, where each state's delegation received a single vote.

Within the White House, a memo from a law professor named John Eastman, who had started working with Meadows's associate, lawyer Cleta Mitchell, before Election Day, argued that the vice president could make a determination not to accept certain states' electors. If enough states were contested in that way, neither candidate would receive the necessary majority, and the House of Representatives—where Republicans, despite being in the chamber's minority, controlled more state delegations than Democrats—could pick between Trump and Biden.

But Trump's outside advisers failed to persuade lawmakers in states to send certificates identifying electors supporting Trump that should be considered on January 6; some Trump allies in various states sent fraudulent certificates to the National Archives. Pence's advisers dismissed the idea that his role at the counting of the electoral votes could be anything other than ceremonial, and a prominent conservative retired judge later backed them up. But Trump's supporters ratcheted up pressure. The vice president's chief of staff, Marc Short, reached out to Kushner between Christmas and New Year's Day, seeking advice on what was becoming an untenable situation with Trump and his allies. Kushner, responding, "I'm trying to solve Middle East peace," declined to be drawn in. Unsolicited memos arguing that Pence could be a decision-maker showed up in Pence's office, including one from McEntee that reached back more than two hundred years for supposed precedent: "JEFFERSON USED HIS POSITION AS VP TO WIN." Jenna Ellis also provided a memo. Meadows had a different approach. Recent administrations had developed a practice of supporting the departing vice president as he set up a postgovernment office, but it was not automatic. The funding had to be approved, and for Pence it was being withheld. Meadows told Pence's aides that it was Trump's decision to impose the delay; Short found the timing suspect. On January 4, Pence was summoned to the Oval Office to meet Trump and Eastman, and the lawyer repeated the arguments he had laid out that Pence had the power to essentially take control of the votes. Pence pushed back on Eastman, who conceded that perhaps the vice president did not have quite the power he claimed. "Did you hear that, Mr. President?" Pence asked, trying to make the point to Trump that Eastman's earlier claims didn't hold up.

Pence began speaking with outside allies who worried as they watched the pressure campaign. Paul Ryan, the former House Speaker, reached out to him. Pence also spoke with Dan Quayle, the former vice president, who underscored that Pence had no wiggle room. McEntee wrote a handwritten note that circulated in the White House, which seemed to acknowledge that Pence did not believe he could dictate the election's outcome. Still, Trump continued to insist to his senior aides that he believed Pence was open to Eastman's pitch.

My colleague Annie Karni received a tip about the meeting with Eastman. Sources told me that Pence had been direct in telling Trump he could not do what Trump was asking of him. Annie and I were already writing about the pressure Pence was under, including Trump trying again the next day to coerce him, to no avail. So we recast the story around Pence's message to Trump. PENCE SAID TO HAVE TOLD TRUMP HE LACKS POWER TO CHANGE ELECTION RESULT read the headline. Trump dictated a response that, without consulting with Pence or his staff, declared, "**The New York Times** report regarding comments Vice President Pence supposedly made to me today is fake news. He never said that. The Vice President and I are in total agreement that the Vice President has the power to act." Short called Jason Miller to complain; Miller said it would have been nastier had he not intervened. Trump called Bannon and his cohort of aides who were stationed at the Willard Hotel, saying Pence had become "arrogant." A few hours after our story was published, Pence's general counsel briefed reporters about the arguments they might hear the next afternoon from Republicans trying to stop the certification, and why those arguments were specious. Short was grappling with another concern. Trump had been escalating his aggression toward several officials, including Pence; Short believed that the tensions the vice president's team had spent weeks trying to tamp down were about to become very public. Earlier on January 5, Short had called Pence's lead Secret Service agent, Tim Giebels, to his West Wing office; Short warned the agent that Trump was going to turn on the vice president, and that they may have a security risk because of it. Short, who had never before flagged a security concern, did not know what that threat might look like, only that, once the fight with Trump was out in the open, there was no turning back.

That was in part because the events of January 6 would not be decided by the dueling arguments of constitutional law experts. An outside group that had supported Trump's presidential campaign, Women for America First, had organized a massive rally to take place hours before the certification, on the Ellipse near the White House. Trump promoted the event—"Big protest in D.C. on January 6. Be there, will be wild!" he wrote on Twitter—and focused on details of the staging as though it were one of his own campaign rallies, while his speechwriting team crafted an address for him to deliver. He met with political aides about what he wanted it to look like, who would be on the speakers' list, what music would be played. Trump knew that there was talk of a march from the rally to the Capitol afterward, and he told his aides he wanted to join his supporters on foot. (Trump was informed that the Secret Service could not protect him in that scenario, but he continued to raise the idea into the evening of January 5.) Trump also told aides he wanted National Guard troops present, to protect his supporters from what he insisted would be Antifa counterprotesters. He met extensively with aides about who would speak at the rally; aides put figures such as Roger Stone and Alex Jones, the conspiracy-minded online talk show host, at a spinoff version of the rally on January 5 instead of at the main event. Sitting in the Oval Office as that rally took place, Trump asked about logistics for the next day and signed paperwork as his staff gathered. He'd opened the side doors leading to the Rose Garden and could hear the crowd of his supporters nearby, cheering for him from afar.

Trump emerged from the White House around 11:30 a.m. on January 6, almost exactly two weeks to the minute before the president-elect would leave the building for the inaugural ceremony at the Capitol. He had just had a final call with Pence, who again resisted Trump's demands. Trump grew belligerent, disturbing his daughter and startling even some of his own aides. (One official rushed out of the Oval Office, saying Trump had told Pence that he could go down in history as a "patriot" or as a "pussy.") Trump held a red campaign hat and headed to the Ellipse, the staging area for the rally, where music played and his family members watched monitors showing the rally in a white backstage tent. After a series of increasingly aggressive speeches—Giuliani, whom Trump struck from the speaking list and then restored to it, called for a "trial by combat"—Trump addressed the crowd of more than ten thousand people. "We're going to have to fight much harder," Trump said of Republicans, mocking those demanding that people be "nice." "And Mike Pence is going to have to come through for us, and if he doesn't, that will be a sad day for our country because you're sworn to uphold our Constitution." He directed his followers to head to the Capitol building.

"We're going to walk down to the Capitol, and we're going to cheer on our brave senators and congressmen and women, and we're probably not going to be cheering so much for some of them," he said. "Because you'll never take back our country with weakness. You have to show strength and you have to be strong. We have come to demand that Congress do the right thing and only count the electors who have been lawfully slated, lawfully slated. I know that everyone here will soon be marching over to the Capitol building to peacefully and patriotically make your voices heard."

Trump, furious that he was told he couldn't join them, went home. Roughly fifty minutes after he arrived back at the White House, the proceedings on the Senate floor were halted by loud noises; a riot had begun, and was swamping the building. Pence, whose aides made public a letter at 1:00 p.m. saying that he did not have the power to do what Trump wanted (they intentionally did not send it internally earlier, distrusting White House aides with any lead time), had begun to reject one of the gambits Eastman outlined in his memo, in which lawmakers would delay the counting of electoral votes by inviting states to investigate their results. Pence had worked on specific language with the parliamentarian to thwart the possibility that false documents would be submitted claiming that Trump had electors in specific states. A mob of people, many who had apparently come to

Washington for the rally on the Ellipse, some with weapons and tactical gear, had swarmed the Capitol, shattering windows to gain entry. Police officers were accosted, doors were smashed, and a small crew of Capitol police officers struggled to beat the mob back. Some rioters chanted "Hang Mike Pence!" as wooden gallows appeared outside the building.

Trump's aides began to receive calls, one after another, from inside and outside the Capitol, demanding that he do something to stop the violence being committed in his name. When House Republican leader Kevin McCarthy told Trump directly that the rioters were breaking into his office, Trump replied that the rioters were more upset about the results than McCarthy was. At 2:24 p.m., as his vice president had been hustled away from the Senate chamber and would be taken to an underground loading dock by a Secret Service detail that feared for his life, Trump wrote on Twitter, "Mike Pence didn't have the courage to do what should have been done to protect our Country."

Trump mostly took to the small dining room off the Oval Office, watching the events on television. Meadows's phone lit up with pleas texted to him by former aides and even the president's son. "He has to lead now. It has gone too far and gotten out of hand," Don Jr. wrote. Trump initially resisted urging, including from his daughter Ivanka, to use his social media platforms to tell the mob to disperse. (A post she drafted for herself, meant partly as positive reinforcement for her father, addressed the rioters as "American Patriots"; "Just send it!" Ivanka told an aide of the tweet as she raced back downstairs to her father, but she deleted it amid an uproar and made clear she intended no harm by it.) Trump never asked about Pence's safety, or tried to reach his vice president, who was taken to a secure area underground and declined to get in the waiting car that his Secret Service detail said they could take to his residence. Pelosi—second in line to the presidency—McConnell, McCarthy, and Schumer were rushed to Fort McNair to protect them from the siege. Trump did not call any government officials to mobilize a response; that fell to Pence, while he was taking shelter. Watching television, Trump told aides that perhaps Pence should be hanged.

It took almost five hours for law enforcement to begin to secure the Capitol and another two hours to restore order; despite several people saying there had been directives to get the National Guard moving (including Meadows, who told West Wing officials he'd reached out to a Defense Department official), they did not begin arriving until after 5:30 p.m. When Short called Meadows in late afternoon to say that Pence and his team were safe, Meadows volunteered unprompted that no one had delayed calling in the Guard. Senators returned to the chamber, at Pence's insistence, to continue voting on states' electoral slates as soon as possible. Their remarks were filled with a mix of defiance, shock, disgust, and shame. "I just think it's a uniquely bad idea to delay this election," said South Carolina Republican Lindsey Graham. "Trump and I, we had a hell of a journey. I hate it being this way. Oh my God, I hate it. From my point of view, he's been a consequential president. . . . All I can say is count me out. Enough is enough."

But he was not out. Almost no one was for very long.

More than two thousand people entered the Capitol building that day. At least five people died in connection with the riot, including a police officer. More than eight hundred people were charged in connection with the riot, including educators, former members of the military, and firefighters. Among those charged were a number of rioters described as members of far-right militia groups advocating violence, such as the Oath Keepers and the Proud Boys. (Roger Stone, who was seen being guarded by some members of the Oath Keepers, including standing outside the Willard Hotel, told people his security was arranged through one of the rally organizers and that he never attended the January 6 rally—he had been kept from speaking by planners and, he insisted, he had no role in what took place at the Capitol.)

When Trump spoke to McCarthy a few days after the riot, he tried to minimize it all, prompting McCarthy to remind him they had spoken as the riot was under way. "I called you to get them out!" McCarthy complained about the rioters.

Across Trump's government, there were resignations, from cabinet secretaries down to junior staffers.
Some of the senior cabinet-level officials, including
those with national security portfolios, remained on
because they feared it could get even worse in their
absence or because they wanted to entrench some of
their personal policy objectives; O'Brien (who had
been assisting the transition to his incoming counterpart, Jake Sullivan, prior to that day), Chris Liddell,
the economic adviser Larry Kudlow, Mnuchin, and
Pompeo all stayed on. (Pompeo would tell several
people a story in which Gene Scalia, the labor secretary, suggested members of the cabinet should speak
with the president to discuss necessary steps to ensure an orderly transition. "How do you think that
conversation is going to go?" Pompeo recounted saying in response.) O'Brien worked with others in the
administration, including Ratcliffe and Pompeo in
particular, to try to cement the Trump administration's policy stance toward China, including through
sanctions; Ratcliffe wrote an op-ed describing China
as the "greatest threat" to the U.S. since the Second
World War and favored a minority view among analysts that the intelligence community understated
China's efforts to influence the 2020 election to damage Trump. Among those who remained, many of
whom had stayed in the White House because they
either believed in Trump's policies or were invested in
him personally, there was a sense that he had undermined all their shared achievements. Now because of

their service in his government they would face questionable career prospects and certain legal bills over investigations that would follow. Democrats began to move quickly to impeach Trump again. In the legislature, Democrats felt their position in terms of the impeachment proceedings was stronger after Senate runoffs that—thanks in part to Trump's sabotage of Republican campaigning in Georgia—saw them win back the Senate.

Almost immediately after January 6, Pence's post-government transition funding was approved. With an eye toward salvaging Trump's legacy, Graham began plotting with Meadows and Kushner to spend his final days in office highlighting his accomplishments. But the plan never materialized; Trump was not especially interested. Nor did he favor a suggestion by O'Brien that Trump award Pence the Medal of Freedom. Instead, he watched the reactions to his behavior on television, including coverage of the social media platforms that had suspended him in the wake of January 6. When asked on Fox News if Trump felt "emasculated" by the Twitter ban, former White House spokesman Hogan Gidley appeared to be confused by the question. "I wouldn't say emasculated," Gidley said. Then he leaned in. "The most masculine person, I think, to ever hold the White House is the president of the United States," Gidley said. Trump called his former adviser to tell him he was correct, and had aides play the video of Gidley speaking several times.

A rapprochement was forged between Pence and Trump by way of Kushner and his wife. (Kushner had been traveling in the Middle East in the days before January 6 to help resolve a years-long regional blockade against Qatar, arriving back in Washington as the events were unfolding.) When Pence and Trump met, Trump asked his vice president if the relationship could go back to the way it had been before. Pence, uninterested in maintaining a conflict, murmured something affirmative. Not everyone felt peaceful; at least one of McEntee's employees stuffed copies of photos of Hunter Biden, the incoming president's son, into vents in an air conditioner unit at the White House complex, breaking it.

Trump's final hours were spent on a frenzy of pardons and grants of clemency, many of them for people connected to the Trumps or their associates. Soon after Election Day, Trump began asking various aides, out of nowhere, if they wanted pardons. Just before Christmas, Trump had issued a crush of pardons, including to Stone, Manafort, and Charles Kushner, his son-in-law's father. (Jared Kushner insisted through aides he had played no role in it, something few if any people believed.) On January 19, he issued 143 more pardons and commutations. One went to Bannon, which Trump spent his final full day in office dithering over, as most of his aides objected to it; Jason Miller ultimately told Trump that if Bannon's trial on fraud charges proceeded, it would play out as a referendum on Trump each day. Stone had pushed for the White House to consider a slew of pardons for people Stone cared about; White House officials said the list included preemptive pardons for members of Congress who'd opposed certifying Biden's win. Cipollone opposed Stone's proposals, along with Trump's considerations of preemptive pardons for himself, Giuliani, and his family; Trump dropped the idea. The last pardon went to Al Pirro, one of his former lobbyists who had spent time in prison for tax evasion, at the behest of his ex-wife, Jeanine, who had become Trump's favorite Fox News anchor. When he scrawled his name in thick black pen on an Executive Grant of Clemency for Pirro, the work of the Trump presidency was done.

Trump was at Joint Base Andrews, where he would depart for Palm Beach. It was a frigid morning, and despite the efforts by White House officials to round up as many attendees as possible, the crowd that gathered was large but not massive. Almost no current or former administration officials showed up.

Trump seemed unsure of exactly what to say, fumbling through his remarks at the podium. "It's been something very special. We've accomplished a lot," he said of his four years. He told the crowd he loved them, before an awkward farewell. "Have a good life, we will see you soon," Trump said. He descended from the dais, and walked the red carpet's length onto Air Force One for the last time. As the plane taxied down the runway, a recording of Frank Sinatra's "My Way" blasted over the speaker system, like a movie finale.

But little else went the way Trump expected it to. He believed he should have been the one preparing for an inauguration, for a second term in which he would finally have the right aides in the right jobs so they would enforce what he asked for. He should have been the one still in charge. This was one of the few times in his life that he was not able to get what he believed was due to him.

Even the final minutes of his time in Washington weren't how he envisioned them. The sendoff featured blasting cannons and a full military band, among the specific requests Trump had made. The band was able to play "Hail to the Chief," but a White House aide told me later that in the frigid winter air some of the instruments froze. It was the last time the song would be played for him while he was president, and it wasn't how he wanted it to be. Almost always there had been a net beneath Donald Trump. But at last, no matter how hard he tried, there was nothing to catch him—no father, no banks, no politicians or judges or customers or voters or his own salesmanship or his power of positive thinking. He had fallen to the ground, at least for a time.

Epilogue

Donald Trump began his attempted comeback, as he had all of his previous ones, by refusing to concede that anything was wrong. On the flight to Florida, Trump spoke with Republican National Committee chair Ronna McDaniel and vented his fury at her party, suggesting he might form one of his own. McDaniel pointed out all the party resources from which he had already benefited and that those would not be available to him as a third-party candidate.

He was facing repercussions in Congress from the members and senators whose lives had been threatened by a swarming mob of his supporters. Trump's second impeachment trial, for "incitement of insurrection," commenced nearly three weeks after he left office. House Democratic impeachment managers presented a detailed account of Trump's actions leading up to the invasion of the Capitol on January 6, and his apparent lack of action during it. This time, seven Republicans voted in support of impeachment. McConnell left open the idea of doing so, although he ultimately voted to acquit Trump. Nevertheless, in a speech immediately after the vote,

McConnell said that Trump was "practically and morally responsible for provoking the events of that day." The ex-president's legal team had triumphed, but at the typical cost for Trump-related projects: internal divisions and hostilities that broke into the open and ended in anger. (One of the lawyers was forced to spend thousands of dollars on new suits because Trump did not like the way he looked on television.)

Several months later, to continue its January 6 investigation, the House of Representatives formed a select committee that would have time and fact-finding powers unavailable to the rushed impeachment. Republicans, given a role in subpoena power but told that the Trump allies they wanted on the committee would be denied appointments, effectively decided not to participate. One exception was Wyoming Republican Liz Cheney, the daughter of a deeply conservative vice president and herself furious over the events of January 6, who became the committee vice chair. Another was Republican Representative Adam Kinzinger, from Illinois. Trump, in retaliation, made eliminating both of them politically a priority of his post-presidency. House Republican leader Kevin McCarthy, who had initially criticized Trump for his role in the January 6 riot and was captured on tape discussing whether he would ask Trump to resign, ultimately looked toward his own political future and chose Trump's side over Cheney. Several former White House officials and outside supporters, taking cues from the former president, refused to comply with the congressional subpoenas. Bannon was indicted for contempt of Congress; he appeared almost giddy about it.

Public interest in the events of January 6 had begun to fade, but Trump's obsession had not. Nor had his nostalgic faith in a long-gone mentor whom he'd banished from his life in his final days. Trump continued to invoke Roy Cohn in conversation: if Cohn was still alive, Trump told advisers once out of office, he would still be president.

He got aggressively involved in 2022 primary races, telling people that his logic in some cases was to make sure he had allies in place if the 2024 election was contested or if he was to be impeached if he won the White House again. One was Dr. Mehmet Oz, a celebrity physician who ran for the U.S. Senate from Pennsylvania and whose greatest political asset, Trump suggested at a rally, was his broadcast fame. "When you're in television for eighteen years, that's like a poll, that means people like you," Trump said. He reflected to me that Richard Nixon was ousted from office in part because he had "treated the Senate and he treated the House unbelievably badly, and he got away with it, and then all of the sudden he had Watergate."

As always, Trump's pursuit of money factored into his behavior and decisions. Some aspects of Trump's family business had suffered while he was in office, as Trump engaged in one politically polarizing fight after another. But the presidency opened up new financial possibilities. Almost immediately after his defeat, he had begun fundraising off his claims of fraud. Plenty of people donated small amounts of money to continue a fight he swore was valid and building toward action. It was difficult to discern whether Trump believed what he was saying about the election. (Despite insisting he was sincere about fraud concerns, he remained silent about reports that his chief of staff, Mark Meadows, had registered to vote from a North Carolina address where he had never lived.)

I learned in the spring that Trump was repeating a claim from one of his most vocal allies, the self-made pillow company CEO Mike Lindell, that Trump would be reinstated as president by August 2021. Trump liked the idea, telling aides he did not want to have to sit through another three and a half years of a Biden presidency. He quietly encouraged some conservative writers to publicize the idea in their own voices, telling **National Review** editor Rich Lowry that he anticipated being reinstated by August 2021. Trump encouraged Lowry to write about it, saying it could help the magazine. When Jenna Ellis, his former adviser, protested on Twitter the notion that Trump could be reinstated to office, Trump told Ellis that her reputation would be damaged. She took that as pressure to reverse her statement. Trump conceded to her that the scenario was "almost impossible," but that he wanted to keep the idea alive.

Other moneymaking opportunities arrived,

ostensibly tied to the reverent memory of the Trump presidency. His son Don Jr. began a publishing company along with an aide; its first book was a coffee-table book of photos of Trump in the White House, which he had personally captioned, selling for seventy-five dollars apiece (his official White House photographer had told Trump's aides that she wanted to do a book of her own; they sought a cut of her advance in exchange for writing a forward and helping to promote it, and then he went ahead with his own). Trump promoted himself as a DJ at Mar-a-Lago, and he hosted a high-dollar fundraiser where candidates for office around the country, charging six-figure donations to one of his own committees; guests also had the option to rent a room at the club. Jared Kushner had separately launched a multibillion-dollar investment fund, believed to be seeded partly from money in the Middle East, where he had engineered meaningful diplomatic breakthroughs that also happened to deepen his personal relationships. (Kushner was not particularly interested in helping some colleagues who sought him out after the White House years ended, complaining, "No good deed goes unpunished.")

The most audacious plan was for a social media company of Trump's own. In the days immediately after January 6, Trump was suspended from Twitter, Facebook, Instagram, and YouTube; he spent most of the next year insisting that he did not care about being banned while suing the companies to get his accounts restored. In October, he announced that he would launch his own social network as part of a merger with a so-called blank-check company, whose stock price shot up when its merger was announced. The funding mechanism, which sparked an SEC investigation prior to the platform's launch, was completely opaque.

Trump had long marveled at whom he attracted, and how. "Can you believe these are my customers?" he had asked once while surveying the crowd at the Taj Mahal casino's poker room. "Look at those losers," he said to his consultant, Tom O'Neil, of people spending money on the floor of the Trump Plaza casino. Visiting the Iowa State Fair as a presidential candidate in 2015, he was astounded that locals fell in line to support him because of a few free rides in his branded helicopter. When in the White House, he was sometimes stunned at his own backers' fervor, telling aides, "They're fucking crazy." Yet they loved him and wanted to own a piece of him, and that was what mattered most.

The highs of Trump's moneymaking efforts were offset by a year of blows to the Trump Organization. During his presidency, some Trump advisers were open about the fact that the office shielded him from prosecution—a reality that would exist again should he return to the presidency. Six months after he left office, however, the Manhattan district attorney Cy Vance formally attached criminality to the Trump name. He indicted Trump's company, alleging that it participated in an extended tax-avoidance scheme, and that its chief financial officer, Allen Weisselberg, had evaded taxes on fringe benefits he had received. Five months later, Atlanta-area district attorney Fani Willis empaneled a special grand jury investigating Trump's efforts to tamper with local election results, including his ominous call demanding the secretary of state "find" votes for him.

And yet, as had happened so often before, someone or something intervened. Alvin Bragg, who in January 2022 succeeded Vance in the Manhattan district attorney's office, let expire a special grand jury exploring whether to indict Trump personally, a decision that infuriated the prosecutors who'd pursued the case. Trump's lawyers were mindful that both Bragg and New York attorney general Letitia James had criticized Trump during their candidacies for their prosecutorial offices in a way that Trump's team could use to argue against their cases in court. Bragg ultimately worried about bringing an indictment and using Michael Cohen, Trump's former fixer, as a key witness. Trump had also begun a new attack against those investigating him. At a point when all three investigations were still active, Trump used a campaign-style rally in Texas to call the prosecutors "racist"— Willis, Bragg, and James are all Black—and urged his supporters to launch protests in Atlanta, Washington, and New York if they did anything "illegal or wrong."

Throughout the year, Trump also tried to manage the stories told of his presidency, speaking to nearly every author writing a book on the topic. I was among them. I had three interviews with Trump for this book, the first of which his team offered and the second two I requested.

Trump typically welcomed visiting authors for interviews in an indoor area at Mar-a-Lago that gets converted to a dining room at night, where a model of the redesigned Air Force One—whose proposed new livery had been an early focus of Trump's after winning the presidency but was to be developed after his term—sat proudly on a low table. Trump had registered to vote in Florida while he was president, something his family said he likely would have done even if he'd lost in 2016. But after the headiness of being at the center of the world's gaze, his time after the White House made him seem shrunken. He often played golf and then went to his newly built office at the club for meetings with whoever traveled down to seek his approval. He would watch television before going to dinner, where club members would sometimes applaud him, and then it would start all over again the next day, so removed from the daily rhythms of the broader world that he was oblivious to holidays on the calendar and staff had to remind him.

When I arrived for the first interview, in March 2021, I was ushered away from that room to a smaller dining area where Trump sometimes dined with guests. The club was empty, but I thought little of it, because it was only around 4:30 p.m. when I arrived;

I learned as we wrapped up that it was empty because it had been closed off after a COVID scare, but Trump decided to have us sit there regardless, without checking to see if I was vaccinated. "COVID," Trump said as he described the club's closure, "turns out, not good."

Trump greeted me cordially before taking a seat across the table from me; he was in sales mode, not combat mode. He wanted to hear from me about news in New York. "How is Cuomo doing?" he asked almost immediately.

Andrew Cuomo, in his third term as New York's governor, had been accused by three women, two of them state employees, of sexual harassment (the number would grow to eleven). Senior Democrats in both Albany and Washington had rushed to demand an investigation. "I was very surprised," Trump said. He was referring not to the sexual harassment allegations, but the fact that members of Cuomo's own party had spoken out about them. (He would be gone within months, resigning in order to avoid impeachment hearings.)

I pointed out that Democrats no longer feared Cuomo, and that many resented how he had treated them over time. By contrast, a number of Republican lawmakers still liked Trump, even after everything that he had foisted upon them, and those who feared him generally did so because of his popularity with their voters. Cuomo never cared about being liked, only about wielding power, but Trump was animated by both.

Talking about Cuomo's difficulties prompted Trump to look back on his own first impeachment trial as a positive memory. "You have to keep a smile," Trump said, calling the experience "different" than the ultimately abandoned impeachment proceedings against Richard Nixon, which had occurred when Trump was twenty-seven. "That was a dark period of time, right?" he asked me. "Mine wasn't dark at all. I was actually having a good time. And my numbers went up every time I got impeached. It cheapened the impeachment process very severely."

His history in New York dominated our interview. He thought back to the first major political figure he had observed up close, Democratic Party boss Meade Esposito, who dominated Brooklyn politics when Trump joined his father's real estate business. "Meade ruled with an iron fist," Trump said. "And he was a very strong leader, to put it mildly. And when I came to Washington, I said, Oh, well, this is now the big league. So as tough as they were, this must be even tougher. But I said, how could anybody be tougher than Meade? Meade had a cane at the end. He used to start swinging the cane at people. I mean, he was wild." Trump had seemed to try to emulate Esposito's style in his post-presidency, receiving visitors who came to kiss his ring, and picking favorites in primaries to try to determine the outcomes of those races.

I asked him if he had expected the presidency to function the same way. Rather, Trump said, that is how he thought congressional leaders would act on his behalf: "Well, I figured that the Mitch McConnells would be like him, in the sense of strength." There were plenty of factual problems with the criticism. In fact, McConnell had kept Republican senators in line over and over to advance Trump's policy and personnel concerns and generally protect his political standing as the leader of the Republican Party. Nevertheless, Trump said to me in another session, using his favorite new nickname for McConnell, "The Old Crow's a piece of shit." Trump also complained to me about senators successfully practicing this type of power politics against him, as Lindsey Graham and Ted Cruz had when they persuaded Trump not to back a challenge to a colleague, Nebraska's Ben Sasse; Trump gave a surprise endorsement to Sasse, who after winning reelection voted to convict Trump during his second impeachment. "Like a schmuck, I went along with it," Trump said.

When I explained that my book would tie together his life in New York with his life in the White House, Trump responded with an elaborate story about friends who years earlier had asked him for help securing a restaurant reservation because he was better known than they were. "Before I did the presidency, but I was famous and rich, and they were rich. And I'd say, they call me up. 'Hi, Don, how you doing? Listen, I'm going to Joe's Stone Crab in Miami. I can't get in. There's a line that's a mile long, could you get me in?' I said, 'Yeah.'" I wasn't really sure where he was going with this, other than to convey that the point of celebrity appeared to be to get preferential treatment in public.

"Sometimes I say, what's the point? You understand. Some people are rich," Trump went on. "They can't get a table at a restaurant. So no, but the job we've done has been amazing."

I recalled that this was almost identical to something he had told **Washington Post** journalist Lois Romano when she interviewed him for a 1984 profile. Her article opened with Trump professing to be uneasy that they had arrived for breakfast at the Plaza Hotel without a reservation. Trump permitted Romano to observe him as he secured one on the basis of his bold-faced name, remarking to her as he did that he knew "one of the most successful men in New York, and he couldn't get a table at a restaurant," until Trump, standing in the same restaurant, swooped in to help, gifting the man an important life lesson. The man had needed for people to know who he was, and not merely to be rich.

Trump's response helped me to answer something I had planned to ask him, which he raised before I got the chance to. "The question I get asked more than any other question: If you had it to do again, would you have done it?" Trump said of running for president. "The answer is, yeah, I think so. Because here's the way I look at it. I have so many rich friends and nobody knows who they are." He then went on to talk about how much easier life would have been had he not run. Yet there it was: reflecting on the meaning of having been president of the United States, his first impulse was not to mention public service, or what he felt he'd accomplished, only that it appeared to be a vehicle for fame, and that many experiences were only worth having if someone else envied them. (When I asked him in a later interview about what he'd liked about the job, he replied, "Getting things done," and listed a few accomplishments.)

Trump was clear he did not believe he would have faced any of the same legal problems that had dogged him if Manhattan's longtime district attorney, Robert Morgenthau, had still been in office. "No. He was a friend of mine. He was a great gentleman. He was a great man. He was highly respected. No. And I run a clean organization. This is a continuation of the witch hunt." He added, "Bob Morgenthau would not have stood for this." The investigation by Morgenthau's successor, he insisted, was part of "an attack on the Republic."

He was perhaps even more dire when describing the threat he had faced from the special counsel investigation into his campaign's ties to Russia. It forced him, he said, to perform "two jobs when I was president, running the country and survival."

We met again for a follow-up interview five weeks later, again at Mar-a-Lago, again in the late afternoon. He was not in a good mood. By way of greeting, he told me, "I'm watching the Arizona situation very carefully." It was shorthand familiar at least to anyone closely following conservative media, but it had not gotten much mainstream attention yet: a private company called the Cyber Ninjas was conducting a so-called audit of Maricopa County ballots and tabulation equipment that had been handed over by the Republican-led State Senate.

He had talked about his claims of widespread fraud in our first interview, but not about trying to undo the results. He seemed to be going backward. I learned later that he'd tried getting the RNC to fund the "audit" in Arizona, to no avail (the "audit" ultimately affirmed the results of the state's election).

He was at his most animated when I asked about why he had trusted Sidney Powell, given the concerns his other advisers had about her. Since then, Powell had faced libel suits from voting-machine manufacturers she had accused of corruption; her defense had been, essentially, that no one should have taken what she had to say seriously. "I was very disappointed in her statement," Trump said. "That is so demeaning for her to say about herself." Then he essentially read stage directions on how to use public claims in lawsuits. "All she had to say," he said, "was 'upon information and belief, I think such and such.' Now all she says there, was take a thousand stories that were written over the last ten years long before all of this, that are bad stories," he said, "and that is information and belief, she read them. And that's the end of that case. That's true for everybody: 'It's upon information and belief and let's go to court to find out if it's true.'"

I pressed him on what, at that point, was one of the persistent mysteries of January 6, which would become central to the congressional select committee's investigation: what he had been doing in the hours when the Capitol was under assault from his supporters. He insisted he was not watching television, despite volumes of witness testimony and other evidence to the contrary. "I didn't usually have the television on. I'd have it on if there was something. I then later turned it on and I saw what was happening," he said. He lied throughout that bit of our interview: "I had heard that afterward and actually on the late side. I was having meetings. I was also with Mark Meadows and others. I was not watching television."

Our third meeting was at the end of the summer, which he had largely spent at the quarters that he kept on the grounds of his New Jersey golf course. When I arrived at the Trump National Golf Club Bedminster, I waited in a small room off the front entrance. I spotted Lindsey Graham outside, in golf pants; it was the second time I had encountered him in Trump's vicinity that year. Trump eventually entered the room, having lost a noticeable amount of weight since I had seen him last. Graham followed a minute later and gestured toward Trump. "The greatest comeback in American history!" Graham declared.

Trump looked at me. "You know why Lindsey kisses my ass?" he asked. "So I'll endorse his friends." Graham laughed uproariously.

It was shortly after the twentieth anniversary of the September 11 attacks. That day, after being nudged by aides to somehow honor the occasion, Trump had grudgingly agreed to visit a Manhattan police station for a brief photo op and visit, at which he gave an abridged version of a rally address. Afterward, he flew to Florida, where he and his eldest son gave color commentary for a boxing match at the Hard Rock Casino, the same venue that Trump had walked away from building twenty-five years earlier, and then engaged in a punishing legal fight with one of his closest former advisers. Meanwhile, in New York, the city's former mayor Rudy Giuliani hosted an annual dinner that had begun as a somber remembrance for people who had worked together on the day of the attacks. Like its host, the event had during the Trump years morphed into something almost unrecognizable. The 2021 dinner featured Steve Bannon, who livestreamed it on the same platforms he and Giuliani had used to promote their plans to overturn the presidential election.

Earlier that day, former president George W. Bush, who had remained largely silent during Trump's presidency, condemned domestic "extremism" and the "malign forces" in the country. "So much of our politics has become a naked appeal to anger, fear and resentment," he said in Shanksville, Pennsylvania, near where one of four hijacked planes had crashed into a field on September 11. He never mentioned Trump directly.

When I asked Trump about his own seeming lack of interest in being part of the informal club of living ex-presidents, he mentioned what had just happened in Shanksville. "I'm glad Bush did the speech the other day," he said, pausing, "because it allows me to talk about him. He did a terrible job as president. And getting into the Middle East, overall."

It was Trump's successor, however, who ultimately delivered on Trump's desires to end the country's twenty-year adventure in Afghanistan. Trump revised history to claim he had a plan in place for withdrawal and that if only Joe Biden had followed it, everything would have been fine. "The Taliban was totally under control" while he was president, Trump insisted. "There was no problem. We could have left. We could have taken a year, two years, or two months. They would have never been anywhere near us. They were not fucking around with me."

There were no simple or easy choices for the United States in Afghanistan, but Trump reduced the aftermath of the departure to managing a construction project. "They say, 'It's easier to build a new building and cheaper than it is to renovate an old one.' Well that's not true, unless you don't know what you're doing," he told me. "I have people that don't know what they're doing in real estate. They say, I mean, you have the foundations, you have the construction, you have the exterior, maybe if you want to use it. It's a lot less expensive to renovate if you know what you're doing. So anyway this reminded me of that."

Trump aimed his criticism at Mark Milley, whom he had appointed as the chairman of the Joint Chiefs of Staff, "who's basically stupid," citing a dispute they had over the cost of removing military equipment from Afghanistan. "I have to tell you, there are two Mark Milleys," Trump explained. "Mark Milley for me was okay. He wasn't a genius, but he was okay. He blew it. When he suggested he walked down to the church, which was just smolder—"

I interrupted him; it was laughable to claim that it was the army general's idea to conduct what became a photo op in front of St. John's Church in the midst of Black Lives Matter protests feet away. "He suggested walking to the church?" I asked, incredulous. "Oh, yeah," Trump said, before backing off the claim. "He said . . . well, let me say that it was at least equal. Because he was with me. We had a ceremony for something. He was there and it was suggested that we walk down. He said, 'That's a good idea.' And we walked down. It was no big deal. Nobody ever thought of it." None of that was what had happened; it had been a Rose Garden speech specifically scheduled so Trump could criticize the unrest in the wake of a brutal murder of a Black man by police. "Then the radical left started calling him and saying, 'He shouldn't have walked.' And instead of saying, 'I'm proud to walk with my president,' or, 'I'm proud to walk with the Office of the President.' It's the Office of the President, it's the presidency. Instead of saying that, Maggie, he started apologizing, and once he apologized, I said, 'Forget that guy. He's a weak sister.'"

Trump had not wanted to be part of the so-called "president's club," and I was curious when he said he kept in touch with other world leaders since leaving office. I asked whether that included Russia's Vladimir Putin and China's Xi Jinping, and he said "no." But when I mentioned North Korea's Kim Jong-un, he responded, "Well, I don't want to say exactly, but," before trailing off. I learned after the interview that he had been telling people at Mar-a-Lago that he was still in contact with North Korea's supreme leader, whose picture with Trump hung on the wall of his new office at his club.

He demurred when I asked if he had taken any documents of note upon departing the White House—"nothing of great urgency, no," he said—before mentioning the letters that Kim Jong-un had sent him, which he had showed off to so many Oval Office visitors that advisers were concerned he was being careless with sensitive material. "You were able to take those with you?" I asked. He kept talking, seeming to have registered my surprise, and said, "No, I think that's in the archives, but . . . Most of it is in the archives, but the Kim Jong-un letters . . . We have incredible things." In fact, Trump did not return the letters—which were included in boxes he had brought to Mar-a-Lago—to the National Archives until after **The Washington Post** reported on it in early 2022; the Justice Department began investigating how the classified material made its way in and out of the White House residence. (In one of our earlier interviews, I had asked him separately about some of the texts between the FBI agent and the FBI official working on the Mueller investigation whose affair prompted the agent's removal from the case; we had learned the night before Biden's inauguration that Trump was planning to make them public. He ultimately didn't, but he told me that Meadows had that material in his possession and offered to connect me with him.)

He said there was a "misconception" that he didn't get along with other Western leaders, as opposed to Putin. Instead of focusing on his vocal undercutting of the central tenet of the North Atlantic Treaty Organization's mission, he talked about his signing of congressionally approved sanctions on the Nord Stream 2 gas pipeline between Germany and Russia. "That was against Russia," Trump insisted. "I mean, he can't be thrilled about that." I asked if Putin had ever asked him to back away from NATO. "No, never. No, he never did," Trump said. "One thing he did say, he said, 'You're killing me in the pipeline.' Despite that," Trump said of the pipeline, "I liked Putin, and Putin liked me."

Six months later, when Putin sent the Russian military to invade Ukraine, Trump initially praised him as "savvy" for recognizing the opportunity before him: a land grab in exchange for paying a fine in the form of international sanctions. "He's taken over a country for two dollars' worth of sanctions, I'd say that's pretty smart," he said during an appearance at Mar-a-Lago. "He's taking over a country—a vast, vast location, a great piece of land with a lot of people—just walking right in." He eventually moved to condemn the invasion, although without criticizing Putin directly. At Mar-a-Lago, he repeated rumors from right-wing news outlets claiming Putin might be cancer-stricken.

I asked why he had been attracted to doing business in Russia over so many years. "I thought building a building in Moscow would be good and would be glamorous," he said. "But the concept is very tough. You know, the ownership position with Russia is not like the ownership position here." It's "much different. You know, when they tell you, you know, 'Build a building, but by the way you don't own it.'" I pressed again on what exactly had appealed to him about building there. Was it the challenge of it? "No, I thought it would be a glamorous project. I do a lot of things for glamour. I like glamour. You know the word 'glamour'?" he said. "I love glamour."

I had long watched the way people drifted in and out of Trump's world, and how he often let back in people he had earlier cut off. In our first interview, he had spoken buoyantly about Bannon, who years after being pushed from a top White House job returned to play a central role in the postelection efforts in

2020. "He was negative and he had a lot of people that he didn't like in the administration, so I understand," Trump had said, noting that Bannon had since become "very positive." (Trump did not mention that two of the people in the administration whom Bannon had been most vocal about not liking were Trump's daughter and son-in-law.) I asked him about others who had been at his side even before he launched his first political campaign. He praised his onetime campaign manager Corey Lewandowski. Former communications director Hope Hicks was "fantastic." Sam Nunberg, an adviser whom he had sued for allegedly violating a campaign nondisclosure agreement and who had then countersued, forcing a settlement, was "very smart politically," he said, adding that Nunberg had said positive things about him recently. (Nunberg had fought the suit, which was eventually settled.) Roger Stone "understood politics better than most," he said.

Over the course of our conversations, he appeared reluctant to take shots at many of those people on whom I knew him to have been toughest behind closed doors. His campaign manager Brad Parscale spent money "unwisely," he said, but he did not criticize him beyond that. "I didn't" give Kushner expansive power, Trump said when I asked why he had done exactly that. When I pressed, Trump said, "Look, my daughter has a great relationship with him and that's very important."

He was not so sanguine about Mike Pence, who had

begun to defend his own actions on January 6 with increasing stridency, prompting Trump to escalate his condemnation of his former vice president's judgment that day. "I said, 'Mike, you have a chance to be Thomas Jefferson, or you can be Mike Pence,'" Trump recounted to me, repeating an inaccurate comparison to the election of 1800. "He chose to be Mike Pence." I brought up another potential future primary rival, by mentioning that he had been compared to New Jersey's feisty governor Chris Christie before the two men faced off in the 2016 primary. Trump replied, "I was compared to him? Why? I didn't know I had that big of a weight problem." A small smirk followed. Then, "He's an opportunist." I heard that Trump was describing Florida governor Ron DeSantis, in similar terms to Christie, calling him "fat," "phony," and "whiny," while claiming credit for making his candidacy in 2018.

Even as he talked about launching another campaign for the presidency, Trump was more comfortable looking back than forward. When I told Trump I wanted to talk about 2024, he asked, "2024 or 2020?"

Trump may have been unlike any president in American history, but the clean break many expected as soon as he left office failed to materialize. Biden, too, struggled to handle the pandemic, and after he condemned Trump's xenophobia during the campaign, the Biden administration enraged immigration advocates by not immediately ending a border-crossing restriction ostensibly related to curbing disease but that served to limit immigration. Aspects of Trump's belligerent posture toward China remained American policy. The political shifts that in 2016 first appeared to be a function of Trump's personality-driven populism began to look like part of a permanent realignment, with party coalitions sorting on the basis of education levels, culture, and a growing urban versus exurban geography, rather than the old divides of religion, income, or even ideology. Those trends polarized issues that once were largely removed from politics; after Trump was booed at rallies for recommending coronavirus vaccines, he complained privately that he couldn't get proper credit for their existence due to opposition from what he called the "radical right."

Some industries are dotted with people who share aspects of Trump's behavior—a messy personal history, a ruthlessness in approaching rivals, complete willingness to submit to the needs of any given moment, a dismissiveness of one's own flesh and blood. But American politics had operated in such a way that certain behaviors were understood to be disqualifying from holding higher office, at least once they became public. Over the course of reporting this book, various Republicans and even some Democrats pointed to the rule-defying Bill Clinton presidency as helping to pave the way for Trump decades earlier. Clinton, too, was criticized for breaching ethical norms and had faced nonstop inquiries into his finances, personal conduct, and political maneuvers throughout his presidency. He shared some of Trump's complaints about congressional probes, independent prosecutors, and media coverage, and some of the same sense of gratification at surviving all three. But the relative volumes of their transgressive behavior, and the overall arcs of their lives, were very different. Clinton grew up working-class, and had spent a lifetime in public service and government generally accepting the frameworks of those systems. Trump, the son of a wealthy man, showed no interest in them. And he had no compunction about being seen as using the government as if it were an extension of himself.

When the tide sank, all boats were lowered. Trump had proven that the majority of Washington Republicans who had initially opposed him were exactly as craven as he had said they were, as he bent them to his will because they saw personal opportunity or necessity for survival, even after the Capitol riot. The ranks of those who had found wealth through new sectors of anti-Trump media and activism exposed a different set of perverse financial incentives driving political behavior in problematic directions.

Trump appeared to be ushering in a new era of behavior, real and expected, from politicians, his relativism seeping into the national fabric. He appeared to make that point during our September interview as we talked about Herschel Walker, the former star of his New Jersey Generals football franchise then running for the U.S. Senate from Georgia. I said that Walker has a "complicated personal history"—namely accusations of assault against women—that worried other Republicans. "He does, but do you know that it's a personal history that, ten years ago, maybe it would have been a problem. Twenty years ago would've been a bigger problem. I don't think it's a problem today," Trump said. "Why is that?" I asked. "Why do you think that's changed?" "Because the world is changing," he said. He did not acknowledge that it was changing because he had helped change it.

The House committee on which Cheney served spent months documenting what happened in the lead-up to the Capitol riot, including Trump's intimate involvement in various efforts to keep himself in power. Among the most disturbing testimony concerned his personal pressure on Justice Department officials to discredit state election results, despite being told repeatedly that his demands exceeded the law. Ultimately, it was a twenty-six-year-old aide to Meadows—the chief of staff whose compulsion to tell different people what they wanted to hear arguably helped pave the way for the events of that day—who first publicly described the president's unhinged behavior on January 6. Cassidy Hutchinson described Trump in a rage, as the crowd in place for his Ellipse speech was thinner than he wanted it to be. Trump blamed Secret Service checkpoints keeping some of his armed supporters out, Hutchinson testified, and demanded metal detectors be taken down even after he was warned that some people were carrying weapons. "They're not here to hurt me," she recalled him saying, before he took to the stage and told them to walk "patriotically and peacefully" to the Capitol. "I'm the fucking president," she related Trump saying as he demanded to be taken there himself.

Trump loyalists quickly began trying to tear down Hutchinson's credibility. Yet even as some contradicted specific elements in her testimony, she had painted a familiar portrait of Trump, one that dozens of people who worked for his company, political campaigns, and government tried masking over four decades: a narcissistic drama-seeker who covered a fragile ego with a bullying impulse and, this time, took American democracy to the brink.

Trump's heart did not seem to be in a return to electoral politics. When the Supreme Court that he reshaped overturned the landmark **Roe v. Wade** abortion decision, Trump—who as president usually outsourced criticism of abortion to Pence—privately had to be coaxed into issuing a statement of praise. "I never like to take credit for anything," he laughably informed my colleague Michael Bender about his silence after a draft of the decision leaked; privately he told advisers the court's move would be "bad for Republicans." As investigations into the post-election schemes to undermine the transfer of power intensified, Trump struggled to find new lawyers he liked, turning to a childhood classmate, Peter Ticktin. He also began more aggressively considering plans for a third presidential campaign.

I had covered Trump as a political figure for many years by then, and little was surprising. And still the choreography of in-person interviews could reveal moments of unintended candor. He started to explain why he doesn't like when audiotapes of his interviews are released. Being on camera was "much different," he said. "Whereas," he said, in a "written interview, I'll repeat it twenty times, because I want to drum it into your beautiful brain. Do you understand that?" He repeated himself again. "One of the things I'll do, if I'm doing, like with you, for the written word, is I got to drum it into your head. So I'll repeat something six times."

His interest in repetition was not news to me, but his self-awareness of it was notable. At another point, he was going on a stemwinder about New York's then outgoing mayor Bill de Blasio canceling a contract with the Trump Organization to manage a public golf course in the Bronx after January 6. De Blasio's choice to replace Trump was deeply controversial, and a judge later ruled in Trump's favor.

"It's like communism," he said, asking what the word was for when someone takes your property. (It came to him twenty minutes later. "'Confiscate' is the word," he declared in the middle of another thought.) I tried redirecting him, but he cut me off. "Let me just finish it," he said. "Just let me do this, and then I'm going to tell you," he said. He seemed to hear himself, and smiled. Then he turned to the two aides he had sitting in on our interview, gestured toward me with his hand, and said, "I love being with her, she's like my psychiatrist."

It was a meaningless line, almost certainly intended to flatter, the kind of thing he has said about the power of release he got from his Twitter feed or other interviews he has given over the years. The reality is he treats everyone like they are his psychiatrists—reporters, government aides, and members of Congress, friends and pseudofriends and rally attendees and White House staff and customers. All present a chance for him to vent or test reactions or gauge how his statements are playing or discover how he is feeling. He works things out in real time in front of all of us. Along the way, he reoriented an entire country to react to his moods and emotions. I spent the four years of his presidency getting asked by people to decipher why he was doing what he was doing, but the truth is, ultimately, almost no one really knows him. Some know him better than others, but he is often simply, purely opaque, permitting people to read meaning and depth into every action, no matter how empty they may be.

Acknowledgments

I owe everything to my husband, my children, my three parents, and my brother and sister for their support and understanding over six tumultuous years of covering a campaign, a presidency by commute, and then writing a book on what had taken place.

Confidence Man would not exist without Sasha Issenberg, who patiently guided me through the process of writing it and worked on the material to make sense of it all. Cameron Peters was an extraordinary research assistant, who went above and beyond in his work for this project. Julie Tate, an incredible researcher and fact-checker, was deeply patient.

Colleagues who covered the beat from other outlets were absolute rocks to me. John Santucci was a dear friend and colleague, throughout the campaign, the White House years, and thereafter. Jonathan Swan and Josh Dawsey were intense and fearsome competitors and also very good friends; Swan's "Off the Rails" series about the final days of the Trump presidency was one of the most significant contributions to the historical record that's been written.

At the **Times,** Michael Schmidt was my ride-or-die

and closest collaborator for several years; he was invaluable then, and invaluable through the book process. He, Mark Mazzetti, Adam Goldman, Julian Barnes, and Matt Apuzzo were good colleagues and good friends who helped me enormously through the Trump presidency and over the last year.

Matt Flegenheimer gave me endless feedback and support since I joined the paper, but particularly during the year of this book, and was incredibly patient along the way. Annie Karni wrote one of the most important stories of the presidency, about how Trump ripped up official documents. Katie Rogers and Zolan Kanno-Youngs helped on reporting and with my thinking on a beat we covered together closely for years. Erica Green and Katie Benner, two excellent collaborators and journalists, kept me sane. Alex Burns and Jonathan Martin were my longtime partners at **Politico** before we all went to the **Times;** they are two of the best political reporters in the country, and they repeatedly carried me over the years. Julie Davis, Peter Baker, Michael Shear, Mark Landler, David Sanger, and the inimitable Doug Mills all were models for me as I learned to navigate the White House beat. So were Ben Protess and Willie Rashbaum in understanding the investigations into Trump. Nick Corasaniti was a true friend in the process.

My terrific editor at Penguin Press, Scott Moyers, was incredibly patient with life and with a changing world, as were members of his team. So were my agents at Javelin, Matt Latimer and Keith Urbahn, who steered me through this process with ease and good humor. My excellent lawyer, Michael O'Connor, guided me through everything else with fortitude.

Outside the paper, Trump chroniclers Tim O'Brien and Neil Barsky and Gwenda Blair and Harry Hurt and Michael D'Antonio were incredibly generous with their time, as was Tom Robbins, one of the greatest New York newspaper veterans around. Wayne Barrett was too; he was a great teacher to those of us who were just coming up, starting when I went on television for the first time in 1999, on a panel with Barrett, and I did so poorly that he took me for coffee afterward. He passed away on the eve of Trump's inauguration.

David McCraw, the **Times**'s main lawyer, was an extensive source of support. So was A. G. Sulzberger, a publisher whom I watched as he pushed back, in the Oval Office, on Trump's language attacking journalists. Dean Baquet and Carolyn Ryan, who hired me for the paper, gave me permission to write the book and time to finish it. Matt Purdy took endless phone calls from me about the White House beat and then the writing of this book. Elisabeth Bumiller, Dick Stevenson, and Bill Hamilton provided me a home in the Washington bureau despite my working for it from afar, and Rebecca Blumenstein offered me extensive support.

Ben Smith, Maureen Dowd, Olivia Nuzzi, Ruby Cramer, Kara Swisher, Andrew Meier, and Brian Koppelman all helped shape my thinking as I worked on this project. At CNN, where Jeff Zucker hired me and gave me a shot on television, I am thankful to Rebecca Kutler, Jamie Zahn, M. J. Lee, Jake Tapper, John Berman, Brianna Keiler, Kaitlin Collins, Alyson Camerota, Wolf Blitzer, and Anderson Cooper. Elsewhere, I'm thankful to Devlin Barrett, Phil Rucker, Steve Holland, Jill Colvin, Jonathan Lemire, John Harris, Jim VandeHei, Mike Allen, Ashley Parker, Lois Romano, Michael Bender, and Jonathan Karl.

I have to thank the person who gave me my first job in journalism, Stuart Marques, and the person he assigned me to work with, the late Jack Newfield, as well as the four people from whom I learned nearly everything: David Seifman, Gregg Birnbaum, Robert Hardt, and Mike Hechtman. I am eternally grateful to my first coauthor, Jeane MacIntosh, as well as Kerri Lyon, Stefan Friedman, Kate Lucadamo, Lisa Colangelo, Dinny Fitzpatrick, Amanda Nelson Mandel, and Danny Kanner. There are also people who helped me think through the changing landscape of the Republican Party; John Ellis, David Kochel, Liam Donovan, and Jim Hobart were a particular help.

There are things to clarify. Because of Trump's fixation on me, I got criticism for pieces that weren't actually mine, but also credit for information that other reporters had first. Alex Burns was the first to learn that Trump had lost his cell phone in a Bedminster golf cart and should have had a byline on our story referencing it (and through an error of mine did not), while Emily Flitter first heard about a Trump parking garage lessee sending him gold bars, but we couldn't confirm it at the time.

And there are things to be grateful for. It was a privilege to cover the White House during a historic presidency, and it has been a privilege to be a reporter as long as I have. To those of you who have read my work, including this book, I thank you.

Notes

PROLOGUE

8 **conceived years earlier:** Tina Nguyen, "Trump Ally Wants Trump Delegates to Sign Loyalty Pledge," **Vanity Fair,** April 13, 2016.

16 **the eternal now:** Michael Gerson, "A Huge Question for Trump's North Korea Crisis," **Washington Post,** August 10, 2017.

22 **about the missteps:** Maggie Haberman, Ashley Parker, Jeremy W. Peters, and Michael Barbaro, "Inside Donald Trump's Last Stand: An Anxious Nominee Seeks Assurance," **New York Times,** November 6, 2016.

CHAPTER 1: THE POWER OF NEGATIVE THINKING

25 **morning of November 21, 1964:** Gay Talese, "Staten Island Link to Sister Boroughs Is Opening Today," **New York Times,** November 21, 1964.

25 **an array of politicians:** Gay Talese, "Verrazano Bridge Opened to Traffic; New Landmark Greeted with Fanfare in Harbor," **New York Times**, November 22, 1964.

25 **drove over the bridge:** Talese, "Verrazano Bridge Opened to Traffic."

26 **disappeared into the grandstand:** Bernard Stamler, "City Lore; New York's Other Master Bridge Builder," **New York Times,** April 16, 2000.

26 **as a "sad experience":** Stamler, "City Lore."

26 **"rain was coming down":** Howard Blum, "Trump: Development of a Manhattan Developer," **New York Times,** August 26, 1980.

26 **Gay Talese's next-day Times dispatch:** Talese, "Verrazano Bridge Opened to Traffic."

27 **emigrated from Switzerland:** Stamler, "City Lore."

27 **"greatest living bridge engineer":** The New York Public Radio Archive Collections, WNYC, "Verrazano Narrows Bridge Dedication," November 20, 1964.

28 **freshman at Fordham:** Sophie Kozub, "Inside Trump's Days at Fordham," **Observer,** January 26, 2017.

28 **toyed with studying film:** Nancy Collins, "Donald Trump Talks Family, Women in Unearthed Transcript: 'When I Come Home and Dinner's Not Ready, I Go Through the Roof,'" **Hollywood Reporter,** October 13, 2016.

29 **practice of pseudonymity:** Marc Fisher, and Will Hobson, "Donald Trump Masqueraded as Publicist to Brag About Himself," **Washington Post,** May 13, 2016.

30 **"barbaric European history":** Gwenda Blair, **The Trumps: Three Generations That Built an Empire** (New York: Simon & Schuster, 2000).

30 **After six years:** Ted Widmer, "An Immigrant Named Trump," **New Yorker,** October 1, 2016.

31 **married in 1902:** Blair, **The Trumps.**

31 **household spoke German:** Blair, **The Trumps.**

31 **"Then he died":** Blair, **The Trumps.**

31 **than a half million dollars:** Blair, **The Trumps.**

32 **work as a carpenter:** Alden Whitman, "A Builder Looks Back—and Moves Forward," **New York Times,** January 28, 1973.

32 **Ku Klux Klan rally:** Philip Bump, "In 1927, Donald Trump's Father Was Arrested After a Klan Riot in Queens," **Washington Post,** February 29, 2016.

32 **Fred ingratiated himself:** Wayne Barrett, **Trump: The Deals and the Downfall** (New York: HarperCollins, 1992).

33 **an appealing addition:** Barrett, **Trump: The Deals and the Downfall.**

34 **influential political clubs:** Barrett, **Trump: The Deals and the Downfall.**

35 **Trump maintain ownership:** Kimberly Pierceall, "Tracing Donald Trump's Financial Ties to Norfolk Starts with Father Fred," **Virginian-Pilot,** August 13, 2016.

35 **pelted by rocks:** Paul Schwartzman and Michael E. Miller, "Confident. Incorrigible. Bully: Little Donny Was a Lot Like Candidate Donald Trump," **Washington Post,** June 22, 2016.

35 **a Scottish immigrant:** Michael Kranish and Marc Fisher, **Trump Revealed: An American Journey of Ambition, Ego, Money, and Power** (New York: Scribner, 2016).

35 **either in Atlantic City:** Blair, **The Trumps.**

35 **an "oasis" from:** Jason Horowitz, "Donald Trump's Old Queens Neighborhood Contrasts with the Diverse Area Around It," **New York Times,** September 22, 2015.

36 **paper delivery route:** Blair, **The Trumps.**

36 **with vanity plates:** Stephen Nessen, "The One Thing Donald Trump Didn't Inherit," WNYC News, August 24, 2015.

36 **might not survive:** Blair, **The Trumps.**

37 **Robert's toy blocks:** Kranish and Fisher, **Trump Revealed.**

37 **the private elementary:** Kranish and Fisher, **Trump Revealed.**

38 **bedsheets in his home:** Peter Brant, "'Trump Revealed': The Reporting Archive," inteview by Michael E. Miller, n.d., **Washington Post,** www .washingtonpost.com/wp-stat/graphics/politics/ trump-archive/docs/peter-brant.pdf.

38 **his son's collection:** Schwartzman and Miller, "Confident. Incorrigible. Bully."

38 **"sent to military academy":** Brant, "'Trump Revealed.'"

39 **promotion to captain:** Schwartzman and Miller, "Confident. Incorrigible. Bully."

39 **did so "at a remove":** Sandy McIntosh, "How Young Donald Trump Was Slapped and Punched Until He Made His Bed," **New York Daily News,** August 11, 2017.

40 **"designation of Ladies' Man":** Peter Ticktin, **What Makes Trump Tick: My Years with Donald Trump**

from New York Military Academy to the Present (Herndon, VA: Mascot Books, 2020).

40 **"where he got in":** Blair, **The Trumps.**

40 **but withdrew as:** Jake Shore, "'A Bit of a Loner,' Former Classmates Remember Donald Trump in the Bronx," **Fordham Ram,** February 4, 2021.

40 **only scattered impressions:** Shore, "'A Bit of a Loner.'"

41 **tracts of land:** Barrett, **Trump: The Deals and the Downfall.**

41 **private financing eluded:** Barrett, **Trump: The Deals and the Downfall.**

42 **Fred Trump found himself:** Barrett, **Trump: The Deals and the Downfall.**

42 **only as "not photographed":** Rebecca Tan and Alex Rabin, "Many of Trump's Wharton Classmates Don't Remember Him," **Daily Pennsylvanian,** February 20, 2017.

42 **"king of New York real estate":** Matt Viser, "Donald Trump Was Brash, Even at Wharton Business School," **Boston Globe,** August 28, 2015.

43 **handed out bricks:** Michael Daly, "How Donald's Dad Fred Trump Tried to Kill Coney Island," **Daily Beast,** July 12, 2017.

43 **undeveloped for years:** Barrett, **Trump: The Deals and the Downfall.**

43 **none of these challenges:** Barrett, **Trump: The Deals and the Downfall.**

44 **a commercial pilot:** Jason Horowitz, "For Donald Trump, Lessons from a Brother's Suffering," **New York Times,** January 2, 2016.

44 **Freddie's drinking problem:** Michael Kranish, "Trump Pressured His Alcoholic Brother About His Career. Now He Says He Has Regrets," **Washington Post,** August 8, 2019.

44 **"I watched him," Trump:** Horowitz, "For Donald Trump, Lessons from a Brother's Suffering."

44 **David Black's office:** Michael Paulson, "For a Young Donald J. Trump, Broadway Held Sway," **New York Times,** March 16, 2016.

45 **after 112 performances:** Paulson, "For a Young Donald J. Trump."

45 **a rent-stabilized apartment:** Barrett, **Trump: The Deals and the Downfall.**

45 **"part of the act":** Rudy Giuliani interview by Michael Kirk, **The Frontline Interview,** PBS, June 12, 2020.

46 **efforts to join:** Anthony Haden-Guest, "Donald Trump's Nights Out at Le Club with Roy Cohn," **Daily Beast,** March 12, 2019.

46 **chose to settle:** Jonathan Mahler and Steve Eder, "'No Vacancies' for Blacks: How Donald Trump Got His Start, and Was First Accused of Bias," **New York Times,** August 27, 2016.

47 **escaped four indictments:** Ken Auletta, "Don't Mess with Roy Cohn," **Esquire,** December 1978.

48 **"bounds of legal propriety":** Auletta, "Don't Mess with Roy Cohn."

48 **"given me a reputation":** Auletta, "Don't Mess with Roy Cohn."

48 **generous with friends:** Albin Krebs, "Roy Cohn, Aide to McCarthy and Fiery Lawyer, Dies at 59," **New York Times,** August 3, 1986.

49 **"go to hell":** Michael Kruse, "'He Brutalized for You,'" **Politico,** April 8, 2016.

49 **"central casting" looks:** Daniel Dale, "'Central Casting': Trump Is Talking More Than Ever About Men's Looks," CNN, August 13, 2019.

CHAPTER 2: WELCOME TO FEAR CITY

51 **taking over as chairman:** Linda Greenhouse, "Legislature Votes U.D.C. $228 Million," **New York Times,** May 1, 1975.

51 **once great but crumbling:** James Nevius, "The Winding History of Donald Trump's First Major Manhattan Real Estate Project," **Curbed New York,** April 3, 2019.

51 **worst fiscal crisis:** Steven R. Weisman, "How New York Became a Fiscal Junkie," **New York Times,** August 17, 1975.

52 **forty thousand public employees:** Lawrence Van Gelder, "Layoffs of 40,000 Ordered as City Ends Fiscal Year," **New York Times,** July 1, 1975.

52 **inspired worker protests:** Kim Phillips-Fein, "Opinion: In Bleak '70s, Salvo of Protest," **New York Times,** October 19, 2011.

53 **"drove me crazy":** Donald J. Trump and Tony Schwartz, **Trump: The Art of the Deal** (New York: Random House, 1987).

53 **to a "massive fleeing":** Barbara Campbell, "Realty Company Asks $100 Million 'Bias' Damages," **New York Times,** December 13, 1973.

53 **such an outcome:** Campbell, "Realty Company Asks $100 Million 'Bias' Damages."

54 **making baseless statements:** Michael Kranish and

Robert O'Harrow Jr., "Inside the Government's Racial Bias Case Against Donald Trump's Company, and How He Fought It," **Washington Post,** January 23, 2016.

56 **hand out pamphlets:** Glenn Fowler, "24 Unions Given Right to Pursue 'Fear' Drive Here," **New York Times,** June 17, 1975.

56 **nickname "Fun City":** Israel Shenker, "Fun City Revisited: Lindsay Glances Backward," **New York Times,** December 6, 1970.

56 **which forced a sell-off:** Linda Charlton, "Penn Central Is Granted Authority to Reorganize Under Bankruptcy Laws," **New York Times,** June 22, 1970.

56 **the company's West Side rail yards:** Wayne Barrett, **Trump: The Deals and the Downfall** (New York: HarperCollins, 1992).

57 **courted executives representing:** Barrett, **Trump: The Deals and the Downfall.**

57 **"my complete backing":** Barrett, **Trump: The Deals and the Downfall.**

57 **Berger informed Trump:** Wayne Barrett, "Donald Trump Cuts the Cards: The Deals of a Young Power Broker," **Village Voice,** January 22, 1979.

58 **his Philadelphia town house:** Barrett, **Trump: The Deals and the Downfall.**

58 **vision of a new hotel:** Barrett, **Trump: The Deals and the Downfall.**

59 **"no particular time limit":** Alan S. Oser, "Hotel Dispute Focuses on Tax Abatements," **New York Times,** April 27, 1976.

59 **only his signature:** Barrett, **Trump: The Deals and the Downfall.**

60 **"a very shallow person":** Barrett, **Trump: The Deals and the Downfall.**

61 **defeat the abatement:** Barrett, **Trump: The Deals and the Downfall.**

61 **won preliminary approvals:** Frank Lombardi, "Commodore Plan OKd After Taxing Study," **New York Daily News,** May 21, 1976.

62 **property tax relief:** Wayne Barrett, "A Seamless Web," **Village Voice,** February 26, 1979.

62 **Trump was the focus:** Judy Klemesrud, "Donald Trump, Real Estate Promoter, Builds Image as He Buys Buildings," **New York Times,** November 1, 1976.

63 **developed the habit:** Gwenda Blair, **The Trumps: Three Generations That Built an Empire** (New York: Simon & Schuster, 2000).

63 **if he met the right woman:** Klemesrud, "Donald Trump, Real Estate Promoter."

63 **set to begin:** John Lewis, "Work Starts on Hyatt Hotel, Replacing Commodore," **New York Daily News,** June 29, 1978.

64 **a competitive skier:** Barrett, **Trump: The Deals and the Downfall.**

64 **Austrian ski instructor:** Harry Hurt%III, **Lost Tycoon: The Many Lives of Donald J. Trump** (New York: W. W. Norton, 1993).

64 **excitedly described her:** Barrett, **Trump: The Deals and the Downfall.**

64 **tried to find evidence:** Jonathan Van Meter, "That's Why the Lady Is a Trump," **Spy,** May 1, 1989.

64 **she blamed others:** Barrett, **Trump: The Deals and the Downfall.**

65 **"ruin your life":** Katie Kindelan, "Ivana Trump Says She Is 'First Lady,'" ABC News, October 9, 2017.

65 **"don't know why you want to do this":** Barrett, **Trump: The Deals and the Downfall.**

65 **a "gold-digger warning":** Barrett, **Trump: The Deals and the Downfall.**

65 **The wedding ceremony:** Barrett, **Trump: The Deals and the Downfall.**

66 **"really brutal father":** Kindelan, "Ivana Trump Says She Is 'First Lady.'"

66 **insisted on the fish:** Kindelan, "Ivana Trump Says She Is 'First Lady.'"

66 **"well-known supermodels getting screwed":** Timothy L. O'Brien, **TrumpNation: The Art of Being the Donald** (New York: Warner Books, 2005).

67 **joined The Village Voice:** Sam Roberts, "Wayne Barrett, Fierce Muckraker at The Village Voice, Dies at 71," **New York Times,** January 19, 2017.

67 **a mentor to Barrett:** Barrett, **Trump: The Deals and the Downfall.**

68 **the phone rang:** Wayne Barrett, "How a Young Donald Trump Forced His Way from Avenue Z to Manhattan," **Village Voice,** January 15, 1979.

CHAPTER 3: FIFTH AVENUE FRIEZE-OUT

69 **on the front page:** Wayne Barrett, "How a Young Donald Trump Forced His Way From Avenue Z to Manhattan," **Village Voice,** January 15, 1979.

69 **two long installments:** Wayne Barrett, "Donald

Trump Cuts the Cards: The Deals of a Young Power Broker," **Village Voice,** January 22, 1979.

69 **opened a criminal investigation:** Wayne Barrett, **Trump: The Deals and the Downfall** (New York: HarperCollins, 1992).

70 **staid masonry front:** Paul Goldberger, "42nd Street Is About to Add Something New and Pleasant: The Grand Hyatt; An Appraisal," **New York Times,** September 22, 1980.

70 **windfall in fees:** Michael Kranish and Marc Fisher, **Trump Revealed: An American Journey of Ambition, Ego, Money, and Power** (New York: Scribner, 2016).

70 **opposition to Trump's proposals:** Barrett, **Trump: The Deals and the Downfall.**

70 **"short and quiet":** Barrett, **Trump: The Deals and the Downfall.**

70 **no improper arrangement:** Barrett, **Trump: The Deals and the Downfall.**

71 **Trump blamed Barrett:** Donald J. Trump with Charles Leerhsen, **Trump: Surviving at the Top** (New York: Random House, 1990).

71 **his 1990 book:** Trump, **Trump: Surviving at the Top.**

71 **father had learned:** Barrett, **Trump: The Deals and the Downfall.**

72 **elected district attorney:** Edith Evans Asbury, "Morgenthau Trounces Kuh in D.A. Race," **New York Times,** November 6, 1974.

72 **a separate connection:** Wayne Barrett, "Peas in a Pod: The Long and Twisted Relationship between

Donald Trump and Rudy Giuliani," **New York Daily News,** September 4, 2016.

73 **made a donation:** Stephanie Mansfield, "The Rise and Gall of Roger Stone; The Political Strategist, Playing Hardball," **Washington Post,** June 16, 1986.

74 **inaugurated a partnership:** Manuel Roig-Franzia, "How Paul Manafort and Roger Stone Created the Mess Donald Trump Said He'd Drain," **Washington Post,** November 29, 2018.

75 **staked a claim:** "N.Y. Building of Famed Store Is Being Sold," Associated Press, January 27, 1979.

76 **calling Tiffany Tower:** Barrett, **Trump: The Deals and the Downfall.**

76 **destroying the frieze:** Robert D. McFadden, "Builder Orders Bonwit Art Deco Sculptures Destroyed," **New York Times,** June 6, 1980.

76 **historic glass pavilion:** Michael Daly, "How Donald's Dad Fred Trump Tried to Kill Coney Island," **Daily Beast,** July 12, 2017.

76 **a false rumor:** "No Trump: British Palace Denies Tower Digs Sought Here," **New York Daily News,** August 3, 1981.

77 **"goodwill of the Establishment":** Marie Brenner, "After the Gold Rush," **Vanity Fair,** September 1990.

77 **employed undocumented Polish immigrants:** Barrett, **Trump: The Deals and the Downfall.**

77 **Genovese crime family:** Barrett, **Trump: The Deals and the Downfall.**

78 **powerful building trades union:** Barrett, **Trump: The Deals and the Downfall.**

78 **FBI agents investigating:** Barrett, **Trump: The Deals and the Downfall.**

79 **stunning and mysterious:** Barrett, **Trump: The Deals and the Downfall.**

79 **swooping into Las Vegas:** Alan S. Oser, "About Real Estate; Waiting," **New York Times,** December 10, 1975.

79 **envisioned slot machines:** Owen Moritz, "Casino Fever—Is It Catching?," **New York Daily News,** May 13, 1979.

79 **legalized gambling in 1976:** Frank J. Prendergast, "New Jersey Voters Approve Casino Gambling in A.C.," **Press of Atlantic City,** November 2, 1976.

80 **started building relationships:** Barrett, **Trump: The Deals and the Downfall.**

80 **Trump's campaign lawyer:** Ben Terris, "Trump's Own Beltway Establishment Guy: The Curious Journey of Don McGahn," **Washington Post,** April 11, 2016.

80 **purchased the property:** Barrett, **Trump: The Deals and the Downfall.**

81 **omitted to inform:** Barrett, **Trump: The Deals and the Downfall.**

81 **a motley trio:** Barrett, **Trump: The Deals and the Downfall.**

81 **a history with Sullivan:** Robert O'Harrow Jr., "Trump's Ties to an Informant and FBI Agent Reveal His Mode of Operation," **Washington Post,** September 17, 2016.

81 **an odd dance:** O'Harrow, "Trump's Ties to an Informant and FBI Agent Reveal His Mode of Operation."

82 **his casino license:** Donald Janson, "Trump Assured Casino License; One Snag Is Left," **New York Times,** March 16, 1982.

82 **Robert pulled strings:** Barrett, **Trump: The Deals and the Downfall.**

82 **a six-figure fine:** Henry Stern, "Casino Fined $200,000 for Moving Black and Female Dealers for High Roller," Associated Press, June 5, 1991.

82 **Trump claimed not to:** Michael Isikoff, "Trump Challenged over Ties to Mob-Linked Gambler with Ugly Past," Yahoo News, March 7, 2016.

83 **demanded an abatement:** Barrett, **Trump: The Deals and the Downfall.**

83 **fight over a subway easement:** Barrett, **Trump: The Deals and the Downfall.**

83 **denying the tax break:** Lee A. Daniels, "Trump Denied Tax Abatement for Fifth Ave. Tower," **New York Times,** March 29, 1981.

84 **"miscarriage of justice being done":** Barrett, **Trump: The Deals and the Downfall.**

85 **continued to fight:** Katharine Schaffer and Owen Moritz, "Court Trumps Trump on 50M Tax Abatement," **New York Daily News,** May 21, 1982.

85 **ruled conclusively that:** David Margolick, "Top State Court Rules Trump Is Entitled to Tax Break for Midtown Tower," **New York Times,** July 6, 1984.

87 **described by newspapers:** Lois Romano, "Donald Trump, Holding All the Cards; The Tower! The Team! The Money! The Future!," **Washington Post,** November 15, 1984.

87 **questionable tax schemes:** David Barstow, Susanne

Craig, and Russ Buettner, "Trump Engaged in Suspect Tax Schemes as He Reaped Riches from His Father," **New York Times,** October 2, 2018.

87 **viewed with credibility:** Barrett, **Trump: The Deals and the Downfall.**

87 **add his signature:** Barrett, **Trump: The Deals and the Downfall.**

88 **about him running for president:** Jason Horowitz, "Fred Trump Taught His Son the Essentials of Showboating Self-Promotion," **New York Times,** August 12, 2016.

CHAPTER 4: BLIND TO THE BEAUTIFUL MOSAIC

89 **a French vehicle:** Olivier Royant, "Donald Trump: 'Je Ne Pourrais Jamais m'Offrir La Tour Eiffel,'" **Paris Match,** June 15, 1989.

89 **convicted of manslaughter:** Jack Newfield, **Only in America: The Life and Crimes of Don King** (New York: William Morrow & Co., 1995).

90 **"fight for themselves":** Al Sharpton, James Brown, and Muhammad Ali interviewed by Tom Snyder, **Tomorrow,** NBC, May 6, 1981.

93 **identify ethnic groups:** Ben Smith, "Trump and the Blacks," **Politico,** April 14, 2011.

93 **five days of riots:** R. W. Apple Jr., "Violence Flares Again in Harlem; Restraint Urged," **New York Times,** July 20, 1964.

94 **the aggressive tactics:** Jon Hurdle and Maria Cramer, "Philadelphia Removes Statue Seen as Symbol of Racism and Police Abuse," **New York Times,** June 3, 2020.

94 **spoken at the time:** "Florida Governor Backs Miami Police in Hoodlum Crackdown," UPI, December 18, 1967.

95 **purchased a team:** Sam Goldaper, "Generals Are Sold to Trump," **New York Times,** September 23, 1983.

95 **"'give me the ball'":** Donald J. Trump and Tony Schwartz, **Trump: The Art of the Deal** (New York: Random House, 1987), 290.

95 **to host prizefights:** John R. O'Donnell with James Rutherford, **Trumped!: The Inside Story of the Real Donald Trump** (Hertford, NC: Crossroad Press, 1992).

96 **professional fighting debut:** Mike Puma, "'Iron Mike' Explosive In and Out of Ring," ESPN, October 10, 2005.

97 **later denied it:** Kate Feldman, "Carla Bruni Again Denies Affair with President Trump," **New York Daily News,** June 18, 2017.

98 **first, brief report:** Lawrence K. Altman, "Rare Cancer Seen in 41 Homosexuals," **New York Times,** July 3, 1981.

99 **require prospective dates:** Harry Berkowitz, "The Donald's Rx for Romance; He Has Dates AIDS-Tested," **Newsday,** June 28, 1991.

100 **"just totally incompatible":** Matt Tyrnauer, **Where's My Roy Cohn?** (Los Angeles: Sony Pictures Classics, 2019).

101 **likely contracted it:** Jonathan Mahler and Matt Flegenheimer, "What Donald Trump Learned from Joseph McCarthy's Right-Hand Man," **New York Times,** June 20, 2016.

101 **of improper conduct:** William A. Reuben and Alexander Cockburn, "Why Roy Cohn Was Disbarred," **Nation,** July 1986.

101 **to his defense:** Marie Brenner, "How Donald Trump and Roy Cohn's Ruthless Symbiosis Changed America," **Vanity Fair,** June 28, 2017.

102 **Cohn told associates:** Wayne Barrett, **Trump: The Deals and the Downfall** (New York: HarperCollins, 1992).

102 **lawyer once recounted:** William Safire, "Essay: About Roy Cohn," **New York Times,** August 4, 1986.

102 **Cohn died in August 1986:** Albin Krebs, "Roy Cohn, Aide to McCarthy and Fiery Lawyer, Dies at 59," **New York Times,** August 3, 1986.

102 **the "whispering campaign":** Joseph Berger, "Admirers Eulogize Roy Cohn as Friend and Ardent Patriot," **New York Times,** October 23, 1986.

102 **at the back:** Barrett, **Trump: The Deals and the Downfall.**

104 **final reelection campaign:** Joyce Purnick, "Koch Tunes Up for Re-Election Drive," **New York Times,** January 6, 1985.

105 **a subway vigilante:** Robert D. McFadden, "A Gunman Wounds 4 on IRT Train, Then Escapes," **New York Times,** December 23, 1984.

105 **A majority of Americans supported:** "A Majority of Americans Support Subway Vigilante Bernhard Goetz . . . ," UPI, March 3, 1985.

105 **a jog through Central Park:** Trisha Meili, "'I Am the Central Park Jogger,'" **New York Times,** May 4, 2003.

105 **roaming the park:** Susan Welsh, Keren Schiffman, and Francis Enjoli, "Looking Back at the 1989 Central Park Jogger Rape Case That Led to 5 Teens' Conviction, Later Vacated," ABC News, May 24, 2019.

105 **sometime around midnight:** Meili, "'I Am the Central Park Jogger.'"

105 **arrested eight teenagers:** Ronald Sullivan, "Park Victim, Out of Coma, Says 'Hello,'" **New York Times,** May 4, 1989.

106 **Koch decried them:** Jim Dwyer, "The True Story of How a City in Fear Brutalized the Central Park Five," **New York Times,** May 30, 2019.

107 **underscore his message:** Reis Thebault, "Donald Trump and Al Sharpton's Relationship Status: It's Complicated," **New York Times,** July 19, 2019.

108 **"has to stop":** Andrew Kaczynski and Jon Sarlin, "Trump in 1989 Central Park Five Interview: 'Maybe Hate Is What We Need,'" CNN, October 10, 2016.

108 **called Trump's ad:** Thomas Collins, "Donald Trump's High-Priced Graffiti," **Newsday** (Nassau and Suffolk edition), May 3, 1989.

109 **convictions were vacated:** Susan Saulny, "Convictions and Charges Voided in '89 Central Park Jogger Attack," **New York Times,** December 20, 2002.

109 **focused on race:** Walter Goodman, "Review/ Television; A Poll of Viewers' Feelings About Racial Issues" **New York Times,** September 8, 1989.

109 **"has a tremendous advantage":** "The R.A.C.E. Part I," NBC News, September 5, 1989, https://tvnews .vanderbilt.edu/broadcasts/891255.

110 **whose recent film:** Vincent Canby, "Review/Film; Spike Lee Tackles Racism in 'Do the Right Thing,'" **New York Times,** June 30, 1989.

110 **"with that garbage":** "The R.A.C.E. Part I," NBC News.

110 **chased and killed:** Ralph Blumenthal, "Black Youth Is Killed by Whites; Brooklyn Attack Is Called Racial," **New York Times,** August 25, 1989.

110 **marched through Bensonhurst:** Nick Ravo, "Marchers and Brooklyn Youths Trade Racial Jeers," **New York Times,** August 27, 1989.

110 **first Black mayor:** Sam Roberts, "Dinkins Defeats Giuliani in a Close Race; Wilder Seems Virginia Winner, Florio In; Voters, 5–4, Approve New York Charter," **New York Times,** November 8, 1989.

111 **In his inaugural address:** "Mayor Dinkins: A Pledge to All the People," **New York Times,** January 2, 1990.

111 **he complained bitterly:** Michael Tomasky, "'They Stole That Election from Me,' Rudy Giuliani Said Decades Ago," **New York Times,** December 1, 2020.

111 **three days of riots:** Rich Schapiro and Ginger Adams Otis, "Crown Heights Erupts in Three Days of Race Riots After Jewish Driver Hits and Kills Gavin Cato, 7, in 1991," **New York Daily News,** August 13, 2016.

112 **leading to violent riots:** James Dao, "Angered by Police Killing, a Neighborhood Erupts," **New York Times,** July 7, 1992.

112 **banging on the windows:** David Weigel, "From a Whisper to a Scream," **Reason,** July 23, 2007.

114 **"I believed her"**: Corey Dade, "The Rev. Al Sharpton, in Six True-False Statements," NPR, January 19, 2013.

114 **a paid adviser:** Phil Berger, "Trump Enters Tyson's Corner," **New York Times,** July 9, 1988.

CHAPTER 5: ON THE WAY UP

117 **Koch's famous routine:** Joseph Berger, "So, How Did Mayor Koch Do?," **New York Times,** February 2, 2013.

118 **let the option expire:** Wayne Barrett, **Trump: The Deals and the Downfall** (New York: HarperCollins, 1992).

118 **a controlling stake:** Barrett, **Trump: The Deals and the Downfall.**

119 **looked down on:** Barrett, **Trump: The Deals and the Downfall.**

119 **his prized option:** Martin Gottlieb, "Trump Set to Buy Lincoln West Site," **New York Times,** December 1, 1984.

119 **not just a new building:** Martin Gottlieb, "Trump Planning 66th St. Tower, Tallest in World," **New York Times,** November 19, 1985.

120 **editorial page observed:** "Opinion: The Next Trump Tower and Its Shadow," **New York Times,** November 21, 1985.

121 **a two-and-a-half-year renovation:** Joyce Purnick, "Trump Offers to Rebuild Skating Rink," **New York Times,** May 31, 1986.

121 **"Dear Ed" letter:** Purnick, "Trump Offers to Rebuild Skating Rink."

121 **rights to operate the rink:** Suzanne Daley, "Trump

to Rebuild Wollman Rink at the City's Expense by Dec. 15," **New York Times,** June 7, 1986.

122 **Koch had written:** Purnick, "Trump Offers to Rebuild Skating Rink."

122 **the construction work:** David Freedlander, "A 1980s New York City Battle Explains Donald Trump's Candidacy," Bloomberg, September 29, 2015.

123 **completion by December:** Daley, "Trump to Rebuild Wollman Rink at the City's Expense by Dec. 15."

123 **half dozen press conferences:** William E. Geist, "About New York; Pssst, Here's a Secret: Trump Rebuilds Ice Rink," **New York Times,** November 15, 1986.

124 **discover a sign:** Susan Heller Anderson and David W. Dunlap, "New York Day by Day; Down at the Wollman," **New York Times,** August 7, 1986.

124 **with remarkable creativity:** Barrett, **Trump: The Deals and the Downfall.**

124 **allegedly forced tenants:** Jose Pagliery, "Trump Was a Nightmare Landlord in the 1980s," CNN, March 28, 2016.

124 **"Some people think":** Sydney H. Schanberg, "New York; Trump for Mayor," **New York Times,** June 4, 1983.

124 **completed their work:** "Wollman Skate Rink Is to Open Thursday," **New York Times,** November 8, 1986.

125 **stopped working with Trump:** Michael Kruse, "The Executive Mr. Trump," **Politico,** July/August 2016.

125 **"He's gotta get":** Janet Babin, "Is Donald Trump Saving NYC Millions, or Making Millions Off Taxpayers?," WNYC News, October 19, 2016.

125 **becoming a priest:** Paul Schwartzman and Ben Terris, "What Happened to 'America's Mayor'? How Rudy Giuliani Became Trump's Attack Dog," **Washington Post,** October 16, 2016.

126 **appointment as U.S. Attorney:** "Man in the News; Nominee for U.S. Attorney," **New York Times,** April 13, 1983.

126 **made his name:** Michael Winerip, "High-Profile Prosecutor," **New York Times Magazine,** June 9, 1985.

126 **made frequent use:** Leigh Jones, "Perp Walk? Blame Giuliani," Reuters, May 18, 2011.

126 **a baroque scandal:** Richard J. Meislin, "The Corruption Scandal: Manes Mystery Is Hub of 8 Inquiries," **New York Times,** February 2, 1986.

126 **Giuliani's biggest trophy:** Richard J. Meislin, "Friedman Is Guilty with 3 in Scandal," **New York Times,** November 26, 1986.

127 **helped a man:** Wayne Barrett, "Rudy's Long History of Quashing Trump Probes," **Village Voice,** October 12, 1993.

128 **delivered satisfactory answers:** Barrett, "Rudy's Long History of Quashing Trump Probes."

129 **he received tickets:** Barrett, "Rudy's Long History of Quashing Trump Probes."

129 **ended up backing:** Barrett, "Rudy's Long History of Quashing Trump Probes."

129 **pet charitable cause:** Steve Eder and Megan Twohey, "Donald Trump the Philanthropist Is Known for

His Reluctance," **New York Times,** September 23, 2016.

130 **a featured tenant:** Barrett, **Trump: The Deals and the Downfall.**

130 **a private letter:** Alan Finder, "Koch Rejects Tax Break for Trump TV City Site," **New York Times,** May 29, 1987.

131 **read aloud praise:** Walter Kravetz, "Mine Games; Abortion Advice; Make-Believe Justice?; Big Apple Brawl," **MacNeil/Lehrer NewsHour,** PBS, August 11, 1987, https://americanarchive.org/catalog/cpb-aacip_507-ws8hd7pp7d.

131 **milk the situation:** Alan Finder, "The Koch-Trump Feud," **New York Times,** June 1, 1987.

132 **"there's no excuse":** Finder, "The Koch-Trump Feud."

132 **"piggy, piggy, piggy":** Gwenda Blair, **The Trumps: Three Generations That Built an Empire** (New York: Simon & Schuster, 2000).

132 **received a letter:** Donald J. Trump and Tony Schwartz, **Trump: The Art of the Deal** (New York: Random House, 1987).

132 **list of the country's wealthiest people:** Timothy L. O'Brien, "What's He Really Worth?," **New York Times,** October 23, 2005.

133 **he purchased Mar-a-Lago:** "Post Foundation Sells Its Mansion to Trump," UPI, January 2, 1986.

133 **superyacht for $29 million:** Roxanne Roberts, "Inside the Fabulous World of Donald Trump, Where Money Is No Problem," **Washington Post,** October 9, 2015.

133 **condominium project in:** Fox Butterfield, "Trump

Hints of Dreams Beyond Building," **New York Times,** October 5, 1987.

133 **Nevada gaming license:** Donald Janson, "Trump Ends His Struggle to Gain Control of Bally," **New York Times,** February 28, 1987.

133 **a "takeover artist":** Laurie P. Cohen and Bryan Burrough, "Merger Juggernaut in U.S. Stalls on Fears of Higher Rates, Proposed Tax Changes," **Wall Street Journal,** October 20, 1987.

133 **barely attending meetings:** Lois Romano, "Donald Trump, Holding All the Cards; The Tower! The Team! The Money! The Future!," **Washington Post,** November 15, 1984.

134 **violated federal law:** David Corn, "The Time Donald Trump Was Hit with a $750,000 Fine by the Feds," **Mother Jones,** June 24, 2016.

134 MADE TRUMP MILLIONS: Michael Shain, "Bail-Out Made Trump Millions," **New York Post,** October 20, 1987.

134 EARLY SELL-OFFS LEAVE: Daniel Heneghan, "Early Sell-Offs Leave Trump in the Black," **Press of Atlantic City,** October 21, 1987.

134 **"very negative instincts":** David E. Pitt, "Just a Paper Loss, the Richest Say," **New York Times,** October 21, 1987.

134 **"sold all my stock":** Randall Smith, "Big Investors Say They Knew Better Than to Overstay: Trump and Others Who Sold Have Small Expectations of Any Turnaround Soon," **Wall Street Journal,** October 20, 1987.

134 **"haven't played the market":** Cohen and Burrough,

"Merger Juggernaut in U.S. Stalls on Fears of Higher Rates."

135 **show of inspecting:** Kirk Johnson, "U.S. Aide Urges Private Industry to Help Bridge," **New York Times,** April 22, 1988.

136 **"This fascinates me":** Peg Byron, "Trump Wants to Handle Williamsburg Bridge Repairs," UPI, April 21, 1988.

136 **him on the cover:** Graydon Carter, "The Secret to Donald Trump's Success," **GQ,** May 1984.

136 **sold so well:** Timothy L. O'Brien, **TrumpNation: The Art of Being the Donald** (New York: Warner Books, 2005).

137 **occasionally leafing through:** Jane Mayer, "Donald Trump's Ghostwriter Tells All," **New Yorker,** July 18, 2016.

137 **claimed when pressed:** Marie Brenner, "After the Gold Rush," **Vanity Fair,** September 1990.

137 **hired a collaborator:** Mayer, "Donald Trump's Ghostwriter Tells All."

138 **Trump assured Romano:** Romano, "Donald Trump, Holding All The Cards."

139 **to discuss denuclearization:** Ron Rosenbaum, "Trump: The Ultimate Deal," **Manhattan, Inc.,** November 1985.

140 **a brief meeting:** Maureen Dowd, "The Summit; As 'Gorby' Works the Crowd, Backward Reels the K.G.B.," **New York Times,** December 11, 1987.

140 **tour Trump Tower:** Paula Span, "From the Archives: When Trump Hoped to Meet Gorbachev in Manhattan," **Washington Post,** December 3, 1988.

141 **already made contributions:** Bill Sternberg, "The Presidential Gambit: New York Contributors Push Favors, Not Ideology," **Crain's New York Business,** November 9, 1987.

142 **to qualify Trump:** "A Trump Presidential Bid?," **New York Times,** July 14, 1987.

142 **for an invitation:** Fox Butterfield, "New Hampshire Speech Earns Praise for Trump," **New York Times,** October 23, 1987.

143 **buy up copies:** John R. O'Donnell with James Rutherford, **Trumped!: The Inside Story of the Real Donald Trump** (Hertford, NC: Crossroad Press, 1992).

143 **a significant philanthropist:** Donald Trump interview by Phil Donahue, **The Phil Donahue Show,** NBC, December 15, 1987.

144 **first crossed paths one:** Nancy Benac, "Trump and Nixon Were Pen Pals in the '80s. Here Are Their Letters," Associated Press, September 23, 2020.

144 **photos of him:** Lisa Gray, "The Night Trump Shook Hands with Nixon in Houston," **Houston Chronicle,** November 10, 2019.

144 **"an expert on politics":** Benac, "Trump and Nixon Were Pen Pals in the '80s."

145 **joining the Republican ticket:** Eric Bradner, "Trump Says Bush 41 Adviser Approached Him About Becoming VP," CNN, November 8, 2015.

146 **Trump was mesmerized:** Michael Kruse, "'This Is What I Want': Why Trump Needs a Packed Convention," **Politico,** May 28, 2020.

149 **for raw dominance:** Adam Davidson, "What Donald Trump Doesn't Understand About 'the

Deal,'" **New York Times Magazine,** March 17, 2016.

CHAPTER 6: ON THE WAY DOWN

151 **a yearlong pursuit:** William H. Meyers, "Stalking the Plaza," **New York Times Magazine,** September 25, 1988.

152 **"don't like auctions":** Meyers, "Stalking the Plaza."

152 **made the front page:** Robert J. Cole, "Plaza Hotel Is Sold to Donald Trump for $390 Million," **New York Times,** March 27, 1988.

152 **Trump's interlocutor with:** Meyers, "Stalking the Plaza."

152 **manage the hotel:** Cole, "Plaza Hotel Is Sold to Donald Trump for $390 Million."

152 **had previously served:** Michael Shnayerson, "Inside Ivana's Role in Donald Trump's Empire," **Vanity Fair,** January 2, 1988.

153 **"lost without it":** Rose Mary Pedersen Budge, "Ivana Trump: Plaza 'Queen' Exudes Grace Under Pressure," **Deseret News,** June 4, 1989.

153 **filming a sequel:** Jason Guerrasio, "Donald Trump 'Bullied' His Way into 'Home Alone' Sequel, Says Director," **Insider,** November 12, 2020.

154 **forceful grassroots opposition:** Thomas J. Lueck, "Celebrities Open Wallets to Fight Trump's Project," **New York Times,** September 30, 1987.

154 **new neighborhood organization:** Gwenda Blair, **The Trumps: Three Generations That Built an Empire** (New York: Simon & Schuster, 2000).

154 **took to dismissing:** Michael Kruse, "The Lost City of Trump," **Politico,** June 29, 2018.

155 **offered $550 million:** Wayne Barrett, **Trump: The Deals and the Downfall** (New York: HarperCollins, 1992).

155 **"between two worlds":** Thomas J. Lueck, "Trump City Site May Be Sold, Developer Says," **New York Times,** October 13, 1988.

155 **the seller's demand:** Barrett, **Trump: The Deals and the Downfall.**

156 **He developed a reputation:** Monci Jo Williams, "Will Donald Trump Own the World?," **Fortune,** November 21, 1988.

156 **acquire the company:** Agis Salpukas, "American Air Gets Trump Bid of $7.5 Billion," **New York Times,** October 6, 1989.

157 **learned from Cohn:** Lois Morgan, "Why Doesn't Roy Cohn Pay His Bills?," **Village Voice,** July 5, 1976.

157 **financing the purchases:** Suzette Parmley, "A Troubled Empire: Trump Gambled on Junk Bonds, and Lost," **Philadelphia Inquirer,** August 11, 2004.

157 **protracted and costly fight:** Nina J. Easton, "Merv Griffin's Outrageous Fortune: When Millionaire Griffin Took on Billionaire Trump, They Said It Was a Mismatch. They Were Wrong," **Los Angeles Times,** July 24, 1988.

158 **retained the law firm:** Wayne Barrett, "The Seduction of Mario Cuomo," **Village Voice,** January 14, 1992.

158 **One story had it:** John R. O'Donnell with James Rutherford, **Trumped!: The Inside Story of the Real Donald Trump** (Hertford, NC: Crossroad Press, 1992).

158 **a poor decision:** Donald Trump and Marla Maples interview by Nancy Collins, **Primetime Live,** March 10, 1994.

159 **he later reflected:** Donald J. Trump with Charles Leerhsen, **Trump: Surviving at the Top** (New York: Random House, 1990).

159 **declare loudly enough:** Maureen Orth, "The Heart of the Deal: The Love Story of Marla Maples and Donald Trump," **Vanity Fair,** November 1990.

159 **secreted into Atlantic City:** Orth, "The Heart of the Deal."

159 **his strange habits:** O'Donnell, **Trumped!**

160 **Trump casino executives:** David Cay Johnston, Michael E. Ruane, and Mike Schurman, "Three Top Trump Casino Executives, Two Others Die in Helicopter Crash," **Philadelphia Inquirer,** October 11, 1989.

160 **Marla was there:** O'Donnell, **Trumped!**

160 **"I love your husband":** Dana Schuster, "Ivana Trump on How She Advises Donald—and Those Hands," **New York Post,** April 3, 2016.

160 **only slowly intervening:** Orth, "The Heart of the Deal."

161 **floated to attend:** O'Donnell, **Trumped!**

161 **Hotel guests reported:** Michael Vitez, "Trump Taj Mahal Opening in 1990: 'It's Beautiful, but It's Too Large,'" **Philadelphia Inquirer,** April 5, 1990.

161 **bluffed his way through:** O'Donnell, **Trumped!**

162 **berated his brother:** O'Donnell, **Trumped!**

162 **quitting his job:** Blair, **The Trumps.**

162 **trouble generating that revenue:** Michael Kranish and Marc Fisher, **Trump Revealed: An American**

Journey of Ambition, Ego, Money, and Power (New York: Scribner, 2016).

162 **refused to recant:** "Securities Analyst Marvin Roffman 'Renegotiates' Life After Trump," **Press of Atlantic City,** July 15, 1990.

163 **twisted the knife:** Trump, **Trump: Surviving at the Top.**

164 **article was devastating:** Dan Alexander, "Why We Took Trump Off the Forbes 400 During His Decade of Tax Losses," **Forbes,** May 8, 2019.

164 **"the sudden ostentation":** David Folkenflik, "Donald Trump Still Tormented by 'Spy' Magazine Founders," NPR, March 7, 2016.

164 **"objets de Trump":** Susan Orlean, "Trumporama on Fifth," **Spy,** September 1987.

164 **mailed checks to:** Bruce Feirstein, "Trump's War on 'Losers': The Early Years," **Vanity Fair,** August 12, 2015.

165 **identified him relentlessly:** Folkenflik, "Donald Trump Still Tormented By 'Spy' Magazine Founders."

165 **discuss the topic:** Walter Kravetz, "Trumpty-Dumpty?; Making Music; 'Crime and Punishment'," **The MacNeil/Lehrer NewsHour,** PBS, June 19, 1990, https://americanarchive.org/catalog/cpb-aacip_507-rn3028q89f.

165 **defamation of character:** Brendan J. O'Reilly, "Abraham Wallach Was Sued, Then Hired, by Donald Trump," **Southampton Press,** August 29, 2018.

166 **head of acquisitions:** Alan Feuer, "For Donald Trump, Friends in Few Places," **New York Times,** March 11, 2016.

166 **$2 billion in debt:** Stratford P. Sherman and Mark D. Fefer, "Donald Trump Just Won't Die," **Fortune**, August 13, 1990.

166 **missed a payment:** Tom Furlong, "Trump Misses a $42-Million Casino Bond Payment: The Developer's Woes Worsened When Japanese Banks Balked at a Bailout Plan. Rescue Talks Continue," **Los Angeles Times,** June 16, 1990.

166 **inflatable Godzilla doll:** "Employees Rally for Trump," **Press of Atlantic City,** June 17, 1990.

167 **foiled the surprise:** Martha Gross, "'The Donald' Revels on His 44th," **South Florida Sun-Sentinel,** June 20, 1990.

167 **"setting every record":** "Employees Rally for Trump."

167 **his current predicament:** Gross, "'The Donald' Revels on His 44th."

167 **"first set of blocks":** Gross, "'The Donald' Revels on His 44th."

168 **Barrett was handcuffed:** Christopher Massie, "A Reporter Spent the Night in Jail for Sneaking into Donald Trump's Birthday Party," **BuzzFeed,** May 13, 2016.

168 **Trump was having an affair:** Liz Smith, "Splitsville?," **New York Daily News,** February 11, 1990.

168 **on her terms:** Marc Fisher, "How Liz Smith Invented Donald Trump," **Washington Post,** November 13, 2017.

168 **before and after Aspen:** Liz Smith, "Liz Smith: I Think I Invented the Trumps, Part II," **New York Social Diary,** August 25, 2015.

169 **security system installed:** Maureen Dowd, "Cindy

Adams, Gossip's G.O.A.T.," **New York Times,** August 7, 2021.

169 **most highly paid:** Fisher, "How Liz Smith Invented Donald Trump."

169 **unending tit for tat:** Howard Kurtz, "Marla Has Her Say About Ivana," **Washington Post,** July 25, 1990.

170 **handed a name:** Kranish and Fisher, **Trump Revealed.**

170 **rail about the publicity:** Trump, **Trump: Surviving at the Top.**

171 **"wanted it both ways":** Sydney H. Schanberg, "When Publicity-Mongers Seek Privacy," **Newsday,** March 6, 1990.

172 **"cruel and inhuman":** James Barron, "Trumps Get Divorce; Next, Who Gets What?," **New York Times,** December 12, 1990.

172 **agreed to settle:** Doug Vaughan and Harry Berkowitz, "Trumps Settle: $14M," **Newsday,** March 24, 1991.

172 **Commission documents revealed:** Neil Barsky, "Negative Net Worth of $294 Million Is Shown for Trump," **Wall Street Journal,** August 16, 1990.

172 **for gaming chips:** "Trump Dad Reportedly Helped Son with $3 Million Chip Buy," Associated Press, January 21, 1991.

173 **to great fanfare that he had met:** "Trump Says Payments Made On Trump Castle," Associated Press, December 17, 1990.

173 **noted Fred's transaction:** "Trump Dad Reportedly Helped Son With $3 Million Chip Buy."

173 **declined to renew:** Michael Kruse, "The 5 People

Who Could Have Stopped Trump," **Politico,** November 1, 2019.

174 **reported bluntly that:** Neil Barsky, "Shaky Empire: Trump's Bankers Join to Seek Restructuring of Developer's Assets," **Wall Street Journal,** June 4, 1990.

174 **a crushing load:** Neil Barsky, "On the Ropes: Trump Could Face Big Personal Liability if Empire Collapses," **Wall Street Journal,** June 18, 1990.

174 **borrow money from Fred Trump:** Neil Barsky, "Trump May Have to Borrow Funds from His Father," **Wall Street Journal,** May 31, 1991.

175 **sign a codicil:** David Barstow, Susanne Craig, and Russ Buettner, "Trump Engaged in Suspect Tax Schemes as He Reaped Riches from His Father," **New York Times,** October 2, 2018.

175 **"going to blast him":** Donald J. Trump and Kate Bohner, **Trump: The Art of the Comeback** (New York: Times Books, 1997).

176 **would be damaging:** Neil Barsky, "Trump, the Bad, Bad Businessman," **New York Times,** August 5, 2016.

176 **"evil, vicious, false":** Howard Kurtz, "Media Notes," **Washington Post,** June 10, 1991.

176 **executive editor, Norman Pearlstine:** Julie Baumgold, "Mr. Lucky and the Champs: Going to the Big Fight with Donald Trump," **New York,** February 15, 1988.

177 **ill with hepatitis:** Shawn Tully, "Donald Trump: An Ex-Loser Is Back in the Money," **Fortune,** July 22, 1996.

177 **later take loans:** Timothy L. O'Brien, **TrumpNation:**

The Art of Being the Donald (New York: Warner Books, 2005).

177 **cleared the way:** David Barstow, Susanne Craig, Russ Buettner, and Megan Twohey, "Donald Trump Tax Records Show He Could Have Avoided Taxes for Nearly Two Decades, The Times Found," **New York Times,** October 1, 2016.

177 **Trump executives departed:** Barrett, **Trump: The Deals and the Downfall.**

178 **taking that flight:** Jack O'Donnell interview by Callie Wiser, **The Frontline Interview,** PBS, September 27, 2016.

178 **final divorce settlement:** Vaughan and Berkowitz, "Trumps Settle: $14M."

178 **for corporate bankruptcy:** "Chapter 11 for Taj Mahal," Reuters, July 18, 1991.

178 **turn over half:** David Carpenter, "Trump Relinquishes Half of Swank Plaza Hotel as Part of Debt Restructuring," Associated Press, March 18, 1992.

178 **the Trump Shuttle:** David S. Hilzenrath and Michelle Singletary, "Trump Went Broke, but Stayed on Top," **Washington Post,** November 29, 1992.

178 **were almost giddy:** Harry Berkowitz, "Strip Poker: Trump Is Running Out of Chips," **Newsday,** April 21, 1991.

CHAPTER 7: NICE AND COMPLICATED

181 **onto the stage:** "Marla Maples Debuts in 'Will Rogers,'" **Washington Post,** August 3, 1992.

181 **played a girlfriend:** Alessandra Stanley, "Maples in

Spotlight on Opening Night," **New York Times,** August 4, 1992.

181 **more than two decades earlier:** Michael Paulson, "For a Young Donald J. Trump, Broadway Held Sway," **New York Times,** March 16, 2016.

181 **"I create stars":** Donald Trump and Marla Maples interview by Nancy Collins, **Primetime Live,** ABC News, March 10, 1994.

182 **won the Tony:** Mervyn Rothstein, "'Yonkers' and 'Will Rogers' Win the Top Tony Awards," **New York Times,** June 3, 1991.

182 **giving out two hundred tickets:** Stanley, "Maples in Spotlight on Opening Night."

182 **"look for a drama critic":** "Marla Maples Debuts in 'Will Rogers.'"

182 **"see the woman":** Stanley, "Maples in Spotlight on Opening Night."

182 **Trump Princess yacht:** Beth Healy, "A Boston Bank Lent Millions to Trump. It Wasn't Smooth Sailing," **Boston Globe,** October 4, 2016.

183 **to convert Mar-a-Lago:** Mark Seal, "How Donald Trump Beat Palm Beach Society and Won the Fight for Mar-a-Lago," **Vanity Fair,** December 27, 2016.

183 **mocking him as "Fat Jerry Nadler":** Michael Daly, "The Guy Trump Called 'Fat Jerry' Is Chairman Nadler Now," **Daily Beast,** March 5, 2019.

183 **effectively bailed out:** David W. Dunlap, "Hong Kong Investors Finance a Trump Project," **New York Times,** July 1, 1994.

183 **in suburban Westchester:** Mary McAleer Vizard, "In the Region/Westchester; Trump Pushes 2 Golf

Projects Long in Negotiation," **New York Times,** April 11, 1999.

183 **seventy-two-story building:** "40 Wall Street Is Sold to Trump," Bloomberg, December 7, 1995.

184 **firing his publicist:** Beth Whitehouse, "Dumped by Trump," **Newsday,** February 11, 2004.

184 **"a very honest guy":** Liz Trotta, "Trump Says Talk of His Demise Is Greatly Exaggerated; As Plaza Slips Away, Lion Roars at Those Who Say He's Finished," **Washington Times,** April 18, 1995.

185 **about selling shares:** Monci Jo Williams, "Trump's Troubles," **Fortune,** December 18, 1989.

185 **back Trump Plaza:** "Company News; Trump Plaza to Sell Notes, in Bid to End Bank Scrutiny," Bloomberg, February 23, 1993.

185 **and the Trump Castle:** "Trump Castle Refinancing," Bloomberg, December 29, 1993.

185 **eventual public offering:** Floyd Norris, "Trump Plaza Casino Stock Trades Today on Big Board," **New York Times,** June 7, 1995.

186 **sued for $250 million:** Brendan J. O'Reilly, "Abraham Wallach Was Sued, Then Hired, by Donald Trump," **Southampton Press,** August 29, 2018.

186 **Trump's former bodyguard:** Allyson Chiu, "Matthew Calamari, Trump's Longtime Bodyguard, Goes Viral After Michael Cohen Hearing. He's Real, and He Loves Trump," **Washington Post,** February 28, 2019.

186 **convicted of taking:** Alex Witchel, "At Home With: Marla Maples; Cinderella, with Both of Her Shoes," **New York Times,** August 20, 1992.

186 **the theme of loyalty:** Donald J. Trump, "I'm Back," **New York Times Magazine,** November 19, 1995.

189 **was for Pizza Hut:** Robert Klara, "Yes, It Was Donald Trump Who First Introduced Pizza Hut's Stuffed Crust to the World," **Adweek,** September 22, 2016.

191 **began trading on Wall Street:** Norris, "Trump Plaza Casino Stock Trades Today on Big Board."

191 **a riverboat casino:** Karen Springen, "The Donald Goes West," **Newsweek,** March 14, 1999.

194 **that he had acquired:** "Trump Buys 3 Beauty Pageants," **Los Angeles Times,** October 24, 1996.

194 **into a model:** Jennifer Steinhauer, "Her Cheekbones (High) or Her Name (Trump)?," **New York Times,** August 17, 1997.

194 **and Maples cohosted:** Nick Kirkpatrick and Justin Wm. Moyer, "How Donald Trump Resurrected Miss USA—and Is Fighting to Keep It Alive," **New York Times,** July 13, 2015.

194 **memberships at Mar-a-Lago:** Don Sider, "Party Time at Mar-a-Lago," **South Florida Sun-Sentinel,** June 18, 1995.

195 **later accused him:** Alexander Alter, "E. Jean Carroll Accuses Trump of Sexual Assault in Her Memoir," **New York Times,** June 21, 2019.

195 **gave Birnbach a tour:** Lisa Birnbach, "Mi Casa Es Su Casa," **New York,** February 12, 1996.

196 **wedding dress in tow:** Wayne Barrett, "Donald Trump's History with Women: Adultery, Objectification," **New York Daily News,** April 17, 2016.

196 **wed in December:** Georgia Dullea, "Vows; It's a

Wedding Blitz for Trump and Maples," **New York Times,** December 21, 1993.

197 **found Maples and:** George Rush and Don Gentile, "A Trump(ed)-Up Story: Marla Denies Tale of Fla. Tryst," **New York Daily News,** April 27, 1996.

197 **a strange tip:** Peter Baker and Maggie Haberman, "'I Don't Talk' That Way, Trump Says. Except When He Does," **New York Times,** September 7, 2018.

198 **set a horizon:** Bruce Weber, "Donald and Marla Are Headed for Divestiture," **New York Times,** May 3, 1997.

199 **upon publication in 1997:** "Best Sellers: December 21, 1997," **New York Times,** December 21, 1997.

199 **sending notes reading:** Peter J. Wilson, "When Donald Trump's Empire Crashed He Was Snubbed by One-Time Friends. Now He's Back on Top . . . With a Thirst for Revenge," **Daily Mirror,** January 25, 1998.

199 **most expansive work:** Mark Singer, "Trump Solo," **New Yorker,** May 12, 1997.

199 **didn't particularly want:** Mark Singer, "Best Wishes, Donald," **New Yorker,** April 26, 2011.

200 **present in New York:** Singer, "Trump Solo."

CHAPTER 8: THE AMERICA WE DESERVE

203 **won the right:** Antonio Fins, "Donald Trump in Palm Beach: A 30-Year Timeline," **Palm Beach Post,** February 3, 2017.

203 **then began aiming:** Mary McAleer Vizard, "In the Region/Westchester; Trump Pushes 2 Golf Projects

Long in Negotiation," **New York Times,** April 11, 1999.

203 **ultimately abandoned it:** Lisa W. Foderaro, "Trump Drops Golf Course in Favor of Homes," **New York Times,** March 27, 2004.

203 **looked more promising:** Elsa Brenner, "In the Region/Westchester; Trump Takes a Golf Project from Rough to Fairway," **New York Times,** June 10, 2001.

204 **for tax fraud:** Joseph Berger, "Westchester Prosecutor's Husband Is Indicted," **New York Times,** February 24, 1999.

204 **"a huge asset":** Devin Leonard, "Trump's Garish Golf Course Plan Disrupts Quiet Westchester Town," **New York Observer,** April 5, 1999.

204 **to strong reviews:** Corey Kilgannon, "Development; The Course That Trump Built," **New York Times,** June 30, 2002.

206 **agreed to return:** Chris Smith, "Clash of the Titans," **New York,** February 16, 1998.

206 **ordered them painted:** Fox Butterfield, "Trump Hints of Dreams Beyond Building," **New York Times,** October 5, 1987.

206 **elderly widow refused:** Manuel Roig-Franzia, "The Time Donald Trump's Empire Took on a Stubborn Widow—and Lost," **Washington Post,** September 9, 2015.

206 **playing for sympathy:** Paul Schwartzman, "She Kicks Sand in Trump's Face; Sneers at the Donald's Bucks," **New York Daily News,** July 26, 1998.

206 **developed a habit:** Russ Buettner and Charles V. Bagli, "How Donald Trump Bankrupted His

Atlantic City Casinos, but Still Earned Millions," **New York Times,** June 11, 2016.

207 **in a deal:** Steve Lohr, "Trump Hotels Settles Case Accusing It of Misleading Investors," **New York Times,** January 17, 2002.

208 **"type of accounting":** Neil Roland, "Trump Hotels Settles Case of 'Misleading' Accounting," Bloomberg, January 17, 2002.

209 **The biggest threat:** David Lightman, "Trump Criticizes Pequots, Casino," **Hartford Courant,** October 6, 1993.

210 **casinos were rife:** Lightman, "Trump Criticizes Pequots, Casino."

211 **asked him to explain:** Lightman, "Trump Criticizes Pequots, Casino."

211 **seeking to partner:** Rosalind S. Helderman, "How Donald Trump Tried—and Failed—to Open a Casino in Florida," **Washington Post,** September 19, 2015.

211 **beat back gaming:** Nancy Plevin, "Trump Suing U.S. Over Indian Gaming Rights," Associated Press, May 3, 1993.

211 **Trump's friend Fields:** Eamon Javers, "Trump's Angry Apprentice," Bloomberg, December 12, 2005.

211 **invited Seminole leaders:** Michael Daly, "The True Story of Donald Trump's Florida Casino Fail," **Daily Beast,** April 14, 2017.

212 **fundraiser for Bush:** Jeremy Diamond, "Jeb Bush: The Man Who Killed Trump's Casino Dreams," CNN, September 1, 2015.

212 **they had misrepresented:** Robert Little, "Trump

Sues Cordish Co. over Fla. Casino Project," **Baltimore Sun,** January 13, 2005.

212 **accepted the cash infusion:** David W. Dunlap, "Hong Kong Investors Finance a Trump Project," **New York Times,** July 1, 1994.

212 **intended to subsidize:** Michael Daly, "The Guy Trump Called 'Fat Jerry' Is Chairman Nadler Now," **Daily Beast,** March 5, 2019.

213 **the dubious basis:** Wayne Barrett, "Peas in a Pod: The Long and Twisted Relationship Between Donald Trump and Rudy Giuliani," **New York Daily News,** September 4, 2016.

213 **"nothing against luxury apartments":** Daly, "The Guy Trump Called 'Fat Jerry' Is Chairman Nadler Now."

215 **his second wife:** Dareh Gregorian, "It's No Peach of a Deal—Marla Settles with Donald for Mere $2M," **New York Post,** June 9, 1999.

215 **He reportedly met:** Julia Ioffe, "Melania Trump on Her Rise, Her Family Secrets, and Her True Political Views: 'Nobody Will Ever Know,'" **GQ,** April 27, 2016.

215 **another beautiful model:** Yamiche Alcindor and Maggie Haberman, "Circling the Square of President Trump's Relationship with Race," **New York Times,** August 17, 2017.

216 **"He was impressed":** Alcindor and Haberman, "Circling the Square of President Trump's Relationship with Race."

217 **it was Melania:** Angela Mosconi, "Trump Patriarch Eulogized as Great Builder," **New York Post,** June 30, 1999.

218 **"everything I know"**: Jason Horowitz, "Fred Trump Taught His Son the Essentials of Showboating Self-Promotion," **New York Times,** August 12, 2016.

218 **"the toughest day"**: Mosconi, "Trump Patriarch Eulogized as Great Builder."

218 **such poor timing**: Gwenda Blair, **The Trumps: Three Generations That Built an Empire** (New York: Simon & Schuster, 2000).

219 **saluting the longevity**: Mosconi, "Trump Patriarch Eulogized as Great Builder."

219 **cut off medical funding**: Heidi Evans, "Inside Trumps' Bitter Battle," **New York Daily News,** December 19, 2000.

219 **toxic family dispute**: Erica Orden, "Mary Trump Sues President and His Siblings for Fraud, Calling It the Family 'Way of Life,'" CNN, September 24, 2020.

219 **renew his ruminations**: David Shiflett, "Trump's No Chump" **American Spectator,** February 2000.

220 **always more libertarian**: Paul Bond, "Roger Stone: There's a Difference Between Dirty Tricks and Just Being Stupid (Q&A)," **Hollywood Reporter,** May 23, 2017.

222 **an early harbinger**: Steve Kornacki, "When Trump Ran Against Trump-ism: The 1990s and the Birth of Political Tribalism in America," NBC News, October 2, 2018.

223 **beat back a challenge**: Gerald Posner, "Perot, Alone," **New York Times Magazine,** September 22, 1996.

223 **when he was elected**: Pam Belluck, "The 1998

Elections: The States—The Maverick; A 'Bad Boy' Wrestler's Unscripted Upset," **New York Times,** November 5, 1998.

223 **the potential candidates:** Kornacki, "When Trump Ran Against Trump-ism."

223 **an exploratory committee: Larry King Live,** Donald Trump interview by Larry King, October 8, 1999.

224 **"enhances the brand":** Joel Siegel, "Perfect Sales Pitch for Trump, Talk of Presidency May Mean Big Bucks," **New York Daily News,** October 14, 1999.

224 **to make money:** Jerry Useem, "What Does Donald Trump Really Want?," **Fortune,** April 3, 2000.

224 **held a reception:** David Freedlander, "An Oral History of Donald Trump's Almost-Run for President in 2000," **New York,** October 11, 2018.

225 **"concept of abortion":** Donald Trump interview by Tim Russert, **Meet the Press,** October 24, 1999.

225 **universal health care:** Donald Trump interview by Larry King, **Larry King Live,** October 8, 1999.

225 **more natural groove:** Francis X. Clines, "Trump Quits Grand Old Party for New," **New York Times,** October 25, 1999.

225 **of Hitler's speeches:** Marie Brenner, "After the Gold Rush," **Vanity Fair,** September 1990.

226 **"a Hitler lover":** Clines, "Trump Quits Grand Old Party for New."

226 **the conservative vote:** Freedlander, "An Oral History of Donald Trump's Almost-Run for President in 2000."

226 **Trump was unhappy:** Useem, "What Does Donald Trump Really Want?"

226 **in years to come:** David Weigel, "Pro-Cruz PAC Resurrects 1999 Trump Support of Abortion," **Washington Post,** January 25, 2016.

226 **few hundred votes:** Michael E. Miller, "'It's Insanity!': How the 'Brooks Brothers Riot' Killed the 2000 Recount in Miami," **Washington Post,** November 15, 2018.

227 **attacked the building:** Dana Canedy and Dexter Filkins, "Counting the Vote: Miami-Dade County; A Wild Day in Miami, with an End to Recounting, and Democrats' Going to Court," **New York Times,** November 23, 2000.

227 **Stone would boast:** Jeffrey Toobin, "The Dirty Trickster," **New Yorker,** May 23, 2008.

227 **foreign policy's fecklessness:** Linda Qiu, "Trump's Misleading Claim That He Warned About Osama Bin Laden," **New York Times,** November 19, 2018.

228 **local TV news broadcast:** Phone interview with Donald Trump, WWOR/UPN 9 News, September 11, 2001.

228 **"Forty Wall Street actually":** Phone interview with Donald Trump, WWOR/UPN 9 News, September 11, 2001.

228 **It wasn't even true:** Philip Bump, "On 9/11, Trump Pointed out He Now Had the Tallest Building in Lower Manhattan. He Didn't," **Washington Post,** September 11, 2018.

228 **"working down here":** Michael Balsamo and Nancy Benac, "Trump's 9/11 Narrative: Memory and Hyperbole, 15 Years Later," Associated Press, April 20, 2016.

229 **"The great thing":** Interview with Donald Trump, NBC News, September 13, 2011.

229 **six firefighters had been:** N. R. Kleinfeld, "A Nation Challenged: The Ladder Company; In Stopping to Save Woman, Rescuers Saved Themselves," September 28, 2001.

229 **there is no record:** Amy Sherman, "Donald Trump Says He Spent a Lot Time with 9/11 Responders. Here Are the Facts," **PolitiFact,** July 30, 2019.

229 **registered in Bermuda:** Aaron Cooper, "Meet Donald Trump's Air Fleet," CNN, July 23, 2015.

230 **two other businessmen:** Jennifer Steinhauer, "Giuliani Used Trump's Plane for Weekend Visit to Israel," **New York Times,** December 11, 2001.

230 **described her return:** Victoria Gotti, "I Was Plane Scared Flying Last Week," **New York Post,** September 23, 2001.

231 **welcomed a visitor:** Abby Ellin, "'Survivor' Meets Millionaire, and a Show Is Born," **New York Times,** October 19, 2003.

231 **Burnett was a fan:** Patrick Radden Keefe, "How Mark Burnett Resurrected Donald Trump as an Icon of American Success," **New Yorker,** December 27, 2018.

232 **cast of tycoons:** Michael M. Grynbaum and Ashley Parker, "Donald Trump the Political Showman, Born on 'The Apprentice,'" **New York Times,** July 16, 2016.

233 **homage to George Steinbrenner:** Allan Smith, "All the President's Yankees: How Trump's Long Affair with the Team Foreshadowed His Presidency," NBC News, October 19, 2019.

233 **hogging the microphone:** Marcia Kramer, "George Trumps Donald," **New York Daily News,** February 9, 1984.

234 **debuted in January:** Bill Carter, "The Challenge! The Pressure! The Donald!," **New York Times,** January 4, 2004.

234 **a fourth bankruptcy:** Suzette Parmley, "A Troubled Empire: Trump Gambled on Junk Bonds, and Lost," **Philadelphia Inquirer,** August 11, 2004.

235 **"something very seductive":** "'Apprentice' May Come to Broadway," Associated Press, January 18, 2005.

236 **an empty floor:** Keefe, "How Mark Burnett Resurrected Donald Trump as an Icon of American Success."

236 **"a crumbling empire":** Keefe, "How Mark Burnett Resurrected Donald Trump as an Icon of American Success."

CHAPTER 9: ASPHALT SURVIVOR

239 **neared a deal:** Charles V. Bagli, "Against All Odds, a Complicated Casino Proposal Advances," **New York Times,** April 17, 2000.

239 **spent on the ads:** Joseph Tanfani, "Trump Was Once So Involved in Trying to Block an Indian Casino That He Secretly Approved Attack Ads," **Los Angeles Times,** June 30, 2016.

239 **investigated the source:** Richard Pérez-Peña, "State Commission Investigates Trump Effort to Stop Casino," **New York Times,** July 18, 2000.

240 **They had met:** "Trump, Associates Detail Campaign," Associated Press, November 29, 2000.

240 **approve new casinos:** Richard Pérez-Peña, "Senate Bill Poses New Threat to Proposed Catskill Casino," **New York Times,** June 13, 2000.

240 **had also hired:** Fredric U. Dicker, "Trump Hired Firm to Probe Gov's Aide: Paid 61G in Casino 'Research,'" **New York Post,** December 29, 2000.

241 **the state's history:** Charles V. Bagli, "Trump and Others Accept Fines for Ads in Opposition to Casinos," **New York Times,** October 6, 2000.

241 **seeking a ninth:** Leslie Eaton, "First Real Challenge in 20 Years for Manhattan District Attorney," **New York Times,** February 24, 2005.

242 **received years earlier:** Wayne Barrett, "Rudy's Long History of Quashing Trump Probes," October 12, 1993.

242 **appointed Chris Christie:** Laura Mansnerus, "Corporate Lawyer in New Jersey Is Chosen as Federal Prosecutor," **New York Times,** December 8, 2001.

242 **asked his sister:** Kate Zernike, "For Chris Christie and Donald Trump, Ties Go Back Years," **New York Times,** March 7, 2016.

242 **an early impression:** Chris Christie, **Let Me Finish: Trump, the Kushners, Bannon, New Jersey, and the Power of In-Your-Face Politics** (New York: Hachette Books, 2019).

242 **Trump called him:** Christie, **Let Me Finish.**

243 **his third wife:** "Melania Knauss and Donald Trump Wed," **New York Times,** January 23, 2005.

243 **two different dresses:** Michael Callahan, "Trump's Wedding to Melania: Bill, Hill and Tons of Stars Hit

the 'Yuuuge' Affair," **Hollywood Reporter,** April 7, 2016.

243 **the royal family:** "The Donald Weds 34-Year-Old Model," **Tampa Bay Times,** January 23, 2005.

244 **who accused him:** Jordyn Phelps, "Flashback: Donald Trump Called Bill Clinton's Accusers 'Terrible' and 'Unattractive' and Former President 'Terrific,'" ABC News, October 9, 2016.

244 **also criticizing his judgment:** Nancy Benac, "Trump and the Fifth Amendment: It's Complicated," Associated Press, May 23, 2017.

244 **their new life:** Maureen Dowd, "When Hillary and Donald Were Friends," **New York Times Magazine,** November 2, 2016.

244 **his new member:** Sam Weinman, "Once upon a Time, When Bill Clinton Needed a Golf Haven, He Turned to Donald Trump," **Golf Digest,** November 4, 2016.

245 **"nine national interviews":** Marc Fisher, "Donald Trump Ignored His Agent and Did 'The Apprentice.' It Changed Everything," **Washington Post,** January 27, 2016.

245 **raised no objections:** Andrew Kaczynski, Chris Massie, and Nate McDermott, "Donald Trump's Decades-Long History of Misogynistic Comments and Crude Sex Talk," CNN, October 9, 2016.

245 **"incredible looking women":** Kaczynski, Massie, and McDermott, "Donald Trump's Decades-Long History of Misogynistic Comments and Crude Sex Talk."

246 **"absolutely not gay":** Donald Trump interview

by Howard Stern, **The Howard Stern Show,** April 2010.

246 **"big thought process":** Donald Trump interview by Howard Stern, **The Howard Stern Show,** April 2010.

246 **recounted the pitch:** Maggie Haberman et al., "Trump Employs an Old Tactic: Using Race for Gain," **New York Times,** July 20, 2019.

247 **name-calling tit for tat:** Mark Dagostino and Brian Orloff, "Rosie Slams Trump, The Donald Fires Back," **People,** December 20, 2006.

247 **marquee Wrestlemania tournament:** Richard Langford, "Donald Trump to Be Inducted into WWE Hall of Fame," **Bleacher Report,** February 25, 2013.

247 **the 2006 installment:** Aaron Oster, "Donald Trump and WWE: From 'WrestleMania' to the White House?" **Rolling Stone,** February 1, 2016.

247 **came back the next year:** Oster, "Donald Trump and WWE."

247 **book about him:** Timothy L. O'Brien, **TrumpNation: The Art of Being the Donald** (New York: Warner Books, 2005).

248 **no more than $250 million:** O'Brien, **TrumpNation.**

248 **$5-billion libel lawsuit:** "Trump Sues Writer and Book Publisher," **New York Times,** January 25, 2006.

248 **one of many:** Nick Penzenstadler and Susan Page, "Exclusive: Trump's 3,500 Lawsuits Unprecedented for a Presidential Nominee," **USA Today**, June 1, 2016.

248 **as inflicting pain:** Paul Farhi, "What Really Gets under Trump's Skin? A Reporter Questioning His Net Worth," **Washington Post,** March 8, 2016.

248 **less than truthful:** David A. Fahrenthold and Robert O'Harrow Jr., "In 2007, Trump Was Forced to Face His Own Falsehoods. And He Did, 30 Times," **Washington Post,** August 10, 2016.

249 **"net worth fluctuates":** Fahrenthold and O'Harrow Jr., "In 2007, Trump Was Forced to Face His Own Falsehoods."

249 **Trump would be investigated:** Ben Protess, William K. Rashbaum, and Maggie Haberman, "Prosecutors Investigating Trump Focus on His Finance Chief," **Baltimore Sun,** March 1, 2021, www.baltimoresun.com/news/nation-world/ct-aud-nw-nyt-prosecutors-investigate-trump-finance-chief-20210302-kzkfrajkaffnlezdjtm3o7niqi-story.html.

250 **one major exception:** David Enrich, "The Money Behind Trump's Money," **New York Times,** February 4, 2020.

250 **to personally guarantee:** David Enrich, "A Mar-a-Lago Weekend and an Act of God: Trump's History with Deutsche Bank," **New York Times,** March 18, 2019.

250 **suddenly paid more than:** Jonathan O'Connell, David A. Fahrenthold, and Jack Gillum, "As the 'King of Debt,' Trump Borrowed to Build His Empire. Then He Began Spending Hundreds of Millions in Cash," **Washington Post,** May 5, 2018.

250 **ground was broken:** Michael Idov, "The Zone-Skirting Scheme and Shadowy Businessmen

Behind the Trump Soho," **New York,** March 28, 2008.

250 **condominium and hotel:** Craig Karmin, "Trump SoHo Hotel Lender Plans to Put Property Up for Sale," **Wall Street Journal,** September 16, 2014.

251 **18 percent equity stake:** Michael Hirsch, "How Russian Money Helped Save Trump's Business," **Foreign Policy,** December 21, 2018.

251 **The majority partner:** Andrew Rice, "Felix Sater: Donald Trump's Original Russia Connection," **New York Magazine,** August 3, 2017.

251 **Sater had been convicted:** Rosalind S. Helderman and Tom Hamburger, "Former Mafia-Linked Figure Describes Association with Trump," **Washington Post,** May 17, 2016.

251 **maintained an office:** Idov, "The Zone-Skirting Scheme and Shadowy Businessmen Behind the Trump Soho."

251 **lent its name:** Ana Swanson, "The Trump Network Sought to Make People Rich, but Left Behind Disappointment," **Washington Post,** March 23, 2016.

252 **try to teach:** Stevenson Swanson, "Trump Wants to School You," **Chicago Tribune,** May 24, 2005.

252 **decided to sell:** Charles V. Bagli, "Trump Group Selling West Side Parcel for $1.8 Billion," **New York Times,** June 1, 2005.

252 **$1 billion in damages:** Farah Stockman and Keith Bradsher, "Donald Trump Soured on a Deal, and Hong Kong Partners Became Litigants," **New York Times,** May 30, 2016.

252 **Trump hurled back:** Shawn Tully, "How Donald Trump Lucked into the Most Lucrative Deal of His Career," **Fortune,** April 27, 2016.

252 **being ripped off:** Jim Tankersley and Mark Landler, "Trump's Love for Tariffs Began in Japan's '80s Boom," **New York Times,** May 15, 2019.

252 **stake in the profits:** Stockman and Bradsher, "Donald Trump Soured on a Deal."

252 **would bring him:** Russ Buettner, Susanne Craig, and Mike McIntire, "Trump's Taxes Show Chronic Losses and Years of Income Tax Avoidance," **New York Times,** September 27, 2020.

253 **monumentally large fine:** Bagli, "Trump and Others Accept Fines for Ads in Opposition to Casinos."

253 **make a public apology:** Bagli, "Trump and Others Accept Fines for Ads in Opposition to Casinos."

253 **replaced him with:** Patrick Healy, "In N.Y. Races, a Historic Sweep," **New York Times,** November 7, 2006.

253 **"roll over you":** "NY Gov. Spitzer Stands by 'Steamroller' Boast," Reuters, January 31, 2007.

254 **to investigate Bruno:** Danny Hakim, "Spitzer's Staff Misused Police, Report Finds," **New York Times,** July 23, 2007.

254 **filed a complaint with a:** Danny Hakim, "Politics Seen in Nasty Call to Spitzer's Father," **New York Times,** August 22, 2007.

254 **as an alibi:** Danny Hakim and Nicholas Confessore, "Political Consultant Resigns After Allegations of Threatening Spitzer's Father," **New York Times,** August 23, 2007.

254 **"ultimate dirty trick":** Hakim, "Politics Seen in Nasty Call to Spitzer's Father."

254 **controversy cost Stone:** Hakim and Confessore, "Political Consultant Resigns After Allegations of Threatening Spitzer's Father."

254 **a "stone-cold loser":** Jeffrey Toobin, "The Dirty Trickster," **New Yorker,** May 23, 2008.

CHAPTER 10: 140 CHARACTERS

257 **a former ballerina:** Amber Phillips, "Who Is Meredith McIver, the Trump Staffer Who Took the Fall for Melania's Speech?," **Washington Post,** July 20, 2016.

259 **value of TRMP stock:** Tami Luhby, "Buffett: A Monkey Could Outperform Those Who Bet on Trump's Stock," CNN, August 3, 2016.

259 **just 31 cents:** Floyd Norris, "Chapter 33 for Trump Casinos," **New York Times,** November 28, 2008.

259 **at his eponymous tower:** David Enrich et al., "How Trump Maneuvered His Way Out of Trouble in Chicago," **New York Times,** October 27, 2020.

259 **fifth casino bankruptcy:** Michelle Lee, "Fact Check: Has Trump Declared Bankruptcy Four or Six Times?," **Washington Post,** September 26, 2016.

259 **acquire the Trump Marina:** "The Donald vs. The Richard," **Forbes,** May 29, 2008.

259 **larger rebranding effort:** "Facelift Changes Name, Theme of Trump's Castle, but Will It Help?," **Las Vegas Sun,** June 25, 1997.

260 **rebrand it Margaritaville:** Wayne Parry, "Ex-Buyer

Sues Trump Casinos for Failed Marina Deal," **Morning Call,** July 29, 2009.

260 **abruptly agreed to:** Jon Burstein, "Seminoles, Developer Settle Disputes," **South Florida Sun-Sentinel,** April 18, 2007.

260 **mere $38 million:** Donald Wittkowski, "Golden Nugget Owner Reveals Details of Trump Marina Purchase and $150 Million in Upgrade," **Press of Atlantic City,** February 15, 2011.

260 **Nick Ribis—had departed:** Paul Tharp, "Trump Takes Lumps—No. 2 Exec, Nick Ribis, Jumps Sinking Ship," **New York Post,** May 31, 2000.

261 **married Jared Kushner:** "Ivanka Trump Weds Jared Kushner," **New York Times,** October 24, 2009.

261 **converted to Judaism:** Lizzie Widdicombe, "Ivanka Trump and Jared Kushner's Power Play," **New Yorker,** August 15, 2016.

261 **he first noticed:** Michael Schwirtz, William K. Rashbaum, and Danny Hakim, "Trump Foot Soldier Sidelined Under Glare of Russia Inquiry," **New York Times,** July 2, 2017.

262 **cut Cohen's salary:** Rebecca Ballhaus et al., "'What's He Doing Here?': Inside Trump's Turbulent Relationship with Michael Cohen," **Wall Street Journal,** June 15, 2018.

263 **very public friendship:** Maureen Dowd, "When Hillary and Donald Were Friends," **New York Times Magazine,** November 2, 2016.

263 **threw his support:** Mike Allen, "Trump Endorses McCain on Larry King," **Politico,** September 17, 2008.

263 **loudest congressional critics:** Michael Daly, "The Guy Trump Called 'Fat Jerry' Is Chairman Nadler Now," **Daily Beast,** March 5, 2019.

263 **had praised Obama:** Aaron Blake, "Obama and Trump: The Ticktock of a Truly Bizarre Relationship," **Washington Post,** March 6, 2017.

264 **country's first Black president:** Michael Tesler, **Post-Racial or Most-Racial? Race and Politics in the Obama Era** (Chicago: University of Chicago Press, 2016).

264 **commission a survey:** McKay Coppins, "Inside the Fraternity of Haters and Losers Who Drove Donald Trump to the GOP Nomination," **BuzzFeed,** July 17, 2016.

264 **a telephone interview:** Lucy Madison, "Donald Trump: I'm 'Absolutely Thinking About' Running for President," CBS News, October 5, 2010.

265 **created an outfit:** Jeffrey Toobin, "The Dirty Trickster," **New Yorker,** May 23, 2008.

265 **right-wing media entrepreneur:** Matthew Goldstein et al., "Bannon Made Millions in Shaping Right-Wing Thought," **New York Times,** March 31, 2017.

266 **promised to fund:** Jeremy W. Peters, "Carl Paladino, a Conservative, Joins Governor's Race," **New York Times,** April 5, 2010.

266 **another gubernatorial candidate:** Danny Hakim, "Roger Stone Plays Role in Two Opposing Campaigns," **New York Times,** August 11, 2010.

266 **Stone's extended orbit:** Hakim, "Roger Stone Plays Role in Two Opposing Campaigns."

267 **"not pedigreed poodles":** Michael Barbaro, "Many Top Paladino Aides Have Checkered Pasts," **New York Times,** September 28, 2010.

267 **the prostitution investigation:** Michael M. Grynbaum, "Spitzer Resigns, Citing Personal Failings," **New York Times,** March 12, 2008.

267 **his own scandals:** Danny Hakim and Jeremy W. Peters, "David Paterson Drops Out of New York Governor's Race," **New York Times,** February 26, 2010.

267 **written a letter:** Amy Driscoll, "Spitzer Miami Tryst Alleged; A GOP Strategist Said He Alerted the FBI Months Ago That New York Gov. Eliot Spitzer Hired Prostitutes," **Miami Herald,** March 22, 2008.

267 **filled with reports:** Kenneth Lovett, "New York State GOP Gubernatorial Hopeful Carl Paladino Has 10-Year-Old Love Child," **New York Daily News,** April 4, 2010.

267 **Paladino had sent:** Nicholas Confessore, "Racist E-Mail Tied to Candidate for Governor," **New York Times,** April 12, 2010.

267 **a full-throated apology:** Jaya Saxena, "Paladino on Emails: 'I'm Not a Racist,'" **Gothamist,** April 13, 2010.

268 **Muslim cultural center:** Ralph Blumenthal and Sharaf Mowjood, "Muslim Prayers Fuel Spiritual Rebuilding Project by Ground Zero," **New York Times,** December 8, 2009.

268 **development—inaccurately dubbed:** Spencer Ackerman, "How the 'Ground Zero Mosque'

Meltdown Set the Table for Trump," **Vanity Fair,** August 9, 2021.

268 **nefarious sources of foreign money:** Rick Lazio, "Who's Paying for the Ground Zero Islamic Center?," CNN, July 23, 2010.

268 **officials in both parties:** Russell Goldman, "Republican Pol Warns of Playing 'Political Football' with 'Ground Zero Mosque,'" ABC News, August 17, 2010.

269 **quickly leaked it:** Sumathi Reddy and Tamer El-Ghobashy, "Donald Trump Offers to Buy Out Investor in Islamic Center and Mosque Near Ground Zero," **Wall Street Journal,** September 9, 2010.

269 **Paladino upset Lazio:** David M. Halbfinger and Michael Barbaro, "Paladino Stuns N.Y. G.O.P. with Victory," **New York Times,** September 14, 2010.

271 **published a column:** Roger Stone, "Why Trump Should Run in 2012," The Stone Zone (blog), December 14, 2010.

CHAPTER 11: RISING ON A LIE

273 **win over major donors:** Jonathan Martin and Maggie Haberman, "Romney Dominates GOP Cash Dash," **Politico,** June 24, 2011.

274 **crash the party:** Chris Moody, "How Gay Conservatives Helped Launch Donald Trump," CNN, March 3, 2016.

274 **a civil union:** Donald J. Trump, "Elton John's Wedding," **The Trump Blog** (blog), December 22, 2005.

275 **until the last minute:** Maggie Haberman and Jonathan Martin, "Surprise! Trump Tees Up," **Politico,** February 10, 2011.

275 **called himself "very pro-choice":** Donald Trump interview by Tim Russert, **Meet the Press,** October 24, 1999.

276 **was first promoted:** Ben Smith and Byron Tau, "Birtherism: Where It All Began," **Politico,** April 22, 2011.

278 **his own effort:** Michael Scherer, "The Men Behind the Dueling Draft Donald Trump Websites," **Time,** April 12, 2011.

278 **quarter century earlier:** "G.O.P. Seeks Out Trump," Associated Press, July 7, 1987.

278 **he was interviewed:** Donald Trump interview by Ashley Banfield, **Good Morning America,** March 17, 2011.

279 **sought out a conversation:** Ashley Parker and Steve Eder, "Inside the Six Weeks Donald Trump Was a Nonstop 'Birther,'" **New York Times,** July 2, 2016.

279 **Stone insisted he did not:** Roger Stone interview by Jason M. Breslow, **The Frontline Interview,** PBS, September 27, 2016.

279 **called a racist:** Michael C. Bender, **"Frankly, We Did Win This Election": The Inside Story of How Trump Lost** (New York: Hachette Books, 2021).

279 **But publicly, he said:** Ben Smith, "Trump's Birther Play," **Politico,** March 28, 2011.

279 **such as Andrew Breitbart:** Dana Milbank, "Andrew Breitbart and the Rifts on the Right," **Washington Post,** April 21, 2011.

280 **and Ann Coulter:** Zachary Pleat, "Coulter Ignores

Conservative Media Promoting Birtherism," Media Matters for America, April 12, 2011.

280 **kept with it:** Jonathan Strong, "Donald Trump's Birth Certificate Strategy," **Daily Caller,** March 24, 2011.

280 **dispatching investigators to Hawaii:** Donald Trump interview by Meredith Vieira, **Today,** April 7, 2011.

280 **released a version:** Jess Henig, "Born in the U.S.A.," FactCheck.org, August 21, 2008.

280 **Trump would headline:** Juana Summers, "The Donald to Headline Iowa GOP Dinner," **Politico,** March 23, 2011.

281 **to a Republican pollster:** Maggie Haberman and Alexander Burns, "Donald Trump's Presidential Run Began in an Effort to Gain Stature," **New York Times,** March 12, 2016.

281 **of white-grievance politics:** Alan Rappeport, "In Philadelphia, a Brash Ex-Mayor Draws Comparisons to Donald Trump," **New York Times,** April 24, 2016.

282 **Trump started calling the:** Haberman and Burns, "Donald Trump's Presidential Run Began in an Effort to Gain Stature."

282 **through her husband:** Josh Dawsey and John Wagner, "George Conway, Kellyanne Conway's Husband, Called 'Total Loser' by Trump," **Washington Post,** March 19, 2019.

282 **offered to connect him:** Maggie Haberman and Ben Smith, "What's Donald Trump Really After?," **Politico,** April 18, 2011.

282 **being notoriously cheap:** David A. Fahrenthold

and Danielle Rindler, "Searching for Evidence of Trump's Personal Giving," **Washington Post,** August 18, 2016.

283 **Stone joined him:** Alex Leary, "That Time Donald Trump Met the Tea Party in Florida and Saw the Path to 2016," **Tampa Bay Times,** September 11, 2016.

284 **entered his limousine:** Leary, "That Time Donald Trump Met the Tea Party in Florida and Saw the Path to 2016."

284 **released a copy:** Michael D. Shear, "Obama Releases Long-Form Birth Certificate," **New York Times,** April 27, 2011.

285 **annual black-tie dinner:** Haberman and Burns, "Donald Trump's Presidential Run Began in an Effort to Gain Stature."

285 **expect some ribbing:** Roxanne Roberts, "I Sat Next to Donald Trump at the Infamous 2011 White House Correspondents' Dinner," **Washington Post,** April 28, 2016.

286 **He left quickly:** Haberman and Burns, "Donald Trump's Presidential Run Began in an Effort to Gain Stature."

286 **was the center of attention:** Helen Kennedy, "Donald Trump Not Amused by Obama's Jokes at White House Correspondents Dinner; 'Honored' by Insults," **New York Daily News,** May 1, 2011.

287 **ended the speculation:** "Trump Not Running for President," CNN, May 16, 2011.

288 **after his win:** Jeff Zeleny, "Romney Wins G.O.P. Primary in New Hampshire," **New York Times,** January 10, 2012.

289 **large Mormon electorate:** "Mormon Voters a Key in Nevada—They're for Romney," Associated Press, February 2, 2012.

289 **"just can't imagine":** Reid J. Epstein, "Trump Endorses Mitt," **Politico,** February 2, 2012.

289 **credited his endorser:** Domenico Montanaro, "#TBT: For Trump and Romney, What Happened in Vegas, Stayed in Vegas," NPR, August 27, 2015.

289 **rejected Trump's request:** McKay Coppins, "Inside the Fraternity of Haters and Losers Who Drove Donald Trump to the GOP Nomination," **BuzzFeed,** July 17, 2016.

289 **actor portraying Obama:** Michael Cohen, **Disloyal: A Memoir** (New York: Skyhorse Publishing, 2020).

289 **hurricane bearing down:** Philip Bump, "2012 Was Closer to Being the Year of Trump Than You Might Remember," **Washington Post,** November 6, 2015.

289 **forced the cancellation:** Emily Schultheis, "Trump's Moment in Fla. Spotlight," **Politico,** August 26, 2012.

290 **a private fundraiser:** David Corn, "Secret Video: Romney Tells Millionaire Donors What He REALLY Thinks of Obama Voters," **Mother Jones,** September 17, 2012.

290 **visited in Las Vegas:** Megan Twohey and Steve Eder, "How a Pageant Led to a Trump Son's Meeting with a Russian Lawyer," **New York Times,** July 10, 2017.

290 **the first time in Russia:** Michael Crowley, "When Donald Trump Brought Miss Universe to Moscow," **Politico,** May 15, 2016.

290 **Agalarov had ties:** Crowley, "When Donald Trump Brought Miss Universe to Moscow."

291 **compile a document:** Kenneth P. Vogel, "The Trump Dossier: What We Know and Who Paid for It," **New York Times,** October 25, 2017.

291 **opened an investigation:** Andrea Bernstein et al., "How Ivanka Trump and Donald Trump, Jr., Avoided a Criminal Indictment," **New Yorker**/ProPublica/WNYC, October 4, 2017.

291 **Vance ultimately returned:** James C. McKinley Jr., "Vance Returned Trump Lawyer's Donation After Reporters' Questions," **New York Times,** October 4, 2017.

291 **not to convene:** Bernstein et al., "How Ivanka Trump and Donald Trump, Jr., Avoided a Criminal Indictment."

292 **launched in 2005:** Alan Feuer, "Trump University Made False Claims, Lawsuit Says," **New York Times,** August 24, 2013.

292 **a civil investigation:** Lauren McGaughy, "Greg Abbott's Top Consumer Attorneys Built a $5.4M Case Against Donald Trump, but It Never Happened," **Dallas Morning News,** June 2, 2016.

292 **abruptly pulled out:** Patrick Svitek, "In Texas, Trump U Shut Down After State Scrutiny," **Texas Tribune,** June 2, 2016.

292 **gave thirty-five thousand dollars:** Jeff Horwitz and Michael Biesecker, "Trump University Model: Sell Hard, Demand to See a Warrant," Associated Press, June 2, 2012.

292 **fully ceased operations:** Feuer, "Trump University Made False Claims, Lawsuit Says."

293 **ethics complaints against:** Michael Gormley, "Donald Trump Files 2 Ethics Complaints

Against N.Y. Attorney General," Associated Press, December 24, 2013.

293 **Trump's foundation donated:** Kevin Sack and Steve Eder, "New Records Shed Light on Donald Trump's $25,000 Gift to Florida Official," **New York Times,** September 14, 2016.

293 **took no action:** David A. Fahrenthold, "Trump Previously Donated $6,000 to Kamala D. Harris's Campaigns," **Washington Post,** August 12, 2020.

293 **other for-profit educational entities:** Matthew Artz, "Trump University Investigation Could Explain Donald Trump's Political Donations to Kamala Harris," **Mercury News,** September 8, 2016.

293 **"As a businessman, I need":** Peter Nicholas, "Donald Trump Walks Back His Past Praise of Hillary Clinton," **Wall Street Journal,** July 29, 2015.

294 **directly to camera:** Ben Schreckinger, "'Oh, No': The Day Trump Learned to Tweet," **Politico,** December 20, 2018.

295 **live-tweet a debate:** Schreckinger, "'Oh, No.'"

295 **compared the moment:** Schreckinger, "'Oh, No.'"

295 **his worst impulses:** Michael Barbaro, "Pithy, Mean and Powerful: How Donald Trump Mastered Twitter for 2016," **New York Times,** October 5, 2015.

296 **received a memo:** Fredric U. Dicker, "GOPers Eye Donald Trump for Governor Run," **New York Post,** October 14, 2013.

297 **polled the race:** Joshua Green, **Devil's Bargain:**

Steve Bannon, Donald Trump, and the Storming of the Presidency (New York: Penguin Press, 2017).

299 **was easily reelected:** Jason Noble, "Terry Branstad Re-Elected to Historic Sixth Term," **Des Moines Register,** November 5, 2014.

299 **a triumphant November:** Jonathan Weisman and Ashley Parker, "Election Results: Republicans Win Senate Control with at Least 7 New Seats," **New York Times,** November 4, 2014.

300 **an "autopsy" report:** Sarah Wheaton and Michael D. Shear, "Blunt Report Says G.O.P. Needs to Regroup for '16," **New York Times,** March 18, 2013.

300 **newly elected senator:** Greg Sargent, "Tom Cotton: Terrorists Collaborating with Mexican Drug Cartels to Infiltrate Arkansas," **Washington Post,** October 7, 2014.

300 **authorities turn away:** David McCabe, "Roberts Links Ebola, ISIS to Border Security," **The Hill,** October 15, 2014.

CHAPTER 12: MAKE OR BREAK

306 **their own trips:** James Hohmann, "Scott Walker Huddles with Donald Trump," **Politico,** February 20, 2015.

306 **the two men spoke that May:** Robert Costa and Anne Gearan, "Donald Trump Talked Politics with Bill Clinton Weeks Before Launching 2016 Bid," **Washington Post,** August 5, 2015.

306 **his advisers knew:** Roger Stone, "Why Trump Should Run in 2012," **The Stone Zone** (blog), December 14, 2010.

306 **about-face on abortion:** David Weigel, "Pro-Cruz PAC Resurrects 1999 Trump Support of Abortion," **Washington Post,** January 25, 2016.

307 **bipartisan bill pairing:** Dean DeChiaro, "On Immigration, McCain Leaves a Roadmap," **Roll Call,** August 27, 2018.

307 **"ripping us off":** Fox Butterfield, "New Hampshire Speech Earns Praise for Trump," **New York Times,** October 23, 1987.

307 **a new way:** Julie Hirschfeld Davis and Peter Baker, "How the Border Wall Is Boxing Trump In," **New York Times,** January 5, 2019.

307 **told by advisers:** Ashley Parker and Steve Eder, "Inside the Six Weeks Donald Trump Was a Nonstop 'Birther,'" **New York Times,** July 2, 2016.

308 **a basketball charity:** "Donald Trump Donates $25,000 to Slam Jam," **New York Amsterdam News,** September 25, 2013.

308 **with David Pecker:** Annie Karni and Maggie Haberman, "Jeffrey Epstein Was a 'Terrific Guy,' Donald Trump Once Said. Now He's 'Not a Fan,'" **New York Times,** July 9, 2019.

308 **"catch and kill":** Ronan Farrow, "Donald Trump, the Playboy Model Karen McDougal, and a System for Concealing Infidelity," **New Yorker,** February 16, 2018.

309 **official campaign kickoff:** Alexander Burns, "Donald Trump, Pushing Someone Rich, Offers Himself," **New York Times,** June 16, 2015.

310 **managed to overshadow:** Michael Barbaro and Jonathan Martin, "Jeb Bush Announces White

House Bid, Saying 'America Deserves Better,'" **New York Times,** June 15, 2015.

310 **his first interview:** Donald Trump interview by Bill O'Reilly, **The O'Reilly Factor,** June 16, 2015.

310 **no longer owned:** David Stout and Kenneth N. Gilpin, "Trump Is Selling Plaza Hotel to Saudi and Asian Investors," **New York Times,** April 12, 1995.

310 **views toward Russia:** Donald Trump interview by Bill O'Reilly, **The O'Reilly Factor,** June 16, 2015.

311 **a private meeting at:** Michael Barbaro, Maggie Haberman, and Jonathan Martin, "Can't Fire Him: Republican Party Frets over What to Do with Donald Trump," **New York Times,** July 9, 2015.

311 **Priebus called Trump:** Karen Tumulty, Philip Rucker, and Robert Costa, "GOP Leaders Fear Damage to Party's Image as Donald Trump Doubles Down," **Washington Post,** July 8, 2015.

312 **gleefully attacked John McCain:** Jonathan Martin and Alan Rappeport, "Donald Trump Says John McCain Is No War Hero, Setting Off Another Storm," **New York Times,** July 18, 2015.

313 **relatively mild criticism:** Nick Gass, "McCain: Trump 'Fired Up the Crazies,'" **Politico,** July 16, 2015.

313 **"being a jackass":** Jean Song, "Sen. Lindsey Graham to Donald Trump: 'Stop Being a Jackass,'" CBS News, July 21, 2015.

313 **and encouraged people:** Nick Gass and Adam B. Lerner, "Donald Trump Gives Out Lindsey Graham's Cellphone Number," **Politico,** July 21, 2015.

313 **Trump was made public:** Daniel Strauss, "Donald Trump 2016: Gawker Publishes Trump's Phone Number," **Politico,** August 3, 2015.

314 **the active disdain:** Julie Pace and Jeff Horwitz, "In Business and Politics, Trump Stokes Internal Rivalries," Associated Press, May 28, 2016.

314 **one political race:** Joshua Green and Sasha Issenberg, "Inside the Trump Bunker, with 12 Days to Go," Bloomberg, October 27, 2016.

314 **almost upon meeting:** Corey R. Lewandowski and David N. Bossie, **Let Trump Be Trump: The Inside Story of His Rise to the Presidency** (New York: Center Street/Hachette, 2017).

315 **years-old Facebook posts:** Hunter Walker, "Sam Nunberg's 'Racist' Facebook Posts," **Insider,** July 31, 2015.

315 **banish their rival:** Gabriel Sherman, "The Trump Campaign Has Descended into Civil War—Even Ivanka Has Gotten Involved," **New York,** August 6, 2015.

315 **week of attacks:** Jonathan Martin and Maggie Haberman, "Hand-Wringing in G.O.P. After Donald Trump's Remarks on Megyn Kelly," **New York Times,** August 8, 2015.

315 **spoke to a reporter:** Robert Costa, "Trump Ends Relationship with Longtime Political Adviser Roger Stone," **Washington Post,** August 8, 2015.

316 **Trump was challenged:** David Folkenflik, "Univision Anchor Jorge Ramos Removed from Trump Press Conference," NPR, August 26, 2015.

317 **insisted in response:** Josh Robin, "Scuffle Between Trump Staffers, Protesters Dims Anticipated

Campaign Announcement," NY1, September 4, 2015.

317 **Bush "low energy":** Ashley Parker, "Jeb Bush Sprints to Escape Donald Trump's 'Low Energy' Label," **New York Times,** December 29, 2016.

317 **as physically unattractive:** Adam Edelman, "Donald Trump Hits Rand Paul on His Looks During GOP 2016 Debate," **New York Daily News,** September 16, 2015.

317 **a private moment:** Paul Solotaroff, "Trump Seriously: On the Trail with the GOP's Tough Guy," **Rolling Stone,** September 9, 2015.

317 **"a big problem":** Gregory Krieg, "Trump Likens Carson's 'Pathology' to That of a Child Molester," CNN, November 12, 2015.

318 **"pledging my allegiance":** Jessica Taylor, "Trump: I'm 'Totally Pledging' My Allegiance to the Republican Party," NPR, September 3, 2015.

CHAPTER 13: MANY PEOPLE ARE SAYING

321 **a coordinated attack:** Alissa J. Rubin and Elian Peltier, "The Paris Attacks, 2 Years Later: Quiet Remembrance and Lasting Impact," **New York Times,** November 13, 2017.

321 **to displace Al-Qaeda:** Eric Schmitt, "As ISIS Loses Land, It Gains Ground in Overseas Terror," **New York Times,** July 3, 2016.

321 **"great Trojan horse":** Editorial Board, "Mr. Trump Spreads Dangerous Lies About Syrian Refugees," **Washington Post,** November 17, 2015.

321 **shutting down mosques:** Gregory Krieg, "Donald

Trump: 'Strongly Consider' Shutting Mosques," CNN, November 16, 2015.

321 **interview shortly thereafter:** Hunter Walker, "Donald Trump Has Big Plans for 'Radical Islamic' Terrorists, 2016 and 'That Communist' Bernie Sanders," Yahoo News, November 19, 2015.

322 **"a lot of systems":** Vaughn Hillyard, "Donald Trump's Plan for a Muslim Database Draws Comparison to Nazi Germany," NBC News, November 19, 2015.

323 **"sign them up":** "CNN Newsroom with Brooke Baldwin," CNN, November 20, 2015, www.cnn .com/TRANSCRIPTS/1511/20/cnr.08.html.

324 **prepared a story:** Maggie Haberman and Richard Pérez-Peña, "Donald Trump Sets Off a Furor with Call to Register Muslims in the U.S.," **New York Times,** November 20, 2015.

324 **supposed "fact check":** Charlie Spiering, "Donald Trump: 'Media Proposed Muslim Database, Not Me,'" **Breitbart,** November 20, 2015.

324 **attacked me personally:** John Nolte, "Muslim Registry: Rope-Me-Hillary-Haberman Lies About Trump on NYT Front Page," **Breitbart,** November 21, 2015.

326 **refused to concede that his account:** Jordyn Phelps, "Donald Trump Again Says He Saw Cheering in New Jersey on 9/11," ABC News, November 22, 2015.

326 **after the 2001 attacks:** Serge F. Kovaleski and Fredrick Kunkle, "Northern New Jersey Draws Probers' Eyes," **Washington Post,** September 18, 2001.

326 **they did not recall:** Glenn Kessler, "Donald Trump's Revisionist History of Mocking a Disabled Reporter," **Washington Post,** August 2, 2016.

326 **one of the authors:** Kessler, "Donald Trump's Revisionist History of Mocking a Disabled Reporter."

327 **another terrorist attack:** Michael S. Schmidt and Richard Pérez-Peña, "F.B.I. Treating San Bernardino Attack as Terrorism Case," **New York Times,** December 4, 2015.

328 **Trump immediately remarked:** Colin Campbell, "Trump: San Bernardino Shooting Looks Like 'Islamic Disaster,'" **Insider,** December 3, 2015.

328 **a policy proposal at the ready:** Patrick Healy and Michael Barbaro, "Donald Trump Calls for Barring Muslims from Entering U.S.," **New York Times,** December 7, 2015.

328 **a notorious Islamophobe:** Philip Bump, "Meet Frank Gaffney, the Anti-Muslim Gadfly Reportedly Advising Donald Trump's Transition Team," **Washington Post,** November 16, 2016.

328 **saw as blatantly unconstitutional:** Jerry Markon, "Experts: Trump's Muslim Entry Ban Idea 'Ridiculous,' 'Unconstitutional,'" **Washington Post,** December 7, 2015.

329 **depth of knowledge:** Alan Rappeport, "Ben Carson Sinks on Doubts About His Foreign Policy," **New York Times,** December 2, 2015.

329 **the misogynistic attack:** Jonathan Martin and Maggie Haberman, "Hand-Wringing in G.O.P. After Donald Trump's Remarks on Megyn Kelly," **New York Times,** August 8, 2015.

330 **apparently durable connection:** Maggie Haberman and Thomas Kaplan, "Evangelicals See Donald Trump as Man of Conviction, If Not Faith," **New York Times,** January 18, 2016.

330 **"Two Corinthians, 3:17":** Nick Corasaniti, "Donald Trump Quotes Scripture, Sort of, at Liberty University Speech," **New York Times,** January 18, 2016.

331 **accused of shooting:** Alice Robb, "When Doug and Ashley Benefield Started a Ballet Company, It Wasn't Supposed to End in Death," **Vanity Fair,** September 2, 2021.

331 **a self-described evangelical:** Haberman and Kaplan, "Evangelicals See Donald Trump as Man of Conviction, If Not Faith."

331 **he attended church:** Sarah Pulliam Bailey, "Donald Trump Almost Put Money in the Communion Plate at a Church in Iowa," **Washington Post,** February 1, 2016.

331 **appeared reasonably engaged:** Maggie Haberman and Thomas Kaplan, "Donald Trump Delivers Flurry of Flattery in Iowa," **New York Times,** January 31, 2016.

333 **inability to offend:** Jenna Johnson, "Donald Trump: They Say I Could 'Shoot Somebody' and Still Have Support," **Washington Post,** January 23, 2016.

333 **he showily announced:** Philip Rucker, Dan Balz, and Jenna Johnson, "Trump Says He Won't Participate in GOP Debate on Fox News," **Washington Post,** January 26, 2016.

333 **previously levied threats:** Mark Joyella, "Fox News

Accuses Trump Campaign Manager of Threatening Megyn Kelly," **Adweek,** January 26, 2016.

333 **a simultaneous event:** David A. Fahrenthold, "What Ever Happened to All That Money Trump Raised for the Veterans?," **Washington Post,** March 3, 2016.

333 **raised $6 million:** Fahrenthold, "What Ever Happened to All That Money Trump Raised for the Veterans?"

334 **gave $1 million:** Peter Eavis, "Putting Donald Trump's $1 Million for Veterans in Context," **New York Times,** June 1, 2016.

334 **the claimed sum:** David A. Fahrenthold, "Trump Said He Raised $6 Million for Veterans. Now His Campaign Says It Was Less," **Washington Post,** May 21, 2016.

334 **began asking questions:** David A. Fahrenthold, "Four Months After Fundraiser, Trump Says He Gave $1 Million to Veterans Group," **Washington Post,** May 24, 2016.

334 **coverage drew interest:** Steve Eder, "New York Attorney General to Investigate Donald Trump's Nonprofit," **New York Times,** September 13, 2016.

334 **"they're not laughing":** Maggie Haberman and Alexander Burns, "Donald Trump's Presidential Run Began in an Effort to Gain Stature," **New York Times,** March 12, 2016.

334 **against imaginary agitators:** Nolan D. McCaskill, "Trump Urges Crowd to 'Knock the Crap out of' Anyone with Tomatoes," **Politico,** February 1, 2016.

336 **"most disgusting things":** Andrew Kaczynski,

"Trump Says He'll Probably Sue Over Iowa Results, Accuses Cruz of 'Voter Fraud,'" **BuzzFeed,** February 3, 2016.

336 **"he stole it":** Tom McCarthy, "Donald Trump Claims Ted Cruz 'Stole' Iowa Caucuses and Calls for New Election," **Guardian,** February 3, 2016.

336 **subsequent South Carolina primary:** Jonathan Martin and Alexander Burns, "Donald Trump Wins South Carolina Primary; Cruz and Rubio Vie for 2nd," **New York Times,** February 20, 2016.

336 **and Nevada caucuses:** Alexander Burns and Nick Corasaniti, "Donald Trump Wins Nevada Caucuses, Collecting Third Straight Victory," **New York Times,** February 23, 2016.

336 **stood any chance:** Katie Glueck and Kyle Cheney, "Cruz and Kasich Team Up to Stop Trump," **Politico,** April 24, 2016.

336 **who dropped out:** Alexander Burns and Maggie Haberman, "Chris Christie Drops Out of Presidential Race After New Hampshire Flop," **New York Times,** February 10, 2016.

337 **his friend's candidacy:** Michael Barbaro, Maggie Haberman, and Ashley Parker, "Chris Christie Endorses Donald Trump and Calls Marco Rubio 'Desperate,'" **New York Times,** February 26, 2016.

337 **"lend my support":** Jeremy Diamond et al., "Chris Christie Endorses Donald Trump," CNN, February 26, 2016.

337 **his own enthusiasm:** Andrew Kaczynski, "David Duke Urges His Supporters to Volunteer and Vote for Trump," **BuzzFeed,** February 25, 2016.

337 **retweeting a post:** Tal Kopan, "Donald Trump

Retweets 'White Genocide' Twitter User," CNN, January 22, 2016.

337 **pressed on the subject:** Glenn Kessler, "Donald Trump and David Duke: For the Record," **Washington Post,** March 1, 2016.

338 **mentioned the Klansman:** Donald J. Trump, "What I Saw at the Revolution," **New York Times,** February 19, 2000.

339 **a "lunatic fringe":** Erick Trickey, "Before QAnon, Ronald Reagan and Other Republicans Purged John Birch Society Extremists from the GOP," **Washington Post,** January 15, 2021.

CHAPTER 14: STOP THE STEAL

341 **"an authoritarian President":** Susan B. Glasser, "Mike Pompeo, the Secretary of Trump," **New Yorker,** August 19, 2019.

342 **estimates soon concluded:** Elizabeth Crisp, "Donald Trump Calls GOP Primary Politics 'Unfair,' Challenges Louisiana Delegate Distribution," **Advocate,** March 29, 2016.

342 **after the Iowa caucuses:** Andrew Kaczynski, "Trump Says He'll Probably Sue Over Iowa Results, Accuses Cruz of 'Voter Fraud,'" **BuzzFeed,** February 3, 2016.

342 **a lawsuit against the state:** Brian Naylor, "Trump's Threat to Sue over Louisiana Delegates Reveals Organizational Weakness," NPR, March 29, 2016.

343 **a candidate debate:** Philip Rucker, Dan Balz, and Jenna Johnson, "Trump Says He Won't Participate in GOP Debate on Fox News," **Washington Post,** January 26, 2016.

343 **traditional campaign functions:** Maggie Haberman and Jonathan Martin, "Donald Trump Scraps the Usual Campaign Playbook, Including TV Ads," **New York Times,** December 24, 2015.

343 **for such infrastructure:** Maggie Haberman, Ashley Parker, and Nick Corasaniti, "Donald Trump, in Switch, Turns to Republican Party for Fund-Raising Help," **New York Times,** May 9, 2016.

343 **call in by phone:** David Bauder, "Trump's Penchant for Phone Interviews Draws Network Ire," Associated Press, March 27, 2016.

344 **effective tax rate:** Robert Farley, "Does Romney Pay a Lower Rate in Taxes Than You?," FactCheck.org, August 3, 2012.

345 **Protesters arrived at the arena:** Mike Lowe, "24-Hour Vigil Precedes Protest at Donald Trump Rally in Chicago," WGN-TV, March 11, 2016.

345 **leading to fights:** Monica Davey and Julie Bosman, "Donald Trump's Rally in Chicago Canceled After Violent Scuffles," **New York Times,** March 11, 2016.

345 **canceling the event:** Davey and Bosman, "Donald Trump's Rally in Chicago Canceled After Violent Scuffles."

345 **the following Tuesday:** Jonathan Martin and Alexander Burns, "Donald Trump Takes 3 States; John Kasich Wins Ohio," **New York Times,** March 15, 2016.

345 **wrest the nomination:** Kyle Cheney, "Chaos Erupts on GOP Convention Floor After Voice Vote Shuts Down Never Trump Forces," **Politico,** July 18, 2016.

346 **allegations of affairs:** Domenico Montanaro, "Tabloid Allegations Again Fly in a Political Campaign—And Why No One Can Look Away," NPR, March 25, 2016.

346 **was somehow proximate:** Glenn Kessler, "Trump's False Claim That the National Enquirer Story on Cruz's Father Was Not Denied," **Washington Post,** May 4, 2016.

346 **He was directed:** Glenn Thrush, "To Charm Trump, Paul Manafort Sold Himself as an Affordable Outsider," **New York Times,** April 8, 2017.

346 **helped to stage:** Warren Weaver Jr. and E. J. Dionne Jr., "Campaign Trail," **New York Times,** May 12, 1998.

346 **a delegate-counting operation:** Alexander Burns and Maggie Haberman, "Donald Trump Hires Paul Manafort to Lead Delegate Effort," **New York Times,** March 28, 2016.

346 **advised Viktor Yanukovych:** Alexander Burns and Maggie Haberman, "Mystery Man: Ukraine's U.S. Fixer," **Politico,** March 5, 2014.

347 **brutal and antidemocratic leaders:** Manuel Roig-Franzia, "How Paul Manafort and Roger Stone Created the Mess Donald Trump Said He'd Drain," **Washington Post,** November 29, 2018.

347 **former Manafort business partner:** Kate Zernike, "'Steady Hand' for the G.O.P. Guides McCain on a New Path," **New York Times,** April 13, 2008.

347 **maintained top posts:** Matthew Mosk, "Top McCain Adviser Has Found Success Mixing Money, Politics," **Washington Post,** June 26, 2008.

347 **from granting Manafort:** Burns and Haberman, "Mystery Man: Ukraine's U.S. Fixer."

347 **whittled down to three:** Tal Kopan, "Marco Rubio Drops Out of Presidential Campaign After Florida Loss," CNN, March 16, 2016.

348 **for one column:** Maureen Dowd, "Opinion: Trump Does It His Way," **New York Times,** April 2, 2016.

348 **declined to answer:** Dowd, "Opinion: Trump Does It His Way."

349 **not actually marketed:** Brett Neely, "Trump Doesn't Own Most of the Products He Pitched Last Night," NPR, March 9, 2016.

350 **class action lawsuits:** Drew Griffin, Nelli Black, and Curt Devine, "Thousands of Trump University Students File to Get Their Money Back," CNN, March 23, 2017.

350 **scheduled for trial:** "Trial Date Set in Trump University Lawsuit," Associated Press, May 6, 2016.

350 **"He's a hater":** Reid J. Epstein, "Trump Attacks Federal Judge in Trump U Case," **Wall Street Journal,** May 27, 2016.

350 **the Indiana-born Curiel:** Maureen Groppe, "What Trump Has Said About Judge Curiel," **Indianapolis Star,** June 11, 2016.

350 **alternately described as:** Eli Rosenberg, "Trump Disparaged 'Mexican Judge' Gonzalo Curiel, Who Will Now Hear a Key Border Wall Case," **Washington Post,** February 5, 2018.

350 **later on CNN:** Rosenberg, "Trump Disparaged 'Mexican Judge' Gonzalo Curiel."

350 **could be biased:** Alan Yuhas, "Trump: 'It's Possible,

Absolutely' Muslim Judges Are Also Biased Against Me," **Guardian,** June 5, 2016.

350 **Republicans publicly condemned:** Laurie Kellman, "GOP Leaders Warning Trump to Drop Attacks on Judge," Associated Press, June 5, 2016.

350 **persuaded him in private:** Chris Christie, **Let Me Finish: Trump, the Kushners, Bannon, New Jersey, and the Power of In-Your-Face Politics** (New York: Hachette Books, 2019).

351 **"I'm not changing":** Kellman, "GOP Leaders Warning Trump to Drop Attacks on Judge."

351 **the well-respected pollster:** Maggie Haberman and Ashley Parker, "Donald Trump Hires Pollster as Campaign Strategist, Sources Say," **New York Times,** May 16, 2016.

351 **who had crafted the:** Alex Isenstadt, "Donald Trump 2016 Team in Talks with Veteran Ad Maker," **Politico,** November 12, 2015.

351 **bugged by Trump:** Ashley Parker and Maggie Haberman, "Donald Trump's Campaign Stumbles as It Tries to Go Big," **New York Times,** May 27, 2016.

351 **for quashing spots:** Alex Isenstadt et al., "Inside Trump's Stunning Upset Victory," **Politico,** November 9, 2016.

352 **left the campaign:** Gabriel Sherman, "The Final Days of Trump's Unprecedented Campaign," **New York Magazine,** October 29, 2016.

352 **succeeded in orchestrating:** Maggie Haberman, Alexander Burns, and Ashley Parker, "Donald Trump Fires Corey Lewandowski, His Campaign Manager," **New York Times,** June 20, 2016.

352 **Lewandowski's appearance on CNN:** Corey R. Lewandowski interview by Dana Bash, CNN, June 20, 2016.

353 **an economic speech:** Neil Irwin, "Donald Trump's Economic Nostalgia," **New York Times,** June 28, 2016.

353 **who used aspects:** Ashley Killough, "Top Aide: Donald Trump Will Channel 1968 Richard Nixon in Speech," CNN, July 18, 2016.

354 **Trump only ever:** Alexander Burns and Maggie Haberman, "How Donald Trump Finally Settled on Mike Pence," **New York Times,** July 15, 2016.

355 **his own support for:** Adam Kelsey, "Possible Trump VP Pick Flynn Supports Abortion Rights: 'Women Have to Be Able to Choose,'" ABC News, July 10, 2016.

355 **At a fundraiser:** Alexander Burns and Maggie Haberman, "After Outbreaks of Violence, Donald Trump Strains to Project Leadership," **New York Times,** July 11, 2016.

355 **San Diego for a fundraiser:** Matt Rascon, Candice Nguyen, and Jaspreet Kaur, "Donald Trump Holds Fundraiser in Rancho Santa Fe," NBC 7 San Diego, July 14, 2016.

356 **the first senator to:** Eli Stokols, "Sen. Jeff Sessions Endorses Trump," **Politico,** February 28, 2016.

356 **was so superstitious:** Christie, **Let Me Finish.**

357 **as he made clear:** Christie, **Let Me Finish.**

358 **"believe me now":** Christie, **Let Me Finish.**

358 **a terrorist attack:** Alexander Burns, Maggie Haberman, and Ashley Parker, "Donald Trump

Postpones Naming Running Mate," **New York Times,** July 14, 2016.

358 **someone leaked word:** Patricia Murphy, "Trump to Pick Mike Pence, Says Source," **Roll Call,** July 14, 2016.

358 **"send out a tweet":** Christie, **Let Me Finish.**

359 **formed a group:** Rosie Gray, "Trump Ally Roger Stone Says He's Planning 'Days of Rage' at the Convention," **BuzzFeed,** April 1, 2016.

359 **"disclose the hotels":** Nick Gass, "Roger Stone Threatens to Send Donald Trump Supporters to Delegate Hotel Rooms," **Politico,** April 5, 2016.

359 **marketed T-shirts accusing:** Oliver Laughland, "Bill Clinton 'Rape' T-Shirt Goes on Sale at Republican National Convention," **Guardian,** July 21, 2016.

360 **as a competitor:** Maggie Haberman, Danny Hakim, and Nick Corasaniti, "How Republicans Are Trying to Use the Green Party to Their Advantage," **New York Times,** September 22, 2020.

360 **still in touch:** Dana Milbank, "The Crazy Face of Trump's GOP," **Washington Post,** July 18, 2016.

360 **interviewed Trump together:** "Transcript: Donald Trump Expounds on His Foreign Policy Views," interview by Maggie Haberman and David E. Sanger, March 26, 2016.

361 **repeatedly took stances:** "Transcript: Donald Trump on NATO, Turkey's Coup Attempt and the World," interview by David E. Sanger and Maggie Haberman, July 21, 2016.

362 **soften the resolution:** Josh Rogin, "Trump

Campaign Guts GOP's Anti-Russia Stance on Ukraine," **Washington Post,** July 18, 2016.

362 **"History isn't kind":** Tim Alberta, **American Carnage: On the Front Lines of the Republican Civil War and the Rise of President Trump** (New York: HarperCollins, 2019).

362 **instructed those listening:** Patrick Healy and Jonathan Martin, "Ted Cruz Stirs Convention Fury in Pointed Snub of Donald Trump," **New York Times,** July 20, 2016.

362 **top of mind:** Jane Mayer, "Donald Trump's Ghostwriter Tells All," **New Yorker,** July 18, 2016.

363 **a cease-and-desist letter:** Nicholas Fandos, "Trump Lawyer Sends 'Art of the Deal' Ghostwriter a Cease-and-Desist Letter," **New York Times,** July 21, 2016.

363 **held their convention:** Patrick Healy and Jonathan Martin, "Democrats Struggle for Unity on First Day of Convention," **New York Times,** July 25, 2016.

363 **of stolen emails:** Michael D. Shear and Matthew Rosenberg, "Released Emails Suggest the D.N.C. Derided the Sanders Campaign," **New York Times,** July 22, 2016.

363 **first reported in July:** Michael S. Schmidt and Matt Apuzzo, "Inquiry Sought in Hillary Clinton's Use of Email," **New York Times,** July 23, 2015.

363 **closed the probe:** Mark Landler and Eric Lichtblau, "F.B.I. Director James Comey Recommends No Charges for Hillary Clinton on Email," **New York Times,** July 5, 2016.

363 **held an extraordinary press conference:** Landler and Lichtblau, "F.B.I. Director James Comey

Recommends No Charges for Hillary Clinton on Email."

364 **chair to step down:** Jonathan Martin and Alan Rappeport, "Debbie Wasserman Schultz to Resign D.N.C. Post," **New York Times,** July 24, 2016.

364 **the apparent hack:** David E. Sanger and Eric Schmitt, "Spy Agency Consensus Grows That Russia Hacked D.N.C.," **New York Times,** July 26, 2016.

364 **"Russia: If you're listening":** Ashley Parker and David E. Sanger, "Donald Trump Calls on Russia to Find Hillary Clinton's Missing Emails," **New York Times,** July 27, 2016.

365 **tamped that down:** Michael Crowley and Tyler Pager, "Trump Urges Russia to Hack Clinton's Email," **Politico,** July 27, 2016.

365 **tape an interview:** Transcript: Donald Trump, Vice President Joe Biden, and Ret. Gen. John Allen interview by George Stephanopoulos, **This Week,** July 31, 2016.

365 **from Khizr Khan:** Maggie Haberman and Richard A. Oppel Jr., "Donald Trump Criticizes Muslim Family of Slain U.S. Soldier, Drawing Ire," **New York Times,** July 30, 2016.

365 **overwhelmed by grief:** Philip Bump, "Donald Trump Responds to the Khan Family: 'Maybe She Wasn't Allowed to Have Anything to Say,'" **Washington Post,** New York **Times,** July 30, 2016.

367 **website published photos:** Isabel Vincent, "Melania Trump Like You've Never Seen Her Before," **New York Post,** July 30, 2016.

367 **scheduled to appear live:** Jason Miller interview by Brian Stelter, **Reliable Sources,** CNN, July 31,

2016, www.cnn.com/TRANSCRIPTS/1607/31/rs.01.html.

CHAPTER 15: THE SCI-FI CAMPAIGN

371 **Trump's campaign chairman:** Maggie Haberman and Ashley Parker, "Trump Aide Paul Manafort Promoted to Campaign Chairman and Chief Strategist," **New York Times,** May 19, 2016.

371 **Manafort sometimes dressed:** Corey R. Lewandowski and David N. Bossie, **Let Trump Be Trump: The Inside Story of His Rise to the Presidency** (New York: Center Street/Hachette, 2017).

371 **was not invited:** Lewandowski and Bossie, **Let Trump Be Trump.**

371 **published a story about:** Alexander Burns and Maggie Haberman, "Inside the Failing Mission to Tame Donald Trump's Tongue," **New York Times,** August 13, 2016.

372 **tearing into Manafort:** Joshua Green, **Devil's Bargain: Steve Bannon, Donald Trump, and the Storming of the Presidency** (New York: Penguin Press, 2017).

372 **Manafort's Ukraine ties:** Andrew E. Kramer, Mike McIntire, and Barry Meier, "The Black Ledger in Ukraine Lists Cash for Trump's Campaign Chief," **New York Times,** August 14, 2016.

372 **elusive father-and-daughter team:** Nicholas Confessore, "How One Family's Deep Pockets Helped Reshape Donald Trump's Campaign," **New York Times,** August 18, 2016.

373 **the Mercers' urging:** Confessore, "How One

Family's Deep Pockets Helped Reshape Donald Trump's Campaign."

373 **political campaign experience:** Michael Barbaro and Michael M. Grynbaum, "Stephen Bannon, a Rookie Campaign Chief Who 'Loves the Fight,'" **New York Times,** August 17, 2016.

373 **bring in Cambridge Analytica:** Matthew Rosenberg, Nicholas Confessore, and Carole Cadwalladr, "How Trump Consultants Exploited the Facebook Data of Millions," **New York Times,** March 17, 2018.

373 **spending on Facebook:** Joshua Green and Sasha Issenberg, "Inside the Trump Bunker, with 12 Days to Go," Bloomberg, October 27, 2016.

373 **David Bossie joined:** Robert Costa, "Trump Enlists Veteran Operative David Bossie as Deputy Campaign Manager," **Washington Post,** September 1, 2016.

374 **had melded uncomfortably:** Alexander Burns and Maggie Haberman, "Tensions Deepen Between Donald Trump and R.N.C.," **New York Times,** September 2, 2016.

374 **a strategic decision:** Matt Flegenheimer, "Hillary Clinton Says 'Radical Fringe' Is Taking Over G.O.P. Under Donald Trump," **New York Times,** August 25, 2016.

374 **making an effort:** Richard Fausset, Alan Blinder, and John Eligon, "Donald Trump's Description of Black America Is Offending Those Living in It," **New York Times,** August 24, 2016.

375 **twenty-year-old characterization of:** Allison Graves, "Did Hillary Clinton Call African-American

Youth 'Superpredators?,'" **PolitiFact,** August 28, 2016.

375 **Old Post Office:** Jonathan O'Connell, "Eleven Things You Should Know About Trump's New D.C. Hotel, Even if You're Not Going to Go There," **Washington Post,** September 14, 2016.

375 **pin the blame:** Maggie Haberman and Alan Rappeport, "Trump Drops False 'Birther' Theory, but Floats a New One: Clinton Started It," **New York Times,** September 16, 2019.

375 **rabid Clinton supporters:** Ben Smith and Byron Tau, "Birtherism: Where It All Began," **Politico,** April 22, 2011.

376 **family leave plan:** Nick Corasaniti and Maggie Haberman, "Donald Trump Unveils Plan for Families in Bid for Women's Votes," **New York Times,** September 13, 2016.

376 **pneumonia-stricken Clinton:** Jonathan Martin and Amy Chozick, "Hillary Clinton's Doctor Says Pneumonia Led to Abrupt Exit From 9/11 Event," **New York Times,** September 11, 2016.

376 **"communicating" with WikiLeaks:** Tamara Keith, "A Timeline of What Roger Stone Said—and When—in Relation to His Indictment," NPR, January 25, 2019.

377 **written a book:** Nick Gass, "Donald Trump 2016: The Candidate Embraces Sensational Anti-Clinton Book by Former Aide Roger Stone," **Politico,** October 14, 2015.

377 **he had installed:** Adam C. Smith, "Donald Trump Shakes Up His Florida Campaign Team, Puts Susie

Wiles in Charge," **Tampa Bay Times,** September 7, 2016.

379 **remained with the campaign:** Marc Caputo and Kyle Cheney, "How Trump Won Florida," **Politico,** November 8, 2016.

380 **invited in guests:** Chris Christie, **Let Me Finish: Trump, the Kushners, Bannon, New Jersey, and the Power of In-Your-Face Politics** (New York: Hachette Books, 2019).

380 **a lawyer friend:** Lewandowski and Bossie, **Let Trump Be Trump.**

381 **got tangled up:** Nick Gass, "Trump: Transgender People Can Use Whatever Bathroom They Want," **Politico,** April 21, 2016.

381 **walked it back:** Reena Flores, "Donald Trump Amends Stance on North Carolina Transgender Bathroom Law," CBS News, April 22, 2016.

382 **about to report:** David A. Fahrenthold, "Trump Recorded Having Extremely Lewd Conversation About Women in 2005," **Washington Post,** October 8, 2016.

383 **acknowledged without hesitation:** Maggie Haberman and Jonathan Martin, "Trump Once Said the 'Access Hollywood' Tape Was Real. Now He's Not Sure," **New York Times,** November 28, 2017.

383 **Kushner nevertheless posited:** Tim Alberta, "'Mother Is Not Going to Like This': The 48 Hours That Almost Brought Down Trump," **Politico,** July 10, 2019.

383 **cache of documents:** Amy Chozick et al., "Highlights from the Clinton Campaign Emails:

How to Deal with Sanders and Biden," **New York Times,** October 10, 2016.

383 **detailing paid speeches:** Amy Chozick, Nicholas Confessore, and Michael Barbaro, "Leaked Speech Excerpts Show a Hillary Clinton at Ease with Wall Street," **New York Times,** October 7, 2016.

384 **this time apologizing:** Alexander Burns, Maggie Haberman, and Jonathan Martin, "Donald Trump Apology Caps Day of Outrage over Lewd Tape," **New York Times,** October 7, 2016.

384 **begun casting ballots:** Brent Griffiths, "When Does Early Voting Start in Every State?," **Politico,** September 21, 2016.

385 **announced himself "sickened":** Jake Sherman, "Ryan 'Sickened' by Trump, Joint Appearance Scrapped," **Politico,** October 7, 2016.

385 **began by addressing:** Alberta, "'Mother Is Not Going to Like This.'"

385 **a joint interview:** Steve Bannon interview by Michael Kirk, **The Frontline Interview,** PBS, March 17, 2019.

386 **made himself unavailable:** Alberta, "'Mother Is Not Going to Like This.'"

386 **represent the campaign:** Christie, **Let Me Finish.**

387 **four surprise guests:** Robert Costa, Dan Balz, and Philip Rucker, "Trump Wanted to Put Bill Clinton's Accusers in His Family Box. Debate Officials Said No," **Washington Post,** October 10, 2016.

387 **legal aid clinic:** Glenn Kessler, "The Facts About Hillary Clinton and the Kathy Shelton Rape Case," **Washington Post,** October 11, 2016.

387 **blocked the move:** Costa, Balz, and Rucker,

"Trump Wanted to Put Bill Clinton's Accusers in His Family Box."

388 **a successful scheme:** Ashley Parker, "Donald Trump, Slipping in Polls, Warns of 'Stolen Election,'" **New York Times,** October 13, 2016.

388 **fraud was rare:** Jonathan Martin and Alexander Burns, "Officials Fight Donald Trump's Claims of a Rigged Vote," **New York Times,** October 16, 2016.

389 **helped seed funding:** Kenneth P. Vogel, "Clinton Campaign and Democratic Party Helped Pay for Russia Trump Dossier," **New York Times,** October 24, 2017.

390 **second October surprise:** Adam Goldman and Alan Rappeport, "Emails in Anthony Weiner Inquiry Jolt Hillary Clinton's Campaign," **New York Times,** October 28, 2016.

CHAPTER 16: NO ONE SMARTER

393 **two days after winning:** Matt Flegenheimer and Michael Barbaro, "Donald Trump Is Elected President in Stunning Repudiation of the Establishment," **New York Times,** November 9, 2016.

393 **scheduled to spend:** Edward-Isaac Dovere, "Obama Meets His Nemesis," **Politico,** November 10, 2016.

394 **given serious thought:** Chris Christie, **Let Me Finish: Trump, the Kushners, Bannon, New Jersey, and the Power of In-Your-Face Politics** (New York: Hachette Books, 2019).

394 **were suddenly eager:** Andrew Restuccia and Nancy Cook, "Trump Advisers Steamroll Christie's Transition," **Politico,** November 15, 2016.

395 **joined transition meetings:** Michael D. Shear, Maggie Haberman, and Michael S. Schmidt, "Vice President-Elect Pence to Take Over Trump Transition Effort," **New York Times,** November 11, 2016.

395 **had the binders:** Nancy Cook, "How Flynn—and the Russia Scandal—Landed in the West Wing," **Politico,** November 11, 2017.

395 **Ivanka asked Flynn:** Jane Mayer, "The Danger of President Pence," **New Yorker,** October 16, 2017.

395 **given a prominent role:** Matthew Rosenberg and Maggie Haberman, "Michael Flynn, Anti-Islamist Ex-General, Offered Security **Post,** Trump Aide Says," **New York Times,** November 17, 2016.

396 **that Cohn agreed:** Nathaniel Popper, "Goldman President Named Trump Adviser, Opening Door for Younger Executives," **New York Times,** December 12, 2016.

396 **hire smart people:** Maggie Haberman and Annie Karni, "Bloomberg Is Taunting Trump, and Trump Is Taking the Bait," **New York Times,** January 27, 2020.

396 **instead ran it:** Drew Harwell and Lisa Rein, "Who's Helping Pay for President-Elect Trump's Transition Effort? You Are," **Washington Post,** November 23, 2016.

397 **a clear violation:** Stephen Castle, "U.K. Rejects Donald Trump's Call for Nigel Farage to Be Made Ambassador," **New York Times,** November 22, 2016.

397 **violated nearly forty years:** Mark Landler and David E. Sanger, "Trump Speaks with Taiwan's

Leader, an Affront to China," **New York Times,** December 2, 2016.

397 **secure its investment:** Susanne Craig, Jo Becker, and Jesse Drucker, "Jared Kushner, a Trump In-Law and Adviser, Chases a Chinese Deal," **New York Times,** January 7, 2017.

397 **rapper Kanye West:** Katie Rogers, "Kanye West Visits Donald Trump," **New York Times,** December 13, 2016.

398 **After their meeting:** Dan Merica, "Trump Team Denies Skeptic Robert F. Kennedy Jr. Was Asked to Head Vaccine Commission," CNN, January 10, 2017.

398 **television executives and anchors:** Michael M. Grynbaum and Sydney Ember, "Trump Summons TV Figures for Private Meeting," **New York Times,** November 21, 2016.

398 **complained about the coverage:** Grynbaum and Ember, "Trump Summons TV Figures for Private Meeting."

398 **to slip away:** Paul Farhi, "Trump Dumps His Press Pool Again, Raising Concerns About Future Access," **Washington Post,** November 16, 2016.

399 **already inserted himself:** Nathan Bomey, "Trump Slams Boeing Deal for New Air Force One," **USA Today,** December 6, 2016.

400 **appointed by Obama:** Benjamin Weiser, "U.S. Attorneys Named for Manhattan and New Jersey," **New York Times,** May 15, 2009.

400 **had been successfully prosecuted:** C. J. Hughes, "Ex-Council President, Andrew Stein, Avoids Prison on Tax Evasion," **New York Times,** March 15, 2011.

400 **a Ponzi scheme:** James Barron, "Ex-Borough President Andrew Stein Indicted," **New York Times,** May 27, 2010.

400 **selecting Rex Tillerson:** Michael D. Shear and Maggie Haberman, "Rex Tillerson, Exxon C.E.O., Chosen as Secretary of State," **New York Times,** December 12, 2016.

400 **had been interviewed:** Manuel Roig-Franzia, "How Alex Jones, Conspiracy Theorist Extraordinaire, Got Donald Trump's Ear," **Washington Post,** November 17, 2016.

401 **in fact authentic:** Maggie Haberman and Jonathan Martin, "Trump Once Said the 'Access Hollywood' Tape Was Real. Now He's Not Sure," **New York Times,** November 28, 2017.

401 **country's top intelligence officials:** John O. Brennan, "The Day I Met Donald Trump," **Atlantic,** October 1, 2020.

402 **Russians had interfered:** Michael D. Shear and David E. Sanger, "Putin Led a Complex Cyberattack Scheme to Aid Trump, Report Finds," **New York Times,** January 6, 2017.

402 **attempting to diminish:** Brennan, "The Day I Met Donald Trump."

402 **was essentially asserting:** Brennan, "The Day I Met Donald Trump."

403 **needed to speak:** James R. Clapper, **Facts and Fears: Hard Truths from a Life in Intelligence** (New York: Penguin Books, 2018).

403 **drafting a press release:** Clapper, **Facts and Fears.**

403 **circulating for months:** Peter Nicholas, "Fusion

GPS Execs Release New Book on Steele Dossier," **Atlantic,** November 21, 2019.

404 **those private conversations:** Evan Perez et al., "Intel Chiefs Presented Trump with Claims of Russian Efforts to Compromise Him," CNN, January 10, 2017.

404 **Clapper called Trump:** Clapper, **Facts and Fears.**

404 **in its entirety:** Ken Bensinger, Miriam Elder, and Mark Schoofs, "These Reports Allege Trump Has Deep Ties to Russia," **BuzzFeed,** January 10, 2017.

404 **stacked high on a long:** Jonathan Lemire, "Contents of Trump's Folders Spark Speculation," Associated Press, January 12, 2017.

CHAPTER 17: WHY IT'S PRESIDENTIAL

407 **hosted a reception:** Michael D. Shear and Emmarie Huetteman, "Trump Repeats Lie About Popular Vote in Meeting with Lawmakers," **New York Times,** January 23, 2017.

407 **real estate business:** Sam Frizell, "Donald Trump: Chuck Schumer Interview on Dealing with Him," **Time,** February 9, 2017.

407 **was not true:** Rebecca Ballhaus, "Topping List of Senators Trump Has Supported: Chuck Schumer," **Wall Street Journal,** November 10, 2016.

408 **a postelection event:** Andrew Rice, "Jared Kushner's Rise to Unimaginable Power," **New York,** January 8, 2017.

409 **national popular vote:** Shear and Huetteman, "Trump Repeats Lie About Popular Vote in Meeting with Lawmakers."

409 **insisted that his evidence:** Glenn Thrush, "Trump's

Voter Fraud Example: A Troubled Tale with Bernhard Langer," **New York Times,** January 25, 2017.

409 **correct the record:** Thrush, "Trump's Voter Fraud Example."

409 **similarly baseless story:** Eli Stokols, "Trump Brings Up Vote Fraud Again, This Time in Meeting with Senators," **Politico,** February 10, 2017.

410 **investigate supposed instances:** Julie Hirschfeld Davis, "Trump Picks Voter ID Advocate for Election Fraud Panel," **New York Times,** May 11, 2017.

410 **employees sign agreements:** Josh Dawsey and Ashley Parker, "'Everyone Signed One': Trump Is Aggressive in His Use of Nondisclosure Agreements, Even in Government," **Washington Post,** August 13, 2018.

410 **were not enforceable:** Julie Hirschfeld Davis et al., "White House Job Requirement: Signing a Nondisclosure Agreement," **New York Times,** March 21, 2018.

411 **come to rely on as a:** Michael D. Shear, Maggie Haberman, and Alan Rappeport, "Donald Trump Picks Reince Priebus as Chief of Staff and Stephen Bannon as Strategist," **New York Times,** November 13, 2016.

411 **White House's chief strategist:** Shear, Haberman, and Rappeport, "Donald Trump Picks Reince Priebus as Chief of Staff and Stephen Bannon as Strategist."

411 **four large whiteboards:** Z. Byron Wolf, "Steve Bannon's White House Whiteboard Revealed," CNN, May 3, 2017.

411 **arrayed under a "Make America Great Again":** Maeve Reston, "Inside Donald Trump's Tumultuous First 100 Days," CNN, April 6, 2017.

412 **filled with objectives:** Matthew Nussbaum et al., "Annotating Steve Bannon's Whiteboard," **Politico,** May 3, 2017.

412 **a permanent seat:** Glenn Thrush and Maggie Haberman, "Bannon Is Given Security Role Usually Held for Generals," **New York Times,** January 29, 2017.

412 **on-the-record interview:** Steven Bertoni, "Exclusive Interview: How Jared Kushner Won Trump the White House," **Forbes,** December 20, 2016.

413 **told corporate executives:** Peter Baker, Glenn Thrush, and Maggie Haberman, "Jared Kushner and Ivanka Trump: Pillars of Family-Driven West Wing," **New York Times,** April 15, 2017.

413 **often described as a shadow:** Glenn Thrush, Maggie Haberman, and Sharon LaFraniere, "Jared Kushner's Role Is Tested as Russia Case Grows," **New York Times,** May 28, 2017.

413 **fleeting family relationship:** Jodi Kantor, "For Kushner, Israel Policy May Be Shaped by the Personal," **New York Times,** February 11, 2017.

414 **soon found themselves:** Maggie Haberman, Jeremy W. Peters, and Peter Baker, "In Battle for Trump's Heart and Mind, It's Bannon vs. Kushner," **New York Times,** April 6, 2017.

414 **came to describe:** Thrush, Haberman, and LaFraniere, "Jared Kushner's Role Is Tested as Russia Case Grows."

414 **to dictate policy:** Rice, "Jared Kushner's Rise to Unimaginable Power."

414 **tried to engage:** Juliet Eilperin and Karen Tumulty, "Is Ivanka Trump a Passionate Political Advocate—or a Businesswoman Building Her Brand?," **Washington Post,** December 11, 2016.

414 **program halting deportations:** Julia Preston and Jennifer Medina, "Immigrants Who Came to U.S. as Children Fear Deportation Under Trump," **New York Times,** November 19, 2016.

414 **broader immigration-reform deal:** David Nakamura, Abby Phillip, and Philip Rucker, "Trump Says He Is Open to Immigration Compromise Including Legal Status," **Washington Post,** February 28, 2017.

415 **not seen as compatible:** Julian Aguilar, "Democrats Say Trump's Plan to Tie DACA Deal to Border Wall Dead on Arrival," **Texas Tribune,** October 9, 2017.

415 **the most impact:** Haberman, Peters, and Baker, "In Battle for Trump's Heart and Mind, It's Bannon vs. Kushner."

416 **policy restricting visitors:** Michael D. Shear and Ron Nixon, "How Trump's Rush to Enact an Immigration Ban Unleashed Global Chaos," **New York Times,** January 29, 2017.

416 **to give input:** Jonathan Blitzer, "How Stephen Miller Manipulates Donald Trump to Further His Immigration Obsession," **New Yorker,** February 21, 2020.

417 **Turnberry golf resort:** Severin Carrell, Heather Stewart, and Ben Jacobs, "Donald Trump to Visit

UK on Day of EU Referendum Result," **Guardian,** June 1, 2016.

419 **phobia about steps:** Tom McTague, "9 Trump Moments over Lunch with Theresa May," **Politico,** January 28, 2017.

419 **call her husband:** Peter Beaumont, "How Donald Trump's Hand-Holding Led to Panicky Call Home by Theresa May," **Guardian,** February 7, 2021.

419 **generating a plan:** Maggie Haberman and Robert Pear, "Trump Tells Congress to Repeal and Replace Health Care Law 'Very Quickly,'" **New York Times,** January 10, 2017.

420 **came under threat:** Michael D. Shear and Maggie Haberman, "From Trump's Mar-a-Lago to Facebook, a National Security Crisis in the Open," **New York Times,** January 13, 2017.

420 **club membership fee:** Steve Eder and Eric Lipton, "'It Is Unacceptable': Ethics Doubts Swirl as Trump Club Doubles Fee," **New York Times,** January 25, 2017.

420 **open-air war room:** Shear and Haberman, "From Trump's Mar-a-Lago to Facebook."

420 **a Supreme Court vacancy:** Julie Hirschfeld Davis and Mark Landler, "Trump Nominates Neil Gorsuch to the Supreme Court," **New York Times,** January 31, 2017.

420 **"central casting," he liked to say:** Daniel Dale, "'Central Casting': Trump Is Talking More Than Ever About Men's Looks," CNN, August 13, 2019.

420 **not been appreciative:** Ashley Parker, Josh Dawsey, and Robert Barnes, "Trump Talked About

Rescinding Gorsuch's Nomination," **Washington Post,** December 19, 2017.

421 **and FBI headquarters:** Jonathan Swan, "Donald Trump Is Obsessed with Revamping the 'Terrible' FBI Building," **Axios,** July 29, 2018.

421 **build a wall:** Julie Hirschfeld Davis, David E. Sanger, and Maggie Haberman, "Trump to Order Mexican Border Wall and Curtail Immigration," **New York Times,** January 24, 2017.

421 **his chosen director:** Karoun Demirjian, "Coats Confirmed as Nation's New Spy Chief," **Washington Post,** March 15, 2017.

421 **and former ambassador:** Jennifer Steinhauer and Michael D. Shear, "Dan Coats, the 'Mister Rogers' Senator Poised to Be Intelligence Chief," **New York Times,** January 5, 2017.

421 **take punitive action:** James Carroll, "Sen. Dan Coats Sponsors Resolution to Penalize Russia for Actions in Ukraine," **Louisville Courier-Journal,** March 5, 2014.

CHAPTER 18: OUT LIKE FLYNN

425 **recommended only placing:** Matt Apuzzo and Emmarie Huetteman, "Sally Yates Tells Senators She Warned Trump About Michael Flynn," **New York Times,** May 8, 2017.

425 **piece of personnel advice:** Michael D. Shear, "Obama Warned Trump About Hiring Flynn, Officials Say," **New York Times,** May 8, 2017.

425 **joined Trump's campaign:** Bryan Bender and Shane Goldmacher, "Trump's Favorite General," **Politico,** July 8, 2016.

425 **first DIA director:** Greg Miller, Adam Entous, and Ellen Nakashima, "National Security Adviser Flynn Discussed Sanctions with Russian Ambassador, Despite Denials, Officials Say," **Washington Post,** February 9, 2017.

426 **focused on Iran:** Matthew Rosenberg, Mark Mazzetti, and Eric Schmitt, "In Trump's Security Pick, Michael Flynn, 'Sharp Elbows' and No Dissent," **New York Times,** December 3, 2016.

426 **had echoed back:** Matthew Rosenberg and Maggie Haberman, "Michael Flynn, Anti-Islamist Ex-General, Offered Security **Post,** Trump Aide Says," **New York Times,** November 17, 2016.

426 **written an op-ed:** Michael T. Flynn, "Our Ally Turkey Is in Crisis and Needs Our Support," **The Hill,** November 8, 2016.

426 **lobbying registration requirements:** Charlie Savage, "How Michael Flynn May Have Run Afoul of the Law," **New York Times,** May 25, 2017.

426 **the younger Flynn:** Matthew Rosenberg, Maggie, and Eric Schmitt, "Trump Fires Adviser's Son from Transition for Spreading Fake News," **New York Times,** December 6, 2016.

427 **so-called Pizzagate conspiracy:** German Lopez, "Pizzagate, the Fake News Conspiracy Theory That Led a Gunman to DC's Comet Ping Pong, Explained," **Vox,** December 8, 2016.

427 **with Russia's ambassador:** David Ignatius, "Why Did Obama Dawdle on Russia's Hacking?," **Washington Post,** January 12, 2017.

427 **resolution condemning Israel:** Kate O'Keeffe and Farnaz Fassihi, "Inside the Trump Team's Push on

Israel Vote That Mike Flynn Lied About," **Wall Street Journal,** January 5, 2018.

427 **sanctions on Russia:** David E. Sanger, "Obama Strikes Back at Russia for Election Hacking," **New York Times,** December 29, 2016.

427 **praise Putin's reaction:** Lauren Gambino and Ben Jacobs, "Trump Praises Putin over US Sanctions—a Move That Puts Him at Odds with GOP," **Guardian,** December 30, 2016.

427 **had a transcript:** Salvador Rizzo, "Understanding the Twists and Turns in the Michael Flynn Case," **Washington Post,** May 7, 2020.

427 **share holiday greetings:** Miller, Entous, and Nakashima, "National Security Adviser Flynn Discussed Sanctions with Russian Ambassador."

428 **fact of an exchange:** Ignatius, "Why Did Obama Dawdle on Russia's Hacking?"

428 **When Pence and:** Mike Pence, Joe Manchin, Newt Gingrich interview by John Dickerson, **Face the Nation** transcript, January 15, 2017.

428 **they repeated what:** Reince Priebus interview by Chuck Todd, **Meet the Press,** January 15, 2017.

428 **met with McGahn:** Apuzzo and Huetteman, "Sally Yates Tells Senators She Warned Trump About Michael Flynn."

428 **protested the propriety:** Apuzzo and Huetteman, "Sally Yates Tells Senators She Warned Trump About Michael Flynn."

428 **a counterintelligence risk:** Apuzzo and Huetteman, "Sally Yates Tells Senators She Warned Trump About Michael Flynn."

428 **subsequently briefed by:** Maggie Haberman,

Michael S. Schmidt, and Michael D. Shear, "Trump Says He Fired Michael Flynn 'Because He Lied' to F.B.I.," **New York Times,** December 2, 2017.

428 **"wise or just":** Michael D. Shear et al., "Trump Fires Acting Attorney General Who Defied Him," **New York Times,** January 30, 2017.

429 **After the story was published:** Miller, Entous, and Nakashima, "National Security Adviser Flynn Discussed Sanctions with Russian Ambassador."

430 **submitted his resignation:** Maggie Haberman et al., "Michael Flynn Resigns as National Security Adviser," **New York Times,** February 13, 2017.

430 **insisted to Christie:** Chris Christie, **Let Me Finish: Trump, the Kushners, Bannon, New Jersey, and the Power of In-Your-Face Politics** (New York: Hachette Books, 2019).

430 **about the dossier:** James R. Clapper, **Facts and Fears: Hard Truths from a Life in Intelligence** (New York: Penguin Books, 2018).

431 **a private dinner:** Michael S. Schmidt, "In a Private Dinner, Trump Demanded Loyalty. Comey Demurred," **New York Times,** May 11, 2017.

431 **refuse any role:** Jeffrey Toobin, "How Rudy Giuliani Turned into Trump's Clown," **New Yorker,** September 3, 2018.

431 **held discussions of his own:** Adam Entous, Ellen Nakashima, and Greg Miller, "Sessions Met with Russian Envoy Twice Last Year, Encounters He Later Did Not Disclose," **Washington Post,** March 1, 2017.

431 **no choice but to recuse himself:** Mark Landler and

Eric Lichtblau, "Jeff Sessions Recuses Himself from Russia Inquiry," **New York Times,** March 2, 2017.

432 **flew to Mar-a-Lago:** Michael S. Schmidt and Julie Hirschfeld Davis, "Trump Asked Sessions to Retain Control of Russia Inquiry After His Recusal," **New York Times,** May 29, 2018.

432 **much freer hand:** Eli Watkins, "'Unmasking,' FISA and Other Terms to Help You Understand the Wiretapping Story," CNN, May 23, 2017.

432 **the original target:** Michael D. Shear and Michael S. Schmidt, "Trump, Offering No Evidence, Says Obama Tapped His Phones," **New York Times,** March 4, 2017.

432 **summarizing these theories:** Joel B. Pollak, "Mark Levin to GOP: Investigate Obama's 'Silent Coup' vs. Trump," **Breitbart,** March 3, 2017.

433 **statement imploring Congress:** Colin Dwyer, "President Donald Trump Tweets Allegations That Obama Wiretapped Trump Tower, Produces No Proof," NPR, March 4, 2017.

433 **a press conference at the Capitol:** Zack Beauchamp, "The Devin Nunes/Trump/Wiretapping Controversy, Explained," **Vox,** May 23, 2017.

434 **draft a letter:** Michael S. Schmidt and Maggie Haberman, "Mueller Has Early Draft of Trump Letter Giving Reasons for Firing Comey," **New York Times,** September 1, 2017.

435 **"has grown unpredictable":** Mike Levine, "In Scathing Draft of Letter Never Made Public, Trump Chided James Comey for 'Erratic,' 'Self-Indulgent' Conduct," ABC News, January 18, 2021.

436 **"They hate him":** Christie, **Let Me Finish.**

436 **Saturday Night Massacre:** Peter Baker, "In Trump's Firing of James Comey, Echoes of Watergate," **New York Times,** May 9, 2017.

437 **recommendation of Rosenstein:** Charlie Savage, "Deputy Attorney General's Memo Breaks Down Case Against Comey," **New York Times,** May 9, 2017.

437 **a private meeting with:** Matt Apuzzo, Maggie Haberman, and Matthew Rosenberg, "Trump Told Russians That Firing 'Nut Job' Comey Eased Pressure from Investigation," **New York Times,** May 19, 2017.

437 **interview to NBC News:** Donald Trump interview by Lester Holt, **NBC Nightly News,** May 11, 2017.

437 **slew of secret memos:** Michael S. Schmidt, "Comey Memo Says Trump Asked Him to End Flynn Investigation," **New York Times,** May 16, 2017.

437 **named a special counsel:** Rebecca R. Ruiz and Mark Landler, "Robert Mueller, Former F.B.I. Director, Is Named Special Counsel for Russia Investigation," **New York Times,** May 17, 2017.

438 **conferring with Trump:** Dareh Gregorian, "Newly Released Documents Shed Light on Mueller-Trump Meeting," NBC News, December 2, 2019.

438 **selected Christopher Wray:** Glenn Thrush and Julie Hirschfeld Davis, "Trump Picks Christopher Wray to Be F.B.I. Director," **New York Times,** June 7, 2017.

438 **was a former member:** Michael S. Schmidt and Maggie Haberman, "Trump Ordered Mueller Fired, but Backed Off When White House Counsel

Threatened to Quit," **New York Times,** January 25, 2018.

438 **by directing McGahn:** Schmidt and Haberman, "Trump Ordered Mueller Fired."

439 **over the recusal:** Michael S. Schmidt and Maggie Haberman, "Trump Humiliated Jeff Sessions After Mueller Appointment," **New York Times,** September 14, 2017.

439 **chased after Sessions:** Veronica Stracqualursi, "Priebus Says He Stopped Sessions from Resigning," CNN, February 14, 2018.

439 **letter of resignation:** Schmidt and Haberman, "Trump Humiliated Jeff Sessions After Mueller Appointment."

439 **"think is very unfair":** "Excerpts from The Times's interview with Trump," interview by Peter Baker, Michael S. Schmidt, and Maggie Haberman, **New York Times,** July 19, 2017.

440 **the Times reported:** Jo Becker, Adam Goldman, and Matt Apuzzo, "Russian Dirt on Clinton: 'I Love It,' Donald Trump Jr. Said," **New York Times,** July 11, 2017.

441 **how to respond:** Ashley Parker et al., "Trump Dictated Son's Misleading Statement on Meeting with Russian Lawyer," **Washington Post,** July 31, 2017.

441 **a search warrant:** Michael S. Schmidt and Adam Goldman, "Manafort's Home Searched as Part of Mueller Inquiry," **New York Times,** August 9, 2017.

441 **agreed to speak to:** Matt Apuzzo and Maggie Haberman, "'I Did Not Collude,' Kushner Says

After Meeting Senate Investigators," **New York Times,** July 24, 2017.

441 **from a Russian state bank:** Matthew Rosenberg, Mark Mazzetti, and Maggie Haberman, "Investigation Turns to Kushner's Motives in Meeting with a Putin Ally," **New York Times,** May 29, 2017.

441 **about his proposal:** Ellen Nakashima, Adam Entous, and Greg Miller, "Russian Ambassador Told Moscow That Kushner Wanted Secret Communications Channel with Kremlin," **Washington Post,** May 26, 2017.

441 **for closer cooperation:** Allison Quinn, "Kushner Details His Wild Idea to Use Russia's Secret Comms," **Daily Beast,** May 7, 2020.

442 **joined her husband:** Maggie Haberman and Rachel Abrams, "Ivanka Trump, Shifting Plans, Will Become a Federal Employee," **New York Times,** March 29, 2017.

442 **addressed the press:** Apuzzo and Haberman, "'I Did Not Collude,' Kushner Says After Meeting Senate Investigators."

CHAPTER 19: EXECUTIVE TIME

445 **decided to remain:** Victoria Bekiempis, Brian Niemietz, and Adam Edelman, "Melania Trump Will Stay in NYC so 10-Year-Old Barron Can Finish School Year," **New York Daily News,** November 20, 2016.

446 **the cost of protecting:** David A. Fahrenthold, Josh Dawsey, and Joshua Partlow, "How Trump's Company Charged the Secret Service More

Than $900,000," **Washington Post,** August 27, 2020.

447 **described as his "secret bathroom":** Maggie Haberman, Glenn Thrush, and Peter Baker, "Inside Trump's Hour-by-Hour Battle for Self-Preservation," **New York Times,** December 9, 2017.

448 **a recording system:** Haberman, Thrush, and Baker, "Inside Trump's Hour-by-Hour Battle for Self-Preservation."

448 **typically return upstairs:** Glenn Thrush and Maggie Haberman, "Trump and Staff Rethink Tactics After Stumbles," **New York Times,** February 5, 2017.

448 **White House's nocturnal chaos:** Thrush and Haberman, "Trump and Staff Rethink Tactics After Stumbles."

449 **that the story was false:** Jordan Fabian, "Spicer: New York Times Owes Trump an Apology," **The Hill,** February 6, 2017.

449 **robe surfaced online:** Elle Hunt, "Images of Donald Trump in a Bathrobe Flood Twitter After Spicer Says He 'Doesn't Own One,'" **Guardian,** February 7, 2017.

450 **tearing up documents:** Annie Karni, "Meet the Guys Who Tape Trump's Papers Back Together," **Politico,** June 10, 2018.

451 **her prenuptial agreement:** Mary Jordan, **The Art of Her Deal: The Untold Story of Melania Trump** (New York: Simon & Schuster, 2020).

451 **resettle in Washington:** Kate Bennett, "Melania Trump Moves into the White House," CNN, June 12, 2017.

451 **Trump had a softer side:** Gary Myers, "Patriots

Owner Robert Kraft Opens Up About Deflategate, Roger Goodell and President Donald Trump," **New York Daily News,** January 29, 2017.

452 **tens of billions:** Julia Edwards Ainsley, "Exclusive—Trump Border 'Wall' to Cost $21.6 Billion, Take 3.5 Years to Build: Internal Report," Reuters, February 10, 2017.

452 **personnel and policy matters:** Isaac Arnsdorf, "The Shadow Rulers of the VA," ProPublica, August 7, 2018.

452 **eager to engage:** Haberman, Thrush, and Baker, "Inside Trump's Hour-by-Hour Battle for Self-Preservation."

453 **had opposed Trump during:** Alexander Burns and Jonathan Martin, "These Wealthy People Refuse to Give Donald Trump Money. Here's Why," **New York Times,** May 21, 2016.

453 **backer of GOProud:** Kent Cooper, "Large 2012 Political Contributions Still Being Disclosed," **Roll Call,** April 10, 2013.

453 **that had helped to:** Chris Moody, "How Gay Conservatives Helped Launch Donald Trump," CNN, March 3, 2016.

454 **been openly critical:** Louis Nelson, "Trump Ramps Up Attacks on Paul Ryan: 'Weak and Ineffective Leader,'" **Politico,** October 11, 2016.

455 **uniting his party:** Emmarie Huetteman, "On Health Law, G.O.P. Faces a Formidable Policy Foe: House Republicans," **New York Times,** March 20, 2017.

455 **made the trek:** Julie Hirschfeld Davis, Thomas Kaplan, and Robert Pear, "Trump Warns House

Republicans: Repeal Health Law or Lose Your Seats," **New York Times,** March 21, 2017.

455 **aimed particular attention:** Susan Davis and Tamara Keith, "Trump Says Republicans Will Lose in 2018 if They Don't Support GOP Health Care Bill," NPR, March 21, 2017.

455 **slow to support:** Deirdre Shesgreen, "Meadows Embraces Trump, Spreads Word at GOP Convention," **USA Today,** July 20, 2016.

456 **pulled the bill:** Robert Pear, Thomas Kaplan, and Maggie Haberman, "In Major Defeat for Trump, Push to Repeal Health Law Fails," **New York Times,** March 24, 2017.

457 **opposed to it:** Rachel Bade and Josh Dawsey, "Inside Trump's Snap Decision to Ban Transgender Troops," **Politico,** July 26, 2017.

457 **threatening to block:** Jonathan Swan, "Transgender Troop Ban Is Victory for Bannon, Social Conservatives," **Axios,** July 27, 2017.

457 **went much further:** Bade and Dawsey, "Inside Trump's Snap Decision to Ban Transgender Troops."

457 **by complete surprise:** Barbara Starr, Zachary Cohen, and Jim Sciutto, "Donald Trump Transgender Ban Tweet Blindsided US Joint Chiefs," CNN, July 27, 2017.

460 **the internal rivalry:** Maggie Haberman, Jeremy W. Peters, and Peter Baker, "In Battle for Trump's Heart and Mind, It's Bannon vs. Kushner," **New York Times,** April 6, 2017.

461 **reach a compromise:** Thomas Kaplan and Robert Pear, "House Passes Measure to Repeal and Replace

the Affordable Care Act," **New York Times,** May 4, 2017.

461 **kill the bill:** Carl Hulse, "McCain Provides a Dramatic Finale on Health Care: Thumb Down," **New York Times,** July 28, 2017.

461 **last much longer:** Andrew Prokop, "Reince Priebus's Ouster as Chief of Staff, Explained," **Vox,** July 28, 2017.

461 **was making changes:** Corey R. Lewandowski and David N. Bossie, **Let Trump Be Trump: The Inside Story of His Rise to the Presidency** (New York: Center Street/Hachette, 2017).

CHAPTER 20: IN THE TANK

465 **auditorium-like room known:** Tyler Rogoway, "Trump Said He Found the Greatest Room He'd Ever Seen Deep in the Pentagon, Here's What He Meant," **The War Zone,** January 3, 2019.

466 **a four-star Marine general:** Dan Lamothe, "New Defense Secretary James Mattis Arrives at the Pentagon, Gets to Work," **Washington Post,** January 21, 2017.

466 **called a "warrior":** Michael R. Gordon and Eric Schmitt, "James Mattis, Outspoken Retired Marine, Is Trump's Choice as Defense Secretary," **New York Times,** December 1, 2016.

466 **Goldman Sachs executive at home:** Nathaniel Popper, "Goldman President Named Trump Adviser, Opening Door for Younger Executives," **New York Times,** December 12, 2016.

467 **a chemical agent:** Anne Barnard and Michael R. Gordon, "Worst Chemical Attack in Years in Syria;

U.S. Blames Assad," **New York Times,** April 4, 2017.

467 **announced the operation:** Michael R. Gordon, Helene Cooper, and Michael D. Shear, "Dozens of U.S. Missiles Hit Air Base in Syria," **New York Times,** April 6, 2017.

467 **positive media coverage:** Christopher Wilson, "Trump's Media Critics Praise Syria Strikes," Yahoo News, April 7, 2017.

467 **lack of internal consensus:** Eliana Johnson, "How Trump Swallowed a Bitter Afghanistan Pill," **Politico,** August 22, 2017.

468 **first foreign trip:** Peter Baker, "Opening First Foreign Trip, Donald Trump Tries to Leave Crisis Behind," **New York Times,** May 19, 2017.

469 **eager to see a:** Michael D. Shear, "Trump Envisions a Parade Showing Off American Military Might," **New York Times,** September 18, 2017.

469 **of wounded veterans:** Jeffrey Goldberg, "Trump: Americans Who Died in War Are 'Losers' and 'Suckers,'" **Atlantic,** September 3, 2020.

471 **When wildfires struck:** Thomas Fuller and Derrick Bryson Taylor, "Trump Reverses Decision to Reject California's Request for Wildfire Relief," **New York Times,** October 16, 2020.

472 **reluctant to dispense:** Tracy Jan and Lisa Rein, "Trump Administration Blocked Investigation into Delayed Puerto Rico Hurricane Aid, Inspector General Says," **Washington Post,** April 22, 2021.

472 **a significant donor:** Steven Allen Adams, "Bob Murray, Murray Energy Big Donors to National,

West Virginia Republicans," **Parkersburg News and Sentinel,** November 1, 2019.

473 **he told a reporter he:** Eric Wolff et al., "Lewandowski Pressed Trump on Aid to Coal Industry," **Politico,** August 25, 2017.

473 **reserved for emergencies:** Jeff Horwitz, Michael Biesecker, and Matthew Daly, "A Coal Country Dispute over an Alleged Trump Promise Unmet," Associated Press, August 22, 2017.

475 **Murray later claimed:** Horwitz, Biesecker, and Daly, "A Coal Country Dispute over an Alleged Trump Promise Unmet."

475 **he had had an extramarital affair:** Marc Caputo, Josh Dawsey, and Alex Isenstadt, "Trump Pick Backs Out of White House Job After Affair Allegations," **Politico,** December 25, 2016.

476 **hoped the appointment:** Michael D. Shear, Glenn Thrush, and Maggie Haberman, "John Kelly, Asserting Authority, Fires Anthony Scaramucci," **New York Times,** July 31, 2017.

476 **plans to depart:** Glenn Thrush and Maggie Haberman, "Sean Spicer Resigns as White House Press Secretary," **New York Times,** July 21, 2017.

477 **event trumpeting arrests:** Maggie Haberman and Liz Robbins, "Trump, on Long Island, Vows an End to Gang Violence," **New York Times,** July 28, 2017.

477 **fired ten days:** Shear, Thrush, and Haberman, "John Kelly, Asserting Authority, Fires Anthony Scaramucci."

477 **Scaramucci spoke disparagingly:** Ryan Lizza, "Anthony Scaramucci Called Me to Unload About White House Leakers, Reince Priebus, and Steve Bannon," **New Yorker,** July 27, 2017.

478 **some overdue maintenance:** John Wagner and Elise Viebeck, "President Trump Settles in for 17-Day Vacation at His Secluded New Jersey Club," **Washington Post,** August 5, 2017.

478 **most of August:** Wagner and Viebeck, "President Trump Settles In for 17-Day Vacation at His Secluded New Jersey Club."

478 **where a far-right organizer:** Dara Lind, "Nazi Slogans and Violence at a Right-Wing March in Charlottesville on Friday Night," **Vox,** August 12, 2017.

478 **a prerally march:** Lind, "Nazi Slogans and Violence at a Right-Wing March in Charlottesville on Friday Night."

478 **young progressive activist:** Christina Caron, "Heather Heyer, Charlottesville Victim, Is Recalled as 'a Strong Woman,'" **New York Times,** August 13, 2017.

480 **for public-works projects:** Lisa Friedman, "Trump Signs Order Rolling Back Environmental Rules on Infrastructure," **New York Times,** August 15, 2017.

481 **cover of Time:** David Von Drehle, "Is Steve Bannon the Second Most Powerful Man in the World?," **Time,** February 2, 2017.

481 **treated his role:** Michael D. Shear, Maggie Haberman, and Michael S. Schmidt, "Critics See Stephen Bannon, Trump's Pick for Strategist, as Voice of Racism," **New York Times,** November 14, 2016.

482 **chatted with us:** Michael D. Shear and Maggie Haberman, "Trump Defends Initial Remarks on

Charlottesville; Again Blames 'Both Sides,'" **New York Times,** August 15, 2017.

484 **thick Boston accent:** Annie Linskey, "John Kelly: The Boston Native in Charge of Bringing Order to President Trump's White House," **Boston Globe,** October 5, 2017.

484 **died during combat:** Greg Jaffe, "Lt. Gen. John Kelly, Who Lost Son to War, Says U.S. Largely Unaware of Sacrifice," **Washington Post,** March 2, 2011.

484 **to impose order:** Glenn Thrush, Michael D. Shear, and Eileen Sullivan, "John Kelly Quickly Moves to Impose Military Discipline on White House," **New York Times,** August 3, 2017.

486 **never fully divested:** Amy Brittain and Jonathan O'Connell, "Kushner Keeps Most of His Real Estate but Offers Few Clues About Potential White House Conflicts," **Washington Post,** May 21, 2017.

486 **criminal justice system:** Gabby Orr and Daniel Lippman, "Trump Snubs Jared Kushner's Signature Accomplishment," **Politico,** September 24, 2019.

487 **Tom and Daisy:** F. Scott Fitzgerald, **The Great Gatsby** (1925; New York: Penguin Classics, 2021).

487 **in the East Wing:** Stephanie Grisham, "How Jared and Ivanka Hijacked the White House's Covid Response," **Politico,** October 1, 2021.

CHAPTER 21: THE GREATEST SHOWMAN

489 **program suspending deportations:** Glenn Thrush, Maggie Haberman, and Julie Hirschfeld Davis, "On DACA, President Trump Has No Easy Path," **New York Times,** September 4, 2017.

490 **threatened a lawsuit:** Ted Hesson, "Texas AG Leads Push to End DACA," **Politico,** June 29, 2017.

490 **aligned with Miller:** Jonathan Blitzer, "A Trump Official Behind the End of DACA Explains Himself," **New Yorker,** November 10, 2017.

490 **eager to end:** Matt Apuzzo and Rebecca R. Ruiz, "Trump Chooses Sessions, Longtime Foe of DACA, to Announce Its Demise," **New York Times,** September 5, 2017.

490 **deliver the news:** Michael D. Shear and Julie Hirschfeld Davis, "Trump Moves to End DACA and Calls on Congress to Act," **New York Times,** September 5, 2017.

491 **"a great heart":** "Trump Says He Has 'Great Heart' for Immigrant 'Dreamers,'" Reuters, September 5, 2017.

491 **she asked him to:** Jenna Johnson, Mike DeBonis, and David Nakamura, "At Pelosi's Request, Trump Tweets 'No Action' Against DACA Recipients for Six Months," **Washington Post,** September 7, 2017.

491 **tried to pin Trump down:** Maggie Haberman and Yamiche Alcindor, "Pelosi and Schumer Say They Have Deal with Trump to Replace DACA," **New York Times,** September 13, 2017.

492 **Party leaders prioritized:** Alan Rappeport, "Dealt a Defeat, Republicans Set Their Sights on Major Tax Cuts," **New York Times,** March 26, 2017.

492 **during a negotiation over:** Josh Dawsey, "'Twenty Is a Pretty Number.' In Tax Debate, Trump Played the Role of Marketer in Chief," **Washington Post,** December 20, 2017.

492 **negotiations ultimately settled at:** Heather Long, "The Final GOP Tax Bill, Explained," **Washington Post,** December 15, 2017.

494 **a weekend visit:** Darlene Superville, "Trump, GOP Congressional Leaders to Meet at Camp David," Associated Press, December 28, 2017.

494 **upon hours of television:** Maggie Haberman, Glenn Thrush, and Peter Baker, "Inside Trump's Hour-by-Hour Battle for Self-Preservation," **New York Times,** December 9, 2017.

494 **a handful of daily newspapers:** Daniel Lippman, "The Print Reader in Chief: Inside Trump's Retro Media Diet," **Politico,** July 29, 2019.

495 **and marker-scrawled notes:** Lippman, "The Print Reader in Chief."

495 **something of a fool:** Jonathan Mahler and Jim Rutenberg, "How Rupert Murdoch's Empire of Influence Remade the World," **New York Times Magazine,** April 3, 2019.

495 **including informal advisers:** Jane Mayer, "The Making of the Fox News White House," **New Yorker,** March 4, 2019.

495 **Trump was thrilled to see:** Brian Ballou and Aric Chokey, "President Trump Surprises Some Supporters by Inviting Them to Mar-a-Lago," **South Florida Sun-Sentinel,** December 31, 2017.

496 **the United Nations, former:** Nahal Toosi and Alex Isenstadt, "Trump Taps Nikki Haley to Be UN Ambassador," **Politico,** November 23, 2016.

496 **fill her seat:** Tim Alberta, **American Carnage: On the Front Lines of the Republican Civil War**

and the Rise of President Trump** (New York: HarperCollins, 2019).

497 **announced a trip:** Maggie Haberman and Katie Rogers, "A White House Challenge: Balancing the Roles of the First Lady and First Daughter," **New York Times,** November 11, 2018.

497 **on a criminal justice reform bill:** Annie Karni, "The Senate Passed the Criminal Justice Bill. For Jared Kushner, It's a Personal Issue and a Rare Victory," **New York Times,** December 14, 2018.

497 **child tax credit:** Jim Tankersley, "Trump Wanted a Bigger Tax Cut for the Rich, Ivanka Went Elsewhere," **New York Times,** November 29, 2017.

497 **passed both houses:** Thomas Kaplan, "House Gives Final Approval to Sweeping Tax Overhaul," **New York Times,** December 20, 2017.

497 **Republican opposition came:** Alexander Burns, "Tax Plan Burdens Blue-State Republicans and Their Districts," **New York Times,** November 5, 2017.

498 **their own lawsuit:** Michael D. Shear, "Napolitano Sues Trump to Save DACA Program She Helped Create," **New York Times,** September 8, 2017.

498 **broader immigration deal:** Michael D. Shear, "White House Makes Hard-Line Demands for Any 'Dreamers' Deal," **New York Times,** October 8, 2017.

499 **specifically singling out:** Josh Dawsey, "Trump Derides Protections for Immigrants from 'Shithole' Countries," **Washington Post,** January 12, 2018.

499 **Two Republican senators:** Josh Dawsey, Robert Costa, and Ashley Parker, "Inside the Tense,

Profane White House Meeting on Immigration," **Washington Post,** January 15, 2018.

499 **federal government shut down:** Sheryl Gay Stolberg and Thomas Kaplan, "Government Shutdown Ends After 3 Days of Recriminations," **New York Times,** January 22, 2018.

499 **had long believed:** Michael D. Shear and Maggie Haberman, "Bannon Mocks Colleagues and 'Alt-Right' in Interview," **New York Times,** August 17, 2017.

500 **the president suffered:** Martin Pengelly, "Steve Bannon Believed Trump Had Early Stage Dementia, TV Producer Claims," **Guardian,** February 16, 2021.

500 **"a wet nurse":** Aidan McLaughlin, "Bannon Reportedly Said of Trump: 'I'm Sick of Being a Wet Nurse to a 71-Year-Old Man,'" Mediaite, February 11, 2018.

500 **published <u>Fire and Fury</u>:** Michael Wolff, **Fire and Fury: Inside the Trump White House** (New York: Henry Holt, 2018).

500 **singling me out:** Erik Wemple, "Kellyanne Conway, Michael Wolff Spar Over New York Times' Maggie Haberman," **Washington Post,** April 12, 2017.

501 **and in an interview:** "'Aberrant President': Author Michael Wolff Tells Mike Hosking That Donald Trump Won't Run Again," **New Zealand Herald,** January 24, 2018.

502 **baseless "witch hunt":** Ashley Parker, "Trump Claims to Be Victim of 'Witch Hunt' Following Justice Department Appointment of Special Counsel in Russia Case," **Washington Post,** May 18, 2017.

502 **had during the campaign:** Jo Becker, Adam Goldman, and Matt Apuzzo, "Russian Dirt on Clinton: 'I Love It,' Donald Trump Jr. Said," **New York Times,** July 11, 2017.

502 **Bannon said in Wolff's book:** Wolff, **Fire and Fury.**

502 **"about money laundering":** Wolff, **Fire and Fury.**

CHAPTER 22: TAKING A BULLET

503 **extending cash bonuses:** Jim Tankersley, "Bonuses Aside, Tax Law's Trickle-Down Impact Not Yet Clear," **New York Times,** January 22, 2018.

503 **a record pace:** Khorri Atkinson, "Trump Has Now Appointed Most Ever Federal Appeals Judges in 1st Year," **Axios,** December 14, 2017.

504 **public and private abuse:** Michael S. Schmidt and Maggie Haberman, "Trump Humiliated Jeff Sessions After Mueller Appointment," **New York Times,** September 14, 2017.

505 **speak with Mueller:** Michael S. Schmidt and Matt Apuzzo, "Mueller Seeks to Talk to Intelligence Officials, Hinting at Inquiry of Trump," **New York Times,** June 14, 2017.

505 **attempt a strategy:** Peter Baker and Kenneth P. Vogel, "Trump Lawyers Clash over How Much to Cooperate with Russia Inquiry," **New York Times,** September 17, 2017.

505 **McGahn revealed the president's:** Michael S. Schmidt and Maggie Haberman, "White House Counsel, Don McGahn, Has Cooperated Extensively in Mueller Inquiry," **New York Times,** August 18, 2018.

505 **amount of time:** Schmidt and Haberman, "White House Counsel, Don McGahn, Has Cooperated Extensively in Mueller Inquiry."

506 **Flynn pleaded guilty:** Michael D. Shear and Adam Goldman, "Michael Flynn Pleads Guilty to Lying to the F.B.I. and Will Cooperate with Russia Inquiry," **New York Times,** December 1, 2017.

506 **helped fund research:** Kenneth P. Vogel, "Clinton Campaign and Democratic Party Helped Pay for Russia Trump Dossier," **New York Times,** October 24, 2017.

506 **refused to yield:** Michael S. Schmidt and Julie Hirschfeld Davis, "Trump Asked Sessions to Retain Control of Russia Inquiry After His Recusal," **New York Times,** May 29, 2018.

507 **venting to advisers:** Jane Mayer, "The Making of the Fox News White House," **New Yorker,** March 4, 2019.

507 **not to make the call:** Mayer, "The Making of the Fox News White House."

507 **the FBI director and:** Michael D. Shear and Matt Apuzzo, "F.B.I. Director James Comey Is Fired by Trump," **New York Times,** May 9, 2017.

507 **the federal prosecutor responsible:** Maggie Haberman and Charlie Savage, "U.S. Attorney Preet Bharara Says He Was Fired After Refusing to Quit," **New York Times,** March 11, 2017.

507 **conducting parallel inquiries:** Matt Flegenheimer and Emmarie Huetteman, "Senate Intelligence Committee Leaders Vow Thorough Russian Investigation," **New York Times,** March 29, 2017.

508 **Trump struggled to find:** Carol D. Leonnig, Josh

Dawsey, and Ashley Parker, "Trump Has Trouble Finding Attorneys as Top Russia Lawyer Leaves Legal Team," **Washington Post,** March 22, 2018.

508 **continued to represent:** Rebecca R. Ruiz and Sharon LaFraniere, "Role of Trump's Personal Lawyer Blurs Public and Private Lines," **New York Times,** June 11, 2017.

508 **veteran Washington attorney:** Maggie Haberman and Matt Apuzzo, "Trump Hires Veteran Lawyer with Deep Experience in Washington," **New York Times,** June 16, 2017.

508 **first presidential pardon:** Julie Hirschfeld Davis and Maggie Haberman, "Trump Pardons Joe Arpaio, Who Became Face of Crackdown on Illegal Immigration," **New York Times,** August 25, 2017.

509 **reforming federal prisons:** Annie Karni, "The Senate Passed the Criminal Justice Bill. For Jared Kushner, It's a Personal Issue and a Rare Victory," **New York Times,** December 14, 2018.

510 **would often praise:** David E. Sanger and Maggie Haberman, "Trump Praises Duterte for Philippine Drug Crackdown in Call Transcript," **New York Times,** May 23, 2017.

510 **his violent crackdowns:** "Philippines President Rodrigo Duterte Urges People to Kill Drug Addicts," **Guardian,** June 30, 2016.

510 **for Rubashkin's release:** Mitch Smith, "President Commutes Sentence of Iowa Meatpacking Executive," **New York Times,** December 20, 2017.

510 **possibility of pardons:** Michael S. Schmidt, Jo Becker, Mark Mazzetti, Maggie Haberman, and Adam Goldman, "Trump's Lawyer Raised Prospect

of Pardons for Flynn and Manafort," **New York Times,** March 28, 2018.

511 **made a payment:** Michael Rothfeld and Joe Palazzolo, "Trump Lawyer Arranged $130,000 Payment for Adult-Film Star's Silence," **Wall Street Journal,** January 12, 2018.

511 **the FBI raided:** Matt Apuzzo, "F.B.I. Raids Office of Trump's Longtime Lawyer Michael Cohen; Trump Calls It 'Disgraceful,'" **New York Times,** April 9, 2018.

511 **called Cohen personally:** Ben Protess, William K. Rashbaum, and Maggie Haberman, "How Michael Cohen Turned Against President Trump," **New York Times,** April 21, 2019.

511 **$130,000 payment to Clifford:** Rothfeld and Palazzolo, "Trump Lawyer Arranged $130,000 Payment for Adult-Film Star's Silence."

512 **prove a real threat:** Matt Apuzzo, Maggie Haberman, and Eileen Sullivan, "Trump Sees Inquiry into Cohen as Greater Threat Than Mueller," **New York Times,** April 13, 2018.

512 **become plainly obvious:** Maggie Haberman, Sharon LaFraniere, and Danny Hakim, "Michael Cohen Has Said He Would Take a Bullet for Trump. Maybe Not Anymore," **New York Times,** April 20, 2018.

513 **had pushed out:** Michael S. Schmidt and Maggie Haberman, "Trump's Lawyer Resigns as President Adopts Aggressive Approach in Russia Inquiry," **New York Times,** March 22, 2018.

513 **to the sidelines:** Michael S. Schmidt, Maggie Haberman, and Matt Apuzzo, "Trump Aides, Seeking

Leverage, Investigate Mueller's Investigators," **New York Times,** July 20, 2017.

513 **adding Rudy Giuliani:** Maggie Haberman and Michael S. Schmidt, "Giuliani to Join Trump's Legal Team," **New York Times,** April 19, 2018.

513 **had repaid Cohen:** Michael D. Shear and Maggie Haberman, "Giuliani Says Trump Repaid Cohen for Stormy Daniels Hush Money," **New York Times,** May 2, 2018.

514 **relentless attacks on:** Dana Bash, "How Rudy Giuliani Wins by Being 'the Craziest Guy in the Room,'" CNN, May 31, 2018.

514 **First Amendment rights:** Joan Biskupic and Clare Foran, "Trump's Call to End Mueller Probe Reignites Obstruction Question," CNN, August 1, 2018.

514 **included a recording:** Matt Apuzzo, Maggie Haberman, and Michael S. Schmidt, "Michael Cohen Secretly Taped Trump Discussing Payment to Playboy Model," **New York Times,** July 20, 2018.

514 **a past affair:** Ronan Farrow, "Donald Trump, the Playboy Model Karen McDougal, and a System for Concealing Infidelity," **New Yorker,** February 16, 2018.

514 **to stop paying:** Protess, Rashbaum, and Haberman, "How Michael Cohen Turned Against President Trump."

514 **giving a detailed account:** Eric Bradner and Maegan Vazquez, "Stormy Daniels Says She Was Threatened to Keep Quiet About Trump," CNN, March 26, 2018.

514 **denied the affair:** Jeremy Diamond, "White House

Says Trump Continues to Deny Stormy Daniels Affair," CNN, March 26, 2018.

515 **list of questions Mueller:** Michael S. Schmidt, "Mueller Has Dozens of Inquiries for Trump in Broad Quest on Russia Ties and Obstruction," **New York Times,** April 30, 2018.

515 **would perjure himself:** Peter Baker, "New Revelations Suggest a President Losing Control of His Narrative," **New York Times,** May 3, 2018.

515 **had already charged:** Matt Apuzzo et al., "Former Trump Aides Charged as Prosecutors Reveal New Campaign Ties with Russia," **New York Times,** October 30, 2017.

515 **bank and tax fraud:** Michael S. Schmidt and Matt Apuzzo, "Mueller Files New Fraud Charges Against Paul Manafort and Rick Gates," **New York Times,** February 22, 2018.

515 **2018 and began cooperating:** Shear and Goldman, "Michael Flynn Pleads Guilty to Lying to the F.B.I. and Will Cooperate with Russia Inquiry."

515 **returned further charges:** Kenneth P. Vogel, "Mueller Adds Obstruction Charge on Manafort and Indicts His Right-Hand Man," **New York Times,** June 8, 2018.

515 **had pleaded guilty:** Eileen Sullivan and Glenn Thrush, "George Papadopoulos, First to Plead Guilty in Russia Inquiry," **New York Times,** October 30, 2017.

516 **an alcohol-infused conversation:** Sharon LaFraniere, Mark Mazzetti, and Matt Apuzzo, "How the Russia Inquiry Began: A Campaign Aide,

Drinks and Talk of Political Dirt," **New York Times,** December 30, 2017.

516 **force their departure:** Mark Landler and Maggie Haberman, "Trump's Chaos Theory for the Oval Office Is Taking Its Toll," **New York Times,** March 1, 2018.

516 **a U.S. prince:** Philip Rucker, Carol D. Leonnig, and Anne Gearan, "Two Princes: Kushner Now Faces a Reckoning for Trump's Bet on the Heir to the Saudi Throne," **Washington Post,** October 14, 2018.

516 **warm relationship with:** David D. Kirkpatrick et al., "The Wooing of Jared Kushner: How the Saudis Got a Friend in the White House," **New York Times,** December 8, 2018.

517 **been unable to secure:** Michael D. Shear and Katie Rogers, "Jared Kushner's Security Clearance Downgraded," **New York Times,** February 27, 2018.

517 **overseas business entanglements:** Shear and Rogers, "Jared Kushner's Security Clearance Downgraded."

517 **accurately or completely:** Kara Scannell, "Background Check Chief Has 'Never Seen' Mistakes Like Jared Kushner Forms," CNN, February 13, 2018.

517 **was walked out:** Michael D. Shear and Maggie Haberman, "John McEntee, Trump Aide, Is Forced Out over Security Issue, but Joins Re-Election Campaign," **New York Times,** May 13, 2018.

518 **his clearance downgraded:** Shear and Rogers, "Jared Kushner's Security Clearance Downgraded."

518 **permanent top-secret clearance:** Maggie Haberman, Adam Goldman, and Annie Karni, "Trump Ordered Officials to Give Jared Kushner a Security Clearance," **New York Times,** February 28, 2019.

518 **ruled against it:** Laura Strickler, Ken Dilanian, and Peter Alexander, "Officials Rejected Jared Kushner for Top Secret Security Clearance, but Were Overruled," NBC News, January 24, 2019.

518 **an unusual move:** Cristiano Lima, "Kushner Gets Permanent Security Clearance, Lawyer Says," **Politico,** May 23, 2018.

518 **installed Brad Parscale:** Katie Rogers and Maggie Haberman, "Trump's 2020 Campaign Announcement Had a Very Trumpian Rollout," **New York Times,** February 27, 2018.

519 **Trump filed notice:** Rogers and Haberman, "Trump's 2020 Campaign Announcement Had a Very Trumpian Rollout."

519 **properties, helping to:** Katie Rogers, "Trump Hotel at Night: Lobbyists, Cabinet Members, $60 Steaks," **New York Times,** August 25, 2017.

519 **often chose it:** Jonathan O'Connell and Mary Jordan, "For Foreign Diplomats, Trump Hotel Is Place to Be," **Washington Post,** November 18, 2016.

519 **became a place:** Zeke Miller and Jonathan Lemire, "Ex-Trump Aides Often Find a Soft Landing for Staying Quiet," Associated Press, August 14, 2018.

519 **pile of money:** Kenneth P. Vogel and Rachel Shorey, "$88 Million and Counting: Trump Amasses Huge

Head Start for 2020 Campaign," **New York Times,** July 15, 2018.

CHAPTER 23: EXTREME ACTION

521 **moved its embassy:** Julie Hirschfeld Davis, "Jerusalem Embassy Is a Victory for Trump, and a Complication for Middle East Peace," **New York Times,** May 14, 2018.

521 **acknowledge Jerusalem's status:** Alexia Underwood, "US Jerusalem Embassy: The Controversial Move, Explained," **Vox,** May 16, 2018.

522 **As a candidate, Trump promised:** Stephen Collinson, "Donald Trump: U.S. Should Rethink NATO Involvement," CNN, March 22, 2016.

522 **former bankruptcy lawyer:** Matthew Rosenberg, "Trump Chooses Hard-Liner as Ambassador to Israel," **New York Times,** December 15, 2016.

522 **tried to steer:** Mark Landler, Lara Jakes, and Maggie Haberman, "Trump's Request of an Ambassador: Get the British Open for Me," **New York Times,** July 21, 2020.

523 **"today's historic event":** Camila Domonoske, "U.S. Dedicates New Embassy in Jerusalem," NPR, May 14, 2018.

523 **58 Palestinians were killed:** Fares Akram and Josef Federman, "58 Dead in Gaza Protests as Israel Fetes US Embassy Move," Associated Press, May 14, 2018.

523 **a massive uprising:** Alastair Jamieson, "Middle East on Edge After Trump's 'Dangerous' Jerusalem Move," NBC News, December 7, 2017.

524 **decried the presence:** Aaron Blake, "Trump's

Afghanistan Strategy Isn't Really a Flip-Flop. But His Entire Foreign Policy Is," **Washington Post,** August 21, 2017.

524 **Camp David meeting:** David Nakamura and Abby Phillip, "Trump Announces New Strategy for Afghanistan That Calls for a Troop Increase," **Washington Post,** August 21, 2017.

524 **a televised address:** Nakamura and Phillip, "Trump Announces New Strategy for Afghanistan That Calls for a Troop Increase."

524 **to impose tariffs on:** "Donald Trump's Economic Promises," BBC, November 9, 2016.

525 **announced the tariffs:** Ana Swanson, "Trump to Impose Sweeping Steel and Aluminum Tariffs," **New York Times,** March 1, 2018.

525 **briefing materials warning:** Carol D. Leonnig, David Nakamura, and Josh Dawsey, "Trump's National Security Advisers Warned Him Not to Congratulate Putin. He Did It Anyway," **Washington Post,** March 20, 2018.

527 **final few weeks:** Mark Landler, "For McMaster, Pomp Under Bittersweet Circumstances," **New York Times,** April 6, 2018.

527 **proposed border wall:** Kristina Peterson, "The Wall Funding Deals Trump Rejected," **Wall Street Journal,** January 14, 2019.

527 **reached a deal:** Dylan Matthews, "Omnibus Spending Bill: Congress's $1.3 Trillion Spending Bill Explained," **Vox,** March 23, 2018.

527 **increase military spending:** Brad Lendon, "What the Massive US Military Budget Pays For," CNN, March 28, 2018.

528 **condemned the bill:** John T. Bennett, "After Self-Created Drama, Trump Signs Omnibus," **Roll Call,** March 23, 2018.

528 **signing the omnibus:** Dylan Matthews, "Omnibus Spending Bill: Congress's $1.3 Trillion Spending Bill Explained," **Vox,** March 23, 2018.

528 **a mental cue:** Julie Hirschfeld Davis and Peter Baker, "How the Border Wall Is Boxing Trump In," **New York Times,** January 5, 2019.

528 **became the centerpiece:** Hirschfeld and Baker "How the Border Wall Is Boxing Trump In."

529 **Trump's funding requests:** Erica Werner, Mike DeBonis, and John Wagner, "Trump Announces Deal to Temporarily Reopen Government, Ending Shutdown," **Washington Post,** January 25, 2019.

529 **whom he recommended:** Ron Nixon, "Kirstjen Nielsen, White House Aide, Is Confirmed as Homeland Security Secretary," **New York Times,** December 5, 2017.

529 **to be painted black:** Nick Miroff and Josh Dawsey, "Trump Wants His Border Barrier to Be Painted Black with Spikes. He Has Other Ideas, Too," **Washington Post,** May 16, 2019.

530 **could shoot migrants:** Michael D. Shear and Julie Hirschfeld Davis, "Shoot Migrants' Legs, Build Alligator Moat: Behind Trump's Ideas for Border," **New York Times,** October 1, 2019.

530 **capable of emitting heat:** Michael D. Shear, "Border Officials Weighed Deploying Migrant 'Heat Ray' Ahead of Midterms," **New York Times,** August 26, 2020.

530 **resisted these proposals:** Shear, "Border Officials

Weighed Deploying Migrant 'Heat Ray' Ahead of Midterms."

530 **had quietly implemented:** Lisa Riordan Seville and Hannah Rappleye, "Trump Admin Ran 'Pilot Program' for Separating Migrant Families in 2017," NBC News, June 29, 2018.

530 **"take away children":** Michael D. Shear, Katie Benner, and Michael S. Schmidt, "'We Need to Take Away Children,' Jeff Sessions Said," **New York Times,** October 6, 2020.

530 **resisted the concept:** Shear, Benner, and Schmidt, "'We Need to Take Away Children,' Jeff Sessions Said."

530 **officials signaled approval:** Julia Ainsley and Jacob Soboroff, "Trump Cabinet Officials Voted in 2018 White House Meeting to Separate Migrant Children, Say Officials," NBC News, August 20, 2020.

531 **signed a memo:** Shear, Benner, and Schmidt, "'We Need to Take Away Children,' Jeff Sessions Said."

531 **repeatedly deflected blame:** Shear, Benner, and Schmidt, "'We Need to Take Away Children,' Jeff Sessions Said."

531 **died by suicide:** Jeffrey C. Mays and Matt Stevens, "Honduran Man Kills Himself After Being Separated from Family at U.S. Border, Reports Say," **New York Times,** June 10, 2018.

531 **a breastfeeding infant:** Ed Lavandera, Jason Morris, and Darran Simon, "Zero-Tolerance Immigration Policy Leads to Surge in Family Separations, Lawyer Says," CNN, June 14, 2018.

531 **"kids in cages":** Alexandra Yoon-Hendricks and Zoe Greenberg, "Protests Across U.S. Call for End to Migrant Family Separations," **New York Times,** June 30, 2018.

531 **about children weeping:** Ginger Thompson, "Listen to Children Who've Just Been Separated from Their Parents at the Border," ProPublica, June 18, 2018.

531 **publicly derided the practice:** "Opinion: Laura Bush: Separating Children from Their Parents at the Border 'Breaks My Heart,'" **Washington Post,** June 17, 2018.

531 **joined the chorus:** Jessica Taylor, "Melania Trump Pressured President Trump to Change Family Separation Policy," NPR, June 20, 2018.

531 **ending the practice:** Dara Lind, "Family Separation: What Trump's New Executive Order Actually Does," **Vox,** June 20, 2018.

531 **he'd previously insisted:** Calvin Woodward and Elliot Spagat, "AP Fact Check: Trump Assails Dems for His Own Migrant Policy," Associated Press, June 15, 2018.

532 **thousands of children:** Miriam Jordan, "Family Separation May Have Hit Thousands More Migrant Children Than Reported," **New York Times,** January 17, 2019.

532 **would remain separated:** Aishvarya Kavi, "Parents of 445 Children Separated by Trump Still Not Found, Filing Says," **New York Times,** April 7, 2021.

532 **incalculable psychological damage:** William Wan, "The Trauma of Separation Lingers Long After

Children Are Reunited with Parents," **Washington Post,** June 20, 2018.

532 **meet with Putin:** Julie Hirschfeld Davis, "Trump, at Putin's Side, Questions U.S. Intelligence on 2016 Election," **New York Times,** July 16, 2018.

532 **no American officials:** Greg Miller, "Trump Has Concealed Details of His Face-to-Face Encounters with Putin from Senior Officials in Administration," **Washington Post,** January 13, 2019.

533 **sanctions for interfering:** David E. Sanger, "Obama Strikes Back at Russia for Election Hacking," **New York Times,** December 29, 2016.

533 **the global deal:** Mark Landler, "Trump Abandons Iran Nuclear Deal He Long Scorned," **New York Times,** May 8, 2018.

533 **nevertheless believed should:** Alex Ward, "Remember When Jim Mattis Was Supposed to Rein in Donald Trump?," **Vox,** May 9, 2018.

533 **meeting with North Korean:** Mark Landler, "The Trump-Kim Summit Was Unprecedented, but the Statement Was Vague," **New York Times,** June 12, 2018.

535 **military had defeated:** Mark Landler, Helene Cooper, and Eric Schmitt, "Trump to Withdraw U.S. Forces from Syria, Declaring 'We Have Won Against ISIS,'" **New York Times,** December 19, 2018.

535 **have to resign:** Helene Cooper, "Jim Mattis, Defense Secretary, Resigns in Rebuke of Trump's Worldview," **New York Times,** December 20, 2018.

535 **a NATO summit:** Cooper, "Jim Mattis, Defense Secretary, Resigns in Rebuke of Trump's Worldview."

535 **Trump tweeted announcing:** Helene Cooper and Katie Rogers, "Trump, Angry over Mattis's Rebuke, Removes Him 2 Months Early," **New York Times,** December 23, 2018.

536 **Sessions's replacement, Acting:** Adam Goldman, Michael D. Shear, and Mitch Smith, "Matthew Whitaker: An Attack Dog with Ambition Beyond Protecting Trump," **New York Times,** November 9, 2018.

536 **the hush-money payments:** Josh Gerstein, Laura Nahmias, and Josh Meyer, "Cohen Says He Paid Hush Money at Candidate Trump's Direction," **Politico,** August 21, 2018.

536 **had recused himself:** Erica Orden and Nicole Hong, "Manhattan Federal Prosecutor Recuses Himself from Cohen Probe," **Wall Street Journal,** April 10, 2018.

536 **active in the Trump campaign:** Alan Feuer, "U.S. Attorney Candidate for Manhattan: A Canny Mind with Humor," **New York Times,** August 14, 2017.

536 **reverse his decision, but:** Mark Mazzetti et al., "Before Mueller's Report, President Waged a Two-Year War Against the Trump-Russia Investigations," **New York Times,** February 19, 2019.

537 **seeking in vain:** Charlie Savage and Maggie Haberman, "Trump Will Nominate William Barr as Attorney General," **New York Times,** December 7, 2018.

537 **had personally contributed:** Michael S. Schmidt, Maggie Haberman, and Matt Apuzzo, "Trump

Aides, Seeking Leverage, Investigate Mueller's Investigators," **New York Times,** July 20, 2017.

537 **had sent an unsolicited:** Sadie Gurman and Aruna Viswanatha, "Trump's Attorney General Pick Criticized an Aspect of Mueller Probe in Memo to Justice Department," **Wall Street Journal,** December 19, 2018.

537 **Trump legal team in 2018:** Ariane De Vogue, "Barr Sent or Discussed Controversial Memo with Trump Lawyers," CNN, January 15, 2019.

537 **his Roy Cohn:** Michael S. Schmidt, "Obstruction Inquiry Shows Trump's Struggle to Keep Grip on Russia Investigation," **New York Times,** January 4, 2018.

CHAPTER 24: PARTY MAN

539 **from brain cancer:** Robert D. McFadden, "John McCain, War Hero, Senator, Presidential Contender, Dies at 81," **New York Times,** August 25, 2018.

539 **two men argued:** David Choi, "'I Gave Money to Your Campaign': Trump Was Frustrated by John McCain After He Ignored Him at a Congressional Hearing, New Book Says," **Insider,** October 16, 2020.

539 **federal tax benefits:** Michael Daly, "The Guy Trump Called 'Fat Jerry' Is Chairman Nadler Now," **Daily Beast,** March 5, 2019.

539 **stirred up "crazies":** Nick Gass, "McCain: Trump 'Fired Up the Crazies,'" **Politico,** July 16, 2015.

540 **unapologetic insult candidacy:** Jonathan Martin and Alan Rappeport, "Donald Trump Says John

McCain Is No War Hero, Setting Off Another Storm," **New York Times,** July 18, 2015.

540 **small but crucial:** Yvonne Wingett Sanchez, "John McCain's Role in Trump Dossier Intrigue Detailed in Deposition," **Arizona Republic,** March 18, 2019.

540 **dooming the health-care bill:** Carl Hulse, "McCain Provides a Dramatic Finale on Health Care: Thumb Down," **New York Times,** July 28, 2017.

540 **on an essay:** Miles Taylor, "Opinion: I Am Part of the Resistance Inside the Trump Administration," **New York Times,** September 5, 2018.

541 **the "steady state":** Taylor, "Opinion: I Am Part of the Resistance Inside the Trump Administration."

541 **went on a hunt:** Michael D. Shear, "Miles Taylor, a Former Homeland Security Official, Reveals He Was 'Anonymous,'" **New York Times,** October 28, 2020.

541 **not be identified:** Shear, "Miles Taylor, a Former Homeland Security Official, Reveals He Was 'Anonymous.'"

542 **receive an invitation:** Katie Rogers, Nicholas Fandos, and Maggie Haberman, "Trump Relents Under Pressure, Offering 'Respect' to McCain," **New York Times,** August 27, 2018.

542 **not been recognized:** Katie Galioto, "Trump Says He Never Got a Thank You for McCain's Funeral," **Politico,** March 20, 2019.

542 **infuriating McCain's daughter:** Cheryl Teh, "Meghan McCain Says Ivanka Trump and Jared Kushner 'Had No Goddamn Business' Being at Her Father's Funeral," **Insider,** October 21, 2021.

543 **unlike some of her peers:** Alex Isenstadt, "Trump Campaign Splits with Top GOP Official in Ohio," **Politico,** October 15, 2016.

543 **wealth of opportunity:** Zeke Miller and Jonathan Lemire, "Ex-Trump Aides Often Find a Soft Landing for Staying Quiet," Associated Press, August 14, 2018.

543 **her family heritage:** Steve Holland, "Republican Romney Calls Trump 'a Fraud,' Creates Pathway to Contested Convention," Reuters, March 2, 2016.

543 **the Romney name:** Jeremy W. Peters, "A Romney Who Is Unfailingly Loyal to Trump," **New York Times,** January 13, 2018.

545 **the nickname ZOTUS:** Maggie Haberman and Nicholas Fandos, "A Top Aide's Exit Plan Raises Eyebrows in the White House," **New York Times,** December 20, 2018.

545 **young political strategist:** Kenneth P. Vogel and Katie Rogers, "Nick Ayers Is Rising Fast in Trump's Washington. How Far Will He Go?," **New York Times,** November 21, 2018.

546 **Alabama special election:** Jenna Johnson, "'I Love Alabama—It's Special': At Rally for Sen. Luther Strange, Trump Vents Frustrations in Rambling Speech," **Washington Post,** September 23, 2017.

546 **the establishment favorite:** Jonathan Martin, "Trump Rewards Loyalty in Alabama Senate Race by Tweeting Endorsement," **New York Times,** August 8, 2017.

546 **Strange lost, which:** Daniel Strauss, "Moore Crushes Strange in Alabama Senate Primary," **Politico,** September 26, 2017.

547 **added a riff:** Johnson, "'I Love Alabama—It's Special.'"

547 **the head of his own:** Steve Bousquet and Emily L. Mahoney, "Shakeup: Ron DeSantis Hires Susie Wiles to Take Over Floundering Campaign," **Tampa Bay Times,** September 26, 2018.

548 **DeSantis spokeswoman countered:** Alex Isenstadt and Marc Caputo, "Trump Rails on Top Florida Ally over Hurricane Maria Flap," **Politico,** September 18, 2018.

548 **after the support:** Isenstadt and Caputo, "Trump Rails on Top Florida Ally over Hurricane Maria Flap."

548 **his own concealed-carry permit:** Lorraine Woellert, "Missing from the Gun Debate: Trump's Own Experience with Concealed Carry," **Politico,** February 28, 2018.

548 **"Second Amendment people":** Nick Corasaniti and Maggie Haberman, "Donald Trump Suggests 'Second Amendment People' Could Act Against Hillary Clinton," **New York Times,** August 9, 2016.

548 **own spending records:** Jon Schuppe, "NRA Sticking with Trump, Breaks Own Record for Campaign Spending," NBC News, October 12, 2016.

548 **profligate outside group:** Mike Spies and Ashley Balcerzak, "The NRA Placed Big Bets on the 2016 Election, and Won Almost All of Them," OpenSecrets, November 9, 2016.

548 **killed seventeen people:** Audra D. S. Burch and Patricia Mazzei, "Death Toll Is at 17 and Could Rise in Florida School Shooting," **New York Times,** February 14, 2018.

548 **host a forum:** Valerie Strauss, "Word for Word: What Everyone Said When Trump Met with Students and Parents to Talk About Guns," **Washington Post,** February 22, 2018.

549 **told Republican lawmakers:** Tara Golshan, "Trump's Madcap, Unscripted Gun Control Meeting with Lawmakers, Explained," **Vox,** February 28, 2018.

549 **observing separately that:** Mike DeBonis and Anne Gearan, "Trump Stops Short of Full Endorsement of Gun Proposals," **Washington Post,** February 26, 2018.

549 **Trump backed off:** Michael D. Shear and Sheryl Gay Stolberg, "Conceding to N.R.A., Trump Abandons Brief Gun Control Promise," **New York Times,** March 12, 2018.

549 **horrific mass shootings:** Campbell Robertson, Julie Bosman, and Mitch Smith, "Back-to-Back Outbreaks of Gun Violence in El Paso and Dayton Stun Country," **New York Times,** August 4, 2019.

549 **among those encouraging:** Elaina Plott, "Trump's Phone Calls with NRA's Wayne LaPierre," **Atlantic,** August 20, 2019.

549 **Again, he did not act:** Annie Karni and Maggie Haberman, "After Lobbying by Gun Rights Advocates, Trump Sounds a Familiar Retreat," **New York Times,** August 19, 2019.

549 **earlier mass shooting:** Alex Ward, "Trump on Pittsburgh Synagogue Shooting: 'Anti-Semitic' and a 'Wicked Act of Mass Murder,'" **Vox,** October 27, 2018.

550 **second Supreme Court vacancy:** Michael D.

Shear, "Supreme Court Justice Anthony Kennedy Will Retire," **New York Times,** June 27, 2018.

550 **young federal appeals court judge:** Mark Landler and Maggie Haberman, "Brett Kavanaugh Is Trump's Pick for Supreme Court," **New York Times,** July 9, 2018.

550 **Kavanaugh was accused:** Sheryl Gay Stolberg, "Kavanaugh's Nomination in Turmoil as Accuser Says He Assaulted Her Decades Ago," **New York Times,** September 16, 2018.

550 **hear her testimony:** Sheryl Gay Stolberg and Nicholas Fandos, "Christine Blasey Ford Reaches Deal to Testify at Kavanaugh Hearing," **New York Times,** September 23, 2018.

550 **Kavanaugh's angry denial:** Mike McIntire et al., "At **Times,** Kavanaugh's Defense Misleads or Veers Off Point," **New York Times,** September 28, 2018.

551 **other nominees overcome:** Anne Gearan et al., "Trump Says Drug Czar Nominee Tom Marino Is Withdrawing After Washington Post/'60 Minutes' Investigation," **Washington Post,** October 17, 2017.

551 **and he mocked:** Josh Dawsey and Felicia Sonmez, "Trump Mocks Kavanaugh Accuser Christine Blasey Ford," **Washington Post,** October 2, 2018.

551 **confirmation was ensured:** Sheryl Gay Stolberg, "Kavanaugh Is Sworn In After Close Confirmation Vote in Senate," **New York Times,** October 6, 2018.

551 **additional ones following:** Steve Eder, Jim Rutenberg, and Rebecca R. Ruiz, "Julie Swetnick Is Third Woman to Accuse Brett Kavanaugh of Sexual

Misconduct," **New York Times,** September 26, 2018.

551 **Trump warned his rally:** Dawsey and Sonmez, "Trump Mocks Kavanaugh Accuser Christine Blasey Ford."

551 **yoked Kavanaugh's plight:** Zeke Miller, Jonathan Lemire, and Catherine Lucey, "Trump Criticizes Rush to Condemn Saudi Arabia over Khashoggi," Associated Press, October 16, 2018.

551 **the CIA concluded:** Julian E. Barnes, "C.I.A. Concludes That Saudi Crown Prince Ordered Khashoggi Killed," **New York Times,** November 16, 2016.

551 **he later bragged:** Bob Woodward, **Rage** (New York: Simon & Schuster, 2020).

552 **a northern-bound caravan:** Dara Lind, "The Migrant Caravan, Explained," **Vox,** October 25, 2018.

552 **active-duty troops just before:** Michael D. Shear and Thomas Gibbons-Neff, "Trump Sending 5,200 Troops to the Border in an Election-Season Response to Migrants," **New York Times,** October 29, 2018.

552 **Election Day passed:** Maggie Haberman and Mark Landler, "A Week After the Midterms, Trump Seems to Forget the Caravan," **New York Times,** November 13, 2018.

552 **biggest financial backers:** Jennifer Jacobs, Alyza Sebenius, and Ryan Beene, "Trump Watched Midterm Election Results with Adelson, Schwarzman," Bloomberg, November 6, 2018.

552 **they were decidedly mixed:** Jonathan Martin and Alexander Burns, "Democrats Capture Control of

House; G.O.P. Holds Senate," **New York Times,** November 6, 2018.

553 **refuse to acknowledge:** Eileen Sullivan, "Takeaways from Trump's Midterms News Conference: 'People Like Me,'" **New York Times,** November 7, 2018.

553 **"And she lost":** Sullivan, "Takeaways from Trump's Midterms News Conference."

554 **the hundredth anniversary:** Peter Baker and Alissa J. Rubin, "Trump's Nationalism, Rebuked at World War I Ceremony, Is Reshaping Much of Europe," **New York Times,** November 11, 2018.

554 **Trump never made it:** Peter Baker, "Trump Assails Macron and Defends Decision to Skip Cemetery Visit," **New York Times,** November 13, 2018.

554 **erupted by phone:** Josh Dawsey and Philip Rucker, "Five Days of Fury: Inside Trump's Paris Temper, Election Woes and Staff Upheaval," **Washington Post,** November 13, 2018.

554 **praised Adolf Hitler:** Michael C. Bender, **"Frankly, We Did Win This Election": The Inside Story of How Trump Lost** (New York: Hachette Books, 2021).

555 **in Kelly's presence:** Jeffrey Goldberg, "Trump: Americans Who Died in War Are 'Losers' and 'Suckers,'" **Atlantic,** September 3, 2020.

555 **the last-minute cancellation:** Baker, "Trump Assails Macron and Defends Decision to Skip Cemetery Visit."

555 **several accounts from staff saying:** Peter Baker and Maggie Haberman, "Trump Denies Calling Fallen Soldiers 'Losers' and 'Suckers,'" **New York Times,** September 4, 2020.

555 **reported much later:** Goldberg, "Trump: Americans Who Died in War Are 'Losers' and 'Suckers.'"

556 **as the "leaker-in-chief":** Maggie Haberman and Katie Rogers, "An Aggrieved Trump Wants Better Press, and He Blames Leaks for Not Getting It," **New York Times,** May 17, 2018.

556 **be leaving the White House:** Josh Dawsey, Seung Min Kim, and Philip Rucker, "Chief of Staff John Kelly to Leave White House by End of Month, Trump Says," **Washington Post,** December 9, 2018.

557 **attempted to lure:** John Haltiwanger and Sonam Sheth, "Trump Told Chris Christie He Leaked Chief of Staff Offer: Book," **Insider,** November 16, 2021.

557 **"It was good for you":** Haltiwanger and Sheth, "Trump Told Chris Christie He Leaked Chief of Staff Offer."

557 **conservative former congressman:** Michael Tackett and Maggie Haberman, "Trump Names Mick Mulvaney Acting Chief of Staff," **New York Times,** December 14, 2018.

557 **the most flawed:** Jake Tapper, "Former White House Chief of Staff Tells Friends That Trump 'Is the Most Flawed Person' He's Ever Met," CNN, October 16, 2020.

558 **often pressed Nielsen:** Jake Tapper, "Trump Pushed to Close El Paso Border, Told Admin Officials to Resume Family Separations and Agents Not to Admit Migrants," CNN, April 9, 2019.

559 **administration began implementing:** Richard Gonzales, "Trump Administration Begins 'Remain

in Mexico' Policy, Sending Asylum-Seekers Back," NPR, January 29, 2019.

559 **Nielsen was visiting:** Rafael Carranza, "Kirstjen Nielsen Vows to Provide Resources to Border Agents in Yuma," **Arizona Republic,** April 4, 2019.

560 **traveled with Trump:** Tapper, "Trump Pushed to Close El Paso Border."

560 **would pardon him:** Tapper, "Trump Pushed to Close El Paso Border."

CHAPTER 25: TOUGHER THAN THE REST

563 **immediately after joining:** Maggie Haberman and Michael S. Schmidt, "Giuliani to Join Trump's Legal Team," **New York Times,** April 19, 2018.

563 **a prisoner swap:** Josh Dawsey, Carol D. Leonnig, and Matt Zapotosky, "Trump Asked Tillerson to Help Broker Deal to End U.S. Prosecution of Turkish Trader Represented by Giuliani," **Washington Post,** October 10, 2019.

563 **client of Giuliani's:** Dawsey, Leonnig, and Zapotosky, "Trump Asked Tillerson to Help Broker Deal to End U.S. Prosecution of Turkish Trader Represented by Giuliani."

565 **repeatedly unspooled stories:** Philip Bump, "A Timeline of Giuliani's Dubious Interactions with the Trump Administration," **Washington Post,** April 28, 2021.

566 **military aid approved:** Caitlin Emma and Connor O'Brien, "Trump Holds Up Ukraine Military Aid Meant to Confront Russia," **Politico,** August 28, 2019.

566 **Trump's foreign-policy views:** Natasha Bertrand,

"Trump's New Intel Chief Was a Trump Critic in 2016," **Politico,** February 21, 2020.

566 **Trump voiced interest:** Michael R. Gordon and Gordon Lubold, "Trump to Pull Thousands of U.S. Troops from Germany," **Wall Street Journal,** June 5, 2020.

566 **as "that bitch":** Carol Leonnig and Philip Rucker, **I Alone Can Fix It: Donald J. Trump's Catastrophic Final Year** (New York: Penguin Press, 2021).

567 **blow everyone up:** Peter Baker and Nicholas Fandos, "Bolton Objected to Ukraine Pressure Campaign, Calling Giuliani 'a Hand Grenade,'" **New York Times,** October 14, 2019.

568 **on votive candles:** Samuel Ashworth, "Mueller's Report Is Done. Is There Still a Point in Having a Prayer Candle with His Image on It?," **Washington Post,** May 13, 2019.

568 **his new role:** Li Zhou and Jen Kirby, "The Senate Confirms Bill Barr as Attorney General," **Vox,** February 14, 2019.

568 **written an unsolicited memo:** Sadie Gurman and Aruna Viswanatha, "Trump's Attorney General Pick Criticized an Aspect of Mueller Probe in Memo to Justice Department," **Wall Street Journal,** December 19, 2018.

570 **broke in 2018:** Michael S. Schmidt and Maggie Haberman, "Trump Ordered Mueller Fired, but Backed Off When White House Counsel Threatened to Quit," **New York Times,** January 25, 2018.

571 **had to remove:** Karoun Demirjian and Devlin Barrett, "Top FBI Official Assigned to Mueller's Russia Probe Said to Have Been Removed After

Sending Anti-Trump Texts," **Washington Post,** December 2, 2017.

571 **piece of surveillance warrant:** Charlie Savage, "Carter Page FISA Documents Are Released by Justice Department," **New York Times,** July 21, 2018.

571 **conduit to WikiLeaks:** Mark Mazzetti, Eileen Sullivan, and Maggie Haberman, "Indicting Roger Stone, Mueller Shows Link Between Trump Campaign and WikiLeaks," **New York Times,** January 25, 2019.

571 **a predawn raid:** Mazzetti, Sullivan, and Haberman, "Indicting Roger Stone, Mueller Shows Link Between Trump Campaign and WikiLeaks."

572 **declared Credico dead:** Josh Gerstein and Darren Samuelsohn, "WikiLeaks, Dog Threats and a Fake Death Notice: Roger Stone's Odd Friendship with Randy Credico," **Politico,** November 8, 2019.

572 **Stone's former partner:** Matt Apuzzo et al., "Former Trump Aides Charged as Prosecutors Reveal New Campaign Ties with Russia," **New York Times,** October 30, 2017.

572 **and began cooperating with Mueller:** Mark Mazzetti and Maggie Haberman, "Rick Gates, Trump Campaign Aide, Pleads Guilty in Mueller Inquiry and Will Cooperate," **New York Times,** February 23, 2018.

572 **campaign polling data:** Sharon LaFraniere, Kenneth P. Vogel, and Maggie Haberman, "Manafort Accused of Sharing Trump Polling Data with Russian Associate," **New York Times,** January 8, 2019.

572 **convicted of all charges:** Andrew Prokop, "Roger Stone Found Guilty on All 7 Counts After Trial," **Vox,** November 15, 2019.

573 **allies brushed off:** Steve Benen, "To Defend Trump, Republicans Scoff at 'Process Crimes,'" MSNBC, November 30, 2018.

573 **basis for impeaching:** Ella Nilsen, "2020 Democrats' Response to Mueller Statement: Impeach Trump," **Vox,** May 29, 2019.

574 **Nancy Pelosi explained:** Joe Heim, "Nancy Pelosi on Impeaching President Trump: 'He's Just Not Worth It,'" **Washington Post Magazine,** March 11, 2019.

574 **investigate the origins:** Michael Balsamo and Eric Tucker, "Barr Appoints Prosecutor to Examine Russia Probe Origins," Associated Press, December 1, 2020.

574 **information-handling policies by:** Adam Goldman, "Comey Is Criticized by Justice Dept. Watchdog for Violating F.B.I. Rules," **New York Times,** August 29, 2019.

576 **Trump was dismissing:** Maggie Haberman, Julian E. Barnes, and Peter Baker, "Dan Coats to Step Down as Intelligence Chief; Trump Picks Loyalist for Job," **New York Times,** July 28, 2019.

579 **between bellicose language:** Mark Landler, "Trump's Twitter Threat vs. Iran: Loud but Hardly Clear," **New York Times,** July 23, 2018.

579 **a retaliatory strike:** Michael D. Shear et al., "Strikes on Iran Approved by Trump, Then Abruptly Pulled Back," **New York Times,** June 20, 2019.

579 **pull back fighter jets:** Shear et al., "Strikes on Iran Approved by Trump, Then Abruptly Pulled Back."

580 **sitting U.S. president:** Peter Baker and Michael Crowley, "Trump Steps into North Korea and Agrees with Kim Jong-Un to Resume Talks," **New York Times,** June 30, 2019.

580 **acquiring Greenland, which had:** Peter Baker and Maggie Haberman, "Trump's Interest in Buying Greenland Seemed Like a Joke. Then It Got Ugly," **New York Times,** August 21, 2019.

580 **hosting the Taliban:** Peter Baker, Mujib Mashal, and Michael Crowley, "How Trump's Plan to Secretly Meet with the Taliban Came Together, and Fell Apart," **New York Times,** September 8, 2019.

581 **wrote on Twitter that he:** Philip Ewing, "Trump Fires John Bolton as National Security Adviser in Final Break over Policy," NPR, September 10, 2019.

581 **killed in Afghanistan:** Baker, Mashal, and Crowley, "How Trump's Plan to Secretly Meet with the Taliban Came Together, and Fell Apart."

581 **would be signed:** Mujib Mashal, "Taliban and U.S. Strike Deal to Withdraw American Troops from Afghanistan," **New York Times,** February 29, 2020.

581 **an "urgent" complaint:** Ellen Nakashima et al., "Whistleblower Complaint About President Trump Involves Ukraine, According to Two People Familiar with the Matter," **Washington Post,** September 19, 2019.

582 **was finally released:** Emily Cochrane and Kenneth P. Vogel, "Amid Bipartisan Outcry, White House Agrees to Release Ukraine Aid," **New York Times,** September 12, 2019.

582 **met in person:** Kevin Liptak and Betsy Klein, "Trump Claims He Put 'No Pressure' on Zelensky Despite White House Transcript," CNN, September 25, 2019.

583 **Trump would maintain that:** Annie Karni, "Trump Claims Texts Prove No 'Quid Pro Quos of Any Kind' with Ukraine. But His Ambassador Suspected One," **New York Times,** October 4, 2019.

583 **Three times in the past:** Adam Willis, "Al Green's Third Attempt to Impeach Donald Trump Fails," **Texas Tribune,** July 17, 2019.

583 **vowed to stop:** Aaron Rupar, "Rashida Tlaib on Trump: 'We're Going to Impeach This Motherfucker!,'" **Vox,** January 4, 2019.

583 **had withheld military aid:** Sharon LaFraniere, Andrew E. Kramer, and Danny Hakim, "Trump, Ukraine and Impeachment: The Inside Story of How We Got Here," **New York Times,** November 11, 2019.

584 **Trump abruptly decided:** Marc Santora, "Poland Had the Royal Castle Ready. Then Trump Canceled His Trip," **New York Times,** August 30, 2019.

CHAPTER 26: ONE STRIKE AND YOU'RE OUT

587 **depart for Europe:** Marc Santora, "Poland Had the Royal Castle Ready. Then Trump Canceled His Trip," **New York Times,** August 30, 2019.

588 **Pence's family had roots:** Sheryl Gay Stolberg, "'I Am an American Because of Him': The Journey of Pence's Grandfather from Ireland," **New York Times,** March 16, 2017.

588 **an unsubtle headline:** Andrew Stein, "Trump-Haley in 2020," **Wall Street Journal,** June 23, 2019.

591 **an elongated cone:** Matthew Cappucci and Andrew Freedman, "President Trump Showed a Doctored Hurricane Chart. Was It to Cover Up for 'Alabama' Twitter Flub?," **Washington Post,** September 5, 2019.

591 **with firing by:** Christopher Flavelle, Lisa Friedman, and Peter Baker, "Commerce Chief Threatened Firings at NOAA After Trump's Dorian Tweets, Sources Say," **New York Times,** September 9, 2019.

591 **had represented bondholders:** Alison Leigh Cowan, "A Bankruptcy Wizard's Coups," **New York Times,** December 7, 1990.

593 **install Brad Parscale:** Katie Rogers and Maggie Haberman, "Trump's 2020 Campaign Announcement Had a Very Trumpian Rollout," **New York Times,** February 27, 2018.

594 **rally finally arrived:** Maggie Haberman, Annie Karni, and Michael D. Shear, "Trump, at Rally in Florida, Kicks Off His 2020 Re-Election Bid," **New York Times,** June 18, 2019.

595 **immediately preceded him:** Madeleine Joung, "Trump Has Now Had More Cabinet Turnover Than Reagan, Obama and the Two Bushes," **Time,** July 12, 2019.

598 **crying on election night:** Tim Alberta, **American Carnage: On the Front Lines of the Republican Civil War and the Rise of President Trump** (New York: HarperCollins, 2019).

598 **an off-the-record dinner:** Daniel Lippman, "Trump's Personal Assistant Fired After Comments About Ivanka, Tiffany," **Politico,** August 30, 2019.

599 **about getting rid of:** Katie Rogers, Annie Karni, and Maggie Haberman, "Trump's Personal Assistant, Madeleine Westerhout, Shared Intimate Details of First Family," **New York Times,** August 30, 2019.

599 **not charging Comey:** Adam Goldman, "Comey Is Criticized by Justice Dept. Watchdog for Violating F.B.I. Rules," **New York Times,** August 29, 2019.

600 **grew more expansive:** David A. Fahrenthold, "Trump's Company Billed the Government at Least $2.5 Million. Here Are the Key Charges," **Washington Post,** October 27, 2020.

600 **the default venue:** David A. Fahrenthold et al., "Ballrooms, Candles and Luxury Cottages: During Trump's Term, Millions of Government and GOP Dollars Have Flowed to His Properties," **Washington Post,** October 27, 2020.

600 **resort outside Miami:** Toluse Olorunnipa, David A. Fahrenthold, and Jonathan O'Connell, "Trump Has Awarded Next Year's G-7 Summit to His Doral Resort," **Washington Post,** October 17, 2019.

600 **allowed to rejoin:** Damian Paletta, Anne Gearan, and John Wagner, "Trump Calls for Russia to Be Reinstated to G-7, Threatens Allies on Trade," **Washington Post,** June 8, 2018.

600 **he mocked Obama:** Felicia Sonmez, "Trump Renews Call for Russia to Be Readmitted to G-7," **Washington Post,** August 20, 2019.

601 **was a quid pro quo:** John Parkinson, "Mulvaney

Admits Quid Pro Quo, Says Military Aid Withheld to Get Ukraine to Probe Democrats," ABC News, October 17, 2019.

602 **a potential crisis:** Jen Kirby, "Trump's Shocking Syria Decision and Confusing Aftermath, Explained," **Vox,** October 8, 2019.

602 **end of September:** Helene Cooper, "How Mark Milley, a General Who Mixes Bluntness and Banter, Became Trump's Top Military Adviser," **New York Times,** September 29, 2019.

602 **Trump had declared:** Zachary Cohen, "Trump Surprises Allies, Claims US-Backed Forces Reclaimed 100% of ISIS Territory in Syria," CNN, March 1, 2019.

603 **"support or be involved":** Eric Schmitt, Maggie Haberman, and Edward Wong, "President Endorses Turkish Military Operation in Syria, Shifting U.S. Policy," **New York Times,** October 7, 2019.

605 **worked to convert:** Catie Edmondson and Maggie Haberman, "Pledging 'Undying Support' for Trump, Jeff Van Drew Becomes a Republican," **New York Times,** December 19, 2019.

605 **an SEC investigation:** "Securities Analyst Marvin Roffman 'Renegotiates' Life After Trump," **Press of Atlantic City,** July 15, 1990.

606 **appearing on Fox News:** Craig Mauger, "Trump Goes After Dingell on Twitter After She Talks Impeachment on TV," **Detroit News,** December 14, 2019.

606 **Dingell wrote an op-ed:** "Opinion: Debbie Dingell: Why I Will Vote to Impeach Trump," **New York Times,** December 17, 2019.

606 **"Merry Christmas" event:** Beth LeBlanc, "Trump to Hold 'Merry Christmas Rally' in Battle Creek," **Detroit News,** December 5, 2019.

CHAPTER 27: ACQUITTED

609 **during a raid:** Rukmini Callimachi and Falih Hassan, "Abu Bakr Al-Baghdadi, ISIS Leader Known for His Brutality, Is Dead at 48," **New York Times,** October 27, 2019.

610 **of Iran-directed attacks:** Falih Hassan, Ben Hubbard, and Alissa J. Rubin, "Protesters Attack U.S. Embassy in Iraq, Chanting 'Death to America,'" **New York Times,** December 31, 2019.

610 **weighed targeting Suleimani:** Michael Crowley, Falih Hassan, and Eric Schmitt, "U.S. Strike in Iraq Kills Qassim Suleimani, Commander of Iranian Forces," **New York Times,** January 2, 2020.

610 **drone-fired missile killed:** Crowley, Hassan, and Schmitt, "U.S. Strike in Iraq Kills Qassim Suleimani, Commander of Iranian Forces."

610 **bases in Iraq:** Alissa J. Rubin, "Missile Strike Damage Appears Limited, but Iran May Not Be Done," **New York Times,** January 8, 2020.

610 **roughly one hundred troops:** Mihir Zaveri, "More Than 100 Troops Have Brain Injuries from Iran Missile Strike, Pentagon Says," **New York Times,** February 10, 2020.

610 **only the third president:** Nicholas Fandos and Michael D. Shear, "Trump Impeached for Abuse of Power and Obstruction of Congress," **New York Times,** December 18, 2019.

611 **deal with China:** Ana Swanson and Alan Rappeport,

"Trump Signs China Trade Deal, Putting Economic Conflict on Pause," **New York Times,** January 15, 2020.

611 **fired in 2017:** Julie Hirschfeld Davis, "White House Aide Forced Out After Claim of Leftist Conspiracy," **New York Times,** August 11, 2017.

612 **had been forced out:** Michael D. Shear and Maggie Haberman, "John McEntee, Trump Aide, Is Forced Out over Security Issue, but Joins Re-Election Campaign," **New York Times,** May 13, 2018.

612 **he took charge:** Michael D. Shear and Maggie Haberman, "Trump Places Loyalists in Key Jobs Inside the White House While Raging Against Enemies Outside," **New York Times,** February 13, 2020.

613 **review of existing employees:** Jonathan Swan and Alayna Treene, "New White House Personnel Chief Tells Cabinet Liaisons to Target Never Trumpers," **Axios,** February 21, 2020.

613 **prepared loyalty questionnaires:** Jeremy Diamond, "White House Questionnaire Adds New Litmus Tests for Prospective Hires," CNN, March 3, 2020.

613 **to serve simultaneously:** Julian E. Barnes and Maggie Haberman, "Trump Names Richard Grenell as Acting Head of Intelligence," **New York Times,** February 19, 2020.

616 **to summon witnesses:** Kyle Cheney, John Bresnahan, and Andrew Desiderio, "Republicans Defeat Democratic Bids to Hear Witnesses in Trump Trial," **Politico,** January 31, 2020.

616 **an upcoming book:** Maggie Haberman and Michael S. Schmidt, "Trump Told Bolton to Help

His Ukraine Pressure Campaign, Book Says," **New York Times,** January 31, 2020.

617 **was one exception:** Ian Millhiser, "Mitt Romney Just Did Something That Literally No Senator Has Ever Done Before," **Vox,** February 5, 2020.

617 **a "con man":** Steve Holland, "Republican Romney Calls Trump 'a Fraud,' Creates Pathway to Contested Convention," Reuters, March 2, 2016.

617 **accepting his endorsement:** Alex Isenstadt, "Trump Endorses Romney for Utah Senate Seat," **Politico,** February 19, 2018.

617 **and criticizing him:** "Opinion: Mitt Romney: The President Shapes the Public Character of the Nation. Trump's Character Falls Short," **Washington Post,** January 1, 2019.

617 **still fell short:** Li Zhou, "President Trump Acquitted by Senate on 2 Articles of Impeachment," **Vox,** February 5, 2020.

618 **laying out the case:** Peter Baker, "Assured of Impeachment Acquittal, Trump Makes Case for Second Term in State of the Union," **New York Times,** February 5, 2020.

618 **"Love your enemy":** Sebastian Smith, "Trump Takes Impeachment Victory Lap over 'Vicious' Democrats," Agence France-Presse, February 6, 2020.

619 **first sitting president:** Elizabeth Dias, Annie Karni, and Sabrina Tavernise, "Trump Gives Speech at 2020 March for Life Rally in Washington, D.C.," **New York Times,** January 24, 2020.

619 **from tortured answers:** Philip Bump, "Donald

Trump Took 5 Different Positions on Abortion in 3 Days," **Washington Post,** April 3, 2016.

619 **a clear statement:** Dan Mangan, "Trump: I'll Appoint Supreme Court Justices to Overturn Roe v. Wade Abortion Case," CNBC, October 19, 2016.

619 **federal funding formula:** Pam Belluck, "Trump Administration Blocks Funds for Planned Parenthood and Others over Abortion Referrals," **New York Times,** February 22, 2019.

620 **Roger Stone was sentenced:** Josh Gerstein and Darren Samuelsohn, "Roger Stone Sentenced to over 3 Years in Prison," **Politico,** February 20, 2020.

620 **lauded Stone's penchant:** Dylan Bank, Daniel DiMauro, and Morgan Pehme, **Get Me Roger Stone** (Netflix, 2017).

620 **commuted the sentence:** Michael D. Shear and Maggie Haberman, "Trump Grants Clemency to Blagojevich, Milken and Kerik," **New York Times,** February 18, 2020.

622 **the Carlson segment:** Timothy Bella, "Trump Tweets Tucker Carlson Segment That Hints of Possible Pardon for Roger Stone," **Washington Post,** February 20, 2020.

622 **social media posts were:** Anne Flaherty, "Barr Blasts Trump's Tweets on Stone Case: 'Impossible for Me to Do My Job,'" ABC News, February 13, 2020.

622 **dropped the charges:** Josh Gerstein and Kyle Cheney, "DOJ Drops Criminal Case Against Michael Flynn," **Politico,** May 7, 2020.

624 **a Gujarat stadium:** Anita Kumar, "India Rolls

Out the MAGA Carpet for Trump," **Politico,** February 24, 2020.

624 **few substantive advances:** Kevin Liptak, "Trump Concludes India Visit Without Major Agreements," CNN, February 25, 2020.

625 **by placing Pence:** Michael D. Shear, Noah Weiland, and Katie Rogers, "Trump Names Mike Pence to Lead Coronavirus Response," **New York Times,** February 26, 2020.

625 **over what information:** Michael D. Shear and Maggie Haberman, "Pence Will Control All Coronavirus Messaging from Health Officials," **New York Times,** February 27, 2020.

CHAPTER 28: GET HEALTHY AMERICA

627 **endorsed narrow limits:** Abby Goodnough, Maggie Haberman, and Sheila Kaplan, "With Partial Flavor Ban, Trump Splits the Difference on Vaping," **New York Times,** January 2, 2020.

627 **novel coronavirus arrived:** Roni Caryn Rabin, "Wuhan Coronavirus: C.D.C. Identifies First U.S. Case in Washington State," **New York Times,** January 21, 2020.

628 **"a great relationship with President Xi":** Donald Trump interview by Joe Kernen, **Squawk Box,** CNBC, January 22, 2020.

628 **two pointed memos:** Jonathan Swan and Margaret Talev, "Peter Navarro Memos Warning of Mass Coronavirus Death Circulated West Wing in January," **Axios,** April 7, 2020.

630 **citizens were exempted:** Stephen Braun, Hope Yen, and Calvin Woodward, "AP Fact Check: Trump and

the Virus-Era China Ban That Isn't," Associated Press, July 18, 2020.

630 **reporter's second book:** Bob Woodward, **Rage** (New York: Simon & Schuster, 2020).

630 **then abruptly rescheduled:** Anita Kumar, "Trump's Back-and-Forth Day: A Rebooked CDC Trip and a Coronavirus False Alarm," **Politico,** March 6, 2020.

630 **of coronavirus tests:** Miriam Valverde, "Donald Trump's Wrong Claim That 'Anybody' Can Get Tested for Coronavirus," KHN and PolitiFact, March 12, 2020.

631 **officially designated the coronavirus:** Donald G. McNeil Jr., "Coronavirus Has Become a Pandemic, W.H.O. Says," **New York Times,** March 11, 2020.

631 **suspended their seasons:** "Coronavirus: NBA, NHL, MLS Suspend Seasons, MLB Delays Start of 2020 Campaign," BBC, March 12, 2020.

631 **tournaments were canceled:** "NCAA Tournaments Canceled over Coronavirus," ESPN, March 12, 2020.

631 **fierce opposition from:** Eric Lipton et al., "He Could Have Seen What Was Coming: Behind Trump's Failure on the Virus," **New York Times,** April 11, 2020.

631 **basic factual errors:** Philip Rucker, Ashley Parker, and Josh Dawsey, "Inside Trump's Failed 10-Minute Attempt to Control the Coronavirus Crisis," **Washington Post,** March 12, 2020.

633 **separately discouraged kindness:** Matthew Choi, "Trump Calls Inslee a 'Snake' over Criticism of Coronavirus Rhetoric," **Politico,** March 6, 2020.

633 **One of the ships:** Ruben Vives, Alex Wigglesworth, and Andrew Dyer, "Hospital Ship Mercy Arrives in L.A. for Coronavirus Relief," **Los Angeles Times,** March 27, 2020.

634 **first at work:** Kathryn Watson, "Mark Meadows Officially Enters Chief of Staff Job amid National Coronavirus Crisis," CBS News, March 31, 2020.

635 **if it became public:** Jonathan Swan, "Scoop: How the White House Is Trying to Trap Leakers," **Axios,** July 12, 2020.

636 **held Trump accountable:** Lipton et al., "He Could Have Seen What Was Coming."

639 **with the hashtag:** Gabby Orr and Marianne Levine, "Trump's #FireFauci Retweet Spurs a Cycle of Outrage and a White House Denial," **Politico,** April 13, 2020.

639 **theoretically insulated from:** Paulina Villegas, "Can President Trump Fire Dr. Fauci?," **Washington Post,** November 2, 2020.

639 **first briefed about:** Ayesha Rascoe and Colin Dwyer, "Trump Received Intelligence Briefings on Coronavirus Twice in January," NPR, May 2, 2020.

640 **by private-sector employees:** Yasmeen Abutaleb, Ashley Parker, and Josh Dawsey, "Kushner Coronavirus Team Sparks Confusion Inside White House Response Efforts," **Washington Post,** March 18, 2020.

641 **evangelized to him:** Peter Baker et al., "Trump's Aggressive Advocacy of Malaria Drug for Treating Coronavirus Divides Medical Community," **New York Times,** April 6, 2020.

642 **bodies piled up:** Michael Rothfeld et al., "13 Deaths

in a Day: An 'Apocalyptic' Coronavirus Surge at an N.Y.C. Hospital," **New York Times,** March 25, 2020.

644 **published a poll:** Steven Nelson, "Democrats Want to Drop Joe Biden for Andrew Cuomo, Poll Finds," **New York Post,** April 10, 2020.

645 **to normalize relations:** Michael Crowley, "Trump Hosts Israel, UAE and Bahrain in Signing Ceremony," **New York Times,** September 15, 2020.

646 **millions of cash cards:** Jonathan Martin and Maggie Haberman, "A Deal on Drug Prices Undone by White House Insistence on 'Trump Cards,'" **New York Times,** September 18, 2020.

646 **"getting away with murder":** Dylan Scott, "Trump: Drug Companies 'Getting Away with Murder,'" Stat, January 11, 2017.

646 **shifting responsibility elsewhere:** J. M. Rieger, "How Trump Has Put the Onus on States amid the Coronavirus Pandemic," **Washington Post,** April 10, 2020.

CHAPTER 29: DIVIDE AND CONQUER

650 **officers had pinned:** Evan Hill et al., "How George Floyd Was Killed in Police Custody," **New York Times,** May 31, 2020.

651 **a racist history:** Katelyn Burns, "'When the Looting Starts, the Shooting Starts': The Racist History of Trump's Tweet," **Vox,** May 29, 2020.

652 **accused of brutality:** Burns, "'When the Looting Starts, the Shooting Starts.'"

652 **first from Frank Rizzo:** Rob Tornoe, "Trump Incorrectly Cites Former Philly Mayor Frank Rizzo

for Racist Phrase Aimed at Protesters on Fox News Interview," **Philadelphia Inquirer,** June 12, 2020.

652 **affixing a warning:** Davey Alba, Kate Conger, and Raymond Zhong, "Twitter Places Warning on Trump Minneapolis Tweet, Saying It Glorified Violence," **New York Times,** May 29, 2020.

653 **compared that exchange:** Amanda Watts and Chandelis Duster, "Philonise Floyd Details the Difference Between His Phone Calls with Trump and Biden," CNN, May 30, 2020.

653 **hustled Trump downstairs:** Peter Baker and Maggie Haberman, "As Protests and Violence Spill Over, Trump Shrinks Back," **New York Times,** May 31, 2020.

653 **at Cape Canaveral:** Lori Rozsa and Seung Min Kim, "Trump Celebrates Successful Space Launch, a Moment of Unity amid Tensions across the Country," **Washington Post,** May 30, 2020.

655 **rioters set fire:** Peter Hermann, Sarah Pulliam Bailey, and Michelle Boorstein, "Fire Set at St. John's Church in D.C. During Protests of George Floyd's Death," **Washington Post,** June 1, 2020.

656 **responsible be "executed":** Michael C. Bender, **"Frankly, We Did Win This Election": The Inside Story of How Trump Lost** (New York: Hachette Books, 2021).

657 **told the governors:** "Read: President Trump's Call with US Governors over Protests," CNN, June 1, 2020.

658 **her television commentary:** Mark Maremont and Corinne Ramey, "How Jenna Ellis Rose from Traffic

Court to Trump's Legal Team," **Wall Street Journal,** December 3, 2020.

660 **belated and belligerent:** Peter Baker et al., "How Trump's Idea for a Photo Op Led to Havoc in a Park," **New York Times,** June 2, 2020.

661 **delivered the rebuke:** Jeffrey Goldberg, "James Mattis Denounces Trump as Threat to Constitution," **Atlantic,** June 3, 2020.

662 **targeted the federal courthouse:** Nicholas Bogel-Burroughs, "Portland Clashes Converge on Courthouse Named for an Antiwar Republican," **New York Times,** July 22, 2020.

664 **suspended the rule:** Glenn Thrush, "Civil Rights Groups Challenge HUD's Fair Housing Enforcement," **New York Times,** May 8, 2018.

665 **helped to secure:** Christina Anderson and Alex Marshall, "ASAP Rocky Is Freed Pending Assault Verdict in Sweden," **New York Times,** August 2, 2019.

665 **As he campaigned:** Hailey Fuchs, "Trump Moves to Roll Back Obama Program Addressing Housing Discrimination," **New York Times,** July 23, 2020.

665 **accept welfare recipients:** Barbara Campbell, "Realty Company Asks $100-Million 'Bias' Damages," **New York Times,** December 13, 1973.

CHAPTER 30: TULSA

667 **the disclaimer issued:** Matt Flegenheimer, "Trump's 'What Do You Have to Lose?' Presidency Is Rallying Again," **New York Times,** June 20, 2020.

667 **exactly a year earlier:** Maggie Haberman, Annie

Karni, and Michael D. Shear, "Trump, at Rally in Florida, Kicks Off His 2020 Re-Election Bid," **New York Times,** June 18, 2019.

667 **worked for months:** Alexander Burns, Jonathan Martin, and Maggie Haberman, "A Bruised Trump Faces Uncertain 2020 Prospects. His Team Fears a Primary Fight," **New York Times,** January 26, 2019.

667 **nearly all in-person:** Matt Pearce and Melissa Gomez, "How Coronavirus Has Changed Political Campaigning," **Los Angeles Times,** March 13, 2020.

667 **make a campaign stop:** Scott Detrow, "Biden Holds 1st In-Person Campaign Event After the Lockdown, Meets Community Leaders," NPR, June 1, 2020.

670 **a limited-liability company:** Shane Goldmacher and Maggie Haberman, "Lara Trump Served on the Board of a Company Through Which the Trump Political Operation Spent More Than $700 Million," **New York Times,** December 18, 2020.

670 **a lap dance:** Natasha Korecki et al., "Inside Donald Trump's 2020 Undoing," **Politico,** November 7, 2020.

670 **boyfriend raised eyebrows:** Korecki et al., "Inside Donald Trump's 2020 Undoing."

670 **documented his lifestyle:** Jose Lambiet, "Exclusive: How Donald Trump's Campaign Manager Brad Parscale Went from Family Bankruptcy to Splashing Out Millions on Mansions, Condos and Luxury Cars Through His Companies That Get a Hefty Cut of the President's $57M Campaign Contributions," **Daily Mail,** August 22, 2019.

671 **its next convention:** Alan Blinder and Maggie Astor, "Republicans Choose Charlotte for Their 2020 Convention," **New York Times,** July 20, 2018.

671 **relax the rules:** Annie Linskey and Josh Dawsey, "Trump Said 'We Can't Do Social Distancing' at Convention as He Made Personal Appeal to North Carolina Governor," **Washington Post,** June 4, 2020.

672 **could get sick:** Linskey and Dawsey, "Trump Said 'We Can't Do Social Distancing' at Convention as He Made Personal Appeal to North Carolina Governor."

672 **Lafayette Square debacle:** Katie Rogers, "Protesters Dispersed with Tear Gas So Trump Could Pose at Church," **New York Times,** June 1, 2020.

672 **DeSantis quietly waved:** Bender, **"Frankly, We Did Win This Election": The Inside Story of How Trump Lost** (New York: Hachette Books, 2021).

673 **country's bloodiest acts:** Emily Stewart, "One of America's Worst Acts of Racial Violence Was in Tulsa. Now, It's the Site of Trump's First Rally in Months," **Vox,** June 16, 2020.

673 **holiday of Juneteenth:** Fabiola Cineas, "Juneteenth, Explained" **Vox,** June 18, 2020.

673 **Black Secret Service agent:** Bender, **"Frankly, We Did Win This Election."**

673 **push it back:** Karl de Vries, "Trump Reschedules Tulsa Rally 'Out of Respect' for Juneteenth," CNN, June 13, 2020.

674 **a "superspreader" event:** Benjamin Siegel, Will Steakin, and Katherine Faulders, "Indoors, Yelling and Packed Crowds: Experts Sound Alarm Ahead

of Trump's Tulsa Rally amid Coronavirus," ABC News, June 16, 2020.

674 **driven media attention:** Kevin Liptak and Kaitlan Collins, "Sick Staff and Empty Seats: How Trump's Triumphant Return to the Campaign Trail Went from Bad to Worse," CNN, June 21, 2020.

674 **force the resignation:** Alan Feuer et al., "Trump Fires Berman at S.D.N.Y. After Tensions over Inquiries," **New York Times,** June 20, 2020.

674 **that very office:** Maggie Haberman and Charlie Savage, "U.S. Attorney Preet Bharara Says He Was Fired After Refusing to Quit," **New York Times,** March 11, 2017.

674 **in Berman's removal:** Feuer et al., "Trump Fires Berman at S.D.N.Y. After Tensions over Inquiries."

675 **dupe the campaign:** Maggie Haberman and Annie Karni, "The President's Shock at the Rows of Empty Seats in Tulsa," **New York Times,** September 9, 2020.

676 **set off wildfires:** Virginia Langmaid and Judson Jones, "Mount Rushmore Hasn't Had Fireworks for More Than a Decade Because It's Very Dangerous. Here's Why," CNN, July 3, 2020.

677 **U.K. state visit:** Meredith McGraw and Tara Palmeri, "Trump Kids Joining President, First Lady for State Visit with the Queen," ABC News, May 23, 2019.

677 **a charter plane:** Eric Lutz, "Kim Guilfoyle, Don Jr. Reportedly Stranded Trump Staffers in South Dakota," **Vanity Fair,** July 24, 2020.

678 **showing Trump's face:** Jonathan Martin and Maggie

Haberman, "How Kristi Noem, Mt. Rushmore and Trump Fueled Speculation About Pence's Job," **New York Times,** August 8, 2020.

678 **ran an article:** Emily Smith, "Ghislaine Will 'Name Names,'" **New York Post,** July 5, 2020.

679 **he had died:** William K. Rashbaum, Benjamin Weiser, and Michael Gold, "Jeffrey Epstein Dead in Suicide at Jail, Spurring Inquiries," **New York Times,** August 10, 2019.

680 **expand the use:** Juliette Love, Matt Stevens, and Lazaro Gamio, "Where Americans Can Vote by Mail in the 2020 Elections," **New York Times,** August 14, 2020.

680 **set by statute:** Rebecca Shabad, "Trump Floats Delaying the Election, But He Can't Do That," NBC News, July 30, 2020.

680 **move Kushner aside:** Maggie Haberman, Jonathan Martin, and Alexander Burns, "Why June Was Such a Terrible Month for Trump," **New York Times,** July 2, 2020.

681 **defrauded Trump supporters:** Maggie Haberman, Michael S. Schmidt, and Jeremy W. Peters, "Arrest Disrupts Bannon's Efforts to Stay Relevant After Leaving White House," **New York Times,** August 20, 2020.

681 **at DeSantis's behest:** Bender, **"Frankly, We Did Win This Election."**

682 **campaign's ad spending:** Shane Goldmacher and Maggie Haberman, "How Trump's Billion-Dollar Campaign Lost Its Cash Advantage," **New York Times,** September 7, 2020.

682 **"land the plane":** Jonathan Swan, "Trump's Advisers Brace for Loss, Point Fingers," **Axios,** October 16, 2020.

683 **willing to host:** Maggie Haberman, Patricia Mazzei, and Annie Karni, "Trump Abruptly Cancels Republican Convention in Jacksonville: 'It's Not the Right Time,'" **New York Times,** July 23, 2020.

683 **settled on staging:** Anita Kumar, "Trump's Prime-Time Convention Plan: A D.C. Ballroom and Government Backdrops," **Politico,** August 13, 2020.

683 **speech from Jerusalem:** Lara Jakes, "Pompeo to Deliver R.N.C. Speech from Israel with Eye on 2024," **New York Times,** August 25, 2020.

683 **long-standing diplomatic protocol:** Isabel Kershner and David M. Halbfinger, "On Mideast Trip, Pompeo Mixes Diplomacy with Partisan Politics," **New York Times,** August 24, 2020.

683 **diffuse broadcast production:** Ella Nilsen, "The Virtual 2020 Democratic National Convention, Explained," **Vox,** August 17, 2020.

684 **announced a pardon:** Peter Baker, "Trump Extends Pardon to Alice Johnson After She Praises Him at Convention," **New York Times,** August 28, 2020.

684 **had previously commuted:** Peter Baker, "Alice Marie Johnson Is Granted Clemency by Trump After Push by Kim Kardashian West," **New York Times,** June 6, 2018.

CHAPTER 31: NOT ONE OF THE DIERS

687 **surpassed two hundred thousand deaths:** Laura King and Henry Chu, "U.S. COVID-19 Deaths

Reach 200,000," **Los Angeles Times,** September 22, 2020.

687 **did not join them:** Bess Levin, "White House on 200,000 Coronavirus Deaths: Call Us When 2 Million of You Are Dead," **Vanity Fair,** September 22, 2020.

687 **by mid-September, indoor venues:** Eric Fiegel et al., "Trump Holds First Entirely Indoor Rally in Nearly Three Months," CNN, September 14, 2020.

688 **who served Trump:** Myah Ward and Daniel Lippman, "Trump's Personal Valet Tests Positive for Coronavirus," **Politico,** May 7, 2020.

688 **a positive result:** Martin Pengelly, "Trump Tested Positive for Covid Few Days Before Biden Debate, Chief of Staff Says in New Book," **Guardian,** December 1, 2021.

688 **the process used:** Ashley Parker et al., "Trump Tested Positive for Coronavirus Before First Debate with Biden, Three Former Officials Say," **Washington Post,** December 1, 2021.

689 **Trump's third appointee:** Peter Baker and Maggie Haberman, "Trump Selects Amy Coney Barrett to Fill Ginsburg's Seat on the Supreme Court," **New York Times,** September 25, 2020.

689 **succumbing to cancer:** Linda Greenhouse, "Ruth Bader Ginsburg, Supreme Court's Feminist Icon, Is Dead at 87," **New York Times,** September 18, 2020.

689 **set by physicians:** Aaron C. Davis, Shawn Boburg, and Josh Dawsey, "Trump's Debate Guests Refused to Wear Masks, Flouting Rules," **Washington Post,** October 2, 2020.

691 **Hunter dropped off:** Andrew Prokop, "Rudy Giuliani Hopes to Use a Hard Drive with Purported Hunter Biden Emails to Help Trump's Reelection Efforts," **Vox,** October 15, 2020.

692 **Bloomberg News reported:** Jennifer Jacobs, "Trump Says He Will Quarantine After Aide Falls Ill with Virus," Bloomberg, October 1, 2020.

694 **a kidney-related issue:** Jordyn Phelps, Devin Dwyer, and Cindy Smith, "President Visits First Lady Melania Trump in Hospital After Kidney Procedure," ABC News, May 14, 2018.

694 **more medical care:** Maggie Haberman and Noah Weiland, "Trump's Blood Oxygen Level in Covid Bout Was Dangerously Low, Former Aide Says," **New York Times,** December 6, 2021.

694 **up from his bed:** Haberman and Weiland, "Trump's Blood Oxygen Level in Covid Bout Was Dangerously Low."

695 **"I could be one of the diers":** Olivia Nuzzi, "The Entire Presidency Is a Superspreading Event," **New York,** October 9, 2020.

695 **liked fast-food restaurants:** Rachel DeSantis, "Donald Trump's Lifelong Love of Fast Food, from His 2002 McDonald's Commercial to 'Hamberders,'" **New York Daily News,** January 15, 2019.

696 **Meadows crept over:** Anita Kumar et al., "White House Triggers Questions and Confusion About Trump's Coronavirus Case," **Politico,** October 3, 2020.

698 **social media posts from:** Tina Nguyen, "Trump

Isn't Secretly Winking at QAnon. He's Retweeting Its Followers," **Politico,** July 12, 2020.

698 **Biden campaign bus:** Cameron Peters, "After Trump Supporters Surround a Biden Bus in Texas, the FBI Opens an Investigation," **Vox,** November 1, 2020.

699 **months insisting publicly:** Reid J. Epstein, Emily Cochrane, and Glenn Thrush, "Trump Again Sows Doubt About Election as G.O.P. Scrambles to Assure Voters," **New York Times,** September 24, 2020.

701 **the first network:** Annie Karni and Maggie Haberman, "How the Trump Campaign Reacted When Fox News Called Arizona for Biden," **New York Times,** November 4, 2020.

CHAPTER 32: TRIAL BY COMBAT

704 **and text-message blasts:** Monica Alba and Ben Kamisar, "New Campaign Filings Show Trump's Fundraising Haul Off Claims of Voter Fraud," NBC News, December 4, 2020.

705 **the mistaken impression:** Olivia Nuzzi, "Four Seasons Total Landscaping: The Full(est Possible) Story," **New York,** December 21, 2020.

705 **the ballot-counting process:** Zach Montellaro and Josh Gerstein, "Pennsylvania Supreme Court Rejects Complaints About Philadelphia Election Observations," **Politico,** November 17, 2020.

705 **replied to a message:** Aaron Blake, "The GOP Plotted to Overturn the 2020 Election Before It Was Even Over," **Washington Post,** December 15, 2021.

706 **launched at the start:** Jeremy W. Peters, "Steve Bannon Has Some Impeachment Advice for Trump," **New York Times,** October 23, 2019.

706 **"Stop the Steal" effort:** Tina Nguyen, "Trump Ally Wants Trump Delegates to Sign Loyalty Pledge," **Vanity Fair,** April 13, 2016.

706 **activists began using:** Sheera Frenkel, "How Misinformation 'Superspreaders' Seed False Election Theories," **New York Times,** November 23, 2020.

707 **directly to the Oval:** Maggie Haberman and Zolan Kanno-Youngs, "Trump Discussed Naming Sidney Powell as Special Counsel on Election Fraud," **New York Times,** December 19, 2020.

707 **positive coronavirus test:** Jennifer Jacobs and Jordan Fabian, "Trump Adviser David Bossie Tests Positive for Coronavirus," Bloomberg, November 9, 2020.

707 **popular vote margin:** Nicholas Riccardi, "Biden Approaches 80 Million Votes in Historic Victory," Associated Press, November 18, 2020.

708 **the massive sums:** Alba and Kamisar, "New Campaign Filings Show Trump's Fundraising Haul Off Claims of Voter Fraud."

709 **case in Arizona:** Maria Polletta, "Trump Lawsuit on Maricopa County Votes Dismissed by Judge as Outcome Wouldn't Affect Races," **Arizona Republic,** November 13, 2020.

710 **beyond some expenses:** Maggie Haberman and Ben Protess, "Giuliani's Allies Want Trump to Pay His Legal Bills," **New York Times,** May 4, 2021.

711 **was trading texts:** Bob Woodward and Robert Costa, "Virginia Thomas Urged White House

Chief to Pursue Unrelenting Efforts to Overturn the 2020 Election, Texts Show," **Washington Post,** March 24, 2022.

713 **that special thermostats:** Zachary Cohen, Paula Reid, and Sara Murray, "New Details Shed Light on Ways Trump's Chief of Staff Pushed Federal Agencies to Pursue Dubious Election Claims," CNN, December 2, 2021.

714 **She was banned:** Michael Balsamo and Zeke Miller, "Trump Aide Banned from Justice After Trying to Get Case Info," Associated Press, December 3, 2020.

715 **afforded online platforms:** Connor O'Brien and Cristiano Lima, "Trump Threatens to Veto Defense Bill over Social Media Rule," **Politico,** December 1, 2020.

715 **"must hate Trump":** Jonathan D. Karl, "How Barr Finally Turned on Trump," **Atlantic,** June 27, 2021.

715 **offered to resign:** William P. Barr, **One Damn Thing After Another: Memoirs of an Attorney General** (New York: William Morrow, 2022).

716 **had changed his mind:** Barr, **One Damn Thing After Another.**

716 **rivulets of sweat:** Dan Zak and Josh Dawsey, "Rudy Giuliani's Post-Election Meltdown Starts to Become Literal," **Washington Post,** November 19, 2020.

716 **deceased Venezuelan leader:** Felicia Sonmez and Josh Dawsey, "Giuliani Releases Statement Distancing Trump Campaign from Lawyer Sidney Powell," **Washington Post,** November 22, 2020.

716 **issued a statement:** Sonmez and Dawsey, "Giuliani

Releases Statement Distancing Trump Campaign from Lawyer Sidney Powell."

717 **different postelection lawsuits:** Jenna Greene, "How Marc Elias Sealed Biden's Win in Court—64 Times," Reuters, January 22, 2021.

717 **retired army colonel:** Alan Feuer, "Phil Waldron's Unlikely Role in Pushing Baseless Election Claims," **New York Times,** December 21, 2021.

717 **released a report:** Philip Bump, "This Might Be the Most Embarrassing Document Created by a White House Staffer," **Washington Post,** December 18, 2020.

718 **hoped to tell:** Jonathan Swan and Zachary Basu, "Off the Rails: Inside the Craziest Meeting of the Trump Presidency," **Axios,** February 2, 2021.

718 **planning to appoint:** Haberman and Kanno-Youngs, "Trump Discussed Naming Sidney Powell as Special Counsel on Election Fraud."

718 **decreeing the seizure:** Zachary Cohen and Paula Reid, "Exclusive: Trump Advisers Drafted More Than One Executive Order to Seize Voting Machines, Sources Tell CNN," CNN, January 31, 2022.

719 **turned his focus:** Alan Feuer, Maggie Haberman, and Luke Broadwater, "Memos Show Roots of Trump's Focus on Jan. 6 and Alternate Electors," **New York Times,** February 2, 2022.

719 **went to Mar-a-Lago:** Kaitlan Collins and Kevin Liptak, "Trump Returns to Washington Early Ahead of Republican Plan to Disrupt Certification of Biden's Win," CNN, December 31, 2020.

719 **Bannon called Trump:** Bob Woodward and Robert Costa, **Peril** (New York: Simon & Schuster, 2021).

721 **an elated crowd:** Marc Caputo and James Arkin, "The GOP's Georgia Boogeyman: Chuck Schumer," **Politico,** November 11, 2020.

722 **join a lawsuit:** Jeremy W. Peters and Maggie Haberman, "17 Republican Attorneys General Back Trump in Far-Fetched Election Lawsuit," **New York Times,** December 9, 2020.

723 **and considered appointing:** Katie Benner, "Trump and Justice Dept. Lawyer Said to Have Plotted to Oust Acting Attorney General," **New York Times,** January 22, 2021.

723 **calling it a "murder-suicide":** Katie Benner, "Report Cites New Details of Trump Pressure on Justice Dept. over Election," **New York Times,** October 6, 2021.

724 **lacked the authority:** Felicia Sonmez, "Georgia Leaders Rebuff Trump's Call for Special Session to Overturn Election Results," **Washington Post,** December 6, 2020.

724 **"All I want":** Amy Gardner, "'I Just Want to Find 11,780 Votes': In Extraordinary Hour-Long Call, Trump Pressures Georgia Secretary of State to Recalculate the Vote in His Favor," **Washington Post,** January 3, 2021.

725 **to congratulate him:** Nicholas Fandos and Luke Broadwater, "McConnell Congratulates Biden and Lobbies Colleagues to Oppose a Final-Stage G.O.P. Effort to Overturn His Victory," **New York Times,** December 15, 2020.

725 **falling under pressure:** Stephen Miller, **Fox & Friends,** Fox News, December 14, 2020.

725 **with Meadows's associate:** Kyle Cheney, "Fighting Jan. 6 Committee, John Eastman Details How He Came into Trump's Post-Election Fold," **Politico,** February 22, 2022.

726 **conservative retired judge:** "The Never-Before-Told Backstory of Pence's Jan. 6 Argument," **Politico,** February 18, 2022.

727 **Pence pushed back:** Michael S. Schmidt and Maggie Haberman, "The Lawyer Behind the Memo on How Trump Could Stay in Office," **New York Times,** October 2, 2021.

727 **pressure Pence was under:** Maggie Haberman and Annie Karni, "Pence Said to Have Told Trump He Lacks Power to Change Election Result," **New York Times,** January 5, 2021.

728 **at the Willard Hotel:** Jacqueline Alemany et al., "Willard Hotel Was Trump Team 'Command Center' for Denying Biden Presidency Ahead of Jan. 6," **Washington Post,** October 23, 2021.

729 **a massive rally:** Hunter Walker, "Jan. 6 White House Rally Organizers Were 'Following POTUS' Lead,'" **Rolling Stone,** November 21, 2021.

729 **join his supporters:** Maggie Haberman and Jonathan Martin, "After the Speech: What Trump Did as the Capitol Was Attacked," **New York Times,** February 13, 2021.

730 **a final call:** Peter Baker, Maggie Haberman, and Annie Karni, "Mike Pence Reached His Limit with Trump. It Wasn't Pretty," **New York Times,** January 12, 2021.

730 **down in history:** Baker, Haberman, and Karni, "Mike Pence Reached His Limit With Trump."

732 **to receive calls:** Haberman and Martin, "After the Speech."

732 **underground loading dock:** Holmes Lybrand, "Secret Service Says Pence Was Taken to Loading Dock Under US Capitol During January 6 Riot," CNN, March 21, 2022.

732 **phone lit up:** Jacqueline Alemany et al., "How Thousands of Text Messages from Mark Meadows and Others Reveal New Details About Events Surrounding the Jan. 6 Attack," **Washington Post,** February 16, 2022.

734 **entered the Capitol:** Ryan Lucas, "Where the Jan. 6 Insurrection Investigation Stands, One Year Later," NPR, January 6, 2022.

734 **five people died:** Jie Jenny Zou and Erin B. Logan, "Jan. 6: By the Numbers," **Los Angeles Times,** January 5, 2022.

734 **seen being guarded:** Christiaan Triebert et al., "First They Guarded Roger Stone. Then They Joined the Capitol Attack," **New York Times,** February 14, 2021.

735 **there were resignations:** "Here Are the Trump Officials Who Resigned over the Capitol Riot," **New York Times,** January 17, 2021.

735 **Ratcliffe wrote an op-ed:** John Ratcliffe, "China Is National Security Threat No. 1," **Wall Street Journal,** December 3, 2020.

736 **impeach Trump again:** Nicholas Fandos, "Trump Impeached for Inciting Insurrection," **New York Times,** January 13, 2021.

736 **win back the Senate:** Richard Fausset, Jonathan Martin, and Stephanie Saul, "Ossoff and Warnock Win in Georgia, Democrats to Gain Control of Senate," **New York Times,** January 6, 2021.

736 **asked on Fox:** Hogan Gidley, interview by Bill Hemmer, Fox News, January 11, 2021.

737 **years-long regional blockade:** Vivian Yee and Megan Specia, "Gulf States Agree to End Isolation of Qatar," **New York Times,** January 5, 2021.

737 **pardons and commutations:** Maggie Haberman et al., "Trump Grants Clemency to Stephen Bannon and Other Allies," **New York Times,** January 20, 2021.

738 **slew of pardons:** Dalton Bennett and Jon Swaine, "The Roger Stone Tapes," **Washington Post,** March 4, 2022.

738 **included preemptive pardons:** Kaitlan Collins, Kevin Liptak, and Pamela Brown, "Trump Talked Out of Pardoning Kids and Republican Lawmakers," CNN, January 19, 2021.

EPILOGUE

741 **he might form:** Josh Dawsey and Manuel Roig-Franzia, "RNC Chairwoman Ronna McDaniel Is Trying to Hold Together a Party That Donald Trump Might Want to Tear Up," **Washington Post,** January 29, 2021.

742 **"practically and morally":** Nicholas Fandos, "Trump Acquitted of Inciting Insurrection, Even as Bipartisan Majority Votes 'Guilty,'" **New York Times,** February 13, 2021.

742 **a select committee:** Luke Broadwater, "Pelosi Says

She Will Create a Select Committee to Investigate the Jan. 6 Assault on the U.S. Capitol," **New York Times,** July 1, 2021.

742 **committee vice chair:** Annie Grayer et al., "Liz Cheney Named Vice Chair of the January 6 Select Committee," CNN, September 2, 2021.

742 **Representative Adam Kinzinger:** Luke Broadwater, "Pelosi Appoints Kinzinger to Panel Scrutinizing Jan. 6," **New York Times,** July 25, 2021.

743 **indicted for contempt:** Katie Benner, and Luke Broadwater, "Bannon Indicted on Contempt Charges over House's Capitol Riot Inquiry," **New York Times,** November 12, 2021.

745 **a coffee-table book:** Kate Bennett, "Donald Trump Quietly Making Millions from Coffee Table Book," CNN, February 7, 2022.

745 **book of her own:** Eric Lipton and Maggie Haberman, "She Took the White House Photos. Trump Moved to Take the Profit," **New York Times,** March 31, 2022.

745 **Trump was suspended:** Cameron Peters, "Every Platform Cracking Down on Trump After the Deadly Capitol Riots," **Vox,** January 10, 2021.

745 **suing the companies:** Shane Goldmacher, "Trump Sues Tech Firms for Blocking Him, and Fund-Raises off It," **New York Times,** July 7, 2021.

746 **so-called blank-check company:** David Enrich, Matthew Goldstein, and Shane Goldmacher, "Trump Takes Advantage of Wall Street Fad to Bankroll New Venture," **New York Times,** October 21, 2021.

746 **formally attached criminality:** Ben Protess,

William K. Rashbaum, and Jonah E. Bromwich, "Trump Organization Is Charged with Running 15-Year Employee Tax Scheme," **New York Times,** July 1, 2021.

747 **special grand jury investigating:** Tamar Hallerman, "Fulton Judges Greenlight Special Grand Jury for Trump Probe," **Atlanta Journal-Constitution,** January 24, 2022.

747 **to indict Trump:** Ben Protess, William K. Rashbaum, and Jonah E. Bromwich, "How the Manhattan D.A.'s Investigation into Donald Trump Unraveled," **New York Times,** March 5, 2022.

749 **grow to eleven:** Michael R. Sisak and Marina Villeneuve, "Cuomo Urged to Resign After Probe Finds He Harassed 11 Women," Associated Press, August 3, 2021.

749 **gone within months:** Luis Ferré-Sadurní and J. David Goodman, "Cuomo Resigns amid Scandals, Ending Decade-Long Run in Disgrace," **New York Times,** August 10, 2021.

752 **she interviewed him:** Lois Romano, "Donald Trump, Holding All the Cards; The Tower! The Team! The Money! The Future!," **Washington Post,** November 15, 1984.

754 **affirmed the results:** Alexa Corse, "Arizona GOP's Election Audit Confirms Biden Win in State," **Wall Street Journal,** September 24, 2021.

754 **faced libel suits:** Alan Feuer, "Dominion Voting Systems Files Defamation Lawsuit Against Pro-Trump Attorney Sidney Powell," **New York Times,** January 8, 2021.

756 **punishing legal fight:** Eamon Javers, "Trump's Angry Apprentice," Bloomberg, December 12, 2005.

756 **condemned domestic "extremism":** Thomas Kaplan, "Violent Extremists at Home and Abroad 'Are Children of the Same Foul Spirit,' George W. Bush Says in Pennsylvania," **New York Times,** September 11, 2021.

757 **who ultimately delivered:** Thomas Gibbons-Neff, "In Afghanistan, an Unceremonious End, and a Shrouded Beginning," **New York Times,** August 30, 2021.

760 **reported on it:** Jacqueline Alemany et al., "National Archives Had to Retrieve Trump White House Records from Mar-a-Lago," **Washington Post,** February 7, 2022.

762 **was eventually settled:** Nolan D. McCaskill, "Trump Settles Legal Dispute with Former Aide," **Politico,** August 11, 2016.

764 **not immediately ending:** Eileen Sullivan, "C.D.C. Confirms It Will Lift Public Health Order Restricting Immigration," **New York Times,** April 1, 2022.

764 **a border-crossing restriction:** Nick Miroff, "Under Trump Border Rules, U.S. Has Granted Refuge to Just Two People Since Late March During Coronavirus Outbreak, Records Show," **Washington Post,** May 13, 2020.

765 **running for the U.S. Senate:** Marc Caputo, "Herschel Walker Files for Georgia Senate Race," **Politico,** August 24, 2021.

766 **accusations of assault:** Brian Slodysko, Bill Barrow,

and Jake Bleiberg, "As Herschel Walker Eyes Senate Run, a Turbulent Past Emerges," Associated Press, July 23, 2021.

768 **canceling a contract:** Emma G. Fitzsimmons, "New York City Will End Contracts with Trump over Capitol Riot," **New York Times,** January 13, 2021.

Illustration Credits

INSERT 1

Page 1: (top) ARCHIVIO GBB/Redux

Page 2: (top) Uli Seit/The New York Times/Redux; (bottom left) Archivio GBB/contrasto/Redux

Page 3: (top left) Barton Silverman/The New York Times/Redux; (top right) NY Daily News Archive via Getty Images; (bottom left) Frank Russo/NY Daily News Archive via Getty Images; (bottom right) AP Photo

Page 4: (top and center) Fred R. Conrad/The New York Times/Redux; (bottom) Marilynn K. Yee/The New York Times/Redux

Page 5: (top) Ron Galella/Ron Galella Collection via Getty Images; (bottom) Tom Gates/Pictorial Parade/Archive Photos/Getty Images

Page 6: (top) Joe McNally/Getty Images; (bottom) Dennis Caruso/NY Daily News Archive via Getty Images

Page 7: (top) Sonia Moskowitz/Getty Images; (bottom) Fred W. McDarrah/MUUS Collection via Getty Images

Page 8: (top) Victor Junco/St. Petersburg Times/Getty Images; (bottom) Jeffrey Asher/Getty Images

Page 9: (top) 3572821 Globe Photos/MediaPunch /IPX/AP Images; (bottom) George Lange

Page 10: (top) Yann Gamblin/Paris Match via Getty Images; (center) Edward Keating/The New York Times/Redux; (bottom) AP Photo/Igor Tabakov

Page 11: (top) AP Photo/Daniel Hulshizer; (bottom) Davidoff Studios/Getty Images

Page 12: (top) Shutterstock; (bottom) Chester Higgins Jr./The New York Times

Page 13: (top) Jean-Louis Atlan/Paris Match via Getty Images; (bottom) Jonathan Becker/Contour by Getty Images

Page 14: George Napolitano/FilmMagic via Getty Images

Page 15: (top) Sabo Robert/NY Daily News Archive via Getty Images; (bottom) Martin H. Simon/Pool via Bloomberg/Getty Images

Page 16: (top) Matthew Cavanaugh/Getty Images; (bottom) AP Photo/Mike Groll

INSERT 2

Page 1: (top) JEWEL SAMAD/AFP via Getty Images; (bottom) Win McNamee/Getty Images

Page 2: (top) Damon Winter/The New York Times/Redux; (center) Paul Hennessy/Alamy Live News; (bottom) Fred Watkins/Disney General Entertainment Content via Getty Images

Page 3: (top) Stephen Crowley/The New York Times/Redux; (center) NICHOLAS KAMM/AFP via Getty Images; (bottom) Drew Angerer/Getty Images

Page 4: (top) Damon Winter/The New York Times/Redux; (bottom) Drew Angerer/Getty Images

Page 5: (top) Andrew Harrer/Bloomberg via Getty Images; (center) Win McNamee/Getty Images; (bottom) Stephen Crowley/The New York Times/Redux

Page 6: (top) Andrew Innerarity/For The Washington Post via Getty Images; (center) AP Photo/Evan Vucci; (bottom) Official White House Photo by Joyce N. Boghosian

Page 7: (top) Win McNamee/Getty Images; (center) Michael Reynolds-Pool/Getty Images; (bottom) AP Photo/J. Scott Applewhite

Page 8: (top) Doug Mills/The New York Times/Redux; (center) Photograph by John Hogan Gidley; (bottom) Doug Mills/The New York Times/Redux

Page 9: (top) Doug Mills/The New York Times/Redux; (center) Erin Schaff/The New York Times/Redux; (bottom) AP Photo/Jacquelyn Martin

Page 10: (top) Caroline Brehman/CQ-Roll Call, Inc via Getty Images; (center and bottom) Doug Mills/The New York Times/Redux

Page 11: (top) T. J. Kirkpatrick/The New York Times/Redux; (bottom) Win McNamee/Getty Images

Page 12: (top) Doug Mills/The New York Times/Redux; (bottom) Official White House Photo by Andrea Hanks

Page 13: (top) NICHOLAS KAMM/AFP via Getty Images; (center) Tasos Katopodis/Getty Images; (bottom) Yuri Gripas/Abaca/Sipa USA (Sipa via AP Images)

Page 16: (top) Yuri Gripas/Abaca/Sipa USA (Sipa via AP Images); (bottom) Anna Moneymaker/The New York Times/Redux

Index

ABOUT THE AUTHOR

MAGGIE HABERMAN is a journalist who joined **The New York Times** in 2015 and was part of a team that won a Pulitzer Prize in 2018 for reporting on the investigations into Donald Trump's, and his advisers', connections to Russia. She has twice been a member of a team that was a finalist for a Pulitzer Prize: in 2021 for reporting on the Trump administration's response to the coronavirus and in 2022 for coverage related to the January 6, 2021, riot at the Capitol. Before joining **The New York Times** as a campaign correspondent, she worked as a political reporter at **Politico** from 2010 to 2015. She previously worked at the **New York Post** and the **New York Daily News.**